The Most Powerful Court in the World

The Most Powerful Court in the World

A History of the Supreme Court of the United States

STUART BANNER

OXFORD
UNIVERSITY PRESS

Oxford University Press is a department of the University of Oxford. It furthers
the University's objective of excellence in research, scholarship, and education
by publishing worldwide. Oxford is a registered trade mark of Oxford University
Press in the UK and certain other countries.

Published in the United States of America by Oxford University Press
198 Madison Avenue, New York, NY 10016, United States of America.

Library of Congress Cataloging-in-Publication Data
Names: Banner, Stuart, 1963– author.
Title: The most powerful court in the world : a history of the Supreme Court
of the United States / Stuart Banner.
Description: New York : Oxford University Press, 2024. |
Includes bibliographical references and index. |
Identifiers: LCCN 2024012852 (print) | LCCN 2024012853 (ebook) |
ISBN 9780197780350 (hardback) | ISBN 9780197780374 (epub) |
ISBN 9780197780381
Subjects: LCSH: United States. Supreme Court—History.
Classification: LCC KF8742 .B36 2024 (print) | LCC KF8742 (ebook) |
DDC 347.73/2609—dc23/eng/20240325
LC record available at https://lccn.loc.gov/2024012852
LC ebook record available at https://lccn.loc.gov/2024012853

DOI: 10.1093/oso/9780197780350.001.0001

Printed by Sheridan Books, Inc., United States of America

Contents

Acknowledgments

For helpful suggestions, thanks to participants in workshops at Northwestern and UCLA, to OUP's two anonymous readers, and to Beth Colgan, Mark Greenberg, Máximo Langer, Aaron Littman, Jim Pfander, Seana Shiffrin, Clyde Spillenger, Adam Winkler, and most of all Laura Kalman. Thanks to David McBride and Alexcee Bechthold for turning a manuscript into a book.

Introduction

Will abortion be legal? Should people of the same sex be allowed to marry? May colleges prefer black applicants over white ones? These are among the most bitterly contested issues in the United States. We answer these questions, and many more like them, by presenting them to nine lawyers, the justices of the Supreme Court of the United States.

The US Supreme Court was the most powerful court in the world when it was established in the late 1700s. Until recently, it had no competitors for the title. (The Court has not lost any of its power, but lately a few other countries have established similarly powerful high courts based in part on the American model.) The Court "is justly regarded by all lawyers as the most august tribunal upon earth," one popular magazine explained more than a century ago. Or as the constitutional scholar Alexander Bickel put it in the mid-twentieth century, the Supreme Court "is the most extraordinarily powerful court of law the world has ever known."[1] This book is about how the Court acquired so much power, how it has retained its power in the face of repeated challenges, whether it has been as powerful in practice as in theory, and what it has done with its power over the years.

Along the way, I hope the book will also offer some useful perspective on today's arguments about the Court. The Court is often in the news. Its decisions are regularly criticized or praised. But these debates sometimes rest, implicitly or explicitly, on dubious ideas about the Court's history.

For instance, many people discuss the Court as if in the past the justices confined themselves to technical legal questions and only recently ventured into deciding contentious "political" issues. This book is an extended demonstration of the contrary. At all times, the Court's docket has included many obscure cases raising technical questions of little interest to most people, but it has also included a smaller number of high-profile cases involving issues that a great many people cared deeply about. We have always presented controversial political questions to the Supreme Court.

The farther we go back in the past, however, the harder this can be to see. Part of the difficulty is that politically controversial cases made up a smaller percentage of the Court's docket before the twentieth century, when the Court gained the discretion to decline to hear most of the cases presented to it. But probably more important is that many of the most hotly contested political issues of the past are no longer divisive today. They look like dry legal questions to us. To pick one famous example, in *McCulloch v. Maryland* (1819) the Court decided that Congress had the authority to establish a national bank and that the states could not tax it. Today these may seem like drearily technical issues. The law students who study the Court's opinion in *McCulloch* in their introductory course on constitutional law may wonder why anyone would care. But people did care, a lot, and not just lawyers. The case was a focus of intense political controversy. It mattered to people in 1819, just like the Court's cases on abortion and same-sex marriage mattered to people two centuries later. One of the tasks of this book will be to reconstruct the political atmosphere surrounding the Court's most famous cases so that modern readers can appreciate what all the fuss was about.

Today, critics on the left accuse the justices of deciding cases on political rather than legal grounds. This book shows that the Court's critics have *always* leveled this criticism at decisions they did not like. These attacks have usually come from the left because the Court has usually been a conservative institution. In the mid-twentieth century, the one brief period in which the justices were more progressive than the center of American politics, the attacks came from the right. But they have been the same critiques for a very long time.

Another common misunderstanding about the Court is that justices were once chosen based on merit, but that now they are chosen for political reasons. Again, this book will demonstrate the contrary. Justices have always been selected for a mix of reasons. "Merit," or a person's stature within the legal profession, has always been an important criterion and it still is today (although, as we will see, conventional ideas about what counts as merit have changed over time). Most lawyers are not, and never have been, plausible candidates to become justices. But presidents have always sought to nominate, and senators have always tried to confirm, justices who will decide cases in accordance with the presidents' and senators' policy preferences. And personal characteristics have always been part of the mix as well. "Diversity," for instance, has always been an important consideration in choosing justices. The specific *kind* of diversity people care about has changed a great deal over the years, so different sorts of people have become justices in different eras, but there was never a time when justices were appointed without regard to their politics or their demographics.

In these respects, the Court has changed much less than is commonly believed.

In other respects, by contrast, the Court has changed much more. Today the justices live year-round in Washington and work in an imposing building across the street from the Capitol. For much of the Court's history, however, the Court had no building of its own, because the justices were not full-time residents of Washington. They spent most of the year traveling around the country conducting trials. Today the Court decides only a tiny fraction of the cases that arrive at its door and the justices usually write multiple lengthy opinions in each case. For much of its history, however, the Court had to decide every case that was appealed to it, so cases were normally decided in short, unanimous opinions. Today the Senate confirmation of a justice is a public process resembling an election campaign that lasts several months and includes televised hearings. For much of the Court's history, however, the Senate confirmed or rejected justices behind closed doors in a matter of days. In many ways, the Court of today looks nothing like the Court of the past.

To foreground these themes, this book emphasizes long-run developments in the Court's history—things about the Court that have changed, or not changed, over the centuries. For just about any of the current Court's attributes, a few questions come immediately to mind. Was it always like this? If not, what was it like before? How and why did it change? These are the kinds of questions this book tries to answer.

For this reason, this book is organized differently from most histories of the Supreme Court. Most books about the Court's history consist almost entirely of summaries of the Court's decisions.[2] This book certainly discusses the Court's decisions, but it covers much more than that. It is also a history of the Court itself—a history of the sorts of people who become justices and the methods by which they are chosen, a history of the Court's physical environment, a history of how the Court does its work, and a history of the relationship between the Court and other parts of the government. The Court's importance lies in its decisions, but one cannot fully understand the decisions without knowing about the institution that produced them. It would be like trying to understand the behavior of a car without a sense of what is happening under the hood.[3]

A second difference is that this book proceeds thematically rather than in strict chronological order. Most books about the Supreme Court are organized by chief justice—a chapter on the Marshall Court, a chapter on the Taney Court, and so on, right up to the current chief justice.[4] This organization would make sense if the chief justice had the power to change the Court's direction like each new president changes the policies and style of the executive branch. But the analogy between a chief justice and a president is a very poor one. As chief justices themselves have lamented, the chief justice has some administrative responsibilities but no more authority than any other member of the Court. "The extent of the power of the Chief Justice is vastly misconceived," Chief Justice Salmon Chase complained in 1868. "In the Supreme Court he is but one of eight Judges"—there were only eight at the time—"each of whom has the same powers as himself. His judgment has no more weight, and his vote no more importance, than those of any other of his brethren." Harlan Fiske Stone, the chief justice in the 1940s, had previously been the dean of Columbia Law School, another job with a prestigious title but no authority over one's colleagues. Stone joked that "the Chief Justice is a good deal like the dean of a law school, who does the various things that the janitor doesn't do."[5] The Court changes a bit with each new justice, but the change is no greater with a new *chief* justice than with any other.

Indeed, some of the personnel changes with the greatest effects have involved justices who were *not* the chief justice, so labeling periods by chief justice can be quite misleading. For instance, the "Warren Court" is conventionally said to be the entity responsible for the liberal law-changing decisions of the mid-twentieth century, while the "Burger Court" is said to be its more conservative successor. But Burger, not Warren, was the chief justice for some of the most famous of these liberal decisions, including *Roe v. Wade* and *Furman v. Georgia*. Likewise, the Court changed direction dramatically in the late 1930s, but the change had little to do with Charles Evans Hughes, who remained chief justice throughout. Another problem with periodizing by chief justice is that the dividing lines sometimes fall inconveniently in places that only obscure our understanding of the Court's history. For example, the transition from Roger Taney to Salmon Chase occurred right in the middle of the Civil War. If we want to get a sense of the role the Court played in the war, it is more useful to do that directly, without dividing the discussion between the two chief justiceships.

Finally, this book focuses on *understanding* the Supreme Court rather than on praising or criticizing it.[6] In many histories of the Court, authors evaluate the Court's work as if they were a super-Supreme Court—the court of history, perhaps—charged with determining whether the justices decided cases correctly or incorrectly. This has always seemed to me to be a pointless exercise, one in which justices are depicted as cardboard heroes or villains based primarily on whether they anticipated changes in conventional thought that took place after they died. Readers learn more about the author and the author's own times than about the Court. This book has no heroes or villains. Instead of judging the Court, I try to help the reader see the cases through the justices' eyes. For example, rather than critiquing *Dred Scott v. Sandford* as wrong, this book tries to understand why it seemed right to most of the justices in the 1850s, even though it looks abhorrent to most readers today. Rather than praising *Brown v. Board of Education* as right, this book tries to understand why it was so difficult for the Court to reach the decision it did and why so many prominent lawyers of the era considered it wrong, even though it seems obviously correct to most people today.

Before we begin, I should say a word about my own experiences of the Court, which have influenced my perspective in some ways of which I am aware and doubtless others of which I am not. Early in my career I worked at the Court for one year as a law clerk for Justice Sandra Day O'Connor. I have since been a lawyer in several cases before the Court. As a law professor, I have taught courses about the Court. One could count these experiences as an advantage to someone writing a history of the Court, just as we might give more credence to a history of music written by a musician than to one written by someone who had never played an instrument. On the other hand, experience working at the Court could be counted as a disadvantage, because it could produce a loss of critical perspective. Some of the justices themselves have written histories of the Court, and while no one knows the Court from the inside better than a justice, readers of these books might be skeptical about their authors' objectivity.[7] Even participating in cases as a lawyer might introduce bias. One of the classic books about the Court, Charles Warren's three-volume *The Supreme Court in United States History*, won the Pulitzer Prize in 1923, but it suffers from the attachment Warren evidently developed for the Court during his years as assistant attorney general, when he argued many cases before it.[8] I hope I have escaped these traps, but if I have not, I would of course be the last to know.

1

Establishing the Court

When Alexis de Tocqueville toured the United States in the 1830s, he was astonished at how much authority Americans gave their Supreme Court. "A more imposing judicial power was never constituted by any people," he marveled. "The Supreme Court is placed at the head of all known tribunals." The key difference between the Supreme Court and its European analogues, Tocqueville explained, was that European courts only decided disputes between individuals, while the Supreme Court also decided disputes between individuals and their government, and sometimes even disputes between governments. "When the clerk of the court advances on the steps of the tribunal, and simply says 'The State of New York *versus* the State of Ohio,' it is impossible not to feel that the court which he addresses is no ordinary body," Tocqueville noted. "The peace, the prosperity, and the very existence of the Union are vested in the hands of the seven judges."[1] This was the most powerful court in the world.

The justices themselves were acutely aware of the Court's unprecedented power. "The predicament in which this court stands in relation to the nation at large, is full of perplexities and embarrassments," Joseph Story acknowledged in 1819. "It is called to decide on causes between citizens of different states, between a state and its citizens, and between different states. It stands, therefore in the midst of jealousies and rivalries of conflicting parties, with the most momentous interests confided to its care."[2] The justices were merely a small group of unelected lawyers, yet they were strong enough to set aside state and federal statutes, the ultimate outputs of the democratic process, by holding them unconstitutional. They could issue orders to states and to the other branches of the federal government. No country had ever given its judges so much authority.

I

During the debates over the new Constitution, one thing everyone agreed on was the need for a Supreme Court. "The propriety of having a Supreme

Court in every government, must be obvious to every man of reflection," explained James Iredell, who would himself become one of the Court's first justices. Each of the states already had its own high court, but without a national Supreme Court, Iredell worried, "there might be otherwise as many different adjudications on the same subject, as there are states." Alexander Hamilton agreed that "thirteen independent courts of final jurisdiction over the same causes, arising upon the same laws, is a hydra in government, from which nothing but contradiction and confusion can proceed." In the previous decade, under the Articles of Confederation, the national government had lacked a Supreme Court, and indeed any courts at all except for one that only heard cases involving the capture of enemy ships. The absence of a Supreme Court was one of the primary "defects of the confederation," Hamilton observed. "All nations have found it necessary to establish one court paramount to the rest."[3]

A Supreme Court would be particularly useful in the new United States to decide lawsuits between residents of different states, who might doubt whether they would be treated fairly in their opponents' home courts. It was also needed to resolve disputes between the states themselves, disputes which had already arisen over state boundaries. For these reasons, even the Constitution's opponents recognized the need for a Supreme Court. The pseudonymous "Federal Farmer" urged New Yorkers to reject the proposed Constitution, but "I confess, I see some good things in it," he conceded, one of which was the establishment of a Supreme Court. He acknowledged that "there ought in every government to be one court, in which all great questions in law shall finally meet and be determined." At the Constitutional Convention, the creation of a Supreme Court was therefore one of the rare measures that garnered unanimous approval.[4]

But if the idea of a Supreme Court was uncontroversial, nearly everything else about the Court was the subject of vigorous debate. Drafting the Constitution required making some important decisions about what the new Court would be like.

For example, would the Supreme Court sit atop a system of lower federal courts, or would it be the only federal court? Both views received considerable support at the Constitutional Convention. John Rutledge, who would be one of the Court's initial justices, argued that the existing state courts could handle all the nation's litigation, and that a Supreme Court was needed only to hear appeals from the highest state courts to provide uniformity in case the state courts should disagree. Roger Sherman added that a system of lower federal courts would be expensive and duplicative of the state courts. On the other side of the debate, James Madison insisted that lower federal courts were necessary to resolve disputes between residents of different states. If one litigant's home state courts were biased, he pointed out, an appeal to the national Supreme Court would be a poor remedy. Either the Supreme Court would have to send the case back to the state courts for a new trial, which would be just as biased as the first one, or the Supreme Court would have to conduct the trial itself, which would require the litigants to bring their witnesses and evidence to the national capital, at great distance and expense. James Wilson, who would be one of the first justices, suggested that lower federal courts were needed at the very least to handle admiralty cases (that is, cases involving shipping), which involved disputes that arose at sea and so might not be within the jurisdiction of any of the individual states. The Constitutional Convention never reached agreement on this issue. Instead, the Constitution kicked the can down the road, by establishing a Supreme Court and "such inferior courts as the Congress may from time to time ordain and establish." Congress would establish lower federal courts at the first opportunity, but it remains true today that the Supreme Court is the only court required by the Constitution. Congress can abolish the lower federal courts at any time.[5]

Another point of controversy involved how the justices of the new Supreme Court would be selected. Some suggested that they should be chosen by Congress, while others favored letting the president choose the justices. Benjamin Franklin even jokingly suggested a third method, which he claimed was used in Scotland, "in which the nomination proceeded from the Lawyers, who always selected the ablest of the profession in order to get rid of him, and share his practice (among themselves)."[6] In the end, the Convention compromised on the method still used today, in which justices and lower federal judges are nominated by the president but must be approved by the Senate. They would "hold their Offices during good Behaviour," removable only by Senate impeachment.

And what kinds of cases would the Court decide? At the time, state high courts spent much of their time conducting trials, unlike today, when they specialize in hearing appeals from the decisions of lower courts. Should the new Supreme Court likewise be primarily a trial court? One common concern was that if the Court conducted trials, it would be inaccessible to all but the wealthiest Americans and those who happened to live near the national capital, because it would be so expensive and time-consuming for litigants and witnesses to travel to the Court, by horse or by boat, from much of the country. A citizen might have a case in the Supreme Court, Luther Martin scoffed, "in which case the citizen must give up his cause, or he must attend to it at the distance of perhaps more than a thousand miles from the place of his residence." Even if he won the case, Martin noted, his victory "must be attended with a *loss of time*, a *neglect of business*, and an *expence* which will be *greater* than the *original grievance*, and *to which* men in *moderate* circumstances would be *utterly unequal.*" How could a typical resident of Maine or Georgia, not to mention the distant western frontier, be expected to litigate in a court so far away? "The trouble and expence to the parties would be endless and intolerable," worried "Brutus," one of the leading antifederalists. Only the well-heeled would have access to the Supreme Court, "and therefore the poorer and middling class of citizens will be under the necessity of submitting to the demands of the rich and the lordly."[7]

One possible solution to this problem was to have the Court move around the country rather than sitting in one place. The state high courts already used this strategy; they rode a circuit, holding court in towns throughout the state. Judges in England did the same. Roger Sherman suggested that the new national Supreme Court could likewise "have a circuit to make trials as convenient, and as little expensive as possible to the parties." But how could the Court complete a national circuit in such a large country? "It is well known that the supreme courts of the different states, at stated times in every year, go round the different counties of their respective states to try issues of fact, which is called *riding the circuits,*" one critic noted. "Now, how is it possible that the supreme continental court, which we will suppose to consist at most of five or six judges, can travel at least twice in every year, through the different counties of America, from New-Hampshire to Kentuckey, and from Kentuckey to Georgia"?[8] The United States was simply too big to bring the Court to the people.

A more promising solution was to focus the Court's caseload on appeals.[9] An appeal might require *lawyers* to appear in the Court, but it would not require the litigants themselves to travel to the Court, nor would it require witnesses or evidence to make the journey. The Convention adopted this strategy. The Constitution gave the Supreme Court "original Jurisdiction"— jurisdiction as a trial court—over only two small sets of cases. One set encompassed the cases that were most likely to implicate foreign policy, those involving "Ambassadors" and "other public Ministers and Consuls." The other set were cases in which a state was a party. These were the cases where there was the greatest reason to worry about the neutrality of any court, state or federal, located in that state. Otherwise, the Supreme Court would be an appellate court.

Rather than defining the scope of the Court's appellate jurisdiction, the Constitution left the task to Congress, by giving the Court "appellate Jurisdiction, both as to Law and Fact, with such Exceptions, and under such Regulations as the Congress shall make."[10] As a result, Congress has the power to reduce or possibly even eliminate the Court's appellate jurisdiction, but not its much smaller original jurisdiction. This congressional power would prove to be important in later years, because it gives members of Congress a club with which to threaten the Court when they don't like the outcomes of cases.

The mention of "Law and Fact" in this last clause—"appellate jurisdiction, both as to Law and Fact"—created a new controversy when the Constitution was up for ratification. It suggested that the Supreme Court would have the power to overturn factual findings made by juries in lower courts, which resurrected the concern that litigants would have to travel to the national capital to present evidence to the Court. And if the Court could second-guess the findings of juries, the right to a jury trial would be much less valuable than before. "What benefit would be received in the suit by having a jury trial in the court below, when the verdict is set aside in the Supreme Court?" wondered Samuel Spencer in North Carolina's ratifying convention. He accused the Constitution's drafters of intending "that the trial by jury should be suppressed." Supporters of the Constitution denied any such nefarious intention. The Court's power to review "Fact," Alexander Hamilton insisted, was meant to apply only to cases decided without a jury, such as admiralty cases.[11] Nevertheless, this threat to the cherished right of trial by jury remained such a concern after the Constitution was ratified that it prompted the enactment of the Seventh Amendment, which specifies that "no fact tried by a jury shall be otherwise re-examined in any Court of the United States."

The Supreme Court would thus be primarily an appellate court that reviewed issues of law rather than questions of fact, and the Court itself would stay put in the national capital rather than traveling throughout the country. But the justices themselves would be on the move. When Congress established the lower federal courts in 1789, it set up a three-tier structure. The Supreme Court was on top. On the bottom were district courts, staffed by one judge in each state (and one judge each for Maine and Kentucky, which were not yet states). The district courts conducted trials in admiralty cases and in minor civil and criminal cases. The middle level of this three-tier system was occupied by the circuit courts. There were three, one for each region of the country, north, middle, and south. The circuit courts heard appeals from the district courts and were also the primary trial courts in the federal system, with the power to hear the most important civil and criminal cases. But there were no separate circuit judges. Rather, the circuit court in each state consisted of two Supreme Court justices and the district judge for that state. The justices would thus spend a considerable portion of their time riding around their circuits, conducting trials and hearing appeals as circuit judges, rather than sitting in the national capital as the Supreme Court.[12]

This plan of double duty had some points in its favor. It was less expensive than staffing the circuit courts with separate judges. It ensured that the justices would stay in touch with the legal community, and to some extent the wider populace, all over the country. One of the critiques of the Constitution had been that Supreme Court justices would be isolated in the national capital. As one Massachusetts critic feared, "the remote Peasants of Massachusetts" would be bound by the Court's decisions without ever getting to see the justices in person.[13] This concern would be assuaged somewhat if the justices spent part of the year holding trials throughout the country.

On the other hand, the plan had some obvious downsides. It required the justices to follow a grueling travel schedule, especially the justices assigned to the southern circuit, where the distances were the greatest and the roads were in the worst condition. While the Judiciary Act was still under consideration in Congress, Edmund Pendleton, the chief justice of Virginia's highest court, already worried that the justices would be unable to overcome "the fatigue of the Circuits." The plan also required the justices, while sitting on the Supreme Court, to hear appeals from cases in which they had already sat as circuit judges. Was it realistic to expect that they would approach the cases with an open mind and possibly even reverse their own decisions? One Boston editorialist insisted that it was not realistic, and that cases would arrive at the Court with two of the justices already committed to a position, which rendered an appeal nearly pointless.[14] Despite these objections, for decades to come the justices would split their time between the Supreme Court and the circuit courts.

The justices' role as circuit judges set their initial number at six—two for each of the three circuits. Today the most striking thing about this figure is that it is an even number. Multi-judge courts today normally have an odd number of judges, to avoid the possibility of a tie vote. In the late eighteenth century, an even number was hardly the norm, but it was not unheard of. Many American lawyers were familiar with law practice in England, and indeed some had been English lawyers themselves. The main courts in England had four judges each. For this reason, an even-numbered Court did not seem as strange at the time as it would today. The problem of tie votes was just as real then as now. Lawyers did not think the law yielded clear answers in every case. They expected judges to disagree sometimes. "There are endless diversities in the opinions of men," Hamilton observed. "We often see not only different courts, but the Judges of the same court differing from each other."[15] But in a judicial system with two justices per circuit, the Supreme Court required an even number of justices.

At the time, the primary criticism of a six-justice Court was not that the number was even but that it was too small. The Massachusetts lawyer Theophilus Parsons, the state's future chief justice, thought "6 Judges will not be enough." John Adams agreed. So did Francis Dana, another future Massachusetts chief justice, who urged an increase to nine justices. "The number of supreme Judges is too small, to make head against eleven state-judiciaries, always disposed to warfare," complained Edmund Randolph, who would shortly become the country's first attorney general. (There were only eleven states at the time, because North Carolina and Rhode Island had not yet ratified the Constitution.) "Nine or perhaps eleven would not transgress the limits of oeconomy too far," Randolph suggested, "and would give an opportunity of gratifying each state with a supreme as well as a district judge." In the Senate, Oliver Ellsworth "rose and made a most elaborate harrangue, on the necessity of a numerous bench of Judges," William Maclay noted in his diary. Ellsworth "enlarged on the importance of the Causes that would come before them, of the dignity it was necessary to Support," and concluded that twelve justices would be an appropriate number. Maclay himself thought six would be too few if the justices had to ride circuit along with performing their Supreme Court duties, but that six would be too many if the justices could be relieved of circuit riding.[16] Despite such critiques, the Court would begin with six justices.

The justices' circuit court responsibilities also influenced the criteria by which justices were chosen. Each justice would have to spend a significant part of the year traveling through one part of the country. The justices would have to be familiar with the state laws in their region, because state law would provide the governing rules in many of the trials before them. It was important, therefore, for a justice to be a resident of the circuit (to ease the travel burden) and to have had some experience practicing law in the circuit.

In selecting the first six justices, George Washington was careful to pick lawyers from six different states, evenly distributed among the three circuits. From the circuit encompassing the northern states, Washington chose John Jay of New York, who became the chief justice, and William Cushing of Massachusetts. Jay had held several positions in the pre-Constitution national government, including secretary of foreign affairs in the late 1780s. Cushing was the chief justice of the Massachusetts Supreme Court. From the middle circuit, Washington chose James Wilson of Pennsylvania and John Blair of Virginia. Wilson was a prominent lawyer who had been a member of the Continental Congress and the Constitutional Convention. Blair had been a Virginia judge since shortly after independence. From the southern circuit, Washington chose John Rutledge of South Carolina and James Iredell of North Carolina. Rutledge was the former governor of his state. Iredell had been a judge and the state attorney general. All six had held public office in their home states, several as judges.[17] All six had supported the new Constitution during the ratification debates. All were within the loose community of shared political views that would soon coalesce as the Federalist party.

For as long as circuit riding remained part of a justice's job duties, this geographic distribution would be an important criterion in the selection of justices. Some geographic balance would likely have existed even without circuit riding, simply as a matter of political prudence, to ensure that no region felt excluded from the Court. But circuit riding made geography a nearly absolute rule. "It has become almost the common law of the land, and is generally expected, that the judge selected should be a resident citizen of the Circuit for which he is appointed," President James Polk reflected in 1846. "No departure from this rule has ever occurred, except in one or two instances, and in them has given great dissatisfaction."[18] When a justice from New England, for example, died or retired, it was understood that his replacement would likewise be from New England, someone who was known to the local bar and who could claim some familiarity with local law.

The new Supreme Court opened for business on February 1, 1790, at the Royal Exchange Building in New York, the temporary national capital. Only three of the six justices were present—Jay, Cushing, and Wilson, the three closest to New York—but this was no hindrance because there were not yet any cases on the Court's docket. When Blair arrived the next day, making a

The Old Royal Exchange Building
Formerly located at the foot of Broad Street in New York City. Sessions of the U.S. Supreme
Court were held here in 1790.
From a rare old drawing in the Emmett Collection now in the New York City Public Library.

Figure 1.1 The Royal Exchange Building in New York was the Court's home in 1790, before the national capital moved to Philadelphia and then Washington. National Archives, 30-N-40-38.

quorum, the Court began swearing in lawyers as members of the Court's bar. The courtroom was "uncommonly crouded" with lawyers eager to see the justices in action and to become bar members, a local newspaper reported. As the Georgia congressman Abraham Baldwin explained, "there is little business but to organize themselves and let folks look on and see they are ready to work."[19] The US Supreme Court was underway.

II

The Supreme Court's power is at its peak when it declares statutes unconstitutional. The Court has exercised this power of "judicial review" in its most famous cases, such as *Brown v. Board of Education* and *Roe v. Wade.* Judicial review can seem profoundly undemocratic, because it allows the justices, a small group of unelected lawyers, to nullify statutes enacted by the people's elected representatives.

How did the Court acquire the power of judicial review? The conventional answer used to be that judicial review did not exist until the Court created it in the famous 1803 case of *Marbury v. Madison*. Although lawyers and historians still sometimes retell this story, recent scholarship has demonstrated that it is incorrect. The Court had the power of judicial review from the very beginning.[20]

State courts already exercised the power of judicial review before the Constitution was drafted. In the 1780s, there were several cases in which state courts refused to enforce statutes on the ground that they were contrary to state constitutions. For example, the New Jersey Supreme Court held unconstitutional a statute providing for a jury of six, because the state constitution required juries of twelve. The North Carolina Supreme Court refused to enforce a statute forfeiting a Loyalist's land because the statute was contrary to the state constitution's protection of property. Because the constitution was "the fundamental law of the land," the court explained, the statute must "stand as abrogated and without any effect." Similar cases were decided in New Hampshire, Connecticut, New York, and Virginia.[21]

At the Constitutional Convention and in the state ratifying conventions, there was thus no debate over whether the new Supreme Court would have the power to declare statutes unconstitutional. Supporters and opponents of the Constitution both assumed that it would, just like the state courts did.[22] For supporters, judicial review was one of the main points in the Court's favor. For opponents, it was a reason to worry that the Court would grow too powerful.

The Constitution's supporters cited judicial review as a reason to vote for ratification. There was no need to fear that Congress would grow too strong at the states' expense, argued the Maryland judge Alexander Contee Hanson. If Congress purported to exceed the scope of the powers it was granted in the Constitution, "every judge in the union, whether of federal or state appointment (and some persons would say every jury) will have a right to reject any act, handed to him as a law, which he may conceive repugnant to the constitution." At the North Carolina ratifying convention, John Steele insisted that "if the Congress make laws inconsistent with the Constitution, independent Judges will not uphold them." Alexander Hamilton, who had been a lawyer in one of the state judicial review cases a few years earlier, provided a thorough discussion of judicial review in *Federalist* 78. Under the new Constitution, he explained, "the courts were designed to be an intermediate body between the people and the legislature, in order, among other things, to keep the latter within the limits assigned to their authority." If Congress enacted a statute that conflicted with the Constitution, "that which has the superior obligation and validity ought of course to be preferred; or in other words, the constitution ought to be preferred to the statute."[23]

On the other side of the debate, the Constitution's opponents cited the Court's power of judicial review as a grave danger, because with the authority to declare statutes void, the Court would become the most powerful part of the government, and with life tenure, the justices would be unaccountable to anyone. The antifederalist Brutus worried that "this power in the judicial, will enable them to mould the government, into almost any shape they please." The Court would dominate the other two branches of the federal government. "The supreme court under this constitution would be exalted above all other power in the government," he predicted, "and subject to no controul." And there was nothing anyone could do about it. "There is no power above them that can correct their errors or controul their decisions," Brutus worried. "The adjudications of this court are final and irreversible." The justices could not even be "removed from office or suffer a diminution of their salaries, for any error in judgement or want of capacity." Brutus provided an ominous assessment of the new Supreme Court: "I question whether the world ever saw, in any period of it, a court of justice invested with such immense powers, and yet placed in a situation so little responsible."[24]

Supporters of the Constitution argued that such concerns were overblown. The Court was, if anything, too *weak*, insisted the Massachusetts lawyer James Sullivan, because the justices could be removed by impeachment if Congress did not like their decisions. Were that to occur, Sullivan worried, "they may be removed by one branch of the Legislative power, and their Seats filled with men who will Act in consort with the other powers of the State." If that should happen, he asked, "where is the Counterpoise which is so much talked of?" Hamilton responded to Brutus's essays by describing the judiciary as the "least dangerous" branch of the government, in that "it may truly be said to have neither FORCE nor WILL, but merely judgment; and must ultimately depend upon the aid of the executive arm even for the efficacy of its judgments."[25] Both sides of this debate over the Court's expected power assumed that the Court would be able to declare statutes unconstitutional and thus unenforceable. They simply drew different conclusions from this premise.

In the Court's first decade the justices exercised the power of judicial review several times. The first occasion was in 1792, when the justices refused to comply with a federal statute requiring them to determine whether disabled veterans of the Revolution were entitled to pensions.

The early federal government employed so few people that Congress repeatedly assigned to federal judges tasks that in later years would be performed by executive branch personnel. For example, when the crew of a ship thought the ship was unsafe, they could ask a judge to hire inspectors "skilful in maritime affairs" to examine the ship and determine whether it needed to be repaired. When a person was fined for a customs violation he claimed was inadvertent, he could ask a judge to gather the facts and transmit them to the secretary of the treasury, who had the authority to reduce or remit the fine.[26] Tasks like these would be classified today as administrative rather than judicial, but in the early republic they were often performed by judges because the federal government lacked other officials to perform them.

The justices drew the line, however, when Congress added to this list of nonjudicial functions that of deciding whether disabled veterans were entitled to pensions. A circuit court was to examine the veteran, determine the severity of his injury, and recommend to the secretary of war the amount that should be paid as a pension. The secretary of war would make the actual decision, which was in turn subject to review by Congress.[27]

The justices, in their capacity as circuit judges, all objected to this scheme. In the Eastern Circuit, John Jay and William Cushing determined that the task the circuit courts had been assigned was not properly judicial because it was subject to review by the other two branches of government. To avoid holding the scheme unconstitutional, they interpreted it to assign the task not to the circuit *court* but to the circuit *judges* in their individual capacities, as commissioners appointed specially to review pension applications rather than as judges. Explaining that they considered themselves "at liberty to accept or decline that Office," they accepted it. In the Middle Circuit, James Wilson and John Blair refused to consider the applications of any veterans on the ground that the statute was unconstitutional. A court's judgments could not be "revised and controuled" by Congress or by an executive officer, they insisted in a letter to President Washington. "Such revision and controul we deemed radically inconsistent with the Independence of that judicial power, which is vested in the Courts." In the Southern Circuit, James Iredell took the same view, which he likewise expressed in a letter to Washington explaining why he would not entertain any applications from veterans.[28]

The following year, Congress amended the pension scheme by relieving the circuit courts of the obligation to evaluate veterans' claims and instead authorizing the district judges to appoint commissioners for that purpose. The result was a system much like the ones already used for administrative tasks like assessing the seaworthiness of ships. The fault the justices found with the original pension scheme was not that it required judges to make decisions outside the frame of ordinary litigation—judges were often called upon to make such decisions in the early republic—but rather that the scheme subjected courts' decisions to the review of the other branches of government. In time, this principle would become an important element of the constitutional doctrine of separation of powers.[29] In 1792, it marked the first occasion for the justices to hold a statute unconstitutional.

Justice William Paterson provided another early statement of judicial review in a jury charge he delivered in 1795 while sitting as a circuit judge. "If a legislative act oppugns a constitutional principle," Paterson instructed the jury, "the former must give way, and be rejected on the score of repugnance. I hold it to be a position equally clear and sound, that, in such case, it will be the duty of the Court to adhere to the Constitution, and to declare the act null and void."[30]

The following year, in *Ware v. Hylton* (1796), the justices wielded the power of judicial review for the first time while sitting as the Supreme Court. The treaty ending the American Revolution included a clause that prohibited both sides from impeding the recovery of debts owed by debtors in one country to creditors in the other. The main beneficiaries of this provision were British creditors, who used the new federal courts to seek repayment from American debtors. In Virginia, debtors defending against these suits invoked state statutes enacted during the war that shielded American debtors from having to pay. One of these suits was filed by John Tyndale Ware, the administrator of a deceased British creditor, against the Richmond merchant Daniel Hylton. When Ware's case reached the Supreme Court, Justice James Iredell called it "the greatest Cause which ever came before a Judicial Court in the World," because, as the congressman Jeremiah Smith observed, "property to an immense amount depends upon the decision & the national Honour & faith are supposed to be involved."[31] But if the Court's decision was of great commercial importance, no one involved in the case, neither the lawyers nor the justices, expressed any doubt about the Court's power of judicial review. The Constitution's Supremacy Clause provides that treaties take precedence over state statutes. The Court held that Virginia's statutes protecting debtors were void because they conflicted with the treaty.

Nearly simultaneously, in *Hylton v. United States* (1796), the Court first reviewed the constitutionality of a federal statute.[32] *Hylton* was a constitutional challenge to a federal tax on carriages. The Constitution requires "direct taxes" to be apportioned among the states according to their populations. The challenger was once again Daniel Hylton, who refused to pay the carriage tax on the ground that it was a direct tax that violated the apportionment requirement. The Court upheld the tax. The justices unanimously held that it was not a direct tax and so did not need to be apportioned. Neither side in the case questioned the Court's power to declare federal statutes unconstitutional. Both sides assumed that if the carriage tax were a direct tax, the Court could properly find it invalid.

The justices had the same assumption. When *Hylton v. United States* was being argued in the circuit court the previous year, the government's lawyer began discussing the power of courts to declare statutes unconstitutional, but Justice James Wilson assured him that it was unnecessary to address the topic, because "it has come before each of the judges in their different circuits, and they have all concurred in opinion." At the Supreme Court, the newly appointed Samuel Chase, who had not yet had confronted any cases involving judicial review, was the only justice who even raised the issue. "As I do not think the tax on carriages is a direct tax," Chase explained, "it is unnecessary, at this time, for me to determine, whether this court, constitutionally possesses the power to declare an act of Congress void, on the ground of its being made contrary to, and in violation of, the Constitution." But Chase would soon overcome this uncertainty about the judicial review of federal statutes, and at the time his hesitancy does not appear to have been widely shared. The congressman and future treasury secretary Albert Gallatin noted in a discussion of the case published soon afterward that "one of the most important consequences, flowing from the principle of a Constitution binding the different branches of government, has been in some instances, not a limitation of the powers of government, but a transfer of those powers from the legislative to the judiciary department." As the Court's decision in *Hylton* demonstrated to Gallatin, "the judges have exercised in all doubtful cases the authority to explain the Constitution, as they explain the laws, and to decide, even in cases of taxation, whether a law was constitutional or not, valid or a dead letter." Chase himself acknowledged in 1800 that "it is, indeed, a general opinion . . . that the Supreme Court can declare an act of congress to be unconstitutional, and, therefore, invalid."[33]

The Court again assumed that it had the power of judicial review in *Calder v. Bull* (1798), in which a Connecticut statute with the effect of overruling a court decision was challenged as contrary to the Constitution's Ex Post Facto Clause. The Court decided that the statute was not unconstitutional, but everyone proceeded on the assumption that the statute would have been invalid if it were. "The sole enquiry," Chase explained, was whether the Connecticut statute "is an ex post facto law, within the prohibition of the Federal Constitution."[34]

By 1803, when the Court decided *Marbury v. Madison*, there was thus nothing new or controversial about judicial review. American courts had been invalidating legislation as unconstitutional for many years. In the debates over the Constitution, both sides had assumed that the new federal courts, including the Supreme Court, would continue to do so. And the Supreme Court assessed the constitutionality of legislation on a few occasions in the 1790s. But *Marbury* would be the first case in which the Court actually used the power of judicial review to strike down a federal statute.

Marbury was also the first case in which the Court discussed judicial review at any length. "Certainly all those who have framed written constitutions contemplate them as forming the fundamental and paramount law of the nation, and consequently the theory of every such government must be, that an act of the legislature, repugnant to the constitution, is void," Chief Justice John Marshall explained. Marshall famously concluded: "It is emphatically the province and duty of the judicial department to say what the law is." Because "the constitution is superior to any ordinary act of the legislature; the constitution, and not such ordinary act, must govern the case to which they both apply."[35]

This thorough defense of judicial review no doubt accounts for much of *Marbury*'s enduring celebrity. Marshall's ringing declaration of the power of the judiciary has been studied by generations of law students, unlike the Court's judicial review cases of the 1790s, which are not well known to lawyers, or the earlier lower court cases, which are even more obscure. It is perhaps understandable that lawyers would become accustomed to thinking of *Marbury* as the origin of judicial review.

At its creation, then, the Supreme Court was handed a great deal of power. It could resolve disputes between states. It could decide cases pitting individuals against the government. It could even declare statutes unconstitutional. Why did Americans create such a powerful Court?

One reason was the new nation's federal structure. Most countries had one national government that was superior to any local authorities, but the United States was organized differently. The national government would exist side-by-side with the thirteen state governments that were already in place. The new country thus had fourteen different governments—the number would soon grow rapidly—none of which were subordinate to any of the others. It was obvious that disputes would arise regarding the limits of each government's authority. "The erection of a new government, whatever care or wisdom may distinguish the work, cannot fail to originate questions of intricacy and nicety," Hamilton observed, "and these may in a particular manner be expected to flow from the establishment of a constitution founded upon the total or partial incorporation of a number of distinct sovereignties."[36] Deciding these intricate questions would be the job of the Supreme Court. Most countries did not need such a powerful court, because most countries had but a single sovereign. A country with fourteen or more sovereigns needed a different kind of court. As we will see, most of the Court's important early cases were precisely of the kind that Hamilton predicted. They were disputes involving the boundary between state and federal power.

A second reason for creating such a powerful court, apart from the problem of multiple sovereigns, was that the Constitution included all sorts of anti-democratic features that needed enforcing. One primary purpose of the Constitution was to serve as a counterweight to democracy.[37] Events of the preceding decade had persuaded many elite Americans of the dangers of populism. State legislatures had enacted statutes shielding debtors from their creditors. They had issued paper currencies that quickly lost much of their value. The year before the Constitutional Convention, in the sequence of events that came to be called Shays's Rebellion, armed mobs in western Massachusetts had succeeded in shutting down the courts to prevent them from seizing debtors' property. One big reason for drafting a Constitution was to prevent such things from happening again.

The Constitution therefore included several anti-democratic features. The Electoral College, as originally conceived, ensured that the president would not be chosen by a public vote. Senators were to be chosen by state legislatures, not by the people. And the Constitution included long lists of things the states and the federal government were not allowed to do. But these paper limits on state and federal authority would be meaningless without some means of enforcement. If a state legislature undertook to relieve debtors, for example, there had to be an institution that could step in and order the state to stop. The Supreme Court was that institution. From the beginning, therefore, the Court was empowered to adjudicate disputes involving governments and to hold statutes unconstitutional. These were powers that no other country gave its courts.

III

On paper, the Supreme Court had a vast authority. But in practice, would anyone listen to it? When the Court ruled against a state, what would happen? When the Court ruled against the president or against Congress, would they obey?

Judicial *review* was established from the beginning, but not judicial *supremacy*, the view that the Court is the final authority on the meaning of the law. That view would be constantly contested in subsequent years, as presidents, members of Congress, and state governments would claim a co-equal power to interpret the Constitution and a corresponding right to refuse to follow Supreme Court decisions with which they disagreed. The Court would never go unchallenged as a constitutional interpreter.[38] This was especially true in the Court's early years, when it had to navigate some difficult challenges to its authority.

The first of these challenges involved suits against states. The states had gone heavily into debt during the Revolution and the succeeding years. To pay these debts was politically tricky for state elected officials, because it would require raising taxes on state residents, who were voters, and sending the money to creditors, who were typically nonresidents and often foreigners. Creditors knew they would face an unfriendly forum if they tried collecting their debts by filing suits against states in the states' own courts. But they had an alternative. The Constitution gave the federal courts jurisdiction over suits "between a State and Citizens of another State," and it gave the Supreme Court original jurisdiction over cases in which a state is a party. Creditors thus turned to the Supreme Court. Several of the Court's first cases were suits filed by people who were owed money by state governments.

The Court's very first case, *Van Staphorst v. Maryland*, was filed by two Dutch bankers, Jacob and Nicolaas van Staphorst. Maryland had borrowed a considerable sum from the van Staphorsts in 1782. The parties argued over the terms of repayment for several years. When the Supreme Court was established, the van Staphorsts promptly used it to sue the state. The dispute was soon settled, so the Court never had the chance to decide it. Another of these early cases, *Oswald v. New York*, was filed by the Philadelphia-based administrator of the estate of John Holt, the late New York state printer, whose salary the state had failed to pay for the last few years of his life. The Court held a jury trial and the jury awarded damages to Holt's estate, which the state eventually paid.[39]

Lurking behind these cases was a politically sensitive question: What would happen if a state refused to acknowledge the Court's authority? The Court was able to avoid the issue in *Van Staphorst* because the case settled, and in *Oswald* because New York, after some hesitation, complied with the Court's judgment. But the Court soon had to confront the question, in what would become the most famous of its early cases, *Chisholm v. Georgia* (1793).

Chisholm involved another debt owed by a state government. In 1777, the South Carolina merchant Robert Farquhar sold a variety of goods to the state of Georgia. Farquhar was never paid. He spent several years trying to collect the debt. When he died, the task fell to his executor, another South Carolina merchant named Alexander Chisholm. The creation of the federal courts gave Chisholm a new forum in which to seek repayment. He filed a lawsuit against Georgia in the Supreme Court.[40]

The government of Georgia was alarmed. Before the case was even argued, the state House of Representatives resolved that the federal courts lacked any power over a state government, and that "the state of Georgia will not be bound by any decree or judgment" issued by the Supreme Court. If the state were to submit to the Court's authority, the Georgia House worried, the state would be drawn into "numberless law-suits" that would "perplex the citizens of Georgia with perpetual taxes." The state refused to send a lawyer to the Supreme Court to represent it. In Philadelphia (then the national capital), "the Great Georgia Question" was the talk of the day, one congressman reported. "If Judgment is rendered against the State, I fear it will much disturb the Publick mind."[41]

The legal question in *Chisholm* pitted a literal interpretation of the constitutional text against a widespread sense among lawyers that the true meaning of the Constitution was something other than what the text seemed to say. The Constitution gave the federal courts jurisdiction over controversies "between a State and Citizens of another State." *Chisholm* was literally that: it was a dispute between Georgia and a citizen of South Carolina. If one read the Constitution literally, the Court clearly had jurisdiction. But many lawyers were certain that the Constitution could not possibly require this outcome, because it was such a dramatic change from prior Anglo-American practice, under which a sovereign could not be sued without its consent. Edmund Pendleton, the Virginia judge, expressed a common view: "I have been taught by all writers on the Subject," he explained, "that there is no Earthly Tribunal before whom Sovereign & independent Nations can be called & compelled to do justice, either to another Nation at large or its individual Citizens." Pendleton concluded that the Constitution's grant of jurisdiction over disputes between states and citizens of other states was intended to include only cases in which states sued individuals, but not cases in which individuals sued states.[42]

A "numerous and respectable audience" came to the Court to hear the justices announce their opinions. There were only five justices, because Thomas Johnson had recently quit and had not yet been replaced. Four of the five decided that the Court had jurisdiction. Each delivered his own opinion, as was the practice at the time. John Blair and William Cushing relied primarily on the literal words of the Constitution. "When a citizen makes a demand against a State," Cushing reasoned, "it is as really a controversy between a State and a citizen of another State, as if such State made a demand against such citizen. The case, then, seems clearly to fall within the letter of the Constitution." John Jay and James Wilson reached the same result by taking a more philosophical view. Jay argued that a sovereign's immunity from suit, even if established in England, should have no place in the legal system of the United States. "Sovereignties in Europe, and particularly in England, exist on feudal principles," he observed. "That system considers the Prince as the sovereign, and the people as his subjects; it regards his person as the object of allegiance, and excludes the idea of his being on an equal footing with a subject, either in a Court of Justice or elsewhere." But matters were different in the United States, where "the sovereignty devolved on the people; and they are truly the sovereigns of the country." Only James Iredell sided with Georgia. Before the Constitution existed, he pointed out, there had been no way to force a state government into court. "Nothing but express words" in the Constitution, "or an insurmountable implication" from them, "would authorise the deduction of so high a power." Iredell did not think the Constitution was clear enough to change the traditional rule.[43]

The Court's decision in *Chisholm* was extraordinarily unpopular. "This decision is pretty generally reprobated here by Gentlemen of the first information," Senator William Few reported from Philadelphia. From North

Carolina, Iredell's brother-in-law informed him that his dissenting opinion "is universally applauded." A New York newspaper asked a pointed question of Chief Justice Jay: What was the Court "to do with the state of Georgia, if (groaning under an Indian war) she should prove insolvent? Send the legislature to gaol?" The Massachusetts legislature resolved that the Court's decision "is inconsistent with the sovereignty which is essential to all Governments." William Cushing's opinion may even have cost him the state's 1794 gubernatorial election. "Judge Cushing might have been chosen by a considerable majority," a member of the state House reflected, "but for his opinion on the suability of States."[44]

Within a short time, several state legislatures called for a constitutional amendment to undo the Court's decision in *Chisholm*. The proposed amendment sailed through both houses of Congress in early 1794 and was ratified by the necessary number of states by early 1795, a pace that suggests just how unpopular the Court's decision was. The Eleventh Amendment provides, in language that precisely contradicts the holding of *Chisholm*: "The Judicial power of the United States shall not be construed to extend to any suit in law or equity, commenced or prosecuted against one of the United States by Citizens of another State, or by Citizens or Subjects of any Foreign State."[45] The Court's first high-profile case had created a storm of protest and a swift rebuke from Congress and the states.

More controversy followed soon after. As political parties coalesced in the 1790s, the Court was drawn into the vicious partisanship that characterized the era.[46] In 1795, Chief Justice John Jay returned from England after negotiating a treaty with Britain. Jay was nearly simultaneously elected governor of New York. When Jay resigned from the Court, President George Washington nominated John Rutledge to take his place. Rutledge had been one of the original six justices in 1790, but he had left the Court the following year to return to South Carolina to become the state's chief judge.

The Jay Treaty quickly became the subject of fierce debate between the two emerging political parties—the Federalists, who supported it, and the party that would soon become known as the Republicans, who believed that Jay had conceded too much to Britain. At a public anti-treaty meeting in Charleston, Rutledge gave a passionate speech in which he denounced the treaty as "a surrender of our rights and privileges." It is unclear whether Rutledge had learned of his nomination to be chief justice when he gave this speech, because the news from Philadelphia may not yet have reached him in South Carolina. The speech caused the Federalists, who held a majority in the Senate, to rally against Rutledge. The Connecticut Congressman Chauncey Goodrich reported that "many of the warmest advocates for the present measures [i.e., the Jay Treaty] are hurt by Mr. Rutledge's appointment, and are difficulted to account for it." Rumors were already circulating that Rutledge was sliding into mental illness, and some Federalists saw Rutledge's speech as evidence that this was so. Secretary of State Edmund Randolph told Washington that "the conduct of the intended Chief Justice is so extraordinary, that [Oliver] Wolcott and [Timothy] Pickering conceive it to be a proof of the imputation of insanity." Attorney General William Bradford predicted that "the crazy speech of Mr. Rutledge joined to certain information that he is daily sinking into debility of mind & body" would "prevent him [from] receiving the appointment." Opponents of the Jay Treaty responded by defending Rutledge in the press. "The late attack upon Judge Rutledge," one paper insisted, "is more licentious than any thing which the pen of faction has yet produced."[47]

The Senate was in recess when Rutledge was appointed as chief justice, so he took his seat as a recess appointment for a few months. When the Senate reconvened, Rutledge's nomination was defeated. The vote correlated almost perfectly with the earlier Senate vote on the Jay Treaty. Every senator who opposed Rutledge had voted in favor of the treaty, and every senator but one who supported Rutledge had voted against the treaty. Rutledge does appear to have been suffering from mental illness, as suggested by his unsuccessful suicide attempt soon after the Senate vote. But the vote indicated that party politics drove the Senate's refusal to confirm Rutledge as chief justice. "I hope that Chief Justices at least will learn from this to be cautious how they go to popular Meetings," John Adams chortled. The Congressman Jeremiah Smith blamed Rutledge's rejection on his speech in opposition to the treaty, which Smith called "a speech which would have disgraced the lips of an Idiot." Robert Livingston, a New York judge, was more sympathetic. He noted that many of the same senators who voted against Rutledge this time had voted in his favor back in 1790, when Washington first appointed him to the Court. "I am sorry for the mortification Rutledge will feel in being made the sport of a party," Livingston sighed. Thomas Jefferson similarly complained that Rutledge's opponents in the Senate "cannot pretend any objection to him but his disapprobation of the treaty. It is of course a declaration that they will receive none but tories hereafter into any department of the government." As one Republican newspaper put it, the Senate's rejection of Rutledge "appears an unparalleld instance of party spirit."[48]

Figure 1.2 John Rutledge, painted by John Trumbull in approximately 1791, a few years before his nomination as chief justice became a casualty of the period's emerging partisan politics. National Portrait Gallery, Smithsonian Institution, NPG.97.190.

Party spirit swirled around the Court even more strongly a few years later. The justices' circuit-riding responsibilities were such a burden that in 1800, Justices William Paterson and Bushrod Washington met with members of Congress and proposed a bill to appoint full-time circuit judges, which would allow the justices to focus on their Supreme Court cases. This proposal was joined with other reforms to the lower federal courts in a package of changes that Congress debated through 1800 and early 1801.[49]

The appointment of circuit judges took on a new meaning, however, after the election of 1800, when the Federalist party led by incumbent President John Adams lost control of the presidency and both houses of Congress to the Republican party led by Thomas Jefferson. The Federalists suddenly had an urgent reason to create the new circuit judgeships quickly, so the positions could be filled by Federalists before Jefferson and the new Congress took office in March 1801. The result was the Judiciary Act of 1801, enacted in February. It divided the country into six circuits, staffed by sixteen circuit judges. Two weeks later, Congress also created several new positions for lower court judges in the District of Columbia. Adams and the lame-duck Federalist Senate promptly filled the sixteen seats in the circuit courts and the additional spots in the lower courts with Federalist judges.[50] For good measure, the Judiciary Act also reduced the size of the Supreme Court from six justices to five. The smaller number may have been justifiable in light of the justices' reduced responsibilities, and one fewer justice partially offset the cost of the sixteen new circuit judges. But a smaller Court would also prevent President Jefferson from appointing a new justice when the first vacancy of his administration occurred.

Jefferson and the Republicans were outraged by the appointment of these "midnight judges." They were already opposed to strengthening the federal judiciary at the expense of the state courts, so the addition of so many new federal judges would have rankled under any circumstances, but the way it was done seemed like a purely partisan maneuver. The Federalist Party "has retired into the judiciary in a strong body where it lives on the treasury & therefore cannot be starved out," James Monroe fumed the day before Jefferson's inauguration. "While in possession of that ground it can check the popular current which runs against them." Jefferson agreed that the Federalists "have retired into the Judiciary as a strong hold." He feared that "from that battery all the works of republicanism are to be beaten down & erased." The Federalists had "multiplied useless judges merely to strengthen their phalanx." The Kentucky Representative John Fowler called the Judiciary Act "a law very extraordinary in its origin," which had "placed the courts of law in the hands of the vanquished" Federalists.[51]

Once Jefferson and the Republican Congress took control, they repealed the Judiciary Act of 1801. The new circuit courts ceased to exist, the new circuit judges lost their jobs, the old circuit courts staffed by traveling justices were reinstated, and the Supreme Court once more had six justices. Now the Federalists were upset, but because they were outnumbered in Congress, their only hope of redress was in the courts. They argued that the repeal of the Judiciary Act of 1801 was unconstitutional, for two reasons: first, because the new circuit judges had life tenure and so could not be deprived of their positions unless they were impeached for committing misconduct; and second, because Congress lacked the authority to require the Supreme Court justices to serve as circuit judges. The Republicans in Congress, worried that the Court would agree with these arguments, quickly enacted a statute that cancelled the Court's 1802 session. The Court would not be able to consider the constitutionality of the repeal until 1803. In the interim, the justices made the difficult decision, after much deliberation, to resume their circuit duties, despite the still-lingering question of the constitutionality of the repeal.[52]

In *Stuart v. Laird*, decided in early 1803, the Court indirectly upheld the constitutionality of the repeal. In a very short opinion delivered by William Paterson, the Court held that Congress has the authority to transfer a case from one court to another, which was what the repeal had accomplished—it had transferred cases from the new circuit courts, staffed by full-time circuit judges, to the reinstated old circuit courts. As for the constitutionality of requiring the justices to ride circuit, the Court briefly explained that the practice had been acquiesced in for several years, ever since the organization of the federal judiciary, and that this was enough to defeat the claim that it was contrary to the Constitution. The Court never directly addressed the Federalists' argument that Congress may not abolish the position of a life-tenured judge, but the Court's clear implication was that Congress may do so.[53]

A week before *Stuart*, the Court decided a much more famous case arising from the same clash of political parties—*Marbury v. Madison*. William Marbury was one of the "midnight judges" who had been appointed to a five-year term as justice of the peace for the District of Columbia, one of the offices created by the Federalists in 1801. Marbury's judgeship had not been abolished by the Republicans in 1802. Rather, in the rush to fill all the new judgeships before John Adams's term as president expired, the Federalists had simply run out of time before they could complete their paperwork. They failed to deliver a commission—the document signifying an office-holder's authority—to some of the new justices of the peace, including Marbury. The Jefferson administration refused to recognize the appointments of the justices of the peace who had not received commissions. The "Madison" in the case's name was James Madison, the secretary of state, whom Marbury sued to receive his belated commission. It was Madison's predecessor as secretary of state—John Marshall, now the chief justice—who had failed to deliver the commission before the expiration of the Adams administration.[54]

In a lengthy opinion by Marshall, the Court held that William Marbury had a legal right to take his office as justice of the peace, and that the Jefferson administration had acted wrongly by not delivering his commission, but that the Court lacked jurisdiction to hear Marbury's case and so could not order Madison to deliver the commission. Marbury had filed his suit directly in the Supreme Court, invoking the Court's original jurisdiction. He relied on the provision of the Judiciary Act of 1789 that authorized the Court to issue writs of mandamus—orders to government officials to perform their duties. The Court held that this provision was unconstitutional. The Constitution gave the Court original jurisdiction only in certain defined circumstances, none of which included Marbury's suit against Madison. The Court concluded that Congress could not expand the Court's original jurisdiction past the boundaries delineated in the Constitution.

As we have seen, today *Marbury* is most famous for the final section of the Court's opinion, in which Marshall sought to justify the power of judicial review. In its own day, however, commentators gave scarcely any notice to this passage, which merely explicated the familiar concept that statutes inconsistent with the Constitution could not be enforced. Contemporaries paid more attention to the Court's implicit criticism of Jefferson for acting unlawfully in failing to deliver Marbury's commission. At the time, the most important thing about *Marbury* was not its discussion of judicial review but rather the way it avoided creating an opportunity for Jefferson to challenge the Court's authority. Had the Court ordered the Jefferson administration to deliver commissions to Marbury and the other midnight judges, Jefferson might well have refused. A few years earlier, Jefferson had authored the Kentucky Resolution in opposition to the Alien and Sedition Acts, in which he asserted that each state had "an equal right to judge for itself" what the Constitution required. A few years later, in discussing *Marbury*, Jefferson took the same view of the three branches of the federal government. "Each department is truly independent of the others," he insisted, "and has an equal right to decide for itself what is the meaning of the constitution."[55] If the Court in *Marbury* had ordered Jefferson to deliver the commissions, and if Jefferson had refused, there was little the Court could have done to enforce its decision. The Jefferson administration would probably have prevailed in the confrontation. Marshall's opinion allowed the Court to assert its authority over the president in the abstract without actually imposing that authority in practice.

The political controversies over *Chisholm v. Georgia* and the Judiciary Act of 1801 were not of the justices' own making. In *Chisholm*, the Court interpreted the Constitution in a literal but unpopular way, while the Judiciary Act and its subsequent repeal were the products of political polarization in Congress, not among the justices. But the most serious political controversy that engulfed the Court in its early years was brought on by the justices themselves.

When the justices were traveling around the country as circuit judges, one of their routine tasks was to instruct grand juries on the law. From the beginning, the justices used these grand jury charges as occasions to give lectures about the new Constitution and the new federal government. John Jay, for instance, explained to grand juries throughout the Eastern Circuit how the three branches of government served as checks on one another. "These Remarks may not appear very pertinent to the present occasion," he acknowledged, "yet it will be readily admitted, that occasions of promoting good will, and good Temper, and the Progress of useful Truths among our Fellow Citizens should not be omitted." James Wilson was in the habit of summarizing the entirety of federal criminal law in grand jury charges that must have lasted for hours. "I offer no apology, gentlemen, for the nature or the length of this address," he remarked at the close of one jury charge. "The criminal laws of the United States, are now first formed. They only begin to be diffused over the wide-spreading regions, for which they are designed. In this situation, in which I have the honor to be placed, I deem it my duty to embrace every proper opportunity of disseminating the knowledge of them *far* and *speedily*." After all, Wilson asked, "can this be done with more propriety than in an address to a Grand Jury[?]"[56]

The justices had a captive audience when they instructed grand juries, so a grand jury charge was a unique opportunity to evangelize on behalf of the new government. The Constitution had only just been ratified, and by a slim margin at that, so popular loyalty to the United States could not be taken for granted. Often the justices provided the text of their grand jury charges to newspapers, which spread the message even more broadly. After discoursing on "the fundamental principles of this government," James Iredell paused to reflect on why he had spoken about much more than the specific cases the grand jury would be considering. "I have troubled you with these observations, Gentlemen, because it is of great importance that the principles of this constitution should be clearly understood, and the more they are so the more highly in general, I am persuaded, it will be approved." Jay urged the necessity of supporting the federal government with taxes, which, he insisted, were nothing like the odious taxes that had been imposed by Britain before the Revolution. "Let it be remembered that this Revenue is the People's Revenue," Jay declared. "The Government it is to support, is the People's Government."[57]

In the mid-1790s, however, these grand jury charges began to take a partisan turn. The immediate impetus was the violent Whiskey Rebellion in western Pennsylvania against the federal excise tax on liquor. Some of the justices, evidently alarmed, began to use their grand jury charges—in cases that had nothing to do with the rebellion—to praise the Washington administration and to criticize its opponents. William Cushing told a grand jury of Rhode Islanders that the Pennsylvania rebels had committed treason and lauded "the unceasing vigilance and severe attention of our chief magistrate," George Washington, who had, for a time, personally led the troops that crushed the rebellion. In Delaware, John Blair instructed a grand jury that "the root of the evil" was "a spirit, which in various parts of the Union has been too much encouraged," a spirit "incompatible with order, and temperate provisions of regular government." Blair spent so much time criticizing the rebels that he forgot to instruct the grand jury on the law relating to the cases it would be considering. As he acknowledged sheepishly, "I have been so absorbed, Gentlemen, by a subject of this magnitude, as to have little room for notice of other subjects." He simply urged the jurors to "pay a proper attention to the whole system of Congressional Legislation" and sent them off to work.[58]

Even when the Whiskey Rebellion subsided, the justices, who were all associated with the incumbent Federalists, continued to take potshots at the Republicans in their jury instructions. These charges regularly drew return fire from the Republican press. When Oliver Ellsworth deplored "the baneful influence of those elements of disorganization, & tenets of impiety, which have been propagated with a zeal that would have done honor to a better cause," it was clear enough to whom he was referring. The Republican *Argus* struck back. "What clause of the constitution gives the federal judiciary cognizance respecting religious tenets?" the *Argus* asked. It was not "fitting at any season, for a Chief Justice of the United States to join the hue and cry of a party." When James Iredell instructed a grand jury not to let "abandoned men . . . disturb the order of society by their crimes," the Republican *Aurora* had a ready reply. It had become "a regular practice of the federal judges, to make political discourses to the grand jurors throughout the United States," the *Aurora* observed. "They have become a band of political preachers, instead of a sage body to administer the law." As another paper put it, in response to another of Iredell's politically inflected charges, "while judges administer the law, they answer the end of their appointment. But when they are degraded into the engines of an executive, they deviate widely from what their duty should prescribe." Iredell and his colleagues had turned their grand jury charges into "merely a political invective, calculated to irritate and inflame." The paper cautioned that a judge "should neither approve the tenets of one party, nor inveigh against the principles of another. He should neither commend the wisdom of an administration, nor mark the virulence of its opponents. Above all, he should be very vigilant, lest he impresses on the public mind that he fosters in his own bosom all the acrimony of a partizan."[59]

The justices' partisan grand jury charges took on an even sharper edge after the enactment of the Sedition Act in 1798, which made criticism of the Adams administration a criminal offense. "We have heard the government as grossly abused as if it had been guilty of the vilest tyranny," Iredell complained to a grand jury in Philadelphia. The Republican press in turn stepped up its criticism of the justices. Iredell "enters into political disquisitions, advances opinions extraneous to his functions, and exhibits himself a disciple of party," the *Aurora* argued. "Can justice be fairly dispensed by a Judge, who permits the sensations of party to intrude themselves upon him?" But Iredell was hardly alone in turning grand jury charges into political speeches. "There are few men in this country of genuine republican principles who have not been disgusted with the charges which are commonly given to juries by the judges of our federal courts," the *Aurora* declared. "Instead of confining themselves to an illustration of the law, applying it to those cases on which the jury are to decide, which is all that the duty requires; we find them often spinning out a charge to an enormous length, in defence of some favorite measure of the government, with which the *jury*, as such, have no more concern than they have with the edicts of the Grand Turk." And when the court proceedings were over, "these charges are afterwards published in all the papers of a certain stamp, and cried up by the devotees of faction, as master pieces of human wisdom." The paper concluded with a note of resignation: "Thus it is that the bench is perverted into an engine of party."[60]

The most partisan justice of all was Samuel Chase. Appointed to the Court in 1796 after a long career as a legislator and a judge in Maryland, Chase was an easily angered man who made enemies everywhere he went. "I have no personal acquaintance with Mr. Chase," the former senator Samuel Johnston remarked to Iredell shortly after Chase's appointment, "but am not impressed with a very favorable opinion of his moral Character whatever his professional Abilities may be."[61] Once on the Court, Chase continued to stir up controversy. He gave campaign speeches for John Adams in the summer of 1800. He presided over the celebrated 1799 treason trial of John Fries in such a partisan manner that Fries's defense attorneys quit in disgust. A similar episode took place the following year at the sedition trial of the pamphleteer James Callender, when Chase refused to let the sole defense witness testify and chastised the defense lawyers so constantly that they refused to continue. In another case, when a grand jury declined to indict a Delaware newspaper publisher for sedition, Chase refused to discharge the grand jurors until they changed their minds. In a widely reproduced grand jury charge in Baltimore in 1803, Chase fulminated against Jefferson and the Republicans. "Our Republican Constitution will sink into a mobocracy," he declared. "Peace and order, freedom and property, shall be destroyed." The Republicans finally had enough. In 1804 the House of Representatives, which was more than 70% Republican, voted to impeach Chase.

Chase's trial in the Senate was a sensation. As one contemporary magazine put it, "no event of a domestick nature has, since the adoption of the federal constitution, excited in the United States a more universal interest, than the impeachment of Judge Chase." The trial took place in early 1805, while the Court was in session. Because the Supreme Court still shared the Capitol with Congress, Chase walked back and forth between the two chambers, a justice in one room and a defendant in the other.[62] The Republicans held more than two-thirds of the seats in the Senate, so a party-line vote would have been enough to convict Chase, but several Republicans voted not guilty, so Chase was acquitted.

The Federalists breathed a sigh of relief, because the successful impeachment of Chase might well have led to more impeachments of Federalist justices. "The acquittal of Judge Chase is considered by the federalists here, as a matter of great triumph," Justice William Paterson's son reported to him from New York. "It was the opinion of some of them, that you would have been the next victim, to the intolerance and persecution of the dominant party."[63] The trial had a sobering effect on Chase himself, who uncharacteristically stayed out of controversy for the rest of his career. It had a similar effect on the other justices, who likewise toned down the partisanship of their jury charges. The episode also had an effect on Congress, in that Samuel Chase remains the only Supreme Court justice ever to be impeached. In the two centuries since, members of Congress have often been displeased with the justices, but, except in a few instances, Congress has used methods other than impeachment to try to bring them into line. All concerned seem to have

Figure 1.3 Samuel Chase, the only Supreme Court justice ever to have been impeached, was acquitted by the Senate in 1805. This portrait was painted by John Wesley Jarvis in 1811, the year Chase died. National Portrait Gallery, Smithsonian Institution, NPG.67.2.

recognized the chaos that would result if the majority party in Congress routinely impeached justices of the other party.

In its first fifteen years, the Court thus weathered some difficult political storms. It emerged a bit less powerful than when it began. The Court lost the jurisdiction to hear suits against state governments. The justices had to acknowledge the power of Congress to reorganize the federal courts, even by abolishing life-tenured judgeships. The Court had to back down halfway in its standoff with the Jefferson administration, by declining to order the administration to seat the judges appointed by Adams, even as it reaffirmed its theoretical authority to issue such an order. The justices were forced to stop delivering partisan jury charges. The Court is sometimes described as having "risen" to power in its earliest years, but it would be more accurate to say that it started with a great deal of power which was then shaved back a little in the early years.

Yet the Court that emerged from these early controversies was still an extraordinary institution, with the most important aspects of its authority intact. It could still declare statutes unconstitutional. It could still resolve disputes involving governments as well as individuals. The Court's power was, of course, hardly unlimited. The justices had to wait for cases to come before them; they could not reach out and decide whatever issues they wanted. The Court could not enforce any of its decisions; it depended on the compliance of the states and the other branches of the federal government, a compliance that could not always be counted on. As Alexis de Tocqueville recognized, however, the Supreme Court of the United States was the most powerful court in the world.

2

Itinerant Judges on a Part-Time Court

Who were the early Court's justices? How were they chosen? What was their work like? In some respects, the Court of the early nineteenth century looked very different from today's Court, while in other respects it looked very similar.

I

Thirty-four people served as Supreme Court justices before the Civil War. All were white men. There would be no nonwhite justice until Thurgood Marshall in 1967 and no female justice until Sandra Day O'Connor in 1981. This uniformity in race and gender was typical of top government positions during the era. There would be no nonwhite members of Congress until after the Civil War and no women in Congress until the early twentieth century. The first nonwhite member of the cabinet took office in 1966 and the first woman in 1933. The demographics of the legal profession were similar. Before the Civil War there were no women lawyers and only a handful of black lawyers.[1] In the nineteenth century there was no realistic possibility of anyone but a white man being appointed to the Supreme Court.

All of the antebellum justices were Christians, but Christianity was not the absolute qualification that race and gender were. Judah Benjamin, a prominent Jewish lawyer from New Orleans who argued several commercial cases in the Court, declined President Millard Fillmore's offer of nomination to the Court in late 1852, because he had just been chosen to represent Louisiana in the Senate.[2] (Eight years later, when Louisiana seceded, Benjamin would resign from the Senate to become the Confederate attorney general.) Apart from Benjamin, however, every other person seriously considered for the Court during this period was Christian. There would not be another Jewish nominee until Louis Brandeis in 1916. To this day, every nominee has been either Christian or Jewish.

Thirty-three of the thirty-four justices were Protestant. The exception was Chief Justice Roger Taney, appointed in 1835, who was Catholic. In an era when there was considerable prejudice against Catholics, Taney's nomination by President Andrew Jackson aroused a great deal of opposition. The *Catholic Telegraph* complained with good reason of "panic invectives against Mr. Taney" and "hackneyed slander against Roman Catholics" in the press. The Protestant religious periodicals were especially egregious. "Roger B. Taney *is a Jesuit*, a member and a sworn supporter of an order founded for political purposes, whose grand aim is to grasp at all the wealth and power in the universe," gasped the *Religious Intelligencer*. "Is it not known that the principles of this order are diametrically opposed to every principle of liberty and justice?"[3] There would not be another Catholic justice until Edward White was appointed in 1894.

The average age of a new justice was forty-eight, a few years younger than the average age of recent appointees.[4] The youngest were Joseph Story and William Johnson, who were both appointed at thirty-two, while the oldest were Thomas Johnson and Gabriel Duvall, who were appointed at fifty-eight. The justices were in office for an average of seventeen years. The shortest-serving was Thomas Johnson, who quit after a few months when he realized that riding circuit was too hard for a fifty-eight-year-old man. The longest-serving included, as one might expect, the justices who had been appointed while still young, including Story and John Marshall, who were both on the Court for thirty-four years (Marshall was appointed at the age of forty-five).

Because justices were expected to come from the circuit to which they would be assigned, the justices were evenly distributed among regions of the country. The thirty-four justices came from sixteen different states, during a period that began with only eleven states and ended with thirty-three. Virginia produced the most justices, but that was only five. New York and Maryland followed with four, and Massachusetts and Pennsylvania had three. As the country expanded westward, so did the Court, with justices appointed from the then-western states of Ohio, Kentucky, Tennessee, and Alabama.

One consequence of the Court's regional balance is that there were always several justices from states with slavery. Of the thirty-four antebellum justices, nineteen came from states where slavery was lawful until the Civil War. To that figure we can add John Jay of New York and William Paterson of New Jersey, who both owned slaves while on the Court, because their home states had not yet abolished slavery. The justices from the southern states were likewise slaveowners, including John Marshall and Roger Taney, who occupied the chief justice's seat from 1801 to 1864. As John Quincy Adams complained in 1842, "from the commencement of this century, upwards of forty years, the office of Chief Justice has always been held by slaveholders."[5] This consistent representation of slaveowners on the Court would have a considerable influence on the Court's decisions.

Twenty-four of the thirty-four justices had been lower court judges at some point in their careers before joining the Court. Most had been judges in the state courts, which is not surprising considering how few lower federal judges there were in the years before the Civil War. More surprising may be the fact that the justices without prior judicial experience were often the ones who were most respected for their ability as judges, including John Marshall and Joseph Story, the Court's intellectual leaders. The lesson may be not that experience is unhelpful, but that as a lawyer one can acquire a vicarious experience in judging without being a judge oneself.

More important than prior judicial experience during this period was prior experience as an elected official. Twenty-eight of the thirty-four antebellum justices held elective office at some point in their careers before joining the Court. Twelve had been members of Congress. Many more held state offices, including three who were former governors—John Rutledge of South Carolina, William Paterson of New Jersey, and Levi Woodbury of New Hampshire. Several also held cabinet positions, including two secretaries of state (Jay and Marshall), two secretaries of the treasury (Taney and Woodbury), two attorneys general (Taney and Nathan Clifford), two secretaries of the Navy (Woodbury and Smith Thompson), and one postmaster general (John McLean). Today, politics and the judiciary tend to be two separate career paths. The last Supreme Court justice with experience as an elected official was Sandra Day O'Connor, who sat in the Arizona state senate from 1969 to 1974. The last appointment of a justice who had previously served in Congress took place in 1949, when Harry Truman appointed his former Senate colleague Sherman Minton. In the early nineteenth century, by contrast, political office was the most common path to the Supreme Court, more common than service as a judge on a lower court.

The fact that justices usually came to the Court from the world of politics meant that nominees were people whose political views were already well known. Nominees were closely affiliated with a political party. They had taken public positions on contested political issues. Unlike today, when the Senate, the press, and the public must infer the political views of nominees from scraps of evidence scattered throughout the nominees' prior lives, the ideologies of nineteenth-century nominees were no secret. Everyone knew what a prospective justice stood for.

For example, when John Marshall died in 1835 and Andrew Jackson nominated Roger Taney to take his place, there was no doubt about Taney's political views. He had spent most of the previous four years in Jackson's cabinet, as attorney general and secretary of the treasury. In the latter position, as a recess appointee, he removed federal deposits from the Bank of the United States and transferred them to state banks, a step so controversial that when the Senate returned from recess it refused to confirm Taney as treasury secretary. Earlier he had been in the Maryland state senate and had served as the state's attorney general. Taney's politics were widely known. "The President will nominate a Democratic Chief Justice—and thus, we hope, give some opportunity for the good old State Rights Doctrines of Virginia of '98–'99 to be heard and weighed on the Federal Bench," the *Richmond Enquirer* predicted. "We believe that Mr. Taney is a strong State-Rights man." It was generally understood that Taney's loyalty to Jackson was the main reason Jackson appointed him as chief justice. Taney "was a sound lawyer of many years practice," remarked Senator Oliver Smith. But "Chief Justice Taney, it was said, received his appointment from Gen. Jackson as a reward for his services in removing the deposits from the Bank of the United States." A New York newspaper agreed that Taney's appointment "was unquestionably given on political consideration."[6]

Because so many justices came to the Court from the world of politics, it was not unusual for justices to think about leaving the Court for a political office. We saw in Chapter 1 that John Jay resigned as chief justice in 1795 to become governor of New York and that William Cushing was a candidate for governor of Massachusetts in 1794. They were not alone. Smith Thompson ran for president in 1824 and for governor of New York in 1828. Levi Woodbury and John McLean were candidates for president in 1848, and then McLean ran again in 1856 and 1860. McLean's biography is appropriately subtitled "A Politician on the United States Supreme Court." "For many years I hoped to have the pleasure to see you in the Presidential Chair," one admirer wrote him toward the end of his career. "That hope I suppose I must now abandon."[7]

When justices came to the Court from political office, they were often on familiar terms with the president, and indeed some had spent many years advising the president. These relationships tended to continue, but only in an informal way. The Court established very early that it would not give the president formal legal counsel. In 1793, President George Washington asked the Court for advice concerning the war between Britain and France. Washington wanted the United States to remain neutral in the war, but a 1778 treaty with France suggested that French ships had to be given certain privileges in American ports. The situation raised legal questions "of considerable difficulty," Secretary of State Thomas Jefferson explained in a letter to the justices. These "questions depend for their solution on the construction of our treaties, on the laws of nature & nations, & on the laws of the land." President Washington "would therefore be much relieved if he found himself free to refer questions of this description to the opinions of the Judges of the supreme court."[8]

At the time it was not clear whether the Court had the power to render advisory opinions—opinions in response to legal questions posed by the president or Congress, as opposed to opinions deciding litigated cases. Some of the state courts had that power, and indeed some still do. In England, the courts had been giving advisory opinions for a long time. But Washington and his cabinet recognized the uncertainty in whether the new federal courts could do likewise. At the constitutional convention, there had been a proposal that "Each Branch of the Legislature, as well as the supreme Executive shall have authority to require the opinions of the supreme Judicial Court upon important questions of law, and upon solemn occasions," but this proposal had been rejected.[9] Jefferson was accordingly careful to ask the justices "whether the public may, with propriety, be availed of their advice on these questions?"

The justices' answer was a firm no. "The Lines of Separation drawn by the Constitution between the three Departments of Government," they explained, "and our being Judges of a court in the last Resort[,] are Considerations which afford strong arguments against the Propriety of our extrajudicially deciding the questions alluded to."[10] The Supreme Court would not give advisory opinions. The Court has held to this view ever since.

But while the Court, as an institution, would not give legal advice to the president, that did not stop individual justices from providing their counsel or even greater assistance. Jay often gave informal advice to Washington about a wide range of matters, including—in one letter alone—Indian policy, the definition of federal crimes, the utility of federally funded post roads, the need for forts in the west, and the importance of securing an adequate supply of timber for ships. In later years, other justices were trusted advisors to presidents. Taney, for instance, was so close to Jackson that he continued advising Jackson even after he became chief justice. President James Polk had a similar relationship with Justice John Catron. The two had been close for years before they became national figures. They had been young Tennessee lawyers involved in state politics at the same time, and they married women from the same family. Catron continued to be one of Polk's confidants when Polk became president. When this kind of informal advice concerned legal matters, it could resemble advisory opinions. In 1822, for example, President James Monroe vetoed a bill to extend the National Road because he believed the Constitution did not authorize the federal government to build roads. In response, Justice William Johnson wrote to Monroe that he and the other justices thought the federal government *did* have the authority to build roads.[11]

When there was a vacancy on the Court, it was generally understood that the president's nominee would be someone within the pool of qualified lawyers with political views matching those of the president's party. Albert Gallatin put it well when Justice Alfred Moore resigned in 1804: Moore's replacement would have to be "a republican & a man of sufficient talents." Two years later, when William Paterson died, Joel Barlow urged Jefferson to replace him with Pierpont Edwards, Connecticut's federal district judge, because the appointment "would be Particularly & highly advantageous to the republican interest in Connecticut, where they stand in great need of as much aid from the government as it is convenient to afford them."[12]

This matter-of-fact focus on the political loyalties of a prospective justice was well illustrated in 1810, when William Cushing, the last of the original justices, announced his intention to retire. Cushing was seventy-eight years old and had been in poor health for some time. The other six justices were evenly divided between the two parties, with three Federalists who had been appointed by Washington or Adams (John Marshall, Samuel Chase, and Bushrod Washington) and three Republicans who had been appointed by Jefferson (William Johnson, Henry Brockholst Livingston, and Thomas Todd). Cushing's departure would give the Republicans a majority on the Court for the first time.

Levi Lincoln, who had been attorney general during Jefferson's first term as president, quickly wrote to President James Madison: "I need not state to you how important it is in the opinion of republicans that his successor should be a gentleman of tried & undeviating attachment to the principles & policy which mark your's [*sic*] and your Predecessor's administration." Cushing died before he could retire. As his obituary put it, "the great Arbiter of events anticipated his intention, and gave him his final discharge." The Republicans rejoiced at this good fortune. "The Judiciary is (I hope) destined to experience a radical Reform," exulted William Claiborne. "Cushing is dead, & in his Successor we may expect to find correct principles." Jefferson agreed that "the death of Cushing is therefore opportune as it gives an opening for at length getting a Republican majority on the supreme bench." He told Madison: "Another circumstance of congratulation is the death of Cushing." For ten years, he complained, the Court had turned itself "into a political body to correct what they deem the errors of the nation." But now "the death of Cushing gives an opportunity of closing the reformation by a successor of unquestionable republican principles."[13]

Cushing was from Massachusetts, so by custom his replacement would likewise have to be from New England. Recommendations concerning a successor poured in, all of which discussed the political views of the person in question. Elbridge Gerry suggested the Boston lawyer George Blake, because of "the pointed opposition of the Anglo-federal party to him, resulting . . . from his firmness & decision on all great republican points & measures." Jefferson suggested appointing Levi Lincoln. "Federalists say that [the Federalist judge Theophilus] Parsons is better," he acknowledged, "but the criticalness of the present nomination puts him out of question." Lincoln was preferable, he advised, because of his "political firmness, & unimpeachable character." Henry Smith urged Madison not to appoint David Howell, the federal district attorney for Rhode Island. "If political fidelity & consistency be considered as qualifications," Smith confided, "this gentleman's pretentions are light indeed," because "he pertinaciously supported all the anti-republican measures of Mr. Adam's [sic] administration." Jefferson expressed a similarly dark view of Joseph Story, the Speaker of the Massachusetts House of Representatives and a former member of Congress. Story was a "pseudo-republican," Jefferson insisted. He was "unquestionably a tory." The Massachusetts Congressman Ezekiel Bacon even assumed that Story would not be a realistic candidate for this reason. Bacon asked Story to support Gideon Granger, the Postmaster General, whose main merit was his loyalty to the Republican party. As Bacon pointedly put it, Granger's claims to a seat on the Court "appear to me in every point of view much stronger than those of any other one in N. England *who would be likely to obtain it.*"[14]

It took Madison four tries to fill the vacancy left by Cushing. He first offered the position to the sixty-one-year-old Levi Lincoln, who turned it down because he was going blind. Lincoln "had determined never again to go out into the bustle of society," his obituary would report a few years later, "and he adhered to his resolution."[15] Madison then nominated Alexander Wolcott, a longtime customs official in Connecticut with no apparent qualifications other than a career of partisanship on behalf of the Republican party. Although the Republicans held an overwhelming majority in the Senate, they refused to confirm Wolcott because he was so clearly unqualified. Madison, seeking to avoid a similar embarrassment, turned to a much more highly regarded New England Republican, John Quincy Adams, who was then serving as ambassador to Russia. The Senate unanimously confirmed Adams—so quickly that word reached Adams only afterward. When he learned about his new job, Adams turned it down, because he had his eye on other positions; he would later become secretary of state and of course president. By this point, more than a year had elapsed since Cushing's death. Madison finally offered the seat to Joseph Story, despite Jefferson's suspicions about him. The Senate confirmed Story a few days later.

As the protracted effort to replace Cushing suggests, having the right political views was necessary to becoming a justice, but not sufficient. One also had to come from the same part of the country as the justice who needed replacing, and one had to have enough intellectual gravity to earn the respect of the relatively small community of leading lawyers and members of Congress. It took some good luck for all three of these requirements to be satisfied at the same time. Some of the most distinguished state court judges of the early Republic never had the opportunity to be placed on the Supreme Court, because the wrong party held the presidency when their turn came around.

Lemuel Shaw, for example, was the highly regarded chief justice of the Massachusetts Supreme Court from 1830 to 1860. But Story occupied New England's seat on the Court from 1812 to 1845, the prime years of Shaw's career. When Story died and the New England seat opened up for the first time in more than thirty years, the Democrat James Polk was the president, and Shaw was a Whig. He received no consideration for Story's seat, which went to the Democratic Senator Levi Woodbury. As New Hampshire's Democratic congressman Edmund Burke observed in urging Polk to nominate Woodbury, the appointment "would be very gratifying to the Democratic party of New England at least, and I believe, of the whole country." The Boston Democrat David Henshaw reminded Polk that as most political appointments "are for but short periods, their influence will be proportionably limited; but the appointment of a Judge is much more important" because of the longer term of office. By the time Woodbury died and the seat opened again, the Whig Millard Fillmore was in office, but now Shaw was seventy years old. The seat went instead to Benjamin Curtis, who was only forty-one. "I am desirous of obtaining as long a lease, and as much moral and judicial power as possible, from this appointment," Fillmore explained. He wanted to appoint a Whig of "a good judicial mind, and such age as gives a prospect of long service."[16]

James Kent of New York, another state judge held in extraordinarily high esteem within the profession, suffered from the same bad timing. Kent was a Federalist and then a Whig, but during the period when Kent was the right age to be put on the Court, a president of the opposing party was in office each time New York's seat opened up. In 1806, Jefferson appointed Henry Brockholst Livingston. When Livingston died in 1823, James Monroe was president. Monroe's attorney general, William Wirt, urged him to overlook party loyalties and appoint Kent. "I know that one of the factions in New York would take it in high dudgeon," Wirt acknowledged. "But Kent holds so lofty a stand every where for almost matchless intellect and learning, as well as for spotless purity and high-minded honor and patriotism, that I firmly believe the nation at large would approve and applaud the appointment." Wirt recognized that his request seemed unrealistic. "I am not so visionary," he assured Monroe, "as to suppose that the thing which is best in the abstract can, in the present state of parties, or perhaps in any state of them which we can hope for under our Government, be always safely and prudently done." But Wirt insisted that the Court "should be set apart and consecrated to talent and virtue, without regard to the shades of political opinion."[17] Monroe ignored Wirt's advice and appointed Smith Thompson, Monroe's secretary of the navy. By the time Thompson died in 1843, Kent was eighty years old.

During this period the Senate acted on nominations to the Court with a speed that would be unimaginable today. When the Senate confirmed a nominee, confirmation typically took place within a few days of nomination. Jefferson's three nominees, for example, were all confirmed within four days or less. Senate confirmation took place so quickly that some nominees learned of their appointment only after they had already been confirmed. This speed was possible because the Senate did not hold public hearings on appointments to the Court. Because the nominees were normally men whose political views were well known, the Senate could simply discuss them in closed session, if at all, and then vote.

The Senate refused to confirm eleven nominees during this period.[18] Eight of the eleven were appointed late in the administration of a president who was of a different party from the Senate majority, when senators could hope that a president of their own party would take office very soon. In December 1828, the lame duck president John Quincy Adams nominated John Crittenden to fill the seat vacated by the death of Robert Trimble, but the Jacksonian majority in the Senate took no action on the nomination, so the vacancy could be filled by Andrew Jackson when he took office in early 1829. In 1844 and 1845, outgoing president John Tyler was so unpopular with the Senate's Whig majority that the Senate refused to confirm four of his nominees. In the closing months of the Fillmore administration in 1852–1853, the Democratic majority in the Senate turned down three of Fillmore's nominees, including one of their own colleagues, the North Carolina senator George Badger. These eight unsuccessful nominations were *all* the nominations made by a president in an election year when the Senate was controlled by the opposing party. By contrast, Senates controlled by the opposing party confirmed all three nominations made by presidents earlier in their terms—Robert Trimble (1826), James Moore Wayne (1835), and Benjamin Curtis (1851).

The remaining three rejected nominees were John Rutledge (1795) and Alexander Wolcott (1811), whose fates we have already seen, and George Woodward (1845–1846), who was nominated by a Democratic president (Polk) but was nevertheless rejected by a Democratic-majority Senate because he was opposed by Simon Cameron, the Democratic senator from Woodward's home state of Pennsylvania, and by James Buchanan, Polk's secretary of state, who was also from Pennsylvania.

The justices sometimes tried to time their retirements to ensure the appointment of a like-minded successor. Of course, this was not always possible. The justices were a group of middle-aged and elderly men in an era when medicine could do little to prolong anyone's life. Like everyone else, they might fall ill or die without much advance notice. After only two years on the Court, for example, Robert Trimble died unexpectedly at the age of fifty-two of what was then called a bilious fever. James Wilson ended a distinguished career by suffering a stroke at fifty-five shortly after his release from debtors' prison, where he was sent when his speculations in land turned out poorly. Even when death or poor health did not come suddenly, the absence of any pension was a powerful reason not to retire. Henry Baldwin, for instance, died penniless in 1844 after fourteen unhappy years on the Court, during most of which he suffered from mental illness. His obituary chari- tably emphasized his pre-judicial career, when, not yet "fevered with the malady which afflicted him some years afterwards, his mental faculties were in the full play of their mature strength."[19] Had Baldwin wished to retire from the Court, he could not have afforded to.

But when justices were fortunate enough to be able to plan their resignations, one factor they considered was the party who would choose their replacements. In the summer of 1831, for instance, John Marshall was nearing his seventy-sixth birthday. His health was failing. He confided to Joseph Story that in deciding when to retire, he was considering the 1832 presidential election. "You know how much importance I attach to the char- acter of the person who is to succeed me," he reminded Story. "Calculate the influence which probabilities on that subject would have on my continuance in office."[20] Marshall's meaning would have been clear to Story. He did not want Andrew Jackson, the incumbent president, to name his replacement, so he would retire only if Jackson were not reelected. As it turned out, Jackson won the 1832 election. Marshall died in office in 1835.

Story himself faced the same decision a few years later. When William Henry Harrison won the 1840 presidential election, Story was sixty-one years old. He had been on the Court for nearly thirty years. According to his son, Story would probably have retired during Harrison's administration, but Harrison died only a month into his term as president. He was succeeded by Vice President John Tyler, "but Mr. Tyler's views and wishes were quite different from those of General Harrison, and from the party by which he was elected," Story's son recalled. To make matters worse, Tyler was reported to have vowed that if he could fill a vacancy on the Court, "no one should be appointed who was of the school of Story." Story hung on until the 1844 elec- tion, when he hoped Henry Clay would be the winner. "If Mr. Clay had been elected," he told a friend soon after, "I had determined to resign my office as Judge, and to give him the appointment of my successor. How sadly I was disappointed by the results of the late election I need not say."[21] From Story's perspective, James Polk, the new president, was little better than Tyler. Like Marshall, Story would die in office before the next presidential election.

Even when justices did not admit to timing their resignations for po- litical reasons, contemporaries often believed that they did. In William Cushing's last years on the Court, Republicans alleged that he was clinging to office, despite "the failure of his powers, lest a Republican should suc- ceed him." Gabriel Duvall was said to have delayed his departure from the Court for several years, despite being so deaf that he could not hear a word of oral argument, until he was assured that Roger Taney would be his replacement.[22]

But if party politics played a role in the selection of justices, so too did that elusive quality called "merit." Each of the major political parties included a great many lawyers, but contemporaries would have considered the vast majority of them unqualified to serve on the Court. One had to have achieved a level of prominence—as a lawyer, a judge, or an elected official, and more likely in two or even all three of these categories—to be in the pool of plausible candidates. The justices appointed before the Civil War were, on the whole, a distinguished group of people.

The early justice who enjoys the highest reputation today is John Marshall, the chief justice from 1801 to 1835. One can get a sense of Marshall's renown simply by reading the titles of some of his recent biographies: "Definer of a Nation." "The Man Who Made the Supreme Court." "The Chief Justice Who Saved the Nation." "The Great Chief Justice." "The Heroic Age of the Supreme Court." Marshall's public image was just as lofty a century ago, when the US Senator-turned-historian Albert Beveridge won the Pulitzer Prize for his fawning four-volume biography of Marshall. "He appears to us as a gigantic figure looming, indistinctly, out of the mists of the past," Beveridge gushed in his first volume. In the preface to volume three, the volume in which Marshall begins serving on the Court, Beveridge extolled his "great Constitutional opinions," which "were nothing less than state papers and of the first rank."[23]

In Marshall's own day his legal skills were held in the same high esteem, although contemporary opinions of his statesmanship, like that of any public figure, could depend on the political party to which one belonged. The Virginia lawyer William Wirt called Marshall "a universal genius," by which he meant that Marshall had "applied a powerful mind to the consideration of a great variety of subjects." Marshall did not *look* impressive, Wirt conceded. He was "tall, meagre, emaciated; his muscles relaxed, and his joints so loosely connected, as not only to disqualify him, apparently, from any vigorous exertion of body, but to destroy every thing like elegance and harmony in his air and movement." But Wirt thought Marshall "deserves to be considered as one of the most eloquent men in the world; if eloquence may be said to consist in the power of seizing the attention with irresistible force, and never permitting it to elude the grasp, until the hearer has received the conviction which the speaker intends." Another admirer was John Adams, the president who appointed Marshall, first as secretary of state and then as chief justice. Shortly before his death, Adams wrote Marshall a letter in which he compared Marshall with four leading English judges of the seventeenth and eighteenth centuries, judges who were then familiar names to American lawyers. "There is no part of my life that I look back upon with more pleasure, than the short time I spent with you," Adams told Marshall. "And it is the pride of my life that I have given to this nation a Chief Justice equal to Coke or Hale, Holt or Mansfield."[24]

Even Thomas Jefferson, who detested Marshall and considered him the very opposite of a statesman, acknowledged Marshall's skill as a judge and a lawyer. Jefferson complained of "the rancorous hatred which Marshal[l] bears to the Government of his country," and "the cunning and sophistry within which he is able to enshroud himself." He accused Marshall of "twistifications in the case of Marbury" and other cases, which "shew how dexterously he can reconcile law to his personal biasses [sic]." But Jefferson could recognize a quality opponent. "When conversing with Marshall, I never admit anything," he told Joseph Story. "So sure as you admit any position to be good, no matter how remote from the conclusion he seeks to establish, you are gone. So great is his sophistry, you must never give him an affirmative answer, or you will be forced to grant his conclusion. Why, if he were to ask me whether it were daylight or not, I'd reply, 'Sir, I don't know, I can't tell.'"[25]

Of course, there were other skilled lawyers of Marshall's era whom no one remembers today. His present-day fame rests in part on his personal qualities, but even more on three facts about his environment. First, and most obviously, Marshall was the chief justice for thirty-four of the Court's first forty-five years. Because the Court decided few cases before he arrived that would prove to be important for later generations, Marshall would eventually be associated with virtually all the Court's foundational cases.

Second, on the primary constitutional issue the Court confronted during Marshall's tenure—the relative powers of the federal government and the states—Marshall tended to side with the federal government, which turned out to be the winning position in the long run. We will look at these cases in the next chapter, but for now it is enough to note that Marshall's opinions in these controversies helped create the vision of the United States that is by and large taken for granted today, according to which the federal government's regulatory power far exceeds that of the states. For most modern readers, Marshall's side of the debate seems the more sensible one, because it is much closer to our world than the state-oriented arguments of his opponents.

Figure 2.1 John Marshall, the chief justice from 1801 to 1835, authored many of the Court's best-known early opinions. This portrait was painted by James Reid Lambdin sometime after 1831. National Portrait Gallery, Smithsonian Institution, NPG.65.54.

Third, and perhaps most important, Marshall joined the Court near the end of an important transition in the way the Court announced its opinions. In the Court's earliest years, the justices followed English practice in announcing their opinions "seriatim." Each justice would express an opinion in each case, even when all the justices agreed on the outcome. After Oliver Ellsworth became chief justice in 1796, the Court gradually adopted the practice it has followed ever since, in which a single opinion, designated as an opinion of the Court, speaks for the majority or all the justices. There were still some seriatim opinions under Ellsworth's leadership, but by 1800 the Court usually issued a single opinion, often delivered by Ellsworth himself. Indeed, in one case that year, when, in Ellsworth's absence, the Court reverted to its earlier seriatim practice, Justice Samuel Chase was caught unprepared. "The Judges agreeing unanimously in their opinion, I presumed that the sense of the Court would have been delivered by the president [that is, the chief justice]," Chase apologized, "and therefore, I have not prepared a formal argument on the occasion."[26]

The practice of speaking with a single voice continued to be the norm after Marshall became chief justice. Under Marshall, in each case the Court typically published just one opinion, designated as the opinion of the Court. Justices who disagreed normally did not publicize their disagreement. They published dissenting opinions only in the cases they considered the most important. As Smith Thompson prefaced one such dissent, "it is with some reluctance, and very considerable diffidence, that I have brought myself publicly to dissent from the opinion of the Court in this case; and did it not involve an important constitutional question relating to the relative powers of the general and State governments, I should silently acquiesce in the judgment of the Court, although my own opinion might not accord with theirs."[27]

A greatly disproportionate number of the Court's opinions were delivered by Marshall himself. During Marshall's tenure, he delivered 547 opinions of the Court. All the other justices combined delivered 574. The skew was greatest before 1811, when Marshall out-opinioned all his colleagues together by 133 to 17. Once Story joined the Court in 1812, the numbers grew less disproportionate, largely because Story himself delivered many of the Court's opinions. But Marshall still had the greatest share, typically between a third and a half of the opinions of the Court each year.[28] There does not appear to be any surviving documentary evidence of the original authorship of most Marshall Court opinions, but this tally is so lopsided that most scholars have concluded that other justices probably wrote some of the opinions that Marshall delivered. Considering the justices' close collaboration during this period (a topic that will be discussed below), the Court's opinions might in any event be best understood as the justices' collective work rather than the output of a single person.

The only justice on the Marshall Court who wrote a significant number of dissents was William Johnson of South Carolina, whose time on the Court, from 1804 to 1834, was nearly coterminous with Marshall's. Our view of the Court's abandonment of seriatim opinions and its practice of normally not publishing dissenting opinions has been heavily influenced by correspondence from the early 1820s between Johnson and Thomas Jefferson, both of whom were fierce political opponents of Marshall. At the time, Jefferson was even more exasperated than usual with Marshall and with the Court.

In the preceding few years, the Court had issued several important opinions buttressing the power of the federal government and restricting that of the states, in cases such as *McCulloch v. Maryland* (1819) and *Cohens v. Virginia* (1821). In a letter to Johnson, Jefferson vented his anger at Marshall for, among other things, the abandonment of seriatim opinions. In Jefferson's view, the Court displayed to the public a false unanimity in the opinions Jefferson so strongly resented. The publication of a single opinion "is certainly convenient, for the lazy the modest & the incompetent," Jefferson complained. "It saves them the trouble of developing their opinion methodically, and even of making up an opinion at all." Jefferson thought the Court should return to the seriatim practice, which "shews whether every judge has taken the trouble of understanding the case, of investigating it minutely, and of forming an opinion for himself instead of pinning it on anothers sleeve."[29]

Johnson enthusiastically agreed. He recalled that "while I was on our State-bench I was accustomed to deliver my seriatim Opinions in our appellate Court." When he was appointed to the US Supreme Court, however, he was "surprised to find our Chief Justice in the Supreme Court delivering all the Opinions in Cases in which he sat, even, in some Instances when contrary to his own Judgment & vote." Johnson was told that this was because "he is willing to take the Trouble, & it is a Mark of Respect to him. I soon however found out the real Cause." In truth, Johnson told Jefferson, it was a sign of the weakness of the other justices: "Cushing was incompetent, Chase could not be thought to think or write—Patterson [*sic*] was a slow man & willingly declined the Trouble, & the other two Judges you know are commonly estimated as one Judge." (This last comment was a dig at Bushrod Washington, who tended to vote the same way as Marshall.) When Johnson published his first dissenting opinion, he recalled, "during the rest of the Session I heard nothing but Lectures on the Indecency of Judges cutting at each other." He stopped publishing dissents for a while. Eventually "I got them to adopt the Course they now pursue, which is to appoint some one to deliver the Opinion of the Majority, but leave it to the Discretion of the rest of the Judges to record their Opinions or not." Johnson explained that he would be happy to return to seriatim opinions "if it would compel incompetent Men to quit the Bench," but he feared that the only result would be that the more enterprising justices would ghost-write opinions for the others: "Others would write their Opinions merely to command their Votes."[30]

Jefferson returned to this theme a few months later. "The very idea of cooking up opinions in Conclave begets suspicion that something passes which fears the public ear," he worried. By making the Court look bad, the single-opinion practice might "produce at some time abridgement of tenure, facility of removal, or some other modification" to the Court's independence. If each justice would instead declare "his opinion seriatim and publicly," the public would be able to see that "he uses his own judgement independently and unbiassed [*sic*] by party views, and personal favor or disfavor."[31]

Historians have sometimes followed Jefferson and Johnson in crediting (or blaming, depending on one's view) John Marshall for causing the Court to switch from announcing seriatim opinions to issuing a single opinion for the Court. But in Jefferson and Johnson's eagerness to criticize Marshall, they overstated Marshall's role in changing the Court's practice. The Court had gone most of the way toward abandoning seriatim opinions before Marshall became chief justice. And the custom of not publishing separate opinions was probably not due to any browbeating by Marshall. He had no authority over the other justices, all of whom had life tenure just like he did. If they had wanted to write separately, they could have, with no negative consequences. Nor was it likely due to the incompetence of the other justices, who were all accomplished lawyers before they joined the Court. As justices they were older men, but the quality of their work could hardly have dropped off so quickly. Marshall's colleagues, other than Johnson, must have agreed with him that the Court should speak with a single voice and that the voice should normally be Marshall's.

The Court's published opinions are its only visible output. When we look back at the Marshall Court's cases, we see a great many opinions under Marshall's name and much fewer under the name of anyone else. It is easy to be fooled into thinking Marshall was doing nearly all the work, because today an opinion bearing a justice's name is understood to have been the work of that justice. Marshall's reputation hardly needs inflating, but it has been artificially inflated by his role as the Court's most frequent spokesman.

This same practice has artificially *deflated* the reputations of some of Marshall's colleagues. Justices are known primarily through the opinions that bear their names, so we know little about the justices who delivered few of the Court's opinions during Marshall's tenure. Gabriel Duvall, who was Marshall's colleague for twenty-three years, is credited with only twelve opinions of the Court during his entire career. Thomas Todd has similar statistics: nineteen years with only fourteen opinions. Bushrod Washington, Henry Brockholst Livingston, and Smith Thompson are likewise obscure figures today, despite long tenures on the Court, because they are credited with few opinions by today's standards. As Thompson's biographer discovered, "upon learning that the author is engaged in writing a biography of Smith Thompson, the usual response of listeners, in varying degrees of politeness, is, 'Who is Smith Thompson?'" Had justices like these lived in an era with different opinion-writing (or opinion-crediting) practices, we would know much more about them.[32]

The meager published output of some of the early justices could make them mysterious figures even to contemporaries. "Little seems to be known of his powers as an advocate or a lawyer," one observer said of Bushrod Washington after Washington had been on the Court for nearly two decades, "and that little does not tend to place him much beyond the grade of mediocrity." Yet those who knew Washington thought otherwise. "Nothing about him indicates greatness; he converses with simplicity and frankness," Joseph Story remarked in 1808, a few years before he joined Washington on the Court. "But he is highly esteemed as a profound lawyer, and I believe not without reason. His written opinions are composed with ability, and on the bench he exhibits great promptitude and firmness in decision." Story offered a conclusion that may have applied just as well to several of the more obscure justices: "It requires intimacy to value him as he deserves."[33]

It says a great deal about the fluky nature of appointments to the Supreme Court that Marshall, talented as he was, joined the Court only because he happened to be in the right place at the right time. Chief Justice Oliver Ellsworth resigned due to his poor health in late 1800, when John Adams had only a few more months as president. Adams offered the position to John Jay, the former chief justice, who was now the governor of New York. Jay declined in January 1801. If Adams waited much longer, Thomas Jefferson would be the one to make the appointment. Indeed, there was an even greater reason to hurry, because the bill that would become the Judiciary Act of 1801 was making its way through Congress. The Judiciary Act would reduce the number of seats on the Court from six to five, so if Adams were to appoint a new justice he would have to get the nominee confirmed by the Senate before the Judiciary Act took effect. John Marshall, as secretary of state, was the person who received Jay's letter declining the nomination. As Marshall later recalled, "when I waited on the President with Mr. Jay[']s letter declining the appointment he said thoughtfully 'Who shall I nominate now?'" Marshall suggested William Paterson, who had served on the Court since 1793 and was second in seniority to William Cushing, who had already turned down the opportunity to be chief justice a few years earlier, when Ellsworth had taken the position. But Adams "said in a decided tone 'I shall not nominate him.' After a moment[']s hesitation he said 'I believe I must nominate you.' I had never even heard myself named for the office and had not even thought of it."[34] Marshall may well have been genuinely surprised, because his appointment would put a second Virginian on the Court. (Adams had appointed Bushrod Washington two years before. This would be the first time there were two justices from the same state. It would not happen again until 1864, when Salmon Chase joined his fellow Ohioan Noah Swayne on the Court, at a time when the southern states had seceded from the Union.) The lame-duck Federalist Senate confirmed Marshall in late January, only two weeks before Congress enacted the Judiciary Act. To be sure, Marshall was not in the same room as Adams by chance. He was secretary of state because he had already excelled as a Richmond lawyer, as a member of Congress, and as a diplomat, and because he belonged to the same party as Adams. But it took an unlikely combination of events for Marshall to be appointed to the position he would come to personify.

Among Marshall's contemporaries on the Court, only Joseph Story has received comparable respect, both then and now. Story served for nearly thirty-four years, from 1812 to his death in 1845. He was, by a wide margin, the most erudite American judge of his era. He was also the most industrious. He wrote more opinions on the Marshall Court than anyone but Marshall. While on the Court he taught each year at Harvard Law School, authored eleven major treatises on various areas of law, and published a variety of shorter works as well. Story did not wear his erudition lightly. His opinions and treatises were stuffed with Latin phrases and citations to English authorities. As John Chipman Gray, one of his successors at Harvard, ambivalently remarked a half-century after Story's death, "he was a man of great learning, and of reputation for learning greater even than the learning itself."[35]

Story was nominally a Republican, appointed, as we have seen, by James Madison only after Madison's first three choices either declined the position or were rejected by the Senate. As a justice, however, he tended to take the same nationalist positions as Marshall, to the dismay of the Republicans and their Jacksonian successors. Jackson himself called Story "the most dangerous man in America."[36] As with Marshall, Story's opinions expressed a view of the federal government's authority much closer to the conventional view today, so his opinions have aged better than those of his more state-oriented colleagues.

Figure 2.2 Joseph Story was a justice from 1812 to 1845, while simultaneously teaching at Harvard Law School and writing several foundational treatises. This daguerreotype, taken in Mathew Brady's studio near the end of Story's life, is the earliest known photograph of a Supreme Court justice. Library of Congress, LC-USZ62-10984.

Of the other justices appointed before the Civil War, the only one who is a familiar name today is Roger Taney, Marshall's successor as chief justice.[37] Taney served nearly as long as Marshall and Story, until his death in 1864, during the Civil War. Today Taney is mostly remembered for the infamous *Dred Scott* decision in 1857, but had he left the Court before then, he would be best known for opinions that often, but not always, turned away from the nationalizing trend of the Marshall years and reasserted the authority of state governments. The Court's movement in this direction was not due to Taney alone. He was just one of the six justices whom Andrew Jackson had the good fortune to appoint. Jackson's likeminded successor Martin Van Buren appointed two more, so during nearly all of Taney's tenure the Court had a solid Jacksonian Democratic majority.

Some of the other pre–Civil War justices are remembered primarily for things they did other than sit on the Supreme Court. John Jay, the first chief justice, was a diplomat, the governor of New York, and the author of some of the *Federalist* papers. James Wilson, another of the original six justices, was a signer of the Declaration of Independence, a participant in the Constitutional Convention, and one of the country's first law professors at the school that would later be the University of Pennsylvania. Benjamin Curtis, a justice in the 1850s, may be better known for his work as a lawyer, including his successful defense of Andrew Johnson during Johnson's impeachment trial. Paterson, New Jersey, is named for William Paterson, but it was named before Paterson joined the Court, while he was still the state's governor. If anyone remembers Bushrod Washington, it is likely to be for being George Washington's nephew or merely for his unusual first name, which was his mother's family name.

Most of the justices appointed before the Civil War are obscure figures today. Scarcely anyone remembers Samuel Nelson or John Catron, even though each spent twenty-eight years on the Court. Justices who served for shorter periods, like Alfred Moore or Levi Woodbury, are even less known. There are no biographies of long-tenured justices like Thomas Todd, Gabriel Duvall, or Henry Brockholst Livingston. Apart from Marshall, Story, and Taney, the justices of the early Court have been largely forgotten.

II

Once the Court's opinions were announced, how did they become known outside the courtroom? Some were published in newspapers. *Marbury v. Madison*, for example, appeared in several New York papers about a month after the decision was announced.[38] But most of the Court's opinions were not of broad enough interest to justify printing in a newspaper. To read them, lawyers had to wait until they were gathered and published in books.

The publication of court opinions in the early United States, unlike today, was a private commercial enterprise. Case reporters were literally reporters; they were lawyers who sat in court and took notes while the judges delivered their opinions orally from the bench. If the reporter was absent from court one day, opinions announced that day might never be published. If the reporter took poor notes, a published opinion might not accurately reflect what the judge had said. The reporter was not a government employee. He was an entrepreneur who hoped to earn money from sales of the opinions he reported.

Case reporting in the early Supreme Court was no different. While the Court sat in Philadelphia in the 1790s, some of its opinions were collected and published by a young local lawyer named Alexander Dallas, in volumes that also included decisions of the Pennsylvania courts. Later in life, Dallas would have a distinguished career that culminated in two years as secretary of the treasury in the Madison administration, but his stint as a case reporter was less successful. He failed to report many cases. In the 1820s, the Philadelphia lawyer Peter DuPonceau recalled a significant admiralty case the Court decided in the 1790s that had never been reported. "I heard the argument & the decision, but it is forgotten," DuPonceau lamented. "There was no reporter at that day, & all who were present at the argument are, I believe, dead, except myself." The cases Dallas did report sometimes included inaccurate accounts of the justices' opinions and the arguments of counsel. Some mistakes were perhaps inevitable, because Dallas had to scribble notes as justices and lawyers were speaking, but the problem was made worse by the fact that Dallas was an advocate in some of the cases he was reporting. As one reviewer of his volumes noted, "he was necessarily therefore the hero of his own tale," who had to "resist the natural impulse to swell his own arguments, and contract those of his antagonists." And even when Dallas reported cases accurately, commercial considerations forced him to wait several years to accumulate enough cases to justify publication. The most important of the Court's early cases, *Chisholm v. Georgia*, was decided in 1793, but Dallas did not publish the justices' opinions until volume two of his reports appeared in 1798. By that time, *Chisholm* had been superseded by the Eleventh Amendment. Dallas's account of *Chisholm* was "no use as a precedent," a reviewer admitted, "yet it will afford matter for interesting observation in the judicial history of the United States."[39] For all the flaws of Dallas's reports, however, they were the only reports of Supreme Court decisions in the 1790s, so lawyers must have been grateful to have them. They were better than nothing.

Dallas stayed behind in Philadelphia when the Court moved to Washington along with the rest of the federal government. The task of reporting the Court's decisions was taken up by William Cranch, who had recently been appointed by his uncle, John Adams, as circuit judge for the

District of Columbia. (Cranch was "to me very much like one of my sons," Adams explained.) Cranch would remain a circuit judge for a remarkable fifty-four years, until his death in 1855. His job as reporter was made much easier by the Court's new practice, apparently instituted by John Marshall when he became chief justice, of producing written opinions in the most important cases. In these cases, one reviewer observed, Cranch's task became "merely that of a copyist." Cranch was succeeded in 1815 by Henry Wheaton, a lawyer and judge from New York, who may be best remembered today for his later service as a diplomat in Europe and for his treatise on international law, which became the standard work in the field for much of the nineteenth century. Wheaton, like Cranch, benefited from the Court's practice of writing opinions rather than merely delivering them orally. "The duty of a reporter was formerly much more arduous and responsible, than it now is," reflected a reviewer of Wheaton's first volume of reports. "He was obliged to catch the words, as they fell from the lips of the judges, and to transfer them to his page." Under these circumstances, "it was not strange, that he should often err, and that many of the limitations and restrictions which accompanied the opinion should be omitted in the report." But opportunities for error had become much fewer. "Of late years," the reviewer continued, "the practice has been for the judges themselves, upon questions of any importance, to reduce their opinions to writing. Very little is left for the reporter, but to give a clear statement of the facts, and an accurate and faithful account of the arguments of counsel."[40]

Case reporting had become simpler, but it was still a private enterprise in which the reporter earned income only from book sales, which gave rise to the perennial problem of delay. Even the most industrious reporter could not publish a volume until he found a publisher who thought the venture would turn a profit. But there was not much of a market for Supreme Court decisions in the early nineteenth century. "Law Reports can have but a limited circulation," John Marshall acknowledged. "They rarely gain admission into the libraries of other than professional gentlemen." And most lawyers found it more useful to have volumes of state court cases than volumes of cases decided by the US Supreme Court. Marshall was resigned to the fact that "only a few of those who practise in the courts of the United States, or in great commercial cities, will often require them." Daniel Webster worried that despite the inherent interest of many of the Court's opinions, "the number of law libraries, which contain a complete set of the Reports of the cases in the Supreme Court of the United States, is comparatively small."[41]

Because of this concern, Marshall and Story repeatedly asked Congress to provide compensation for the Court's reporter. This effort bore fruit in 1817, when the job became a salaried position. The former problems associated with reporting the Court's cases "have been entirely avoided," one happy lawyer remarked, "by the official station of the reporter," who no longer needed to find enough customers to make reporting worthwhile. For many years, however, it would still be a part-time position. When Henry Wheaton left to become a diplomat in Denmark, the Maine lawyer Simon Greenleaf considered replacing him as reporter. Greenleaf was already the reporter for the Maine Supreme Court, while maintaining his law practice, and, as he explained to Story, he anticipated that he would "retain my practice in the U. States courts & perhaps in the Sup. Jud. Court of this state . . . & at the same time discharge that of Reporter in the Sup. Ct. of the U. States." He expected that the job "must be much less laborious & more delightful than the drudgery to which a state reporter must submit." Greenleaf did not get the job—it went instead to the Philadelphia lawyer Richard Peters—but a few years later he would become one of the first professors at Harvard Law School. In 1843, when Benjamin Howard took over from Peters, he inserted in his first volume an advertisement for "his professional services, in arguing causes before the Supreme Court." As Howard explained, he was already going to be in the courtroom each day, so clients could be sure that their cases would not be overlooked. "Cases are often brought up from distant courts," Howard advised, "and from the uncertainty of the time at which they may be called, as well as the small amount in controversy, it is inconvenient or impossible for the counsel who argued them below to follow them. The daily presence of the Reporter in court will ensure his attention to any cases that may be confided to him."[42]

Once the Court's reporter was paid by the government, the reporting of the Court's opinions became routine and dependable. In 1874, the government would take over the role of publisher as well. It no longer mattered so much who the reporter was, a fact that would be acknowledged when the reporter's name was taken off the covers of the volumes. Early nineteenth-century lawyers cited the volumes of reports with names like "2 Cranch" for Cranch's second volume or "3 Wheaton" for Wheaton's third. After 1874, they stopped using the reporter's name. William Otto's first volume as the Court's reporter in 1875 was not called "1 Otto." It was "91 U.S.," meaning the ninety-first volume of reports since Alexander Dallas had published his first volume back in 1790. The task of reporting the Court's cases still required proofreading, proposing corrections, and preparing brief summaries of the Court's opinions, but it became an anonymous job conducted behind the scenes. Everyone who read Supreme Court opinions in the 1790s knew Alexander Dallas's name. Today, only the very closest observers of the Court could identify the Court's reporter.

III

Until the late nineteenth century, the justices sat in the nation's capital as the Supreme Court for only a few months each year. They spent most of the year riding around the country from city to city, conducting trials and hearing appeals as circuit judges.

It was obvious right away that riding circuit was a crushing obligation, requiring extensive travel under difficult conditions. John Blair complained in July 1790, after only a few months on the job, that his time was "constantly employed in riding." John Jay groused that riding circuit "takes me from my Family half the Year, and obliges me to pass too considerable a part of my Time, on the Road, in Lodging Houses, & Inns." Most of the justices traveled alone, leaving their wives and children at home, but William Cushing was often accompanied by his wife Hannah. "We are traveling machines," Hannah Cushing told one of her relatives, with "no abiding place in every sense of the word."[43]

The justices assigned to the southern circuit had the worst of it, because of the poor roads, the great distances between cities, and the meager accommodations along the way. "I suffered very much the first night, having to sleep in a room with five People and a bed fellow of the wrong sort," James Iredell told his wife in 1791.[44] Iredell was traveling through Salisbury, North Carolina, on his way to hold court in Augusta, Georgia. On another trip he reported from Richmond that "the town was so full that for three or four nights I was obliged to lodge in a room where there were three other beds." On one journey to Savannah, Iredell found that the bridges across a swamp had all been washed away. "We got through the swamp with some difficulty, having in some places to plunge through very deep holes where the bridges had been," he explained. But the water soon grew too deep to continue, and Iredell had to turn back. The court session in Savannah had to be cancelled. The constant travel wore on Iredell. "It is impossible I can lead this life much longer," he lamented. "To lead a life of perpetual travelling, and almost a continual absence from home, is a very severe lot."[45]

Iredell repeatedly complained to his colleagues that his travel burden was greater than theirs. "I will venture to say no Judge can conscientiously undertake to ride the Southern Circuit constantly, and perform the other parts of his duty," he grumbled in a 1791 letter to Jay, Cushing, and Wilson. "Besides the danger his health must be exposed to, it is not conceivable that accidents will not often happen to occasion a disappointment of attendance at the Courts. I rode upon the last Circuit 1900 miles; the distance from here and back again is 1800. Can any Man have a probable chance of going that distance twice a year, and attending at particular places punctually on particular days?" Jay acknowledged that "your Share of the Task has hitherto been more than in due proportion," but he did nothing about the inequity. The following year, Iredell proposed rotating the circuits among the justices, to even out the workload. "I can no longer undertake voluntarily so very unequal a proportion of duty," he complained. Again, Jay took no action. Rotating the circuits would have defeated one of the main purposes of the system—to ensure that a justice who decided cases in any given region of the country was a resident of that region who was familiar with local law. Perhaps more importantly, Jay and the other justices from the northern and central states could not have been eager to ride the southern circuit themselves. Iredell then turned to Congress, where he found success. Congress enacted a statute mandating that no justice, without his consent, would have to ride any given circuit until all the other justices had ridden that circuit. The justices further evened the burden by reaching an agreement among themselves to each give $100 to whoever was assigned to the southern circuit, a meaningful sum at a time when the justices' annual salary was just $3,500 ($4,000 for the chief justice).[46]

Circuit-riding was hard enough to make some justices quit and to cause other lawyers to decline appointments to the Court. Robert Harrison, one of George Washington's first six appointees, explained to Washington that he could not accept the position because "the duties required from a Judge of the Supreme Court would be extremely difficult & burthensome, even to a Man of the most active comprehensive mind; and vigorous frame." Harrison was already in poor health. If he became a justice, Harrison worried, he would risk "the loss of my health, and sacrifice a very large portion of my private and domestic happiness." John Rutledge left the Court after only a year to become chief justice of the South Carolina Court of Common Pleas, in large part because of all the travel. His replacement, Thomas Johnson, quit even sooner. Johnson apologized to Washington that "the Office and the Man do not fit. I cannot resolve to spend six Months in the Year of the few I may have left from my Family, on Roads at Taverns chiefly and often in Situations where the most moderate Desires are disappointed: My Time of Life Temper and other Circumstances forbid it." John Jay resigned in 1795 to become governor of New York. When his term as governor ended, Jay declined re-appointment as chief justice because of "the fatigues incident to the office." John Blair of Virginia left after five and a half years, Alfred Moore of North Carolina after less than four, both because their poor health would no longer permit the rigors of travel.[47] It was a grueling job.

The justices persistently lobbied the other two branches of government to improve their lot. In the fall of 1790, after only a few months in office, they wrote a collective letter to President Washington pleading to be re-lieved from their circuit obligations. Attorney General Edmund Randolph proposed the same relief to Congress. Nothing happened. A couple of years later the justices tried to formulate a proposal to Congress in which each justice would give up $500 of his salary to help pay for the appointment of full-time circuit judges. The plan apparently foundered when Jay expressed reluctance to participate, which Iredell attributed to Jay's expectation that he would soon leave the Court to become governor of New York. The justices nevertheless combined to send another round of letters to Washington and to Congress in the summer of 1792, again urging them to put an end to cir-cuit riding. "We really, Sir, find the burthens laid upon us so excessive that we cannot forbear representing them in strong and explicit terms," the justices informed Washington. "We cannot reconcile ourselves to the idea of existing in exile from our families." To Congress, the justices lamented having "to pass the greater part of their days on the road, and at Inns, and at a distance from their families." They added that "some of the present Judges do not enjoy health and strength of body sufficient to enable them to undergo the toilsome Journies through different climates and seasons, which they are called upon to undertake." They doubted "that any set of Judges however robust, would be able to support and punctually execute such severe duties for any length of time."[48]

In response, Congress cut the burden of circuit riding in half. The Judiciary Act of 1793 required the attendance of only one justice, not two, at each session of the circuit courts. The grateful justices thanked Congress for this measure, which "afforded them great relief, and enabled them to pass more time at home and in studies made necessary by their official duties."[49]

The law did not otherwise change the composition of the circuit courts, so it gave rise to a new problem. Each circuit court now consisted of only two judges—one district judge and one Supreme Court justice—which allowed for the possibility of a tie vote. To resolve such deadlocks, Congress provided that in the event of a tie, the case would be held over until the next year, when a different justice would arrive to hold circuit court. If the vote was tied again, the view of the two justices would prevail over that of the district judge. But this tiebreaking method broke down in 1802, when Congress ended the rotation of circuits and reverted to the original system under which each justice rode the same circuit year after year. The solution from 1802 onward was to give the Supreme Court jurisdiction to hear cases in which the two circuit judges were divided.[50]

By the late 1790s, as the caseload grew, even this halved obligation became burdensome. The justices obtained relief for a short time when Congress enacted the Judiciary Act of 1801, which established full-time circuit judges to staff the circuit courts. As we saw in the last chapter, however, this reform was swiftly undone by party politics, when the outgoing Federalists seized the opportunity to appoint all the new circuit judges and the incoming Republicans retaliated by repealing the law. The Court went on as before, with justices who spent most of their time riding circuit.

For decades thereafter, the justices continued in their dual roles. As the country expanded westward, Congress added new circuits, and each time the Supreme Court grew larger to accommodate new circuit-riding justices. The Court grew to seven justices in 1807 when Congress created a new seventh circuit for Kentucky, Tennessee, and Ohio. The new position was filled by Thomas Todd, the chief justice of the Kentucky Court of Appeals. The Court acquired an eighth and a ninth justice in 1837, when Congress created two new circuits to encompass Michigan, Indiana, Illinois, Missouri, Arkansas, Louisiana, Mississippi, and Alabama. The new justices were John Catron, the former chief justice of Tennessee, and John McKinley, a senator from Alabama. The Court reached its peak size of ten justices in 1863, when Congress added a tenth circuit for California and Oregon.[51] Abraham Lincoln appointed Stephen Field, the chief justice of California. In the era of circuit-riding, the size of the Court was dictated by the number of circuits.

These expansions of the Court all took place when a single party held the presidency and controlled both houses of Congress. During periods of divided government, neither party would authorize the creation of a new seat on the Court to be filled by its opponent. The 1807 expansion occurred in

Jefferson's second term, when his party had large majorities in both houses. The 1837 expansion took place on the last day of Andrew Jackson's presidency, when Jackson's Democratic party controlled both houses. The results of the 1836 election were in, and it was known that the Democrat Martin Van Buren would succeed Jackson and that the Democrats would retain their majorities in both houses. The 1863 expansion occurred during the Civil War, when, in the absence of the southern states, both houses of Congress had large majorities from Lincoln's Republican party.

Riding the new western circuits was even more onerous than riding the old southern circuit had been, because the distances were even greater and the transportation and accommodations even more rudimentary. John McKinley had the worst of it. His Ninth Circuit required him to hold court sessions in Little Rock, Arkansas, beginning on the fourth Monday of March; in Mobile, Alabama, beginning on the second Monday of April; in Jackson, Mississippi, beginning on the first Monday of May; in New Orleans beginning on the third Monday of May; and in Huntsville, Alabama, beginning on the first Monday of June. Then he had to make the trip all over again in October and November. In between, of course, he was a Supreme Court justice who had to hear cases in Washington, DC, between January and March. In 1838, after his first year on the job, McKinley estimated that he had traveled 10,000 miles during the preceding year, by boat, stagecoach, and horseback. And McKinley had never even made it to Little Rock, which was just too hard to reach in the time allotted.[52]

In 1842 McKinley petitioned Congress to change this system. He "found the business of the circuit greatly beyond the physical capacity of any one man to perform," he explained. Once his fall circuit was complete, he had so little time "to reach Washington so as to avoid the ice in the Ohio river" that some years he could not visit his family. When the Supreme Court session ended, he could not get back to his circuit in time for the first session. "Is it proper that a judge should have no time allowed him for attending to his private concerns? no time for relaxation? no time for reading and study?" McKinley asked in despair. "Is it just to the suitors in the ninth circuit to deprive them of the services of the judge, by requiring more of him than he can possibly perform?" Congress took pity on McKinley and reorganized the circuits to even out the workload.[53]

Now the duty of traveling through the undeveloped old southwest fell to the newest justice, Peter Daniel of Virginia, who hated it just as much as McKinley had. On his way to hold court in Little Rock in 1851, Daniel found himself stuck in tiny Napoleon, Arkansas, on the Mississippi River. "I reached this delepidated [sic] and most wretched of wretched place at twelve oclock today," he complained in a letter to his daughter. He had been on a steamboat scheduled to reach Napoleon a few days earlier, but the captain had stopped at every town along the way in the hope someone would pay him to transport freight, and then he had lingered two whole days in Memphis, causing Daniel to miss the mail boat that would have carried him to Little Rock. "This miserable place consists of a few slightly built wood houses, hastily erected no doubt under some scheme of speculation, and which are tumbling down without ever having been finished," he told his daughter. "To give an idea of the condition of things, I will state that the best hotel in the place, is an old dismantled Steam Boat." While he waited for another boat to Little Rock, Daniel was "serenaded by muschetos [mosquitos], who are not deterred from their attack [by] the motion of my fingers, on which they constantly fasten." Even worse than the mosquitos were "clouds of what in this region is called the Buffalo Gnat; an insect so fierce & so insatiate, that it kills the horses & mules bleeding them to death." Another slow journey to Little Rock a couple of years later took so long that "in the same time I might have been to Liverpool & half way back." He had been riding all the while "on very small and unsafe boats; filthy too beyond description & crowded with rude dirty people, & with scarcely any thing eatable."[54]

And that was just the waterborne portion of the trip. To get to the western rivers from Washington, Daniel first had to endure an arduous westward journey by stagecoach. This part of the trip got easier when the railroads were built, but it could still be an ordeal. In the early 1850s, Daniel had to take a train from Washington to Wheeling. The Baltimore & Ohio Railroad promised "to convey passengers from Washington or Baltimore to Wheeling in nineteen hours," Daniel griped, but "the speed of the Cars was generally slow—stoppages frequent, and the trip of 19 hours *promised* proved to be of two nights and a day. During all this time the travellers were confined to the cars without sleep and without food."[55] Adding insult to injury, the justices had to pay for their own travel expenses, unlike members of Congress, who received travel allowances.

And that was just the travel. When the justices finally arrived and held circuit court in remote western towns, they had to work in conditions markedly inferior to those back east. Statute books and case reports were scarce. Local lawyers were often unskilled. John Catron had spent his legal career in Tennessee, so he was accustomed to practice in the west, but even Catron was aghast when he presided over his first circuit session in Frankfort, Kentucky. "The most important causes are heard & decided without reference to a single book, and any knowledge where the law is to be found," he complained. The most highly regarded lawyers in Frankfort had reputations based on "Stump oratory," Catron despaired. "Whether the Judge is right or wrong they have no knowledge."[56]

Riding circuit was much easier in the northeast, where the cities were larger and closer together, and where working conditions were nicer. "My circuit is not only not unpleasant to me," Joseph Story admitted to his brother-in-law, "but it is greatly preferable to a second annual journey to Washington." Story was from Massachusetts, and his circuit brought him to Boston twice a year, as well as cities in Maine, New Hampshire, and Rhode Island. While in Boston he even found time to teach at Harvard Law School each fall and spring. When Congress was considering another bill to put an end to circuit-riding, Story urged Daniel Webster, who was then the chair of the House Judiciary Committee, not to do so. "You know very well my own notion as to the Judges of the Supreme Court performing such duties. I am quite sure it is a great advantage to them in quickening their diligence," he told Webster. "I am sure that I am a better Judge for my circuit labors."[57] That was easy for him to say, John McKinley or Peter Daniel might have pointed out. Story didn't have to slog through Arkansas and Mississippi.

One complaint about the justices' circuit obligations was that the travel occupied so much of their time. Another was that they had to review their own decisions when a case was appealed from a circuit court to the Supreme Court. "The disadvantages of such a system in practice can hardly be estimated, except by those who have had some experience in them," Henry Brockholst Livingston observed. Livingston had just that experience— eleven years on the Court, reviewing his own circuit decisions and those of his colleagues. He was well aware of how hard it was to consider both sides of a legal question once he had already decided the question on circuit. "It is certainly desirable that judges of an appellate court should form no opinion in an inferior tribunal," Livingston insisted, "or otherwise, the benefit of consultation [with the other justices], without any previous bias, will be in a great measure lost."[58]

This concern did not figure nearly as prominently in the debates over circuit-riding as the complaint that circuit-riding took up too much of the justices' time, because the Court was actually quite willing to reverse decisions of its own members as circuit judges. Between 1801 and 1835, the

Court heard 519 such cases and reversed in 211 of them—a remarkably high reversal rate of 40%. Even John Marshall and Joseph Story, the intellectual leaders of the Court during this period, had their decisions reversed 26% and 38% of the time respectively. Because the Court's custom during most of this period was normally not to write dissenting opinions, we don't know how often the justices themselves personally agreed with the reversal of their own decisions. It did happen sometimes. As Justice John McLean noted in 1853, "there are some cases to be found, where a judge writes the opinion of the court reversing his own decision on the circuit."[59] But lawyers had visible proof that the Court was not deferential to individual justices' circuit court opinions. That must have relieved much of the profession's anxiety about the fairness of the system.

Bills to end circuit-riding were repeatedly introduced in Congress in the first half of the nineteenth century. There was a great amount of debate, but none of the bills was enacted. Proponents of reform emphasized the difficulty of travel and the drain on the justices' time entailed by riding circuit. "I am not quite convinced that riding rapidly from one end of this country to the other is the best way to study law," scoffed Gouverneur Morris. "I am inclined to believe that knowledge may be more conveniently acquired in the closet than in the high road." Alexander Hamilton observed that stationary circuit judges could better handle the burgeoning caseload of the circuit courts than itinerant justices. "The necessity of visiting, within a given time, the numerous parts of an extensive circuit, unavoidably rendered the sessions of each Court so short," he noted, "that where suits were in any degree multiplied, or intricate, there was not time to get through the business." In his annual message for 1816, President James Madison urged Congress to end circuit-riding and appoint full-time circuit judges for these reasons. The opposition press was quick to note that Madison and his party had opposed the identical measure back in 1801, when the Federalists were the ones appointing the judges. But Madison could not get the bill through Congress, even when both houses were controlled by his own party. "The demagogues in Congress as well as in the state legislatures are clamorous for economy & the abolition of what they conceive to be useless & unnecessary offices," lamented Justice Thomas Todd. "I therefore almost despond of any change in the Judiciary within any short period."[60]

Concern about the justices' workload grew more intense as the Court developed a backlog of cases awaiting argument in the brief period each year when the justices were all in Washington. Some years, travel accidents and delays prevented the justices from returning to Washington from their circuit duties in time for the beginning of the Court's session, which further reduced the time available for hearing the cases that were piling up. The Court had to cancel the 1811 term for lack of a quorum, because William Cushing had died and had not yet been replaced, Samuel Chase was ill, and Thomas Todd and William Johnson were unable to get back to Washington in time. In 1829, the Court lost a full week because Robert Trimble had died and had not yet been replaced, William Johnson was seriously injured in a stagecoach accident, Smith Thompson was too ill to work, and John Marshall and Gabriel Duvall were late in returning from their circuits. At the start of the session, Joseph Story and Bushrod Washington were the only justices present. The newspapers feared "that the loss of a week's time of the Court will have the effect to postpone, for a year or two the hearing of some of the causes now on the docket." Indeed, had either Marshall or Duvall not arrived, or had one of the four justices present become sick, "the whole of the present term of the Court would have been lost."[61] Nevertheless, Congress consistently declined the opportunity to relieve the justices of the burden of circuit riding.

One perennial obstacle to reform was that it would have required the appointment of a new cohort of circuit judges, at least one judge per circuit. At any given time, the political party that was out of power had no interest in handing this opportunity to its opponents. Meanwhile, there was always one party whose core ideological commitment was opposition to any increase in the power of the federal government at the expense of the states, including any strengthening of the capacity of the federal judiciary. Every attempt to end circuit-riding was therefore guaranteed to draw substantial political opposition. When Congress was considering such a measure in 1819, Joseph Story correctly predicted that it would fail. The Federalists would vote against it because "the new Judges will be exclusively selected from the Republican party." And many Republicans would be opposed as well, because "among the Republicans, it is well known that there are many hostile in the highest degree to any scheme, which changes or gives more effect to the jurisdiction of the Courts of the United States."[62] This political configuration would not change for many years to come.

The standard arguments in favor of circuit-riding, moreover, had not lost their appeal. The justices still needed familiarity with the laws of the states, especially in the many cases involving disputed western land titles that turned on state property law. "By compelling the Judges of the Supreme Court to hold the Circuits," Martin Van Buren declared in the Senate while opposing reform in 1826, "the knowledge they have acquired of the local laws will be retained and improved, and they will thus be enabled, not only the better to arrive at correct results themselves, but to aid their brethren of the Court who belong to different Circuits." State law was printed in books obtainable in Washington, but members of Congress repeatedly insisted that reading books was no substitute for personal acquaintance with local conditions. The justices "might acquire abstract principles from the books, it was true," acknowledged Representative James Bowlin of Missouri, "but it required more than that for the judges. . . . It required a practical knowledge of the operations of systems, which could only be obtained where they prevailed. Books could do much, but they could not do everything." This argument always had its skeptics, including Senator Andrew Butler of South Carolina, himself a former state judge, who mocked the notion "that it is an advantage to a judge to travel through a country, that he may imbibe something of the spirit of popular jurisprudence." Butler concluded: "Sir, I would much prefer that he should imbibe the law in his library here."[63]

Some of the other claimed benefits of circuit-riding were less easy to dismiss. Daniel Webster, one of the leading Supreme Court advocates of the era, thought it was important for justices to sit regularly as trial judges so they could understand the practical effects of their decisions. "However beautiful may be the theory of general principles," Webster noted, "such is the infinite variety of human affairs, that those most practiced in them, and conversant with them, see at every turn a necessity of imposing restraints and qualifications on such principles." Service as trial judges "will necessarily inspire Courts with caution," he observed, "and, by a knowledge of what takes place upon the Circuits, and occurs in constant practice, they will be able to decide finally, without the imputation of having overlooked, or not understood, any of the important elements and ingredients of a just decision." Stephen Douglas thought the justices gained respect from the bar and the public by mingling with local lawyers and judges. Sitting aloof in Washington would make them "mere paper judges," he predicted. "I think they will lose that weight of authority in the country which they ought to have." Senator William Allen of Ohio worried that if the justices no longer made regular visits to the rest of the country, they would develop what would much later come to be called an inside-the-beltway mentality. "What will be the effect of the existence of a fixed, central tribunal, seated in this Capitol, composed of men who hold their places for life, cut off from all communication with the States and the people of the States?" Allen asked. The Court would become "a Washington city star chamber, under the influences which act upon the capital where the political powers of the nation are all concentrated."[64] There was never any shortage of arguments for retaining the justices' obligation to serve as circuit judges.

The main reason to end circuit-riding was to free up the justices' time for their Supreme Court cases. Many suggested that the same goal could be accomplished if the justices would simply work harder. If one counted only the time they spent in court, the justices did not seem to be working very hard at all. "Oh! What an amount of humbug there is in the world!" Allen exclaimed. While sitting in Washington, "these venerable gentlemen" did not commence court sessions until "eleven o'clock every morning, except on Saturday, when they take some relief from their labors." Allen "thought it not becoming in this Senate to extend the time for them to sit here and enjoy the dignity of indolence." The Connecticut Jeffersonian Abraham Bishop counted up the number of days a justice spent in scheduled court sessions, including the Supreme Court and the circuit court, and found that it totaled only 153 days per year, which Bishop considered proof that riding circuit was scarcely any burden. Lawyers knew that much of a judge's work—most notably the reading of records and briefs and the writing of opinions—took place out of court, but the justices seemed to have it easy in this respect as well. The Court had the luxury of printed records and skilled counsel, one critic insisted, "and thus it is that the labor of the judges of the Supreme Court is exceedingly small when compared to that to which the judges of the State courts are subjected."[65]

Even if riding circuit *was* a burden, others suggested, it was a burden well worth bearing. "Even if each judge try but half a dozen criminal and patent cases a year," one lawyer reckoned, the work "more than repays him for the trouble and inconvenience; and the consequent mingling and association with the bar all over the circuit keeps up an acquaintance and understanding between it and the bench which we should be sorry to see at all lessened."[66] Because of views like these, bills to relieve the justices of their circuit court duties consistently failed to get through Congress. Congress would eventually end circuit-riding, but not until after the Civil War. Until then, the justices spent most of their time serving as circuit judges rather than as members of the Supreme Court.

During the era of circuit-riding, some of the justices' most important opinions were written in the circuit courts, not in the Supreme Court. A disproportionate number of the influential circuit opinions were written by Joseph Story. Story was the most learned of his colleagues and, at least as important, he took the greatest care to arrange for the publication of his opinions, at a time when circuit opinions were not published by the government. "If my fame shall happen to go down to posterity," Story once remarked, "my character as a Judge will be more fully & accurately seen in the opinions of the circuit Court than in the Supreme Court." Other justices were less interested in publishing their circuit opinions. At the opposite extreme from Story was John Catron, who refused to publish any of his circuit opinions, because, he said, if an issue on which he had written later reached the Supreme Court, he wanted to have an open mind and not be tempted to adhere to a position he had already taken in print.[67]

The best known of Story's circuit opinions, because the most useful to other judges and the bar, were those that offered encyclopedic treatments of technical but fundamental points of law. For example, in *DeLovio v. Boit* (1815), Story provided a 27,000-word treatise on the scope of the federal courts' admiralty jurisdiction, a recurring issue that marked one important division of authority between state and federal courts. In *Sherwood v. Sutton* (1828), he authored a similarly exhaustive, if shorter, analysis of when a judge should start the clock on a limitations period where a fraud is so successful that it takes some time before the victim even realizes he has been injured. In *Folsom v. Marsh* (1841), a suit involving infringement of the copyright in the collected writings of George Washington, Story established the principles underlying the "fair use" doctrine of copyright law. Story's circuit opinions were quite influential in their day, and indeed some are still cited as authority two centuries later.[68]

The justices were usually not together when they wrote their circuit opinions, but they sought each other's help by mail. In 1814, for instance, Bushrod Washington was in Philadelphia, working on his circuit opinion in *Golden v. Prince*, which raised the thorny question of whether the Constitution allowed a state to enact a bankruptcy law relieving debtors of their contractual obligations. Washington wrote to John Marshall, who was in Richmond, for advice. The case presented "a question of considerable difficulty," Marshall replied. "I have not thought of the question long enough, nor viewed it in a sufficient variety of lights to have a decided opinion on it, but the biass [sic] of my mind at the moment is rather in favor of the validity of the law." A few years later, Marshall was in a quandary of his own. He was in Richmond, having difficulty with an opinion in an admiralty case. "I have so little experience in admiralty proceedings," he wrote to Story, "that

I sometimes doubt in cases which are probably quite of common occurrence and are thought very plain by those who have much practice of that description." Story, many of whose circuit cases arose in the active port of Boston, was an old hand at admiralty. He offered his advice, which Marshall adopted in his opinion.[69]

As circuit judges, the justices also presided over some of the most high-profile criminal trials of the era. Perhaps the most famous was the 1807 treason trial of Aaron Burr, the former vice president, who was accused of plotting to separate the western states and territories from the United States and to create a new nation under his control. The presiding judge was Chief Justice John Marshall, in his capacity as circuit judge. Marshall called the Burr trial "the most unpleasant case which has ever been brought before a Judge in this or perhaps in any other country."[70] The case required difficult decisions about what constituted treason and how the offense could be proved, and it was as politically charged as a trial could be, because Burr had long been a rival of President Thomas Jefferson, who was the driving force behind the prosecution. When Burr was acquitted, in part because of legal rulings made by Marshall, the chief justice was burned in effigy.

Justices conducted several other criminal trials that were well known at the time but have since been largely forgotten. When the celebrated mail robbers Joseph Hare, Lewis Hare, and John Alexander were convicted in Baltimore in 1818, the presiding judge was Justice Gabriel Duvall, serving in his capacity as circuit judge. A few years later, when another group of notorious mail robbers was tried in Philadelphia, Justice Henry Baldwin was the judge.[71] When cases like these were in the headlines, the justices were probably more familiar to the public as circuit judges than for their work on the Supreme Court.

IV

The justices' circuit obligations had important practical consequences for the Supreme Court. Because the justices were not in Washington very much, the Court had no building of its own. A courthouse would have sat vacant most of the year. In 1790, when New York was briefly the national capital, the Court sat in the Exchange Building, a covered marketplace with a meeting hall on the second floor. In Philadelphia, the temporary national capital in the 1790s, the Court shared space with the Pennsylvania state courts. When the capital moved to Washington in 1800, the new city included buildings for Congress and the president, but none for the Court. In January 1801, just as the Court was about to conduct its first session in Washington, the commissioners responsible for laying out the new city asked Congress if the Court could be given some space in the Capitol. Fortunately, Congress consented. The Court moved into what Benjamin Latrobe, the Architect of the Capitol, called a "half-finished Committee room, meanly furnished, & very inconvenient." In 1807, when the Senate needed this room, the court-room was moved to the Capitol's library, but in 1808, Latrobe reported, "the library became so inconvenient & cold that the supreme court preferred to sit at Lang's tavern." Finally, in 1810, the Court moved into a more per-manent courtroom in the Capitol building, directly beneath the Senate chamber. A few years later, when the Capitol was burned by British soldiers during the War of 1812, the Court had to move temporarily to its clerk's own private home, an arrangement that one lawyer, the future literature professor George Ticknor, found "uncomfortable, and unfit for the purposes for which it is used."[72] Once the Capitol courtroom was repaired, the Court would stay there until 1860.

The courtroom had a low arched ceiling and was broken up by pillars helping to support the Senate chamber directly above. (Building a court-room beneath the Senate was so difficult that the project's on-site supervisor, John Lenthall, was crushed to death when the ceiling collapsed during con-struction.) The justices sat at separate mahogany desks, lined up in a row, with the chief justice in the center. The windows were behind the justices, so during arguments the sun shone directly on the face of the attorney who was addressing the Court. This necessitated curtains, which made the courtroom quite dark when they were closed. The Attorney General sat to the right of the justices, the clerk and the marshal to the left. There was a section for members of the bar, with desks and armchairs, and a separate section with cushioned chairs and sofas for members of the public. The justices had a pri-vate room off to the side, but it was not large enough for any work or even for the justices to put on their robes, so the justices had to enter and robe them-selves while everyone watched.[73]

Tourists who visited the courtroom were usually disappointed. The English traveler Francis Hall thought it resembled a prison because it was so low and cramped. "It is by no means a large or handsome apartment," agreed a Scottish visitor, "and the lowness of the ceiling, and the circum-stance of its being under ground, give it a certain cellar-like aspect, which

Figure 2.3 The Court held oral argument in this courtroom beneath the Senate from 1810 to 1860, except for a few years after the burning of the Capitol during the War of 1812. The courtroom was restored and opened to the public in 1975. This photograph was taken by James W. Rosenthal in 2008. Library of Congress, HABS DC-38-B-22 (CT).

is not pleasant." It left him with "the impression of justice being done in a corner." The courtroom's poor lighting and ventilation were common objects of criticism. One lawyer joked that while "wandering one day in the basement story of the Capitol, which resembles, in some respects, the crypt" of a cathedral, he "got lost amongst the numerous and stunted pillars which support the dome of the edifice." When he opened a door looking for a way out, he found himself in the Supreme Court of the United States, where Daniel Webster was arguing a patent case. Even the courtroom's rare defenders were aware of the room's poor reputation. "It is, indeed, small for such a Court," a Boston lawyer acknowledged, "but certainly not so small, or so mean, as from report we expected to see it." He concluded that "everything about it, is neat and legal looking—nothing gaudy or showy." Another lawyer felt "indignant, at first," about the Court's modest accommodations, "but I found the judges liked it, as they preferred to have no crowd in the galleries for the lawyers to talk to," and "they are out of the way of the idlers about the rotunda." The courtroom was beneath the Senate, a journalist explained, but that only served to "symbolize a great truth—that the principles of *justice* and *rectitude* should be the basis of legislative enactments."[74]

When the Court was in session, the justices spent much of the day in this courtroom listening to lawyers. In the early nineteenth century, litigation before the Court consisted of oral presentations by the lawyers on each side, who normally did not file written briefs. The justices let lawyers go on at length. Argument was "full and thorough," one lawyer noted. "Counsel are not interrupted and catechized like schoolboys."[75] A single case could last for days.

Because of the time and expense required to travel to Washington from most parts of the country, a small group of local lawyers dominated practice in the Court. Several of the leaders of the early Supreme Court bar—in an era before there were any conflict-of-interest rules preventing government officials from representing private clients on the side—were prominent political figures. William Wirt, the attorney general between 1817 and 1829, appeared in the Court on behalf of paying clients far more often than he appeared on behalf of the United States. Daniel Webster, perhaps the most famous advocate in the country, argued in many of the Court's celebrated cases while simultaneously representing Massachusetts in Congress. Henry Clay appeared in several cases while representing Kentucky. As one admirer of Clay's advocacy put it, a spectator at the Court "is constantly called upon to listen to arguments from senators and representatives, whose eloquence upon national topics has attracted the retainers of constituents with personal or pecuniary interests appealed before the highest legal tribunal of their country." After years of listening to arguments from such well known people, Justice Gabriel Duvall understandably advised his son that "a knowledge of the law, which can best be matured & perfected by practice, [is] the shortest & most certain road to fame."[76]

But this small group of Supreme Court practitioners also included some lawyers who were not famous, lawyers who gained renown for their legal work rather than for politics. The all-time record for most arguments before the Court—more than 300—is still held by Walter Jones, who never sought elective office. Jones racked up some of that total as US Attorney for the District of Columbia in the first two decades of the century, because at the time the Supreme Court served as the equivalent of a state supreme court for the District, but most of his cases were in private practice. Jones was simply a talented lawyer who made the smart decision to move to Washington and open a law practice soon after the city became the national capital.[77]

In an era when oratory was a form of entertainment, arguments often drew large audiences, especially when a famous lawyer was scheduled to speak. "The court-room was thronged" to hear William Wirt argue one case, he proudly told a friend. Among the spectators were "fifteen or twenty ladies" and "many members of Congress," who heard Wirt deliver an address *"four hours and half long!"* "It is the fashion for ladies to attend the Supreme Court when any interesting cases are to be argued," one traveler reported, "and their entrée produces some sensation in the court. But the most strict order and decorum are observed, the most profound silence." A journalist likewise emphasized the utter silence in the courtroom. "Those who attend either for business or as mere spectators and auditors, are seemingly loath even to whisper to one another," he observed, "and, though many persons were coming in or going out, I never heard the bailiff, or by whatever other name the officer in attendance is called, cry out 'order' or 'silence,' as such seem to do almost half their time in some ordinary courts." The Court was "certainly the most dignified body that I ever saw."[78]

As the Court's caseload grew, there was no longer time for such leisurely oral arguments. The Court amended its rules in 1821 to require lawyers to submit printed briefs summarizing the facts and the legal arguments before a case could be heard. In 1833, the Court even invited lawyers to submit cases entirely in writing, to be decided without any oral argument at all. In 1848, the Court limited each lawyer to two hours of argument.[79] The style of litigation before the Court was gradually shifting, as oral performance began to give way to arguments presented in writing. This shift made it less necessary for an advocate to be in Washington, so it opened the Supreme Court bar to lawyers in other cities. At the same time, improvements in transportation made it easier for lawyers in other cities to come to the Court. There was no longer as much need to hire a lawyer resident in Washington. By mid-century, Supreme Court practice was no longer dominated by a small group of local lawyers.

Because the justices of the early nineteenth century were in Washington for only a short time each year, few had a home or an office in the city. The justices lived together in a boardinghouse, where they ate their meals, discussed their cases, and wrote their opinions. They typically did not bring their wives or children with them. When Joseph Story arrived in Washington as a new justice in 1812, he loved the camaraderie. "We live very harmoniously and familiarly," he told a friend. "We moot questions as they are argued, with freedom, and derive no inconsiderable advantage from the pleasant and animated interchange." He enjoyed his colleagues, "with whom I live in the most frank and unaffected intimacy. Indeed, we are all united as one, with a mutual esteem which makes even the labors of Jurisprudence light." Living and eating together broke down the wall between the justices' personal and professional lives. "Two of the Judges are widowers, and of course objects of considerable attention among the ladies of the city," Story told his wife after barely a month in Washington. "We have fine sport at their expense, and amuse our leisure with some touches at match-making. We have already ensnared one of the Judges"—it was Thomas Todd—"and he is now (at the age of forty-seven) violently affected with the tender passion."[80] The object of Todd's passion was a widow named Lucy Washington, whose older sister was Dolley Madison, the first lady. When Todd married Washington, President James Madison became his brother-in-law.

The Court's sessions in Washington settled into a routine: oral arguments in the Capitol courtroom during the day, followed by discussions of the cases among the justices in the boardinghouse each evening. "My time was never passed with more uniformity," John Marshall told his wife in 1831. "I rise early, pore over law cases, go to court and return at the same hour and pass the evening in consultation with the Judges." On one occasion in 1816 Marshall had to apologize for declining a dinner invitation, because, he explained, "the Judges have pledged themselves to each other to continue at home for the purpose of conferring on the causes under consideration, & I cannot absent myself from our daily consultation without interrupting the course of the business & arresting its progress."[81]

Sunday dinners were set aside for socializing with others. The future Senator Charles Sumner was a young Boston lawyer when he visited Washington in 1834. "All the judges board together," he wrote home to his parents. "I dined with them yesterday, being Sunday. Judges Marshall, Story, Thompson, and Duval were present." Sumner was impressed by the justices' informality. "No conversation is forbidden, and nothing which goes to cause cheerfulness, if not hilarity. The world and all its things are talked of." The only justice who did not join in the fun was Gabriel Duvall, who "is eighty-two years old, and is so deaf as to be unable to participate in conversation."[82] A decade later, Richard Henry Dana, another young Boston lawyer, had a similar experience when he called upon Story at the justices' boardinghouse. Story "came down into the parlor, & brought with him Judges McLean & McKinley, who, he said, wished to see me," Dana noted with evident surprise. "These judges are the pleasantest set of fellows I met in Washington.

Having no politics on their mind, & no fear of the people, & no ends to gain either in society or from the public, they are easy & natural, & having gone thro' a heavy day's work are very glad to relax themselves. We had a great deal of pleasant conversation, & loud laughing."[83]

Like Story, Marshall placed great value on the justices' living together during the Court's annual session. While Marshall was chief justice, Bushrod Washington was the justice who lived closest to the national capital—he inherited Mount Vernon, the estate of his uncle George, after Martha Washington died in 1802—so the responsibility of finding a boardinghouse each winter fell to him. "If it be practicable to keep us together you know how desirable this will be," Marshall urged Washington one year. "If that be impracticable, we must be as near each other as possible. Perhaps we may dine together should we even be compelled to lodge in different houses."[84]

This communal living arrangement began to break up in the late 1820s and early 1830s. John McLean, appointed to the Court in 1829, had been Postmaster General since 1823, so he and his family already lived in Washington. As Marshall remarked to Story in discussing the justices' accommodations, "our brother McLain [sic] will of course preserve his former position" rather than joining the other justices. William Johnson, who had previously boarded with his colleagues, apparently stopped doing so in the Court's 1832 term, perhaps emboldened by McLean's example. The other five justices stayed together for the time being. "I suppose, that we shall be for the future separated, as (I cannot but believe) has been the design of some of our Brethren," Story complained to Marshall. In later years, living arrangements continued to splinter. By the late 1830s, McLean and his wife had apparently left their house and were sharing a boardinghouse with Story, but Story's correspondence suggests that none of the other justices lived with them. "But for the companionship of Judge McLean, who lodged in a contiguous room, I should scarcely have known what to do," Story admitted after the 1838 term. "His friendship and society were a great solace to me." In 1842, Story and the McLeans took rooms in the house of a family named White, again apparently without any of their colleagues. "It will afford me the most sincere pleasure to board in the same house with Mrs. McLean & yourself next winter at Washington," Story wrote to McLean in the fall of 1843. "I give up all expectation that the judges will ever live together, as in former times."[85]

The justices continued to live and work in boardinghouses and hotels, often in small groups, until the 1870s. In the early 1840s, John McKinley spent one term with John Catron and the McLeans in a home owned by a Mr.

Treacle, another term sharing a boardinghouse with Story and the McLeans, and another in a boardinghouse with Story, the McLeans, and Chief Justice Roger Taney. An 1850 city directory listed Taney, Peter Daniel, and Robert Grier living at a boardinghouse called Brenner's; James Moore Wayne, Catron, and Levi Woodbury at Gadsby's Hotel; McLean at a boardinghouse called Mrs. Carter's; and Samuel Nelson at one called the Potomac House. When Benjamin Curtis arrived in Washington as a new justice in 1851, he moved into "Brown's new hotel," where the McLeans, the Catrons, and Wayne also stayed. "There are some pleasant people in the house," Curtis happily reported. When David Davis was appointed in 1862, he lived in a boardinghouse with several of his colleagues.[86] The justices would continue to share temporary accommodations in Washington for as long as their circuit responsibilities forced them to spend most of the year on the road.

The justices' living and working arrangements in Washington most likely contributed to their practice of speaking with a single voice in their opinions. They all worked, socialized, and ate together while they served on the Court. They were in one another's company all day and evening. They had to get along. As anyone who has lived with other people knows, publicizing disagreements is not always conducive to good relationships. It is telling that William Johnson, the first frequent dissenter, was also the first justice to break with the custom of living together in a boardinghouse while in Washington. Already a maverick at work, he became one in his choice of home as well.[87]

Firsthand accounts of the Court's decision-making process in this period, other than Johnson's, emphasize the friendly collaboration of the justices. We have already seen Story's enthusiastic descriptions from the 1810s. John McLean, who was on the Court from 1829 to 1861, left a similar account, which he apparently wrote in 1853. "Before any opinion is formed by the court," he explained, "the case after being argued at the bar, is thoroughly discussed in consultation. Night after night this is done," back at the boardinghouse, "until the mind of every judge is satisfied, and then each judge gives his views of the whole case, embracing every point in it." Once a case had been fully discussed, "the chief justice requests a particular judge to write, not his opinion, but the opinion of the court." At a later meeting, after the opinion had been written, "it is read to the judges, and if it do not embrace the views of the judges, it is modified and corrected."[88] Living together seems to have encouraged the justices to downplay their differences and to speak with one voice most of the time.

In many ways, then, the Supreme Court of the early nineteenth century was very different from the Court of today. It sat for only a few months each year because the justices had to spend most of the year out on their circuits, conducting trials. While in Washington, the justices lived, ate, drank, and worked together. The Court had no courthouse and hardly any employees apart from the justices themselves. The justices came mostly from political offices, not lower courts. This was a Court that scarcely resembled the institution it would become.

On the other hand, there are some things about the Court that have not changed in two centuries. In particular, the political calculations that went into the selection of justices were much like those of today. Presidents tried to appoint, and senators tried to confirm, justices who belonged to their political party and who would implement their preferred views. Senate confirmation was virtually assured when the president's party controlled the Senate, but when the Senate was controlled by the opposing party, the Senate did not confirm any of the president's nominees during the final year of his administration. Justices tried, with varying success, to time their retirements to let presidents of their party appoint their successors. All of this looks quite familiar today. Ironically, the use of political considerations in selecting justices is the aspect of the Court that is most often deplored today as a modern innovation, in contrast to an imagined past in which justices were chosen on merit rather than politics. But there was never any such past. The political divides of the nineteenth century are easy to overlook today because they are not our divides. But they were just as important then as ours are now. The justices of the early nineteenth century, men like John Marshall and Joseph Story, were the objects of the same kind of result-oriented praise and criticism as are the justices of today. They were chosen for the same reasons as today's justices. If there is anything about the Court that has remained the same since the 1790s, this is it.

3

Federal and State Power

Between 1801 and 1860, the Supreme Court decided 2,548 cases, or around forty-two per year. The caseload grew steadily over this period, in approximate proportion to the growth in the country's population, until by 1851–1860 the Court decided seventy-seven cases each year, roughly the same figure as in the early twenty-first century.[1] But this apparent similarity conceals an enormous difference. In the 1850s, the justices still spent most of their time traveling around the country as circuit judges. They gathered in Washington as the Supreme Court for only a few months each year.

Most of the Court's cases were of little interest to anyone but the litigants. The Court lacked any control over its own docket. If a case arrived at the Court and it was within the Court's jurisdiction, the Court had to hear it regardless of the case's unimportance. As one reviewer of a volume of the Court's published opinions noted in 1824, "they consist for the most part of obvious applications of well known principles."[2] Even lawyers had no need to read many of them.

Many more of the Court's cases addressed technical legal questions that were of modest importance within the legal profession at the time but that lack any enduring significance today. To pick just one example, *Blake v. Doherty* (1820) was a dispute over a parcel of land in Tennessee.[3] Blake claimed the land by virtue of a grant from Tennessee, while Doherty claimed it under an earlier grant from North Carolina. Doherty had won at trial. In the Supreme Court, Blake argued that Doherty's grant was too ambiguous to be valid, because the corners of the parcel were described as a certain hickory tree, a certain white oak, and two stakes. Blake also argued that the trial judge had erred in allowing the jury to consider a survey of the land prepared by Doherty. In a short opinion by Chief Justice John Marshall, the Court rejected Blake's first argument but agreed with his second. The Court decided that a description of land based on trees and stakes was good enough, so long as there was adequate proof of which trees and stakes were the ones intended. "Almost all grants of land call for natural objects which must be proved by testimony," noted Marshall, who was himself a substantial landowner and a speculator in western land. But the trial judge should not have let the jury consider a survey prepared by one of the litigants, Marshall continued, because of the risk that it might not be accurate. William Johnson dissented: he thought there was no harm in allowing the jury to consider Doherty's survey.

A case like *Blake v. Doherty* was worth knowing about, if you were a lawyer who handled such cases. Litigation over land titles was a major part of law practice at the time, especially in the West. It was not unusual for parcels of land to be delineated by features of the landscape like trees or streams. Nor was it unusual for landowners to prepare surveys of their own land. A well-informed lawyer might have wanted a copy of the Court's opinion in *Blake v. Doherty* so he would be prepared if either of these issues arose in one of his own cases. *Blake v. Doherty* would go on to be cited as authority in sixty-four subsequent cases, most of which were similar land disputes in state courts in the nineteenth century. In this sense, *Blake v. Doherty* was an important case for some lawyers of the era. But it was not of much importance to anyone else at the time. It received no attention in the press or in legislatures. Even among lawyers it lost its significance long ago. Lengthy books about the Marshall Court do not mention it. *Blake v. Doherty* was a typical Supreme Court case of its era, but today it has been forgotten.

By contrast, there is a small group of atypical Supreme Court cases from the period that form the canon of "great" cases on which all accounts of the Court focus. These cases involved politically controversial issues such as slavery, relations with American Indians, the power of the federal government, and the extent to which the states could regulate the economy. These were the cases that were of interest to people other than lawyers. They were the ones discussed in the contemporary press and in Congress. They were the cases the justices themselves considered the most important. And some of these cases still influence the law today.

We will likewise focus on the Court's famous cases, but it bears remembering that this choice comes at a cost. It can leave us with a misleading picture of what the Court actually did during this period. The great cases were exceedingly rare. Most of the Court's work consisted of humdrum disputes that today's Court would never decide, precisely because of their insignificance. If one forgets that the great cases are unrepresentative, it is easy to lapse into the hazy reverence that sometimes mars accounts of this period of the Court's history. If one reads only the great cases, the early nineteenth century can seem like a golden age when the justices were wise statesmen who grappled with fundamental questions of the new nation's constitutional structure. They *did* do that occasionally. But most of the time, the Supreme Court was an ordinary court that decided banal legal disputes with no political implications.

I

Most of the Court's celebrated cases during this era were a product of the country's federal structure. England had governed North America as a group of small colonies rather than a single large one. When some of England's colonists—the ones south of Canada and north of the Caribbean—declared independence, they found themselves living in thirteen independent states rather than one. And when the thirteen states agreed to unite, they preserved much of the states' sovereignty and institutions of government. The United States thus ended up with an unusual system of dual sovereignty in which every resident was governed by two entities at once, a state government and the federal government.[4] The Constitution enumerated the powers of the federal government and placed some restrictions on the state governments, but only in the most general terms, so questions constantly arose about the division of authority between the two. Such questions still arise today.

This federal structure often gave the loser of a political battle a second chance for victory in the courts. If one side lost in Congress, it could go to court and argue that Congress had exceeded its authority by regulating a matter the Constitution left to the states. If one side lost in a state legislature, it could go to court and contend that the state had exceeded its authority by regulating a matter the Constitution reserved for the federal government. And there was no need to wait for a political defeat before making these arguments. If one expected to lose in Congress eventually, that was reason enough to tout the sovereignty of the states, and vice versa. Arguments about the balance of power between the federal government and the states were (and still are) often presented in abstract terms, divorced from the substantive results that would flow from favoring one or the other, but few people have ever been primarily motivated by a theoretical preference for the level of government at which a decision is made. Then as now, most people cared much more about the outcome of the decision itself.

Slavery pushed these concerns to the forefront. White southerners worried that one day they would lose the political battle over slavery at the national level, in the form of nationwide policies, especially regarding taxes and tariffs, that would reduce the profitability of plantation slavery and perhaps even eliminate it entirely. White southerners thus had an ever-present reason for interpreting the Constitution to limit the power of the federal government. One foreign visitor to the United States noticed "the general leaning of the South to an interpretation of the constitution most favourable to the sovereignty of the States." Representative John Randolph of Virginia put it rather more bluntly, in opposing a bill to use federal funds to build roads and canals. "If Congress possesses the power to do what is proposed by this bill," Randolph warned, "they may emancipate every slave in the United States."[5] Opponents of slavery had the opposite incentive to favor an interpretation of the Constitution that vested broad power in the federal government. But sometimes the tables were turned. When the South prevailed in Congress—for instance, in the enactment of a fugitive slave law that required the northern states to return runaway slaves to their owners—it was the northerners who now became champions of state sovereignty, and it was the southerners who now insisted on the primacy of federal authority.

The Supreme Court was not the only or even the primary forum for these battles between state and federal authority, which were fought even more conspicuously in the realm of politics. But part of the struggle took place at the Court, which confronted a series of cases raising questions about the boundary between state and national power.

The best-known of these cases is *McCulloch v. Maryland* (1819), in which the Court held that the federal government had the authority to establish a national bank and that the states lacked the power to tax it. Banking had been a subject of controversy almost from the moment the Constitution was ratified.[6] In 1790, when Treasury Secretary Alexander Hamilton proposed the creation of the first Bank of the United States, the idea drew objections from Secretary of State Thomas Jefferson and Attorney General Edmund Randolph, who insisted that the bank was unconstitutional because the Constitution nowhere authorizes the federal government to establish banks. Hamilton's response persuaded President George Washington of the bank's constitutionality. Hamilton argued that the bank was simply a means of regulating commerce and levying taxes, tasks the Constitution delegates to the federal government, and that the Constitution was most reasonably interpreted to allow the federal government to employ means that were useful in accomplishing these ends. The first Bank of the United States existed from 1791 to 1811, when Congress declined to renew its charter.

McCulloch v. Maryland involved the second Bank of the United States, which was established in 1816. Like the first bank, it was owned in part by the federal government and in part by private stockholders. Like the first bank, it would hold the government's funds, issue paper currency, and make loans. Like the first bank, it could establish branches in cities all over the nation. Unlike the first bank, however, it entered a market already crowded with banks. There were scarcely any banks in the country in 1791, but by 1816 there were hundreds of banks that likewise made loans and issued paper notes that served as currency. From their perspective, the second Bank of the United States—by far the largest corporation in the country—was a gigantic competitor with an unfair advantage in its government backing.

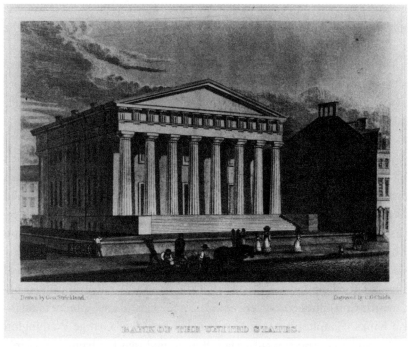

Figure 3.1 The Second Bank of the United States, headquartered in this building in Philadelphia, was the largest corporation in the country when it was established in 1816. In *McCulloch v. Maryland* and *Osborn v. Bank of the United States*, the Court rejected the attempts of Maryland and Ohio to tax the bank. This 1828 engraving is by C. G. Childs, based on a drawing by George Strickland, the architect. Library of Congress, LC-USZ62-26336.

Several states, including Maryland, struck back at the Bank of the United States by taxing its local branches. These taxes served two purposes. On one hand, they somewhat levelled the playing field. Other banks in the state already paid state taxes, so the advantage enjoyed by the Bank of the United States would be even greater if it were the only bank exempt from taxation. On the other hand, state taxes, if high enough, could be a method of driving the national bank out of the state. To test the constitutionality of Maryland's tax, James McCulloch, the cashier of the bank's Baltimore branch, refused to pay it, which prompted a suit by the state to recover the tax.

In the Supreme Court, Maryland was represented by the Philadelphia lawyer and former congressman Joseph Hopkinson, who had successfully represented Samuel Chase in his Senate impeachment trial in 1805. Hopkinson's first argument was that the bank itself was unconstitutional. The Constitution authorizes Congress to make laws "necessary and proper" for executing its assigned powers. Perhaps a bank had been necessary back in Hamilton's day, Hopkinson acknowledged, when "there were but three banks in the United States, with limited capitals, and contracted spheres of operation." But "very different is the case now," he continued, "when we have a banking capital to a vast amount, vested in banks of good credit," and any purpose served by a national bank could be served just as well by existing banks. Daniel Webster, representing the bank, argued that "necessary and proper" could not mean "necessary" in the strict sense. It had to include "such powers as are suitable and fitted to the object; such as are best and most useful in relation to the end proposed. If this be not so, and if congress could use no means but such as were absolutely indispensable to the existence of a granted power, the government would hardly exist."[7]

The Court agreed with Webster. In strong language that would be quoted repeatedly over the next two centuries, John Marshall explained that a broad conception of the federal government's power should be implied from a seemingly restrictive constitutional text. "A constitution," he suggested,

to contain an accurate detail of all the subdivisions of which its great powers will admit, and of all the means by which they may be carried into execution, would partake of the prolixity of a legal code, and could scarcely be embraced by the human mind. It would, probably, never be understood by the public. Its nature, therefore, requires, that only its great outlines should be marked, its important objects designated, and the minor ingredients which compose those objects, be deduced from the nature of the objects themselves.

Constitutions were inherently worded in general terms, leaving the details to be filled in by later generations. "In considering this question," Marshall declared, "we must never forget that it is a *constitution* we are expounding."[8]

Marshall conceded that the Constitution nowhere mentioned banks or corporations as tools Congress could use to achieve its goals. But the Constitution did give Congress power to collect taxes, to regulate commerce, and to fight wars. "Is that construction of the constitution to be preferred, which would render these operations difficult, hazardous and expensive?" Marshall asked. "Can we adopt that construction (unless the words imperiously require it), which would impute to the framers of that instrument, when granting these powers for the public good, the intention of impeding their exercise, by withholding a choice of means?" He concluded that the word *necessary* "imports no more than that one thing is convenient, or useful, or essential to another. To employ the means necessary to an end, is generally understood as employing any means calculated to produce the end, and not as being confined to those single means, without which the end would be entirely unattainable."[9] Maybe a bank was not, strictly speaking, *necessary*. But it was useful and convenient, and that was enough to bring it within the power of the federal government.

Maryland's second argument was that even if the bank was constitutional, the state had the power to tax it like any other bank. Despite the bank's name, Hopkinson pointed out, it was not in fact an agency of the United States. It was a corporation in which the United States owned some of the shares. Webster countered by emphasizing the dangers of letting states tax property owned by the federal government, which would, in effect, allow the states to drive the federal government away. What if states taxed the federal courts or the federal customs houses? Again, the Court agreed with Webster. "The power to tax involves the power to destroy," Marshall declared, in another phrase that would be quoted again and again over the next two centuries. He followed Webster in imagining the dire consequences of permitting Maryland to tax the bank. "If the states may tax one instrument, employed by the government in the execution of its powers, they may tax any and every other instrument," Marshall fretted. "They may tax the mail; they may tax the mint; they may tax patent-rights; they may tax the papers of the custom-house; they may tax judicial process; they may tax all the means employed by the government, to an excess which would defeat all the ends of government."[10]

Contemporaries recognized that *McCulloch* was a strong statement of the federal government's supremacy over the states. "A deadly blow has been struck at the *sovereignty of the states*," complained one shocked reviewer in the press. The Virginia judge William Brockenbrough, using a pseudonym, wrote two sharply critical essays about the case in the *Richmond Enquirer* in which he argued that Marshall's reasoning had no stopping place. If the federal government could do anything it found useful in exercising one of its enumerated powers, Brockenbrough charged, there was nothing it could not do. The essays clearly got under Marshall's skin, because he took the extraordinary step of defending *McCulloch* in his own series of pseudonymous essays that were published in newspapers in Philadelphia and Alexandria. A few weeks later, Spencer Roane, another Virginia judge, published another series of pseudonymous critiques of *McCulloch* in the *Richmond Enquirer*. Like Brockenbrough, Roane worried about the case's implications. The Court's decision had "tread under foot all those parts and articles of the constitution which had been, heretofore, deemed to set limits to the power of the federal legislature," Roane maintained. "That man must be a deplorable idiot who does not see that there is no earthly difference between an unlimited grant of power, and a grant limited in its terms but accompanied with *unlimited* means of carrying it into execution." Marshall responded yet again with two more essays defending his decision. Brockenbrough and Roane were, like Marshall, part of a very small circle of elite Virginia lawyers. Marshall knew the identities of Brockenbrough and Roane, despite their pseudonyms, and they most likely knew his identity as well.[11] Marshall and Roane were neighbors. They had gone to school together. Their willingness to do battle in print demonstrates how important the issue was to them.

McCulloch provoked a different form of resistance in Ohio, which openly defied the Court by continuing to try to tax the local branch of the Bank of the United States. When the bank wouldn't pay, state officials took the money by force. "This opinion of the Supreme Court of the United States must have been well known in the commonwealth of Ohio; but it appears to have been disregarded," remarked one dismayed editorialist. "If the example spreads, anarchy will follow." The dispute reached the Supreme Court a few years later as *Osborn v. Bank of the United States* (1824). Once again, in another

Marshall opinion, the Court held that Congress had the authority to establish a bank and that the states could not tax it.[12] Ohio backed down.

In the long run, *McCulloch v. Maryland* would become the canonical expression of the view that the federal government can wield broad powers implied by, but not explicitly set forth in, the Constitution. Nearly 150 years later, Felix Frankfurter, one of Marshall's successors on the Court, would refer to the opinion's famous line—"it is a *constitution* we are expounding"—as "the single most important utterance in the literature of constitutional law." By that time, the federal government's constitutional authority had expanded far beyond anything that Marshall or his contemporaries could ever have envisioned, but lawyers looked back to *McCulloch* as the basis for the expansion. In the 1960s, for example, when the Court upheld the power of Congress to ban discrimination in hotels, restaurants, and other places of public accommodation, it relied on *McCulloch*.[13]

McCulloch was a strong assertion of federal *legislative* power. In a pair of cases decided shortly before and after *McCulloch*, the Court provided equally strong, and equally controversial, assertions of federal *judicial* power.

The first of these cases was *Martin v. Hunter's Lessee* (1816). At its root, *Martin* was a long-running dispute over the ownership of a large area of land in northern Virginia. In 1813, the Supreme Court had reversed a decision of the Virginia Court of Appeals, the state's highest court, in the land dispute. But the Virginia Court of Appeals refused to acknowledge the Supreme Court's authority. Instead, the state court held that the statute authorizing the Supreme Court to hear appeals from state courts was unconstitutional. When the case returned to the Supreme Court, it was no longer about real estate but about the Court's power over state courts. "The questions involved in this judgment are of great importance and delicacy," Justice Joseph Story recognized in his opinion for the Court. "Perhaps it is not too much to affirm, that, upon their right decision, rest some of the most solid principles which have hitherto been supposed to sustain and protect the constitution itself."[14]

The Court rebuked the Virginia judges for their declaration of independence. Story pointed out that the Constitution explicitly gave the federal courts jurisdiction over all issues of federal law and explicitly authorized Congress to delineate the Supreme Court's appellate jurisdiction, without placing any limits on which lower courts the Supreme Court could supervise. "It is the *case*, then, and not *the court*, that gives the jurisdiction," Story concluded. He then turned from the Constitution's text to its history. "Strong as this conclusion stands upon the general language of the constitution," he continued,

> it may still derive support from other sources. It is an historical fact, that this exposition of the constitution, extending its appellate power to state courts, was, previous to its adoption, uniformly and publicly avowed by its friends, and admitted by its enemies, as the basis of their respective reasonings, both in and out of the state conventions. It is an historical fact, that at the time when the judiciary act was submitted to the deliberations of the first congress, composed, as it was, not only of men of great learning and ability, but of men who had acted a principal part in framing, supporting, or opposing that constitution, the same exposition was explicitly declared and admitted by the friends and by the opponents of that system. It is an historical fact, that the supreme court of the United States have, from time to time, sustained this appellate jurisdiction in a great variety of cases, brought from the tribunals of many of the most important states in the union, and that no state tribunal has ever breathed a judicial doubt on the subject, or declined to obey the mandate of the supreme court, until the present occasion.

Story concluded, in no uncertain terms: "This weight of contemporaneous exposition by all parties, this acquiescence of enlightened state courts, and these judicial decisions of the supreme court through so long a period, do, as we think, place the doctrine upon a foundation of authority which cannot be shaken."[15]

A similar case arose a few years later, when a different branch of Virginia's government once again challenged the Court's authority. *Cohens v. Virginia* (1821) was an appeal from the criminal conviction of two brothers, Philip and Mendes Cohen, for selling District of Columbia lottery tickets in Virginia, which violated a state law barring the sale of tickets to out-of-state lotteries. Virginia argued that the Supreme Court could not even consider the Cohens' appeal, on the theory that the Court lacked the power to hear appeals from state courts in criminal cases. The Court rejected Virginia's argument once again. "The words of the constitution," Marshall declared, "give to the Supreme Court appellate jurisdiction in all cases arising under the constitution, laws, and treaties of the United States. The words are broad enough to comprehend all cases of this description, in whatever Court they may be decided." Characteristically, Marshall relied not just on the Constitution's text but on first principles. "Let the nature and objects of our

Union be considered," he noted; "let the great fundamental principles, on which the fabric stands, be examined; and we think the result must be, that there is nothing so extravagantly absurd in giving to the Court of the nation the power of revising the decisions of local tribunals on questions which affect the nation." As in *Marbury v. Madison*, the Court declared its power without actually exercising it, because the Court ended up agreeing with the state courts by affirming the Cohens' convictions.[16]

The Virginia legal community was nevertheless up in arms once again, just as it had been after *McCulloch* a few years before. *Cohens* "is attacked with a degree of virulence superior even to that which was employed in the Bank question," Marshall complained while in Richmond. Story sent Marshall his encouragement. "The opinion of our best lawyers is unequivocally with the Supreme Court, heartily & resolutely," he reported from Massachusetts. "They consider your opinion in Cohens v. Virginia as a most masterly & convincing argument." But he was apprehensive about the attacks on the Court he had seen in the Virginia press. "The truth is that the whole doctrine of Virginia on the subject of the constitution appears to me so fundamentally erroneous, not to say absurd, that I have a good deal of difficulty in reading with patience the elaborate attempts of her political leaders to mislead & deceive us," he told Marshall. "I am not without my fears for the future." In Congress, Representative Andrew Stevenson of Virginia introduced a resolution to repeal section 25 of the Judiciary Act, the provision that authorized the Supreme Court to review the judgments of state courts. Nothing came of it in the end. As one northern law journal scoffed, Stevenson's resolution was "the last desperate struggle of the new school of Virginia jurists." Marshall's opinion in *Cohens* continued to rankle Virginia lawyers for many years thereafter. "Since the case of Cohen vs. Virginia, I am done with the Supreme Court," John Randolph lamented. "No one admires more than I do the extraordinary powers of Marshall's mind," he continued. "I cannot, however, help thinking that he was too long at the bar before he ascended the bench," and that so many years of making arguments for paying clients "had injured, by the indiscriminate defense of right or wrong, the tone of his perception (if you will allow so quaint a phrase) of truth or falsehood."[17]

One major theme of the Court's cases in the early nineteenth century was thus the reinforcement of the power of the federal government. When states challenged that power, the Court rebuffed the challenges. At the time, the federal government was tiny and quite weak by today's standards, but it would have been even weaker had these cases come out the other way. The Court's decisions, however, were merely words on paper. They would have had no effect unless the states complied with them. The states *did* comply, eventually. They stopped trying to tax the Bank of the United States and they stopped denying the Court's authority to review the judgments of state courts. These outcomes suggest that the Court's decisions in these cases could not have cut too much against the grain of elite national opinion, for if they had, local resistance to the decisions would likely have been much stronger, and the net result might well have been the been the opposite of the one the Court intended to reach.

II

The opposite side of the federalism coin involved the power of *state* governments. In several politically charged early nineteenth-century cases, the Court held that a few different clauses of the Constitution barred the states from regulating the economy in various ways. The Court's conception of these limits on state power would be at its strongest in the early 1820s, but then, after a rapid turnover in personnel, the Court would change course.

The first of these cases, and the first case in which the Court held a state statute unconstitutional, was *Fletcher v. Peck* (1810).[18] In 1795, the government of Georgia approved a sale of the state's western land, now much of Alabama and Mississippi, to a consortium of land companies. It soon became apparent that the sale price was far below the land's market value. The land companies had bribed Georgia's legislators with shares in the companies, which encouraged the legislators to make the price as low as possible so the companies' profit would be greater when they sold the land on to others. Outraged Georgians voted for new legislators at the next election, who promptly repealed the statute authorizing the sale. By then, however, the land companies had already sold much of the land to innocent third parties throughout the country. The result was decades of litigation and political contestation, of which *Fletcher v. Peck* was just one part.

In *Fletcher*, the Court addressed the argument of third-party purchasers that the new legislature's repeal of the land sale violated the Constitution's Contracts Clause, which prohibits the states from enacting any "Law impairing the Obligation of Contracts." The Constitution includes this clause because in the 1780s several states passed legislation relieving debtors from having to repay their creditors, and one purpose of the Constitution was to prevent such a thing from happening again. The Contracts Clause clearly barred states from undoing contracts between private parties, but did it also bar a state from undoing its own land grants? "In considering this very interesting question," Marshall asked in his opinion for the Court, "we immediately ask ourselves what is a contract? Is a grant a contract?" The Court held that the initial sale of lands was indeed a contract between Georgia and the land companies. And did the Contracts Clause prohibit a state from impairing its own contracts, as well as those between private parties? Again, the Court's answer was yes. "The words" of the Clause "contain no such distinction," Marshall reasoned. "They are general, and are applicable to contracts of every description," including contracts to which the state was a party. Once a state made a grant, the Constitution barred the state from altering any of its terms.[19]

In later years, the Court expanded this principle to prevent states from intervening in the economy in other ways. In *New Jersey v. Wilson* (1812), the Court held that a state could not repeal a tax exemption. In *Dartmouth College v Woodward* (1819), the Court held that a state could not alter the terms of a corporate charter. The case involved New Hampshire's effort to transform Dartmouth into a quasi-public university by transferring to the governor the power to appoint trustees, but, far more significantly, the same principle—that once having created a corporation, the state could not change its basic attributes—applied to the proliferating business corporations that would soon dominate the economy. "Perhaps no judicial proceedings in this country, ever involved more important consequences, or excited a deeper interest in the public mind, than the case of Dartmouth College," exclaimed the Boston lawyer Warren Dutton. Dartmouth's charter "is plainly a contract" governed by the Contracts Clause, Marshall's opinion asserted. "It is more than possible," he acknowledged, "that the preservation of rights of this description was not particularly in the view of the framers of the constitution, when the clause under consideration was introduced into that instrument." They had worried that states would intervene in contracts between private parties, not that states might alter the terms of corporate charters. But "it is not enough to say, that this particular case was not in the mind of the convention, when the article was framed, nor of the American people, when it was adopted," Marshall continued. "It is necessary to go further, and to say that, had this particular case been suggested, the language would have been so varied, as to exclude it, or it would have been made a special exception." And there was certainly no evidence of that, as the question simply hadn't arisen.

"The case being within the words of the rule," Marshall concluded, "must be within its operation likewise."[20]

More controversial yet was *Green v. Biddle* (1823). After decades of less-than-meticulous land grants in what were then remote regions, Kentucky was plagued by disputes involving overlapping claims to land. The state addressed the problem with legislation that favored people actually occupying the land, who voted in state elections, over claimants who did not occupy the land, many of whom lived in other states. When the Court first heard the case in 1821, it held that Kentucky's statutes violated the Contracts Clause because they impaired the land grants of the nonoccupants. The decision caused an uproar in Kentucky. Richard Johnson, one of Kentucky's senators, proposed a constitutional amendment allowing the Senate to override Supreme Court decisions invalidating state statutes. He accused the Court of wielding political rather than judicial power. If the Court "can declare the laws of a State unconstitutional and void, and, in one moment, subvert the deliberate policy of that State for twenty-four years, as in Kentucky, affecting its whole landed property, even to the mutilation of the tenure upon which it is held, and on which every paternal inheritance is founded; is not this the exercise of political power?" Johnson asked. "If this is not the exercise of political power, I would be gratified to learn the definition of the term, as contradistinguished from judicial power."[21]

The Court agreed to rehear the case and it subsequently published a new opinion, but the gist was the same: Kentucky's legislation still violated the Contracts Clause. Now Richard Johnson proposed legislation adding three new circuits in the west and increasing the size of the Court from seven justices to ten, which would allow the appointment of three new western justices who would presumably be more sympathetic to Kentuckians. Johnson's legislation would also have required the votes of seven of the ten justices before reaching any decision on the constitutionality of a law. John Marshall promptly wrote to Kentucky's other senator, Henry Clay, urging that Johnson's ideas were impractical. "When we consider the remoteness, the number, and the age of the Judges," Marshall suggested, "we cannot expect that the assemblage of all of them, when they amount to ten, will be of frequent recurrence. The difficulty of the questions, and other considerations, may often divide those who do attend. To require almost unanimity, is to require what cannot often happen, and consequently to disable the court from deciding constitutional questions." In the end nothing came of any of Johnson's proposals, but the sentiment they embodied seems to have been widely felt. "Some plan should be adopted, as it were, to try the *opinions* of the judges of the supreme court," recommended the Baltimore newspaper *Niles' Weekly Register* (italicizing "opinions" to suggest they were no more than that). "I cannot believe that it is composed of infallible men, or that the rights of tens of millions of people should be vested in the discretion of five or six men, who are essentially appointed to office for life."[22]

The Contracts Clause had been included in the Constitution to prevent states from passing laws to protect debtors. In *Sturges v. Crowninshield* (1819), the Court considered a New York bankruptcy statute allowing debtors to be relieved of their debts. The Court held that the Contracts Clause prohibits states from enacting such laws. In his opinion for the Court, Marshall recalled the "general dissatisfaction with that lax system of legislation which followed the war of our revolution," which prompted the Constitution's drafters "to establish a great principle, that contracts should be inviolable." The Contracts Clause accordingly did not permit the states to enact "any law discharging a contract, without performance," which was just what a bankruptcy law did. There was no federal bankruptcy law at the time, so several states had enacted bankruptcy laws of their own, all of which had the same constitutional flaw as New York's. *Sturges* threatened to bring chaos. "Much uneasiness has arisen, in many parts of the Union, from this opinion of the Supreme Court," remarked one Washington newspaper. "Individuals who, years ago, have taken the benefit of insolvent acts, by virtue of state enactments, and who, either by good luck, or attention to business, have become rich, may well fear for their property, for it now lies, naked and exposed, to the sheriffs or the marshals, under antiquated claims, which will doubtless revive with alacrity against them." Another newspaper expected the case to "make some great revolutions in property, and raise up many from penury whose 'eyes have been blinded by the dust of the coach wheels of those that ruined them,' and cause others to descend to the condition that becomes *honest men*, by compelling payment of their debts." Whatever happened, the paper predicted, "the decision will afford a golden harvest to lawyers and sheriffs."[23]

Green v. Biddle and *Sturges v. Crowninshield* represented the peak of the Court's reliance on the Contracts Clause to curb state authority over the economy. For the next decade, members of Congress, especially those from the affected states, fought back by repeatedly introducing legislation to limit the Court's ability to assess the constitutionality of state laws. In 1824, for example, the New York Senator (and future President) Martin Van Buren proposed requiring a supermajority of five of the seven justices before a state law could be held unconstitutional. In 1829, the Virginia Representative (and future Justice) Philip Barbour introduced a bill to the same effect. The power to hold state laws unconstitutional was "one of great magnitude and most extensive operation," Barbour argued. "A power so tremendous should be fenced around with proper guards." In 1831, as sentiment for the state nullification of federal law was brewing in South Carolina, the House Judiciary Committee favorably reported a bill to abolish the Court's jurisdiction over cases arising from state courts. If the Court lost the power to judge the constitutionality of state laws, "the Constitution is practically gone," Story worried.[24]

None of these proposals was adopted, perhaps because it was soon clear that none would be needed. The Court that decided these controversial cases had seen no personnel changes since Story joined the Court in 1812. The gap of eleven and a half years before the next appointment is still the longest in the Court's history. With the death in 1823 of Henry Brockholst Livingston, however, the Court began to turn over very quickly. There would be four new justices in slightly over six years (although only three of the Court's seven seats were affected, due to the early death of Robert Trimble). After a few more years of stability, there was an even greater turnover. Between 1835 and 1837, five new justices were appointed by Andrew Jackson and Martin Van Buren, including two to new seats created by the Court's expansion to nine justices. The new appointees took a more benign view of state power over the economy than the men they replaced.[25]

The first sign of change was *Ogden v. Saunders* (1827), another case involving New York's bankruptcy law. The debt discharged in *Ogden*, unlike the one in *Sturges*, was incurred in a contract that was entered into *after* the state's bankruptcy law went into effect. A bare 4–3 majority of the Court, including the two newcomers, Smith Thompson and Robert Trimble, held that the timing made all the difference. The four justices in the majority each wrote separate opinions, the clearest of which was by Bushrod Washington, in one of his rare disagreements with Marshall. States had all kinds of laws that affected contracts, Washington pointed out, including usury laws, laws limiting the fees that merchants could charge, and so on. The Contracts Clause clearly could not have been meant to invalidate all these laws. These preexisting state laws, he concluded, did not "impair the obligation" of a contract, which is what the Contracts Clause forbad the states from doing. Rather, these state laws *shaped* the obligation of a contract. As Washington put it, the state law in existence when a contract is created forms "a part of the contract, and travels with it."[26] States could have bankruptcy laws, or indeed any laws, that applied prospectively to affect subsequent contracts, but not retrospectively to already-existing contracts.

Marshall dissented—his only published dissent in a constitutional case in his entire career—joined by fellow old-timers Joseph Story and Gabriel Duvall. He argued that the obligation of a contract "is intrinsic, that it is created by the contract itself," rather than being "dependent on the laws made to enforce it." The purpose of the Contracts Clause, he reasoned, was to prevent states from reenacting the debtor relief legislation of the 1780s. The majority's interpretation of the Clause, by contrast, "would change the character of the provision, and convert an inhibition to pass laws impairing the obligation of contracts, into an inhibition to pass retrospective laws." If such had been the intent of the Constitutional Convention, he asked, "is it not reasonable to believe that it would have been so expressed?" The Contracts Clause would have been worded to prohibit merely "the passage of any retrospective law. Or, if the intention had been not to embrace all retrospective laws, but those only which related to contracts, still the word would have been introduced, and the State legislatures would have been forbidden 'to pass any *retrospective* law impairing the obligation of contracts,' or 'to pass any law impairing the obligation of contracts previously made.'" The effect of *Ogden*, as Marshall recognized, was to weaken the force of the Contracts Clause as a means of restricting state regulation of the economy.[27]

The Court continued in this direction in *Charles River Bridge v. Warren Bridge* (1837).[28] In 1785, Massachusetts had granted a charter to one company to build a bridge over the Charles River and to collect tolls from users of the bridge. In 1828, a second company was given the right to build a competing bridge nearby, which would greatly reduce the first company's toll revenue. The first company argued that the state violated the Contracts Clause by destroying the value of its contract. Fifteen or twenty years earlier, the Court would likely have agreed. But a new generation of justices had largely replaced the group that decided the earlier Contracts Clause cases. Bushrod Washington died in 1829, William Johnson in 1834, and John Marshall in 1835. Gabriel Duvall finally retired in 1835 after spending his last few years on the Court completely unable to hear any of the arguments. President Andrew Jackson replaced them with Henry Baldwin, James Moore Wayne, Roger Taney, and Philip Barbour, all political allies of Jackson. Of the justices who had decided *Green v. Biddle* and *Sturges v. Crowninshield*, only Joseph Story remained.

Jacksonians rejoiced at these personnel changes, especially the departure of Marshall. "Of Judge Marshall's spotless purity of life, of his many estimable qualities of heart, and of the powers of his mind, we record our hearty tribute of admiration," wrote the Jacksonian journalist William Leggett in the *New York Evening Post*, three weeks after Marshall's death. "But sincerely believing that the principles of democracy are identical with the principles of human liberty, we cannot but experience joy that the chief place in the supreme tribunal of the Union will no longer be filled by a man whose political doctrines led him always to pronounce such decision of Constitutional questions as was calculated to strengthen government at the expense of the people. We lament the death of a good and exemplary man, but we cannot grieve that the cause of aristocracy has lost one of its chief supports." Observers from the other side of the political divide braced for the worst. They even missed Gabriel Duvall, whose work on the Court was the least visible of any of his colleagues. Duvall's resignation was "lamented by all who consider that tribunal the only refuge left to us, the only protection in the political tempest that is now sweeping off in its ravages, all those principles that the founders of our government considered as the only basis of its continuance," sighed Richard Peters, the Court's reporter.[29]

In *Charles River Bridge*, the Court construed the Contracts Clause more narrowly than in previous cases and held that the state had not violated the terms of its contract with the first bridge company. Taney's opinion for the Court emphasized that the first company's charter did not explicitly say that it would have the *only* bridge across the river, or that the state would refrain from allowing competitors to build more bridges. "Upon all these subjects, the charter is silent," Taney insisted, "and nothing is said in it about a line of travel, so much insisted on in the argument, in which they are to have exclusive privileges." Taney argued that accepting the first company's claim of an implied exclusivity would bring progress to a halt, because it would prevent the construction of new roads or bridges everywhere an old one already existed. "If this court should establish the principles now contended for," he asked,

> what is to become of the numerous railroads established on the same line of travel with turnpike companies; and which have rendered the franchises of the turnpike corporations of no value? Let it once be understood, that such

charters carry with them these implied contracts, and give this unknown and undefined property in a line of travelling; and you will soon find the old turnpike corporations awakening from their sleep, and calling upon this court to put down the improvements which have taken their place. The millions of property which have been invested in railroads and canals, upon lines of travel which had been before occupied by turnpike corporations, will be put in jeopardy. We shall be thrown back to the improvements of the last century, and obliged to stand still, until the claims of the old turnpike corporations shall be satisfied.

For this reason, the Court concluded, the Contracts Clause should be interpreted narrowly, to bar only a state's impairment of an explicit term of a contract.[30]

Story was horrified. "I can conceive of no surer plan to arrest all public improvements," he charged in his dissent, "than to make the outlay of that capital uncertain and questionable" by allowing states to renege on their implied promises of exclusivity. "If the government means to invite its citizens to enlarge the public comforts and conveniences, to establish bridges, or

Figure 3.2 The Charles River Bridge, shown in 1795, ten years after it was built. The Court's 1837 decision allowing the construction of a competing bridge marked a generational change in the justices' views of the extent of states' power over the economy. Engraving by John Scoles. Boston Public Library, 08-02-000195.

turnpikes, or canals, or railroads, there must be some pledge, that the property will be safe; that the enjoyment will be co-extensive with the grant; and that success will not be the signal of a general combination to overthrow its rights and to take away its profits." Story was certain that the original charter of the first bridge company included exactly this kind of implied promise. "Now, I put it to the common sense of every man," he posited,

> whether if, at the moment of granting the charter, the legislature had said to the proprietors; you shall build the bridge; you shall bear the burdens; you shall be bound by the charges; and your sole reimbursement shall be from the tolls of forty years: and yet we will not even guaranty you any certainty of receiving any tolls; on the contrary; we reserve to ourselves the full power and authority to erect other bridges, toll or free bridges, according to our own free will and pleasure, contiguous to yours, and having the same *termini* with yours; and if you are successful, we may thus supplant you, divide, destroy your profits, and annihilate your tolls, without annihilating your burdens: if, I say, such had been the language of the legislature, is there a man living, of ordinary discretion or prudence, who would have accepted such a charter, upon such terms? I fearlessly answer, no. There would have been such a gross inadequacy of consideration, and such a total insecurity of all the rights of property, under such circumstances, that the project would have dropped still-born.

Story was utterly incredulous that his colleagues would construe the Contracts Clause so narrowly. His views on the states' power to impair contracts had not changed, but the Court had changed around him.[31]

Nearly simultaneously, a similar transition took place in the way the Court interpreted a clause of the Constitution that is less familiar to lawyers today, the provision that says states may not "emit bills of credit." A bill of credit was a form of paper money, representing the issuer's promise to pay the amount stated on the bill. This clause, like the Contracts Clause, was put in the Constitution to prevent the states from reenacting the economic policies of the 1770s and 1780s, a period in which several states issued bills of credit. As Marshall recalled in his opinion for the Court in *Craig v. Missouri* (1830), "during the war of our revolution, we were driven to this expedient; and necessity compelled us to use it to a most fearful extent." Some of the states experienced spikes of inflation and deflation. States quarreled about accepting each other's bills of credit. The problem with this form of money, Marshall explained, was that "its value is continually changing; and these changes, often great and sudden, expose individuals to immense loss, are the sources of ruinous speculations, and destroy all confidence between man and man. To cut up this mischief by the roots, a mischief which was felt through the United States, and which deeply affected the interest and prosperity of all; the people declared in their constitution, that no state should emit bills of credit."[32] *Craig* was a constitutional challenge to paper certificates issued by Missouri which could be used to pay taxes and other obligations owed to the state. Looked at one way, Missouri was simply borrowing from its residents, who paid for the certificates on an installment plan. Looked at another way, however, the certificates were bills of credit, because residents could use them to transact with each other. The federal government did not yet issue paper money; rather, banks did, in the form of bank notes redeemable at the bank for gold or silver coins. Missouri was replacing a form of paper money backed by the credit of a hodgepodge of private businesses, some of which were not very dependable, with a more uniform and stable form of paper money backed by the state itself.

By a 4–3 vote, the Court held that Missouri's certificates were unconstitutional because they were bills of credit. "The denominations of the bills, from ten dollars to fifty cents, fitted them for the purpose of ordinary circulation," Marshall explained, "and their reception in payment of taxes, and debts to the government and to corporations, and of salaries and fees, would give them currency." They were not *called* bills of credit, but they looked just like bills of credit. "Had they been termed 'bills of credit,' instead of 'certificates,'" Marshall pointed out, "nothing would have been wanting to bring them within the prohibitory words of the constitution."[33] Johnson, Thompson, and McLean dissented.

But only seven years later, after some personnel changes, the Court reached the opposite conclusion. Kentucky issued certificates like Missouri's; the only difference was that Kentucky set up a state-owned bank to issue the certificates. In *Briscoe v. Bank of Kentucky* (1837), the Court held that Kentucky's certificates did not violate the Constitution, because, in a formal sense, the issuer was the bank, not the state. The effect was to overrule *Craig v. Missouri* as a practical matter. States could now issue paper money, so long as they did so indirectly, through a state-owned bank. Once again Story dissented, again with dismay. "After the decision of the case of *Craig v. State of Missouri,*" he complained, "I had not supposed, that this was a matter which could be brought into contestation, at least, unless the authority of that case was to be overturned; and the court were to be set adrift from its former moorings."[34] Between *Craig* and *Briscoe*, the Court had lost two of the four justices who had formed the *Craig* majority (Marshall and Duvall). They had been replaced by Taney and Barbour, who had a greater solicitude for the authority of the states. Because the federal government had lost its own bank the previous year, when the charter of the second Bank of the United States had been allowed to expire, *Briscoe* empowered the states to take the lead in banking matters until the Civil War, when the federal government would reassert itself.

Perhaps the most difficult question involving the relative powers of the states and the federal government over the economy involved the regulation of economic matters that spilled over state lines. The Constitution's Commerce Clause authorizes the federal government to "regulate commerce ... among the several states," but it does not say whether, or how much, the states may also regulate interstate commerce. Everyone agreed that each state retained its traditional power to govern economic activity that stayed within the state, and everyone agreed that the federal government had no regulatory power over such purely intrastate activity. But when business crossed state lines, what was the relationship between state and federal power? Could the states and the federal government *both* regulate interstate commerce? Were the states completely disabled from regulating it? Or was the answer somewhere in the middle?

Gibbons v. Ogden (1824) was the first case in which the Court grappled with this question. One group of steamboat operators—including Robert Fulton, the inventor of the first commercially successful steamboat—had an exclusive license from the state of New York to run steam ferries in New York harbor between landings in New York and New Jersey. A competing group of steamboat operators—whose boat was captained by a young Cornelius Vanderbilt, later to be one of the wealthiest Americans in history—had a license from the federal government to carry goods and passengers from one domestic port to another. The Vanderbilt group argued that New York lacked the power to grant an exclusive license for the route between New York and New Jersey, because only the federal government could regulate interstate commerce. The Fulton group responded that the states and the federal government could regulate interstate commerce simultaneously, just like they both imposed taxes simultaneously. In his opinion for the Court, Marshall went out of his way to suggest that the Court agreed with the Vanderbilt group that interstate commerce was off-limits to the states. "There is great force in this argument," he noted, "and the Court is not satisfied that it has been refuted."[35] The Court decided in favor of the Vanderbilt group, but on the narrower ground that the state license conflicted with the federal license. The Court left for another day the broader question of whether the states could regulate interstate commerce where Congress had not acted.

Three years later, in *Brown v. Maryland* (1827), the Court again strongly suggested that Congress's power over interstate commerce implicitly rendered the subject off-limits to state regulation, even where Congress had not enacted any laws contrary to state law. In *Brown*, the Court held that a license fee imposed by Maryland on merchants importing goods from out of state was tantamount to a tax on the imported goods themselves and was thus prohibited by the clause of the Constitution that bars states from taxing imports. The Court then went on to explain that Maryland's fee also violated the Commerce Clause. "The power claimed by the State is, in its nature, in conflict with that given to Congress" to regulate interstate commerce, Marshall reasoned. "If the States may tax all persons and property found on their territory, what shall restrain them from taxing goods in their transit through the State from one port to another, for the purpose of re-exportation?" he asked. This kind of state regulation, he concluded, "would obviously derange the measures of Congress to regulate commerce."[36] Had the Court's personnel not changed, it is likely that the Court would have continued to move toward the view that the Constitution implicitly divested the states of the power to regulate interstate commerce.

Once again, however, the Court reversed course in 1837, after several of the justices, including Marshall, had been replaced by Jackson appointees. *New York v. Miln* (1837) was a Commerce Clause challenge to a New York statute intended to keep poor immigrants out of the state. The statute required the master of any ship arriving in New York City from another state or another country to provide a list of all the passengers as well as a bond for each, to indemnify the city in case any of the passengers required public support. Philip Barbour's opinion for the Court emphasized the long tradition of state regulation of the poor. In Barbour's view, New York's law governed the movement of people, not goods, and so was not a regulation of commerce at all. But Smith Thompson took the opportunity in a concurring opinion to reject the contention that the states lacked the power to regulate interstate commerce. "The mere grant of the power to congress," he insisted, "does not necessarily imply a prohibition of the states to exercise the power, until congress assumes to exercise it." As was becoming Story's custom, he dissented alone. He found it "impossible to maintain the doctrine, that the states have a concurrent jurisdiction with congress on the regulation of commerce, whether congress has or has not legislated upon the subject."[37] But by 1837 Story was the only justice left who took this view. The Marshall Court's tentative conception of an exclusive federal power over interstate commerce would never be realized.

The Court's 1837 term, Roger Taney's first as chief justice, was thus a pivotal year in the Court's understanding of the Constitution's limits on state regulation. In *Charles River Bridge*, the Court loosened the constraints of the Contracts Clause. In *Briscoe*, the Court allowed states to issue paper currency. And in *Miln*, the Court came close to repudiating the notion that the states were barred from regulating interstate commerce. A group of nationalist-minded justices had been replaced by justices more willing to leave space for the states, due to the political triumph of Andrew Jackson and his party. Joseph Story, the lone holdover from the old Court, dissented each time. "I am the last of the old race of Judges," Story sighed. "I stand their solitary representative, with a pained heart, and a subdued confidence." Daniel Webster told his wife that Story was in "bad spirits. He thinks the Supreme Court is *gone*, & I think so too." A few years later, Story reflected that "new men and new opinions have succeeded. The doctrines of the Constitution, so vital to the country, which in former times received the support of the whole Court, no longer maintain their ascendency. I am the last member, now living, of the old Court."[38]

There was a widespread sense in the late 1830s, not just among lawyers but also in the general-interest press, that the Court had passed from one era to another. Whether this was good or bad depended on the author's politics. "We have fallen under a new dispensation in respect to the judiciary," despaired one critic in the *North American Review*. "What was the law of the court upon some important points remains so no longer. Within a brief space we have seen the highest judicial corps of the Union wheel about in almost solid column, and retread some of its most important steps. It is quite obvious, that old things are passing away." He complained that in elevating the power of the states relative to that of the federal government, the Court "has already capitulated to the spirit of the old confederation" and to "anti-federal doctrines." The *American Monthly Magazine* excoriated "the flippant, ultra-radical tirades of those friends of the [Van Buren] administration, who exult in the complete revolution which the judiciary has undergone, and the prospect that a new system of jurisprudence will be established on the ruins of long-settled doctrines." Jackson's appointees to the Court have "such an utter disregard for the collected wisdom of the past," the magazine charged, "that hereafter no party who brings suit to their bar, can calculate the probability of success by any fixed principles; but must find that the 'glorious uncertainty of the law' is not a mere fiction of the vulgar fancy, at least as regards questions involving points at issue between different political parties."[39]

The saddest lamentation of all was written anonymously in the Whig *New York Review* by the elderly James Kent, a contemporary of Marshall and Story, who had retired from a long career in the New York judiciary. The justices of the past "shed immortal lustre over the jurisprudence of the nation, by their ability and learning, and the purity and dignity of their character," Kent began. But not "the Supreme Court under the new dynasty," from which Kent perceived "an altered tone and a narrower spirit. . . . The change is so great and so ominous, that a gathering gloom is cast over the future. We seem to have sunk suddenly below the horizon, to have lost the light of the sun." As Kent read the cases of 1837, the Court had shredded the provisions of the Constitution intended to keep the states from rivaling the federal government in regulatory power. The Contracts Clause had been "essentially expunged from the Constitution." The Commerce Clause had been "alarmingly impaired, by admitting the States to exercise a concurrent power." The clause barring the states from emitting bills of credit had been "in effect repealed." Kent concluded with a dark prediction. "When we consider the revolution in opinion, in policy, and in numbers that has recently changed the character of the Supreme Court, we can scarcely avoid being reduced nearly to a state of despair of the commonwealth," he declared. "If the Constitution be destined prematurely to perish, and the last refuge of justice, and the last hopes of temperate and civilized freedom to be destroyed, the expiring struggle will be witnessed in the decisions of that Court."[40]

Of course, there was another side to this debate. The Jacksonian *United States Magazine and Democratic Review* published a blistering response to Kent. "How is it that a court so extravagantly lauded yesterday has fallen into such unmeasured odium today?" the *Review* asked. The answer: politics. "The anxious inquirer after political truth sees at every turn some new attempt to bend the Constitution to the views of one or the other of the numerous sects into which the Whig party is divided; and it is not strange, that in such attempts we often hear the most shallow nonsense." Most politicians tried to "conceal their bias under moderate language," but in Kent's article he "boldly denounces the whole Supreme Court of the nation, because, forsooth, his political friends are no longer in the ascendant." There was nothing wrong with the Taney Court, the *Review* concluded. The problem was "all the ultra notions of those who, for a splendid government, would reason away the Constitution and all its checks and balances; who would, with one breath, make corporations override all individual and public interests, [and] hold in check the power of the States."[41] Each side was certain that it was being true to the Constitution and that its opponents were using the Constitution illegitimately to advance their political goals.

III

In 1837, after *Charles River Bridge*, *Briscoe*, and *Miln*, it looked like the Court was veering sharply toward an interpretation of the Constitution that favored the states at the expense of the federal government in the realm of economic regulation. But things did not turn out that way. Over the next two decades, even with a firm Jacksonian majority, the Court continued to restrict the states' ability to govern the economy. These cases involved a variety of different subjects and different parts of the law, but the common theme was the Court's consistent determination to ensure that the United States remained a single common market free from state-erected barriers to trade.

The first of these cases was *Bank of Augusta v. Earle* (1839), which raised the question whether corporations chartered in one state could lawfully conduct business in another. They often did, especially banks, so a vast amount of money was riding on the Court's answer. The contracts at issue in *Earle* were debts owed by Alabama merchants to out-of-state banks with offices in Alabama, debts which, during the Panic of 1837, the merchants did not pay. "Money is frequently borrowed in one state, by a corporation created in another," Taney explained in his opinion for the Court. "The numerous banks established by different states are in the constant habit of contracting and dealing with one another." This had been normal business practice for so long, the Court concluded, that it established a consensus in favor of the legality of such transactions. "We think it is well settled, that by the law of comity among nations, a corporation created by one sovereignty is permitted to make contracts in another," the Court held. "The same law of comity prevails among the several sovereignties of this Union." The nation was still in the midst of the economic depression that began in 1837.[42] A contrary decision would have gone a long way toward balkanizing the national economy into insular state economies, a result none of the justices could stomach, with the exception of the Court's newest member, John McKinley. McKinley would prove to be one of the Court's most ardent proponents of state authority, but probably just as important, he was an Alabaman himself, who must have found it easier to see the dispute from the point of view of local merchants than that of out-of-state banks.

A few years later, in *Swift v. Tyson* (1842), the Court once again defended the national marketplace against idiosyncratic state rules that formed potential trade barriers. *Swift* involved a technical issue of commercial law on which the New York courts had developed their own rule different from the rule prevailing in other states. The question before the Supreme Court was whether, in a case litigated in a federal court located in New York, the court should apply the state's unique rule or the general rule in force elsewhere. The Judiciary Act required the federal courts to apply the "laws" of the host state in this situation, but the Court nevertheless held that the federal court should not apply New York's unique rule, on the ground that by "laws" the Judiciary Act meant only statutes enacted by the legislature, not the decisions of courts. Lurking not far below the surface was the concern that for financial instruments to circulate effectively in a national and indeed international market, these instruments had to be governed by a uniform body of law. "The true interpretation" of commercial law, Story declared in his opinion for the Court, is "to be sought, not in the decisions of the local tribunals, but in the general principles and doctrines of commercial jurisprudence." Story quoted Lord Mansfield, the famous English judge, to the effect that commercial law was "in a great measure, not the law of a single country only, but of the commercial world." If the courts of each state could invent their own rules of commercial law, the result might be a hodgepodge of inconsistent regimes. The effect of *Swift* was to ensure that the federal courts would enforce a nationally uniform body of law in commercial cases, despite the nonuniformity of state doctrines.[43]

The Court achieved a similar result by expanding its definition of the federal courts' admiralty jurisdiction—their authority to hear cases involving shipping, most of which were commercial disputes. Admiralty cases often had an international flavor. They were governed by their own set of rules, separate from the common law rules governing ordinary land-based commercial disputes, because of the special need for national and even international uniformity in admiralty cases. This was why the Constitution allocated admiralty cases to the federal courts, while leaving ordinary commercial disputes to the state courts. But where exactly was the dividing line between the two categories of cases? The traditional line, inherited from England, was that admiralty jurisdiction extended only to bodies of water large enough to be affected by the tide. Disputes that arose on smaller internal waterways, unaffected by the tide, were governed by the common law rather than by the rules of admiralty. At first, the Court followed this rule. In *The Thomas Jefferson* (1825), Story explained that "the Admiralty never pretended to claim, nor could it rightfully exercise any jurisdiction, except in cases where the service was substantially performed, or to be performed, upon the sea, or upon waters within the ebb and flow of the tide. This is the prescribed limit which it was not at liberty to transcend." Because the dispute in *The Thomas Jefferson* arose on the Missouri River, where there was no tide, the federal courts lacked jurisdiction.[44]

But the ideal of a uniform commercial law exercised a force stronger than the tide. By the middle of the nineteenth century there was considerable shipping on the Great Lakes and the western rivers. Idiosyncratic state common law threatened to balkanize water-based commerce. In *The Genesee Chief* (1851), the Court overruled *The Thomas Jefferson* and extended the admiralty jurisdiction to all navigable waters, with or without the tide. The case involved a ship collision on Lake Ontario, an incident that previously could not have given rise to an admiralty case because of the lack of any tide. But the Great Lakes "are in truth inland seas," Taney reasoned for the Court. "Different states border on them on one side, and a foreign nation on the other. A great and growing commerce is carried on upon them between different states and a foreign nation, which is subject to all the incidents and hazards that attend commerce on the ocean." The same need for an internationally uniform law on the Atlantic Ocean "applies with equal force to the lakes." It no longer made sense to divide authority between court systems based on the tides. "There is certainly nothing in the ebb and flow of the tide that makes the waters peculiarly suitable for admiralty jurisdiction, nor any thing in the absence of a tide that renders it unfit," Taney contended. "If it is a public navigable water, on which commerce is carried on between different states or nations, the reason for the jurisdiction is precisely the same." Just as *Swift* empowered the federal courts to develop a uniform commercial law for disputes on land, *Genesee Chief* empowered them to develop one for disputes on water.[45]

Most important of all, after some years of uncertainty, the Court settled into an interpretation of the Commerce Clause that barred the states from regulating the economy in areas where nationally uniform regulation would be especially useful in facilitating a national common market. The period of uncertainty began in three consolidated cases collectively known as the *License Cases* (1847), involving state laws limiting the sale of liquor, in which the Court produced a cacophony of six separate opinions, with no clear outcome apart from the bottom line that the laws did not encroach on Congress's power to regulate interstate commerce. On the broader question of whether the Commerce Clause limited state regulatory authority over interstate commerce where Congress had not spoken, Taney explained, "it is well known that upon this subject a difference of opinion has existed, and still exists, among the members of this court." Taney himself thought that congressional silence meant that the states were free to regulate as they wished. If the Constitution "was intended to forbid the States from making any regulations of commerce," he reasoned, "it is difficult to account for the omission to prohibit it, when that prohibition has been so carefully and distinctly inserted in relation to other powers, where the action of the State over the same subject was intended to be entirely excluded." Three years later the Court was even more splintered. In two consolidated cases known as the *Passenger Cases* (1849), the Court produced eight separate opinions, occupying (along with the arguments of counsel) nearly three hundred pages in the reports.[46] Again there was little common ground apart from the conclusion, by a 5–4 vote, that the states could not tax passengers arriving from foreign ports.

The Court finally resolved this question in *Cooley v. Board of Wardens* (1852).[47] A Pennsylvania statute required ships entering the Philadelphia harbor either to hire a local pilot or to pay half the cost of hiring one. Many ships were completing interstate voyages, so to that extent the state law governed interstate commerce. If the states lacked any power over interstate commerce, the law would violate the Commerce Clause. Or if one understood the law primarily as a form of state protectionism—a method of creating jobs for Pennsylvania's pilots at the expense of pilots from other states—one might conclude that it violated the Commerce Clause even if one interpreted the Clause to allow some measure of state regulation. On the other hand, states often regulated local economic activity by means that incidentally affected interstate commerce, including with laws regarding navigation through harbors. Every harbor was a bit different, and one could hardly expect Congress to enact precise regulations for each one. Indeed, as the harbor's governing body pointed out, there was a long maritime tradition of requiring local pilots to guide ships safely into port, because only the locals knew where the hidden dangers lay. If one looked at the case this way, Pennsylvania's law was not forbidden protectionism but rather a sensible safety measure.

In the Court's earlier cases assessing the validity of state regulation under the Commerce Clause, the justices had tended to express their views in absolute terms, either by declaring interstate commerce off-limits to the states or by denying that the Commerce Clause imposed any limits at all on state regulation where Congress had not legislated to the contrary. In *Cooley*, three of the justices clung to such absolute views. On one side, John McLean and James Moore Wayne insisted that the power to regulate pilotage belonged exclusively to Congress. On the other side, Peter Daniel argued that it belonged exclusively to the states. But the Court's newest justice, Benjamin Curtis, garnered a majority for a compromise position in the middle. Curtis was a highly regarded Boston lawyer who had replaced Levi Woodbury as New England's justice only a couple of months before the case was argued. He was the only member of the Court who could consider the issue afresh because he had not already expressed an opinion about it in one of the Court's earlier cases. Curtis had an unusual career in a couple of respects—he was the only justice appointed by a president belonging to the Whig Party (Millard Fillmore), and, as we will see in the next chapter, he resigned from the Court after only a few years, while still in his forties, in part because of his unhappiness with the Court's handling of the *Dred Scott* case. Curtis's opinion for the Court in *Cooley v. Board of Wardens* would be the enduring contribution of his short judicial career.

Curtis began by noting that some of Congress's powers, like the power to tax, were necessarily shared with the states. The Constitution's grant of the taxing power to the federal government could not have deprived the states of the power to impose taxes of their own. Other powers of Congress, by contrast, were necessarily exclusive. The Constitution gave Congress the power to legislate for the District of Columbia, for instance, and while it did not explicitly deny such power to the states, it would hardly make sense for the states to legislate for the District too. Some kinds of regulation, like taxation, could be undertaken simultaneously by the federal government and the states without causing any trouble, while others, like governing the District of Columbia, could not. Commerce encompassed a wide range of disparate topics, some of which were amenable to simultaneous state and federal regulation, and others of which were not. Where common sense suggested the need for a single national rule, the Commerce Clause would bar state regulation to leave the field clear for the federal government, but where simultaneous state and federal regulation would be feasible, as with the pilotage rules governing local ports, the states would be allowed to regulate. "Now the power to regulate commerce, embraces a vast field," Curtis explained, "containing not only many, but exceedingly various subjects, quite unlike in their nature; some imperatively demanding a single uniform rule, operating equally on the commerce of the United States in every port; and some, like the subject now in question, as imperatively demanding that diversity, which alone can meet the local necessities of navigation."[48]

After *Cooley*, rather than trying to apply the Commerce Clause the same way in all cases, the Court would proceed case by case, deciding in each situation whether the Commerce Clause left room for states to regulate. The Court's adoption of this intermediate method broke the impasse at which the justices had found themselves in their earlier Commerce Clause cases. This method left a great deal of work for the future, in delineating precisely when state regulation would be allowed and when it would be prohibited. In later years the Court would confront many more cases raising the question. It still confronts them today. Over time, the result would be a mix of cases that imposed greater restrictions on the states than seemed likely in the late 1830s, when the Court appeared to be on the cusp of holding that the Commerce Clause was merely an affirmative grant of power to Congress that placed no limits on state power.

By the 1850s, the dire predictions of Story, Kent, and other Whigs had not come true. They had feared that Taney and his colleagues would interpret the Constitution's restraints on the states so narrowly as to empower the states to fragment the national economy and bring back the evils that had prompted the ratification of the Constitution in the first place. Some of the members of the Taney Court, especially Peter Daniel and John McKinley, might well have taken the Court in that direction if they could have. But they lacked the votes. Most of their colleagues, despite the states'-rights rhetoric of their political party and the presidents who appointed them, proved to be moderate nationalists so far as the economy was concerned. In this sense, most of the Jacksonian justices had a similar experience to that of Jackson himself: holding high national office tends to make the benefits of strong national power easier to see.

IV

Looking back at these cases today, what stories do they tell?

One story is that in the first half of the nineteenth century the Court solidified its own power and the power of the federal courts generally relative to the state courts. The justices successfully defended their turf against repeated challenges. In each of these showdowns the Court could have been the one that blinked, but it was not. By the 1850s, the Court was just what the people who debated the Constitution in the 1780s had expected it to be—the highest court in the land, with the power to reverse the decisions of state courts and to declare state laws unconstitutional.

A second story involves the Court's role in establishing the constitutional structure undergirding the American economy, a structure composed of a federal government with the authority to regulate the national market free from state interference and state governments with power only over local markets. We should be careful not to overstate the Court's contribution. The main parts of this constitutional structure were uncontroversial and were not the subject of litigation, so the Court had no opportunity to say anything about them. No one doubted, for example, that the federal government but not the states could impose tariffs on goods imported from other countries, or that the states but not the federal government could regulate the countless intra-state transactions that made up the vast majority of the economy. The issues that reached the Court involved the structure's finer details— important details, to be sure, especially to the people whose fortunes depended on them, but details all the same. One could write a thorough economic history of the antebellum United States without even mentioning the Supreme Court.[49] But it is impossible to write a history of the antebellum Supreme Court without saying a great deal about the economy, because that was the subject of so many of the Court's high-profile cases.

Before the Civil War, the Court's decisions limiting the states' power over the economy were more important as a practical matter than its decisions endorsing the federal government's power, because the states tested the limits of their authority more often than the federal government did. Between 1800 and 1860, despite changes in the configurations of political parties, there was always one party that favored a less active federal government, and that party held the presidency for all but eight years (or twelve, depending on how one counts John Tyler). Major public works like canals and roads were mostly undertaken by states, not the federal government. After the demise of the second Bank of the United States, the states took over the field of banking as well. During this period the federal government tended to limit its commercial regulation to fields in which its authority could not be reasonably doubted, such as foreign trade and interstate shipping. That would change after the Civil War, when the federal government would become more active in the economy, and the Court would once again be called upon to define the outer bounds of the federal government's authority.

Finally, a third story is about how contemporaries understood these decisions. People today sometimes think of the early nineteenth century as a golden age, before "politics" corrupted the Court. Such a view would have seemed laughable to people at the time. They knew as well as we do that the justices' policy views profoundly affected their decisions in politically inflected cases. If anything, they would have known it even more, because so many of the justices came to the Court after years in Congress, in the cabinet, or in state legislatures, and had plainly been appointed because of their political opinions rather than their skill at judging. Whether contemporaries agreed or disagreed with a decision, they frankly discussed the politics of the arguments on both sides. When a decision was contrary to the policy views of members of Congress, members were not shy about proposing legislation to curtail the Court's authority.

The Court's decisions were also sharply criticized in the press, to a degree that could make the justices uncomfortable. "I had no doubt when the opinion was given it would be attacked, not by reasoning, for that I did not fear, but by abuse," Benjamin Curtis complained after one of his opinions was published. "No doubt, the members of the judiciary department of the government must make up their minds to being treated hereafter by the press with very little deference." On another occasion he groused that the position of the justices "exposes them to attack, such as no honest judiciary, in any country within my knowledge, have been subject to." The press, Curtis believed, made "the grossest charges against those who administer the judicial power."[50] There was never a time when the Court's decisions were understood as based purely on law as distinct from politics. In the early nineteenth century, people understood that the two were always intertwined.

But it would be equally wrong to conclude that the justices' political views were the *only* determinants of their decisions in politically charged cases. The law was malleable, but not completely so. Professional norms defining what counted as a reasonable argument were powerful constraints—so powerful that normally they did not need to be stated. No justice, for example, could have written an opinion denying the federal government's authority over interstate commerce, or forbidding the states from regulating transactions within their borders, without provoking the derision of his colleagues and of the profession as a whole. These professional norms were social conventions one internalized during a legal career. They expressed the bar's prevailing view of the meaning of the constitutional provisions the Court was called upon to interpret. When the Court decided politically charged cases, justices had some room to implement their policy preferences, but only within a range of options bounded by these norms. Then as now, the Court wielded extraordinary power, but within a tightly constrained space.

4

Slaves and Indians

In the twentieth century, some of the Supreme Court's most famous cases would involve the right to equal treatment regardless of race. In the early nineteenth century, by contrast, race discrimination was legal and pervasive. The Court decided several important cases involving the rights of African Americans and American Indians before the Civil War, but these cases did not challenge the subordinate position of these groups. Litigants did not argue, for example, that slavery was unconstitutional or that members of minority groups were entitled to be treated like white people. Arguments like these would have been doomed to failure at the time, so they were not made in the Supreme Court. Rather, the Court's cases involving slaves and Indians tended to implicate questions of federalism like those we saw in in the previous chapter. In cases involving Indian land, for instance, the issue was not whether the Indians could halt white settlement, but rather which level of government, federal or state, would take the Indians' land from them. In cases involving fugitive slaves, the question was not whether black people had the same right to freedom as white people, but whether federal law regulating the recapture of escaped slaves took precedence over state law. Discrimination was such an ordinary part of American life that the Court's cases in this area, important as they were, concerned the details of how discrimination would be implemented, not the lawfulness of discrimination itself.

I

In most of the cases in which the Court adjudicated the rights of American Indians, there were no Indians before the Court. These cases typically involved white litigants on both sides, who claimed rights for Indians only to the extent such rights would advance their own arguments. If rights for Indians would not help either side, no one asserted them.

For example, in *Fletcher v. Peck* (1810), the Court's first important case discussing the rights of Indians, the two litigants were white land speculators.[1]

We saw *Fletcher* in the previous chapter, because it was also the first case in which the Court discussed the Constitution's Contracts Clause at any length. The enormous tract of land that had been fraudulently sold by the Georgia legislature, like all the land in the United States, had originally belonged to the Indians, but this land had never been purchased from them. Indeed, the Creeks, Choctaws, Chickasaws, and Cherokees lived there still. If representatives from any of these tribes had been invited to participate in the litigation, they might have raised a plausible objection under then-existing law to the lawfulness of the state's sale of their land to white purchasers without their consent.

But neither side had any incentive to invite them. The case was collusive: the litigants, white speculators named Robert Fletcher and John Peck, both wanted the Court to uphold the Georgia legislature's corrupt 1795 sale of the land. They agreed to stage the suit in the federal Circuit Court in Boston, where Peck lived. Fletcher lived just across the state line in New Hampshire, which gave the federal courts jurisdiction, since the parties were from different states. Even if the tribes had known about the case, it would have been impractical for them to participate in litigation so far away. The suit alleged that Peck had breached a contract with Fletcher for the sale of land within the disputed territory, on the ground that Peck did not really own the land he claimed to own, because Peck's chain of title began with the 1795 sale. Both sides wanted Peck to win. When the case reached the Supreme Court, Peck was represented by a team of the best lawyers in the country, including John Quincy Adams and Joseph Story, who would join the Court himself soon after. Fletcher was represented by Luther Martin, who was nearing the end of a distinguished legal career but who was declining into alcoholism and who was being paid to lose. No one on either side argued that the land in question had belonged to the Indians before Georgia sold it. Peck argued that it was owned by Georgia, while Fletcher argued that it was owned by the United States.

As a result, John Marshall's opinion for the Court did not even consider whether the Indians were the land's true owners. The Court held that the land belonged to Georgia, and that the state thus had the right to sell it on to speculators. Only William Johnson, writing separately, argued that the Indians owned their land. "To me it appears that the interest of Georgia in that land amounted to nothing more than a mere possibility" of ownership, he explained. The current owners were the tribes who lived on the land. "The uniform practice of acknowledging their right of soil, by purchasing from them, and restraining all persons from encroaching upon their territory, makes it unnecessary to insist upon their right of soil," Johnson continued. Because the Indians owned the land, Georgia did not. "If the Indian nations be the absolute proprietors of their soil," he concluded, "no other nation can be said to have the same interest in it."[2] Johnson, however, was the only member of the Court who took this view. The other justices all decided that the Indians' land could be sold to white speculators by a state government before it had even been purchased from the Indians, in a case in which no Indian voices were heard.

Thirteen years later, when the Court addressed the nature of Indian property rights at length in *Johnson v. M'Intosh* (1823), the Indians were likewise absent from the case. *Johnson* was another collusive suit between two land speculators seeking to establish the validity of two massive purchases of land in the 1770s by private land companies from Indian tribes in present-day Illinois and Indiana. Neither side in the case had any reason to speak up for the Indians' rights to their land. In another opinion by Marshall, the Court held that the "discovery" of North America by European nations vested ownership of all the land in the discovering nation. The Indians had merely a "right of occupancy" in their land, not ownership of it. They could "use it according to their own discretion; but their rights to complete sovereignty, as independent nations, were necessarily diminished, and their power to dispose of the soil at their own will, to whomsoever they pleased, was denied by the original fundamental principle, that discovery gave exclusive title to those who made it." The United States, as the successor to Great Britain, had inherited this rule, so the land in question was owned by the United States, not by the Indian tribes who inhabited it. As Marshall concluded, "conquest gives a title which the Courts of the conqueror cannot deny."[3]

Marshall then ventured a justification for this conclusion, one that surely would have been contested had any Indians been involved in the litigation. "The tribes of Indians inhabiting this country were fierce savages," he reasoned, "whose occupation was war, and whose subsistence was drawn chiefly from the forest. To leave them in possession of their country, was to leave the country a wilderness; to govern them as a distinct people, was impossible, because they were as brave and as high spirited as they were fierce." Conquest, as Marshall saw it, was the only alternative. "The Europeans were under the necessity either of abandoning the country, and relinquishing their pompous claims to it," he argued, "or of enforcing those claims by the sword." So the sword it was.[4]

The Court's conclusion that the Indians did not own their land accorded with the conventional view among lawyers of the era. Marshall himself was a speculator in western land on which Indians still lived, as were many affluent white Americans at a time when the country lacked much of a stock market or any other alternative vehicle for investment. For this reason, the Court's decision was not surprising. It nevertheless came in for sharp criticism. William Wirt, who was the attorney general when *Johnson* was decided, called it "the strangest absurdity. It is said they have no other title [to their lands] than that of having chased their game over them," he observed, "and yet, we contend that an English, Spanish or French ship, having sailed along the coast, or entered the mouth of a river, gains a complete title by discovery to the sovereign of the navigator—not only to the coast seen, but to the unseen interior." The minister Calvin Colton, who visited Indian tribes in the Midwest, argued that the doctrine elaborated in *Johnson* was "an unatoneable outrage." The Creeks expressed what was doubtless the prevailing of view of *Johnson* among Indians. They realized "that we now hold our lands by right of occupancy only," they told federal officials. But "from all the traditions which have been handed down to us from our forefathers, we have been impressed with the belief that we are the original and sole proprietors of the soil."[5]

The Court's most politically salient case involving the rights of Indians, *Cherokee Nation v. Georgia* (1831), was one of the rare cases in this period in which an Indian tribe was a party. Beginning in the 1820s, the Georgia legislature enacted a series of statutes intended to force the Cherokees out of the state. Georgia declared all Cherokee laws void and subjected the Cherokees to state law instead, much of which discriminated against them, such as by denying them the right to vote, to testify in court, and to enter the non-Cherokee parts of the state without a permit. In an earlier era, the Cherokees might have looked to the federal government for protection from Georgia, but that possibility ended with the election of Andrew Jackson as president in 1828. Jackson, an ardent supporter of Indian removal, sided with Georgia.[6] The Cherokees turned to the Supreme Court. They retained William Wirt, the former attorney general, to represent them.

Wirt's first attempt to get a case before the Supreme Court was a challenge to Georgia's indictment of a Cherokee man named George Tassel for murdering another tribe member. Tassel's prosecution was under one of Georgia's new statutes replacing Cherokee law with state law, so the case offered a chance for Wirt to argue that the new statutes were unconstitutional. After the state court rejected this argument, Wirt sought review in the Supreme Court, which scheduled the case for its 1831 term. But Georgia defied the Court by abruptly executing Tassel before the Court could hear his case.[7] Wirt thus turned to a different strategy, one that would not allow the state to block the case from reaching the Supreme Court. The Cherokee Nation sued Georgia directly in the Supreme Court, invoking the Court's original jurisdiction.

Cherokee Nation v. Georgia became one of the Court's best-known cases of the nineteenth century, because the Court took the opportunity to discuss the nature of Indian tribal sovereignty at length. For the Court to have jurisdiction, the Cherokees' suit had to be filed by a "foreign state." Marshall's opinion for the Court began by acknowledging that the Cherokee Nation was clearly a "state." The United States had entered into several treaties with the Cherokees based on that assumption. Indian tribes were obviously not states in the domestic sense, like Georgia or Vermont. Did that make them "foreign" states, as that term was used in the Constitution?

The Court held that tribes were not foreign states either. "It may well be doubted whether those tribes which reside within the acknowledged boundaries of the United States can, with strict accuracy, be denominated foreign nations," Marshall reasoned. Rather, they were in a category of their own. "They may, more correctly, perhaps, be denominated domestic dependent nations," he continued. "They occupy a territory to which we assert a title independent of their will, which must take effect in point of possession when their right of possession ceases. Meanwhile they are in a state of pupilage. Their relation to the United States resembles that of a ward to his guardian." As a result, "the framers of our constitution had not the Indian tribes in view, when they opened the courts of the union to controversies between a state or the citizens thereof, and foreign states." Marshall expressed compassion for the Cherokees. "If courts were permitted to indulge their sympathies," he noted, "a case better calculated to excite them can scarcely be imagined. A people once numerous, powerful, and truly independent, found by our ancestors in the quiet and uncontrolled possession of an ample domain, gradually sinking beneath our superior policy, our arts and our arms, have yielded their lands by successive treaties, each of which contains a solemn guarantee of the residue, until they retain no more of their formerly extensive territory than is deemed necessary to their comfortable subsistence." But they could not sue in the federal courts because they were neither a domestic state nor a foreign state.[8]

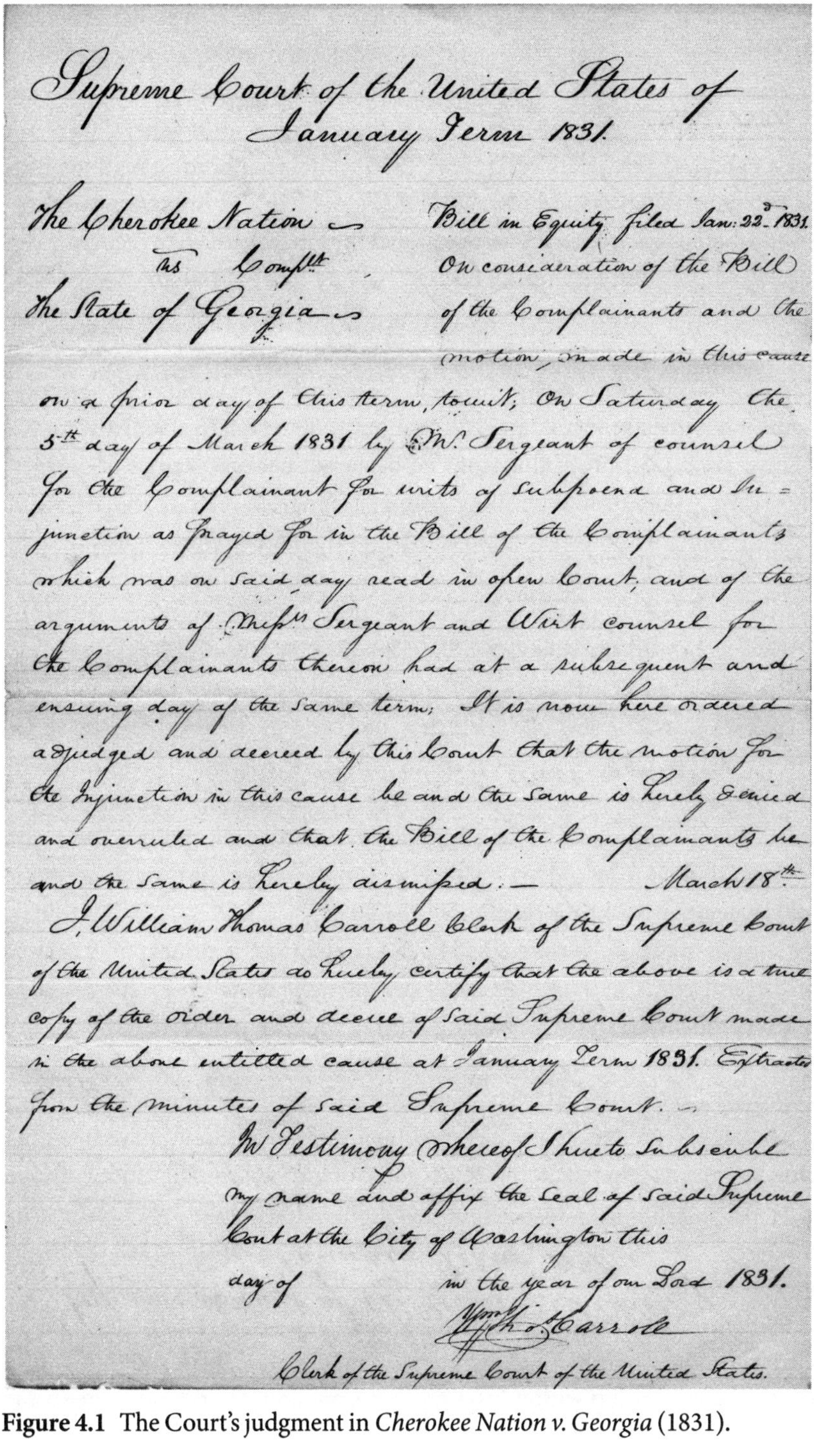

Supreme Court of the United States of
January Term 1831.

The Cherokee Nation   Bill in Equity filed Jan: 22ª 1831.
        vs   Complᵗ   On consideration of the Bill
The State of Georgia   of the Complainants and the
                                                  motion, made in this cause
on a prior day of this term, towit; On Saturday the
5ᵗʰ day of March 1831 by J. M. Sergeant of counsel
for the Complainant for writs of subpoena and In =
junction as prayed for in the Bill of the Complainants
which was on said day read in open Court, and of the
arguments of Mess.ʳˢ Sergeant and Wirt counsel for
the Complainants thereon had at a subsequent and
ensuing day of the same term; It is now here ordered
adjudged and decreed by this Court that the motion for
the Injunction in this cause be and the same is hereby denied
and overruled and that the Bill of the Complainants be
and the same is hereby dismissed. —   March 18ᵗʰ
        I, William Thomas Carroll Clerk of the Supreme Court
of the United States do hereby certify that the above is a true
copy of the order and decree of said Supreme Court made
in the above entitled cause at January Term 1831. Extracted
from the minutes of said Supreme Court. —
            In Testimony whereof I hereto Subscribe
            my name and affix the seal of said Supreme
            Court at the City of Washington this
            day of   in the year of our Lord 1831.
                            Wm Tho. Carroll
            Clerk of the Supreme Court of the United States.

Figure 4.1 The Court's judgment in *Cherokee Nation v. Georgia* (1831).
National Archives, RG 267, Original Jurisdiction Case Files, Case File for
Cherokee Nation v. the State of Georgia, National Archives Identifier 38895559.

William Johnson concurred. In his view, Indians were so uncivilized that the tribes were not states at all. "I cannot but think that there are strong reasons for doubting the applicability of the epithet *state*, to a people so low in the grade of organized society as our Indian tribes most generally are," he reasoned. They were "nothing more than wandering hordes, held together only by ties of blood and habit, and having neither laws or government, beyond what is required in a savage state." If the Cherokees were recognized as a state, where would it stop? "Must every petty kraal of Indians, designating themselves a tribe or nation, and having a few hundred acres of land to hunt on exclusively, be recognized as a state?" Johnson wondered. "We should indeed force into the family of nations, a very numerous and very heterogeneous progeny." Henry Baldwin also concurred, in equally dismissive terms. "There is no plaintiff in this suit," he declared, because "tribes of savages" were simply not juridical entities capable of suing.[9]

Only Smith Thompson and Joseph Story dissented. They argued that the Cherokees *were* a foreign state, that the Court thus had jurisdiction, and that Georgia's statutes were unconstitutional. Story was profoundly influenced by his immersion in the case. He met with two Cherokee leaders soon afterward, who "conversed with singular force and propriety of language upon their own case, the law of which they perfectly understood and reasoned upon," he told his wife. "I never in my whole life was more affected by the consideration that they and all their race are destined to destruction. And I feel, as an American, disgraced by our gross violation of the public faith towards them. I fear, and greatly fear, that in the course of Providence there will be dealt to us a heavy retributive justice."[10]

The plight of the Cherokees had been a contentious national political issue for several years, so the Court faced considerable criticism for its refusal to address the merits of their claims. "The decision of the Court has been frequently assailed, and found few, if any, defenders in the press," the *American Quarterly Review* reported. The *North American Review* thought it "certainly much to be regretted, that a case of this importance should have been decided upon any other principle than that of doing substantial justice between the parties."[11] But the Court's opinion left open the possibility of addressing the Cherokees' arguments if they could be raised in a case in which the Court had jurisdiction.

William Wirt and the Cherokees found such a case soon after. One of Georgia's anti-Cherokee statutes barred white people from residing within the Cherokee Nation without the state's permission. Shortly after the Court decided *Cherokee Nation*, a Congregationalist missionary named Samuel Worcester was convicted under this statute and sentenced to four years in the state penitentiary. Wirt appealed the case to the Supreme Court. The Cherokees won this round. In *Worcester v. Georgia* (1832), Marshall provided a stirring declaration of Indian tribes' inherent sovereignty. "The Indian nations," he insisted, were "distinct, independent political communities, retaining their original natural rights, as the undisputed possessors of the soil." Within the boundaries of the Cherokee Nation, he concluded, "the laws of Georgia can have no force." The Georgia statute under which Worcester was convicted was void. "Thanks be to God," Story wrote to his wife. "The Court can wash their hands clean of the iniquity of oppressing the Indians, and disregarding their rights."[12]

The Court's hands may have been clean, but *Worcester* did nothing to help the Cherokees. There is a widely reprinted story that Andrew Jackson responded disdainfully to *Worcester* by saying "well, John Marshall has made his decision, now let him enforce it." The story originated in Horace Greeley's 1864 book *The American Conflict*, in which Greeley says he heard it from the Massachusetts lawyer George Briggs, who was a member of Congress when *Worcester* was decided.[13] Whether or not Jackson actually said these words, they do reflect his attitude toward the conflict between Georgia and the Cherokees. *Worcester* required Georgia to let Samuel Worcester out of prison, which the state eventually did. In *Worcester* the Court did not, and could not, require the federal government to "enforce" anything. But the Jackson administration continued to do nothing to protect the Cherokees from continuing harassment by the government of Georgia and by white settlers. Within a few years the US Army would round up the Cherokees and force them to leave Georgia for present-day Oklahoma. In the end, the Cherokees gained nothing from the Court's decision in their favor.

These three cases—*Johnson v. M'Intosh*, *Cherokee Nation v. Georgia*, and *Worcester v. Georgia*—expressed the foundational principles defining the sovereignty and property rights of American Indians, principles that still govern the field today. The Court accorded Indian tribes a degree of sovereignty, but not to the extent possessed by states, and a degree of property rights, but not to the extent enjoyed by white property owners. In both respects, Indians' rights were enforceable in theory against states and against individuals, but in practice those rights depended on the federal government to assist in their enforcement, and the federal government was often uninterested in doing so. The Indians' relationship with the federal government was understood as a political or even a military matter in which courts were powerless to intervene, so the Indians had few if any legal rights enforceable against the United States.

Subsequent cases followed this pattern. In *United States v. Rogers* (1846), for example, the Court considered the extent of the federal government's jurisdiction to prosecute crimes that took place in "Indian country," the territory still governed by Indian tribes. William Rogers was a white man who had married into the Cherokee Nation. After his wife's death, he and their children continued to live among the Cherokees, where he was treated as a Cherokee. He had no intention of ever leaving. The federal government charged Rogers with murdering Jacob Nicholson, another white man in the same situation. Nicholson had also married a Cherokee woman and had made his home among the Cherokees. The case raised a fundamental question of jurisdiction: Was this crime an internal Cherokee matter, to be dealt with by the tribe according to its own law? Or could the United States prosecute Rogers?[14]

The Court made clear that the federal government was in full control of its dealings with Indian tribes and that courts had no business interfering. "The native tribes who were found on this continent at the time of its discovery have never been acknowledged or treated as independent nations," Chief Justice Roger Taney declared for a unanimous Court. "On the contrary, the whole continent was divided and parcelled out, and granted by the governments of Europe as if it had been vacant and unoccupied land, and the Indians continually held to be, and treated as, subject to their dominion and control." Courts had no authority "to inquire whether the principle thus adopted is just or not; or to speak of the manner in which the power claimed was in many instances exercised." Whatever the United States did to the Indians was unreviewable by the judiciary. Taney insisted that the government "has exercised its power over this unfortunate race in the spirit of humanity and justice, and has endeavoured by every means in its power to enlighten their minds and increase their comforts, and to save them if possible from the consequences of their own vices." But whether the government had acted with charity or with malice was no concern for the courts. "Had it been otherwise," he concluded, "and were the right and the propriety of exercising this power now open to question, yet it is a question for the law making and political department of the government, and not for the judicial." The United States thus had jurisdiction over any offenses in Indian country it wished to prosecute, regardless of the nominal sovereignty of the tribes.[15]

In the statute under which Rogers was prosecuted, Congress exempted offenses committed by one Indian against another. Rogers argued that this exemption included his crime, but to no avail. "We think it very clear," Taney continued, "that a white man who at mature age is adopted in an Indian tribe does not thereby become an Indian." The Court held that "Indian" was a racial status, not a political one. A person was or was not an Indian by birth, regardless of the political community in which he or she was a member. Rogers might have "become entitled to certain privileges in the tribe," Taney reasoned, "yet he is not an Indian." It was Congress, not the tribe, that had the power to determine which individuals would fall on one side or the other of the jurisdictional divide.[16]

But while the Court deferred to Congress in its dealings with the tribes, the Court was willing to recognize the rights of Indians against private parties. In *Fellows v. Blacksmith* (1856), representatives of the Ogden Land Company evicted a member of the Seneca Nation from land in western New York that the federal government believed it had acquired by treaties from the Senecas as part of the government's removal policy, under which the tribe would be relocated to Kansas. Because of disputes over the treaties' validity and their implementation, many of the Senecas refused to move, to the annoyance of the land company, which had been granted their land. The Court held that even assuming the validity of the treaties, and even assuming that the Ogden Land Company was the rightful owner of the land, the company could not evict the Senecas from the land. Only the federal government could do that. The land company "derived no power, under the treaty, to dispossess by force these Indians," declared Justice Samuel Nelson, who was himself from the region. "A forcible removal must be made, if made at all, under the direction of the United States." Nelson noted that in the long history of pushing the Indians from one place to another to free up land for white settlement, the federal government had always been the sole authorized pusher. "Indeed," he concluded, "it is difficult to see how any other mode of a forcible removal can be consistent with the peace of the country, or with the duty of the Government to these dependent people."[17]

During this period, the Court's cases involving American Indians were thus not about whether Indians would enjoy the same rights as white people. Discrimination against Indians was too engrained a part of American life for it to be questioned in the courts. Rather, the cases were concerned with identifying precisely who—private parties, states, or the federal government—would override the sovereignty and the property rights of tribes.

II

The Court's cases involving slavery were likewise confined to the details of how slavery would be implemented, as opposed to the lawfulness of slavery itself. It was generally understood that each state could allow or forbid slavery as it saw fit, without interference from the federal government or the courts. Some abolitionist lawyers in the decades before the Civil War did contend that the Constitution prohibited slavery, but this argument was never widely accepted and it never reached the Supreme Court, which would surely have rejected it. Nor did any justice consider the morality of slavery to be a question appropriate for the Court to address. The Court would take no "account of the supposed inexpediency and invalidity of all laws recognizing slavery or any right of property in man," Justice Levi Woodbury declared for a unanimous Court in *Jones v. Van Zandt* (1847). "That is a political question."[18]

Instead, the Court's slavery cases involved only a very narrow range of the legal issues that arose from slavery. The law that governed the relationship between slaves and their owners was almost entirely state law, on which the southern state supreme courts had the final word. When slaves were sold, rented, inherited, freed, punished, abused, raped, or even killed, litigation often followed, but such suits rarely reached the Supreme Court.[19] The slavery cases that did reach the Court involved slaves in transit—either from foreign countries to the United States or between slave states and free states—because these were the cases that raised questions of international law or federal law. Although these cases involved only a narrow subset of the legal questions surrounding slavery, it was such an important subset, and slavery was so controversial a topic, that the cases attracted a great deal of attention.

The Court's first prominent slavery cases involved the international slave trade. Congress prohibited the importation of slaves into the United States in 1808, the earliest date permitted by the Constitution. But that did not stop slave traders from trying. When a slave ship was caught entering the country, what would be the fate of its captives, the people who were being brought to the country to be sold into slavery? The Court first ventured an answer to this question in *The Antelope* (1825), when a Spanish ship transporting approximately 280 Africans ostensibly belonging to citizens of Spain and Portugal was captured off the coast of Georgia. The governments of Spain and Portugal claimed the Africans on behalf of their alleged owners. The government of the United States opposed these claims and argued that the Africans should be freed.[20]

The case was one in which "the sacred rights of liberty and of property come in conflict with each other," Marshall observed in his opinion for a unanimous Court. Although he called the slave trade "abhorrent," Marshall insisted that the justices' opinions of slavery had nothing to do with its task, because "this Court must not yield to feelings which might seduce it from the path of duty." Slavery had "been sanctioned in modern times by the laws of all nations who possess distant colonies, each of whom has engaged in it as a common commercial business." Whatever one's views of the morality of slavery, it was lawful in much of the world and in half the United States, so the Court "must obey the mandate of the law."[21]

It is worth pausing a bit over Marshall's suggestion that the Court might have freed the captured Africans if the justices could have indulged their sentiments. Because the allocation of circuits required a regional balance on the Court, most of the early nineteenth-century justices were slaveowners.[22] Whether they were from slave states or free states, the justices all lived for part of the year in the District of Columbia, where slavery was lawful and ubiquitous, including in the White House and around the Capitol, where the Court sat. The justices all experienced slavery as part of everyday life. Four of the six justices who decided *The Antelope* owned slaves—Marshall, Bushrod Washington, William Johnson, and Gabriel Duvall. (The absent seventh justice, Thomas Todd, missed the 1825 term due to illness. He owned slaves as well.) Whatever sympathy they felt for slaves, it was evidently not strong enough to prompt them to free their own slaves.

Some of the justices who owned slaves ventured justifications for slavery. "Certain it is," Johnson told an audience of fellow South Carolina plantation owners, "that at present slaves are the only laborers that can be had to cultivate the country that produces rice, sugar and the long staple cotton. Medical men inform us that there exists a specific difference in secretions of men of the opposite colors" that enabled the descendants of Africans to endure working conditions that would be fatal to the descendants of Europeans. Yet Johnson also left evidence that he was uneasy about the morality of slavery. He remarked to the same audience that "the Christian, who considers all conditions with a view to a state of probation, will often see more to be envied in the life of the slave than in that of the master"—that is, that slaves were more likely to enter heaven than their owners. Marshall evidently shared Johnson's ambivalence about slavery, despite profiting from the ownership and sale of slaves. Yet it seems implausible that the slaveholding justices' doubts concerning the morality of slavery would have caused them to decide cases any differently even if the justices had possessed a broader conception of their own roles as judges. Indeed, four years before the Court decided *The Antelope*, Bushrod Washington sold fifty-four of his approximately ninety slaves to new owners in Louisiana, a world away from the Valley Forge estate he inherited from his uncle George. The sale was widely criticized in the newspapers, which noted that George Washington had treated his own slaves far better by providing in his will for their emancipation upon his wife's death.[23] Marshall suggested at the beginning of his opinion in *The Antelope* that the justices' "feelings" about slavery conflicted with the law, but if we consider the justices' actions rather than their words as the best guide to their feelings, it is hard to avoid some skepticism.

Marshall then reviewed the English cases involving similar captures of slave ships. He concluded that they established a clear principle: if the ship belonged to a nation in which the slave trade was lawful, the slaves would be restored to their owners, but if the ship belonged to a nation in which the slave trade had been abolished, they would not. Nations could either permit or forbid the slave trade, and other nations had to respect that choice. That slavery "is contrary to the law of nature will scarcely be denied," Marshall acknowledged. "Every man has a natural right to the fruits of his own labour," he reasoned, and "no other person can rightfully deprive him of those fruits, and appropriate them against his will." But international law consisted of "the usages, the national acts, and the general assent" of the community of nations, which had engaged in the slave trade for centuries. "Both Europe and America embarked in it; and for nearly two centuries, it was carried on without opposition, and without censure," Marshall noted. "A jurist could not say, that a practice thus supported was illegal."[24]

The justices thus agreed that if the Spanish and Portuguese claimants could prove their ownership of the Africans, the Africans would have to be restored to them as slaves. But the justices were evenly divided on whether the claimants had proven their ownership. After further litigation, thirty-nine of the Africans were designated as Spanish-owned and were sold into slavery, while the remaining Africans were deemed free and were shipped back to Africa.[25] The latter group were not returned to their homes. They were brought instead to Liberia, the new colony founded by the American Colonization Society, an organization devoted to ridding the United States of free black people by sending them to Africa. The president of the Colonization Society was Bushrod Washington.

A similar case, *United States v. The Amistad* (1841), came to the Court sixteen years later.[26] The captured Africans on board the Amistad, another Spanish ship, revolted and took control of the ship, which was eventually seized by the US Navy off the coast of Long Island. Once again, the Spanish government sought to have the Africans returned to their ostensible owners. This time, the United States government took the side of Spain on the ground that a treaty with Spain required the return of ships and cargo seized by pirates, and that the Africans became pirates when they took over the ship. The growing abolitionist community retained John Quincy Adams, the ex-president then serving in Congress, to represent the Africans in the Supreme Court.

Joseph Story's opinion for the Court acknowledged that if the Africans had been lawfully held as slaves under Spanish law, the treaty would require that they be returned to their Spanish owners. But Story determined that the Africans were not slaves under Spanish law. Rather, "they are natives of Africa, and were kidnapped there, and were unlawfully transported to Cuba," in violation of Spanish law. The Africans were free. Donations from abolitionist organizations funded a return trip home.[27]

Neither *The Antelope* nor *The Amistad* involved the domestic law of slavery, which was a much more controversial topic in the United States than the international law governing the slave trade. The Court addressed a few important domestic slavery issues in a series of cases in the 1840s and 1850s.

One set of issues involved the sale of slaves from one state to another. The Constitution gave Congress the power to regulate interstate commerce. Could Congress prohibit interstate commerce in slaves? Did Congress's authority over interstate commerce deprive the southern states of the power to regulate transactions in slaves where the buyer and seller lived in different states? These issues loomed behind the Commerce Clause cases discussed in the previous chapter. They provided a powerful incentive for white southerners to favor a narrow view of the federal government's power and a broad view of the states' power. These questions reached the Court in *Groves v. Slaughter* (1841). A provision of the Mississippi Constitution authorized the state legislature to bar the introduction into the state of slaves for the purpose of sale, while allowing slave owners to bring their own slaves

Figure 4.2 Sengbe Pieh (often called Joseph Cinqué in the United States) led the revolt on the Amistad, which resulted in one of the Court's important slavery cases. This is an engraving by John Sartain based on a portrait painted by Nathaniel Jocelyn in 1840 while Pieh was in prison in New Haven, CT, awaiting trial. National Portrait Gallery, Smithsonian Institution, NPG.69.66.

into the state. Other states in the deep South had similar laws, because white southerners feared that too rapid an increase in the number of slaves might lead to a slave rebellion. *Groves* was a suit to recover a debt that derived from the sale of a slave into Mississippi, in which the debtor argued that the debt was void because the sale had violated this provision of the state constitution. The Court, in an opinion by Smith Thompson, did not address the Commerce Clause. The Court simply held that the state constitution did not itself prohibit interstate slave trading, but merely empowered the Mississippi legislature to do so. The legislature had not yet prohibited the trade, so the Court determined that the transaction was lawful and that the debt was thus valid.[28]

Had the case ended there, *Groves* would have been of little interest outside Mississippi. But Justice John McLean, an opponent of slavery who also believed that the states could not regulate interstate commerce, took the opportunity to expound on his views at some length, even though, as he admitted, "the question I am to consider, is not necessary to a decision of the case." McLean argued that if slaves were considered merely as property, Congress would have the exclusive power to regulate interstate slave sales. But he also argued that the states had the exclusive power to decide the terms on which they would allow slaves to enter the state. He reconciled these two propositions by concluding that "the constitution treats slaves as persons" rather than as property.[29]

McLean's opinion provoked responses from his colleagues. Roger Taney explained that he "had not intended to express an opinion upon the question," but that "as my brother McLean has stated his opinion upon it, I am not willing, by remaining silent, to leave any doubt as to mine." Taney insisted that "the power over this subject is exclusively with the several states," which could decide for themselves the terms on which they would allow the entry of slaves, and that "the action of the several states upon this subject cannot be controlled by congress, either by virtue of its power to regulate commerce, or by virtue of any power conferred by the constitution of the United States." Henry Baldwin agreed with McLean that Congress's power over interstate commerce was exclusive but disagreed with him about the nature of slaves. He thought they were property, that the states could not regulate interstate transactions in slaves, and that the clause of the Mississippi Constitution that purported to do so was void. The other members of the Court found it necessary to take sides in this dispute. They briefly noted their view that the Commerce Clause did not bar Mississippi from regulating the importation of slaves into the state. In this odd way, in a case that did not raise the issue, the Court removed any doubts as to the southern states' ability to govern interstate transactions in slaves.[30]

Another important issue involved the recapture of fugitive slaves. The Constitution's Fugitive Slave Clause required free states to return runaway slaves to their owners. In the Fugitive Slave Act of 1793, Congress established a procedure for doing so, under which a slaveowner or his agent could seize an alleged runaway slave in a free state and take the slave before a judge to prove his ownership. The Fugitive Slave Act prohibited interference with this process, such as by hiding or rescuing the slave. As abolitionist sentiment grew in the north, however, the return of fugitive slaves became a matter of intense controversy. It required judges in free states to, in effect, enforce the slavery laws of the southern states. It gave rise to the considerable risk that free black people in the north might falsely or mistakenly be labeled run-away slaves and sold into slavery in the south. Because of such concerns, Pennsylvania enacted a statute that prohibited taking any black person out of the state for the purpose of making him or her a slave. The state law allowed slaveowners to retrieve their own slaves, but it imposed stricter evidentiary requirements on slaveowners than the Fugitive Slave Act did, to ensure that the people alleged to be runaway slaves truly were.

In *Prigg v. Pennsylvania* (1842), the Court held Pennsylvania's statute un-constitutional. The facts of the case are murky, because the Court did not discuss them in any detail.[31] Margaret Morgan, the ostensible slave, left northern Maryland in 1832 with her husband and their children. The family moved just a few miles away, across the state line to southern Pennsylvania. Morgan's parents had been slaves, so she may have been a slave as a legal matter, but she appears to have been treated as a free person. She and her family lived in Pennsylvania for five years without anyone claiming that she was a fugitive. This period of peace ended in 1837, when a group of men, in-cluding a relative of her former owner, kidnapped her and her children and took them to Maryland, where they seem to have been sold into slavery. The kidnappers were charged with violating the Pennsylvania statute.

"Few questions which have ever come before this court involve more del-icate and important considerations," Story observed in his opinion for the Court, "and few upon which the public at large may be presumed to feel a more profound and pervading interest." He began by noting that the pur-pose of the Constitution's Fugitive Slave Clause was "to guard against the doctrines and principles prevalent in the non–slave-holding states, by preventing them from intermeddling with, or obstructing, or abolishing the rights of the owners of slaves." In Story's view, the Constitution thus did not allow any state regulation of the process of capturing and returning fugitive slaves. The Fugitive Slave Clause "manifestly contemplates the existence of a positive, unqualified right on the part of the owner of the slave, which no state law or regulation can in any way qualify, regulate, control or restrain," he concluded.[32]

Story's opinion made clear that the northern states could not place any obstacles in the path of southern slavecatchers, even for the purpose of ensuring that slavecatchers did not kidnap free black people on false pre-tenses. But by holding that Congress's power over fugitive slaves was exclusive, Story implied that states also lacked the power to pass legislation *helping* southern slavecatchers. Roger Taney, Peter Daniel, and Smith Thompson all wrote separately to quarrel with this point. Daniel emphasized that help from state governments would often be needed to apprehend slaves in free states, because there were many more state officials than federal officials.[33] Taney and Daniel were both sensitive to the practicalities of capturing slaves who had fled to free states, because both were slaveowners in the upper South—Taney in Maryland and Daniel in northern Virginia.

The question whether Congress's authority over fugitive slaves was truly exclusive reached the Court ten years later, in *Moore v. Illinois* (1852). Illinois had convicted the abolitionist Richard Eells of harboring a fugitive slave. Eells was the president of the Illinois Anti-Slavery Party and the party's candidate for governor in 1846. He lived in Quincy, just a few blocks from the Mississippi River, across which lay the slave state of Missouri. His house was the first stop on the Underground Railroad for slaves escaping from Missouri.[34] In 1842, Eells was caught trying to hide a slave named Charley, who had swum across the river. He was convicted in state court—the trial judge was a young Stephen Douglas—and fined $400. (Eells died while the case was pending in the Supreme Court. The case became known as *Moore v. Illinois* because Moore was his executor.)

The case attracted a great deal of attention, in part because Eells was so well known, and in part because of the controversy surrounding the question of fugitive slaves. In the Supreme Court, Eells was represented by Salmon Chase, who was perhaps the most prominent abolitionist in the country. Chase had been elected to the Senate as one of the leaders of the Free Soil Party, which opposed the expansion of slavery in the West. He would go on to be governor of Ohio and secretary of the treasury, and in 1864 he would replace Roger Taney as the Court's chief justice. The state was represented by a sitting senator as well, James Shields of Illinois, who had been a member of the Illinois Supreme Court and indeed had written the opinion affirming Eells's conviction.[35]

Chase relied on *Prigg* to argue that Illinois could not prohibit the harboring of fugitive slaves, because Congress had exclusive power to regulate the subject. The Court rejected the argument, on the ground that Congress's power was not exclusive, and that the states could accordingly pass laws forbidding assistance to fugitive slaves. The Illinois statute "does not interfere in any manner with the owner or claimant in the exercise of his right to arrest and recapture his slave," Justice Robert Grier reasoned. "It neither interrupts, delays, or impedes the right of the master to immediate possession. It gives no immunity or protection to the fugitive against the claim of his master." Grier, whose home state of Pennsylvania shared a long border with the slave state of Maryland, had no sympathy for abolitionists who sought to protect fugitive slaves. In *Moore*, he endorsed the northern state laws such as the one under which Eells had been convicted. In Grier's view, they served the important goal of keeping black people out of the North. "Some of the States, coterminous with those who tolerate slavery, have found it necessary to protect themselves against the influx either of liberated or fugitive slaves," he declared, "and to repel from their soil a population likely to become burdensome and injurious, either as paupers or criminals."[36] The northerners on the Court were not abolitionists. Indeed, Grier might be called an anti-abolitionist.

The southerners on the Court were slaveowners themselves. "These Judges, able and learned as they are, are yet men," Salmon Chase observed in 1853, a year after losing *Moore v. Illinois*. "Five out of the nine are from the Slave States, and cannot be quite exempt from bias. Three of the remaining four were appointed, no doubt, with express reference to their 'soundness' on the slavery question, and are therefore not absolutely impartial."[37] From the perspective of a justice who was accustomed to slavery as part of everyday life, the legal issues involving slaves were no different from the legal issues involving any other kind of property. A federalism case was a federalism case, for example, whether the item in interstate transit was a steamboat, a bushel of wheat, or a human being.

III

The issues of fugitive slaves and interstate slave sales were controversial enough, but the question that would provoke the most controversy involved the status of slaves who were brought by their owners temporarily to free states or territories. Did the slaves become free when they reached a jurisdiction that prohibited slavery? When a slaveowner traveled to a free state with a slave, could the slave simply walk away? Or could the slaveowner compel him to return home? And what if the slave returned home but later claimed to be free? These questions all involved the circumstances under which one state was obliged to respect the contrary laws of another. Was slavery a permanent status that stuck with a person wherever he went? Or did a person's status as a slave change as he traveled from state to state?

This set of questions gave rise to an enormous amount of litigation in the state courts. The Supreme Court first addressed the issue in the narrowest possible way. In *Strader v. Graham* (1850), the Court held that slaves from Kentucky who had been sent by their owner temporarily to Ohio to perform as musicians were not free when they returned to Kentucky, because such was the law of Kentucky. "Every state has an undoubted right to determine the *status*, or domestic and social condition, of the persons domiciled within its territory," Taney explained in a short opinion. "There is nothing in the Constitution of the United States that can in any degree control the law of Kentucky upon this subject. And the condition of the negroes, therefore, as to freedom or slavery, after their return, depended altogether upon the laws of that state, and could not be influenced by the laws of Ohio."[38] Neither state had to yield to the other. Whether or not the musicians could have stayed in Ohio as free men under the laws of Ohio, their return to Kentucky subjected them once again to the laws of Kentucky, under which they were slaves.

Dred Scott v. Sandford (1857) involved a similar question and could have been decided in a similarly narrow manner.[39] Dred Scott was a slave owned by John Emerson, an army doctor who lived in St. Louis. When Emerson was transferred to a post in Illinois, a free state, he took Scott with him. A couple of years later, Emerson was transferred to Fort Snelling in present-day Minnesota and he again took Scott with him, even though Fort Snelling was in a federal territory in which Congress had prohibited slavery. After two years at Fort Snelling and a brief period in Louisiana, Emerson and Scott returned to St. Louis. Back in Missouri, Scott sued for his freedom and that of his wife and children, on the ground that they had become free by virtue of his periods of residence in Illinois and Minnesota. By then, Emerson had died. John Sanford (the case caption misspelled his name as "Sandford") was Emerson's brother-in-law and the executor of his will.

Scott's case took a complicated path to the Supreme Court, at one step of which the Missouri Supreme Court held that under Missouri law, Scott remained a slave despite having lived in places where slavery was illegal.[40] Had the justices wished to write narrowly, the Missouri court's decision would have been enough to decide the case against Scott, using the template set by *Strader v. Graham* a few years before. The Court could simply have said that whether a person was free or enslaved was a question for each state to decide for itself under its own law, and that even if Scott had been a free man in Illinois and Minnesota, Missouri was entitled to make him a slave once more when he returned to the state. An opinion along these lines would not have changed the law or even have attracted much notice. No one today would remember Dred Scott or his lawsuit.

That was the Court's initial plan. After oral argument, Justice Samuel Nelson wrote a short opinion along these lines, explaining that the issue was one of Missouri law, under which Scott was a slave. But the Court soon changed course. The five southern justices decided to use the case to declare that black people were not US citizens and that Congress lacked the authority to prohibit slavery in federal territories.[41] Both propositions, especially the latter, were widely disputed at the time. The Court's decision was welcomed by those in favor of slavery and deplored by slavery's opponents. The North-South dispute over slavery was nearing its peak—the Civil War would begin just a few years later—and the *Dred Scott* decision only fueled the fire.

All nine justices wrote opinions in *Dred Scott*, but Taney's was the one designated as the opinion of the Court. He addressed the issue of black citizenship first. Scott's lawsuit had been filed in federal court because federal courts had jurisdiction to hear suits between citizens of different states. But were black people *citizens* as the word was used in the Constitution? Taney concluded they were not. African Americans "are not included, and were not intended to be included, under the word 'citizens' in the Constitution," he reasoned. "On the contrary, they were at that time considered as a subordinate and inferior class of beings, who had been subjugated by the dominant race, and, whether emancipated or not, yet remained subject to their authority, and had no rights or privileges but such as those who held the power and the Government might choose to grant them." Back in 1832, as Andrew Jackson's attorney general, Taney had expressed the same view in advising Jackson that South Carolina could lawfully imprison free black seamen who entered the state's ports. In *Dred Scott*, he again concluded that the "subordinate and inferior" status of black people meant they were not considered citizens when the Constitution was ratified. "They had for more than a century before been regarded as beings of an inferior order, and altogether unfit to associate with the white race, either in social or political relations; and so far inferior, that they had no rights which the white man was bound to respect," Taney observed. He accordingly concluded that "the court is of opinion, that . . . Dred Scott was not a citizen of Missouri within the meaning of the Constitution of the United States, and not entitled as such to sue in its courts."[42]

In an ordinary case, that would have been the end. If a court lacks juris-diction to decide a case, the court normally does not decide it. But Taney and the Court went on to decide Dred Scott's case anyway.

In the next portion of Taney's opinion, the Court held that Scott was still a slave while he was in Minnesota, on the ground that the federal statute ban-ning slavery in the territory was unconstitutional. This was a surprising con-clusion, because Congress had been prohibiting slavery in federal territories since 1789, when the first Congress prohibited slavery in the Northwest Territory. The prohibition of slavery in Minnesota was part of the Missouri Compromise of 1820, a package that included the admission of Maine and Missouri as states and a ban on slavery in the territories to the north and west of Missouri. Whether Congress *should* prohibit slavery in the territories had been a hotly disputed political issue for decades, but it was generally accepted that Congress *could* prohibit slavery in the territories. The Court held that such measures had been unconstitutional all along because they deprived slaveowners of their property without due process. "An act of Congress which deprives a citizen of the United States of his liberty or property, merely because he came himself or brought his property into a particular Territory of the United States, and who had committed no offence against the laws, could hardly be dignified with the name of due process of law," Taney rea-soned. And a slave was just like any other kind of property. "No word can be found in the Constitution which gives Congress a greater power over slave property, or which entitles property of that kind to less protection than prop-erty of any other description," he continued. "Upon these considerations," Taney concluded, "it is the opinion of the court that the act of Congress which prohibited a citizen from holding and owning property of this kind in the territory of the United States north of the line therein mentioned, is not warranted by the Constitution, and is therefore void; and that neither Dred Scott himself, nor any of his family, were made free by being carried into this territory."[43] With these words, the Court opened the entire West for slavery and undid decades of carefully negotiated North-South compromise.

At the very end of his opinion, Taney noted in a few brisk paragraphs that Scott's years in Illinois did not make him free in Missouri, because that was a question of Missouri law.[44] This passage only underscored how unneces-sary it was for the Court to hold that Congress could not ban slavery in the territories, because if Missouri law governed Scott's status upon his return from Illinois, Missouri law also governed his status upon his return from Minnesota, regardless of whether Scott had been free in Minnesota.

Each justice wrote separately in *Dred Scott*. The four southern justices besides Taney—James Moore Wayne, Peter Daniel, John Archibald Campbell, and John Catron—all agreed that Congress could not ban slavery in the territories, as did one of the northerners, Robert Grier. Samuel Nelson published his original narrow opinion based on Missouri law, so he expressed no view on whether Congress could ban slavery in federal territories. John McLean and Benjamin Curtis dissented on this point. Three justices—Wayne, Daniel, and Grier—agreed with Taney that black people were not citizens.[45] Campbell, Catron, and Nelson did not discuss the issue, while McLean and

Figure 4.3 Dred Scott's 1857 case produced one of the Court's most reviled decisions—criticized at the time primarily because it opened the West to slavery but criticized in our own era mostly because of the Court's holding that black people were not citizens. This portrait of Scott was painted by Louis Schultze between 1888 and 1897, based on a photograph taken by John H. Fitzgibbon in 1857. Scott died of tuberculosis in 1858. Missouri Historical Society, 1897-009-0001.

Curtis again dissented. Six of the nine justices—the five southerners plus Grier—thus used *Dred Scott* as a vehicle for forcing the federal government to allow slavery in the territories, while four of the justices used it to declare that black people were not citizens, in a case that could easily have been decided without addressing either issue.

In retrospect, the Court's eagerness to reach out and decide these questions unnecessarily has been nearly universally condemned as a serious mistake. What did the six justices in the *Dred Scott* majority think they were accomplishing?

One goal they shared was to discourage the abolition of slavery. The most extreme supporter of slavery among the justices was Peter Daniel, who hated the North so passionately that he refused even to visit the region from 1847 to his death in 1860. Daniel was, in effect, a very early secessionist. His biographer concludes that Daniel "believed that the southern people should not cooperate with the northern states in the selection of a President or, for that matter, in any political activities at all. As far as he was concerned, every northerner was an abolitionist and an enemy of the South." Daniel insisted in *Dred Scott* that "the African negro race . . . has been by all the nations of Europe regarded as subjects of capture or purchase; as subjects of commerce or traffic; and that the introduction of that race into every section of this country was not as members of civil or political society, but as slaves, as *property* in the strictest sense of the term." When the Court decided *Dred Scott*, Daniel was in his mid-seventies and in poor health. He would die within three years. Soon before oral argument, his wife suffered a painful, horrific death at their home when a candle ignited the robe she was wearing, leaving him with two small children he knew he would not live long enough to raise.[46] After a lifetime in public office, he must have seen *Dred Scott* as his last chance to exert some influence in the world, for a cause in which he zealously believed.

The other justices in the *Dred Scott* majority may not have been as ardent in their support for slavery as Daniel was, but they too considered the abolition of slavery a dangerous prospect. Roger Taney had freed his own slaves thirty years earlier, while he was in his forties, but his views on race hardened as he aged. Shortly after *Dred Scott*, he wrote to a friend: "Every intelligent person whose life has been passed in a slaveholding State, and who has carefully observed the character and capacity of the African race, will see that a general and sudden emancipation would be absolute ruin to the negroes, as well as to the white race." In Taney's experience, "freedom has been a serious misfortune to the manumitted slave," who lacked "the capacity and fitness for freedom."[47] Taney seems to have been convinced that in ensuring the spread of slavery in the western territories he was performing a valuable public service.

John Archibald Campbell took the same dim view of abolition. "The inevitable consequence of any act of immediate emancipation," he predicted in an 1847 article in the *Southern Quarterly Review*, would be "the abandonment of existing plantations; the sacrifice of all the capital that has been expended upon them; the cessation of field labor and the cultivation of staple productions." As the former slaves dispersed to the "careless cultivation" of small farms of their own, the South would end up with "millions of Robinson Crusoes, without improvement, social ties, public obligations, or private morality." To prevent these dangers, Campbell urged slaveowners not to "yield the destinies of this people to the enterprises even of well meaning projectors;—much less to visionary and unreasoning fanatics," by which he meant abolitionists. He concluded: "We must maintain our ascendancy and control over this institution."[48]

James Moore Wayne likewise saw only danger in abolition. "When slavery has become habitual," he told the American Colonization Society in an 1854 speech, "safety may not permit the dissolution of the evil all at once." Wayne believed that the sudden abolition of slavery "has always produced bloodshed, massacre and war." John Catron agreed that the slaves were better off under slavery. Once they were freed, he insisted, "the black man is degraded by his color, and sinks into vice and worthlessness from want of motive to virtuous and elevated conduct." For this reason, he believed that "the slave who receives the protection and care of a tolerable master holds a condition here superior to the negro who is freed from domestic slavery." The final member of the *Dred Scott* majority was the Pennsylvanian Robert Grier, who although of course not a slaveowner, shared his southern colleagues' scorn for abolitionists. He called them "infuriated fanatics and unprincipled demagogues" who "counsel a bloody resistance to the laws of the land."[49]

The justices in the *Dred Scott* majority thus had a strong interest in preventing the abolition of slavery. The issue of slavery in the territories was very much in the public eye at the time. The previous few decades had demonstrated that territories with slavery usually ended up as states with slavery, while free territories usually ended up as free states. The future balance of power in Congress and the future character of the nation thus depended on the extent to which slavery would be permitted in the territories. Contemporaries were well aware of this, which is why slavery in the territories was such a contentious political issue, despite the relatively small number of slaves actually present there. At midcentury, meanwhile, many more settlers were moving to the northern parts of the West where slavery was unlawful than to the southern parts where slavery was permitted. Southerners worried that emigration patterns alone would harm southern interests in the near future.[50]

The justices had reason to think their intervention would be welcomed, because prominent southern members of Congress had recently called upon the Court to resolve the issue. In 1850, during debate over the status of slavery in the territory newly acquired from Mexico, Henry Clay suggested that an answer "satisfactory to both sides of the question, to the free States and to the slaveholding States," could be provided "by the only competent authority that can definitely settle it forever, the authority of the Supreme Court of the United States." Jefferson Davis, who was then a US senator, likewise declared that "we are entitled to a decision of the Supreme Court of the United States" as to whether "we should be allowed to try the institution of slavery" in California and New Mexico. The Court's majority-southern composition no doubt gave congressional supporters of slavery confidence that the outcome of a decision on the issue would be to their liking. In *Dred Scott*, some of the justices indicated that they too thought the Court was the appropriate forum for resolving the legality of slavery in the territories. Taney feared that "the silence of the court might lead to misconstruction or future controversy." Wayne thought there was "such a difference of opinion" on the issues "that the peace and harmony of the country required the settlement of them by judicial decision." Daniel declared "there never has been submitted to any tribunal . . . questions surpassing in importance those now claiming the consideration of this court."[51] The justices in the *Dred Scott* majority thus believed that by reaching out to decide that Congress had to allow slavery in the territories, they were resolving an important question that needed to be answered and that they were uniquely well placed to answer.

The justices well understood the politics swirling around the case. Catron and Grier both took the extraordinary step of giving James Buchanan, the new president, advance notice of the outcome in time for Buchanan to discuss the case in his inaugural address, two days before the opinions were announced. Buchanan had been the candidate of the Democratic party, which opposed abolition in the territories, and his support had come primarily from the South. In his inaugural address, Buchanan noted that the issue of slavery in the territories was "a judicial question, which legitimately belongs to the Supreme Court of the United States, before whom it is now pending." Without letting on that he already knew the result, Buchanan confidently declared: "To their decision, in common with all good citizens, I shall cheerfully submit, whatever this may be."[52]

Equally extraordinary was Taney's conduct after the opinions were announced. Normally, once the justices read their opinions orally from the bench, the opinions were filed with the Court's clerk, to be printed and made available to the press. After the announcement of *Dred Scott*, however, Taney refused to file his opinion with the clerk. The other justices duly filed their opinions, but Taney kept his. He spent the next few weeks adding a great deal of new material to it, in response to the dissents of Curtis and McLean. Most of the justices, including Curtis, had left Washington to attend to their circuit obligations. Curtis wrote to the Court's clerk, requesting a copy of Taney's revised opinion when it had been printed, but Taney ordered the clerk not to let anyone see the opinion until it had been published in the Court's official reports. When Curtis asked Taney for a copy, Taney sent an angry reply in which he accused Curtis of seeking to use the opinion for improper political purposes. A vituperative series of letters between the two justices followed, culminating in Curtis's resignation from the Court.[53]

Curtis had been thinking about quitting for some time. Unlike most of his colleagues, he came to the Court from a lucrative private practice, so he took a substantial cut in pay. The job was "in a high degree onerous," he complained in 1854, after three years on the Court. The justices' "salaries are so poor that not one judge on the bench can live on what the government pays him." He had trouble supporting his wife and their twelve children. He could not afford a second house in Washington along with his Boston home, so "I must either live apart from my family from four to six months every year while I go there, or subject them to a kind of vagrant life in boarding-houses, neither congenial nor useful." Taney's rudeness in *Dred Scott* was the last straw. "I cannot again feel that confidence in the court, and that willingness to co-operate with them, which are essential to the satisfactory discharge of my duties," he confided to his uncle.[54] He resigned at the age of forty-seven to resume his private practice.

If the justices in the *Dred Scott* majority thought their decision would settle the debate over the status of slavery in the territories, they were badly mistaken. *Dred Scott* was harshly criticized in the northern press. The New York *Tribune* called Taney's opinion a "collation of false statements and shallow sophistries," while the Chicago *Tribune* deplored its "inhuman dicta" and "the wicked consequences which may flow from it." "The opinion of the Chief Justice has disappointed everyone," the lawyer-diplomat John Appleton told Benjamin Curtis. "Whether its mistakes as to fact or its perversions as to law are the more remarkable may well be a matter upon which intelligent men may differ. That history has been falsified through ignorance or mistake— that the law has been disregarded or rather trampled under foot—few will doubt." As one newspaper summarized the reception of Taney's opinion, "the Republican press has been constant in its abuse of Chief Justice Taney ever since the decision of the Supreme Court in the Dred Scott case. He has been characterized as a slavery propagandist, wedded to the exclusive interest of the slave holder of the South, and ready to bow to the behests of that institution at any cost."[55] Court opinions rarely, if ever, settle political controversies. They merely provide more material for the disputants to fight over.

Dred Scott would remain a topic of controversy until it was rendered irrelevant by the onset of the Civil War a few years later. Some writers have claimed that the Court's opinion was one of the causes of the war, but this seems unlikely. If the case had never been decided, or if it had been decided in the narrow fashion the Court initially contemplated, the conflict between the North and the South over slavery would almost certainly have proceeded in just the same way. There is nothing the Court could have done to prevent a war from starting.

In terms of the law, the effect of *Dred Scott* did not last long. The Court's conclusion that Congress could not ban slavery in the territories was superseded by the ratification of the Thirteenth Amendment in 1865, which banned slavery throughout the country. The Court's other conclusion, that black people were not citizens, was superseded in 1866 by the Civil Rights Act and then again in 1868 by the Fourteenth Amendment. Within a decade after *Dred Scott* was decided, it had no impact on the law.

But *Dred Scott* had a lingering effect on the Court itself. When the opinions were published, people already worried that in reaching out to opine unnecessarily on such politically charged questions, the Court had done significant damage to its own reputation. "By grasping at too much, the court have lost the whole," declared the Boston lawyer Timothy Farrar. "The country will feel the consequences of the decision more deeply and more permanently, in the loss of confidence in the sound judicial integrity and strictly legal character of their tribunals, than in anything beside; and this perhaps may well be accounted the greatest political calamity which this country, under our forms of government, could sustain." The Court's decisions had always come in for criticism by those on the losing side, but to its critics, *Dred Scott* seemed like such a nakedly political document that it constituted error of an entirely different order—not just a poor performance as a court but an unseemly eagerness to step outside a court's normal role. "The Supreme Court of the United States has degenerated into a mere partisan and sectional instrument," charged one Massachusetts newspaper. "If we cannot secure a Supreme Court immeasurably above the base partisan uses to which the present court degrades itself, then it were better that the whole thing should be rooted up."[56]

This eventually became the conventional understanding of *Dred Scott*, even within the Court, as mainstream attitudes toward racial equality moved farther away from the views expressed by Taney and the other justices in the majority. In the 1920s, Charles Evans Hughes (then between stints on the Court) described *Dred Scott* as a "self-inflicted wound" from which the Court "suffered severely." In the 1990s, Antonin Scalia recalled how "the Court was covered with dishonor and deprived of legitimacy" by *Dred Scott*.[57] The case became a cautionary tale of the dangers of judicial overreaching.

Dred Scott also rendered Taney an object of scorn throughout much of the North. When Taney died in 1864, the New York lawyer George Templeton Strong wrote in his diary: "The Hon. old Roger B. Taney has earned the gratitude of his country by dying at last. Better late than never." Strong noted the irony that Taney died just as Maryland was finally abolishing slavery. A proposal in the Senate for a bust of Taney to be placed in the courtroom gave rise to an angry debate over whether he deserved the honor. Senator Benjamin Wade insisted that he would not "take money from the pockets of my constituents to commemorate the merits of him who pronounced the Dred Scott decision." John Hale likewise denounced the proposal, because to posterity, "Judge Taney and the Dred Scott decision will go together; the name of Dred Scott will bring up Roger B. Taney, and the name of Roger B. Taney will bring up Dred Scott."[58] Taney would not get his bust until the death of his successor, Salmon Chase, when Congress appropriated funds for busts of both.

By the late twentieth and early twenty-first centuries, when debates about slavery in the territories had long since been forgotten but the issue of racial equality was as salient as ever, the portion of Taney's opinion that seemed the most blameworthy was the section denying citizenship to black people on the ground that they were "considered as a subordinate and inferior class

Figure 4.4 Chief Justice Roger Taney toward the end of his life, photographed in the late 1850s or early 1860s, when his decision in the *Dred Scott* case had caused his reputation to decline in the North. Library of Congress, LC-BH82-402A.

of beings" who "had no rights which the white man was bound to respect." Taney came to be remembered, if at all, as a racist. His statue was removed from the grounds of the Maryland State House in 2017 after a white supremacist rally in Charlottesville, Virginia, focused public attention on monuments to historical figures who expressed views about race that are abhorrent today. Removing Taney's statue was "the right thing to do," explained Maryland Governor Larry Hogan. "The time has come to make clear the difference between properly acknowledging our past and glorifying the darkest chapters of our history."[59]

If *Dred Scott* had been decided narrowly, like the Court's other slavery cases and as the Court originally planned, our memory of Roger Taney would be completely different. When he died in 1864, an obituary observed that "Judge Taney would have left behind him a fame worthy in all respects of his high position, but for his decision in the Dred Scott case, when he reversed the policy of his predecessors and the doctrines of all our wisest statesmen, and acted far more as the advocate of a bad cause than as an impartial Judge."[60] Today, Taney might be almost as obscure as the chief justices who succeeded him—Salmon Chase, Morrison Waite, Melville Fuller, and Edward White—judges who were famous in their own time but who are hardly household names today, except in the households of historians. If Taney would be remembered at all today, it would be for cases like *Charles River Bridge*, involving issues of economic regulation that have faded in importance. So far as race is concerned, Taney might even be viewed positively, as one of the rare slaveowners who emancipated his slaves during his own lifetime. But *Dred Scott* has cast a long shadow, over Taney and over the Court itself.

5

The Court and the Civil War

Like other American institutions, the Supreme Court was profoundly affected by the Civil War and Reconstruction. The war altered the Court's personnel, the kinds of cases it decided, and even its size. The Court, in turn, influenced the war and its aftermath, because in several cases the Court was asked to address the constitutionality of the Union's conduct of the war and of Reconstruction.

The cases arising from the Civil War illustrated the tension at the heart of the Court's role in American government. On one hand, the Court possessed an extraordinary degree of authority. It was called upon, in case after case, to judge whether a war and the subsequent occupation of a defeated opponent were being carried on lawfully. Issues that were considered purely military questions in most of the world were cast as constitutional questions in the United States. On the other hand, the Court was reluctant to use this power anywhere close to its full extent, in part because of the concern that Congress or the president might ignore the Court's orders. The Court did rule against the government on some occasions, but in several of these cases, including the ones that might have had the most significant consequences, the Court avoided having to reach a decision by taking a narrow view of its own jurisdiction and by writing its opinions carefully to avoid casting doubt on the military's activities. We might say that the Court conserved its power by declining to exercise it. Or we might conclude that the Court was stronger in theory than it was in practice.

I

The war had an immediate personal impact on the Court. Three justices were from states that seceded and joined the Confederacy: John Archibald Campbell of Alabama, John Catron of Tennessee, and James Moore Wayne of Georgia. (Peter Daniel of Virginia would have been a fourth, but he died in May 1860 and had not yet been replaced.) They faced a difficult choice. For many years they had been senior members of the government of the United States. Wayne had been on the Court since 1835, Catron since 1837, and Campbell since 1853. All three had opposed secession. "The cause of the South is not lost," Campbell insisted after Lincoln's election. The South "would be strong and powerful in the Union if we had wise counsels among our representatives and people."[1] But all three had deep personal and professional relationships in their home states. Because of the justices' circuit court obligations, they spent more time in the South than they did in Washington. Their families were there. When the Civil War began, Campbell, Catron, and Wayne had to choose sides.

Campbell resigned from the Court in the spring of 1861 and returned to Alabama. Because of his opposition to secession, he was met with "coldness" and "aversion," he later recalled. He played no role in the Confederate government until late 1862, when he became assistant secretary of war. In early 1865 he was part of a delegation of Confederate commissioners who met with Abraham Lincoln and Secretary of State William Seward on a ship docked in Hampton Roads, Virginia, in an unsuccessful effort to negotiate an end to the war. Like other Confederate officials, Campbell was imprisoned after the war, but he was released after a few months, in part because of the intervention of Benjamin Curtis, his former colleague on the Court. Campbell "was not only clear of all connection with the conspiracy to destroy the Government," Curtis reminded the new president, Andrew Johnson, "but incurred great odium in the South and especially in his own State, by his opposition to it." Curtis urged that if Campbell were freed, "he can undoubtedly exert an important influence over Southern opinion" to "promote the pacification of the Country, and the conciliation of Southern opinion to the necessities of their condition."[2] After the war, Campbell became a prominent lawyer in New Orleans. He argued many cases before the Court on which he had once served, including *The Slaughterhouse Cases* (1873) and *United States v. Cruikshank* (1876).

James Moore Wayne and John Catron chose to stay with the Union and continue serving on the Court. Both were considered traitors in the South. The Confederate government charged Wayne as an enemy alien and confiscated all his property in Georgia. He could not go home until after the war. By then he was seventy-five years old. He died two years later. Catron's life was threatened when he tried to return to Tennessee early in the war, but because the Union army gained control of Tennessee soon after, he was able to return to Nashville in 1862, when he resumed holding sessions of the circuit court.³ He died a few weeks after the war ended.

Chief Justice Roger Taney was from Maryland, a slave state but one that did not secede, so he did not face the agonizing choice his southern colleagues had to make. The war nevertheless had a significant impact on Taney as well. An opponent of the war and of ending slavery, he repeatedly found himself at odds with the Lincoln administration and with his colleagues on the Court. One telling instance occurred right at the start of the war, when the governor of Maryland ordered the state militia to destroy several bridges to prevent Union soldiers from traveling through the state. The Union army imprisoned John Merryman, a Maryland farmer, for participating in the destruction of the bridges. Lincoln suspended the writ of habeas corpus, an act that authorized the army to keep Merryman in prison without charging him with any offense. When Merryman challenged the suspension of the writ as unconstitutional, the case came before Taney in his capacity as circuit judge. Taney held that only Congress, not the president, could suspend the writ of habeas corpus. "I had supposed it to be one of those points of constitutional law upon which there was no difference of opinion," he observed, "that the privilege of the writ could not be suspended, except by act of congress." But Lincoln simply disregarded Taney's decision. "Are all the laws *but one* to go unexecuted," he famously asked, "and the Government itself go to pieces lest that one be violated?" He continued suspending the writ of habeas corpus on several occasions over the next two years until Congress finally authorized him to do so in 1863.⁴

The onset of war also had a significant impact on the Court as an institution. The secession of the southern states left the northern states in control of Congress, which allowed for changes to the Court that would not have been possible in earlier years. Senator John Hale suggested getting rid of the Court and creating an entirely new one. The Court "has utterly failed," he charged. "It is bankrupt in everything that was intended by the creation of such a tribunal. It has lost public confidence." The justices "have not been put there because they were learned in the law," Hale insisted. "They have been put there as politicians. This Supreme Court has been a part of the machinery of the old Democratic party." Congress did not go that far, but it did reorganize the circuits to redistribute seats on the Court from the South to the North. Since 1837, five of the nine circuits had consisted of slave states, which ensured that most of the justices were from the South. But the northern states had been gaining population faster than the southern states, so there was a growing

imbalance in the workload of the circuit courts. "Even if there were no rebellion in the country," the *New York Tribune* complained, "the number of
Supreme Judges in the Northern States would not be more than half enough
to transact the business of the Circuits, while at the South there would be
twice as many as were necessary for this purpose. The present"—the absence
of the southern states from Congress—"is a favorable opportunity to restore
a just equilibrium between the sections." Congress seized that opportunity
in 1862 by consolidating the southern states into three circuits rather than
five, to be staffed by the three remaining southern justices, Taney, Wayne,
and Catron.[5]

This reorganization coincided with several vacancies on the Court, so
Lincoln was able to transform the Court within a couple of years. When
Lincoln took office in 1861, the Court already had one vacancy due to the
death of Peter Daniel the previous year. John McLean's death in April 1861
created a second, and then John Archibald Campbell's resignation the same
month created a third. A fourth vacancy opened in 1863, when Congress,
again taking advantage of the absence of the southern states, added a tenth
justice to the Court to cover a circuit including California and Oregon.
Lincoln was thus able to remake the Court by appointing four new justices
in quick succession, all from the North or the West—Noah Swayne (Ohio),
Samuel Miller (Iowa, replacing the Virginian Peter Daniel), David Davis
(Illinois, replacing John Archibald Campbell of Alabama), and Stephen Field
(California). Swayne, Miller, and Davis were politically active Republicans,
and indeed Davis had been Lincoln's campaign manager in 1860. Field
was a Democrat, but as the chief justice of the California Supreme Court
he was the most prominent judge in the new Pacific states, and his brother,
the New York lawyer David Dudley Field, was close to Lincoln.[6] Except for
Swayne, the new justices were in their mid-forties, nearly forty years younger
than Roger Taney. They would all remain on the Court for lengthy periods—
more than thirty-four years in Field's case, which was then a record and is
still the second-longest tenure of any justice.

Taney remained on the Court, despite his worsening health, until his death
in 1864 at age eighty-seven. In an era before the justices received pensions,
Taney was too poor to retire, a problem made worse by the fact that most of
his meager savings were invested in Virginia state bonds, which secession
rendered nearly worthless. After his death, the members of the Supreme
Court bar established a fund to help support his daughters. Taney's replacement, Lincoln's fifth appointment to the Court in three years, was Salmon

Chase, who had been a leading antislavery advocate, one of the founders of the Republican Party, a senator from Ohio, the governor of Ohio, and most recently Lincoln's secretary of the treasury, a position with even more responsibility than usual due to the crushing fiscal burden of the war. Before the war, a person with Chase's record of opposing slavery might never have been confirmed by the Senate, but in the absence of the southern states, Chase was confirmed within hours of his nomination. Lincoln appointees now made up half the ten-justice Court. "I regard your appointment as a matter of profound importance," one Republican lawyer told Chase, because of the Court's expected role "in upholding the legislative & executive policy demanded for the suppression of the Rebellion."[7]

The Court continued to sit during the war, although its caseload declined due to the absence of cases from the South. The Court occupied a new, much more spacious courtroom in the Capitol, the former Senate chamber directly above the old courtroom, which became available in 1860 when the Capitol was enlarged and the Senate moved to a new wing of the building. "The members of this Court have suffered much" from the poor ventilation of the old basement courtroom, the Architect of the Capitol explained. "The death of some of our most talented jurists had been attributed to this location of the court-room." Whether or not the new courtroom was life-prolonging, it was certainly more comfortable. There were skylights in the high domed ceiling. The justices now sat in big chairs behind a long straight elevated desk. There was space for a library and a "retiring-room" behind the desk, from which the justices could emerge fully robed. There were still sofas for spectators.[8] Oral arguments would be conducted in this courtroom until the 1930s, when the Court finally acquired a building of its \.

While the war was ongoing, the Court heard two important cases challenging the methods by which the Lincoln administration was conducting the war.[9] In both cases the Court sided with the administration.

In *The Prize Cases* (1863), the Court rejected a challenge to the Union blockade of southern ports.[10] The vote was 5–4 (the Court had not yet been expanded to ten justices), with the three Lincoln appointees supporting the administration, joined by the Democrats James Moore Wayne and Robert Grier. The four dissenters were all Democrats—Roger Taney, John Catron, Samuel Nelson, and Nathan Clifford. In *The Prize Cases*, the Court confronted a fundamental question about the legal nature of the Civil War. Lincoln never asked Congress for a formal declaration of war because a declaration of war would have implicitly recognized the Confederacy as a

Figure 5.1 Oral arguments were held in this courtroom in the Capitol from 1860, when the Court moved upstairs into the former Senate chamber, until 1935, when the Court got its own building. Library of Congress, LC-H25-18819-CH.

separate country. The administration's position was that secession was impossible and that the states claiming to have seceded were still part of the Union. To fight effectively, however, the Union had to do all the things that nations do when they are at war, such as blockading ports and capturing ships. In the absence of a war, most of these activities would have been clearly beyond the authority of the federal government, which had no power in peacetime, for example, to seize property or to blockade ports. The onset of the Civil War created a legal dilemma for the Lincoln administration, which tried to fight a war without formally acknowledging the existence of one.

This dilemma quickly gave rise to litigation. In April 1861, shortly after the Confederate attack on Fort Sumter marked the beginning of fighting, Lincoln proclaimed a blockade of southern ports. In July, Congress prohibited all trade between the Union and the Confederacy. Union vessels began capturing ships that violated these provisions, including the four merchant ships involved in *The Prize Cases*, which were captured in May, June, and July. The owners of the ships argued that the captures were unlawful because there was no war as a legal matter. Everyone agreed that the ships could not be captured unless a state of war existed. The Court thus confronted a very unusual kind of legal question: When, precisely, did the Civil War begin? Had it even begun at all? Could the Union conduct a war without formally recognizing that it was doing so?

Robert Grier's majority opinion treated the existence of war as a factual question. "To legitimate the capture of a neutral vessel or property on the high seas, a war must exist *de facto*," he began. "Let us enquire whether, at the time this blockade was instituted, a state of war existed." He determined that it did. "As a civil war is never publicly proclaimed, *eo nomine* [by that name], against insurgents, its actual existence is a fact in our domestic history which the Court is bound to notice and to know," Grier reasoned. "When the regular course of justice is interrupted by revolt, rebellion, or insurrection, so that the Courts of Justice cannot be kept open, *civil war exists* and hostilities may be prosecuted on the same footing as if those opposing the Government were foreign enemies invading the land." The Court held that a state of war existed as soon as the fighting began. "This greatest of civil wars was not gradually developed by popular commotion, tumultuous assemblies, or local unorganized insurrections," Grier recalled. "However long may have been its previous conception, it nevertheless sprung forth suddenly from the parent brain, a Minerva in the full panoply of *war*. The President was bound to meet it in the shape it presented itself, without waiting for Congress to baptize it with a name" by formally declaring war. Nor was the Union required to recognize the Confederacy as a country before a state of war could exist. "It is not the less a civil war, with belligerent parties in hostile array, because it may be called an 'insurrection' by one side, and the insurgents be considered as rebels or traitors," Grier explained. "It is not necessary that the independence of the revolted province or State be acknowledged in order to constitute it a party belligerent in a war according to the law of nations." When a war existed in actual fact, it existed as a matter of law. The Court would not "affect a technical ignorance of the existence of a war, which all the world acknowledges to be the greatest civil war known in the history of the human race, and thus cripple the arm of the Government and paralyze its power by subtle definitions and ingenious sophisms." The five-justice majority upheld the captures of the ships as lawful, on the ground that a state of war existed in fact at the time they were captured.[11]

Samuel Nelson's dissent, by contrast, began with the premise that the legality of the captures depended on whether a war existed as a legal matter, not on whether it existed in fact. "In the case of a rebellion or resistance of a portion of the people of a country against the established government," he explained, "there is no doubt, if in its progress and enlargement the government thus sought to be overthrown sees fit, it may by the competent power recognize or declare the existence of a state of civil war, which will draw after it all the consequences and rights of war." But to trigger those consequences, Nelson continued, the government had to formally declare war. "Before this insurrection against the established Government can be dealt with on the footing of a civil war," he argued, "it must be recognized or declared by the war-making power of the Government. No power short of this can change the legal status of the Government or the relations of its citizens from that of peace to a state of war." Nelson acknowledged that there was obviously a war taking place as a factual matter, but in his view that was not the relevant question. "In one sense, no doubt this is war, and may be a war of the most extensive and threatening dimensions and effects," he recognized. But to decide the lawfulness of the capture of a ship, "the question is what constitutes war in a legal sense, in the sense of the law of nations, and of the Constitution of the United States? For it must be a war in this sense to attach to it all the consequences that belong to belligerent rights." The United States did not acquire the rights of a belligerent simply by fighting. First it had to create a state of war by formally recognizing the existence of one. Nelson concluded that Congress's act of July 1861, which authorized Lincoln to prohibit trade with the Confederacy, constituted such a formal recognition of a state of war. In the view of the four dissenters, captures after that date were lawful, but captures beforehand, including those of the ships before the Court, were not.[12]

The mere existence of *The Prize Cases* underscored the remarkable power wielded by the Supreme Court. In any other nation, it would have been unthinkable for a court to assume the responsibility of deciding whether the nation's government would be allowed to wage war. Yet everyone involved in the case seems to have assumed that the Court had the authority to decide the question. "In all States but ours," remarked Richard Henry Dana shortly before the case was argued, "the function of the judiciary is to interpret the acts of the government. In ours, it is to decide upon their legality." Dana, one of the lawyers representing the government, was acutely aware of the magnitude of the issue the Court would be deciding. "Contemplate, my dear sir," he wrote to Charles Francis Adams, "the possibility of a Supreme Court declaring that this blockade is illegal!" If the government lost the case, Dana worried, "it would end the war, and where it would leave us with neutral powers is fearful to contemplate! Yet such an event is legally possible."[13] The Court is sometimes said to have suffered a loss of authority because of its decision in *Dred Scott* six years earlier, but it is hard to see any evidence of such a loss in *The Prize Cases.*

The government won *The Prize Cases,* but it was a close call. If Lincoln had not had the good fortune to appoint three new justices in the previous year, the case would likely have gone the other way, because it is hard to imagine Peter Daniel or John Archibald Campbell voting for the government. Nelson's dissent reached a relatively mild conclusion in dating the legal start of the war to Congress's statute of July 1861, which provided a basis for captures thereafter. Given the reasoning in Nelson's opinion, it would also have been plausible for the dissenters to have concluded that no state of war existed even in 1863, for lack of a formal declaration of war from Congress. If Nelson's opinion had reached that conclusion, and if there had been one more vote for it, the Court might have seriously hindered the Union's conduct of the war. The result might well have been a constitutional crisis because it is not at all clear that Lincoln would have obeyed the Court.

The other important war-related case decided by the Court during the war was *Ex parte Vallandigham* (1864). The federal government arrested and imprisoned thousands of people for disloyalty during the war. Some were never tried at all; others were tried by military commissions rather than the regular courts. Clement Vallandigham was one of the best known. He was a member of Congress from Ohio who fiercely opposed the war. He gave antiwar speeches throughout the North, to the irritation of the War Department. In the speech for which he was arrested, Vallandigham argued that "the present war was a wicked, cruel, and unnecessary war, one not waged for the preservation of the Union, but for the purpose of crushing out liberty and to erect a despotism." He contended that it was "a war for the freedom of the blacks and the enslavement of the whites" that "could have been honorably terminated long ago." He accused the government of using the war as an excuse "to restrain the people of their liberties, and to deprive them of their rights and privileges," and he urged his listeners to "defeat the attempts now being made to build up a monarchy upon the ruins of our free government." For these words, Vallandigham was convicted by a military tribunal and sentenced to be confined in a military fortress for the duration of the war.

Lincoln commuted the sentence by ordering that Vallandigham be taken to Tennessee and handed over to the Confederate forces there.[14] Vallandigham continued his colorful career once he had been freed. He somehow managed to reach Ontario, from where he ran for governor of Ohio in absentia. He lost, but he remained active in politics, even venturing to Chicago to take part in the 1864 Democratic convention.

Meanwhile, fellow antiwar Democrats attempted to use Vallandigham's case to bring a challenge in the Supreme Court to the government's use of military commissions to try opponents of the war. Vallandigham was represented by Ohio Senator George Pugh, who asked the Court to overturn the military conviction. The Court unanimously held that it lacked jurisdiction to do so. "Whatever may be the force of Vallandigham's protest, that he was not triable by a court of military commission," Wayne held in his short opinion for the Court, the statutes delineating the Court's jurisdiction did not allow it "to review or pronounce any opinion upon the proceedings of a military commission." The Court could only review the decisions of lower *courts*, and a military commission was not a court.[15]

The Court thus avoided deciding, during the war, whether civilians could be tried in military commissions rather than in the regular courts. If the Court had reached the question and had decided in Vallandigham's favor, the decision would have mandated a significant change in the way the Lincoln administration conducted the war. There is no way to know whether Lincoln would have complied with the decision. Perhaps this consideration played some role in the Court's willingness to find that it lacked jurisdiction to review the decisions of military commissions. The issue would come before the Court again two years later, shortly after the war ended, when the immediate consequences of a decision against the government were very different.

In January 1865, as the war neared its end, John Swett Rock applied for admission to the Supreme Court bar. Rock was a prominent lawyer, physician, and public speaker in Boston. He was also black, and the Court had never received an application from a black lawyer before. When Chase asked his colleagues what they thought the Court should do, the justices unanimously agreed that Rock's application should be granted. "We adjourned with the understanding that colored men qualified could be admitted without regard to complexion," Chase noted in his diary. "Progress!" Rock was admitted to the Court's bar the next week—the same week that Congress approved the Thirteenth Amendment, which prohibited slavery. "And here has the Supreme Court of the United States just been admitting a colored person one of its attorneys," marveled the New York lawyer George Templeton Strong. "I can scarce believe the evening papers. The dust that was Roger B. Taney must have shivered in its tomb when the motion was granted."[16]

II

The Civil War ended in April 1865. A week later, Andrew Johnson became president after the assassination of Abraham Lincoln. Johnson's term in office would be marked by repeated conflict with Congress over Reconstruction, the process of readmitting the southern states to the Union. Part of this conflict involved the Supreme Court, which would decide several cases involving the constitutionality of aspects of Reconstruction.

To prepare for these cases, Congress shrank the Court. Johnson's nominee to replace the deceased John Catron was the Ohio lawyer Henry Stanbery, a close ally of Johnson's. Stanbery had advised Johnson in some of his battles with Congress, including Johnson's veto (which Congress overrode) of the Civil Rights Act of 1866. Stanbery "is with us thoroughly, earnestly," Johnson confided to Gideon Welles, the secretary of the navy. He would be "a sound man on the bench" who would be "right on constitutional questions." Members of Congress were also familiar with Stanbery's constitutional views regarding Reconstruction, and they could foresee similar nominations from Johnson in the future. Johnson had nearly three years left as president. There were likely to be more vacancies during that time, because the longest-serving justices—James Moore Wayne, Samuel Nelson, and Robert Grier—were all in their seventies, and Grier was in poor health. Rather than acting on the nomination of Stanbery, Congress quickly enacted a statute reducing the size of the Court through attrition from ten justices to seven, which would prevent Johnson from making any appointments until three additional vacancies emerged. Chief Justice Salmon Chase favored the legislation and even conferred with members of the House Judiciary Committee while it was being prepared. Justice David Davis explained to his brother-in-law that "the bill was passed simply to prevent the President from appointing Supreme Judges."[17]

This maneuver would have a major effect on the Court. When Wayne died in 1867, only eight justices were left. The Court never got down to seven. In April 1869, once Johnson's term as president ended, Congress increased the size of the Court back to nine justices, where it has remained ever since.[18]

The new president, Ulysses Grant, would solidify Republican control of the Court by appointing four new justices, two of whom would have been Johnson appointments had Congress not temporarily downsized the Court.

The Republicans in Congress were particularly concerned about the Court's personnel because the Court was soon called upon to decide some fundamental questions involving the constitutionality of Reconstruction. The first of these cases was *Ex parte Milligan* (1866). Lambdin Milligan, an Indiana lawyer who opposed the war, was convicted and sentenced to death in 1864 by a military commission for conspiring against the government. In the Supreme Court, he argued that the Constitution prohibited the government from using military commissions to try civilian opponents of the war. In a narrow sense, *Milligan* was a challenge to the Union's conduct of the

Figure 5.2 The first group photograph of the justices, taken in February 1867. Congress had recently reduced the Court's size from ten to seven through attrition to prevent Andrew Johnson from appointing any new justices. There are nine justices in this picture, which was taken a few months before the death of James Moore Wayne reduced their number to eight. D. W. Middleton, the clerk of the Court, is standing at the left. Seated from left to right are David Davis, Noah Swayne, Robert Grier, James Moore Wayne, Salmon Chase, Samuel Nelson, Nathan Clifford, Samuel Miller, and Stephen Field. Library of Congress, LC-USZ62-9906.

war rather than to Reconstruction. But under Reconstruction, the military was governing the South at the time. It was trying civilians before military commissions. The case was thus generally understood as a test of the constitutionality of this aspect of Reconstruction.[19]

All nine justices agreed that Milligan's trial had been unlawful. "During the late wicked Rebellion," David Davis observed in his opinion for a five-justice majority, "the temper of the times did not allow that calmness in deliberation and discussion so necessary to a correct conclusion of a purely judicial question. *Then*, considerations of safety were mingled with the exercise of power; and feelings and interests prevailed which are happily terminated. *Now* that the public safety is assured, this question, as well as all others, can be discussed and decided without passion." Davis concluded that the government could not try civilians in military courts when the regular civilian courts were open. "This court has judicial knowledge," he explained, "that in Indiana the Federal authority was always unopposed, and its courts always open to hear criminal accusations and redress grievances." The Constitution guaranteed defendants the right to be tried before a normal court, where one was available. "One of the plainest constitutional provisions was, therefore, infringed when Milligan was tried by a court not ordained and established by Congress, and not composed of judges appointed during good behavior." Davis cautioned "that this is not a question of the power to proclaim martial law, when war exists in a community and the courts and civil authorities are overthrown. Nor is it a question what rule a military commander, at the head of his army, can impose on states in rebellion to cripple their resources and quell the insurrection." In such circumstances, the military had full power to use tribunals of its own. But Indiana was not in rebellion in 1864. Its courts were open for business, including for the prosecution of people like Lambdin Milligan. "If in Indiana he conspired with bad men to assist the enemy," Davis concluded, "he is punishable for it in the courts of Indiana," not in a military tribunal.[20]

Chase wrote a concurring opinion, joined by Wayne, Swayne, and Miller. They agreed that Milligan should not have been tried by a military commission, but they were evidently concerned about the implications of Davis's opinion for Reconstruction. The majority seemed to have concluded "not only that the military commission held in Indiana was not authorized by Congress," Chase explained, "but that it was not in the power of Congress to authorize it." In Chase's view, Congress *did* have the power to authorize trials before military commissions, as it had done in Reconstruction. The fault in

Milligan's trial, they concluded, was merely that Congress had never author-ized them in Indiana.[21]

Many years later, *Milligan* would be hailed as "one of the great landmarks" of individual liberty against government oppression, for affirming "the tra-dition of military subordination to civil authorities and institutions" by holding that the government cannot use military tribunals to try civilians where the regular courts are functioning. At the time, however, *Milligan* was generally understood as a blow to Reconstruction, because it cast doubt on the constitutionality of military trials in the South. David Davis, the au-thor of the Court's opinion, was baffled by its reception. "Not a word is said in the opinion about reconstruction," he complained. "Yet the Republican press everywhere has denounced the opinion as a second Dred Scott." Davis thought the two cases were completely different, because "the Dred Scott opinion was in the interest of slavery, & the Milligan opinion is in the interest of liberty." To another correspondent he declared: "If that decision is not law there is an end of Constitutional liberty." He was amazed at the criticism he received. "The people are mad," he exclaimed. "Cowardice is the vice of the times. Do the people want to legalize military commissions?"[22]

In the view of many, however, military commissions were badly needed in the South, to protect black people from violence on the part of whites, who would almost certainly be acquitted by all-white juries in the southern state courts. *Milligan* seemed to imperil this project, so it was deplored in the northern press. The *New York Times* summed up this understanding of the case: "The Supreme Court, we regret to find, throws the great weight of its influence into the scale of those who assailed the Union." Davis's professed inability to comprehend this concern may have been due to his skepticism about Reconstruction, which he thought was doomed to failure. "Negro suf-frage ... may prove a measure of wisdom and good statesmanship, but I doubt it," he remarked during a trip to the South. "I was raised among negroes. I have a great kindness for their race & in my soul I believe the insisting on their political rights is to their injury," in light of "the degraded ignorance of the poor creatures." In the long run, *Milligan* would be seen as a strong statement of constitutional liberty against military rule, but when the case was decided, its primary beneficiaries were thought to be southern whites, who seemed to have gained the liberty to be tried in their own racially biased court systems rather than in courts run by the Union army.[23]

Soon after, in a pair of 1867 cases, the Court held unconstitutional another key aspect of Reconstruction, the disqualification of former Confederates from positions of responsibility in the rebuilt southern states. *Cummings v. Missouri* (1867) was a challenge to a provision of the new Missouri constitution that limited voting, political office, and several professions, including the ministry, to those who swore an oath that they had always supported the United States against its enemies. The case involved a Catholic priest convicted of preaching without having taken the oath. *Ex parte Garland* (1867) was a challenge to a federal statute that imposed a similar oath requirement for attorneys before they could practice in the federal courts. The suit was brought by Augustus Garland, a former Confederate senator from Arkansas who had been one of the many Confederate officials pardoned by President Andrew Johnson. (In the 1870s and 1880s he would become the governor of Arkansas, a US senator, and finally attorney general in the Grover Cleveland administration.) Garland, like most prominent lawyers in the South, was excluded from practicing in the federal courts because of his former support for the Confederacy.[24]

In both cases, by the same 5–4 party-line vote, the Court held that the loyalty oath requirement violated the Ex Post Facto Clause of the Constitution, because it retrospectively increased the punishment for past acts. "The disabilities created by the constitution of Missouri must be regarded as penalties—they constitute punishment," Stephen Field explained for the Democratic majority in *Cummings*. "The deprivation of any rights, civil or political, previously enjoyed, may be punishment." In *Garland*, Field likewise concluded that the exclusion of attorneys from the federal courts "imposes a punishment for some of the acts specified which were not punishable at the time they were committed." In both cases, the four dissenters were Lincoln's Republican appointees—Chase, Swayne, Miller, and Davis. They viewed the loyalty oaths not as punishment but merely as qualifications for the privilege of practicing a profession, of the kind that governments had always imposed. "The act which has just been declared to be unconstitutional," Miller argued in *Garland*, "is nothing more than a statute which requires of all lawyers who propose to practise in the national courts, that they shall take the same oath which is exacted of every officer of the government, civil or military." He concluded that "fidelity to the government under which he lives, a true and loyal attachment to it, and a sincere desire for its preservation, are among the most essential qualifications which should be required in a lawyer."[25]

Cummings and *Garland* were roundly criticized in the North for allowing former Confederates back into positions of power. *Harper's Weekly* decried "the disposition of the Court to withstand the national will and to reverse the results of the war." The *New York Herald* wondered: "How is Congress to make any discriminations between loyal citizens and rebels in the work of Southern reconstruction?" Representative Thomas Williams of Pennsylvania introduced a bill forbidding the Court from declaring a statute unconstitutional unless the Court was unanimous.[26] As in *Milligan*, the Court seemed sympathetic to the South when considering the constitutionality of Reconstruction.

For this reason, as soon as Congress passed the first two Reconstruction Acts in March 1867, providing for military governance of the southern states, Mississippi immediately filed a suit against President Andrew Johnson directly in the Supreme Court in which it asked the Court to enjoin Johnson from enforcing the statutes. "For the first time in the history of any nation," one astonished spectator observed, "the legal representatives of the participants in an organized rebellion, defeated in the field, were permitted to appear in court, not to defend their clients on trial, but to arraign and deny the authority of the law-making power, and plead anew the issue of the cause already decided by the sword."[27] Courts in other countries were not understood to have the authority to decide how the winner of a war should treat the loser. That was a military issue, not a legal question for courts to decide. Only in the United States did lawyers litigate the terms of military occupation in the aftermath of a war.

In *Mississippi v. Johnson* (1867), a unanimous opinion by Chase announced only ten days after Mississippi asked leave to file the suit and only three days after oral argument, the Court held that it could not enjoin the president from administering the Reconstruction Acts. Although courts could order executive branch officials to perform or refrain from performing acts that were merely ministerial, Chase explained, they could not enjoin the president regarding acts that were "executive and political," such as the governance of the South. "The impropriety of such interference will be clearly seen upon consideration of its possible consequences," Chase reasoned. "Suppose the bill filed and the injunction prayed for allowed. If the President refuse obedience, it is needless to observe that the court is without power to enforce its process. If, on the other hand, the President complies with the order of the court and refuses to execute the acts of Congress, is it not clear that a collision may occur between the executive and legislative departments of the government? May not the House of Representatives impeach the President for such refusal?" He concluded that "this court has no jurisdiction of a bill to enjoin the President in the performance of his official duties."[28]

The very same day, the southern states tried again to have the Court decide the constitutionality of Reconstruction. Georgia filed a similar suit, but this time against Edwin Stanton, the secretary of war, and Ulysses Grant, who commanded the Army. Once again, Georgia asked the Court to enjoin the enforcement of the Reconstruction Acts. In *Georgia v. Stanton* (1868), the Court again found that it lacked jurisdiction. For a case to be "appropriate for the exercise of judicial power," Samuel Nelson's opinion held, the case must involve "rights of persons or property, not merely political rights, which do not belong to the jurisdiction of a court." Georgia claimed to have suffered a loss to its sovereignty, but that kind of injury, the Court reasoned, was not the kind that courts could redress. Georgia's grievances presented "political questions," not legal ones. The Court could consider the constitutionality of Reconstruction only in a suit alleging the loss of property, liberty, or some similar right, not in a suit alleging harm to a state's political power.[29]

It did not take long to find such a case. The Mississippi journalist William McCardle, editor of the *Vicksburg Times*, had been imprisoned by the military for publishing editorials in which he urged whites not to vote in elections for a state constitutional convention. His appeal to the Court, after having been denied a writ of habeas corpus, challenged the constitutionality of Reconstruction in precisely the way the Court had said a case should be framed, as one alleging the loss of liberty. The Court held oral argument in McCardle's case in March 1868. Congress, fearing that the Court would declare Reconstruction unconstitutional, hurriedly repealed the statute giving the Court jurisdiction to hear appeals in habeas corpus cases. Now the case raised a new question: Could Congress deprive the Court of jurisdiction to decide a pending case? In *Ex parte McCardle* (1869), the Court held unanimously that Congress indeed could. The Constitution provided that the Court's jurisdiction was subject to "such exceptions . . . as Congress shall make," Chase pointed out in his opinion for the Court. "It is quite clear, therefore, that this court cannot proceed to pronounce judgment in this case, for it has no longer jurisdiction of the appeal." By withdrawing the Court's jurisdiction, Congress prevented the Court from determining the constitutionality of Reconstruction.[30]

At nearly the same time, the Court eschewed one more opportunity to address the issue. Strictly speaking, *Texas v. White* (1869) was not about whether Reconstruction was constitutional.[31] The suit was filed by the Reconstruction government of Texas, invoking the Court's original jurisdiction, to recover US bonds the state had unlawfully sold during the war. The main question before the Court was whether Texas was a "state," despite being governed by the military, because the relevant component of the Court's original jurisdiction extended only to suits by states. But this jurisdictional issue bled into the question of the constitutionality of Reconstruction. If Texas was a state, did that mean the Constitution barred the federal government from controlling it? To uphold Reconstruction, did the Court have to conclude that Texas was not a state?

In a majority opinion by Chase, the Court scrupulously avoided saying anything about the constitutionality of Reconstruction. The Court held that Texas had always been a state. The Union was perpetual and secession was a nullity. In Chase's famous words, "the Constitution, in all its provisions, looks to an indestructible Union, composed of indestructible States." It was still a state despite having been governed by the military since the war's end. "Whether the action then taken was, in all respects, warranted by the Constitution, it is not now necessary to determine," Chase declared. "The power exercised by the President was supposed, doubtless, to be derived from his constitutional functions, as commander-in-chief; and, so long as the war continued, it cannot be denied that he might institute temporary government within insurgent districts." Chase carefully skirted any discussion of the Reconstruction Acts. "We do not inquire here into the constitutionality of this legislation so far as it relates to military authority, or to the paramount authority of Congress," he insisted. "It suffices to say, that the terms of the acts necessarily imply recognition of actually existing governments" capable of filing suits on behalf of states. Grier, Swayne, and Miller dissented, on the ground that Texas had not been a state since secession because it was not represented in Congress or in the Electoral College, but they too avoided discussing the constitutionality of the Reconstruction Acts.[32]

The Court never did decide whether Reconstruction was unconstitutional. Part of the responsibility lies with Congress, which, having already reduced the size of the Court to ensure that no new anti-Reconstruction justices could be appointed, manipulated the Court's jurisdiction when it seemed that a change in size would not be enough to prevent an adverse decision. But much of the responsibility lies with the justices themselves. In three cases—*Johnson*, *Stanton*, and *McCardle*—in three consecutive years, for three different reasons, the Court found that it lacked the jurisdiction to address the constitutionality of Reconstruction. In a fourth case, *White*, in which the Court found that it did have jurisdiction, it wrote narrowly to avoid the issue. Any of these cases could have been decided differently, had the justices been eager to decide the question. But they evidently were not. A decision against the constitutionality of Reconstruction would have been widely perceived as another *Dred Scott*—another example of the Court gratuitously seizing the right to decide the country's most divisive political issue. And a decision in *favor* of Reconstruction's constitutionality was unnecessary, because, by simply declining to address the question, the Court preserved Congress's authority to legislate as it saw fit.

Despite their efforts to stay out of the political controversy surrounding Reconstruction, at times the justices found themselves sucked in. Chase spent the spring of 1868 presiding over the impeachment trial of Andrew Johnson. He hated it. Although Chase was no supporter of Johnson, he did not think impeachment was justified. "My position is particularly difficult," he complained to Gerrit Smith, a former abolitionist colleague from his days in Congress. "To me the whole business seems wrong and if I had any option under the Constitution I would not take part in it."[33] Chase's participation in the trial was the first use of the provision in the Constitution requiring the chief justice to preside at the impeachment trial of a president, rather than the Senate's normal presiding officer, the vice president, who would have an obvious interest in the conviction of the president. It would not happen again until 1999, when Chief Justice William Rehnquist presided over the impeachment trial of Bill Clinton.

David Davis, like Chase, was not a supporter of Johnson, but he was "sick at heart about the impeachment," he told his wife. "I need not say to you that I am opposed to impeachment." Davis worried that Congress might also seek to impeach other officials for impeding Reconstruction, including some of the justices themselves. "Congress has ordered an inquiry into a report that a judge of the Supreme Court has been making intemperate remarks about the Reconstruction acts," he noted in early 1868. "The matter is aimed at Judge Field," who had recently authored the opinions in *Cummings* and *Garland* invalidating the loyalty oaths that excluded former Confederates from office. "We have fallen on strange times," Davis said. "I keep quiet, unexcited, and hold my tongue."[34]

For Chase, the only virtue of presiding over Johnson's impeachment was that it delayed a task he dreaded even more—presiding over the treason trial of Jefferson Davis, the president of the Confederacy. After more than two years of debate over whether to prosecute Davis, the Johnson administration determined to try him in Virginia, which was within Chase's circuit. Chase did what he could to prevent the trial from taking place. The consensus in the press was that Chase was planning to run for president and that he feared antagonizing southern voters. As the trial neared, Chase took the extraordinary step of meeting privately with Davis's defense counsel to suggest that section 3 of the recently ratified Fourteenth Amendment, which barred former Confederates from holding federal office, might be interpreted to be Confederates' exclusive punishment and thus to preclude a prosecution for treason. The astonished lawyer promptly moved to dismiss the indictment on that ground. Chase voted to grant the motion, but his colleague on the circuit court, the district judge John Underwood, voted to deny it. The difference of opinion gave the Supreme Court jurisdiction to decide the question. Before the Court could take any action, however, Andrew Johnson issued a blanket pardon to everyone who had sided with the Confederacy. Davis was now immune from prosecution for treason. Chase was free to seek the presidency without being known as the man who had sentenced Jefferson Davis to hang.[35]

III

Many of the Court's cases over the next few decades involved other lingering effects of the war. The wartime confiscation of Confederates' property gave rise to numerous postwar cases involving issues such as the rights of Confederates who had been pardoned and the claims of heirs to the property. Even slavery had an afterlife at the Court, in the form of suits to recover under prewar contracts for the sale of slaves, because the Court held that such contracts were still enforceable despite the abolition of slavery. "Whatever we may think of the institution of slavery viewed in the light of religion, morals, humanity, or a sound political economy," Swayne noted for the Court in *Osborn v. Nicholson* (1871), "as the obligation here was valid when executed, sitting as a court of justice, we have no choice but to give it effect."[36] But the Civil War issue that focused the greatest attention on the Court, once the war was over, involved money.

To pay for the war, the Union issued paper currency for the first time. The currency was initially backed by gold, but the war proved so expensive that in 1862 the Union went off the gold standard. That caused the currency's value relative to gold to plummet, which made people reluctant to accept it. Congress responded with the Legal Tender Act of 1862, which made the paper currency, popularly called "greenbacks," a legal tender for all debts—that is, Congress required people to accept the greenbacks as payment.[37] The statute was an unwelcome surprise to creditors who had made contracts before the currency became legal tender, who stood to receive less than they thought they had bargained for. The inevitable lawsuits raised the question whether the Legal Tender Act was within the federal government's constitutional authority. The Court decided the issue twice. At first it found the Legal Tender Act unconstitutional, but the following year, after the addition of two new justices, it overruled the first decision and held the Act constitutional.

The issue first reached the Court in *Hepburn v. Griswold* (1870). The Court still had only eight justices, one of whom, Chief Justice Salmon Chase, had been secretary of the treasury when greenbacks were made legal tender. Yet Chase joined the Court's four Democrats in a 5–3 decision declaring the Legal Tender Act unconstitutional. Toward the end of his opinion for the Court, Chase acknowledged the inconsistency in the positions he took as treasury secretary and as chief justice. "It is not surprising that amid the tumult of the late civil war, and under the influence of apprehensions for the safety of the Republic almost universal, different views, never before entertained by American statesmen or jurists, were adopted by many," Chase recalled. "The time was not favorable to considerate reflection upon the constitutional limits of legislative or executive authority. If power was assumed from patriotic motives, the assumption found ready justification in patriotic hearts." He suggested that he had changed his mind. "Not a few who then insisted upon its necessity," he continued, "have, since the return of peace, and under the influence of the calmer time, reconsidered their conclusions."[38]

The *Hepburn* majority concluded that the authority to make currency legal tender could not be implied from any of the powers the Constitution grants to Congress—not the power to coin money, nor the power to declare and carry on war, nor the power to regulate interstate commerce, nor the power to borrow money. Nor was the power to make currency legal tender consistent with what Chase called "the spirit of the Constitution." One of the "great cardinal principles of that instrument," he declared, was "the establishment of justice." He found this principle expressed in the Constitution's Contracts Clause, which barred the states from impairing the obligations of contracts. The Contracts Clause restricted only the states, not the federal government, Chase conceded, but he concluded that the Legal Tender Act violated the clause's spirit by modifying the terms of contracts to the detriment of creditors. The Legal Tender Act also violated the Due Process

Clause, Chase continued, by depriving creditors of property. "A very large proportion of the property of civilized men exists in the form of contracts," he declared. "These contracts almost invariably stipulate for the payment of money." Before Congress compelled creditors to accept greenbacks in payment, contracts for the payment of money were, in effect, "contracts to pay the sums specified in gold and silver coin. And it is beyond doubt that the holders of these contracts were and are as fully entitled to the protection of this constitutional provision as the holders of any other description of property." Congress thus lacked the authority to make currency legal tender.[39]

At the end of Chase's majority opinion was an unusual sentence explaining that Robert Grier, who had retired the week before the opinion was announced, was nevertheless being counted in the Court's five-justice majority. Grier had been in very poor condition, both physically and mentally, for some time. A couple of years earlier, Samuel Miller had remarked that Grier "is getting a little muddy." The dissenting justices believed that Grier had actually voted in favor of the Legal Tender Act's constitutionality, which made the real vote 4–4, but that Chase had taken advantage of Grier's dementia to persuade him that he voted against it.[40] Whether or not Grier understood his vote while he was still a justice, he was no longer one when the decision was announced. Yet Chase counted him in the majority so the vote would be 5–3 rather than 4–3.

Miller, Swayne, and Davis dissented. They emphasized the fiscal emergency of the war, which in their view made the Legal Tender Act necessary and therefore within Congress's power to carry on the war. "With the spirit of the rebellion unbroken, with large armies in the field unpaid, with a current expenditure of over a million of dollars per day, the credit of the government nearly exhausted, and the resources of taxation inadequate to pay even the interest on the public debt," they recalled, "Congress was called on to devise some new means of borrowing money on the credit of the nation." The Legal Tender Act "furnished instantly a means of paying the soldiers in the field, and filled the coffers of the commissary and quartermaster. It furnished a medium for the payment of private debts, as well as public, at a time when gold was being rapidly withdrawn from circulation, and the State bank currency was becoming worthless." They concluded that "this law was a necessity in the most stringent sense in which that word can be used."[41]

Grier's resignation left two vacancies on the Court, one to replace Grier and the other to fill the new seat created when Congress increased the Court's size back to nine. Grant had already tried to fill the latter seat twice, but Edwin Stanton, the former secretary of war, died four days after being confirmed, and the Senate narrowly rejected Ebenezer Hoar, Grant's attorney general. On the same day that *Hepburn* was announced, Grant sent two new nominees to the Senate: William Strong, a former justice on the Pennsylvania Supreme Court, and Joseph Bradley, a New Jersey lawyer. Both were confirmed quickly. The Court then set for argument two more cases raising the same question the Court had just decided in *Hepburn*. This time, in a pair of cases known as *The Legal Tender Cases*, the Court held that the Legal Tender Act was constitutional. A 5–3 majority against the Act had flipped into a 5–4 majority in its favor, due to the retirement of one justice and the appointment of two new ones.[42]

Strong's majority opinion tracked Miller's dissent from *Hepburn* in holding that the Legal Tender Act had been necessary to fight the war. Chase reprised his majority opinion, this time as a dissent. Strong insisted that there was nothing untoward about the Court's U-turn. *Hepburn* had been "decided by a divided court, and by a court having a less number of judges than the law then in existence provided this court shall have," he pointed out. By contrast, "these cases have been heard before a full court, and they have received our most careful consideration." Strong added that "it is no unprecedented thing in courts of last resort, both in this country and in England, to overrule decisions previously made. We agree this should not be done inconsiderately, but in a case of such far-reaching consequences as the present, thoroughly convinced as we are that Congress has not transgressed its powers, we regard it as our duty so to decide." Chase, unsurprisingly, took a darker view of the Court's proceedings. "This reversal, unprecedented in the history of the court, has been produced by no change in the opinions of those who concurred in the former judgment," he reminded readers. "But the vacancy caused by the resignation of Mr. Justice Grier having been subsequently filled and an additional justice having been appointed," the former majority of five justices had become a minority of four. Field expressed the same dismay. "I shall not comment upon the causes which have led to a reversal of" *Hepburn*, he noted. "They are patent to every one. I will simply observe that the Chief Justice and the associate justices, who constituted the majority of the court when that judgment was rendered, still adhere to their former convictions."[43] Both sides of this argument were right, in their own way. The Court does sometimes overrule its past decisions. But it does not usually overrule them so quickly, when it is so clear that nothing has changed in the interim but the Court's personnel.

It was widely observed at the time that regardless of how one stood on the legal tender issue, there was something unsettling about the sudden reversal. "Independent of the right of thing," remarked the Harvard law professor Emory Washburn, "it is certainly to be lamented that an abstract principle of constitutional law is to shift by a mere change of majorities, from time to time, among the members of the court of the last resort." Even a supporter of the Court's about-face acknowledged that it would "hazard the respect and confidence with which all good citizens desire to regard its judgments." The Court seemed to have pulled the curtain back to reveal that its decisions were driven primarily by the power of a president to choose justices who shared his policy preferences. Rumors had already circulated, even before the Court decided *The Legal Tender Cases*, that Grant had put Strong and Bradley on the Court specifically to overrule *Hepburn*. One law journal accused Strong of lobbying for his own confirmation by telling senators how he would vote on the legal tender issue. Years later, these rumors would still be so pervasive that participants in the case felt the need to defend themselves in print. In 1896, after Attorney General Ebenezer Hoar died, his brother, Senator George Hoar, published a forty-five-page pamphlet refuting the charge that Grant and Ebenezer Hoar had packed the Court to secure the overruling of *Hepburn*. A few years later, after the death of all the justices involved in the cases, Bradley's son published an account making the same argument.[44]

Grant's appointment of Strong and Bradley was probably not as Machiavellian as critics suggested. They were his third and fourth choices for the Court. No one seems to have thought that Hoar and Stanton, his first two choices, were also appointed because of their views on the legal tender issue. Grant must have chosen to nominate Strong and Bradley before the Court even decided *Hepburn*, because their nominations were forwarded to the Senate on the same day the Court's decision was announced. That said, Grant and the senators who confirmed Strong and Bradley likely had a good idea where they stood on the issue, which was much in the public eye at the time, and on which views tended to correlate with party affiliation. Grant and the Republican senators could not have been surprised when the Court overruled *Hepburn*, even if Strong and Bradley had not been appointed specifically for that purpose.

IV

The Civil War also had some longer-run effects on the Court. Six of the justices were involved in one of the strangest after-effects of the war, the disputed presidential election of 1876 between Rutherford Hayes, the Republican governor of Ohio, and Samuel Tilden, the Democratic governor of New York. Because the votes of four states—Florida, Louisiana, South Carolina, and Oregon—were in dispute, both candidates claimed to have won. The Constitution does not specify how to resolve such an impasse, so Congress appointed a fifteen-member Electoral Commission to determine the winner. The commission consisted of five members of the House of Representatives, five senators, and five Supreme Court justices. There were five commissioners of each party from Congress. The justices on the commission included two Republicans, Samuel Miller and William Strong, and two Democrats, Nathan Clifford and Stephen Field. The fifth justice was supposed to be David Davis, who was generally thought to be independent of both parties.

Before the commission could meet, however, the Illinois legislature, which had a Democratic majority, voted to make Davis a US senator. Davis had not tried to obtain the office. "It came to me entirely unsought and unexpected," he was to say. "The first notice I had of my name being presented to the Legislature, was in the telegraphic dispatches to the press." The Illinois Democrats appear to have intended to turn Davis into a Democrat so he would side with Tilden. But the tactic backfired badly. As soon as the state legislature's vote was announced, Davis resigned from the Court. He was eager to start his new job in the Senate. "I accepted the Senatorship because I had been anxious for two years previously to retire from the bench," he explained, "on account of the enforced sedentary life." Davis was also happy to get off the Electoral Commission. "I never believed in the Electoral Commission as a mode of determining the Presidential election," he recalled. "My name was proposed as the fifth Justice, against my declared wishes."[45]

When Davis resigned from the Court, he was no longer eligible to serve on the Electoral Commission. The commission needed a new fifth justice. But the remaining justices were all Republicans. The previous nine appointments to the Court had been made by Abraham Lincoln and Ulysses Grant, Republican presidents, because Congress had prevented Andrew Johnson from making any appointments by temporarily reducing the size of the Court. The only two Democrats on the Court were already on the commission. Joseph Bradley took Davis's place. The commission voted 8–7 on straight party lines to award the election to Hayes.

"I was so happy when I saw that you was appointed as the fifth judge for counting the Electoral Vote," a Republican colleague wrote to Bradley—addressing him as "The President-Maker." "You are recognized as the man who saved our country in the greatest hour of its peril." Among Democrats, by contrast, Bradley was demonized for letting his political affiliations dictate his vote. "You are the most thoroughly abused man here in the South that ever lived," a friend reported from Georgia. "We have denounced, despised, and slandered many a man in this section of the country since the war, but it has fallen to your lot to receive as much as all the rest together."[46] There would be more negotiation between the two parties, resulting in a compromise in which the Republicans agreed to various concessions, including most importantly the ending of Reconstruction. But the Supreme Court— and in particular Congress's manipulation of the Court's size in 1866 and 1869—turned out to be the deciding factor in the 1876 election.

The 1869 statute increasing the size of the Court back to nine justices included two other provisions that would have a significant effect on the Court over the long term.

The first was a pension. Federal judges never had one before, but now, once a federal judge had served at least ten years and was at least seventy years old, he could resign and continue receiving his salary for life. Before they were given a pension, justices normally died in office, because their salaries were too low to accumulate enough savings to retire. Of the twenty-three justices who left the Court between 1806 and 1869, twenty died in office. The three who resigned were Gabriel Duvall, who became deaf, Benjamin Curtis, who quit in anger after *Dred Scott*, and John Archibald Campbell, who resigned to join the Confederacy. Other than Duvall, not a single justice retired because of old age or poor health.

But that changed once the justices had a pension. Robert Grier's colleagues persuaded him to retire in 1870. Grier had been senile for a few years, but he apparently could not have retired without a pension, as he had been living on a justice's salary for twenty-three years. Samuel Nelson retired in 1872, at the age of eighty. He had been a judge for nearly half a century, first in the New York state courts and then for twenty-seven years on the Supreme Court. He too suffered from poor health—"he is failing," David Davis had told his wife five years earlier—but Nelson would likely have found retirement impractical without a pension. William Strong retired in 1880, as soon as he reached ten years of service. Strong lived for another fifteen years, a period of retirement that was almost unthinkable before the justices had pensions. Some justices still died in office, and some still hung on long after their mental faculties had deteriorated, but the new possibility of a comfortable retirement offered at least a partial solution to what had been a perennial problem associated with life tenure, the inability of elderly or ill justices to leave office. Henry Billings Brown, who tendered his resignation on his seventieth birthday after thirty-one years as a federal judge, including more than fifteen years on the Supreme Court, cited the pension as the reason. He "only wondered that more judges have not availed themselves of it."[47]

In 1869, when the House of Representatives was debating whether to provide pensions, one version of the bill would have empowered the president to appoint a new justice to the Court for each justice who turned seventy but did not retire. Representative John Bingham justified this provision as an additional encouragement for justices to retire. "It is well known," he declared, "that one of the most eminent members of that bench is not able to-day to reach the bench without being borne to it by the hands of others." Bingham was referring to Grier. The appointment of a new justice to serve alongside Grier "will be giving him notice that it is the will of a great people that he should be permitted in his old age to retire."[48] Bingham did not need to add that this provision would also allow President Grant immediately to appoint two extra Republican justices to the Court. The only justices who were then over seventy were Grier and Nelson, both Democrats. This provision was left out of the final version of the statute, but the idea of adding justices to the Court when existing justices reached a certain age would return in Franklin Roosevelt's Court-packing plan of 1937.

Why did Congress take this sudden interest in judicial pensions in 1869 after ignoring the issue for the previous eighty years? The likely reason was to speed the departure of Grier, Nelson, and Clifford. They were the three oldest justices, the ones appointed by presidents before Lincoln, the justices who were Democrats and who were most hostile to Reconstruction. All three had been part of the Court's 5–4 majorities in *Ex parte Milligan*, *Ex parte Garland*, and *Cummings v. Missouri*. The Court was cleanly divided along party lines by age, so pensions had a political slant that favored the Republicans.

The other important change made in 1869 was a substantial reduction in the justices' circuit-riding responsibilities. As we saw in Chapter 2, circuit-riding had been a controversial topic ever since the creation of the federal court system. These debates continued through the 1860s. The difficulty of holding circuit courts was magnified by the addition of a circuit encompassing California and Oregon, which required Stephen Field to travel back and forth between Washington, DC, and the Pacific coast. Before there was a transcontinental railroad and long before the Panama Canal, Field's trip from Washington required taking a boat down to Panama, crossing the isthmus by land, and taking another boat up to Los Angeles, where he held a session of the circuit court before traveling north to San Francisco and Portland for more court sessions. Then he had to turn around and make the journey in reverse to get back to Washington.[49]

Meanwhile, once the war ended the Court's caseload resumed increasing, as it had before the war, until by 1869 the Court decided 169 cases, more than in any prior year. The justices needed to be "relieved from performing circuit duties," declared Senator Lyman Trumbull of Illinois, so "they will have the more time to attend to their duties in the Supreme Court."[50] Congress accordingly established a new kind of judge called a circuit judge, one for each circuit. The circuit courts, formerly held by a Supreme Court justice and a district judge sitting together, would now be held by either the justice, the circuit judge, or the district judge sitting individually, or by any two of them sitting together. The justices were still required to attend court in their circuits, but only once every two years.

This was a huge burden lifted from the justices' shoulders. Although they were not completely relieved from circuit-riding, their travel had been cut substantially, and when they made their biannual trips to the circuit there was another judge to share the work. This measure was possible because after the election of Grant, the Republicans controlled the presidency and both houses of Congress. When similar ideas had been proposed before, it was either during periods of divided government, when the party controlling Congress had no interest in giving the president a batch of new judges to appoint, or when the presidency and Congress were both controlled by the party ideologically committed to minimizing the size of the federal government.

One consequence of the reduction in circuit-riding was that the justices, for the first time, became nearly permanent residents of Washington. Before 1869, they had lived in boardinghouses and hotels during the two or three months of each Court term. After 1869, they bought houses. Stephen Field bought one in 1870, across the street from the Capitol, on the block now occupied by the Supreme Court. Samuel Miller bought a house on Massachusetts Avenue, not far from the Capitol, in 1872. Joseph Bradley, appointed in 1870 to the Court's newly restored ninth seat, promptly bought a house. Because the justices would not have to spend much time in their circuits, he reflected, "it would be most convenient now for a judge to reside in Washington City." He later recalled that all the other justices bought houses as well, except

Clifford and Davis, who continued to board in hotels.[51] The judges no longer lived together, and because they had no offices in the Capitol, they no longer worked together either, except while holding oral argument. For decades the justices had discussed the cases every night over dinner, but now each justice worked in his own home, and discussions were limited to scheduled conferences before or after oral argument.

The Court's caseload continued to balloon after the war, so although the justices had shed much of their obligation to their circuits, they nevertheless fell behind in their work. Part of the expanded caseload was simply a product of the country's commercial growth and greater population, but much of it was caused by Congress's enactment of several statutes in the 1860s and 1870s that greatly expanded the jurisdiction of the lower federal courts, provisions that shunted into the federal system many cases that were previously within the sole jurisdiction of the state courts. "I think we shall dispose this term of over six hundred cases—four hundred and seventy-one being the largest number ever reached before," David Brewer explained to his daughter in 1891. Each year, more cases came to the Court than the Court could dispose of, so they began to pile up. In 1870, the Court began its term with 636 cases waiting to be decided. In 1880, the Court began with 1,212 cases. By 1890, the figure was 1,816. The backlog of cases kept growing, to the point where it took more than three years before the Court could even begin considering a case that had been appealed to it. The justices pleaded for something to be done. The backlog was "not attributable to any fault of this court," William Strong insisted. The justices "work from an early hour in the morning to a late hour at night, not less than from eight to twelve hours a day," but they could not prevent "a steady accumulation of undecided cases from term to term." At the New York bar association's 1890 banquet commemorating the centennial of the federal courts, Stephen Field urged attendees to do something about the Court's caseload. "Surely it has a right to call upon the country to give it assistance and relief," Field declared. "Something must be done in that direction and should be done speedily."[52]

Several solutions were proposed, including increasing the number of justices and dividing the Court into multiple sections, each with authority over different kinds of cases. Congress instead reorganized the federal court system in 1891. The federal courts had mostly been a two-tier system, but now they would be a three-tier system, with an intermediate appellate layer between the trial courts and the Supreme Court. The old Circuit Courts, which had been the primary trial courts, were converted into Circuit Courts

Figure 5.3 Joseph Keppler's illustration of "Our Overworked Supreme Court" appeared in the humor magazine *Puck* in 1885. The Court's ballooning caseload prompted Congress to reorganize the federal court system in 1891. Library of Congress, LC-DIG-ppmsca-28151.

of Appeals. They became the intermediate appellate courts. The District Courts, which had been the less important of the trial courts, now became the only trial courts. The new Circuit Courts of Appeals, staffed by newly appointed circuit judges, absorbed the appeals that had once gone straight to the Supreme Court. Only the most ardent or deep-pocketed litigants would pursue a second appeal, from the Court of Appeals to the Supreme Court. As with prior legislation increasing the size of the federal judiciary, the Judiciary Act of 1891 was possible because the same party controlled the presidency and both houses of Congress, so the majority party in Congress, in this case the Republicans, could be confident of the political views of all the new judges who would be given life tenure.[53]

The reorganization of the federal courts had two important consequences for the justices. One was an immediate, drastic reduction in the number of cases arriving at the Court. In 1890, the last full year before the change, the Court took in 636 new cases, but in 1892, the first full year afterward, that number plummeted to 290. The Court began whittling away at its backlog of cases. At the end of the 1890 term, the backlog's highest point, there were 1,199 cases still left for decision, but that number began falling each year, until by 1908 it was down to 308, which was less than a year's worth of cases.[54] The caseload had dropped to a manageable level—for a time.

The other result of the new court organization was, at long last, the elimination of the justices' circuit-riding responsibilities. The justices were no longer needed to staff the Circuit Courts, because the new Circuit Courts of Appeals had judges of their own. After 101 years of divided service between two very different kinds of courts, the justices could finally devote their full attention to their work on the Supreme Court.

V

With the death of James Moore Wayne in 1867, there were no longer any southern justices on the Court. The Court had always been regionally balanced, in part because of the justices' circuit responsibilities and in part for political reasons, but when Wayne died, the country had, for the first time in its history, an entirely non-Southern Court.

The justices were still responsible for their circuits, however, and once Reconstruction ended, the political concern for regional balance was as strong as ever. The process of readmitting the South to the Court began gingerly in 1877, shortly after the disputed presidential election, when President Hayes nominated John Marshall Harlan of Kentucky to fill the seat vacated by David Davis when Davis was elected to the Senate. Although Harlan had been a slaveowner, he supported the Union during the Civil War. He joined the Republican Party after the war, was twice the party's gubernatorial candidate, and helped Hayes gain the party's presidential nomination at its 1876 convention. At that point, Harlan was one of the most prominent Republican politicians in the South. Hayes initially planned for the first southern justice to be someone "from one of the extreme Southern States," but he was talked out of it. The Pennsylvania lawyer Wayne MacVeagh, a close associate in Republican politics (and the future attorney general, under Hayes's successor, James Garfield), advised Hayes that "in view of the political history of the country for the thirty years preceding the Rebellion, as well as of the sixteen years since," it would be safer to appoint "a thoroughly sound Republican . . . living in the more Northern States of the South." MacVeagh suggested nominating Harlan to fill the current vacancy and waiting for a second opening before venturing "the appointment of a gentleman from the cotton-growing States."[55] The Senate confirmed Harlan by acclamation.

Although he was the first southern justice appointed in twenty-four years, Harlan would turn out to be the Court's strongest proponent of civil rights for African Americans during his long tenure.

Hayes appointed the second postwar southern justice, William Burnham Woods, three years later in 1880. Woods was indeed from one of "the cotton-growing States," but he was about as un-southern as a southerner could be. Woods spent the first forty-two years of his life in Ohio. He was a high-ranking officer in the Union army during the war. After the war, he settled in Alabama and then Georgia, where he was part of the first cohort of federal circuit judges appointed under the Judiciary Act of 1869. The return of southern justices thus began slowly, with two justices who had sided with the Union in the Civil War.

The first former Confederate appointed to the Court was Lucius Q. C. Lamar of Mississippi, who was nominated by Grover Cleveland in 1888— twenty-three years after the war ended—to replace Woods, who died after only six years in office. A member of the House of Representatives in the 1850s, Lamar was one of the leaders of Mississippi's secession in 1860– 1861. He fought for the Confederacy and traveled to Europe as an envoy in an unsuccessful effort to persuade European nations to recognize the Confederacy. Lamar returned to the House of Representatives in 1872, was elected to the Senate in 1876, and became Cleveland's secretary of the interior in 1885. Lamar's confirmation was a close call because of his service to the Confederacy. The Senate Judiciary Committee voted 5–4 against the nomination on straight party lines, but Lamar was nevertheless confirmed by a whisker, 32–28, when two Republican senators voted in his favor.[56]

As far as the Supreme Court was concerned, Lamar's appointment was the final battle of the Civil War. Subsequent southern justices were appointed without any similar controversy. When Lamar died in 1893, after only five years on the Court, his replacement, Howell Jackson of Tennessee, was confirmed by acclamation. Jackson had been one of Tennessee's senators until 1886, when he became a circuit judge. In the Civil War, Jackson had worked in the Confederate court system as a receiver of property, administering assets confiscated from northerners, but this was no hindrance to his confirmation as a justice. "Among all the Democrats in the South," Harlan remarked shortly after Jackson was nominated to succeed Lamar, "he was my choice for this place." In 1894, Edward White, one of Louisiana's senators, was likewise confirmed by acclamation, on the same day his nomination was sent to his colleagues in the Senate. White had fought for the Confederacy as a teenager, thirty years earlier, but the war was receding ever farther into the past. Horace Lurton of Tennessee, appointed in 1909, also fought for the Confederacy, but he too was confirmed without recorded dissent. Lurton was sixty-five years old when he was appointed. He was the last justice to join the Court who had played any role on either side of the Civil War.[57]

By the 1910s, the war was a distant memory at the Court. Solicitor General John W. Davis was in the middle of one of his many oral arguments when he noticed that "there was Holmes, who was a federal soldier with two bullets in his body, flanked on the bench by White on one side and Lurton on the other, both confederates." The elderly Georgia lawyer James C. C. Black took great satisfaction in contemplating how the South had regained a place at the Court. Black was around the same age as Edward White and Horace Lurton. Like them, he had been a Confederate soldier as a young man. He recalled how "we all thought" that losing the war "would be an irretrievable disaster," because "the most sagacious among us felt convinced that the overthrow of the Confederacy would consign the Southern people to perpetual serfdom." But everything had turned out fine. "A Confederate soldier is Chief Justice of the Supreme Court," he marveled, referring to White, who had become chief justice in 1910. "And other Confederate soldiers have been associated with him." Black was writing to Joseph Lamar, another Georgia lawyer (and Lucius Lamar's cousin), who had himself been appointed to the Court in 1911.[58]

In some respects, the war changed the Court irrevocably, but in others, the Court snapped back to its prewar state. The Court would never again have a southern majority as it did before the Civil War, but the South would be well represented on the Court until the late twentieth century, when regional diversity would be eclipsed in importance by other kinds of diversity.

6

Life at the Court, 1870–1930

"We shall all be glad to see you," Ward Hunt wrote to his new colleague, Morrison Waite. In the winter of 1874, Waite and his family would be moving from Toledo, Ohio, where he had been a prominent local attorney, to Washington, where Waite would begin a more challenging job as chief justice of the Supreme Court. "I am in the occupation of a large house," Hunt continued, "and should be glad to have you stay with me, until you can make the necessary arrangements for Mrs. Waite and your family to be with you. It would be no inconvenience whatever and Mrs. Hunt joins me in the invitation." Noah Swayne, another of Waite's new colleagues, advised him that although the Court was not in session, "most of your brethren will be here and ready to give you a hearty welcome." Swayne offered "to call on you to go round with you and introduce you" to the other justices. Hunt assured Waite that he would acclimate quickly. "There will of course be many details in the position in regard to which information will be needed," Hunt counseled, "but there will be nothing that cannot be readily learned, and nothing that will give you serious difficulty."[1] Hunt knew more than anyone about the transition from pre-Court life to the world of a Supreme Court justice, because he had entered that world himself only the year before.

This chapter is about the institution into which Ward Hunt and Noah Swayne welcomed Morrison Waite. Who were the Supreme Court justices of the late nineteenth and early twentieth centuries? How were they chosen? What was their work like?

I

Forty-one justices took office between 1862, when Abraham Lincoln appointed Swayne, and 1932, when Herbert Hoover appointed Benjamin Cardozo. All were white men; racial and gender diversity still lay well in the future. But the Court became more diverse regarding religion. In 1894, Edward White became the second Catholic justice and the first since Roger

Taney had died thirty years before. Taney had drawn substantial opposition on religious grounds when he was appointed in 1836, but anti-Catholicism, although certainly still present in the United States, had subsided enough by the 1890s that White's religion was not nearly as prominent an issue. To the extent White provoked any opposition, it was not for being Catholic but rather for being from a state other than New York, because White replaced the New Yorker Samuel Blatchford in a seat that had been held by New Yorkers for nearly a century. Indeed, President Grover Cleveland was even accused of *favoring* a Catholic for the position as a ploy to gain the support of Catholic voters. Nor was White's Catholicism much of an issue when in 1910 he was the first sitting justice to be confirmed by the Senate as chief justice (not counting William Cushing, who was confirmed in 1796 but who declined the appointment). Soon after White became chief justice, a profile in a popular magazine paid no attention to his religion but emphasized instead that White was "the only man on the Federal bench who can argue a case in French," because he was from Louisiana.[2]

By the time White became chief justice, there was already another Catholic justice, Joseph McKenna of California, who was appointed in 1898 to replace the Californian Stephen Field. McKenna's nomination drew considerable opposition, but not because of his religion. He had attributes that were disliked much more, particularly his connections with the Southern Pacific Railroad and his dreadful performance as a court of appeals judge. ("His associates in the Circuit Court of Appeals were under the necessity of revising his opinions and correcting his syntax and mistakes of grammar," reported the Oregon district judge Charles Bellinger. "He left more than thirty cases undecided that had been taken under advisement by him, and these reached back over a period of some two and a half years.") There would be two Catholic justices until White's death in 1921. The Court would rarely lack a Catholic justice thereafter. McKenna retired in 1925, but he had already been joined on the Court by Pierce Butler in 1923. From then on, the Court was informally said to have a "Catholic seat," because there was nearly always one Catholic justice. When Butler died in 1939, he was followed by Frank Murphy. In 1949, when Murphy died, the press assumed his replacement would be Catholic as well. "Sound policy calls for some balance on the Court as to religious affiliations," the *Washington Post* editorialized. "Fortunately, there are plenty of able jurists adhering to the Catholic faith." The position went to Sherman Minton, who was not Catholic but who, coincidentally, converted to Catholicism after he retired.[3] The tradition of a

Catholic seat resumed in 1956, when Minton retired and was replaced by William Brennan. There has been at least one Catholic justice ever since.

Louis Brandeis became the first Jewish justice in 1916. He was not the first Jewish lawyer to be offered a seat on the Court; that was Judah Benjamin of New Orleans, who declined Millard Fillmore's offer in 1853 because he preferred to remain in the Senate. But President Woodrow Wilson and his advisors were well aware that Brandeis's religion would arouse opposition. In Wilson's papers is a 1916 list of the eight sitting justices and the Christian denominations to which they belonged. Sure enough, the Boston politician William Fitzgerald was aghast that "a slimy fellow of this kind by his smoothness and intrigue, together with his Jewish instinct," could merit a seat on the Court. But much of the opposition to Brandeis was attributable instead to his career as a progressive reformer, which placed him squarely in opposition to many of the most powerful lawyers of the era. "He is a muckraker," complained the ex-president (and future chief justice) William Howard Taft, "a socialist, prompted by jealousy, a hypocrite."[4] A more conservative Jewish lawyer would likely have provoked much less opposition.

Then again, it is hard to be certain of this, because in polite circles by the early twentieth century, anti-Semitism was put into practice more often than it was spoken out loud. As the Jewish banker Otto Kahn bitterly remarked, "a 'kike' is a Jewish gentleman who has just left the room." It was far more respectable to oppose Brandeis for his politics than for his Judaism. While Brandeis's confirmation was still in doubt, Chief Justice Edward White confided to Justice William Day that he would prefer that Brandeis went "to a summer climate for his health" rather than joining them in Washington. White did not elaborate on his reasons, but Day presumably knew already. "So far as the B. matter is concerned," White told Day, "I try to hold my tongue." White's circumspection was not shared by Justice James McReynolds, who made no effort to conceal his bigotry. "McReynolds was a hater," Felix Frankfurter recalled. "He had primitive anti-Semitism." McReynolds refused even to speak with Brandeis—and the two worked together for nearly twenty-three years.[5]

In 1932, Benjamin Cardozo joined Brandeis as the second Jewish justice. Cardozo had been an extraordinarily well-regarded state court judge for some time, but many considered the presence of Brandeis on the Court an obstacle to appointing Cardozo as well. "It may not be thought wise to name a second judge of the Jewish race," advised Nicholas Murray Butler, the president of Columbia University, when Calvin Coolidge was considering

Figure 6.1 Men labeled "Privilege," "Wall Street," and "Monopoly" bewail the appointment of Louis Brandeis to the Court. The caption reads "Chorus of Grief-Stricken Conservatives: Oh, what an associate for such a pure and innocent girl! And we have tried to bring her up so carefully, too!" The cartoon was drawn by Nelson Greene and published in *Puck* magazine on February 19, 1916. Library of Congress, LC-USZ62-52581.

Cardozo and a few other candidates for the seat that went to Harlan Fiske Stone in 1925. When Cardozo was again one of the contenders in 1932, Justices Pierce Butler and Willis Van Devanter joined McReynolds in urging President Herbert Hoover not to "afflict the Court with another Jew," according to well-placed journalists.[6] Hoover nevertheless chose Cardozo. The Court would have at least one Jewish justice for the next few decades. When Cardozo died, he was succeeded in the informal "Jewish seat" by Frankfurter (1939–1962), Arthur Goldberg (1962–1965), and Abe Fortas (1965–1969).

The emergence of Catholic and Jewish seats was not a jurisprudential matter; there was no uniform Catholic or Jewish position on the issues the

Court decided. Rather, the growing significance of religious diversity on the Court in the early twentieth century was, in large part, a consequence of the declining importance of regional diversity. Before 1891, the justices served as circuit judges, one in each circuit. It made sense for the justice to come from the circuit to which he would be assigned, because he already had a home there, and he would already be known to the local legal community. The abolition of circuit-riding began to cut this local connection. The change took place very gradually at first, because presidents still often found it politically prudent to ensure that there were justices from all parts of the country. The first few justices appointed after 1891 were from the same regions as their predecessors, with the conspicuous exception of Edward White in 1894, and even then, regional balance was restored the following year when Rufus Peckham of New York replaced the southerner Howell Jackson. But the tradition of regional diversity eventually began to weaken. In 1903, Theodore Roosevelt appointed William Day of Ohio, which was in the Sixth Circuit, to replace George Shiras of Pennsylvania, which was in the Third. A few years later, when Henry Billings Brown of Michigan retired, Roosevelt took the bolder step of choosing William Moody of Massachusetts as Brown's replacement. Now there were two justices from Massachusetts, because Roosevelt had already appointed Oliver Wendell Holmes to the Court in 1902. Moody retired after only a few years, but Massachusetts gained a second justice again when Brandeis joined Holmes on the Court in 1916. The same year, John Hessin Clarke of Ohio replaced Charles Evans Hughes of New York, and when Clarke retired in 1922, his replacement was George Sutherland of Utah, who would eventually be succeeded by Stanley Reed of Kentucky. It was no longer automatic that a departing justice would be replaced by someone from the same region. With the appointment of Cardozo in 1932, the Court, for the first time, had *three* justices from a single state, because Cardozo joined fellow New Yorkers Charles Evans Hughes and Harlan Fiske Stone.

Concern for regional diversity never completely disappeared. "The slightest suspicion of sectional or local flavor in the Supreme Court must militate against the universal respect and confidence with which its decisions should be received by the American people," Senator Thomas du Pont insisted in 1922. Du Pont was upset that Massachusetts had two justices while his home state of Delaware had never had any. He thought the appointment of two justices from a single state could never be "successfully defended on the grounds of wise statesmanship or good politics."[7] But regional diversity was beginning to seem less important in the early twentieth century, and its importance would continue to decline thereafter.

Freed from the constraint of replacing an outgoing justice with someone from the same part of the country, presidents could begin to take other political priorities into account. Religion was an obvious one. Because of immigration from Catholic countries, there were more than seventeen million Catholics in the country by 1920, making up about one-sixth of the population. Jews were a much smaller minority but one that was gaining representation in the legal profession, the source of nominees and the group that paid the closest attention to judges. The strategic appointment of Catholic and Jewish justices allowed presidents to use nominations to the Court as a means of seeking electoral support. "Now I am for you whether you are a Unitarian, a Catholic, a Presbyterian, an Agnostic, or a Mormon, and I resent the suggestion that a man's religion should play any part in the primary reasons for selecting him for our Court," Chief Justice William Howard Taft explained to the Catholic nominee Pierce Butler. But "politicians refuse to adopt" his view, Taft continued, "and are quite willing to piece out a man's indifferent qualifications for our Bench by the pleas that we need a Catholic or a Jew."[8]

As the Court grew more religiously diverse, it also grew older. The average age of a new justice between 1862 and 1932 was fifty-five, seven years older than the average age before the Civil War. (This is the average age at first appointment, so it does not include justices or ex-justices reappointed to become chief justice.) It was no longer possible to be appointed while in one's early thirties, as Joseph Story and William Johnson had been in the early nineteenth century. Even justices appointed in their forties, common through the early 1860s when Lincoln appointed three in succession, became rarities. Of the thirty justices who took office between 1880 and 1932, only two were under fifty: Edward White was forty-nine and Charles Evans Hughes was forty-eight. Many more justices were appointed in their sixties, including the sixty-five-year-old Horace Lurton, who is still the oldest justice ever to be appointed for the first time, and Hughes, who was sixty-seven when he rejoined the Court as chief justice. The Court's average age grew accordingly. In 1800 the average justice had been fifty-three years old. In 1850 the average justice was sixty-four. By 1937 he was seventy-two.[9]

People were living a bit longer, so perhaps this aging trend is not surprising. In 1850, the average forty-year-old white man died at sixty-six, while in 1930 he could expect to live until sixty-nine.[10] But life expectancy was not the only cause. With the end of circuit-riding, the job became less physically taxing, as the justices never had to hold court anywhere but Washington. At the same time, the pool of candidates was growing much larger, as the country's population and the number of lawyers ballooned, and as vacancies on the Court came to be filled by national rather than regional searches. In the competition that took place with each appointment, it was taking longer to amass the kind of resumé that qualified one to be a justice.

As the Court grew older, it increasingly confronted a delicate problem— justices who were losing their mental capacities with age but who, for that very reason, were unable to perceive their own decline. Nathan Clifford's dementia appears to have started in the mid-1870s. By 1880 it was obvious to anyone who encountered him. "Judge Clifford reached Washington on the 8th October a babbling idiot," Samuel Miller noted of his seventy-seven-year-old colleague. "I saw him within three hours after his arrival, and he did not know me or any thing, and though his tongue framed words there was no sense in them."[11] Clifford refused to retire. He was eligible for a pension but he could not understand the need to take advantage of it. Clifford remained on the Court throughout the 1880–1881 term and died in office the following summer.

In 1896, as Stephen Field's once-sharp mind deteriorated, his colleagues tried without success to persuade him to retire. Field replied with a stern "denial of the charges about his failing," David Brewer reported to Chief Justice Melville Fuller. "Still, we know he is getting old." Fuller took the precaution of not assigning any opinions to Field, which infuriated him all the more. The following year, as the eighty-year-old Field continued to fade, Brewer even considered enlisting President William McKinley in the effort to persuade Field to step down.[12] There is a well-known story in which the justices delegated John Harlan to try once again to convince Field to retire by reminding Field that nearly thirty years earlier he had been among a group of justices who made the same suggestion to the elderly Robert Grier. When Harlan asked Field if he recalled the episode, the story goes, Field fired back: "Yes! And a dirtier day's work I never did in my life!" The story originated with Harlan, who may have misremembered the detail about Grier, because Field may not have been one of the justices who persuaded Grier to retire.[13] Nevertheless, Field's colleagues, probably including Harlan, did try fruitlessly for two years to convince him to retire, but he hung on until he had broken John Marshall's record for longevity on the Court and until Grover Cleveland, whom he disliked, was no longer the president.[14]

It was Harlan's turn soon enough. In his early sixties, Harlan had joked that he would not retire until 1927, his fiftieth anniversary on the Court, when he would have been ninety-five years old. But as he reached his mid-seventies, his colleagues began to view his behavior in court with alarm. "On the Bench he was restless, talking a good deal to himself, sleeping somewhat," Edward White worried. While cases were being argued, Harlan began "sending for various persons to speak to, his tone of voice being so loud as to attract considerable attention."[15] Harlan died soon after.

The problem would recur regularly, as justices consistently failed to retire before they lost the ability to know when they should. "Our court is not in a strong condition," Taft reported to his brother in 1922. Oliver Wendell Holmes, then eighty-one years old and suffering from asthma and possibly a heart condition, was the least of his worries, because "Holmes does his work with just as much dispatch as ever." The Court's weak members were Mahlon Pitney, who "had a nervous breakdown last year" and who "has a good many cases on his hands which he is not getting rid of"; William Day, who had become so feeble that Taft could no longer assign him any opinions; and "the worst and most embarrassing member," Joseph McKenna, who was approaching eighty. "I don't know what course to take with respect to him, or what cases to assign to him," Taft despaired. "In case after case assigned to him he will write an opinion, and bring it into conference, and it will meet objection because he has missed a point in one case, or, as in one instance, he wrote an opinion deciding the case one way when there had been a unanimous vote the other, including his own." Taft confessed that McKenna "wrote an opinion in an Oklahoma case that we let through the other day, which brought a petition for rehearing that is most humiliating to the Court, and I think we shall have to grant it."[16] As the justices' average age continued to climb, mental decline among the Court's oldest members would be a persistent problem.

The standard items on a prospective justice's resumé were the still the same as before the Civil War, but the emphasis was beginning to shift from elective office to a judgeship on a lower court. Of the forty-one justices appointed between 1862 and 1932, twenty, or slightly less than half, had held elective office. This is a much higher figure than today, but it was a much lower figure than before the Civil War, when 82% of the justices were former elective officeholders. Ten of these twenty had been members of Congress, and one had even been president—William Howard Taft, the only former president ever to serve on the Supreme Court. Two more had been state governors,

Salmon Chase and Charles Evans Hughes. Several others had engaged in the political world by holding cabinet positions, including four who served as attorney general (Joseph McKenna, William Moody, James McReynolds, and Harlan Fiske Stone), two secretaries of state (William Day and Hughes), one secretary of the treasury (Chase), one secretary of war (Taft), one secretary of the interior (Lucius Q. C. Lamar), and one secretary of the Navy (Moody).

The appointment to the Court of so many people with experience in Congress and the executive branch indicates that such experience was generally understood as a useful background for a justice, which in turn suggests that the work of the justices was understood to include an element of pragmatic governance along with its distinctly legal aspects. "I do not minimize at all the importance of having Judges of learning in the law on the Supreme Bench," Taft remarked to George Sutherland after Sutherland joined the Court. "But the functions performed by us are of such a peculiar character that something in addition is much needed to round out a man for service upon that Bench." Sutherland had represented Utah in the Senate for twelve years, but he had never been a judge on any court. He must have been gratified to hear from Taft that more important than judicial experience was "a knowledge of how Government is carried on, and how higher politics are conducted," as well as an understanding of "the actual situation in the country."[17] Taft was in a unique position to know, having served as a federal circuit judge for eight years, secretary of war for four, and of course president for four more. But his view must have been widely shared, or else political office would not have been such a common path to the Court.

As before the Civil War, one consequence of the recruitment of justices from the world of politics is that most nominees to the Court were men whose political views were well known before they were nominated. There was no need to hold hearings or conduct investigations to find out what Taft or Sutherland thought about this or that issue, because senators had worked with them for years. For this reason, the Senate confirmed Taft and Sutherland on the same day they were nominated. Sutherland was in Europe on his nomination/confirmation day, so he only found out afterward. Not all confirmations were as fast, but most took place within a week or two. The occasional confirmations that took longer all involved some circumstance that made the nominee unusually controversial. Brandeis's nomination, for instance, prompted the Senate Judiciary Committee to hold public hearings, a step it had never taken with any prior nominee to the Court. Brandeis was not confirmed until four months after his nomination. It took the Senate nearly three months to confirm Melville Fuller as chief justice in 1888, because Fuller, a Chicago lawyer and a Democrat, was not a familiar figure beyond Illinois, and because some of the Republicans who formed the majority in the Senate wanted to delay until after the presidential election.[18]

Some of the justices who had come from the political world tried to return. Salmon Chase, a former senator and governor, spent most of his tenure as chief justice (1864–1873) strategizing about running for president. "My duties as Judge are rather irksome," he complained. "If I had been appointed younger, & before becoming so deeply concerned in political matters & so largely identified with political measures, I should have liked the position better." His colleague David Davis called Chase the second-most ambitious man he had ever met, behind only Stephen Douglas. "As long as the Presidency is not reached," Davis said of Chase, "everything else that he has obtained is as dust and ashes." But this was hardly intended as criticism, because Davis too was contemplating a run for president. Justice Samuel Miller once remarked of Davis that "every act of his life" was planned to satisfy his "hope of the Presidency." A few months before the 1872 election, a Thomas Nast cartoon on the cover of *Harper's Weekly* magazine depicted Chase and Davis with the caption "The Presidential Fever on the Supreme Bench." Davis would satisfy his political itch a few years later by resigning to become a senator. Other justices likewise ran for president while on the Court. Stephen Field tried to secure the Democratic nomination in 1880 and 1884. Charles Evans Hughes was the Republican candidate in 1916. He resigned from the Court only after the party's convention in June. And these were merely the justices who advertised their hopes for political office. There may well have been others who shared such hopes only with confidants. "In times past," Holmes said during Hughes's campaign, "if several Justices haven't been candidates it was not because they didn't want to be I suspect."[19]

The sight of justices running for president raised the unsettling possibility that a justice might craft his opinions to seek votes or the favor of political patrons. Field's 1880 campaign "is a very disagreeable spectacle," one critic observed. Politics was "a business of intrigue and dicker and engagement which necessarily leaves a candidate upon the bench covered with suspicion." Chief Justice Melville Fuller even turned down Grover Cleveland's offer to become secretary of state for this reason. Taking the job "would be distinctly injurious to the Court," Fuller worried, because it might look like a reward for taking positions favorable to Cleveland. Leaving the Court "for

Figure 6.2 In this 1872 cartoon, Thomas Nast mocked "the presidential fever on the supreme bench" by depicting Salmon Chase and David Davis, who were both maneuvering to run for president. At Chase's feet are the words "A lifelong CHASE after the presidency." Above his shoulder is a sign reading "Beware of political aspirations in this Court." *Harper's Weekly*, April 6, 1872. Library of Congress, LOT 14012, no. 46.

a political position, even though so eminent, would tend to distract from the dignity and weight of the tribunal. We cannot afford this."[20]

While many of the justices during this period had held elective office, more of them—twenty-four out of forty-one—had served as lower court judges. Some, like Oliver Wendell Holmes and Benjamin Cardozo, were well known for their work on state supreme courts. Others, including Willis Van Devanter and Horace Lurton, came from the new federal courts of appeals that had been established in 1891. As the state and federal court systems expanded, and as the number of states increased, there was an ever-larger pool of sitting judges from which to choose a Supreme Court justice. Judicial experience was not yet considered a prerequisite for an appointment, but it was beginning to rise in importance.

While many of the justices had served on lower courts or held elective office, the one experience virtually all shared was a stint as an attorney in private practice. Commercial litigation was the standard fare of a successful private law practice in the late nineteenth and early twentieth centuries. Any attorney who aspired to be a leader of his local legal community—normally the first step in a career that could culminate at the Supreme Court—had to have local businesses as his clients. As a result, most of the justices had some experience as a lawyer representing the corporations that were starting to dominate the American economy, experience that brought them into frequent social and professional contact with prominent businesspeople in their hometowns. In smaller cities like Toledo and Canton, Morrison Waite and William Day represented local banks, railroads, and utilities. In New York, Charles Evans Hughes hobnobbed with John D. Rockefeller.[21] It would be too simple to draw a direct line from justices' early careers as lawyers to their attitudes on the Court. Attorneys did not yet specialize as narrowly as would become the norm later, so lawyers who represented corporations in some cases also typically represented individuals in other cases, sometimes in lawsuits *against* corporations. But their common background representing corporations and socializing with business leaders made it natural for many of them to see things from a business point of view, a perspective that would become important in some of the Court's best-known cases. If experience in government shaped a future justice's worldview, so did experience in the private sector.

Virtually all nominees belonged to the same political party as the president. "The Supreme Court has been usually regarded as an important political vantage-ground," *Harper's Weekly* explained. "Its decisions have been greatly helpful in the carrying out or defeating of party principles," so "appointments to the Supreme Bench have been partisan." But there were some conspicuous exceptions. As we have seen, Lincoln appointed the pro-Union and pro-war Democrat Stephen Field in 1863. Benjamin Harrison, a Republican, appointed Howell Jackson, a Democrat, at the very end of his term in February 1893. The incoming president, Grover Cleveland, was a Democrat, the new Senate would have a Democratic majority, and Jackson was replacing the Democrat Lucius Q. C. Lamar. The press suggested that "under the circumstances the appointment of a Republican would have been looked upon as indicative of an unworthy partisan eagerness to take advantage of an accident," the death of Lamar in January, after Cleveland's election but before his inauguration. In 1932, Herbert Hoover, a Republican, appointed Benjamin Cardozo, a Democrat who had overwhelming support from the legal profession.[22] But these were atypical appointments. Normally, the pool of candidates was limited to those of the president's party.

When the death or retirement of a justice opened a seat on the Court, the president could expect to be inundated with recommendations of suitable nominees. One could not openly lobby for one's own candidacy, but behind the scenes, hopeful would-be justices organized campaigns in their own behalf. In 1906, for example, when Henry Billings Brown retired, Horace Lurton snapped into action. Lurton was a judge on the Court of Appeals for the Sixth Circuit. A former colleague on the Sixth Circuit, William Howard Taft, was the secretary of war, while another former Sixth Circuit colleague, William Day, had been appointed to the Supreme Court three years before. Taft advised Lurton to have Day contact President Theodore Roosevelt before it was too late. Lurton sent Day an urgent telegram: "Matters now ripe for your active interference. At once press on president wisdom of my appointment." Day did just that. He received a bemused thank you note in reply from Roosevelt, who said "curiously enough, Taft had spoken of Judge Lurton exactly in the same way." Roosevelt nominated William Moody instead of Lurton, but when Taft became president, Lurton would be his first nominee to the Court. From his chambers in Nashville, Lurton once again organized a campaign to convince the Senate to confirm him. "Get Wallace Woodruff and Judge Sanford to wire Senator Hughes," he instructed a friend. "If a real fight comes on I may ask you to go personally to Washington. Governor McMillin and Mr. Bryan are going on from here and will be there the most of next week. John Wesley Gaines has already gone, and will land there tomorrow."[23] Lurton's hard work paid off. He would serve as a justice until his death in 1914.

Not long after Lurton was appointed, Willis Van Devanter mounted a similar campaign. Van Devanter, a federal circuit judge in Wyoming, had the assistance of Francis Warren, one of Wyoming's senators, who lobbied Taft and several of Warren's Senate colleagues. Warren's help proved crucial. In a conversation with Charles Nagel, the secretary of commerce and labor, Warren learned that the supporters of one of Van Devanter's competitors for the seat, the Minnesota circuit judge Walter Sanborn, had told Taft that Van Devanter was unable to keep up with his caseload on the court of appeals. Van Devanter had to acknowledge that this was true, but he explained that there were good reasons: his wife had been ill, and then he had taken ill himself, and the cases assigned to him had been more complex than average. If one counted all the opinions written by all the circuit judges over the past several years, he pointed out, his output was right around average. This response evidently satisfied Taft, who nominated Van Devanter rather than Sanborn. Once on the Court, however, Van Devanter once again had trouble keeping up with the pace of the job. Charles Evans Hughes recalled that Van Devanter "was slow in getting out his opinions, having what one of his most intimate friends in the Court (Justice Sutherland) described as 'pen paralysis.' This difficulty increased with the years." In bad-mouthing Van Devanter, Sanborn's supporters had merely told the truth. The same cannot be said of Arthur Rugg, the long-serving chief justice of the Massachusetts Supreme Court in the early twentieth century. According to Oliver Wendell Holmes, Rugg so coveted Holmes's seat on the Court that he falsely spread the rumor that Holmes was soon to retire. One morning in 1925, Fanny Holmes read of her husband's retirement in the newspaper.[24] He would not retire for another seven years.

The Senate confirmed all but six of the president's nominees during this period. Most of the time the president's party was the majority party in the Senate and the nominee sailed through with little opposition. There were only five nominations that took place when the Senate was controlled by the opposing party, but the Senate confirmed all five nominees. Two of these confirmations—Lucius Lamar and Melville Fuller, both nominated by the Democrat Grover Cleveland and both confirmed in 1888—even took place in an election year, when the Republicans who held a majority in the Senate had an incentive to delay in the hope that Cleveland would be defeated by a Republican, as actually happened. William Burnham Woods, nominated by the lame duck Republican Rutherford Hayes after the 1880 presidential election, was promptly confirmed by a Democratic Senate. The Senate let Hayes's January 1881 nomination of the Ohio senator Stanley Matthews lapse until the end of the legislative session, but the Democrats had no party advantage in doing so, because the incoming president, James Garfield, was also a Republican, and the Democrats would lose their majority in the next Senate. The opposition to Matthews was bipartisan, based on senators' familiarity with their colleague's close connections with the large railroads. Garfield quickly re-nominated Matthews, who was confirmed by a one-vote margin, with senators from both parties on both sides of the vote.[25] The other nominee confirmed by a Senate controlled by the opposing party was Rufus

Peckham, nominated in 1895 by Grover Cleveland and confirmed with little ado by a Senate with a slight Republican majority. Partisanship had played a bigger role before the Civil War, when there were eight nominees in an election year when the President and Senate were of opposing parties, and the Senate had declined to confirm the nominee on all eight occasions.

When the Senate rejected a nominee during this period, it was not for partisan reasons but rather because a bipartisan majority found fault with the nominee. The first three instances took place in the Grant administration. In 1870, the Senate narrowly rejected Ebenezer Hoar, Grant's attorney general. Some senators were angry that Hoar had given them no opportunity for patronage before he and Grant filled the nine new circuit judgeships Congress had created the year before, while other senators may have resented Hoar's opposition to the impeachment of Andrew Johnson. When Salmon Chase died three years later, Grant had even more trouble appointing a replacement. His first choice, the New York senator Roscoe Conkling, declined the offer. "He expects to be President," David Davis remarked, "and in the Senate he has a better chance to work for that than on the bench." Grant then nominated George Williams, the attorney general. Williams was not highly regarded as a lawyer. Davis expressed a common opinion when he noted that "the appointment is a great falling off from the standard of the office." According to Davis, "no nomination was ever received with more disfavor, & in some quarters it is not considered respectable." One senator had told Davis "that there were not six men in the senate that were *per se* in favor of his confirmation." Meanwhile, rumors were already circulating about the scandal that would eventually force Williams out of office, involving the use of government money for personal expenses, including a luxurious carriage for his wife. When it became evident that the Senate would not confirm Williams, Grant withdrew the nomination. Next Grant nominated Caleb Cushing, an even more curious choice. Cushing was nearly seventy-four years old. He was a Democrat who had been James Buchanan's attorney general in the 1850s and who had opposed the Civil War. His nomination aroused considerable skepticism, which became outright hostility when senators learned of a letter Cushing had written to Jefferson Davis in March 1861 that seemed to accept the legitimacy of the Confederacy. Grant withdrew Cushing's nomination as well. Grant finally filled the vacancy by nominating Morrison Waite, an Ohio lawyer who had never held any public office and who was not well known outside the state, but who was within the administration's field of vision at that moment because he had recently served as a lawyer for the

United States in Geneva in a successful arbitration proceeding against the United Kingdom for allowing Confederate warships to be built in England. The Senate immediately confirmed Waite, doubtless with more relief than enthusiasm. "Mr. Waite stands in the front rank of second-rate lawyers," one journalist observed. But "on the whole, considering what the President might have done, and tried to do, we ought to be very thankful."[26]

Grover Cleveland had a different kind of difficulty replacing Samuel Blatchford, who died in 1893. Blatchford was from New York, so Cleveland sought to appoint a New York Democrat as his successor, but he ran up against a schism in the state's Democratic Party, where Cleveland's own political career had begun. The New York senator David Hill, who had battled against Cleveland when both were politicians in New York, persuaded his colleagues to reject Cleveland's first two nominees, the New York lawyers William Hornblower and Wheeler Peckham, because they been on Cleveland's side rather than Hill's. "You have been made the victim of the 'pea nut' politics of the Senate," commiserated a colleague in the New York legal community when Peckham's nomination was defeated. "Hill hated you," the New York minister Richard Heber Newton told Peckham. "But he hated Cleveland worse—so he struck at him through you."[27] This is why the Louisianan Edward White was appointed to the seat that had traditionally been held by a New Yorker; Cleveland was getting back at Hill. Cleveland would appoint Rufus Peckham, Wheeler's younger brother, to the next vacant seat on the Court nearly two years later.

The last of the rejected nominees during this period was John J. Parker, who was nominated by Herbert Hoover in 1930. Parker was a federal court of appeals judge from North Carolina who had been the unsuccessful Republican candidate for a House seat, for state attorney general, and for governor. At forty-four, if confirmed he would have been the youngest justice since John Harlan more than a half-century before. Hoover had been advised that Parker was a "progressive" who "represents the new South." But Parker had at least one foot planted in the old South. While running for governor, he had argued that "the participation of the negro in politics is a source of evil and danger to both races and is not desired by the wise men in either race or by the Republican party of North Carolina." His nomination was opposed by an array of African American organizations ranging from the National Association for the Advancement of Colored People to the Kansas City Negro Bar Association. He was also opposed by organized labor because of an opinion he had written upholding an injunction against the United Mine

Workers' effort to organize miners in West Virginia. Parker "does not possess the requisite qualifications to serve in such a responsible position," declared the president of the American Federation of Labor. Parker lamely replied that while running for governor he had merely "called attention to the fact that the colored people as a class were not trying to enter politics," while the Hoover administration defended his opinion in the mine workers' case as compelled by Supreme Court precedent.[28] But the damage had been done. He lost in the Senate by two votes.

Parker's defeat reflected an important change in how the Senate considered nominees to the Court. Before 1916, the Senate discussed nominees behind closed doors. Normally the Senate Judiciary Committee met in executive session, and sometimes it did not meet at all. There were no hearings. The newspapers typically reported which senators spoke for and against the nominee, but journalists knew only what a senator had told them, so these reports were not always accurate. "The newspapers do not get the executive sessions quite as correctly as they are fond of saying," Senator Henry Cabot Lodge remarked in 1906, in assuring William Moody that he had given a speech supporting Moody's confirmation despite press reports to the contrary. But the Senate was transformed in 1913 with the ratification of the Seventeenth Amendment. Now that senators were popularly elected rather than chosen by state legislatures, they had to be more attentive to public opinion. When Woodrow Wilson nominated the controversial Louis Brandeis to the Court in 1916, the Senate Judiciary Committee held public hearings on the nomination for the first time. Parker's nomination was the second in which there were public hearings. After Parker, the Judiciary Committee held public hearings more often than not for the next couple of decades, but public hearings were not standard until the late 1940s. Harold Burton, who joined the Court in 1945, was the last nominee confirmed without a public hearing.[29]

Because of these changes in the Senate, John J. Parker became the first nominee to the Court who was defeated by interest groups that placed pressure on senators to vote no.[30] This strategy was scarcely conceivable before the 1910s, when senators could avoid taking public positions on Supreme Court appointments and when senators were in any event not directly accountable to the voters. Nominations to the Court had always been a matter of politics, but it had been politics conducted behind closed doors by a small group of powerful people. Now that senators were directly elected and the Senate was beginning to hold public hearings, however, the politics moved out into the open and came to involve many more people. In this new context, Parker's defeat was the first demonstration of the power of a well-organized campaign to influence the composition of the Court. It would not be the last.

II

Unlike in the pre–Civil War years, the Court's chief justices in the late nineteenth and early twentieth centuries were not its intellectual leaders. Morrison Waite, the chief justice from 1874 to 1888, was a successful but undistinguished lawyer. A few weeks after Waite became chief justice, his colleague Samuel Miller described him as "pleasant" but "*mediocre.*" After working with Waite for a couple of years, Miller grew exasperated. "I can't make a silk purse out of a sow's ear," he complained. "I can't make a great Chief Justice out of a small man." When Waite died, the kindest thing an obituary in the *American Law Review* could say was: "That he should develop any great strength as a judge was not to be expected of him, and the public expectation was not disappointed."[31]

Waite's successor, the Chicago lawyer Melville Fuller, made scarcely more of a mark than Waite. "Melville W. Fuller of Chicago!" exclaimed Justice Joseph Bradley when he heard of Fuller's nomination. "Mr. Fuller has appeared before us in several private cases, respectably, and nothing more. I have no doubt that he is a very estimable man, and a successful practitioner at the local bar. But this hardly fits the public's expectation for the place of Chief Justice of the United States." Bradley confided to his colleague Stephen Field that he was "greatly disappointed in the nomination." When Fuller died after twenty-two years as chief justice, his obituaries emphasized his warm personal relationships with the other justices rather than the opinions he wrote. He was "perhaps the most popular, though not the strongest or most famous Chief Justice," one magazine explained. Outside the Court, Fuller was perhaps best known for his luxuriant mustache, which gave him a resemblance to Mark Twain. According to a widely told story, Twain was once stopped on the street by an autograph-seeker who thought he was Fuller. Twain obliged by signing "It is delicious to be full, but it is heavenly to be Fuller. I am cordially yours, Melville W. Fuller."[32]

Fuller was succeeded as chief justice in 1910 by Edward White, who came to the Court from the Senate in 1894 and who would serve as chief justice until his death in 1921. White "thinks more as a legislator than as a pure lawyer," noted Oliver Wendell Holmes when White became chief justice. "His writing leaves much to be desired."[33] White's successor as chief justice was William Howard Taft, the ex-president. Taft used his considerable talents as an executive to help transform the Court into the institution that exists today, as we will see in Chapter 9, but he did not stand out to the same degree as a judge. Waite, Fuller, White, and Taft were skillful administrators, but they have never been ranked among the most respected or most influential justices, not even in their own day.

In the late nineteenth century, the Court's intellectual leaders were three justices who all served for a very long time: John Marshall Harlan, Stephen Field, and Samuel Miller. Harlan (a justice from 1877 to 1911) is the one with the greatest reputation today, because his dissenting opinions in cases involving race discrimination anticipated the shift in white sentiment regarding race relations that would take place long after his death. In the *Civil Rights Cases* (1883), Harlan was the only member of the Court who concluded that the Constitution authorized Congress to prohibit discrimination in public facilities like hotels, restaurants, theaters, and trains. In *Plessy v. Ferguson* (1896), he was the only justice who viewed state-mandated segregation as unconstitutional.[34] Although he was a southerner and a former slaveowner, Harlan's views on race discrimination were closer to today's prevailing views than those of any other justice of his era.

If Harlan is today's hero on the late nineteenth-century Court, Stephen Field is today's villain. Harlan is best known for interpreting the post–Civil War constitutional amendments as protections against discrimination, while Field is best known for interpreting the same amendments as protections for businesses against regulation. Harlan's view only became accepted long after he died, while Field's view was accepted during his lifetime. When Field retired in 1897, after more than thirty-four years on the Court, his tenure was the longest in the Court's history. (His record was broken by William Douglas in the 1970s, but Field is still in second place.) Field's expansive view of the constitutional protections for business did not command a majority of the Court at first. In the *Slaughterhouse Cases* (1873), he unsuccessfully urged the Court to use the new Fourteenth Amendment to prohibit a city government from restricting where butchers could carry on their trade. In *Munn v. Illinois* (1877), he disagreed with the Court's decision allowing the state to set maximum rates for grain storage. Toward the end of his career, however, Field's view became orthodoxy. In *Allgeyer v. Louisiana* (1897), a unanimous Court held that the "liberty" protected by the Due Process

Clause of the Fourteenth Amendment included the right of a person "to live and work where he will; to earn his livelihood by any lawful calling; [or] to pursue any livelihood or avocation."[35] This would be the Court's view for the next forty years.

Samuel Miller is not as easy to pigeonhole. Contemporaries thought he was the most distinguished justice of the late nineteenth century. Salmon Chase, the chief justice during most of Miller's first decade on the Court, declared that "beyond question, the dominant personality now upon the bench, whose mental force and individuality are felt by the Court more than any other, is Justice Miller." When Miller died in 1890, one professional journal called him "the most conspicuous legal figure in the United States" and the only American judge comparable in stature to John Marshall. Miller was the author of some of the Court's most significant opinions during his tenure, including the *Slaughterhouse Cases*, *Ex parte Yarbrough* (1884), in which the Court held that Congress had the power to prosecute Ku Klux Klan members for using violence to prevent African Americans from voting, and *Wabash v. Illinois* (1886), in which the Court held that only Congress, not the states, could regulate the rates of interstate railroads.[36] Perhaps because his opinions cannot be distilled into a simple political position for today's approval or disapproval, Miller is less well known today than Harlan and Field, even if he enjoyed a higher reputation during his lifetime.

In the years surrounding the turn of the century, the Court's most visible justice may have been David Brewer, Field's nephew, who served from 1889 to 1910. Brewer spent a large percentage of his time on the lecture circuit. He would "go almost anywhere to address an audience," the historian Gordon Hylton observes. "He spoke to bar associations, to missionary groups, to churches, to life insurance agents, at public health conferences, at conferences on international arbitration, at graduation ceremonies of prestigious and not-so-prestigious colleges, at all-black colleges, and at football dinners." When Brewer died, Holmes noted that "he had the itch for public speaking," which Holmes chalked up to Brewer's desire "to make a little money for his wife." Between lecture tours, Brewer succeeded Field as the Court's most prominent defender of property rights against government regulation. In light of Brewer's deep religious convictions, it is fitting that his best-remembered opinion may be *Holy Trinity Church v. United States* (1892), in which the Court unanimously held that a statute barring the importation of foreigners to perform work of any kind could not possibly have been intended to forbid the hiring of a foreign minister. Brewer declared that the United States "is a Christian nation," a statement that is often misunderstood: Brewer's point was not that Christianity enjoyed any special legal status, but merely that most Americans were Christians.[37]

The leading figure on the Court in the early twentieth century was Oliver Wendell Holmes. Holmes was already well known among lawyers and in wider intellectual circles when he joined the Court in 1902, after twenty years on the Massachusetts Supreme Court. His 1881 book *The Common Law* is still read today, as are several of his many articles. By the later part of his nearly thirty years on the Court, he was such a revered figure that his eighty-fifth birthday was celebrated on the cover of *Time* magazine and his ninetieth birthday was commemorated with a nationwide radio broadcast. Holmes was lionized as the Court's great "liberal," not because he personally favored outcomes preferred by the political left, but because he was less inclined than any of his colleagues to interpret the Constitution as countermanding legislative choices, in an era when most of the statutes the Court found unconstitutional embodied progressive policies.[38]

Holmes's politics, not his status as an intellectual, put him on the Court. President Theodore Roosevelt was simply looking for "a party man, a constructive statesman," who would take the Republican side on the issues that came before the Court. "The majority of the present Court," he noted, who had "upheld the policies of President McKinley and the Republican party in Congress, have rendered a great service to mankind and to this nation." But a four-justice minority "have stood for such reactionary folly" that they seemed interested only in hampering the government "in doing efficient and honorable work for the national welfare." Roosevelt was willing to concede that "without doubt they are men of excellent personal character; but this no more excuses them than the same conditions excused the various upright and honorable men who took part in the wicked folly of secession in 1860 and 1861." Holmes would be replacing Horace Gray, whom Roosevelt considered "one of the most valuable members of the Court." Roosevelt declared: "I should hold myself as guilty of an irreparable wrong to the nation if I should put in his place any man who was not absolutely sane and sound on the great national policies for which we stand in public life."[39]

If anything, Holmes's intelligence and broad interests *hindered* his appointment. George Hoar, one of the senators from Holmes's home state of Massachusetts, recognized that Holmes "is a man of learning," with "an excellent style," who had "been a very faithful student of the origin of the

Figure 6.3   Oliver Wendell Holmes, photographed here in 1913, was the most highly regarded justice of the early twentieth century and is considered by many to be the greatest justice in the Court's history. Library of Congress, LC-USZ62-8099.

English law." But Hoar reported that "the best lawyers in Massachusetts, almost without exception, think that while he has these excellent qualities," he was too intellectual to be an effective judge. "His opinions carry with them no authority, merely because they are his," Hoar insisted. "We have contributed from New England some very tough oak timbers to the Bench, State and National. Our lawyers in general, especially those in the country, do not think that carved ivory is likely to be as strong or enduring, although it may seem more ornamental." When Roosevelt nevertheless nominated him, Holmes noted with dismay that the press "says that I have not been a great Judge, being brilliant rather than sound."[40] Holmes would indeed develop a reputation as the Court's best stylist. His opinions are read today as much for their literary quality as for their substance.

Holmes began his tenure on the Court with relish. He was "more absorbed, interested and impressed than ever I had dreamed I might be," he told a friend shortly after joining the Court. He loved "the variety and novelty to me of the questions" that came before him. In only a few months, he had written opinions "on the constitutionality of part of the Constitution of California, on the powers of the Railroad Commissioners of Arkansas, on the question whether a law of Wisconsin impairs the obligation of the plaintiff's contract," and on "fifty other things as remote from each other as these." But he missed the Harvard-centered intellectual world of Boston where he had spent most of his first sixty years, in the company of thinkers like William James and Charles Sanders Peirce. On the Court, "I am very much alone," he told the Harvard professor John Chipman Gray in 1914. Referring to his colleagues, he explained: "The brethren are kind, friendly, able men, but for the most part the emphasis of their interests and their ideals are not the same as mine." Gray would have understood what Holmes meant, because his half-brother was Horace Gray, the justice Holmes replaced. Holmes would compensate for his intellectual isolation on the Court by maintaining a voluminous correspondence with thinkers all over the world, some of which would be published after his death, and by forming friendships with the younger progressive intellectuals who flocked to Washington in the 1910s and 1920s and who considered Holmes a hero.[41]

Apart from Holmes, the early twentieth-century justice with the greatest reputation today is Louis Brandeis, who was already famous as a progressive lawyer when he joined the Court in 1916. Brandeis was involved in a wide range of reforms, including the break-up of large corporations, the Zionist movement, and the promotion of legislation to protect employees and labor unions. He is credited with pioneering a new kind of legal argument—still called a "Brandeis brief"—filled not with the usual legal authorities but with statistics and other facts about the matter under consideration. In the best-known example, *Muller v. Oregon* (1908), Brandeis successfully defended the constitutionality of Oregon's ten-hour maximum workday for women in factories by filing a brief that contained only a few pages of legal argument but more than a hundred pages of data detailing what were then believed to be the uniquely harmful physical effects on women of overwork.[42] In his nearly twenty-three years on the Court, Brandeis's opinions tended to fulfill the expectations generated by his work as a lawyer. He was a voice for judicial deference to legislative experimentation in the realm of business and labor, but an early proponent of judicial enforcement of individual rights in other realms, such as the freedom of speech.

None of the remaining justices of the late nineteenth and early twentieth centuries are as well-remembered today. Some did not remain on the Court long enough to leave much of a mark. Ward Hunt, appointed in 1872, was "broken down with gout" five years later, according to his colleague Samuel Miller. Hunt was paralyzed by a stroke the following year, which prevented him from doing any work. He nevertheless remained on the Court because he had not yet served the ten years required for a pension. Congress had to pass a special statute giving Hunt an early pension to persuade him to retire. A similar statute was needed for William Moody, who developed rheumatism soon after he joined the Court in 1906 and resigned four years later after spending the last eighteen months of his tenure lying in bed, unable to attend any court sessions. John Hessin Clarke, perhaps the most progressive justice of the early twentieth century apart from Brandeis, quit after only six years because he was bored. "The mere bone labor of the Supreme Court work," he explained, "coupled with the fact that more than one-half of the cases are of no importance in the world except to the parties to them and their lawyers, had become so insupportably irksome to me that it was not difficult for me to lay down the great office." It was "a dog's life," he told his successor, George Sutherland, although he acknowledged that "most men do not think so ill of it." Clarke resigned in 1922 to spend his time on something he thought was more important—persuading Americans that the United States should join the League of Nations. Clarke lived until 1945. Had he remained on the Court through the 1920s and 1930s, some of the big cases of the period would likely have come out the other way, because Clarke's vote would almost certainly have been the opposite of Sutherland's. "Clarke is a good fellow," Taft remarked shortly before Clarke left the Court, "but he has such prejudices that he decides quite a number of cases as he reads the title to the case."[43] What Taft called "prejudices" might also be called political views that Taft did not share.

The Court was generally quite conservative during this era. Several of the justices were simply conventional conservative lawyers who wrote conventionally conservative opinions. As Holmes said of Mahlon Pitney, his colleague from 1912 to 1922, "he had not wings and was not a thunderbolt, but he was a very honest hard working Judge." When these justices are remembered today, it is usually because they happened to write the Court's opinion in a famous case. Henry Billings Brown wrote hundreds of opinions during his fifteen years on the Court, but if his name is known at all, it is for *Plessy v. Ferguson* (1896). Rufus Peckham was on the Court for nearly fourteen years, but had he not written the Court's opinion in *Lochner v. New York* (1905), he would likely be an obscure figure today. When Holmes was asked what Peckham was like intellectually, he replied "Intellectually? I never thought of him in that connection. His major premise was 'God damn it!'" (Then again, Holmes could be a tough critic. Of Harlan he said "Harlan's mind was like a vise, the jaws of which did not meet. It only held the larger objects.") The four most conservative justices of the 1920s and 1930s— Willis Van Devanter (on the Court from 1911 to 1937), James McReynolds (1914–1941), George Sutherland (1922–1938), and Pierce Butler (1923– 1939), known then and now as "the Four Horsemen"—are remembered today primarily for invalidating several of the New Deal economic programs of Franklin Roosevelt's first few years in office. But they were no less conservative, and no less frustrating to progressive lawyers, when Coolidge and Hoover were president. "They don't even try to understand the arguments presented to them on the other side," groused the law professor Robert Hale in 1929. "They have that dangerous combination of ignorance with assurance that they are right."[44]

Before the Civil War, the two major political parties had different views on the main issue that came before the Court, the relative power of the federal government and the states. Beginning in the mid-twentieth century, divisions within the Court on the most salient issues would likewise be aligned with divisions between the political parties. This connection was much weaker in the late nineteenth and early twentieth centuries. The Four Horsemen, for example, were appointed by Taft, Wilson, and Harding, two Republicans and a Democrat. Holmes and Brandeis, the liberal icons of the era, were appointed by Roosevelt and Wilson, one Republican and one Democrat. To some extent, the Republicans were the party of big business during this period. The presidency was occupied by a Republican for fifty-three of the seventy-two years between 1861 and 1933, and Republicans appointed thirty-four of the forty-one justices, so it is tempting to hypothesize that the Court's general conservatism was a product of Republican electoral success. But some of the Democratic appointees were more conservative in this respect than many of the Republican appointees. They included Fuller, White, and Peckham, who were all appointed by Grover Cleveland, and McReynolds, who was appointed by Wilson. The Republicans were the party of Reconstruction and the Democrats the party of southern whites, but in cases involving race discrimination there was little difference in the voting records of Republican and Democratic appointees. This weak connection between a justice's political party and his vote on the most salient issues before the Court helps explain why the Senate was consistently willing to confirm nominees of the opposite party during this era, even in an election year, and why some presidents were willing to nominate justices of the opposite party.

III

Until 1925, the Court, with only a few exceptions, could not choose which cases it would hear. If a lawyer wanted to take a case to the Supreme Court, and if the case was within the Court's jurisdiction, the Court had to decide it. The justices found themselves swamped with cases of no conceivable importance to anyone but the litigants. The Court is "burdened with many cases which never ought to be brought here," George Sutherland complained. For this reason, when Sutherland became a justice, he received an ambivalent letter from John W. Davis, one of the leading lawyers of the era. "In view of the constant grind of the position," Davis half-joked, "I sometimes wonder whether those chosen for it are to be congratulated." Justice Samuel Miller sent a similar note to Horace Gray when Gray joined Miller on the Court. "I sat down to congratulate you," Miller admitted, "but I hesitate to assume that it is a matter to be congratulated about." As we have seen, the glut of inconsequential cases drove John Hessin Clarke off the Court. "The first impression made upon me by my service as a member of the Supreme Court was that of surprise at the great number of cases finding their way into that Court which are of entirely negligible importance," Clarke remarked in a speech to the alumni of New York University Law School. "There seems to be a type of lawyer in every part of the county," he suggested, "who, once he is retained in a cause, no matter how trivial, sets to work with all the ingenuity he possesses to import into the record a federal question which he thinks may enable him to carry it to the Supreme Court." The result was "a great waste of the time of the Supreme Court judges."[45]

The Court had to decide hundreds of these cases each year. The caseload dropped by more than half after the creation of the circuit courts of appeals in 1891, but the numbers soon began to mount again. In 1901, 386 new cases were filed in the Court. In 1911, there were 532 new cases. By 1921, that figure was up to 673. Simply holding oral argument in all these cases took up an enormous amount of time. The Court's practice at the turn of the century was to allow each side two hours of argument, but that soon proved unsustainable. When Edward White became chief justice, the Court created a "summary docket" for the least substantial cases, in which each side was given only thirty minutes. When even this short period proved too long, the Court adopted an even more abbreviated mode of argument. After the lawyer for one side spoke, if it was clear that he would not prevail, the Court would announce that there was no need to hear the other side at all, a shortcut that allowed the justices to move on promptly to the next case. "This was a great relief to the respondent" (the winning side), recalled Charles Henry Butler, the Court's long-serving reporter of decisions, "although it was often a disappointment not to be able to address the Supreme Court of the United States."[46]

The only way the justices could plow through so many cases was to decide them quickly in short opinions. In volume 222 of the *United States Reports*, for example, there are opinions in eighty-eight cases decided between October 1911 and January 1912. Nearly all were published within a few weeks of oral argument. (The exceptions had been argued the previous April and were not yet completed when the Court took its summer recess.) Each case occupies only a few pages, and much of the page count is taken up with summaries of the arguments of counsel. There are only a handful of cases that would have been of interest to contemporary lawyers. In *Kalem Company v. Harper Brothers*, for instance, the Court held that a film of the popular novel *Ben Hur* infringed the copyright in the novel. Movies were new enough that Oliver Wendell Holmes felt obliged to explain what they were. "By means of them anything of general interest from a coronation to a prize fight is presented to the public with almost the illusion of reality," he marveled. In *Southern Pacific v. Kentucky*, the Court held that steamships owned by the Southern Pacific Railroad, a corporation chartered in Kentucky, could be taxed by Kentucky but not by New York, even though the ships were never in Kentucky but regularly docked in New York. In *City of Chicago v. Sturges*, the Court upheld the constitutionality of an Illinois law compensating property owners for damages caused by riots.[47] Cases like these have been forgotten today, but some people would have thought them important when they were decided.

Most of volume 222, however, provides ample support for the justices' complaints about the insignificance of many of the cases they had to decide. In *Blinn v. Nelson*, the Court needed only three paragraphs to explain why

Massachusetts could lawfully distribute property belonging to a person who had been missing for fourteen years. In *Gring v. Ives*, the Court dismissed as frivolous the contention of a tugboat owner that he should not be liable for damages caused by his tugboat in a collision. In *Porto Rico Sugar Company v. Lorenzo*, a case arising from one of the new colonies recently acquired from Spain, the Court briskly affirmed a lower court decision awarding damages for the breach of a contract to grind sugar.[48] Humdrum cases like these, by the hundreds, occupied most of the justices' time.

It would have been impossible to decide so many cases if the justices closely edited one another's work, so they did not. In reading draft opinions by his colleagues, Joseph Bradley explained, "I never bother with language or style or punctuation—that is the business of the writer of the opinion." So long as an opinion reached the desired result, that was good enough. Another time-saving technique the justices adopted was to specialize in the topics they knew best. Henry Billings Brown recalled that "by reason of his previous experience as Secretary of the Interior, Justice Lamar's assignments were chiefly confined to land cases." For similar reasons, Chief Justice Melville Fuller typically assigned himself cases involving procedural issues, while Brown, Joseph Bradley, and Samuel Blatchford got the patent and admiralty cases, and Horace Gray was assigned a disproportionate share of cases raising questions of commercial law.[49]

The Court could not have handled such a huge caseload if justices wrote dissenting opinions whenever they disagreed with the majority, so they generally did not. "I shall not write a dissent," Mahlon Pitney said on one typical occasion, "as I have not time to do so." The infrequency of dissenting opinions was not due to the infrequency of disagreement. When Morrison Waite was chief justice, for example, a justice expressed a dissenting view at the justices' private conference in 40% of the cases, but a justice published a dissenting opinion in only 9% of the cases. The norm was to write a dissenting opinion only in the rare cases where expressing dissent seemed particularly important. "I always write a dissent with real reluctance, and often acquiesce in opinions with which I do not fully agree," Harlan Fiske Stone noted. He wondered on another occasion "whether dissenting has any utility beyond enabling the dissenter to live comfortably with himself."[50] The norm against expressing dissent was in large part a method of saving the justices' scarce time for more important tasks.

The norm also reflected a sense shared by some of the justices that the Court's authority would be weakened by publicizing the justices' disagreements. "The continuity and weight of our opinions on important questions of law should not be broken any more than we can help by dissents," William Howard Taft argued after a divided vote on whether a labor union violated the Sherman Antitrust Act by ordering its members not to work for certain employers. Published dissents from "decisions of the Court, while they must sometimes occur, don't help the weight of its judgment." This concern would never disappear. But once the Court gained the power to choose which cases it would hear, the norm against expressing dissent evaporated.[51] This timing suggests that the norm was primarily a labor-saving technique that was abandoned once it was no longer needed.

The Court still held oral argument in its courtroom in the Capitol, where it would remain until it acquired a building of its own in the 1930s. The justices sat behind their long straight elevated bench, normally for four hours each day. (For several years around the turn of the century, adjoining seats were occupied by Justices Gray, Brown, and White, a color streak that would never be replicated.) For many years the Court took no break for lunch. Instead, while the argument was ongoing, one or two justices at a time would go to a small room right behind the bench, where they could listen to the argument while they were eating. The lunchroom was so close to the courtroom that lawyers could hear the clinking of silverware on the plate. There are conflicting accounts of why the Court instituted a lunch break. According to a 1910 magazine story, the change was in response to a lawyer's protest during one argument that "the personnel of the court has been twice entirely changed on me since I began." In a more colorful version of the story, as a lawyer paused in his argument, everyone could hear dishes clatter and a justice call out "More coffee please, my man, and have it hot!"[52] One or both of these tales might be apocryphal, but they reveal how little space in the Capitol was available to the Court. The justices had a courtroom but not much else.

There was no room for the justices to have offices in the Capitol, so when the Court was not hearing argument they worked in their homes. In principle, the Court supplied each justice with a basic collection of published case reports, but "you would be disappointed if you were to see the imperfect and dilapidated set of books which they tendered to me," Willis Van Devanter noted. "Half of them were returned as utterly of no value. Even the set of the Federal Reporter is incomplete." Van Devanter rejoiced when he learned that the house owned by Emma Brewer, the widow of Justice David Brewer, was available to be rented, in part because "there would be real satisfaction in

Figure 6.4 Oral argument in 1888. Drawing by Carl J. Becker published in *Harper's Weekly*, June 28, 1888. Library of Congress, LC-USZ62-1249.

occupying the house where the Justice and Mrs. Brewer lived," but primarily because he hoped to use the book collection that he hoped Brewer had left behind. "I take it that the house has a study and a library room where I could do my work?" Van Devanter inquired. "Is the Justice's library still there, and how extensive is it?"[53]

Scarce office space in the Capitol did become available every so often, but it was controlled by Congress, not by the Court. In the mid-1920s, Justices Edward Sanford and George Sutherland managed to secure offices in the Capitol. Sutherland's twelve years in the Senate may have given him an insider's knowledge of how rooms were allocated. Harlan Fiske Stone borrowed office space from a Senate committee while the Senate was in recess, but he had to vacate it when the Senate reconvened. Stone had been attorney general, the dean of Columbia Law School, and a New York lawyer, so he was accustomed to working in a comfortable office. "What I need, and need very badly, is a room lighted by daylight, with sufficient wall space to hold a complete set of Federal reports and reference books most commonly used, and a room nearby for the use of my clerical assistants," Stone informed Chief Justice William Howard Taft. "There are a number of rooms in the dome of the Capitol which are ideal for this purpose." Taft had to remind

Stone that the offices were not within his power to dole out. He advised Stone to hold fast to the committee room he was occupying and hope for the best, because "it is a good deal easier to keep one Senator out than it is to put out one or more."[54] The lack of office space in the Capitol would be the one of the primary reasons Taft lobbied Congress for the construction of the Supreme Court building.

Like virtually all senior federal officials before the advent of air conditioning, the justices left the heat and disease of Washington each summer. "Washington City is full of typhoid fever," John Harlan observed in 1902, from the safety of his summer home in Quebec. "I would not wish to go there before I am compelled to." Harlan kept up a bantering correspondence with William Day, who summered on Mackinac Island, Michigan, in which each justice proclaimed the superiority of his own location. "It is a singular state of mind in which any one can be when he affects to believe Mackinaw air can be compared to the pure, delicious atmosphere of this region," Harlan declared. He told Day that in Quebec there was but a single mosquito, whose "face was turned westward as if he were seeking the company of his companions in the Mackinaw country." The justices took their work with them to their summer homes, but their summer schedules were part work and part vacation. "I have had the briefs in the Chicago Drainage case," Taft reported from Quebec, where he too spent the summers. "But I have been just too lazy and too much out of touch to attempt to write." The case had been argued in April, but Taft's opinion for a unanimous Court would not be published until January.[55]

In Washington, the justices spent most of their working hours in their home offices, but there was a constant flow of documents among the justices and between each justice and the Court's small staff. When a justice wrote an opinion, he sent it to the Court's printer, who sent page proofs to each justice. Often the justices had to send notes to each other. To deliver all these documents, each justice was assigned a "messenger" soon after the Judiciary Act of 1869 turned the justices into permanent residents of Washington. The messengers quickly became all-purpose valets who performed a wide range of tasks besides delivering documents. Because the justices worked in their homes, the messengers worked there too, so they were household servants as much as they were office employees. John Harlan's messenger, James Jackson, "was not only a most faithful attendant," Malvina Harlan recalled, "but served my husband with an affectionate loyalty that endeared him to every member of our family. He was with my husband when he died, and he shared our grief as one who was in a real sense a member of our household."

Figure 6.5 Justice Owen Roberts relaxes at his summer home, a dairy farm in Pennsylvania, in the mid-1930s. The justices, like many government officials, fled the heat and disease of Washington during the summer. Library of Congress, LC-DIG-hec-33614.

Justice William Burnham Woods was less happy with his messenger, but his frustration likewise indicates how closely the messengers were involved in their employers' home lives. His messenger "is the most annoying thing I have ever experienced," Woods complained. "The fellow is the first man I see in the morning and the last man I see at night. He forces his way into my bedroom in the morning and orders me down to breakfast, and then asks what I will have for breakfast, taking my order himself to the cook. I cannot get rid of him in any way. He haunts me all the time. I try to think of places to send him, but he is back again as quick as lightning. That fellow will be the death of me."[56]

The messengers were all black men. The relationship between a justice and his messenger had echoes of the prewar relationship between the southern justices and the slaves they brought to Washington to attend to them during Court sessions. Indeed, some of the early messengers were former slaves. Malvina Harlan praised James Jackson's "dignified and courtly manners," which she thought "were undoubtedly acquired from the fine 'Old Maryland' family in which he was brought up as a slave in the ante-bellum days." Joseph McKenna's daughter Isabel looked back fondly on her father's messenger, William Joice, who she called "the old black Joe of our family." She attributed Joice's "gentle civility" to his childhood as a slave "under the influence of a wise master and a great gentleman." These echoes of slavery were amplified by the fact that messengers normally held the job for life and were transferred from one justice to another when a justice died or retired. William Joice, for instance, started work at the Court as Salmon Chase's messenger. When Chase died, Joice became Stephen Field's messenger. McKenna replaced Field, so he acquired Joice's services. Messengers sometimes even passed the job along to their sons. Joice died in 1898. His son Edward became McKenna's messenger, and when McKenna retired, Edward Joice became the messenger for McKenna's replacement, Harlan Fiske Stone. Edward's son Harold also became a messenger. Between 1870 and 1963 there was always at least one Joice in service to a justice.[57]

Of course, the job of a messenger was nothing like slavery. It was stable government employment, in an era when African Americans were largely excluded from more lucrative pursuits. The justices often took a paternalistic interest in facilitating these transitions of messengers from one justice to another. When Horace Gray replaced Nathan Clifford, David Davis wrote to inform Gray that the justices "have each a servant provided for them. Judge Clifford's servant—William H. Bruce—has been unassigned since his death. He is the best servant I ever saw, and withal a good barber. Judge Clifford was much attached to him, and once, when in good health he requested me (should I outlive him) to speak to his successor for his retention." Davis assured Gray that Bruce "is a colored man of good address, good habits, and good timber."[58]

When Gray joined the Court in 1882, he brought another staffing innovation with him. During his years on the Massachusetts Supreme Court, Gray began hiring a recent Harvard Law School graduate each year or two as a law clerk. His half-brother, the Harvard professor John Chipman Gray, selected the clerks for him. One of these early clerks was Louis Brandeis, who worked for Horace Gray from 1879 to 1881. Gray paid for the clerks out of his own pocket. When he moved to the US Supreme Court, he continued this practice. The other justices must have been impressed, because in 1886, Congress began paying for the justices to hire one "stenographic clerk" each.[59]

At first, the justices varied widely in how they used their clerks. Clerks to some justices were primarily stenographers, who took shorthand notes of the justices' dictated correspondence and opinion drafts and then typed them up. "I have a first-class start in my shorthand," William Day's son Rufus proudly told his father. "I spend all my time at shorthand and typewriting," Rufus explained, so he could "be with you and mother a few years longer." Rufus, who had no legal training at the time, would spend several years as his father's clerk, succeeding two of his older brothers who had already served their father in that capacity.[60] Other justices, including Holmes and Brandeis, followed Gray's model of hiring recent law graduates annually or biannually and using them as primarily as legal assistants.

But even the clerks who had been to law school performed many secretarial tasks, because the justices had no secretaries. The clerks hired by Charles Evans Hughes "were fine young men who had been admitted to the bar," he recalled, "but as I kept them busy with dictation, hating to write in longhand, they had little or no time to devote to research and whatever was necessary in that line I did myself." Charles Wilson, a lawyer who clerked for Henry Billings Brown, explained that "my duties with Judge Brown consisted in examining all petitions for certiorari, motions to dismiss or affirm, and all submitted cases, and cases that were argued but involved complicated facts. I sometimes wrote a statement of facts for use in his opinions." This list of tasks suggests that Brown delegated to Wilson some of the most routine aspects of a justice's job, the parts that required the least judgment and skill, but these were a lawyer's tasks nonetheless. Yet Brown also used Wilson as a stenographer. "He dictated to me all his opinions and private correspondence," Wilson added, "and I also attended to some of his private business. I am now attending to his mail and his private affairs while he is in Europe." Francis Biddle recalled that working for Holmes required the clerk to "balance his checkbook, and listen to his tall talk." Holmes "did his own work," Biddle explained, "even checking the citations, and wrote his opinions in longhand" without much help from his clerk. Although the job was not very difficult, Holmes preferred to hire unmarried men, because they had no competing obligations.[61]

The clerks themselves were as widely varied as their duties. The roster of Holmes and Brandeis clerks includes several who would go on to distinguished careers, such as Biddle, who was attorney general during the Second World War; Dean Acheson, the future secretary of state, who clerked for Brandeis from 1919 to 1921; and Henry Friendly, later a prominent circuit judge, who was a Brandeis clerk during the Court's 1927–1928 term. Other clerks were less eminent. Ashton Embry, who spent nearly a decade as a clerk to Joseph McKenna, had to resign in 1919 when he was caught leaking the results of cases to speculators, who used the information to profit on Wall Street. He went into the bakery business. Alger Hiss, a Holmes clerk in the 1929–1930 term, began passing confidential government information to Soviet agents a few years later. He would be convicted of perjury in 1950 for denying it.[62]

This heterogeneity in how the justices used their clerks gradually diminished after 1920, when Congress appropriated funds for separate "stenographic clerks" and "law clerks" for each justice. Once the justices had secretarial help, they could use their law clerks purely as legal assistants.[63] The once-solitary job of reading briefs and writing opinions started to become a collective endeavor. Later expansions of the justices' staffs would push farther in this direction, until by the 1970s each justice presided over, in effect, a miniature law firm consisting of four law clerks, two secretaries, and the messenger, who was still called by that name but who turned into a general office assistant when the Court moved into its own courthouse and there was no longer any need to travel all over the city to deliver messages.

For most of the late nineteenth and early twentieth centuries, however, the justices pumped out hundreds of opinions each year largely on their own, each justice assisted only by a messenger and a single clerk. Most of the time there was nothing particularly awe-inspiring about the Court's work. The Court decided some important cases, as we will see in the next two chapters, but most of the Court's cases were not important at all, even at the time, and even to the justices. Oral argument, the only part of the justices' work carried out in impressive surroundings, was usually a tedious march through the backlog of minor matters. Otherwise, the justices worked in their own homes, where they read briefs and, in the large majority of cases, dashed off short opinions that would be read only cursorily by their colleagues before being published and quickly forgotten by everyone but the litigants. This was still the most powerful court in the world, but on any given day it could not have felt that way to the justices or to close observers of the Court. When we read the Court's most famous opinions from this era, we should be careful to remember how different the Court was from the institution it would later become. Today, the Court decides a small number of cases, many of which are important to the general public and nearly all of which are important to lawyers. In this respect the Court feels quite unlike an ordinary lower court, which has to decide a great number of cases few people care about. In the late nineteenth and early twentieth centuries, by contrast, the Court was much more like an ordinary court. The cases that were considered important, whether to the public or to the legal community, were the exceptions. They emanated only occasionally from a Court that was otherwise thoroughly mundane in its caseload and its working life.

7

The Jim Crow Court

In the decade after the Civil War, there was a remarkable flurry of new laws intended to ensure that the former slaves would enjoy legal equality with white people. The Thirteenth Amendment to the Constitution, ratified in 1865, abolished slavery. The Fourteenth Amendment, ratified in 1868, included a clause guaranteeing all Americans equal protection of the laws. The Fifteenth Amendment, ratified in 1870, barred the states from denying African Americans the right to vote. All three amendments included clauses giving Congress the power to pass legislation to enforce these guarantees. Congress wasted little time in doing so. In statutes enacted in 1870 and 1871 in response to campaigns of terror mounted by whites throughout the South, Congress made it a federal crime to use force or intimidation to prevent black people from voting. The newly created Department of Justice prosecuted white southerners for violating these statutes.[1] In 1875, Congress even passed a far-reaching civil rights act that prohibited discrimination in public transportation, theaters, and hotels. Within a short time, the nation had acquired an array of laws requiring equality between the races.

A few years later, however, most of this project lay in ruins, thanks in part to the Supreme Court, which interpreted the new constitutional amendments extremely narrowly and held the new statutes unconstitutional. By the mid-1880s, the federal government was left with little legal authority to do anything about race discrimination. Meanwhile, when Reconstruction ended and white supremacy resumed in the South, the southern states enacted a wide range of blatantly discriminatory laws of their own. These state laws were repeatedly challenged as unconstitutional, but the Court rejected nearly all the challenges. The Supreme Court was thus partly responsible for the Jim Crow era of the late nineteenth and early twentieth centuries.

This chapter will explore the Court's discrimination cases during this period. How can we explain the justices' hostility to the federal government's enforcement of the post–Civil War constitutional amendments? Why, by contrast, was the Court so deferential to southern state laws that mandated discrimination on the basis of race?

I

The Court first considered the federal government's authority to enforce civil rights in a pair of 1876 cases, *United States v. Reese* and *United States v. Cruikshank*. *Reese* was a federal prosecution of white Kentucky election officials for refusing to count votes cast by black voters. The officials were prosecuted under the Enforcement Act of 1870, which made it a crime to deny the vote to any citizen who was entitled to vote. Congress enacted the Enforcement Act shortly after the ratification of the Fifteenth Amendment, to enforce the Amendment's guarantee of black suffrage. The Court nevertheless held that the Enforcement Act exceeded Congress's authority. "The Fifteenth Amendment does not confer the right of suffrage upon any one," reasoned Chief Justice Morrison Waite. The Amendment merely prevented states "from giving preference, in this particular, to one citizen of the United States over another on account of race." But the Enforcement Act, as the Court saw it, went beyond these bounds. The Act contained "no words of limitation, or reference even, that can be construed as manifesting any intention to confine its provisions to the terms of the Fifteenth Amendment." Rather, the Act punished *everyone* who prevented someone from voting, whether or not race discrimination was the motive for doing so. A statute with such a broad sweep, Waite concluded, could not be justified as a method of enforcing the Fifteenth Amendment.[2]

Justice Ward Hunt was the only dissenter. In the majority's interpretation of the Enforcement Act, he argued, "good sense is sacrificed to technical nicety." He pointed out that although sections 3 and 4 of the statute, the sections under which the officials had been indicted, did not themselves require race discrimination to be the motive for denying the vote, these sections prohibited denying the vote in circumstances "as aforesaid," which was obviously a reference to the preceding sections of the statute, which *did* require race discrimination to be the motive. Only under the most hyper-technical reading of the Enforcement Act could it be thought to prohibit depriving someone of the vote for nondiscriminatory reasons. In any event, Hunt continued, it was hardly plausible to think that Congress's target had been anything but race discrimination. "An examination of the surrounding circumstances," he reminded his colleagues, along with "a knowledge of the evil intended to be prevented," made it plain that Congress meant to ensure that African Americans could vote just like whites could.[3] But Hunt was the only member of the Court who believed that the Fifteenth Amendment empowered Congress to enact the Enforcement Act.

Cruikshank, decided the same day as *Reese*, had a similar outcome. The case arose from the 1873 Colfax massacre, the worst incident of racial violence during Reconstruction, in which a mob of white men in Grant Parish, Louisiana, murdered approximately a hundred black people (accounts of the death toll varied widely) in order to seize control of the local government.[4] Some of the perpetrators were prosecuted under section six of the Enforcement Act, which made it a federal crime to injure or intimidate a person to prevent him from exercising any of his constitutional rights. In another opinion by Waite, the Court held that the charges had to be dismissed. Waite began with the premise that Congress could only enforce rights "granted or secured by the constitution." All other rights, he reasoned, could be enforced only by the state. Waite then picked apart, one by one, the charges against the Colfax defendants. They were accused of interfering with the victims' First Amendment right of assembly, but that right was not granted by the Constitution, Waite explained, because it "existed long before the adoption of the Constitution of the United States. In fact, it is, and always has been, one of the attributes of citizenship under a free government." The Colfax perpetrators were also charged with interfering with the black victims' Second Amendment right to bear arms, but that right was not granted by the Constitution either, in Waite's view. The Constitution merely protected it against infringement by the federal government.

Waite proceeded in this manner, knocking out right after right, until at last he came to the real cause of the Colfax massacre, the effort of whites to prevent African Americans from exercising their right to vote. The defendants were charged with violating the victims' Fourteenth Amendment right to the equal protection of the laws, but this was yet another right that Waite deemed not to be secured by the Constitution. "The equality of the rights of citizens is a principle of republicanism," he suggested. All the Fourteenth Amendment had added was a prohibition on the *states'* infringement of equal protection, not the right to equal protection itself, which had existed ever since the founding of the nation. The Colfax perpetrators were also charged with violating the victims' Fifteenth Amendment right to vote, but Waite rejected this charge as well. "The Constitution of the United States has not conferred the right of suffrage upon any one," he insisted. The Fifteenth Amendment merely protected African Americans "from discrimination in the exercise of the elective franchise on account of race." But the indictment of the Colfax defendants did not specifically allege that the victims' race was the reason for the massacre. "We may suspect that race was the cause of the hostility; but it is not so averred," Waite lectured. "This is material to a description of the substance of the offence, and cannot be supplied by implication." With all the charges against them dismissed, the perpetrators of the Colfax massacre were set free.[5]

The result of *Reese* and *Cruikshank* was to gut most of Congress's power to enforce the Fourteenth Amendment's guarantee of racial equality and the Fifteenth Amendment's assurance of the right to vote. The violence and intimidation that prevented black people from voting in the South was mostly carried on by white individuals (while state government officials looked on with approval), not by state governments themselves. If Congress lacked the authority under the Fourteenth and Fifteenth Amendments to regulate the conduct of individuals, there was little Congress could do to halt the campaigns of terror that white southerners were mounting against black people who tried to exercise their constitutional rights.

A few years earlier, Court decisions like these, with the obvious effect of undermining Reconstruction, would have drawn considerable opposition in Congress. For this reason, as we saw in Chapter 5, the Court went to considerable lengths in the late 1860s to avoid casting any doubt on Reconstruction's constitutionality. By 1876, however, the political environment had changed. In the 1874 elections, the Democrats won a majority in the House of Representatives for the first time since before the Civil War. It was clear that no additional civil rights legislation would be forthcoming from Congress. When the Court decided *Reese* and *Cruikshank*, the justices knew they would not provoke any reaction from the other branches of government.

The change in Congress reflected a broader change in public opinion. Northern whites were becoming more interested in sectional reconciliation with southern whites than in enforcing the rights of the former slaves. Decisions like *Reese* and *Cruikshank* might have drawn criticism in the northern press just a few years earlier, but in 1876 the press portrayed them as sensible and inevitable. The decisions "render still more firm the confidence of the people in the impartiality and wisdom of the court," the *New York Times* declared. The Court's decisions "may be regarded as a respectful but vigorous warning to Congress against the passage of hasty and loosely-worded laws." The *Independent* agreed that for Congress "to assume state powers as the method of punishing and preventing wrong in the states would be an experiment with our political system that had better be omitted. The ostensible end will not justify it. Southern questions, so far as they are purely state questions, must be left to the states themselves." The *Chicago Tribune* acknowledged that the Court's decisions would "open up the opportunity for serious abuses and perhaps terrorism in the South." But the decisions were "fortunate," the *Tribune* concluded, in that they restrained "Congress from enacting penal legislation in elections beyond the power conferred upon it by the Constitution."[6] Of course, the decisions were greeted even more warmly by southern whites.

A few years later, in *United States v. Harris* (1883), the Court used the same reasoning to strike down the Ku Klux Klan Act of 1871, which made it a federal crime to "go in disguise upon the highway" to deprive a person of the equal protection of the laws. In a unanimous opinion by William Burnham Woods, the Court held that the Ku Klux Klan Act was not authorized by the Thirteenth, Fourteenth, or Fifteenth Amendments, because it punished private conduct rather than the conduct of a state. The decision was once again praised in the northern press. "The sound opinion of the Court," gushed *Harper's Weekly*, "commends itself to every intelligent mind." *Harris* was "another illustration of the singular wisdom of our constitutional system."[7] *Reese*, *Cruikshank*, and *Harris* may have left some room, in theory, for Congress to enact statutes drafted more narrowly to punish only racially motivated misconduct with state backing. But everyone knew that further legislation protecting African American voting rights was very unlikely. Once the Republicans lost control of Congress in 1874, there was no longer any realistic possibility that Congress would pass any new statutes to enforce the Civil War amendments. The moment had passed. *Reese*, *Cruikshank*, and *Harris* killed off the federal enforcement of voting rights in the South. Congress would not resume the effort in earnest for nearly a century.

One of the last acts of the lame duck Republican Congress in early 1875 was a statute forbidding race discrimination in hotels, public transportation, and theaters. The constitutionality of the Civil Rights Act of 1875 reached the Court in a group of consolidated lawsuits known collectively as the *Civil Rights Cases* (1883). One of the cases was a prosecution for excluding black patrons from the better seats of a theater in San Francisco; another was a prosecution for barring them completely from New York's Grand Opera House; a third was a civil suit against the Memphis & Charleston Railroad Company for not allowing black women to ride in the ladies' cars of their trains. The Court held that the Civil Rights Act of 1875 exceeded the power of Congress. Once again, the statute's fatal flaw was that it regulated the conduct of private parties rather than states. The Fourteenth Amendment "does not authorize Congress to create a code of municipal law for the regulation of private rights," Joseph Bradley insisted in his opinion for the Court. It merely empowered Congress "to provide modes of redress against the operation of State laws, and the action of State officers." Congress could prohibit discrimination by state officials, Bradley reasoned, but "the wrongful act of an individual" was "simply a private wrong" that could only "be vindicated by resort to the laws of the State for redress." Of course, the southern states had no such laws prohibiting race discrimination by individuals. To the extent southern laws governed the topic, it was to *require* discrimination rather than to proscribe it. That was the reason for the federal statute. But the Court had already established in *Reese*, *Cruikshank*, and *Harris* that the Fourteenth Amendment did not allow Congress to prohibit discrimination by anyone other than a state.[8]

Nor was the Civil Rights Act of 1875 authorized by the Thirteenth Amendment's ban on slavery, Bradley continued. Bradley conceded that the Thirteenth Amendment did not merely ban slavery in the literal sense, but also the "badges and incidents" of slavery. But he did not agree that race discrimination was a badge or incident of slavery. "Is there any similarity between such servitudes and a denial by the owner of an inn, a public conveyance, or a theater, of its accommodations and privileges to an individual, even though the denial be founded on the race or color of that individual?" he asked. "Where does any slavery or servitude, or badge of either, arise from such an act of denial?" Discrimination might be wrong, "but what has it to do with the question of slavery?" Bradley concluded that "it would be running the slavery argument into the ground to make it apply to every act of discrimination which a person may see fit to make as to the guests he will entertain, or as to the people he will take into his coach or cab or car, or admit to his concert or theater."[9]

While asserting this distinction between slavery and mere discrimination, Bradley betrayed considerable impatience with the notion of using the law to enforce racial equality. "When a man has emerged from slavery," he remarked, "and by the aid of beneficent legislation has shaken off the inseparable concomitants of that state, there must be some stage in the progress of his elevation when he takes the rank of a mere citizen, and ceases to be the special favorite of the laws."[10] In Bradley's view, civil rights legislation was not merely beyond the power of Congress. It was misguided as well, because it was time for black people to stand on their own two feet and to stop receiving preferential treatment from the government. In this respect the Court was representative of northern white opinion. Nearly two decades after the Civil War had ended and slavery had been abolished, northern whites were losing interest in racial equality.

Joseph Bradley had long been skeptical about laws requiring racial integration. "Surely Congress cannot guarantee to the colored people admission to every place of gathering and amusement," he had noted several years earlier, shortly after the passage of the Civil Rights Act. "To deprive white people of the right of choosing their own company would be to introduce another kind of slavery." He shuddered at the consequences. "Surely a white lady cannot be enforced by Congressional enactment to admit colored persons to her ball or assembly or dinner party," he fretted. "It never can be endured that the white shall be compelled to lodge and eat and sit with the negro." Bradley believed that civil rights legislation would be fruitless in any event, because "the antipathy of race cannot be crushed and annihilated by legal enactment." He concluded that "it is no deprivation of civil rights to give each race the right to choose their company."[11] This view was most likely shared by most of the other justices, who, like Bradley, were unaccustomed to associating as equals with black people in hotels and restaurants.

The only dissenter in the *Civil Rights Cases* was John Marshall Harlan, the only member of the Court at the time who had personal experience of slavery, as a slaveowner in Kentucky before the war. "The opinion in these cases proceeds, as it seems to me, upon grounds entirely too narrow and artificial," Harlan began. "The substance and spirit of the recent amendments of the Constitution have been sacrificed by a subtle and ingenious verbal criticism." As Harlan saw it, "the power of Congress under the Thirteenth Amendment is not necessarily restricted to legislation against slavery" in a literal sense, "but may be exerted to the extent at least of protecting the liberated race against discrimination." The amendment's purpose had been to abolish slavery, "and since that institution rested wholly upon the inferiority, as a race, of those held in bondage, their freedom necessarily involved immunity from, and protection against, all discrimination against them." Harlan took issue with Bradley's claim that it was high time for African Americans to stop seeking special favors from the government. "It is, I submit, scarcely just to say that the colored race has been the special favorite of the laws," he protested. "The statute of 1875, now adjudged to be unconstitutional, is for the benefit of citizens of every race and color." But Harlan was the only justice who took this view.[12]

Harlan would dissent, typically alone, in many more of the Court's cases involving race discrimination. Within the Court, his dissents were treated with the conviviality characteristic of a small organization in which interpersonal frictions had to be smoothed over or else working life would be grim indeed. After the *Civil Rights Cases*, Harlan's colleague Stanley Matthews joked that Harlan had been afflicted with "dis-sent-ery." Harlan responded with equal good humor. "That the attack was, for a time, serious, is due to the *nauseous* character of the medicine which produced it," he replied. "At the out-set the discharges were all very highly *coloured*." In the world outside, Harlan was recognized as the Court's sole proponent of a vision of civil rights that seemed to be weakening every year. Harlan was "the one great

Figure 7.1 John Marshall Harlan, photographed in 1906, was the only justice of his era who believed that the federal government had the power to prohibit race discrimination by private parties. Library of Congress, LC-USZ62-31223.

calm voice of protest against wasting the riches of civil liberty which a past generation earned for all those which have followed," exulted the Iowa senator J. P. Dolliver toward the end of Harlan's career. "Your votes in the civil rights cases," he told Harlan, were "the chief guide and monitor of these confused times, directing the social progress of the nation."[13]

The Court's decision in the *Civil Rights Cases* seems once again to have reflected northern white opinion, at least as revealed in the press. The Civil Rights Act only "tended to irritate public feeling" and "to keep alive antagonism between the races," the *New York Daily Tribune* editorialized. The statute, "though sincerely intended to benefit the colored people, has really done them more harm than good." The *Nation* summed up the prevailing reaction in the national press. "The calm with which the country receives the news that the leading sections of the celebrated Civil-Rights Act of 1875 have been pronounced unconstitutional by the Supreme Court, shows how completely the extravagant expectations as well as the fierce passions of the war have died out," the magazine recognized.[14] Northern whites were no longer much interested in protecting black civil rights.

A few days after the Court's decision was published, Frederick Douglass provided a very different perspective on the case. "The Supreme Court is the autocratic point in our National Government," Douglass noted. "No monarch in Europe has a power more absolute over the laws, lives and liberties of his people, than that Court has over our laws, lives, and liberties." Douglass was speaking at a "civil rights mass meeting" in Washington, DC. He observed that "this decision has inflicted a heavy calamity upon seven millions of the people of this country, and left them naked and defenceless against the action of a malignant, vulgar, and pitiless prejudice." The Court, he argued, "presents the United States before the world as a Nation utterly destitute of power to protect the rights of its own citizens upon its own soil." Douglass yearned "for a Supreme Court of the United States which shall be as true to the claims of humanity, as the Supreme Court formerly was to the demands of slavery!" He acknowledged that the Civil Rights Act of 1875 had not been frequently enforced because its requirements were so contrary to the customs of white Americans, but he suggested that there was more to the Act than its mere enforcement. "That bill, like all advance legislation, was a banner on the outer wall of American liberty, a noble moral standard, uplifted for the education of the American people," Douglass declared. "This law, though dead, did speak. It expressed the sentiment of justice and fair play, common to every honest heart. Its voice was against popular prejudice

THE JIM CROW COURT 225

and meanness. It appealed to all the noble and patriotic instincts of the American people. It told the American people that they were all equal before the law; that they belonged to a common country and were equal citizens."[15] This was a vision of American law that would not garner much support at the Supreme Court for more than half a century.

In later years, the Court continued to hold that Congress's authority under the Fourteenth and Fifteenth Amendments extended only to punishing discrimination by state governments. Discrimination by private individuals could be regulated only by the states themselves. In *Ex parte Yarborough* (1884), for example, the Court unanimously permitted the federal prosecution of Ku Klux Klan members who had attacked a black man to prevent him from voting in Georgia's congressional elections, because Congress's authority to enact the statute under which the KKK members were prosecuted was not based on the Fourteenth or Fifteenth Amendments. It was based on a different part of the Constitution—article I, section 4, which authorizes Congress to regulate congressional elections. By contrast, in *James v. Bowman* (1903), the Court invalidated a federal statute prohibiting private individuals' interference with the vote on account of race, because for this statute Congress purported to derive its authority from the Fifteenth Amendment. A white Kentucky man was prosecuted for preventing black people from voting, but he was apparently acting in his private capacity, not on behalf of the state government. "This indictment charges no wrong done by the state of Kentucky, or by anyone acting under its authority," Justice David Brewer reasoned in his opinion for the Court. "The matter complained of was purely an individual act of the defendant." That was enough to conclude that the statute under which he had been prosecuted was unconstitutional. As Brewer summarized the Court's cases on the point, "a statute which purports to punish purely individual action cannot be sustained as an appropriate exercise of the power conferred by the 15th Amendment upon Congress."[16]

By then, Congress had long ceased enacting statutes that protected black people in voting or indeed in any other activity. White northerners had largely given up the project of trying to use the federal government to enforce the Civil War amendments, a project to which most white southerners had been opposed from the start. As Justice Henry Billings Brown observed shortly after his retirement, "the qualification of voters had better have been left to the people of each State. The history of the Fifteenth Amendment is a forcible illustration of the futility of legislation which runs counter to a strong popular sentiment."[17] Given the political climate, federal civil rights enforcement would almost certainly have declined after the mid-1870s even without the Supreme Court's intervention. But there can be little doubt that the Court hastened the decline by repeatedly holding the federal civil rights statutes unconstitutional. By the turn of the century, black people in the South were largely on their own, with no prospect of any help from the federal government.

II

As Congress stopped trying to enforce racial equality, the southern states, now fully self-governing and run largely by white supremacists, enacted discriminatory legislation of their own. Many of these statutes were challenged as contrary to the Fourteenth Amendment's Equal Protection Clause and other provisions of the Constitution, and many of these cases reached the Supreme Court. The Court rejected most of the challenges. In the late nineteenth and early twentieth centuries, the Court looked far more benignly on state laws requiring discrimination than it did on federal laws prohibiting it.

For example, the Court upheld state laws requiring racially segregated railroad cars. In the first of these cases, *Louisville, New Orleans & Texas Railway Company v. Mississippi* (1890), the constitutional challenge to Mississippi's law was brought not by a passenger but by a railroad, which contended that the law unconstitutionally interfered with interstate commerce because its trains traveled through Mississippi on interstate routes. The Court rejected the railroad's argument on the ground that the law required separate cars only while the trains were in Mississippi, not while they were in other states. In a short dissenting opinion, Harlan noted that a few years earlier the Court had struck down, as an unconstitutional interference with interstate commerce, a Louisiana law *prohibiting* segregation on steamboats traveling through the state on interstate routes. If a law banning segregation affected interstate commerce, he wondered, how could a law requiring segregation not do the same? He concluded: "I am unable to perceive how the former is a regulation of interstate commerce, and the other is not."[18]

One practical difference between the two cases was that to most white people of the era, likely including most of the justices, segregation seemed the more sensible policy. As Justice Nathan Clifford observed in the steamboat case, "it is not an unreasonable regulation to seat passengers so as to preserve order and decorum, and to prevent contacts and collisions arising from natural or well-known customary repugnancies which are likely to breed disturbances, where white and colored persons are huddled together without their consent." Whether segregation was required by law or optional, it was the norm throughout the South. To let passengers sit wherever they liked, "whether colored or white, is impossible," Clifford declared.[19] Because segregation was the norm, a state law requiring it would not subject a railroad to inconsistent requirements in different states. It was the norm in neighboring states too.

A few years later, in *Plessy v. Ferguson* (1896), the Court again upheld the constitutionality of segregated railway cars, this time in a suit filed by a black passenger. The Court held that compulsory segregation violated neither the Thirteenth Amendment, because segregation was not slavery, nor the Equal Protection Clause of the Fourteenth Amendment, because segregation was not inequality. "In the nature of things," Henry Billings Brown reasoned in his opinion for the Court, the Equal Protection Clause "could not have been intended to abolish distinctions based upon color, or to enforce social, as distinguished from political, equality, or a commingling of the two races upon terms unsatisfactory to either. Laws permitting, and even requiring, their separation, in places where they are liable to be brought into contact, do not necessarily imply the inferiority of either race to the other." Brown cited as an example "the establishment of separate schools for white and colored children, which have been held to be a valid exercise of the legislative power even by courts of states where the political rights of the colored race have been longest and most earnestly enforced."[20] The Constitution, as the Court understood it, required equality but not integration.

Brown briskly dismissed the contention that segregation was tantamount to inequality because everyone knew that whites were excluding blacks and not the other way around. "We consider the underlying fallacy of the plaintiff's argument to consist in the assumption that the enforced separation of the two races stamps the colored race with a badge of inferiority," Brown explained. "If this be so, it is not by reason of anything found in the act, but solely because the colored race chooses to put that construction upon it." African Americans simply needed more self-confidence. In any event, Brown continued, it was hopeless to expect that racial integration could be accomplished through legislation. "If the two races are to meet upon terms of social equality, it must be the result of natural affinities, a mutual appreciation of each other's merits, and a voluntary consent of individuals," he reasoned. "Legislation is powerless to eradicate racial instincts, or to abolish distinctions based upon physical differences, and the attempt to do so can only result in accentuating the difficulties of the present situation." The law could not counteract whites' "natural" disdain for blacks. "If one race be inferior to the other socially," Brown concluded, "the constitution of the United States cannot put them upon the same plane."[21]

Harlan again dissented. He faulted his colleagues for ignoring the obvious social context of segregation. "Every one knows that the statute in question had its origin in the purpose, not so much to exclude white persons from railroad cars occupied by blacks, as to exclude colored people from coaches occupied by or assigned to white persons," he observed. For this reason, he concluded that laws requiring segregation denied equal protection of the laws to African Americans. "The white race deems itself to be the dominant race in this country," Harlan noted. "But in view of the constitution, in the eye of the law, there is in this country no superior, dominant, ruling class of citizens. There is no caste here. Our constitution is color-blind, and neither knows nor tolerates classes among citizens. In respect of civil rights, all citizens are equal before the law." He predicted that "the judgment this day rendered will, in time, prove to be quite as pernicious as the decision made by this tribunal in the Dred Scott Case."[22]

Harlan's prediction would eventually come true. Many years later, *Plessy*, like *Dred Scott*, would be a case infamous for its expression of racial inequality. But while *Dred Scott* was enormously controversial in its own day, *Plessy* was not. The press paid scarcely any attention to it. Most lawyers treated the outcome as obvious. The decision conformed to the conventional wisdom.[23] When *Plessy* was decided, segregation was such a ubiquitous part of everyday life that a contrary result would have been astonishing. The justices were men of their time. It is unlikely that any of them, apart from Harlan, saw anything wrong with segregation. Even if they had, they would have realized that a decision barring segregation would have been extraordinarily difficult to enforce in the South, because it would have been so contrary to prevailing sensibilities among whites. Half a century later, when the Court finally began condemning segregation, the difficulty of enforcing such decisions would become even more apparent.

As the Court recognized in *Plessy*, segregation was also ubiquitous in public schools. As one contemporary lawyer explained, school officials "have power, in the best interest of education, to cause different races and nationalities, whose requirements are manifestly different, to be educated

Figure 7.2 A dispensary in Washington, DC, operated by the US Public Health Service, with signs for separate waiting rooms for whites and nonwhites. Segregation was so commonplace in the late nineteenth and early twentieth centuries that it would have been astonishing for the Court to find it unconstitutional. This photograph was taken between 1909 and 1932; the exact date is unknown. Library of Congress, LC-USZ62-108282.

in separate places." Indeed, school segregation was so much the norm that when a case challenging the practice finally reached the Court, the challenge was brought not by black parents but by a Chinese man, whose argument was not that segregation was unconstitutional but rather that his daughter should have been assigned to the white school rather than to the black one. He lost.[24] Public schools would remain segregated for many years to come.

In *Berea v. College v. Kentucky* (1908), the Court upheld a Kentucky law prohibiting even private schools from offering integrated classrooms. Berea College, founded by abolitionists shortly before the Civil War, was the first integrated college in the South, until Kentucky forced it to expel its black students. Harlan dissented once more, this time joined by William Day. "Have we become so inoculated with prejudice of race," Harlan asked, "that an American government, professedly based on the principles of freedom, and charged with the protection of all citizens alike, can make distinctions between such citizens in the matter of their voluntary meeting for innocent purposes, simply because of their respective races?"[25] The answer, as he knew, was yes.

Plessy's "separate but equal" principle remained the law until the mid-twentieth century. In practice, however, the Court repeatedly gave its blessing to segregated arrangements that did not treat the races equally. In *Cumming v. Board of Education* (1899), for example, the Court unanimously approved a Georgia county's decision to close its black high school while maintaining a high school for white students. The opinion was written by Justice Harlan, who, just three years after his impassioned *Plessy* dissent, accepted with equanimity the school board's justification that it could only afford to educate black children through primary school.[26] Southern schools would be separate and unequal for a very long time.

The Court likewise permitted separate but unequal railway cars. In *McCabe v. Atchison, Topeka & Santa Fe Railway* (1914), the Court considered an Oklahoma statute that allowed trains to maintain sleeping cars and dining cars for white passengers but no comparable cars for black passengers. The rationale for the statute was that there was not enough demand among black passengers for the sleeping and dining cars because they were more expensive. In an opinion joined by only four other justices, Charles Evans Hughes rejected this justification, because it "makes the constitutional right depend upon the number of persons who may be discriminated against, whereas the essence of the constitutional right is that it is a personal one." If there were enough passengers of any race willing to purchase tickets in sleeping and dining cars, "substantial equality of treatment of persons traveling under like conditions cannot be refused." But the black plaintiffs lost the case anyway because the Court found that they had not proven that they would have bought tickets in the sleeping or dining cars had the tickets been available. Nor had they shown that damages would be an inadequate remedy if they ever were denied access to the sleeping and dining cars. The Court thus refused to bar Oklahoma from enforcing the statute. And even that empty declaration of equality was too strong for Oliver Wendell Holmes and the Court's three southern justices, Edward White, Joseph Lamar, and James McReynolds. The four noted in a single sentence that they concurred only in the result, a statement implying that they would have found the statute constitutional even if the plaintiffs had demonstrated that they would have purchased tickets if given the opportunity.[27]

While the Court was allowing the southern states to maintain segregation in public spaces, it also stood by while the southern states effectively barred black people from voting. In *Williams v. Mississippi* (1898), the Court considered Mississippi's laws governing voter registration, which did not explicitly mention race but which required payment of a poll tax and passage of a literacy test and which delegated a great deal of discretion to local officials to determine who was eligible to vote. The state supreme court explained that the purpose of this scheme was "to obstruct the exercise of suffrage by the negro race," because the race was "careless, landless, migratory within narrow limits, without forethought, and its criminal members given to furtive offenses." The Court nevertheless unanimously upheld Mississippi's voting laws, because "they do not on their face discriminate between the races, and it has not been shown that their actual administration was evil; only that evil was possible under them."[28]

In principle, *Williams* left open the possibility of invalidating this sort of voting scheme if it could be proven to have suppressed the black vote, but the Court soon choked off even this possibility. Alabama's voting rules were similar to Mississippi's and were enacted for the same purpose. Before 1903, voters had to be "persons who are of good character" as determined by local officials. Anyone who qualified under this standard was exempt for life from a new requirement that went into effect in 1903, which required would-be voters to be employed and to be able to "read and write any article of the Constitution of the United States." In *Giles v. Harris* (1903), a black plaintiff argued that the intent and the effect of these requirements was to limit voting to whites. Even if this allegation were true, the Court concluded, there was nothing that could be done. The suit contends that "the great mass of the white population intends to keep the blacks from voting," Oliver Wendell Holmes noted. But "to meet such an intent something more than ordering the plaintiff's name to be inscribed upon the lists of 1902 will be needed. If the conspiracy and the intent exist, a name on a piece of paper will not defeat them. Unless we are prepared to supervise the voting in that state by officers of the court, it seems to us that all that the plaintiff could get from equity would be an empty form." The Court considered itself powerless to intervene. Only Congress or the southern states themselves could reform southern elections to allow African Americans to vote. "Relief from a great political wrong," Holmes concluded, "if done, as alleged, by the people of a state and the state itself, must be given by them or by the legislative and political department of the government of the United States."[29] Black people would not vote in significant numbers in the South for many years.

The Court also upheld southern state laws that prohibited interracial marriage and cohabitation. These anti-miscegenation laws were needed, the Alabama Supreme Court explained, to prevent "the amalgamation of the two races, producing a mongrel population and a degraded civilization." In *Pace v. Alabama* (1883), the US Supreme Court considered a pair of Alabama statutes that punished adultery and fornication by up to six months in prison but increased the sentence to seven years in prison where the parties were of different races. In a very short unanimous opinion, the Court held that such laws did not violate the Equal Protection Clause because they applied "the same punishment to both offenders, the white and the black."[30] The southern states prohibited miscegenation for nearly a century thereafter.

The Court did invalidate some of the most blatantly discriminatory southern state laws, but these decisions proved to have little practical effect, because they were nullified by southern resistance and the Court's own acquiescence. In *Strauder v. West Virginia* (1880), for instance, the Court struck down a West Virginia law allowing only white people to serve on juries. But a statute was not the only way to discriminate in jury selection. The same goal could be accomplished by local officials exercising their discretion. In Bolivar County, Mississippi, for example, African Americans constituted a majority of the population, but the county's juries were all white for many years. Although the disparity could not have arisen by chance, the Court held that it did not violate the Equal Protection Clause. The Court also allowed southern states to limit jury service to those eligible to vote, a pool from which black people were largely excluded. As a result, despite the Court's decision in *Strauder*, southern juries were virtually all white during this period.[31]

Equally ineffectual were a pair of 1915 decisions in which the Court struck down the "grandfather clauses" adopted by Oklahoma and Maryland, which imposed stringent voting requirements but exempted the male descendants of people who were eligible to vote before 1866 (in Oklahoma) or 1868 (in Maryland). "It is true," Chief Justice Edward White acknowledged in the Oklahoma case, that the law did not expressly exclude anyone from voting "on account of race, color, or previous condition of servitude." But black people could not vote in Oklahoma before 1866, so it was clear enough that the date was chosen to exclude them from voting a half-century later. But the demise of the grandfather clauses had little effect on the ability of

African Americans to vote. Election officials had other tools to suppress the black vote, including poll taxes and literacy tests, which worked just as well. And the southern states were imaginative in finding new tools. Indeed, when the Court held Oklahoma's grandfather clause unconstitutional, the state promptly enacted a new one that enfranchised only those who were eligible to vote before the Court's decision—a meta-grandfather clause that remained in effect until 1939.[32]

Two years after holding grandfather clauses unconstitutional, the Court reached the same conclusion about discriminatory zoning laws. *Buchanan v. Warley* (1917) was a challenge to a Louisville zoning ordinance enacted, as its title explained, "to prevent conflict and ill-feeling between the white and colored races in the city of Louisville, and to preserve the public peace and promote the general welfare, by making reasonable provisions requiring, as far as practicable, the use of separate blocks, for residences, places of abode, and places of assembly by white and colored people respectively." The ordinance prohibited members of each race from moving to a block where a majority of the residents were of the other race. The suit challenging the ordinance was engineered by a relatively new organization, the National Association for the Advancement of Colored People, which had been founded only a few years before. To prepare for the suit, William Warley, a black resident of Louisville and an NAACP member, signed a contract to purchase a house in a white neighborhood from Charles Buchanan, a white real estate agent who shared the NAACP's goal of invalidating the ordinance. Warley then refused to proceed with the purchase because of its illegality. Buchanan, represented by the NAACP, sued Warley to compel him to purchase the house, on the ground that the ordinance was unconstitutional. The suit was cleverly constructed to enforce the constitutional rights of a white person denied the ability to sell to a black purchaser rather than the constitutional rights of a black person denied entrance to a white neighborhood.[33]

The justices did not object to the ordinance's purpose. "It is said," Justice William Day acknowledged for a unanimous Court, that "such legislation tends to promote the public peace by preventing racial conflicts; that it tends to maintain racial purity; that it prevents the deterioration of property owned and occupied by white people, which deterioration, it is contended, is sure to follow the occupancy of adjacent premises by persons of color." These were all worthy goals, Day explained. "That there exists a serious and difficult problem arising from a feeling of race hostility which the law is powerless to control, and to which it must give a measure of consideration, may be freely admitted," he conceded. But that was not reason enough to deny "the civil right of a white man to dispose of his property if he saw fit to do so to a person of color." The Court concluded that the Louisville ordinance infringed the property rights of the white seller.[34]

Warley was thrilled. "I cannot help thinking it is the most important decision that has been made since the *Dred Scott* case," he exulted, "and this time it came out the right way." But *Buchanan* proved to have little or no effect on residential segregation, which was maintained by pervasive social pressures that did not need to be enforced by zoning ordinances. Segregation was also increasingly enforced by covenants among white homeowners not to sell their property to nonwhites. A few years after *Buchanan*, the Court rejected a constitutional challenge to such covenants for the familiar reason that the post–Civil War amendments restricted only state governments and did not bar private parties from discriminating.[35] Residential neighborhoods remained segregated in much of the country.

The Court also struck down the peonage statutes that southern states adopted in the late nineteenth and early twentieth centuries. These statutes created a system of labor relations that came close to slavery without constituting slavery in a formal sense. In Alabama, for example, an agricultural laborer who failed to work for the full term of his annual contract was guilty of a crime, for which he was punished by a fine so large that he could not hope to pay it. Strictly speaking, laborers were guilty only if they intended to defraud their employers, but the statute provided that a breach of the contract was enough to prove intent to defraud, and laborers were not permitted to testify as to their true intent, so anyone who left his employment before the year was up committed a crime. These statutes applied in principle to all employment contracts, but in practice they were applied to black farmworkers, who were, as a result, bound to their white employers for up to a year at a time and who were liable to be leased out as convicts to other white employers to pay off their fines. Laborers were not formally owned by their employers, as in the days of slavery, but otherwise this system of peonage looked very much like slavery.[36]

In *Bailey v. Alabama* (1911), the Court held that Alabama's peonage statute violated the Thirteenth Amendment's ban on involuntary servitude. Charles Evans Hughes, the newest justice, began his opinion by denying the relevance of race. "We at once dismiss from consideration the fact that the plaintiff in error is a black man," Hughes declared. "The statute, on its face, makes no racial discrimination, and the record fails to show its existence in fact. No question of a sectional character is presented, and we may view the legislation in the same manner as if it had been enacted in New York or in Idaho."[37] Of course, everyone knew that New York and Idaho had no similar statutes, because the purpose of the statutes was to force black people to work on white-owned farms in the South. Hughes, the former governor of New York, knew this as well as anyone. His disavowal of any interest in alleviating race discrimination may have been a prudent strategic decision to make the opinion as inoffensive as possible to southern whites, perhaps to garner the support of one or more of his colleagues, or perhaps to smooth the public reception of the Court's decision in the South.

The Thirteenth Amendment did not merely ban slavery, Hughes continued. "While the immediate concern was with African slavery," he recalled, "the Amendment was not limited to that." Rather, the intention of the Thirteenth Amendment was "to render impossible any state of bondage; to make labor free, by prohibiting that control by which the personal service of one man is disposed of or coerced for another's benefit, which is the essence of involuntary servitude." He concluded that the Alabama statute created a form of coerced labor.[38]

Three years later, the Court invalidated another aspect of Alabama's peonage system. When black people were convicted of minor offenses, they would enter into contracts with white employers, who would pay the fines and court costs in exchange for a commitment to labor for a certain period. If they ceased laboring before the end of the period, that was another criminal offense, which would yield another fine to be paid by another white employer in exchange for another commitment to labor. The result was "an everturning wheel of servitude," William Day observed in his opinion for the Court in *United States v. Reynolds* (1914). The Court concluded that this arrangement was another form of involuntary servitude forbidden by the Thirteenth Amendment. Despite these cases, however, peonage remained common in the South until the mid-twentieth century.[39] Compelled labor could take many forms, so the Court's invalidation of just two of them left ample alternatives for the southern states to implement.

In short, even when the Court ruled in favor of black people, its decisions had little effect. And these cases were among the Court's rare efforts to enforce the Civil War amendments. The Court normally acquiesced in the southern states' establishment of the Jim Crow regime of race discrimination. Meanwhile, the Court repeatedly prevented Congress from doing anything about it.

III

Why did the Court play this role in the establishment and perpetuation of Jim Crow?

Supreme Court justices have always been well within the mainstream of conventional thought among educated white Americans. A person with unconventional views would be very unlikely to travel along the pathway of jobs that culminates in an appointment to the Supreme Court—a route that during this era included a period as a locally prominent lawyer and often service as an elected official, as a lower-court judge, or as a member of the cabinet. The nomination and confirmation process provided another stage for winnowing out any remaining candidates with unorthodox opinions. Anyone who became a justice in the late nineteenth and early twentieth centuries, as in any other era, thus shared most of the views prevailing among educated white Americans of the period.

At the time, one of these conventional views was the superiority of whites over nonwhites. "Now as to the Negroes!" Theodore Roosevelt wrote while president, "as a race and in the mass they are altogether inferior to the whites."[40] Whether nonwhites' inferiority was a biological fact, as the growing influence of Darwinism persuaded many, or whether nonwhites merely trailed behind whites by some distance in the progression from savagery to civilization, as others supposed, educated white Americans in the late nineteenth and early twentieth centuries generally did not consider the races equal. The justices of the Supreme Court shared this view as well.

The Court's acceptance of discrimination was facilitated by the fact that the South was well represented on the Court from the late 1870s onward. Had any southern justice been inclined to press for racial equality, he would have become a pariah in his home community. They were not, in any event, so inclined. Chief Justice Edward White was, according to different accounts, a member of either the Ku Klux Klan or a Klan-like organization as a young man in Louisiana. Many years later, as chief justice, White complimented the author Thomas Dixon on his novel *The Clansman*, a positive portrayal of the Klan that served as the basis for D. W. Griffith's unabashedly racist film *Birth of a Nation*. After the film was screened at the White House for President Woodrow Wilson and members of the cabinet, White arranged for another screening at the National Press Club for the justices, members of Congress, and their families. The film's producer even cited White's endorsement in the publicity materials for *Birth of a Nation* until White insisted that he stop.[41]

Figure 7.3   Chief Justice Edward White was a member of the Ku Klux Klan or a Klan-like organization as a young man in Louisiana. As chief justice, he arranged a private screening for the justices of D. W. Griffith's film *Birth of a Nation*, which glorified the Klan. Library of Congress, LC-DIG-hec-16425.

The other southern justices had similar views. When Lucius Lamar was a member of Congress from Mississippi, he gave speeches extolling "the supremacy of the unconquered and unconquerable Saxon race." Like the other southern members of Congress, he voted against the Civil Rights Act of 1875. As Reconstruction came to an end, Lamar proudly reported that "the negroes are almost as well disciplined in their silence and inactivity as they were before in their aggressiveness." Horace Lurton of Tennessee considered it important "to preserve the gap between the white and the negro race," as he explained to Theodore Roosevelt. Lurton's successor, James McReynolds, also from Tennessee, was famous for his bigotry. "Tell me," McReynolds once asked the Court's African American barber, referring to Howard University, "where is this nigger university?" During an oral argument presented by

Charles Hamilton Houston, at the time the most distinguished black lawyer in the country, McReynolds ostentatiously turned his chair to face the curtain behind the bench, so he would not have to look at Houston.[42] These were not men who could be expected to call a halt to discrimination.

But the justices from other parts of the country exhibited scarcely more interest in racial equality than their southern colleagues. The issue was not high on the agenda of any member of the Court. Nor was it a priority for any of the presidents who appointed the justices. At the Court, as in white society generally, racial inequality was simply a fact of life about which government could do little beyond ameliorating the worst excesses. It was part of "the nature of things," as Henry Billings Brown declared in *Plessy*. "Antagonisms of race," Stephen Field averred, "will always operate, in a greater or less degree, as impediments to the full enjoyment and enforcement of civil rights."[43]

In this respect the justices were like their contemporaries who sat on lower courts, in both the South and the North. As a Kentucky judge explained in upholding the state's requirement that all schools be segregated—the decision the Court affirmed in *Berea College v. Kentucky*—"the separation of the human family into races, distinguished no less by color than by temperament and other qualities, is as certain as anything in nature." The feeling that "some call race prejudice" was merely "nature's guard to prevent the amalgamation of the races." Northern courts reached the same conclusion. New York's highest court, for example, upheld the state's requirement of segregated schools on the ground that "in the nature of things there must be many social distinctions and privileges," including distinctions between the races. In Pennsylvania, the state supreme court approved a railroad's policy of segregating its train cars for the same reason. "Why the Creator made one black and other white, we know not, but the fact is apparent, and the races distinct, each producing its own kind," the court explained. The court determined that it should defer to "the natural law which forbids their intermarriage and their social amalgamation."[44]

Even John Harlan, the lone dissenter in many of the Court's discrimination cases, held this view. Harlan is a hero to many today for his dissenting opinions, and he was a hero to many in his own era as well. Yet even Harlan's dissents remained within the boundaries of conventional thought about the relationship between whites and people of other races. In *Plessy*, after noting that "the white race deems itself to be the dominant race in this country," he continued: "And so it is, in prestige, in achievements, in education, in wealth, and in power. So, I doubt not, it will continue to be for all time." In arguing against separate train cars for blacks and whites, Harlan wondered why Louisiana had not enacted a similar law for "a race so different from our own that we do not permit those belonging to it to become citizens of the United States. . . . I allude to the Chinese race."[45] Harlan's argument in *Plessy* was not that blacks deserved to ride in the same train cars as whites because members of the two races were equals. Nor was his argument that blacks compared more favorably to whites than the Chinese did. Rather, Harlan was merely arguing that whites' superiority to the other races was not a good reason for segregating trains, because the Constitution required treating the races identically regardless of their differing capacities.

Indeed, as Harlan's reference to Chinese immigrants suggests, he held the same view about the relationship between whites and Asians. Two years after *Plessy*, in *United States v. Wong Kim Ark* (1898), the Court held that everyone born in the United States is an American citizen. The decision was a literal interpretation of the Fourteenth Amendment, which provides: "All persons born or naturalized in the United States, and subject to the jurisdiction thereof, are citizens of the United States." But Harlan and Chief Justice Melville Fuller dissented. The case involved a US-born child of immigrants from China. Harlan and Fuller were appalled by the possibility that people "of the Mongolian, Malay, or other race, were eligible to the presidency" by virtue of their citizenship. They insisted for that reason that the Fourteenth Amendment could not be interpreted literally.[46]

The only justice during this era to display any interest in racial equality was David Brewer, the son of missionaries, who had been born in present-day Turkey and had been an ardent abolitionist as a young man before the Civil War. While he was a justice, some of his speeches exhibited compassion for African Americans and a desire to promote their welfare. Yet one would never know this side of Brewer from his opinions in the Court's discrimination cases, which were indistinguishable from those of most of his colleagues. Brewer did not join Harlan's dissents in any of these cases.[47]

The justices' conventional views about the superiority of whites played the same role in cases that did not involve black people. For example, the Court was just as willing to acquiesce in discrimination against the Chinese.[48] In the Chinese Exclusion Act of 1882, Congress prohibited immigration from China. The Scott Act of 1888 made this ban even stricter by providing that Chinese people already in the United States could not reenter the country after leaving. Just a few years before *Plessy*, a unanimous Court upheld the Scott Act, in an opinion by Stephen Field that described ubiquitous anti-Chinese prejudice in the United States without any suggestion that this prejudice might have been unfounded. "They remained strangers in the land," Field said of the Chinese, "residing apart by themselves, and adhering to the customs and usages of their own country. It seemed impossible for them to assimilate with our people, or to make any change in their habits or modes of living." Field, the Court's only Californian, explained that white Californians believed that "their immigration was in numbers approaching the character of an Oriental invasion, and was a menace to our civilization." This view was so widely held by whites at the time that it led to pervasive anti-Asian discrimination.[49] Again, the justices were men of their times.

The idea that white people were superior to members of other races was also in the forefront when the Court decided cases involving the rights of people in the territories acquired in the Spanish-American War, including Puerto Rico, Guam, and the Philippines. The first and best-known of these were the *Insular Cases* (1901). The narrow question in the *Insular Cases* was whether Congress could tax trade between Puerto Rico and the mainland, but the answer depended on the much broader question whether the Constitution "followed the flag" into the new territories. In an opinion by Henry Billings Brown, the author of *Plessy*, the Court expressed incredulity that Puerto Ricans or Filipinos, "whether savages or civilized," might be "entitled to all the rights, privileges and immunities of citizens. If such be their status, the consequences will be extremely serious." The Constitution thus did not protect the nonwhite residents of the new colonies. Harlan dissented, but it was not because he perceived equality between white Americans and the nonwhite occupants of the distant reaches of the new empire. It was because he thought the United States should never have annexed places populated by nonwhites in the first place. "Whether a particular race will or will not assimilate with our people," Harlan lectured, "and whether they can or cannot with safety to our institutions be brought within the operation of the Constitution, is a matter to be thought of when it is proposed to acquire their territory."[50]

The *Insular Cases* prompted two well-known quips. When Elihu Root, the secretary of war (and a distinguished lawyer before that), was asked about the murky reasoning of the Court's opinion, he replied: "As near as I can make out the Constitution follows the flag—but doesn't quite catch up with it." The humorist Finley Peter Dunne, famous for his fictional Irish bartender "Mr. Dooley," had Mr. Dooley say that "no matter whether th' Constitution follows th' flag or not, th' Supreme Court follows th' election returns."[51] Mr.

Dooley was no doubt correct, in the sense that imperial conquest was popular, but equal rights for the nonwhite people in the colonies were not.

The issue arose even more starkly in *Dorr v. United States* (1904), when the Court considered whether the constitutional right to a trial by jury was in force in the Philippines. William Day reasoned that Filipinos "were wholly unfitted to exercise the right of trial by jury." Because the natives were not qualified to serve as jurors, Day concluded, it would make no sense for there to be any right to a jury trial. The United States, a growing imperial power, had taken on the governance of disparate kinds of people, some of whom, in the Court's estimation, were not equipped for the civic obligations taken for granted at home. "If the United States, impelled by its duty or advantage, shall acquire territory peopled by savages," Day suggested, it could hardly "establish there the trial by jury. To state such a proposition demonstrates the impossibility of carrying it into practice."[52]

The inferiority of nonwhites was likewise a basis for the Court's decisions involving American Indians. In *Ex parte Crow Dog* (1883), the Court held that American courts had no jurisdiction over crimes committed in Indian country by one Indian against another. The Indians were "members of a community, separated by race, by tradition, by the instincts of a free though savage life," Justice Stanley Matthews explained in his opinion for the Court. If they were tried in American courts by white judges and jurors, the Indians' conduct would be evaluated "by superiors of a different race, according to the law of a social state of which they have an imperfect conception, and which is opposed to the traditions of their history, to the habits of their lives, to the strongest prejudices of their savage nature; one which measures the red man's revenge by the maxims of the white man's morality." In the Court's view, Indians were not civilized enough to participate in the white justice system. Congress thought differently and promptly established federal jurisdiction over certain crimes committed by Indians. The Court upheld the constitutionality of this new regime, but with no less condescension. Now the Indians *needed* the shelter of the white justice system because of "their very weakness and helplessness." The federal government's paternal authority "over these remnants of a race once powerful, now weak and diminished in numbers, is necessary to their protection."[53] The Indians' inferiority could justify prosecuting them in the federal courts as much as it could justify not prosecuting them.

Similarly, in *Elk v. Wilkins* (1884) the Court held that American Indians, alone among residents of the United States, were not entitled to citizenship simply by virtue of having been born in the country. "The alien and dependent condition of the members of the Indian tribes could not be put off at their own will," Horace Gray argued. They could become citizens only upon providing "satisfactory proof of fitness for civilized life." In *Lone Wolf v. Hitchock* (1903), the Court allowed the federal government to abrogate its treaties with Indian tribes and take their land, in light of "the status of the contracting Indians and the relation of dependency they bore and continue to bear towards the government of the United States."[54] In an era when racial hierarchy was an established part of life, the justices of the Supreme Court held conventional views about the differences between the races.

Distinctions between the races seemed just as natural as distinctions between the sexes, another topic that reached the Court during this period. In *Bradwell v. Illinois* (1873), Myra Bradwell sought to practice law, and in *Minor v. Happersett* (1875), Virginia Minor sought to vote. Both based their claims on the recently ratified Fourteenth Amendment, which barred the states from abridging "the privileges or immunities of citizens of the United States." Bradwell and Minor lost their cases. Women were citizens but had long been barred from practicing law and voting, so the Court held that neither practicing law nor voting was a privilege of citizenship. The differences between men and women, Joseph Bradley explained, were found in "nature herself," which "has always recognized a wide difference in the respective spheres and destinies of man and woman. Man is, or should be, woman's protector and defender. The natural and proper timidity and delicacy which belongs to the female sex evidently unfits it for many of the occupations of civil life." Women could not be lawyers because "the constitution of the family organization, which is founded in the divine ordinance, as well as in the nature of things, indicates the domestic sphere as that which properly belongs to the domain and functions of womanhood. The harmony, not to say identity, of interest and views which belong, or should belong, to the family institution is repugnant to the idea of a woman adopting a distinct and independent career from that of her husband." Bradley hastened to clarify that he was no blind follower of tradition. "The humane movements of modern society, which have for their object the multiplication of avenues for woman's advancement, and of occupations adapted to her condition and sex, have my heartiest concurrence," he declared. "But I am not prepared to say that it is one of her fundamental rights and privileges to be admitted into every office and position, including those which require highly special qualifications and demanding special responsibilities. In the nature of things it is not every citizen of every age, sex, and condition that is qualified for every calling and position." Sex differences, like the hierarchy of races, seemed in the late nineteenth and early twentieth century to be part of "the nature of things."[55]

One reason, then, for the Court's facilitation of Jim Crow was the justices' lack of interest in doing anything about it. Like most educated white Americans of the period, the justices considered racial inequality an ineradicable fact of life rather than a condition to be transcended.

Their apathy toward discrimination was reinforced by the layer of federalism through which racial questions were understood at the Court and in the wider legal community. One legacy of slavery, lasting long after the Civil War, was that the vast majority of black people lived in the southern states. In 1890, for instance, they made up 60% of the population of South Carolina and 58% of that of Mississippi. Northern states, by contrast, had tiny black populations—only 1% in New York and Massachusetts. It was easy for lawyers and judges to think of race relations as a southern problem for southern state governments to handle rather than as a national problem demanding intervention by the federal government. By their training, lawyers and judges were accustomed to thinking of the federal government as possessing limited powers that did not include matters relating to the internal governance of a state. The Civil War amendments had of course altered this relationship between the federal government and the states, but the extent of the alteration was precisely the question that was being contested. It is not surprising that the justices would err on the side of preserving the conception of federalism to which they were accustomed. This tendency toward supporting the authority of state governments nudged the Court even further toward invalidating Congress's civil rights legislation while upholding the contrary legislation of the states.[56]

Finally, even if the justices had been inclined to intervene to prevent the establishment of Jim Crow, they would have realized the futility of any such effort. Without the backing of Congress and the executive branch, the Court had no realistic hope of changing conditions on the ground in the South. The Court did take a few small steps in the direction of civil rights, but they made no difference. The Court held unconstitutional the exclusion of black people from juries, but they were excluded all the same. The Court invalidated peonage, but peonage persisted. The Court struck down grandfather clauses and discriminatory zoning ordinances, but black people could not vote or live in integrated communities. Had there been a justice who was eager to eradicate race discrimination, he would have had to recognize the limits of the Court's practical power.

It took a near-consensus of northern and southern whites to establish and maintain Jim Crow, a near-consensus that included virtually every member of the Court. That consensus would break down in the mid-twentieth century. When it did, the Court would be at the center of change. The words in the Constitution would still be the same, but they would be interpreted by justices who, like other white Americans, thought differently about race relations than their predecessors had a few decades before.

8

The *Lochner* Era

The Supreme Court of the late nineteenth and early twentieth centuries is remembered primarily as a pro-business Court. In several high-profile cases between the 1890s and the 1930s, the Court struck down state and federal regulation as an infringement of the constitutional rights of business enterprises. The name often given to this period—"the *Lochner* era"— comes from one of these cases, *Lochner v. New York* (1905), in which the Court invalidated a state law setting maximum working hours in bakeries. At the time, critics charged that the Court was biased in favor of employers and against labor, that the Court was preventing the country from making progress in dealing with new industrial problems, and that the Court was inventing constitutional doctrines nowhere to be found in the document's text.[1] This kind of criticism would only grow in volume over the years, to the point where today the word "Lochner" has become shorthand for a judicial activism that virtually all judges disclaim.

There is a long-running debate about how best to explain these cases.[2] Some historians have echoed the critique prevalent during the era—that the justices were hostile to regulation and that they adopted constitutional theories that allowed them to implement their laissez-faire philosophy. Other historians have argued that this method of interpreting the Constitution had deep roots in American legal thought, and that the justices were merely applying traditional principles to new factual circumstances.

Each explanation is true in its own way. Several of the justices of the late nineteenth and early twentieth centuries genuinely *were* hostile to some forms of regulation. They feared that socialism was at the gates. They worried that the federal government was amassing far too much concentrated power. They believed that the Court was the last line of defense against these frightening developments. The justices *did* choose constitutional theories that produced results consonant with their views of sound government. But they did not pluck these theories from thin air. Rather, the Court drew upon legal traditions under which some, but not most, of the era's regulation was beyond the authority of legislatures to enact. This way of thinking would lose most of its professional respectability in the mid-twentieth century, so it can seem quite strange today, when many of the types of regulation the Court struck down as unconstitutional, such as minimum wage and maximum hours laws, have become standard features of the legal landscape. At the time, however, the justices could sincerely believe they were following the law when they used the Constitution to shield business from regulation.

I

Some of the late nineteenth-century justices were fierce opponents of government efforts to improve the lives of workers and the poor, which they saw as the entering wedge of socialism. "The present assault upon capital is but the beginning," Stephen Field predicted when Congress tried to establish an income tax in the 1890s. "It will be but the stepping-stone to others, larger and more sweeping, till our political contests will become a war of the poor against the rich." Field believed the Court was the strongest barrier against this radical assault. As "angry menaces against order find vent in loud denunciations," he warned a gathering of lawyers in 1890, "it becomes more and more the imperative duty of the court to enforce with a firm hand all the guaranties of the Constitution." Based on pronouncements like these, Field's biographer concludes with good reason that "at times, Stephen Field seemed not so much a judge as an advocate, and he appeared to be guided not so much by a philosophy as an agenda."[3]

Samuel Miller's political views were more nuanced than Field's, but he too was nervous about radicalism on the horizon. "There are dangers threatening the principles lying at the foundation of our social fabric," Miller warned the graduating class of Iowa State University in 1888. "Under the various cognomens of anarchists, nihilists, socialists, or communists, these men are banded together into clubs or associations, and sometimes into communities, whose object, avowedly in some cases, and in most of them apparently, is the destruction of organized society."[4] Miller and Field, both born in 1816, had seen enormous changes in their lifetimes. Like many conservative lawyers of their generation, they worried that their way of life was coming under attack.

David Brewer likewise worried about socialism. One of the standard themes of his speeches was the importance of the judiciary in protecting property from being expropriated in the guise of regulation. "Private property is subject to governmental attack," Brewer declared at Yale Law School's graduation ceremony. "The demands of absolute and eternal justice forbid that any private property, legally acquired and legally held, should be spoliated or destroyed." In an address to the New York Bar Association, Brewer warned of "the black flag of anarchism, flaunting destruction to property," and "the red flag of socialism, inviting a redistribution of property rights." But "the salvation of the nation," he advised, "rests upon the independence and vigor of the judiciary," which was needed "to stay the waves of popular feeling" and "to restrain the greedy hand of the many from filching from the few that which they have honestly acquired."[5]

Field, Miller, and Brewer may have been more outspoken than their colleagues about the danger that radicals would use the government as a tool to seize the property of the affluent, but their concerns seem to have been shared by many of the justices of the late nineteenth and early twentieth centuries. "If it were possible to establish socialism as the basis of society," Henry Billings Brown advised the members of the American Bar Association at their 1893 annual meeting, "no greater calamity could overtake civilization." Without the courts, affirmed Stanley Matthews, "everything we hold to be dear and sacred as personal right is at the mercy of a monarch or a mob." George Shiras observed that "it is growing more and more apparent that the safety and welfare of the country depend largely on the integrity and firmness of the courts." Chief Justice William Howard Taft expressed a similar view, only half in jest, toward the end of his career. "I am older and slower and less acute and more confused," he confided to his brother. "However, as long as things continue as they are, and I am able to answer in my place, I must stay on the Court in order to prevent the Bolsheviki from getting control."[6]

In the most politically salient cases pitting labor unions against their employers, the justices sided unanimously with the employers. In *In re Debs* (1895), the Court approved the government's actions in breaking a nationwide strike of railway workers. In *Loewe v. Lawlor* (1908), the Court held that a union-led boycott was an unlawful restraint of trade.[7] From the justices' perspective, one primary purpose of courts was to protect property from the depredations of legislative majorities, by ensuring that legislatures did not side with labor over capital. This understanding would have a profound influence on the Court's decisions.

It was no simple matter, however, to translate a worry about socialism into the vocabulary of constitutional law. On one hand, commercial regulation was hardly new. State and local governments had always regulated markets,

Figure 8.1 A parade in support of socialism in New York on May Day 1914. The sign in the center of the photo reads "Women for Socialism and Socialism for Women." Many of the justices of the era considered the Court to be the final line of defense against socialism and other radical movements. Library of Congress, LC-USZ62-117461.

often quite intensively, such as by setting prices and mandating standards of quality. In light of this history, it would not have been plausible to maintain that the Constitution required "free" markets. On the other hand, ante-bellum courts had often said that legislation must be for the public good, and that "class legislation"—regulation intended to benefit some at the expense of others—was beyond the authority of a legislature. "It is manifestly contrary to the first principles of civil liberty and natural justice, and to the spirit of our constitution and laws, that any one citizen should enjoy privileges and advantages which are denied to all others," the Massachusetts Supreme Court declared in 1814. "Class legislation," the Georgia Supreme Court agreed a few decades later, was contrary to "the great fundamental principles of human rights." As Justice Samuel Chase had famously written way back in *Calder v. Bull* (1798), "a law that takes property from A. and gives it to B. . . . cannot be considered a rightful exercise of legislative authority."[8]

It was regulatory favoritism, not regulation alone, that raised constitutional concerns. Regulation to benefit the public was beyond reproach, but the redistribution of wealth or power from one group to another was, on this way of thinking, outside the proper role of government.

The difficulty was that much regulation that was ostensibly for the public good also had redistributive effects. One stark instance of this dilemma was the *Slaughter-House Cases* (1873), the Court's first occasion to apply the new Fourteenth Amendment to economic regulation. The *Slaughter-House Cases* were a group of three lawsuits challenging a Louisiana statute that required most New Orleans slaughterhouses to be located outside the city limits. Slaughtering within the city was consolidated in a single large slaughterhouse to be built and owned by a private company, which other butchers could use upon payment of a set fee. Viewed one way, this was a classic public health regulation. "It cannot be denied," Samuel Miller pointed out in his opinion for the Court, "that the statute under consideration is aptly framed to remove from the more densely populated part of the city, the noxious slaughter-houses, and large and offensive collections of animals necessarily incident to the slaughtering business of a large city." In an era before refrigeration, governments had always closely regulated the location of urban slaughterhouses to minimize the smells and diseases produced by live animals and the leftover parts of dead ones. Miller was a former physician from Keokuk, Iowa, where pig-slaughtering was the leading industry, so he had personal experience with the health risks of slaughterhouses.[9]

Viewed another way, however, the law was a blatant act of favoritism that enriched one group of butchers—the corporation whose slaughterhouse was granted a local monopoly—at the expense of all the others. This was how Stephen Field saw it. "The act is a mere grant to a corporation created by it of special and exclusive privileges by which the health of the city is in no way promoted," he complained in his dissent. "It is plain that if the corporation can, without endangering the health of the public, carry on the business of landing, keeping, and slaughtering cattle . . . it would not endanger the public health if other persons were also permitted to carry on the same business within the same district under similar conditions." In a separate dissent, Noah Swayne contended that "a more flagrant and indefensible invasion of the rights of many for the benefit of a few has not occurred in the legislative history of the country."[10] The Louisiana law protected the public health, but it also made some butchers richer and others poorer. Did the Constitution allow the state legislature to enact such a law?

The law's challengers, butchers unaffiliated with the slaughterhouse company that received the monopoly, argued that the law was inconsistent with several provisions of the Constitution, but their principal contention was that it violated the new Fourteenth Amendment, which included a clause prohibiting states from abridging "the privileges or immunities of citizens of the United States." The challengers, represented by the former Justice John Archibald Campbell, insisted that the right to practice their trade was one such privilege. By a 5–4 vote, however, the Court disagreed. The Privileges or Immunities Clause protected only those privileges specifically attributable to United States citizenship, the Court held, not privileges attributable to state citizenship. In an era when most law was produced by states, not by the national government, this was a small category of privileges indeed. It included such rarely exercised privileges as the right to transact business with the federal government and the right to claim the protection of the United States while abroad, but not the right to practice a trade, which did not depend upon the federal government for its existence.[11]

In dissent, Field scolded the majority for construing the new Privileges or Immunities Clause so narrowly as to deprive it of any effect. Properly interpreted, he reasoned, the clause "assumes that there are such privileges and immunities which belong of right to citizens as such, and ordains that they shall not be abridged by State legislation." If the clause protected only "such privileges and immunities as were before its adoption specially designated in the Constitution or necessarily implied as belonging to citizens of the United States, it was a vain and idle enactment, which accomplished nothing."[12] The Fourteenth Amendment had been ratified only five years earlier. Everyone could remember that its primary purpose had been to prevent the reemergence in the South of a two-caste society in which white people enjoyed privileges denied to black people. This purpose could never be achieved if the clause was as toothless as the majority suggested it was. After the *Slaughter-House Cases*, the Privileges or Immunities Clause would be just as useless to the freed slaves as it was to the excluded butchers of New Orleans.

The Court's 5–4 decision in the *Slaughter-House Cases* cut across political lines. Of Lincoln's five appointees, two were in the majority and three in the dissent. Grant's three appointees split two to one. The Court's two Democrats were on opposite sides. The divide between the two camps was more pragmatic than partisan. All commercial regulation restricts someone's ability to practice their trade to some extent. If the right to engage in a business was to be a "privilege" protected by the Fourteenth Amendment, how could a court distinguish between the familiar everyday sort of regulation that satisfied the Constitution and the exceptional regulation that did not? The majority's view threatened to drain the Privileges or Immunities Clause of any meaning, but the dissenters' view threatened to make all commercial regulation unconstitutional.

Because the Privileges or Immunities Clause lacked much utility to litigants after it was interpreted into insignificance in the *Slaughter-House Cases*, litigation was diverted into alternative doctrinal channels. Claims of race discrimination would rely instead on the Fourteenth Amendment's Equal Protection Clause—with no success, as we saw in the last chapter. And challenges to economic regulation would rely on the Fourteenth Amendment's Due Process Clause, which prohibits states from depriving anyone of liberty or property without "due process of law." The Fourteenth Amendment had been intended to protect black people against discrimination, but for nearly a century after it was ratified, the Court used it primarily to protect white-owned business corporations from regulation.[13]

The Court repeatedly upheld regulation against due process challenges through the 1870s and 1880s, but Field's dissenting opinions in each case prefigured the change that would come. In *Munn v. Illinois* (1877), the Court considered an Illinois statute setting the maximum rates that could be charged to store grain in Chicago's grain warehouses. A seven-justice majority rejected the argument that the price cap deprived the warehouse operators of property without due process. As Chief Justice Morrison Waite emphasized in his opinion for the Court, there was a long history of price regulation in the United States and England. When "one devotes his property to a use in which the public has an interest," Waite reasoned, "he, in effect, grants to the public an interest in that use, and must submit to be controlled by the public for the common good." The warehouses in Chicago had an effective monopoly on the transit of grain through the largest grain market in the world. Just as the government could regulate the prices charged by other local monopolists, such as ferries, it could limit the fees charged by the grain warehouses.[14]

Once again, where the majority saw regulation advancing the public good, Stephen Field saw favoritism, because by reducing the prices charged by grain warehouses, the Illinois law transferred wealth from the warehouse owners to their customers, the farmers and grain dealers who had to pay for storage. In his dissent, Field provided the first extended argument by any justice for why this kind of regulation amounted to a deprivation of property without due process. "If the legislature of a State, under pretence of providing for the public good, or for any other reason, can determine, against the consent of the owner, the uses to which private property shall be devoted, or the prices which the owner shall receive for its uses, it can deprive him of the property as completely as by a special act for its confiscation or destruction," Field warned. And the public interest in grain was no greater than the public interest in any other item that was bought and sold. "The public is interested in the manufacture of cotton, woollen, and silken fabrics, in the construction of machinery, in the printing and publication of books and periodicals, and in the making of utensils of every variety, useful and ornamental; indeed, there is hardly an enterprise or business engaging the attention and labor of any considerable portion of the community, in which the public has not an interest in the sense in which that term is used by the court in its opinion." If the government could fix the price of grain storage, it could fix the price of anything.[15]

Field dissented again in *Powell v. Pennsylvania* (1888) from a decision upholding a state law prohibiting the sale of margarine. The rest of the Court was willing to accept the law's stated rationale, which was to protect the public from being deceived by margarine's close resemblance to butter. Once again, Field thought this ostensible justification was a sham, to cover the statute's real aim of favoring dairy farmers over margarine producers. A state certainly had the right to protect the health and safety of its residents, he acknowledged. But when a law "is passed under the pretense of such regulation, as in this case, by a false title, purporting to protect the health, and prevent the adulteration of dairy products," the task of a court, as Field saw it, was to look through the pretense to ascertain the law's true purpose. If the true goal was to benefit one group at the expense of another, the law was inconsistent with due process.[16]

Field was not arguing that the Constitution required the government to keep its hands off the economy. All members of the Court thought that regulation for the public good was constitutional. In *Davidson v. New Orleans* (1877), Miller complained on behalf of a unanimous Court that too many lawyers were making frivolous due process claims on behalf of businesses. "It would seem, from the character of many of the cases before us," he groused, "that the clause under consideration is looked upon as a means of bringing to the test of the decision of this court the abstract opinions of every unsuccessful litigant in a State court of the justice of the decision against him."

In *Davidson* the Court briskly rejected a due process challenge to a tax on real estate for the purpose of draining swamps. A few years later, even Field cautioned lawyers that a statute's mere "lessening the value of the property affected, does not bring it under the objection of depriving a person of property without due process of law." He warned the bar: "This court is not a harbor where refuge can be found from every act of ill-advised and oppressive state legislation."[17]

Field's disagreement with his colleagues was less about the value of regulation in the abstract than it was about judicial technique: How deferential should a court be in accepting a legislature's stated reason for enacting a law? Through the 1870s and 1880s, the other justices were more willing than he was to defer to a law's ostensible public-regarding justification even if there was reason to suspect that the law's true purpose was to benefit one group at another's expense. As John Harlan said on behalf of all the justices but Field in *Powell*, "every possible presumption . . . is in favor of the validity of a statute, and this continues until the contrary is shown beyond a rational doubt."[18] But deference had its limits. The justices all agreed that a law would be unconstitutional if lacked *any* claim to advance the public good—if its *only* rationale was to transfer wealth from one person to another. And Field's skepticism had limits as well. He agreed that a law would be constitutional, even if it destroyed the value of someone's property, if the law could genuinely be said to be for the public benefit. The dispute was over how much independent judgment a court should exercise in ascertaining a law's true objective.

In *Mugler v. Kansas* (1887), for example, Field joined his colleagues in upholding Kansas's ban on alcoholic beverages, a law that was part of the wave of state-by-state prohibition that preceded national prohibition. In an opinion by Harlan, the Court unanimously explained that while a state could legislate to protect the public health and safety, "it does not at all follow that every statute enacted ostensibly for the promotion of these ends is to be accepted as a legitimate exertion of the police powers of the state." A court could not defer completely to the stated justification of a law. "The courts are not bound by mere forms, nor are they to be misled by mere pretenses," Harlan cautioned. "They are at liberty, indeed, are under a solemn duty, to look at the substance of things, whenever they enter upon the inquiry whether the legislature has transcended the limits of its authority. If, therefore, a statute purporting to have been enacted to protect the public health, the public morals, or the public safety, has no real or substantial relation to those objects . . . it is the duty of the courts to so adjudge." The Court, including Field, had little trouble concluding that the prohibition of alcohol was genuinely intended to protect the public health, so the Court unanimously found the law constitutional, even though the state's alcohol producers lost their livelihoods.[19]

Field's view on this question of deference finally prevailed in the late 1890s, just when Field himself retired. Nine new justices joined the Court between 1888 and 1898. Most of the new arrivals had significant experience representing large corporations. All were conservative men nominated by business-friendly presidents—Grover Cleveland, Benjamin Harrison, and William McKinley. None had much sympathy for legislation intended to curb the power of business enterprises.

The first sign of change was *Allgeyer v. Louisiana* (1897), a short opinion in which the Court unanimously struck down a state law prohibiting the purchase of marine insurance from out-of-state insurance companies. The case was an easy one for all the justices, no matter how much or how little deference one paid to a statute's stated rationale, because this statute was a transparently protectionist measure intended for the benefit of in-state insurance companies and lacking any plausible benefit for anyone else. The long-term significance of *Allgeyer* lay in the broad definition of "liberty" adopted for the Court by Rufus Peckham, the newest justice. Peckham explained that the "liberty" protected by the Due Process Clause "means, not only the right of the citizen to be free from the mere physical restraint of his person," but something far more capacious. It included a person's right "to live and work where he will; to earn his livelihood by any lawful calling; to pursue any livelihood or avocation; and for that purpose to enter into all contracts." This broad definition of liberty had first appeared in an influential treatise by the Michigan judge Thomas Cooley and had already been adopted by some state courts, including Peckham's own former court, the New York Court of Appeals.[20] In *Allgeyer*, the Court concluded that the state insurance law was a deprivation of liberty in this sense, because it denied Louisiana residents the ability to enter into otherwise lawful contracts.

By the turn of the century, the Court had established: first, that any curtailment of a person's ability to work and enter into contracts constituted a deprivation of liberty; second, that class legislation was contrary to due process; and third, that courts should make their own independent determinations of whether statutes truly served a public end or merely amounted to class legislation in disguise. For the next forty years, many of the Court's cases involved claims that a statute enacted ostensibly for the public benefit was really a form of class legislation. In case after case, the justices tried to peer behind the stated rationale for a statute to figure out what was really going on.

II

We can get a good sense of what these cases were like by comparing three famous ones decided within the span of a decade: *Holden v Hardy* (1898), *Lochner v. New York* (1905), and *Muller v. Oregon* (1908).

Holden v. Hardy was a challenge to a Utah statute that limited the workday of miners to eight hours. Seven of the justices upheld the statute as a legitimate effort to mitigate the unhealthy effects of working underground for long periods. "While the general experience of mankind may justify us in believing that men may engage in ordinary employments more than eight hours per day without injury to their health," Henry Billings Brown observed, "it does not follow that labor for the same length of time is innocuous when carried on beneath the surface of the earth, where the operative is deprived of fresh air and sunlight, and is frequently subjected to foul atmosphere and a very high temperature." The majority was willing to credit the judgment of the state legislature that eight hours was a reasonable line to draw. The Court noted that the result might not be the same for other kinds of employees who worked at less perilous jobs. "The question in each case," Brown explained, "is whether the legislature has adopted the statute in exercise of a reasonable discretion, or whether its action be a mere excuse for an unjust discrimination, or the oppression or spoliation of a particular class." Brewer and Peckham dissented without writing an opinion. They most likely believed that the statute was unnecessary as a health measure and was enacted instead to benefit miners at the expense of their employers.[21]

Lochner v. New York also involved a state law setting the maximum hours in a workday, but this time it was bakery employees rather than miners, and that made all the difference. By a 5–4 vote, the Court decided that this was class legislation, not a genuine effort to protect workers' health, because bakers needed no special care. "There is, in our judgment, no reasonable foundation for holding this to be necessary or appropriate as a health law to safeguard the public health, or the health of the individuals who are following the trade of a baker," Peckham declared for the majority. "The trade of a baker, in and of itself, is not an unhealthy one." All work might be unhealthy to some extent if carried on for too long, Peckham acknowledged, but that would not justify legislative interference with the liberty of contract, or else "a printer, a tinsmith, a locksmith, a carpenter, a cabinetmaker, a dry goods clerk, a bank's, a lawyer's, or a physician's clerk, or a clerk in almost any kind of business, would all come under the power of the legislature."[22]

If the law was not needed to protect the health of bakers, why was it enacted? Peckham never answered this question explicitly, but he included several dark hints. The law "gives rise to at least a suspicion that there was some other motive dominating the legislature than the purpose to subserve the public health or welfare," Peckham suggested. He added, ominously, that "it is impossible for us to shut our eyes to the fact that many of the laws of this character, while passed under what is claimed to be the police power for the purpose of protecting the public health or welfare, are, in reality, passed from other motives." He described the legislature's claimed interest in the health of bakers as "a pretext" for the law's true purpose.[23] Peckham's meaning was clear despite the vagueness of his words. The law's real motive, he was implying, was to benefit bakery employees at the expense of bakery owners. This was class legislation masquerading as a health measure. The employees wanted a shorter working day but they could not obtain one by negotiating with their bosses, so they persuaded the legislature to force the shorter working day on the bakery owners.

John Harlan dissented, joined by Edward White and William Day. In their view, the work of a baker really was unhealthful if pursued for too many hours in a day. They quoted from studies of bakeries that emphasized the dangers of inhaling flour, working near hot ovens, and losing sleep (because bakers often worked at night). They agreed with the majority that courts should closely scrutinize the claimed rationale for a statute, and they agreed that a supposed health measure would be contrary to due process if it was actually redistribution in disguise, but they thought New York's law was a genuine health measure.[24]

A dissenting opinion normally discusses the errors of the majority opinion, but Harlan's dissent in *Lochner* does not refer at all to Peckham's majority. When the Court's reporter of decisions, Charles Henry Butler, received Harlan's manuscript, he thought it read more like a majority opinion, which made him suspect that the justices had originally voted to uphold the New York law, that Harlan's opinion had originally been the majority, and that one of the justices had changed his vote. A few years later, after Harlan's death, Harlan's son told Butler that this was indeed the case. Butler never learned which justice changed his mind.[25] If Harlan's opinion had remained the majority, *Lochner* would not have become the iconic case it is today. It would have been one of the many cases, like *Holden v. Hardy*, in which the Court upheld regulation on the ground that it genuinely served the public interest. The period known today as the *Lochner* era might instead have been called the *Adair* era or the *Coppage* era, after other cases (to be discussed below) in which the Court struck down regulation for serving the interest of a class rather than the public as a whole.

Oliver Wendell Holmes dissented as well, in what would become one of his best-known but most often misunderstood opinions. Holmes argued in favor of granting more deference to the stated purposes of a statute than any of his colleagues thought appropriate. "This case is decided upon an economic theory which a large part of the country does not entertain," Holmes charged. "Laws may regulate life in many ways which we as legislators might think as injudicious, or if you like as tyrannical, as this, and which, equally with this, interfere with the liberty to contract. Sunday laws and usury laws are ancient examples. A more modern one is the prohibition of lotteries." All governments had laws that prohibited some kinds of contracts. "Some of these laws embody convictions or prejudices which judges are likely to share," Holmes continued. "Some may not. But a Constitution is not intended to embody a particular economic theory, whether of paternalism and the organic relation of the citizen to the state or of *laissez faire*. It is made for people of fundamentally differing views, and the accident of our finding certain opinions natural and familiar, or novel, and even shocking, ought not to conclude our judgment upon the question whether statutes embodying them conflict with the Constitution." If the voters of a state, speaking through their legislature, thought it a good idea to limit the hours of bakers, judges had no business second-guessing that decision. "I think that the word 'liberty,' in the 14th Amendment, is perverted when it is held to prevent the natural outcome of a dominant opinion," Holmes concluded, "unless it can be said that a rational and fair man necessarily would admit that the statute proposed would infringe fundamental principles as they have been understood by the traditions of our people and our law. It does not need research to show that no such sweeping condemnation can be passed upon the statute before us."[26]

Holmes had a knack for aphorisms. His dissent in *Lochner* includes a famous one: "The 14th Amendment does not enact Mr. Herbert Spencer's Social Statics." Although this line is still often quoted today, its meaning has been obscured by the passage of time. Herbert Spencer was a prolific English writer in the second half of the nineteenth century, whose work encompassed a wide variety of fields, including philosophy, biology, and sociology. He was one of the most famous intellectuals of the era. *Social Statics*, published in England in 1851 and in the United States in 1865, was his first book. Today Spencer tends to be pigeonholed as a social Darwinist—he coined the phrase "survival of the fittest" to argue that death and disease were beneficial in the long run—so Holmes's reference to Spencer is often interpreted as accusing the *Lochner* majority of social Darwinism. But most of *Social Statics* is about liberty, not evolution. Spencer argued against government regulation in terms that sound very much like the doctrine of liberty of contract that the Court would adopt a few decades later. "To secure for each man the fullest freedom to exercise his faculties, compatible with the like freedom of all others, we find to be the state's duty," he declared. "Now trade prohibitions and trade restrictions not only do not secure this freedom, but they take it away. So that in enforcing them the state is transformed from a maintainer of rights into a violator of rights."[27] These were words that could have been written by Rufus Peckham. In writing that "the 14th Amendment does not enact Mr. Herbert Spencer's Social Statics," Holmes was not accusing his colleagues of social Darwinism. Rather, he was accusing them of reading libertarian views like Spencer's into the Due Process Clause.

Holmes's deference to the legislature would eventually become orthodoxy, but not until after his death. For many years he would be the only justice to disagree with the prevailing conception of the Court's role in evaluating regulation. His dissent in *Lochner* is still quoted frequently because it so accurately prefigures the change in constitutional thought that would take place in the mid-twentieth century. But one aspect of his dissent has caused lawyers and historians to misunderstand the views that he was criticizing. Holmes accused his colleagues of interpreting the Constitution to embody "laissez-faire" principles. Many later readers have taken him at his word, but this accusation was not quite right. The other members of the Court did not think the Constitution prohibited *all* government intervention in the economy, as cases like *Holden v. Hardy* demonstrated. Rather, they understood the Constitution to prohibit legislatures from playing favorites, by enacting legislation for the purpose of helping one group at the expense of another.

Indeed, just three years after invalidating a maximum-hours statute in *Lochner*, the Court unanimously upheld another maximum-hours statute in *Muller v. Oregon*. The difference was that in *Muller* the statute applied only to women. The justices all agreed that women genuinely did need the state's protection against overwork. They may have been influenced by the brief filed by the future justice Louis Brandeis, who was then a well-known progressive lawyer. His brief was filled with data ostensibly demonstrating that women's health and that of their children would suffer if women had to work as long as men did. But they may not have needed Brandeis's statistics to persuade them, because this view was so congruent with the gender stereotypes of the era. "That woman's physical structure and the performance of maternal functions place her at a disadvantage in the struggle for subsistence is obvious," David Brewer explained in his opinion for the Court. "This is especially true when the burdens of motherhood are upon her. Even when they are not, by abundant testimony of the medical fraternity continuance for a long time on her feet at work, repeating this from day to day, tends to injurious effects upon the body, and, as healthy mothers are essential to vigorous offspring, the physical well-being of woman becomes an object of public interest and care in order to preserve the strength and vigor of the race." Maximum hours legislation was not needed to protect the health of a male worker, Brewer reasoned, but a female worker "is properly placed in a class by herself, and legislation designed for her protection may be sustained, even when like legislation is not necessary for men, and could not be sustained." A state law setting the maximum hours of work for men was redistribution masquerading as health protection, but the same law for women was truly health protection.[28]

In cases like these, the division among the justices again had no correlation with political party. In *Holden*, the two dissenters, Brewer and Peckham, were of different parties. In *Lochner*, the Court's two Democrats, White and Peckham, were on opposite sides. *Muller* was unanimous. Before the Civil War, political party had been a reliable predictor of justices' votes in the most politically salient cases, and it would be again in later periods, but not during the *Lochner* era.

The Court decided many similar cases over the next thirty years. In most, the Court upheld the constitutionality of regulation even where it had large detrimental effects on the regulated parties, because the justices found that the claimed public benefit of the regulation was genuine. For instance, in *Hadacheck v. Sebastian* (1915), the Court unanimously upheld a Los Angeles ordinance prohibiting the operation of brickyards within the city. The ordinance ruined J. C. Hadacheck's brick business and caused the value of his land to plummet from $800,000 to $60,000. But "the fumes, gases, smoke, soot, steam, and dust arising from petitioner's brickmaking plant have from time to time caused sickness and serious discomfort to those living in the vicinity," the Court noted. The city had the authority to protect the public health, regardless of the losses suffered by any individual. In *Block v. Hirsch* (1921), the Court upheld rent control in Washington, DC. The rent control law profoundly affected the property rights of landlords, but the Court found it justified by a temporary wartime housing shortage in the city. In *Village of Euclid v. Ambler Realty Co.* (1926), a case with enormous long-term implications that could scarcely have been perceived at the time, the Court upheld the then-new practice of zoning. The zoning ordinance at issue, from a suburb of Cleveland, prevented a landowner from using his land for commercial purposes. The land was worth only a quarter of its former value. But the Court determined that zoning was for the public good. The Court found that zoning "will increase the safety and security of home life, greatly tend to prevent street accidents, especially to children, by reducing the traffic and resulting confusion in residential sections, decrease noise and other conditions which produce or intensify nervous disorders, [and] preserve a more favorable environment in which to rear children." That was enough for zoning to satisfy the Constitution despite its obvious effects on property rights and the liberty to enter into contracts.[29]

The Court likewise upheld a considerable amount of regulation that was alleged to infringe liberty in a more personal sense. Just two months before *Lochner*, for example, the Court sounded positively collectivist in rejecting the claim of anti-vaccine activists that the Constitution barred the states from enacting compulsory vaccination laws. "There are manifold restraints to which every person is necessarily subject for the common good. On any other basis organized society could not exist with safety to its members," the Court declared in *Jacobson v. Massachusetts* (1905).[30] The *Lochner* Court was far more receptive to government intervention than its later reputation would suggest.

Even at the peak of the *Lochner* era, the Court upheld much more regulation than it struck down.[31] Counting cases can be a poor measure of the Court's influence, however, because it takes no account of (a) statutes that were never enacted for fear that they would be held unconstitutional, (b) statutes that *were* enacted but were held unconstitutional by lower courts relying on Supreme Court precedent, or (c) long-shot constitutional challenges the Court rejected that were brought by parties emboldened by the Court's decisions. In addition, the cases in which the Court found regulation inconsistent with due process were some of the best-known decisions of the period, because they involved statutes that were the product of high-profile political battles in state legislatures and in Congress. These cases had a cultural impact on the legal profession disproportionate to their number.

One early example was *Smyth v. Ames* (1898), in which the Court unanimously invalidated a Nebraska statute capping the fares railroads could charge for passengers and freight. States could limit prices, John Harlan reasoned in his opinion for the Court, but only up to a point. "If the company is deprived of the power of charging reasonable rates for the use of its property," he explained, "it is deprived of the lawful use of its property, and thus, in substance and effect, of the property itself, without due process of law." The courts, then, had to review each prescribed rate to determine whether it was reasonable. But how was a judge to know whether a rate was unreasonably low? "Undoubtedly, that question could be more easily determined by a commission composed of persons whose special skill, observation, and experience qualifies them to so handle great problems of transportation," Harlan conceded. One needed to know quite a bit about the relevant industry to understand whether a particular price would yield a reasonable return on the stockholders' investment. "But, despite the difficulties that confessedly attend the proper solution of such questions," Harlan continued, "the court cannot shrink from the duty to determine whether it be true, as alleged, that the Nebraska statute invades or destroys rights secured by the supreme law of the land."[32]

In the Midwest, railroads and farmers were recurring foes. The railroads were large corporations mostly owned by eastern shareholders. Farmers, who needed the railroads to reach their markets, were often at the mercy of the nearest railroad. *Smyth v. Ames* evoked "strong feeling on both sides," one contemporary account reported. "Many public men and journals in the West are denouncing Justice Harlan's decision, while the financial journals of New York and the conservative press in general are upholding its doctrines." *Smyth v. Ames* was even worse than *Dred Scott*, declared one critic of "our corporation-controlled courts."[33]

The task of determining whether a rate was reasonable required the Court to examine page after page of detailed financial information about the company in question. Some of this information is reproduced in the opinion in *Smyth v. Ames*, which includes, for several railroads, tables of statistics concerning such matters as their annual revenue per ton of freight hauled and their ratio of revenue to expenses. To assess whether a railroad would receive an adequate return, Harlan observed, a court needed to consider "the original cost of construction, the amount expended in permanent improvements, the amount and market value of its bonds and stock, the present as compared with the original cost of construction, the probable earning capacity of the property under particular rates prescribed by statute, and the sum required to meet operating expenses," along with any other matters that might be relevant.[34] This was a task better suited to accountants than judges, but it was one the justices found themselves performing in many more cases over the next few decades.

The Court also persisted in striking down statutes that the justices perceived as favoring employees over employers. In *Adair v. United States* (1908), the Court invalidated a federal statute that required railroad companies to allow their employees to unionize. The law was biased, Harlan complained in his majority opinion, because while it criminalized discrimination against an employee "because of his being a member of a labor organization, it does not make it a crime to unjustly discriminate against an employee of the carrier because of his *not* being a member of such an organization." Holmes dissented, in a short opinion reminiscent of his *Lochner* dissent a few years before. The law "simply prohibits the more powerful party to exact certain undertakings, or to threaten dismissal or unjustly discriminate on certain grounds against those already employed," he observed. While his colleagues saw unconstitutional favoritism, Holmes was willing to defer to the evident view of Congress that labor unions were in the public interest. "The question what and how much good labor unions do, is one on which intelligent people may differ," he explained. "I could not pronounce it unwarranted if Congress should decide that to foster a strong union was for the best interest, not only of the men, but of the railroads and the country at large."[35]

A few years later, in *Coppage v. Kansas* (1915), the Court struck down a similar state statute for the same reason. Justice Mahlon Pitney's opinion for the Court emphatically rejected the notion that it was a proper function of government to redistribute wealth or power from one sector of society to another. "No doubt, wherever the right of private property exists, there must and will be inequalities of fortune," Pitney acknowledged, "and thus it naturally happens that parties negotiating about a contract are not equally unhampered by circumstances. This applies to all contracts, and not merely to that between employer and employee." There was simply nothing the government could do about it without violating the Constitution. "It is from the nature of things impossible to uphold freedom of contract and the right of private property without at the same time recognizing as legitimate those inequalities of fortune," Pitney continued. Thus a law placing the government's thumb on one side of the scale, by requiring employers to let their employees form unions, impermissibly transferred bargaining power from one side to the other. Since the state could not reduce inequality directly, through a transfer of property from the rich to the poor, "it is clear that it may not do so indirectly, as by declaring in effect that the public good requires the removal of those inequalities that are but the normal and inevitable result" of economic life. Pitney concluded with a ringing statement of the principle underlying this whole line of cases—that redistribution was lawful as the byproduct of some other goal but it was not a lawful goal in itself. "The 14th Amendment debars the states from striking down personal liberty or property rights, or materially restricting their normal exercise, excepting so far as may be incidentally necessary for the accomplishment of some other and paramount object, and one that concerns the public welfare," he declared. "The mere restriction of liberty or of property rights cannot of itself be denominated 'public welfare.'" Holmes dissented yet again. "Whether in the long run it is wise for the workingmen to enact legislation of this sort is not my concern," he noted, "but I am strongly of opinion that there is nothing in the Constitution of the United States to prevent it."[36]

The Court's suspicion of redistributive legislation reached its apex in *Adkins v. Children's Hospital* (1923), in which the Court, by a 5–3 vote, invalidated the District of Columbia's minimum wage for women.[37] Fifteen years earlier, in *Muller v. Oregon*, the Court had upheld a maximum-hours law for women on the ground that women needed more protection than men from the rigors of the workplace. But the Court saw two distinctions between the old case and the new one.

First, the Court found that the differences between men and women had diminished so much that special treatment for women was no longer necessary. "These differences have now come almost, if not quite, to the vanishing point," George Sutherland asserted in his majority opinion. The Nineteenth Amendment, which gave women the right to vote, had been ratified just three years before. Sutherland was a former senator known for supporting women's equality, and indeed he had introduced the Nineteenth Amendment in the Senate. "We cannot accept the doctrine," Sutherland continued, "that women of mature age . . . require or may be subjected to restrictions upon their liberty of contract which could not lawfully be imposed in the case of men under similar circumstances."[38]

Second, the Court held that while maximum-hours legislation might be justified as protecting the health of workers, the same could not be said of minimum-wage legislation, which was pure redistribution from employers to employees. "It is simply and exclusively a price-fixing law," Sutherland charged.[39] A minimum wage was a naked transfer of money from one person to another, which under the prevailing definition of due process was beyond the authority of the government.

This distinction between a maximum-hours law and a minimum-wage law was too fine a line for Holmes, Edward Sanford, and William Howard Taft. Hours and wages were the two components of a laborer's earnings, they pointed out; if the government could regulate one, why couldn't it regulate the other? "If it be said that long hours of labor have a more direct effect upon the health of the employee than the low wage," Taft observed, "there is very respectable authority from close observers, disclosed in the record and in the literature on the subject quoted at length in the briefs that they are equally harmful in this regard. Congress took this view and we cannot say it was not warranted in so doing." Holmes was just as puzzled. "I perceive no difference in the kind or degree of interference with liberty, the only matter with which we have any concern, between the one case and the other," he noted. "The bargain is equally affected whichever half you regulate."[40]

It was cases like these, in which the Court blocked legislation intended to improve the lives of workers, that provoked the most controversy. From the right, the Court was praised for upholding the principle that the government should remain neutral between competing interest groups, siding neither with one nor the other but legislating only for the common good. "The decision gives us personally intense satisfaction," one law journal remarked of *Lochner*. "The individual is superior to the legislature in every respect except as to those limitations which reasonably tend to conserve the health, safety and morals of the whole community." From the left, the Court was condemned for being biased against labor and for lacking an appreciation of the social ills that motivated labor legislation. The law has "not kept pace with the rapid development of our political, economic and social ideals," Louis Brandeis charged in a 1916 speech, shortly before he would join the Court himself.[41] The Court was either a hero or a villain, depending on one's views of redistributive legislation and the proper role of the courts.

III

This debate over redistribution was only half of the story. During this same period, the federal government began regulating matters that had previously been left to the states. These new federal statutes gave rise to "entirely novel" constitutional questions, remarked Attorney General Charles Bonaparte, questions that involved "the extension of principles whose limits are yet to be wholly defined."[42] Each expansion of the federal government's grasp was met with arguments that the federal government had crossed the line separating federal from state power. Here too, the Court decided several well-known cases in which it concluded that the Constitution protected business from regulation. And here too, the justices were motivated by a combination of policy preferences and legal tradition.

Some of the justices were apprehensive about the centralization of governmental power, a development they considered dangerous. "Was there ever seen such a mad scramble on the part of every one, believing in the existence of some wrong, for Congressional legislation in redress?" David Brewer asked in one of his many speeches. He worried about the consequences "if this tendency towards centralization is not stayed." Stephen Field's correspondence is littered with despair over the federal government's accumulation of power relative to the states. Senator Thomas Bayard complained to Field about the "complete centralization" he saw taking place. The lawyer Joseph Choate expressed his hope that if President Cleveland had the opportunity to appoint a new justice, he would choose someone like Field, "who will resist the extreme spirit of centralization and irresponsibility."[43] Regulation was worrisome enough, but *federal* regulation was doubly so.

This concern was reinforced by the Court's traditional role of policing the boundary between state and federal authority. Like all American lawyers of the period, the justices believed that the Constitution imposed serious limits on the activities the federal government could undertake. Until the late nineteenth century, these limits were only rarely tested. But when Congress began testing them more frequently, the Court's own past decisions provided ample material with which to hold federal statutes unconstitutional.

There were several reasons for the expansion of the federal government's regulatory efforts, including improved technologies of transportation and communications, as well as the rapid increase in the size of business enterprises, which now operated on a national scale. But one cause was the Court itself. As business increasingly transcended state boundaries, the effects of state regulation were often felt in other states. The Court confronted a series of cases in which interstate businesses challenged state regulation as beyond the state's authority.

The most important of these cases was *Wabash Railway v. Illinois* (1886), in which the Court held that states could not regulate the fares charged by railroads on interstate routes, because that would interfere with the power of Congress to regulate interstate commerce. The Constitution's Commerce Clause "would be a very feeble and almost useless provision," Samuel Miller worried, "if, at every stage of the transportation of goods and chattels through the country, the state within whose limits a part of this transportation must be done could impose regulations concerning the price, compensation, or taxation, or any other restrictive regulation."[44] The railroads were the largest and most commercially important businesses in the country, and in *Wabash Railway* the Court exempted them from a wide swath of state law. Congress quickly filled the gap by establishing the Interstate Commerce Commission, the first significant federal regulatory agency, which took over from the states much of the task of regulating the railroads.

There was no doubt about the federal government's power over interstate railroads. As the federal government continued to expand into new regulatory domains, however, the new statutes drew repeated constitutional challenges. The Sherman Antitrust Act of 1890, for example, established a new federal prohibition on certain monopolistic business practices. How much power did the federal government have to ban monopolies? In 1894, Congress enacted a new federal income tax. Did it have the authority to do so? Questions like these began arriving at the Court regularly.

The Court would decide many cases involving the Sherman Act. The first important one was *United States v. E. C. Knight Co.* (1895), in which the federal government sued to prevent the impending consolidation of the country's major sugar producers into a single firm that would control 98% of the manufacture of sugar. The Court held that the federal government lacked the power to interfere, because its authority extended only to interstate *commerce*, and manufacturing was something different from commerce. "Commerce succeeds to manufacture, and is not a part of it," Chief Justice Melville Fuller reasoned in his majority opinion. To manufacture something was to make it; to engage in commerce was to sell it after manufacture was complete. "The fact that an article is manufactured for export to another state does not of itself make it an article of interstate commerce," Fuller explained. "The functions of commerce are different. The buying and selling, and the transportation incidental thereto, constitute commerce." Perhaps more important than linguistic precision was the dire result he foresaw if the federal government could regulate the manufacture of all the countless items that were destined to be sold in interstate commerce. The government would gain authority not just over sugar, "but also agriculture, horticulture, stock-raising, domestic fisheries, mining; in short, every branch of human industry. For is there one of them that does not contemplate, more or less clearly, an interstate or foreign market?"[45] To preserve the traditional line between federal and state authority, the federal government's power to regulate monopolies could not extend to manufacturing.

The Court's narrow definition of commerce in *E. C. Knight* led to many more antitrust cases raising similar questions, because the line separating commerce from other pursuits could be a fine one. Did the government have the authority to break up a monopoly of meatpackers? Yes, the Court held in *Swift & Co. v. United States* (1905). Meatpacking was commerce, because meatpackers did not *manufacture* meat; they *sold* it. What about the Standard Oil Company and the American Tobacco Company, which had monopolies in oil refining and tobacco production—were they engaged in commerce or merely in manufacturing? In *Standard Oil Co. of New Jersey v. United States* (1911) and *United States v. American Tobacco Co.* (1911), the Court classified both firms as engaged in commerce. Both would be broken up into smaller companies after they were determined to have violated the Sherman Act. In the years after *E. C. Knight*, the Court's definition of commerce seemed to be gradually expanding, at least for antitrust purposes, because the nation's largest enterprises engaged in both manufacturing and selling, and it proved difficult to keep the two functions apart. But the definition of commerce could expand only so far during this period. Were the major league clubs that monopolized professional baseball engaged in commerce? In *Federal Baseball Club of Baltimore v. National League of Professional Base Ball Clubs* (1922), the Court concluded that they were not. The business of baseball consists of displays of effort and skill, Oliver Wendell Holmes reasoned, but "personal effort, not related to production, is not a subject of commerce." The games were not commerce, so they did not become interstate commerce when the players crossed state lines. No one outside the baseball business considered *Federal Baseball Club* an important decision at the time, but it would have a more enduring effect than most of the others. To this day, baseball is the only professional sport that is not governed by federal antitrust law.[46]

Large corporate combinations were more controversial during this era than they would be in later periods, so the Court's antitrust cases were among its most important to nonlawyers. For example, in *Northern Securities Co. v. United States* (1904), a 5–4 majority allowed the government to break up a corporation that controlled multiple railroads. Holmes, who wrote the dissenting opinion, thought the majority had been unduly influenced by the public's "immediate overwhelming interest" in the case. All the public attention, he worried, exerted "a kind of hydraulic pressure which makes what previously was clear seem doubtful, and before which even well settled principles of law will bend." As Holmes famously put it, "great cases, like hard cases, make bad law." President Theodore Roosevelt was also paying close attention. Roosevelt had put Holmes on the Court just two years before. He was so angry with Holmes's dissent that he is said to have exclaimed: "I could carve out of a banana a judge with more backbone than that!"[47]

It was big news when the Court limited the federal government's power to break up monopolies, but it was even bigger news when, in *Pollock v. Farmers' Loan & Trust Co.* (1895), the Court struck down the federal income tax. The income tax had been established the previous year. It was not the first federal income tax in American history—the Civil War had been financed in part by an income tax that ended in 1872—but it was the first that was not an emergency wartime measure. It was a tiny tax by today's standards. Taxpayers paid a flat rate of 2% of their income. The first $4,000 of income—worth well over $100,000 today—was exempt from tax, so only the wealthiest had to pay. The federal government was still funded primarily by tariffs, and the income tax was meant as a moderately progressive measure that would allow tariffs to be reduced slightly without causing any loss in federal revenue. But the fact that the tax fell only on the wealthy was what made it so pernicious to its opponents. To them, this was class legislation with a vengeance.[48]

The new tax was quickly attacked on several constitutional grounds, but the one that reached the Supreme Court involved the clause of the Constitution that requires all "direct" taxes to be "apportioned among the several States" according to their population. That is, if state A has twice the population of state B, the revenue collected from the tax in state A must be twice the revenue collected in state B. This requirement was a by-product of slavery. At the Constitutional Convention, the northern and southern states disagreed over whether slaves should count as part of a state's population in determining the state's representation in Congress. The southern states wanted to include slaves, although they could not vote, because including them would give the southern states more representatives. The northern states wanted to exclude slaves for the opposite reason. The Convention would eventually compromise by counting each slave as three-fifths of a person. But this compromise was initially rejected by most of the northern states because it promised to encourage the expansion of slavery in the South. The requirement that direct taxes, like representatives, be apportioned by population was added to the Constitution as an incentive in the opposite direction. If slavery expanded, the southern states would gain more representatives, but they would also be liable for a heavier tax burden.[49]

The income tax did not satisfy this apportionment requirement, because the wealthy people who had to pay the tax lived disproportionately in cities like New York and Boston. The only kind of income tax that *could* satisfy the requirement would be regressive, because residents of the poorer states would have to pay a higher percentage of their incomes in tax than residents of the richer states. But the apportionment requirement applies only to "direct" taxes, not to all taxes. *Pollock* thus turned on a definitional question: Was an income tax a direct tax?

In an earlier case challenging the Civil War income tax, the Court had unanimously decided that the only direct taxes were capitation taxes and taxes on real estate. (A capitation tax, also called a head tax, requires each person to pay the same amount.) All other taxes were indirect taxes. In *Pollock*, however, the Court held that a tax on the rent or income from real estate is equivalent to a tax on the real estate itself, so it is also a direct tax. When *Pollock* was first argued, the justices split 4–4 as to whether taxes on other kinds of income are also direct taxes. (Howell Jackson missed the argument because he was ill with tuberculosis.) The case was reargued when Jackson could attend, and this time the Court invalidated the entire income tax. By a vote of 5 to 4, in an opinion by Melville Fuller, the Court determined that if a tax on the income from real estate was a direct tax, the same had to be true of a tax on the income from other kinds of property, including stock dividends and the payment of interest on bonds. "The constitution does not say that no direct tax shall be laid by apportionment on any other property than land," Fuller reasoned. "On the contrary, it forbids all unapportioned direct taxes; and we know of no warrant for excepting personal property from the exercise of the power." That was enough for the Court to strike down the entire income tax, even the parts that taxed income from other sources (such as wages), on the ground that the constitutional parts of the tax could not be severed from the unconstitutional parts.[50]

Figure 8.2 A dog labeled "income tax," with a can reading "decision Supreme Court" tied to its tail, runs out of the Court as a brick labeled "abuse" is thrown at it. The cartoon represents the Court's invalidation of the federal income tax in *Pollock v. Farmers' Loan & Trust Co.* At the rear is Benton McMillin, the Tennessee congressman who sponsored the income tax legislation. This cartoon was drawn by George Yost Coffin and was published in the *Washington Post* on May 21, 1895. Library of Congress, LC-DIG-acd-2a07285.

One curiosity about *Pollock* is that Jackson, whom everyone expected to break the 4–4 tie, was one of the four dissenters from the Court's second opinion. One of the other justices must have changed his mind between the first opinion and the second. Who? This question attracted much speculation at the time, and the debate still goes on. It could not have been Edward White or John Harlan, who wrote dissents on both occasions. Nor could it have been Henry Billings Brown, who wrote a dissent from the Court's second opinion, or Fuller, who wrote both majority opinions. It could not have been Stephen Field, who wanted to go even farther than the majority and hold that any kind of tax was unconstitutionally redistributive unless everyone paid at the same rate. It is unlikely to have been David Brewer, who was such a consistent vote against regulation of all kinds that it is hard to imagine him finding the tax constitutional after the first argument. That leaves George Shiras and Horace Gray. We will probably never know.[51]

The income tax was so important to so many people that when the case was argued for a second time, the Court departed from its ordinary practice and allowed extra spectators to stand in the space between the lawyers who were arguing and the front row of seats. As one journalist explained, "this rare indulgence was granted only because of the popular interest in the litigation, which probably exceeds that felt in any case before the same court since the last legal-tender decision was rendered." The Court's decision provoked a storm of both praise and criticism, depending, of course, on what one thought about the tax. The conservative law professor Christopher Tiedeman had "no doubt whatever" that an income tax was a direct tax. He thought Fuller's majority opinion was "unanswerable from that standpoint." On the other side of the debate, one lawyer complained that *Pollock* was "contrary to what has been accepted as law for nearly one hundred years." Another called it a "wound" the Court "has inflicted upon the rights of the American people" severe enough to "out-balance all the good it has done in twenty years." Sylvester Pennoyer, the former governor of Oregon, was so upset that he argued that judicial review should be abolished.[52]

At the Democratic convention the following year, the party's presidential candidate, William Jennings Bryan, included a critique of *Pollock* as part of his famous "cross of gold" speech. "The income tax was not unconstitutional when it was passed," Bryan declared. "It did not become unconstitutional until one judge changed his mind; and we cannot be expected to know when a judge will change his mind." The Democratic platform condemned *Pollock* and urged the appointment of justices who would overrule it, "to the end that wealth may bear its due proportion of the expenses of government." *Pollock* would indeed be overruled, but not until 1913, and not by the Court, but by the ratification of the Sixteenth Amendment to the Constitution, which authorizes Congress to tax incomes without regard to apportionment among the states.[53]

A similar controversy erupted when the Court held in *Hammer v. Dagenhart* (1918) that the federal government lacked the power to prohibit child labor. Child labor had been abolished in most states by the early twentieth century. It persisted primarily in the textile factories of the South. The federal Child Labor Act of 1916 received overwhelming support in both houses of Congress. The abolition of child labor was a genuinely popular measure. The Child Labor Act was carefully drafted so that it did not ban child labor itself—this was a subject that few lawyers of the era would have considered within the authority of the federal government—but merely the sale in interstate commerce of goods produced in factories that used child labor. This was already a tried-and-true tactic for satisfying the Supreme Court that a statute lay within Congress's power. The Court had recently approved of several similarly crafted statutes, including the Lottery Act of 1895 (which banned interstate commerce in lottery tickets), the Pure Food and Drug Act of 1906 (which banned interstate commerce in adulterated food and drugs), and the Mann Act of 1910 (which banned the interstate transportation of women for the purpose of prostitution). To its proponents, the Child Labor Act seemed like just one more statute along the same lines. William Draper Lewis, the dean of the University of Pennsylvania law school, declared that the Child Labor Act's constitutionality "can hardly be seriously questioned."[54]

But the Court did question it. To the dismay of Lewis and likeminded progressives, the justices voted 5–4 that the Child Labor Act exceeded the power of Congress. In previous cases, William Day explained in the

Figure 8.3 Children at work in a Georgia textile mill in 1909. Congress tried twice to prohibit child labor, but the Court held both statutes unconstitutional. Photograph by Lewis Wickes Hine. Library of Congress, LC-DIG-nclc-05394.

majority opinion, the Court had upheld federal statutes governing inter-state commerce where "the use of interstate transportation was necessary to the accomplishment of harmful results." Lottery tickets, adulterated food, prostitutes—these were harmful things that Congress could keep out of interstate commerce. But there was nothing harmful about the things produced with child labor; the evil lay in the method of production, not in the things themselves. "The act in its effect does not regulate transportation among the states," Day reasoned, "but aims to standardize the ages at which children may be employed in mining and manufacturing within the states. The goods shipped are of themselves harmless." Commerce was for Congress to govern, but production was for the states, and the majority classified the Child Labor Act as a statute regulating production. "Over interstate transportation, or its incidents, the regulatory power of Congress is ample," Day concluded, "but the production of articles, intended for interstate commerce, is a matter of local regulation."[55]

This was too fine a distinction for the dissenting justices. "The Act does not meddle with anything belonging to the States," Oliver Wendell Holmes insisted. "They may regulate their internal affairs and their domestic commerce as they like. But when they seek to send their products across the State line they are no longer within their rights."[56] But the fine line between production and commerce, a line motivated by a longstanding apprehension of centralizing power in the federal government, stood firm.

The Court's decision in *Hammer v. Dagenhart* was extraordinarily unpopular. "The Supreme Court has destroyed a law enacted by Congress in response to a rudimentary national need," the *New Republic* complained. Progress in legislation was being blocked by "a judiciary immune not only from popular control but also from influence of those vital forces which govern and must govern the nation." In the Senate, the Oklahoma Republican Robert Owen urged the enactment of a law stripping the Court of the power to declare statutes unconstitutional. "Child labor should not be exploited for money-making purposes," he declared. Because the Court's decision had been by a single vote, "one man has nullified the opinion, the matured public opinion, of the country." Congress tried a different tactic to ban child labor. It quickly enacted a new statute imposing a 10% tax on the profits of any person employing child labor. But in *Bailey v. Drexel Furniture Co.* (1922), the Court struck down the new statute too, on the ground that it was not truly a tax but rather a disguised way of prohibiting child labor.[57] *Bailey* prompted Congress to propose an amendment to the Constitution barring child labor, as had been done to overrule the Court's invalidation of the income tax. The amendment gained the support of more than half the states within a few years, but the ratification effort would fizzle out in the late 1930s, when it became unnecessary due to the Court's own change in view regarding the power of the federal government.

For the justices, however, *Hammer* and *Bailey* were not primarily cases about child labor. They were cases about where to draw the line between federal and state authority. Every justice probably favored the abolition of child labor, but the vote in *Bailey* was 8–1 against the constitutionality of a child labor tax. John Hessin Clarke was the only dissenter. Even Louis Brandeis and Oliver Wendell Holmes joined the majority. Many of the lawyers who practiced in the Court understood the cases the same way. James Beck, the solicitor general, was the government lawyer tasked with defending the child labor tax in the Court, but even Beck hoped the Court would hold the tax unconstitutional. "Although I presented the Government's contention in the Child Labor Cases as strongly as I was able," Beck told Chief Justice William Howard Taft after the Court's opinion was published, "yet none who heard you deliver the opinion may have welcomed the decision more than I." Had he won the case, Beck worried, "our form of Government would have sustained a serious injury." Taft received even more effusive congratulations from the New York lawyer Frederic Coudert. "Bravo, my dear Chief Justice!" Coudert wrote after reading Taft's opinion in *Bailey*. "We are thankful to learn that the old ship is still afloat!" Coudert thought that efforts to expand the domain of federal regulation were the work of "a persistent minority, inspired by prejudice, ignorance, or fanaticism in translating their hobbies into law."[58]

IV

In the first decades of the twentieth century, the policy preferences expressed in state legislatures and in Congress were increasingly constricted by the traditional constitutional doctrines to which most of the justices still subscribed. The economy was growing more complex. Businesses were consolidating into ever-larger units that operated on a national and even international scale. Workers were unionizing.[59] Legislatures enacted more regulation than the Court's anti-redistributive view of due process would permit. Congress wanted a more active federal government than the Court's conception of federal power would allow. In both respects, it was often said that the Court was preventing the law from changing to suit the times.

Critics charged that the justices were out of touch with the demands of modern life. While running for president in 1912, Theodore Roosevelt complained that "the whole movement for good may come to naught, and festering wrong and injustice be perpetuated, because certain judges, certain courts, are steeped in some outworn political or social philosophy, and totally misapprehend their relations to the people and to the public needs." The Court was blocking "our orderly development as a nation in accordance with our economic and social needs," agreed the law professor and political scientist Frank Goodnow, because the justices were "confined within the political and legal conceptions of a century or more ago." Roscoe Pound, another law professor, accused the Court of employing a "mechanical jurisprudence" under which "rules have been deduced that obstruct the way of social progress."[60] On this view, the justices were stuffy old men clinging to the doctrines of the past because they were unable to understand the changes taking place all around them.

Another line of criticism depicted the justices as tools of the wealthy. "The Supreme Court of the United States is continually encroaching upon the legislative powers of the States, on the one hand, and upon that of the general government, on the other," the *American Law Review* editorialized, "and it does not escape popular attention that it is doing it in almost every case in the interest of the rich and powerful, and against the rights and interests of the masses of the people." The *Review* concluded that the justices could not see beyond their own class prejudices. "A majority of them are, like the British House of Lords, in sympathy with the sentiments of the wealthy, the cultivated, and the influential classes; and that is about all there is in it." As an angry Ohioan complained to Woodrow Wilson, the justices "wore the brand of Standard Oil."[61]

The justices might talk of traditional legal doctrines in their opinions, critics alleged, but the doctrines were window dressing. The justices were merely implementing conservative policy preferences contrary to those of the voting public. In the justices' hands, one law professor contended, the Constitution was "simply a means of vesting judges with power to declare unconstitutional any laws of which they disapprove." Robert La Follette, the progressive Wisconsin senator, lamented that the justices' "detachment from the vital, living facts of the present day" and "their constant thinking on the side of the rich and powerful and privileged classes have brought our courts into conflict with the democratic spirit and purposes of this generation."[62]

Members of Congress attempted to retaliate by curbing the justices' power. In 1907, for instance, Representative Gordon Russell of Texas proposed a constitutional amendment to limit justices to a twelve-year term in office. In 1911, Representative William Wilson of Pennsylvania introduced a bill that would have required a unanimous vote of the justices before the Court could hold a federal or state statute unconstitutional. In 1912, Senator Joseph Bristow of Kansas proposed a constitutional amendment stating that whenever the Court found a federal statute unconstitutional, Congress could submit the statute to the voters in a nationwide referendum at the next congressional election, and if the voters approved the statute, it would be the law despite the Court's decision.[63] But none of these measures progressed very far.

The *Lochner* era would end abruptly in the late 1930s and early 1940s. Cases like *Lochner v. New York* and *Hammer v. Dagenhart* would be overruled, some explicitly and others implicitly. The Court would largely abandon the project of using the Constitution to block economic regulation. It was not until the 1970s, however, that this period would be called "the *Lochner* era." The first law journal articles using the phrase appeared only in 1971, and not until 1977 would it appear in a published court opinion. The term was not a compliment. *Lochner*, like *Dred Scott*, had come to stand for improper judicial activism. In *Obergefell v. Hodges* (2015), for example, when the Court found a constitutional right to same-sex marriage, Chief Justice John Roberts, in dissent, accused his colleagues of returning to "the debacle of the *Lochner* era." In *Epic Systems v. Lewis* (2018), when the Court held that a wide range of labor disputes could be decided by arbitrators rather than by courts, it was Justice Ruth Bader Ginsburg's turn to argue that the decision "ushers us back to the *Lochner* era."[64] *Lochner* had become an equal opportunity epithet, available to criticize decisions from the left or from the right.

But this sort of criticism misunderstands the thinking behind *Lochner* and similar decisions. The justices of the late nineteenth and early twentieth centuries did not believe that judges should be activists. They did not think judges should implement laissez-faire economic policies. Rather, they subscribed to a nineteenth-century conception of government as empowered to advance the public good but not the private good of any individual or group. On this understanding, a law that took money or power from one group and handed it to another, for the purpose of benefiting the second group at the expense of the first, was out of bounds. We no longer think this way. Today we conceive of politics as a clash of interest groups. We understand the transfer of wealth or influence from one group to another as the normal output of the legislative process. If government taxes the rich to help the poor, or if government strengthens the bargaining position of employees by placing restrictions on employers, we see ordinary governance. The judges of the *Lochner* era saw pathology. In their view, the deliberate redistribution of wealth or power was unconstitutional.

9

The Birth of the Modern Court

The Supreme Court, like any institution, has undergone constant change from the moment of its founding. But three particularly important changes took place nearly simultaneously in the 1920s, while William Howard Taft was the chief justice. It is not an exaggeration to say that the combination of these three developments created the modern Supreme Court.

First, the Court gained the power to choose which cases it would hear. Before the 1920s, with modest exceptions, the Court had to decide every case that litigants presented to it. Most of these cases, as we have seen, were of no importance to anyone besides the parties and their lawyers. Like any other court, the Supreme Court spent most of its time on humdrum disputes, deciding little more than who would win. Beginning in the 1920s, however, the Court became what it is today—an institution that primarily decides important questions of law and only incidentally resolves disputes between the litigants who happen to appear before it.

Second, the Court got its own building, the one it still occupies today. The Court had previously held oral argument in a small courtroom in the Capitol. The justices did the rest of their work in their own homes. Once the Supreme Court building was completed, however, the justices had a large courtroom of their own and spacious offices in which to read briefs and write opinions. The building's design presented the justices to the public as distant oracles rather than as human beings temporarily occupying positions of power, while its location and its massive scale signified the Court's equality with the other two branches of government.

Third, the Court gradually began to enforce the noneconomic constitutional rights of individuals against the government. Virtually all the Court's most famous cases in recent times are in this vein. They have involved, for example, the right of criminal defendants to fair trials, the freedom to speak in unpopular ways, and the right to practice one's religion. Before the 1920s, by contrast, scarcely any of the Court's cases were like this. This change would be much more gradual than the first two, but the Court took its first steps in this direction in the 1920s.

As the result of these three changes, the Court of 1935, when construction on the Court's building was finally complete, looked very different from the Court of 1920. It had become much more like the Court we know today.

I

The creation of the Courts of Appeals in 1891 had relieved the congestion in the Supreme Court's docket, but relief proved temporary. Approximately three hundred cases per year were filed in the Court in the early 1890s. This figure topped four hundred in the next decade, and in the 1910s it was regularly above five hundred. By the early 1920s it was above seven hundred.[1] The Court once again began accumulating a backlog.

What could be done to alleviate the burden? There were plenty of possible solutions. Taft worked behind the scenes to prevent all but one of them from being implemented. A committee of the American Bar Association proposed enlarging the Court to twelve justices and letting it decide cases in groups as small as six, in the hope of reducing each justice's workload by as much as half. The justices all hated this idea. One member of the committee happened to be Taft's brother Henry, so the Bar Association's proposal was quietly dropped after Taft conveyed the justices' disapproval. James Beck, the solicitor general, suggested dividing all the cases into two categories, Class A and Class B. The Class A cases, the important ones, would be decided the normal way, but the other cases, in Class B, would be decided by panels of only five justices. Taft spoke privately with Beck and nothing more was ever heard of this suggestion. The Montana senator Thomas Walsh wanted to cut from the Court's docket all the cases turning on what was then called general common law, as distinct from federal law. "Senator Walsh belongs to that character of lawyer who is obstructive and not constructive," Taft grumbled to Louis Brandeis. "He gives an appearance of constructive views by suggesting things that there is no possibility of having, but when there is anything practical, he is always against it." Nothing further came of Walsh's idea at the time, although the Court itself would reach the same outcome by a different route a few years later, by concluding in *Erie Railroad v. Tompkins* (1938) that there is no such thing as general common law but only the common law of individual states.[2]

Taft quickly squelched all these suggested methods of reducing the Court's caseload because he had another plan, one he had been considering for many years. Taft had dreamed of becoming chief justice all his adult life. He was a state court judge at the age of twenty-nine, solicitor general at thirty-two, and a federal circuit judge before his thirty-fifth birthday. He resigned his judgeship in 1900 to become governor general of the new American colony in the Philippines, after being assured by President William McKinley that in return, McKinley would nominate Taft to fill the next vacancy on the Court. McKinley was assassinated the following year, before a vacancy arose, but Theodore Roosevelt, McKinley's successor, offered Taft a seat on the Court in 1902 when George Shiras retired. Taft declined on the ground that he preferred to complete his work establishing the Philippine colonial government. "The Governor, of course, wants to be a Supreme Judge," remarked an American colleague in Manila, "but if he can safely stay here a while yet and be appointed later I think he would be quite content." Taft's aspiration to be chief justice was well known in Washington as well. At a dinner party held by Chief Justice Melville Fuller and his wife Mary, when a young military officer informed the guests that he was soon to leave for Manila, Mary Fuller told him "when you get to the Philippines, you tell Willie Taft not to be in too much of a hurry to get into my husband's shoes."[3] Taft turned down another offer to join the Court in 1906, when Henry Billings Brown retired, because he was already considering a presidential campaign. When Fuller died in 1910, Taft was president. He prudently appointed the sixty-five-year-old Edward White as the new chief justice, which ensured that when Taft left the presidency it would not be too long before the position would be open again.

While he was planning to become chief justice, Taft was also thinking about a major change in the Court's role. His first public discussion of the subject came during his 1908 presidential campaign, when he urged that the Court should be relieved of most of its cases so it could focus on deciding legal questions of broad importance. "So far as the litigant is concerned, one appeal is all that he should be entitled to; the community at large is not interested in his having more," Taft argued. This one appeal would be to the Court of Appeals or to a state appellate court. The job of the Supreme Court should be "to lay down general principles of law in the interpretation of State or Federal constitutions or statutes, or in the application of the common law, for the benefit and guidance, not of the particular litigant affected, but of the communities at large." For this reason, Taft proposed that the "jurisdiction of the Supreme Court should generally be limited to those cases which are typical and which give an opportunity to the court to cover the whole field of the law upon the subject involved." The Court's job would be to clarify the law,

Figure 9.1 William Howard Taft, dressed in a child's suit, looks in on Chief Justice Melville Fuller and says, "Well he's no quitter yet." Taft's hope of becoming chief justice was well known in Washington. This cartoon was drawn by Clifford Berryman and was published in the *Washington Post* on January 14, 1907. National Archives 6010685.

not to resolve disputes between litigants. Similar reforms had recently been put into practice in some of the largest states, whose highest courts faced the same problem of swelling caseloads.[4] Taft urged the federal courts to do the same.

Taft returned to this proposal as president. "The proper and chief usefulness of a supreme court," he insisted in one of his annual messages to Congress, is "to expound the law." He continued: "Therefore, any provisions for review of cases by the Supreme Court that cast upon that court the duty of passing on questions of evidence and the construction of particular forms of instruments, like indictments, or wills, or contracts, decisions not of general application or importance, merely clog and burden the court and render more difficult its higher function." Taft concluded that "the Supreme Court is now carrying an unnecessary burden of appeals of this kind, and I earnestly urge that it be removed." After his presidency, when Taft was a law professor at Yale and president of the American Bar Association, he continued to urge this reconceptualization of the Court's role.[5]

When Taft finally became chief justice in 1921, his long-simmering plan to transform the Supreme Court became something more than a policy proposal; now it affected him personally as well. He was more than ready. A few months after joining the Court, he informed Albert Cummins, the chair of the Senate Judiciary Committee, that "we are preparing a bill which we hope to bring before your committee, to reduce the obligatory jurisdiction of the Supreme Court." The bill was drafted by the justices themselves—primarily Willis Van Devanter, William Day, James McReynolds, and Taft.[6] All had experience in dealing with Congress. Van Devanter was a former assistant attorney general, Day had been secretary of state, McReynolds had been attorney general, and of course Taft had been president.

The justices' bill gave the Court the authority, in most circumstances, to decide for itself which cases it would hear. There would still be some cases the Court would have to hear, including those in which a lower court had held a statute unconstitutional, but otherwise the Court would gain the power to sift through the cases presented to it and determine which ones justified its attention. Previous legislation in 1914 and 1916 had authorized the Court to decline to hear certain categories of cases, but the justices' proposal was a major expansion of this discretion.[7]

Once the bill was written, Taft used all his political skills to get it passed. "I don't think former Chief Justices had so much to do in the matter of legislation as I have," he remarked, correctly, to his brother Horace. "I don't object to it, because I think Chief Justices ought to take part in that." Taft met with members of Congress and the Justice Department to explain the bill's importance and to defend it against opponents. "Suggestions in respect to this bill of ours will never cease until we get it into final form," he complained to Van Devanter. When a group of New York criminal defense lawyers expressed opposition, Taft made sure that members of Congress understood why. "One of the circumstances that I think should be brought out," he told them, "is that there is no field of the law in which there are more frivolous appeals attempted than in that covered by so-called constitutional questions, and the necessity for winnowing out appeals is perhaps greater in such cases than in any others." The criminal defense lawyer leading the opposition to the bill, Taft argued, "seems to be the kind of man who can manufacture constitutional questions of that sort that you can blow out as you would a candle."[8]

Four of the justices—Taft, Van Devanter, McReynolds, and George Sutherland—testified in congressional hearings in support of the bill. (Day, the other justice who helped write it, had recently retired.) Taft emphasized the importance of reducing the Court's caseload. "The business of the court is rapidly increasing," he reported, "and unless the cases that are not important enough to occupy the time of the court are summarily disposed of it is impossible for the court to dispatch promptly, as it should, the important questions which it is organized to settle." He explained that the Court had built up such a large backlog that it took eighteen to twenty-four months after a case had been filed for the justices to hear oral argument. "If you give us a little more leeway in this matter," he promised, "I am quite sure we can catch up and keep up with the docket."[9]

Van Devanter assured senators that the Court would give serious consideration to each petition for certiorari, the document in which a litigant asked the Court to hear a case. The Court already received some of these petitions, Van Devanter observed. The Court "examines the matter in the petition, record, and briefs, each member of the court making his own examination," he explained. "In our conference a vote is taken on the question whether the petition shall be granted or refused, in the same way that we vote in other cases. If there be occasion for discussion, the discussion is had as in other matters." And review would be liberally granted, Van Devanter promised, because "whenever the vote is relatively close the conference makes it a practice to grant the petition." He explained that "we proceed upon the theory that when as many as four members of the court, and even three in some instances, are impressed with the propriety of our taking the case the petition should be granted." Van Devanter hastened to clarify that although the Court would have discretion in determining which cases to hear, it was not a discretion that would be exercised whimsically or at random. "I do not mean, of course, that the Supreme Court merely exercises a choice or will in granting or refusing the writ," he insisted, "but that it exercises a sound judicial discretion, gives careful thought to the matter in the light of the supporting and opposing briefs, and resolves it according to recognized principles."[10]

The only person who testified against the bill was Benjamin Salinger, a former judge on the Iowa Supreme Court. Salinger worried that if lower courts' errors were no longer all corrected by the Supreme Court, different lower courts were likely to interpret the law differently. "With all the State courts virtually free from Federal review, chaos will exist as to Federal questions," Salinger predicted. And if the Court had discretion over which cases to select, he added, litigants had no way to know whether it was worth the expense of asking the Court to hear their cases. But Salinger was fighting a losing battle. Few members of Congress had strong opinions on what seemed to be a technical question of the Supreme Court's jurisdiction. No interest group opposed the bill. It passed by a vote of 76–1 in the Senate and by a voice vote in the House. After four years of lobbying, Taft had engineered the enactment of the Judiciary Act of 1925, or "the Judges' Bill," as it was often called, in reference to its unusual origin as legislation drafted and pressed upon Congress by the justices themselves.[11]

The Judiciary Act worked exactly as the justices hoped it would. The Court's backlog dwindled to zero within a few years. "Not for a hundred years has the Court reached for argument on the regular calendar cases docketed during the term," a pair of law professors reported in 1928. "Last term it achieved this dispatch in its business." At a meeting of the American Law Institute, Taft joked that "we have made such progress with business that I think members of the Bar are beginning to be a little embarrassed by the proximity of the Court to them." The change had been necessary, Louis Brandeis explained, to keep the caseload "within such narrow limits that the nine men, each with one helper, can do the work as well as can be done."[12]

From the justices' point of view, the only downside was that the drudgery of deciding insignificant cases had been replaced by a different sort of drudgery, the task of plowing through hundreds of petitions for certiorari to choose the cases the Court would hear. It was not long before the justices were complaining of "my grind with the certioraris," as Harlan Fiske Stone described it. "I too find the certs mostly dreary," Felix Frankfurter agreed. Frankfurter grew so exasperated with what he called "utterly baseless petitions for certiorari" that he even proposed requiring the parties who filed groundless petitions to pay damages to their opponents, a suggestion that was never adopted.[13] But none of the justices wanted to bring back the old mandatory docket. A pile of certiorari petitions was a small price to pay for the freedom of choosing the cases they would hear.

The Judiciary Act of 1925 was a testament to Taft's political experience and skills. "I suppose you might call Taft's a political appointment," Oliver Wendell Holmes reflected shortly after the bill got through Congress, but "taking everything into account it was the best that could have been made." It was Taft's "political associations," Holmes explained, that "made it easier to get passed a bill remodelling our jurisdiction (drawn by the judges) that was very important and I think will work well."[14]

Holmes was right: the bill *was* very important—not just in immediately cutting the Court's workload, but in several other ways do not seem to have been anticipated at the time.

First, now that the justices could focus their attention on a small number of cases, their opinions grew longer and they began to publish more concurring and dissenting opinions. Throughout the 1910s and 1920s, the median majority opinion was approximately two thousand words, about the same as it had been since the 1820s. By the 1950s it was around three thousand words, and by the 1980s it was around four thousand words. Even more striking was the rapid change in the frequency of concurring and dissenting opinions. In 1910, 1920, and 1930, more than 80% of the Court's opinions were unanimous. But that figure dropped to 72% in 1940, and then it plummeted to 37% in 1950. Dissenting opinions had once been rarities. A justice published a dissenting opinion in only 6% of the cases in 1925, but that number grew to 14% in 1935, and then 50% in 1945.[15]

The Judiciary Act of 1925 was not the only cause of these developments, but it was an important one, because it allowed the Court to avoid deciding hundreds of insignificant cases each year. Minor cases—those with simple legal issues or where one party should obviously win—can be disposed of in short opinions, but major cases—where the legal issues are more difficult and where both sides have good arguments—require longer opinions. In unimportant cases, the justices are more likely to be unanimous, and where they are not, they are less likely to find it worth the trouble to write a separate opinion. In important cases, by contrast, the justices are more likely to disagree, and when they do disagree, they are more likely to feel compelled to explain why. Even apart from these mechanisms, the Court, like most institutions in which the work product is writing, is governed by a version of Parkinson's Law under which documents grow longer as more time is available to write them. All the pages that the justices no longer had to crank out in the humdrum cases were shifted into longer opinions and more separate opinions in the cases the Court did hear. The Judiciary Act was thus the first step in the transformation of Supreme Court opinions. In 1925 a typical case involved one opinion that was short and unanimous. In 1950 a typical case involved more than one opinion and the opinions were much longer.

Second, the Judiciary Act began to change the Court's role. Most cases in most courts are of little interest to anyone but the litigants. That was once true of the Supreme Court as well. But not any longer. Today, almost every case the Supreme Court decides is important to many people, because if that were not so, the Court would not have heard it in the first place. A conventional court resolves disputes between parties, but the Supreme Court has become an institution that specializes in resolving fundamental legal questions that transcend the parties who happen to be before it. Lawyers who practice in the Court have a revealing jargon that reflects this change. They speak of cases as "vehicles" with which the Court can decide this or that legal issue. The abstract legal question is now the important thing; the dispute between the parties is merely a vessel that transports the question into the Court's domain. In this sense, the Supreme Court is a different kind of institution from other courts. The Judiciary Act of 1925 set this change in motion.

Third, the Judiciary Act gave the justices a valuable new tool for shaping the law. The justices no longer had to decide whatever cases came along. Now they could intervene in the development of the law wherever they thought an intervention was warranted. If a justice thought the lower courts were going astray on one issue but not on another, he could vote to hear cases involving the former but not the latter. If a justice had a view about what the law in a particular area should be, and if some cases were more amenable to that view than others (for example, if some litigants were more sympathetic than others), he could vote to hear only the cases that offered the greatest chance of implementing his view. Every justice had policy goals to a greater or lesser extent. The Judiciary Act allowed for the strategic molding of the Court's docket to advance these goals. The justices were transformed from passive recipients of cases to active participants in the making of the law.

Fourth, and perhaps most important in the long run, the Judiciary Act freed the justices to recognize new constitutional rights without increasing their caseload.[16] When the Court had to hear every case that came before it, the justices had a strong incentive not to decide cases in a way that would make their docket much more crowded than it already was. For example, if, before 1925, the Court had held that the Bill of Rights constrains the states as well as the federal government, the Court's own caseload might have ballooned with vast numbers of litigants newly able to assert constitutional claims. The Judiciary Act removed much of this connection between the content of the law and the justices' daily work life. The few decades after the Judiciary Act would see the biggest burst of new constitutional rights in the Court's history. The Judiciary Act was not the primary reason the justices recognized all these new rights, but it removed what would have been a major impediment to their recognition.

The Judiciary Act of 1925 was thus an important step in the creation of the modern Supreme Court. It seemed like a minor technical change, and for that reason it drew scarcely any opposition, but it began the Court's transformation into the institution that it is today.

II

Long before Taft became chief justice, there were serious conversations about giving the Court its own courthouse. In 1890, while the Library of Congress's first building, the Jefferson building, was under construction, the Senate debated whether to purchase the block to the north of the Jefferson building for the Court. "Accommodations for the Supreme Court appear to be a pressing necessity," urged Senator Justin Smith Morrill, the chair of the Senate Committee on Public Buildings and Grounds. "It is clear that the rooms now occupied in the Capitol by the Supreme Court are deplorably inadequate both in size and number for its proper accommodation—being inferior to what our people often offer to their county courts." Morrill had been the driving force behind the construction of the Jefferson building, and he aimed to do for the Court what he had already done for the Library of Congress. Other countries had built courthouses for their highest courts, Morrill continued, "and we can hardly do less, to show our respect to a branch of our Government which from its earliest days has contributed so greatly to the honor of the country." But Morrill's bill could not get through Congress, and when he introduced it again in 1893, it failed again. It could hardly have helped that the justices did not want their own building. "The court is conservative, and it does not desire elegant surroundings," the *New York Times* explained. "The Justices do not care for a courtroom that will accommodate larger audiences, and they do not want to be turned out of the Capitol. The cramped apartments now occupied by them, divided as they are by a public hall across which the robed Justices must pass on their way to and from the bench, have a charm for them that would be lost in new rooms."[17]

Similar proposals returned every few years. In 1896, as the Library of Congress's new building neared completion, it became clear that the building would be far too big for the library's collection. Joseph Cannon, the chair of the House Appropriations Committee, offered to let the Court use the portion of the building that the library did not need. The justices voted unanimously to decline. In 1898, President William McKinley's annual message to Congress included a request for an appropriation for a courthouse "upon available ground near the Capitol." Nothing was done. A Senate report published in 1902 declared: "Facing the Capitol grounds on the east stands the Congressional Library; and it is contemplated that at no distant day the Supreme Court of the United States shall be accommodated in a building constructed for the exclusive use of that tribunal, on the square directly north of the Library."[18] But no such building would be constructed for some time.

The principal obstacle was the justices' reluctance to move. In 1905, Charles Littlefield, a member of the House Judiciary Committee, informed Chief Justice Melville Fuller of his "intention at the next session of Congress to make an earnest effort to secure the erection of an appropriate building (to be a companion building to the Library of Congress, balancing that square) for the Supreme Court." Littlefield believed that the Court needed "suitable accommodations for the Justices and officers of the Court and the profession having business before the Court." But Littlefield knew that the justices had opposed previous efforts, and that there was no point in trying again if they still felt the same way. They still did, so Littlefield gave up. A similar effort stalled a few years later. "We could have had a new building when Taft was president [1909–1913], as he was eager to have one provided, but Chief Justice [Edward] White strongly opposed," recalled Charles Evans Hughes, who joined the Court in 1910. White "thought that if the Court sat away from the Capitol, the public would lose interest in it." In 1917, Representative James Mann of Illinois brought the issue up yet again. "Everybody who has anything whatever to do with the Supreme Court, or made any investigation relating to the Supreme Court, has known that the quarters which they have are very scant and insufficient," he declared. Mann's speech drew applause on the floor of the House. But Congress did not appropriate any funds, because, as Mann acknowledged, the justices wanted to stay in the Capitol.[19]

The outlook for change brightened considerably when Taft became chief justice in 1921, because it was well known that he favored a new building. But Taft would not accept just any building. In 1922 he rejected a proposal to build the new courthouse in a spot south of the White House, on the present site of the Jefferson Memorial (which was built in the early 1940s). The pro-posal would have created a triangular relationship between the Court, the Capitol, and the White House, to symbolize the independence of the three branches of government. Taft turned the idea down, because "the Court would prefer to be nearer the Capitol."[20]

A better opportunity soon came along. In the Public Buildings Act of 1926, Congress appropriated $50 million for the construction of gov-ernment office buildings in Washington. As the bill made its way through Congress, Taft lobbied to get the Court a share of the money. He succeeded in having a sentence inserted in the law specifically authorizing the acqui-sition of a site for a courthouse. Before he could negotiate with Congress, however, Taft had to negotiate with his own colleagues. He was "uncertain whether we can get a majority of our Court to favor the construction of a new building," he explained to Harlan Fiske Stone. Taft was "very much in favor of it," he told Stone, but he "would like to have the authority of the Court" so he could tell members of Congress that the Court wanted a court-house. Taft got his majority, but just barely. Only four other justices wanted to leave the Capitol—Stone, Willis Van Devanter, Pierce Butler, and Edward Sanford. The other four—Oliver Wendell Holmes, James McReynolds, Louis Brandeis, and George Sutherland—preferred to stay. "I haven't heard that the U.S.S.C. building project has been killed," Brandeis wrote shortly before Congress voted on the Public Buildings Act. "I hope so."[21] But Taft prevailed.

The government condemned the site that had long been contemplated for the courthouse, the block north of the Library of Congress. One of the buildings on the block was the "Old Brick Capitol," the temporary home of Congress in 1814 after the British burned the Capitol. The building had been at various times a boardinghouse and a private home. In the late nineteenth century it was the home of Justice Stephen Field, who could simply cross the street to get to the courtroom in the Capitol. When the government acquired it, the building was the headquarters of the National Woman's Party, an organization that advocated for women's right to vote, and once that was achieved, for other forms of gender equality. At the condemnation trial, the National Woman's Party was represented by Burnita Shelton Matthews, a party member, who would later become the first woman to serve as a federal district judge. Matthews secured com-pensation of nearly $300,000, which was considered a remarkably high figure. The NWP was able to purchase a similar building nearby for only $100,000.[22]

Taft ensured that the architect would be Cass Gilbert, who had designed many well-known buildings, including the Woolworth building in New York, the St. Louis Art Museum, and the Department of Commerce building in Washington. Taft and Gilbert were social acquaintances. They were both conservative men around seventy years old. At that stage of his career, Gilbert was known for designing buildings that looked old-fashioned. He produced sketches of an enormous four-story marble temple, nearly four hundred feet in length and more than three hundred in width, that would occupy the entire block and match the scale of the Library of Congress to the south. The building's size raised eyebrows in Congress, because it seemed far too large for nine justices and the Court's small staff. The Massachusetts representative Frederick Dallinger reported that many of his colleagues thought "it would be a good deal larger building than the Supreme Court alone would probably want" and wondered whether the building should house the Justice Department as well. "We do not want the Department of Justice in that building," Taft replied. "They are parties in every Government case coming before the court, and those comprise about two-fifths of all the cases we have. We seek to hold ourselves independent of the Department of Justice, and to be tied up with them would be a good deal worse than to be tied up with the Senate." Congress should "give us a monumental building there," Taft continued. "Why are we not entitled to it, if we are one of the three branches of the Government?" He suggested that the extra space could be used for a law library and for exhibits displaying the Court's history. Recently, he noted, the descendants of John Jay, the Court's first chief justice, had offered to donate Jay's robe to the Court, but "we did not have any room for it." Taft had to decline the offer, because "the only place we could put it would be in our robing room, and nobody comes into the robing room."[23]

The courtroom in the center of the building was 60% larger than the one in the Capitol. It could accommodate approximately three hundred attorneys and spectators combined.[24] At the time, no one seems to have thought that more space for spectators would be needed, so no one suggested expanding the courtroom at the expense of the building's other features, such as the spacious internal courtyards that were accessible only to Court employees. In later years, when would-be spectators would sleep on the sidewalk in front of the Court in the hope of gaining entrance the next day, and when long lines of disappointed people would have to be turned away from most arguments, the courtroom would come to seem far too small.

In the building's early years, by contrast, the main problem with the court-room was that it was too big for spectators and members of the press to hear what the justices were saying. It was even harder to hear the lawyers, who spoke facing the justices, with their backs to the audience. The justices, who all faced the same direction, had trouble hearing one another. "When Mr. Justice Roberts at one end of the bench leans forward to ask a question," *Time* magazine reported after one of the first arguments in the new court-room, "Mr. Justice Cardozo at the other end can hardly hear him." The Court called in acousticians from the Department of Commerce, who proposed supplying the justices and lawyers with microphones. For several years the justices rejected this solution, because they sometimes spoke to one another during the arguments and they were afraid that microphones would make their comments audible to spectators. The Court's marshal suggested that the microphones could "have a pistol-like grip that must be squeezed to make the instrument operate," but at first even this plan was considered too risky. In 1955, the justices finally agreed to install microphones they could turn on and off, except for Felix Frankfurter, who refused to use one. But it took some time to iron out the wrinkles. "The Supreme Court Chamber," one journalist complained in 1959, was "the room with the most miser-able acoustics hereabouts." Frankfurter still would not use a microphone, and his colleagues often neglected to turn theirs on before speaking. As a result, "words seldom penetrate beyond the first few rows in the chamber." When Frankfurter retired in 1962, his successor, Arthur Goldberg, accepted a microphone—Goldberg had just been secretary of labor, so he was ac-customed to them—and the Court was fully miked. The justices eventually learned to operate their microphones. Despite the public address system, however, the justices still had trouble hearing one another, so in 1972, the straight bench behind which they sat was sawed into three parts, which were arranged at an angle so the justices could see their colleagues.[25] After thirty-seven years in the courtroom, the Court's audio problems were finally solved.

The courtroom was in the interior of the building. Around the outside were the justices' offices, each consisting of three rooms and two bathrooms. Each had a fireplace with a black marble mantel, ceiling-high bookshelves, a rug, a mahogany desk, a black leather couch, blue curtains, and a thermostat. The offices were identical, except for the chief justice's office, directly behind the courtroom, which was larger.[26]

Gilbert designed the building with an eye toward stage management. In the Capitol, the justices had to enter a public corridor to walk from their robing room into the courtroom and back again. In the new building, by contrast, the justices would be sealed off from the public. "The plan is so arranged," Gilbert explained, "that any justice may pass from his own chambers to those of the other justices for conference, or to the court room, the conference room, or to the library without passing through the public corridors." The justices could even enter and exit the building without being seen, because they parked their cars in a garage beneath the building and took an elevator to their offices. They would appear in the courtroom as if by magic, from behind the bench, and they would depart the same way. Unless a justice wished to enter the building's public area, no member of the public would ever catch a glimpse of him except while he was on the bench.[27]

Neither Taft nor Gilbert lived to see the Supreme Court building completed. Taft died in 1930, when construction had just begun. As mourners filed past his coffin in the Capitol rotunda, they could see, forty feet away, a plaster model of the building. Flowers had been placed around the model for the occasion. Gilbert died in 1934, about a year before construction ended. The pediment above the west side of the building, the front entrance, included sculptures of nine figures representing concepts such as "liberty" and "order." When Robert Aitken, the sculptor, finished his work, the justices were astonished to see that Taft and Gilbert were models for two of the figures, as were Charles Evans Hughes, the new chief justice, and Aitken himself.[28]

Below the sculpted figures on the west side of the building was the inscription "Equal Justice Under Law." On the east side, the corresponding inscription read "Justice the Guardian of Liberty." These were not quotations from any legal or historical documents. "Equal Justice Under Law" was suggested by the architects because it fit the space and sounded right. The architects' proposal for the east side was "Equal Justice is the Foundation of Liberty," but Hughes, after consulting with Willis Van Devanter, came up with "Justice the Guardian of Liberty" as a substitute. There would be occasional complaints that "Equal Justice Under Law" is either redundant (where justice requires equality) or incorrect (where it requires making distinctions). The journalist Herbert Bayard Swope raised this issue, half in jest, in a letter to Hughes when the building was completed. Ralph Owen Brewster, an ardently anticommunist senator from Maine, repeatedly complained about it in the early 1950s, apparently because he objected to the association of justice with equality. But "Equal Justice Under Law" remained above the Court's front entrance, and indeed the phrase took on a life of its own. Justice Robert

Jackson used it in an opinion in 1948, and since then, it has appeared in forty-two more of the Court's cases.[29] It was not a quotation when the courthouse was built, but it is now.

At the laying of the building's cornerstone in 1932, Hughes recognized Taft's indispensable role in shepherding the project through Congress. "We are indebted to the late Chief Justice William Howard Taft more than to anyone else," Hughes declared. "This building is the result of his intelligent persistence." Hughes explained that the building would be far more convenient for the justices and for lawyers than the Court's old, cramped quarters in the Capitol, but he acknowledged that for most people, who did not work at the Court, the building's value would lie in what it represented. "It symbolizes

Figure 9.2 The new courthouse in 1936, soon after it opened. The building transformed the justices' working environment and the way the Court presented itself to the public. Photograph by Arthur Rothstein. Library of Congress, LC-USF34-005615-E.

the national ideal of justice," Hughes said. "This building is the symbol of the distinctive character of the Republic."[30]

Several of the justices were less pleased. "Personally, I should have preferred to have remained in our old quarters," George Sutherland grumbled when the building opened in 1935. "The new building has cost an immense amount of money." To a journalist he wondered if the justices would look like "nine beetles in the Temple of Karnak." Louis Brandeis continued working at home rather than moving into the new building. "He thought it a great mistake," recalled one of Brandeis's law clerks, that the Court was set "apart in a palace of its own." When his wife took a tour of the vacant offices set aside for Brandeis, she remarked that "they showed me the running ice water and the shower bath, two things my husband never uses." Harlan Fiske Stone complained that "the interior of our building is like a vault or a mausoleum." He told his sons that "the place is almost bombastically pretentious" and that the building was "wholly inappropriate for a quiet group of old boys such as the Supreme Court." Benjamin Cardozo joked that the building was so ostentatious that the justices should enter on white elephants. Brandeis made a similar joke: "On the first day we hold court there, the Chief should go in on an elephant and the rest of us on stilts." Even Hughes, despite his exuberant remarks at the cornerstone ceremony, used his large office only for meetings. Otherwise, he too continued working at home. Only Sutherland and Owen Roberts moved in right away.[31] The veteran justices' unease with the building was not shared by the justices appointed after the building opened, who had no experience with the old way of doing things, and who were accustomed in their previous jobs to work in offices rather than at home. Eventually, after the great turnover in personnel that took place in the late 1930s and early 1940s, all nine justices used their chambers at the courthouse.

The size of the building required more than tripling the Court's small staff. In 1934 the Court had fifty-one employees, but in 1936 it had 163, most of whom were hired to service the building. These included a forty-three-person cleaning staff and thirty-three police officers, as well as some elevator attendants, a laundress, and a cabinetmaker. The building was so enormous that it included a cavernous storage area on the top floor that turned out not to be needed. It was later converted into a nearly full-size basketball court that would be dubbed "the highest court in the land" because it sat atop the Supreme Court.[32]

The new building completely changed the justices' working environment, especially once the nine sets of chambers were all occupied. Not since the boardinghouse days of the early nineteenth century had the justices all worked in the same place. To communicate, they no longer had to send letters by messenger between one another's houses; now they could walk down the hall and speak in person. These conversations were not always welcome. The justices of the 1940s were a famously cantankerous group, who might have loathed one another a bit less if they could have spent more time apart. In later years, however, the justices almost always claimed to get along well. A good working relationship is important for a small group of people who work in the same building and often have the same coworkers for decades. It was far less important when the justices worked primarily in their homes and came together only for oral argument and conferences.

The change of working environment was even more significant for the justices' secretaries, law clerks, and messengers. When they worked in the justices' homes, they were, in effect, simultaneously Court employees and household staff. Howard Westwood, who was Harlan Fiske Stone's law clerk in 1933–1934, recalled that Gertrude Jenkins, Stone's secretary, "became to some extent a personal secretary for Mrs. Stone." Westwood himself had to assist Agnes Stone when she entertained at home each Monday afternoon. He went to the courtroom in the Capitol only on rare occasions, when there was an especially interesting argument. Otherwise, he spent the workweek in the Stones' house, in a room next to Jenkins, while "the Negro messenger assigned to the Justice was ordinarily posted in the basement," waiting for assignments. "The Justice's work and his home life had become integrated during the days of the 'old Court,'" Westwood remembered. But when a justice began working in his chambers at the new Court, so did his staff. They no longer had to spend as much of their time on the justice's personal matters. Work became a more sociable place, with all the secretaries, law clerks, and messengers in a single building, along with the Court's librarians, police officers, and other employees. The nonpublic parts of the building "made up a small self-contained village where the clerks wandered freely, carts loaded with cert petitions were rolled along, and a relaxed atmosphere prevailed," remembered Charles Reich, who clerked for Hugo Black in the early 1950s.[33]

Working together in one building was more enjoyable for the law clerks than working alone in a justice's house had been, but the new arrangement gave rise to a new concern. Now that the law clerks were no longer isolated, they could discuss the Court's cases among themselves. They could reach agreements about whether a certiorari petition should be granted, for example, or about how a case should be decided, before even discussing the case with their justices. "I have heard," worried the lawyer Graham Claytor, a former Brandeis clerk, "that some law clerks have gone so far as to campaign to get others to join them in certain recommendations" to the justices.[34] The fear that the justices' clerks were exerting an improper influence on the Court's decisions, a fear that did not exist before the Court had its own building, would only intensify in later years.

The new building's effect on the Court's public reputation is harder to pin down, but the sheer size and grandeur of the building, along with the careful stage management of the justices' entrances and exits, made the Court seem like a more august institution. The justices now inhabited a "gleaming white ten-million-dollar structure" that was "literally blinding to look at in the brilliant Washington sun," as one popular magazine described it, a building "majestically simple in its Corinthian design."[35] The Supreme Court building became a massive physical representation of the judicial branch of the federal government, like the Capitol and the White House had long been for the other two branches. As the composition of the Court's caseload shifted from mostly humdrum cases to mostly important ones, the Court's physical surroundings changed to match.

III

While the Court was acquiring a building and gaining control of its caseload, it was also beginning to do something else new. For decades, the Court had protected the freedom of businesses from regulation, but it had done little to protect the constitutional rights of individual people in other domains. Areas of the law that occupy a substantial percentage of the Court's attention today, such as the freedom of speech and the rights of criminal defendants, were almost entirely absent from the Court's cases. That began to change, slowly, in the 1920s.

The Court heard scarcely any cases involving the freedom of speech before the 1920s. When it did, the Court interpreted the First Amendment narrowly and the speaker always lost. In *Patterson v. Colorado* (1907), for example, the Court affirmed the criminal conviction of US Senator Thomas Patterson, the publisher of the *Denver Post*. Patterson's offense was publishing editorials and cartoons that criticized the judges of the Colorado Supreme Court. The US Supreme Court held that punishing him for his speech did not violate the First Amendment, even if the critiques were true, because the freedom of speech meant only a freedom from censorship *before* one speaks, not an exemption from punishment *after* one speaks. In *Mutual Film Corporation v. Industrial Commission of Ohio* (1915), the Court unanimously allowed the government to censor films, on the ground that film and other forms of entertainment were not protected by the First Amendment. In the justices' view, cinema, like the theater and the circus, was not speech at all, but merely "a business, pure and simple, originated and conducted for profit, like other spectacles." The Court allowed Boston to prohibit all speeches in public parks. "For the legislature absolutely or conditionally to forbid public speaking in a highway or public park," the Court reasoned in *Davis v. Massachusetts* (1897), "is no more an infringement of the rights of a member of the public than for the owner of a private house to forbid it in his house."[36] The freedom of speech was a dormant part of the Constitution. None of the justices showed any interest in bringing it to life.

The federal government became much more aggressive in punishing speech when the United States entered the First World War in 1917. Congress promptly enacted the Espionage Act, which made it a crime to circulate information intended to interfere with the armed forces or to assist the enemy. The government began prosecuting people who spoke out against the war. At first, the Court did nothing to interfere. In *Schenck v. United States*, decided in March 1919, the Court unanimously affirmed the convictions of Charles Schenck and Elizabeth Baer, two leaders of the Socialist Party, for printing and distributing leaflets arguing that military conscription was a form of despotism and urging draftees to resist. "We admit that in many places and in ordinary times the defendants in saying all that was said in the circular would have been within their constitutional rights," Oliver Wendell Holmes acknowledged in his opinion for the Court. "But the character of every act depends upon the circumstances in which it is done." He reasoned—in what would become a frequently quoted passage—that "the most stringent protection of free speech would not protect a man in falsely shouting fire in a theatre and causing a panic. . . . The question in every case is whether the words used are used in such circumstances and are of such a nature as to create a clear and present danger that they will bring about the substantive evils that Congress has a right to prevent." Holmes concluded that Schenck and Baer had, in effect, shouted fire in a theater. "When a nation is at war," he explained, "many things that might be said in time of peace are such a hindrance to its effort that their utterance will not be endured so long as men fight." A week later, in another opinion by Holmes, the Court unanimously affirmed the Espionage Act conviction of Eugene Debs, the Socialist Party's candidate in several presidential elections, for giving antiwar speeches.[37] First Amendment claims had lost decisively yet again.

The first glimmer of change appeared a few months later, however. *Abrams v. United States*, decided in November 1919, was another Espionage Act prosecution. Five Russian immigrants had been convicted of printing a leaflet that praised the Russian Revolution and urged a similar revolution in the United States. In a short opinion, seven of the justices rejected the defendants' argument that their advocacy was protected by the First Amendment. This time, however, Holmes dissented, joined by Louis Brandeis. "I do not doubt for a moment," Holmes acknowledged, "that by the same reasoning that would justify punishing persuasion to murder, the United States constitutionally may punish speech that produces or is intended to produce a clear and imminent danger." But he concluded that the defendants' pamphlet posed no such danger. "Congress certainly cannot forbid all effort to change the mind of the country," Holmes insisted. "Nobody can suppose that the surreptitious publishing of a silly leaflet by an unknown man, without more, would present any immediate danger." Holmes finished with an extended discussion of the rationale for the freedom of speech—the first ever to appear in a Supreme Court opinion. "Persecution for the expression of opinions seems to me perfectly logical," he explained.

> If you have no doubt of your premises or your power and want a certain result with all your heart you naturally express your wishes in law and sweep away all opposition. To allow opposition by speech seems to indicate that you think the speech impotent, as when a man says that he has squared the circle, or that you do not care whole heartedly for the result, or that you doubt either your power or your premises. But when men have realized that time has upset many fighting faiths, they may come to believe even more than they believe the very foundations of their own conduct that the ultimate good desired is better reached by free trade in ideas—that the best test of truth is the power of the thought to get itself accepted in the competition of the market, and that truth is the only ground upon which their wishes safely can be carried out. That at any rate is the theory of our Constitution.[38]

This was an unorthodox view at the time, when many were fearful of violence on the part of radical political movements. Just a few months before, anarchists had set off bombs in eight cities simultaneously, including one at the house of A. Mitchell Palmer, the attorney general. Many additional bombs had been discovered in packages waiting to be mailed, including one that was addressed to Holmes himself. In *Abrams*, Holmes's rousing defense of the freedom of speech was joined only by Brandeis. Many years later, it would become the conventional understanding of the First Amendment.

Holmes and Brandeis continued to dissent in similar cases for most of the 1920s. In *Gitlow v. New York* (1925), the Court affirmed the conviction of the journalist Benjamin Gitlow for publishing an editorial urging a socialist revolution. The First Amendment "does not protect publications prompting the overthrow of government by force," Edward Sanford declared in his majority opinion. "A State may punish utterances endangering the foundations of organized government." Holmes reprised the theme of his *Abrams* dissent. "It is said that this manifesto was more than a theory, that it was an incitement," he noted. But "every idea is an incitement. It offers itself for belief and if believed it is acted on." Holmes had only scorn for Gitlow's political goals. As he wrote to Felix Frankfurter, his dissent in *Gitlow* came out "in favor of the right to drool on the part of believers in the proletarian dictatorship." But Holmes believed that the marketplace of ideas should be open to the advocacy of revolution, just like the advocacy of any other idea. Holmes concluded: "If in the long run the beliefs expressed in proletarian dictatorship are destined to be accepted by the dominant forces of the community, the only meaning of free speech is that they should be given their chance and have their way."[39]

Holmes and Brandeis dissented again in *Whitney v. California* (1927), when the rest of the Court affirmed the conviction of the activist Anita Whitney, a member of a prominent California family and the niece of the former justice Stephen Field. Whitney's offense was helping to establish the Communist Labor Party of America. This time it was Brandeis who penned a lengthy defense of the freedom of speech. "Those who won our independence," he declared, "believed that the final end of the state was to make men free to develop their faculties." The best way to prevent the spread of bad ideas, Brandeis insisted, was to allow them to be aired fully and to be rebutted in open debate, because "discussion affords ordinarily adequate protection against the dissemination of noxious doctrine." He concluded: "Fear of serious injury cannot alone justify suppression of free speech and assembly. Men feared witches and burnt women. It is the function of speech to free men from the bondage of irrational fears."[40]

In the long run, the most important thing about *Gitlow* and *Whitney* was not the outcome, but the Court's willingness to apply the First Amendment to the states. Benjamin Gitlow was prosecuted by New York, Anita Whitney by California. When the Bill of Rights was written and ratified, it was understood to protect individual rights against infringement only by the federal government, not by the states. In the twentieth century, the Court would gradually conclude, one right at a time, that most of these rights are "incorporated" into the Fourteenth Amendment as aspects of due process, and that they are therefore protected against infringement by states as well. In *Gitlow* and *Whitney*, the freedom of speech became the first right the Court treated this way. The Court incorporated the freedom of the press a few years later in *Near v. Minnesota* (1931).[41]

The view of free speech first taken on the Court by Holmes and Brandeis finally prevailed in the late 1920s and early 1930s, toward the end of Holmes's career, when the Court began reversing the convictions of defendants whose only offense was to be members of radical organizations. In *Fiske v. Kansas* (1927), the Court unanimously reversed the conviction of a member of the International Workers of the World, a then-prominent labor union. In *Stromberg v. California* (1931), the Court reversed the conviction of Yetta Stromberg, a student at the University of Southern California, whose crime was to fly a red flag that signified her membership in the Communist Party. "The opportunity for free political discussion," the Court declared, "is a fundamental principle of our constitutional system."[42] These were modest victories for the freedom of speech, compared with the cases that would follow in later years, but they were the first in the Court's history in which individuals prevailed against governments bent on suppressing unpopular political opinions. In the second half of the twentieth century, when the freedom of speech expanded to protect many more kinds of expression, lawyers would look back to the dissenting opinions of Holmes and Brandeis as the origin of the modern conception of the First Amendment.

At the same time, the Court began to take a greater interest in the constitutional rights of criminal defendants. The Bill of Rights includes much more about criminal trials than any other topic, but before the 1920s, it was rare for the Court to reverse a criminal conviction on constitutional grounds, no matter how unfairly a trial was conducted. The Court's reluctance to get involved in such questions was exemplified by the famous case of Leo Frank, a Jewish man convicted of murdering a thirteen-year-old girl who worked at the Atlanta factory where Frank was a supervisor. Frank was almost certainly innocent, but the courtroom was dominated by an anti-Semitic mob who threatened violence if the jury acquitted him. In *Frank v. Mangum* (1915), the Court affirmed Frank's conviction on the ground that Georgia had provided him the opportunity to appeal, which was all that the Constitution required. Holmes dissented, joined by Charles Evans Hughes. "Whatever disagreement there may be as to the scope of the phrase 'due process of law,'" Holmes remarked, "there can be no doubt that it embraces the fundamental conception of a fair trial, with opportunity to be heard. Mob law does not become due process of law by securing the assent of a terrorized jury." After the Court affirmed Frank's conviction, the governor of Georgia commuted his death sentence to life in prison, a decision so unpopular that a lynch mob kidnapped Frank from prison and hanged him from a tree.[43] From the Court's perspective, criminal procedure was a matter for the state courts, even in an extreme case like Leo Frank's.

In the 1920s, however, the Court began reversing unfair state criminal convictions on constitutional grounds. The first occasion, *Moore v. Dempsey*

Figure 9.3 Leo Frank was lynched in Georgia in 1915 after the Court declined to overturn his conviction, which was obtained at a trial dominated by an angry mob. The Court would begin to intervene in state criminal cases soon after. Atlanta History Center, VIS 71.456.02.

(1923), involved a trial similar to the one Leo Frank received. Five black men had been convicted in Arkansas of murdering a white man, after a hasty trial in which the courtroom was surrounded by a white mob who threatened violence if the defendants were not convicted. The defense lawyer was so frightened that he did not dare to call any witnesses. The jury took less than five minutes to return a guilty verdict. As Holmes put it, "there never was a chance for the petitioners to be acquitted; no juryman could have voted for an acquittal and continued to live in Phillips County and if any prisoner by any chance had been acquitted by a jury he could not have escaped the mob." As in the Leo Frank case, the defendants' convictions were affirmed on appeal in the state courts. This time, however, the Court reversed the convictions. "If the case is that the whole proceeding is a mask," Holmes reasoned, and "that counsel, jury and judge were swept to the fatal end by an irresistible wave of public passion, and that the State Courts failed to correct the wrong, neither perfection in the machinery for correction nor the possibility that the trial court and counsel saw no other way of avoiding an immediate outbreak of the mob can prevent this Court from securing to the petitioners their constitutional rights."[44] *Moore v. Dempsey* was the first case in which the Court reversed a state criminal conviction on constitutional grounds.

The Court did it again four years later. In *Tumey v. Ohio* (1927), the defendant had been fined for violating Ohio's law banning the possession of alcohol. The town in which the trial took place encouraged its judges to enforce the state's prohibition law by giving them a share of the fines collected from offenders. As Taft pointed out, this payment scheme was hardly conducive to a fair trial, because the judge would be paid for convictions but not for acquittals. The Court unanimously reversed the conviction as inconsistent with due process.[45]

In the next few years, the Court reversed convictions in a few more cases like *Moore v. Dempsey*, in which black defendants had received trials that were scarcely fairer than lynchings. The case that received the most attention was *Powell v. Alabama* (1932), involving the trial of the "Scottsboro Boys," black teenagers convicted of raping two white women on a train in Alabama. Despite their innocence, they were convicted after perfunctory trials in a courtroom packed with hostile white spectators. Their only defense lawyer was a local attorney with no experience in criminal cases who was appointed on the spot by the judge and who thus had no time to prepare. In light of "the ignorance and illiteracy of the defendants," George Sutherland wrote for the Court, "we think the failure of the trial court to give them reasonable time and opportunity to secure counsel was a clear denial of due process." When the Scottsboro defendants were retried, they were convicted a second time, and the case returned to the Court as *Norris v. Alabama* (1935) and *Patterson v. Alabama* (1935). The Court reversed yet again, this time because the county had systematically excluded African Americans from serving on juries for as long as anyone could remember.[46]

The following year, in *Brown v. Mississippi* (1936), the Court reversed the convictions of three black farmers who had been tortured into confessing to the murder of a white man. The police hanged one defendant by the neck from a tree. They whipped the other two with a leather strap with buckles on it. These confessions were the only evidence of the defendants' guilt. When the state supreme court nevertheless affirmed their convictions, a dissenting judge observed that "the transcript reads more like pages torn from some medieval account than a record made within the confines of a modern civilization." The Supreme Court unanimously reversed. "It would be difficult to conceive of methods more revolting to the sense of justice than those taken to procure the confessions of these petitioners," Hughes concluded, "and the use of the confessions thus obtained as the basis for conviction and sentence was a clear denial of due process."[47] This was a new role for the Court—protecting the constitutional rights of criminal defendants.

While the Court was beginning to protect the freedom of speech and the fairness of criminal trials, it was also beginning to delineate a constitutional right of personal liberty. In *Meyer v. Nebraska* (1923), the Court struck down a Nebraska law that prohibited the teaching of foreign languages through the eighth grade. During and immediately after World War I, many states enacted similar laws restricting or even prohibiting the teaching of foreign languages, some directed specifically at German and others proscribing all languages besides English. Robert Meyer, who taught in a one-room schoolhouse at the Zion Lutheran Church in Hampton, Nebraska, was convicted of teaching a ten-year-old boy to read the Bible in German. The Court held that the law banning foreign language instruction was an unconstitutional infringement of Meyer's liberty. Liberty "denotes not merely freedom from bodily restraint but also the right of the individual to contract" and "to engage in any of the common occupations of life," James McReynolds explained, in what was already a familiar exposition of the reason for shielding business enterprises from redistributive regulation. But McReynolds then added liberties of a very different kind—the right "to acquire useful knowledge, to marry, establish a home and bring up children, to worship God according to the dictates of his own conscience, and generally to enjoy those privileges long recognized at common law as essential to the orderly pursuit of happiness by free men." This was liberty in the domain of personal life, not business, and it suggested that the Due Process Clause of the Fourteenth Amendment could be as much of a shield against government intrusions into one's private affairs as it was against government interference with commercial endeavors. McReynolds concluded that the teaching and learning of languages was encompassed within this understanding of liberty and thus could not be prohibited by the government. "Mere knowledge of the German language cannot reasonably be regarded as harmful," he reasoned. "Heretofore it has been commonly looked upon as helpful and desirable." Meyer's "right thus to teach and the right of parents to engage him so to instruct their children, we think, are within the liberty of the amendment."[48] Two decades earlier, the Court had determined in *Lochner* that work as a baker was not harmful enough to require government intervention. In *Meyer*, the Court reached the same conclusion about learning foreign languages. The Constitution now barred the government from unduly interfering with personal liberty as well as economic liberty.

Two years later, in *Pierce v. Society of Sisters* (1925), the Court found a constitutional right to send one's children to private school. An initiative enacted by the voters of Oregon required all children to attend public schools. The law was motivated largely by anti-Catholicism, and Catholic schools were among its chief victims, but it applied to all private schools, not just parochial schools. In another opinion by McReynolds, the Court unanimously held the law unconstitutional—not because it infringed the right to practice one's religion, a right that would not be incorporated against the states until the 1940s, but because it deprived parents of the liberty to choose where their children would attend school. Private schools "are engaged in a kind of undertaking not inherently harmful, but long regarded as useful and meritorious," McReynolds suggested, just as he had in *Meyer* regarding the learning of foreign languages. He concluded that the state had no power "to standardize its children by forcing them to accept instruction from public teachers only. The child is not the mere creature of the state."[49] Once again, the Court had adopted a view of the Due Process Clause that carved out a zone of private life immune from government interference.

Many years later, when the Court interpreted the Due Process Clause to bar government interference in private choices concerning matters like contraception and abortion, the school cases of the 1920s would be understood as early steps in this direction. At the time, however, the school cases did not lead to any further development of a general right of privacy. Indeed, just a couple of years after *Pierce*, the Court held in *Buck v. Bell* (1927) that the Due Process Clause did not prevent the state from forcibly sterilizing people determined to be "feeble-minded." Like many states at the time, Virginia had a eugenic program providing for the sterilization of the mentally disabled. "Carrie Buck is a feeble-minded white woman" who had been committed to a state institution, Holmes explained in his opinion. "She is the daughter of a feeble-minded mother in the same institution, and the mother of an illegitimate feeble-minded child." It took him just a few sentences to dismiss the argument that the liberty protected by the Due Process Clause included a right not to be sterilized against one's will. "We have seen more than once that the public welfare may call upon the best citizens for their lives," Holmes declared, a few years after the First World War. "It would be strange if it could not call upon those who already sap the strength of the State for these lesser sacrifices, often not felt to be such by those concerned, in order to prevent our being swamped with incompetence." Holmes himself supported measures like the one at issue in *Buck*. As his biographer remarks, eugenics was the rare "legislative 'reform' about which Holmes did not have his customary skepticism." This view came through clearly in his short opinion for the Court. "It is better for all the world," he insisted, "if instead of waiting to execute degenerate offspring for crime, or to let them starve for their imbecility, society can prevent those who are manifestly unfit from continuing their kind. The principle that sustains compulsory vaccination is broad enough to cover cutting the Fallopian tubes." He concluded with what has become one of the most infamous lines in any Supreme Court opinion: "Three generations of imbeciles are enough."[50]

Eugenics would fall from favor in the mid-twentieth century, and, as it did, so would *Buck v. Bell*. The decision would join *Dred Scott* and *Lochner* in the small anti-canon of Supreme Court cases that law students are taught to deplore. The Court would follow this change in thought and effectively overrule *Buck v. Bell* in the 1940s. In the 1920s, however, most contemporaries found nothing objectionable. The Harvard law professor Felix Frankfurter, who would join the Court himself soon after, included *Buck v. Bell* on a short list of Holmes's most stellar opinions. "The judicial function here reaches its highest exercise," Frankfurter proclaimed. A Virginia lawyers' magazine approved of the decision because "more and more, thinking people have come to realize the necessity of bettering the breed of men."[51] In its own day, *Buck v. Bell*, at least among lawyers, was not the monstrosity it would later become. But it did indicate the limits of the domain of personal liberty the justices were prepared to find in the Constitution. As with the freedom of speech and the right to a fair trial, the individual rights the Court was newly willing to recognize were substantial relative to earlier periods but restrained compared with what would come later.

National attitudes were slowly shifting in favor of individual rights in the 1920s and early 1930s, but how did such cultural developments influence the Court? One important mechanism was that progressive lawyers were engaging in constitutional litigation more than ever before. The National Association for the Advancement of Colored People, formed in 1909, litigated on behalf of the rights of African Americans. The NAACP was involved in some of the Court's early criminal cases, including *Moore v. Dempsey*. The American Civil Liberties Union was founded in 1920 in large part to litigate free speech claims, especially those of radical labor organizations. The ACLU was involved in several of the important cases of the period, including *Gitlow v. New York, Whitney v. California, Stromberg v. California*, and *Pierce v. Society of Sisters*. The International Labor Defense, the litigating arm of the Communist Party, was established in 1925. The ILD helped represent the Scottsboro Boys in *Powell v. Alabama*. Organizations like these, devoted to litigation in support of progressive political causes, did not exist in earlier periods. It takes an infrastructure of lawyers and funding and a deliberate program of litigation to get an issue before the Supreme Court repeatedly.[52] These began to fall into place in the 1920s.

A litigation support structure can get an argument before the Court, but whether the justices will be persuaded depends on who the justices are. A second factor that contributed to the Court's new receptiveness to individual rights arguments in the 1920s was that during the Coolidge and Hoover administrations, a series of new appointments moved the Court decisively to the left. This may sound surprising in light of the two presidents' conservative reputations, but the justices they picked were not particularly conservative, unlike the justices who left the Court, who were.

When Joseph McKenna retired in 1925, Coolidge replaced him with Harlan Fiske Stone, Coolidge's attorney general and former Amherst College classmate. Stone was far to the left of McKenna. He had "a reverence for Holmes and Brandeis," recalled Herbert Wechsler, Stone's law clerk in the early 1930s. Taft retired in 1930 and died a few weeks later. Hoover made Charles Evans Hughes the new chief justice. Hughes had left the Court in 1916 to run unsuccessfully for president. In the intervening years he had been secretary of state and had returned to private practice. Hughes was not nearly as conservative as Taft. As a lawyer in New York, Hughes had been president of the Legal Aid Society, which assisted indigent criminal defendants, and he had represented members of the Socialist Party who had been expelled from the state legislature.[53] Another shift to the left took place later in 1930, when Edward Sanford died and was replaced by the moderate Philadelphia lawyer Owen Roberts, after the Senate rejected Hoover's first nominee, John J. Parker, because of the racist views Parker had expressed while running for governor of North Carolina. The Court could have moved back to the right when Holmes retired in 1932, but Hoover replaced him with the distinguished New York judge Benjamin Cardozo, who joined Brandeis and Stone on the Court's liberal wing. By the early 1930s, the Court was not as conservative as it had been a few years before.

Both these trends would intensify in later years. There would be more progressive organizations conducting litigation campaigns for political ends, campaigns that were based on establishing individual constitutional rights. The Court would move farther to the left, because Franklin Roosevelt was president for so long that by his death he had appointed nearly every justice. In the 1950s and 1960s, the Court would recognize all sorts of constitutional rights that were barely imaginable in the 1920s. But the 1920s was the period when the Court took its first steps in this direction.

On Monday, October 7, 1935, the Court held its first session in the new building. Nothing much happened that day. A few lawyers were admitted to the Court's bar and the justices heard motions in several cases. There would have been time to reflect on how much the Court had changed in the previous decade. The Court now controlled its own docket; it decided only a small fraction of the cases presented to it, the ones raising important legal questions. The Court occupied a massive new courthouse that projected weight and power. And the Court was gradually beginning to hear new kinds of cases. One of the motions it considered that day was filed by the National Association for the Advancement of Colored People, which requested permission to file an amicus brief in support of Angelo Herndon, a black union organizer represented by the International Labor Defense. Herndon had been convicted in Georgia of an offense the state called "insurrection," which was in fact nothing more than the possession of Communist literature. The justices would reverse Herndon's conviction on the ground that it infringed his freedom of speech.[54] In its outward trappings and in the substance of its work, the Court was becoming a different kind of institution.

10

Court-Packing and Constitutional Change

The Supreme Court's understanding of the Constitution changed dramatically in the late 1930s. When the decade began the Court still closely scrutinized economic regulation, as it had done for decades, to determine whether the regulation was consistent with the Court's strict interpretation of the Constitution. If a law was meant to redistribute wealth or power from one sector of society to another, it was a violation of the liberty of contract protected by the Due Process Clause. If Congress tried to regulate economic activity that lacked a direct connection to interstate commerce, the legislation exceeded the federal government's power under the Commerce Clause. In a series of high-profile cases decided during Franklin Roosevelt's first term as president, the Court used these doctrines to strike down several of Roosevelt's New Deal programs, along with similar state regulation. By the end of the decade, however, the Court's approach had changed completely. Now the Court *upheld* virtually all regulation, even laws that were openly redistributive and laws that extended federal control into domains previously reserved to the states. The Court overruled several of its prior decisions and explicitly disclaimed any power to second-guess the propriety of regulation. Rarely has constitutional law been so thoroughly transformed in so short a time.

How can we explain this change?

The most common explanation focuses on a narrow slice of time in 1937, when Roosevelt announced his Court-packing plan. After Roosevelt's landslide reelection in 1936, his administration proposed legislation that would have allowed him to appoint as many as six new justices in addition to the existing nine. The stated justification for the proposal was that the justices needed help because they were old and behind on their work, but it was clear to everyone that the real purpose of the plan was to fill the Court with justices who would interpret the Constitution to allow the New Deal to be implemented. Just when the plan was being debated in Congress, however, the Court shocked everyone. Justice Owen Roberts switched his vote from the conservative to the liberal side of the Court, which converted

5–4 majorities against the New Deal into 5–4 majorities in its favor. As the journalist Cal Tinney quipped, in a line that would be quoted countless times, it was the "switch in time that saved nine."[1] The Court-packing plan had never been popular, and now it was unnecessary as well, so it was defeated in Congress. But the plan had done its work, the story goes, because it persuaded Roberts to change his vote. The result has often been called the constitutional revolution of 1937—an abrupt change in the Court's attitude toward economic regulation.

This story is so incomplete as to be misleading, but it does contain two grains of truth. While these events were taking place, it *was* widely believed that Roberts changed his vote in a deliberate effort to derail the Court-packing plan. One person who believed it was the Harvard law professor Felix Frankfurter, who had long been an informal advisor to Roosevelt and who continued to offer advice during the Court-packing controversy. Frankfurter complained to Roosevelt that "with the shift by Roberts, even a blind man ought to see that the Court is in politics." This accusation turned out to be wrong, at least in its specifics, because although the Court's first decision expressing its new interpretation of the Constitution was published in the midst of the debate over Court-packing, the justices had actually voted in the case several months earlier, before Roosevelt even announced the Court-packing plan. When Roberts changed his mind about the Constitution, he likely did not yet know what the administration had in store. But this revelation did not stop contemporaries from claiming that Roberts had still changed his vote for political reasons, on the theory that after the 1936 election he recognized the popularity of the New Deal. As the journalists Joseph Alsop and Turner Catledge speculated in their 1938 bestseller *The 168 Days*, a blow-by-blow account of the Court-packing plan from its conception to its defeat in Congress, "Roberts may have made his decision to take a hint from the election returns." Roberts insisted for the rest of his life that he had not been influenced by politics. But that is what any judge would say. Historians have been arguing ever since about why Roberts changed his vote.[2]

The other grain of truth is that some of the Court's 1937 decisions cannot be reconciled with decisions from just a year or two earlier. Roberts's change of heart had real consequences. The clearest examples are the minimum wage cases. In June 1936, the Court, by a 5–4 vote, held that New York's minimum wage law was unconstitutional, but in March 1937, after Roberts switched sides, the Court, by another 5–4 vote, upheld the constitutionality of a virtually identical minimum wage law from Washington.[3] Whether or not there was a constitutional "revolution" in 1937, there was certainly a change.

But this tight focus on the events of 1937 obscures as much as it explains, for three reasons. First, the revolution in the Court's approach to the constitutionality of regulation began several years before 1937 and continued several years after. It was a lengthy process, not a sudden event. Second, the change was not unidirectional. It was more of a zigzag than a straight line. At the outset of Roosevelt's first term, the Court was *more* receptive to economic regulation than it would be later. Finally, while Roberts's switch was significant in 1937, it would soon be overwhelmed in importance by personnel changes on the Court. There were no vacancies on the Court during Roosevelt's first five years in office, but between 1937 and 1943 Roosevelt appointed eight new justices, all of whom approved of the New Deal's constitutionality. If Roberts had continued to vote with the conservatives in the spring of 1937, it would have made no difference by the fall, when Roosevelt's first appointee, Hugo Black, took his seat on the Court, because even without Roberts there would have been a 5–4 majority to uphold the New Deal. By 1943, if Roberts still had not changed his mind, he would have been outvoted 8–1. The Court's interpretation of the Constitution would have changed exactly as it did, even if the dramatic events of 1937 had never taken place.[4]

I

As Congress enacted a flurry of legislation in the first few months of Franklin Roosevelt's presidency in an effort to lift the country out of the Great Depression, lawyers within the administration were justifiably wary of how the Supreme Court would treat some of the new statutes. The New Deal rested on a broad conception of the federal government's power over the economy, but most of the justices did not share that conception. Just a few years earlier, for example, the Court had held that Congress lacked the authority to prohibit child labor. Some New Deal programs contemplated restrictions on wages and prices, but the Court had long been skeptical of such limitations, and indeed it had recently invalidated a minimum wage law. The Court's most recent cases offered little hope that the New Deal statutes would receive a more favorable reception. A few months before the 1932 election, the Court struck down a federal tax on gifts and an Oklahoma law requiring a permit to sell ice. Decisions like these did not bode well for the New Deal. Progressives had to "await with ill-concealed concern the decision of the nine old men," observed the Chicago lawyer Mitchell Dawson, to find out whether the New Deal could be put into practice.[5]

The early news from the Court, however, was surprisingly favorable to supporters of the New Deal. The first case to reach the Court after Roosevelt took office involved a state law rather than an initiative of the Roosevelt administration, but it was a state law that was very much in the spirit of the New Deal, in that it was a significant intervention in the economy intended to ameliorate the worst effects of the Depression. Because so many Minnesota homeowners could not make payments on their mortgages, the state legislature declared a two-year moratorium on foreclosures. The moratorium did not relieve borrowers of their debts, but it allowed them to stay in their homes for up to two years if they paid the lender a monthly rental that was set by a judge. In *Home Building & Loan Association v. Blaisdell* (1934), by a 5–4 vote, the Court rejected a lender's argument that the moratorium violated the Constitution's Contracts Clause, which prohibits states from impairing the obligations of contracts. Chief Justice Charles Evans Hughes declared in his opinion for the Court that the meaning of the Constitution should change along with changing circumstances. "There has been a growing appreciation of public needs and of the necessity of finding ground for a rational compromise between individual rights and public welfare," he argued. "If by the statement that what the Constitution meant at the time of its adoption it means to-day, it is intended to say that the great clauses of the Constitution must be confined to the interpretation which the framers, with the conditions and outlook of their time, would have placed upon them, the statement carries its own refutation." The Depression, Hughes concluded, was an "economic emergency which threatened the loss of homes," an emergency "which furnished a proper occasion for the exercise of the reserved power of the state to protect the vital interests of the community." Although the moratorium literally prevented lenders from enforcing a term of their contracts with borrowers, the moratorium did not violate the Contracts Clause.[6]

Justice George Sutherland deplored the result, but he deplored even more the notion that the Constitution's meaning could change over time. "The effect of the Minnesota legislation, though serious enough in itself, is of trivial significance compared with the far more serious and dangerous inroads upon the limitations of the Constitution which are almost certain to ensue," he predicted. The Constitution "does not mean one thing at one time and an entirely different thing at another time." The Contracts Clause had been put into the Constitution during another period of hard times for borrowers, Sutherland explained, precisely to prevent states from succumbing to the inevitable pressure to relieve borrowers from their debts at the expense of lenders. "The provisions of the Federal Constitution, undoubtedly, are pliable in the sense that in appropriate cases they have the capacity of bringing within their grasp every new condition which falls within their meaning," he acknowledged. "But," he insisted, "their meaning is changeless."[7]

Sutherland was joined by the Court's other three most conservative members, Willis Van Devanter, James McReynolds, and Pierce Butler. The four justices would vote together so consistently against the constitutionality of economic regulation that the lawyers in the Roosevelt administration began calling them the "Four Horsemen," after the Biblical Four Horsemen of the Apocalypse. This was a common nickname at the time for groups of four powerful people or forces. One especially well-known example was the backfield of the undefeated 1924 Notre Dame football team, famously dubbed the Four Horsemen by the sportswriter Grantland Rice. (Don Miller, one of Notre Dame's Four Horsemen, became a lawyer in Cleveland after his football career ended and would be appointed by Franklin Roosevelt as the US Attorney for the Northern District of Ohio.) Roosevelt himself was fond of the "four horsemen" metaphor. On the campaign trail in 1932, for instance, he repeatedly referred to "the four horsemen of the present Republican leadership"—Destruction, Delay, Deceit, and Despair.[8]

Two months after *Blaisdell*, by an identical 5–4 vote with the Four Horsemen again in dissent, the Court upheld another state law that closely resembled a New Deal program. Prices were falling in the early 1930s because consumers could not buy as much as before. One common regulatory response was to set price floors. New York, for example, established a Milk Control Board that fixed the price of milk at nine cents per quart. It was unlawful to sell milk for less. Leo Nebbia, a grocer in Rochester, violated the law by selling two quarts of milk plus a loaf of bread for eighteen cents. On appeal, Nebbia challenged the law as inconsistent with due process.[9]

In *Nebbia v. New York* (1934), the Court upheld New York's price floor. The Court had long held that states could regulate prices only in businesses that were "affected with a public interest." In his majority opinion in *Nebbia*, however, Justice Owen Roberts abandoned the public/private distinction in favor of a rule allowing states to set prices in virtually any business. If an "industry is subject to regulation in the public interest," Roberts asked, "what constitutional principle bars the state from correcting existing maladjustments by legislation touching prices? We think there is no such principle. The due process clause makes no mention of sales or of prices." He recast the distinction between businesses that were or were not affected with a public interest as "merely another way of saying that if one embarks in a business which public interest demands shall be regulated, he must know regulation will ensue," a description from which few industries, if any, would be excluded. Roberts concluded that "a state is free to adopt whatever economic policy may reasonably be deemed to promote public welfare, and to enforce that policy by legislation adapted to its purpose."[10] The Court seemed poised to abandon decades of precedent and to allow the government to regulate the economy far more intensively than before.

In his dissent for the Four Horsemen, James McReynolds recognized the astonishing implications of what Roberts had written. "Is the milk business so affected with public interest that the Legislature may prescribe prices for sales by stores?" he asked. Of course not, he concluded: "This Court has approved the contrary view; has emphatically declared that a state lacks power to fix prices in similar private businesses." If the government could set prices for milk, McReynolds pointed out, it could do the same "for farm products, groceries, shoes, clothing, all the necessities of modern civilization, as well as labor, when some Legislature finds and declares such action advisable and for the public good." He concluded: "To adopt such a view, of course, would put an end to liberty under the Constitution."[11]

In *Blaisdell* and *Nebbia*, both decided in early 1934, the Court approved of regulation it would almost certainly have held unconstitutional just a few years before. Contemporaries thought they were seeing the first stage of a permanent change in the Court's approach to the Constitution, a transformation that would see the Court uphold the New Deal measures that were already being challenged in the lower courts. "While Mr. Roosevelt is President," the *New York Times* counseled, "the liberal tendency of the court is certain to be preserved." Within the Roosevelt administration, the *Times* reported, "officials were heartened by the court's decision, which, close as it was, nevertheless indicated to them that the court would sympathize with future legislation, drastic as it might seem." The *Literary Digest* agreed that "the Minnesota and New York cases clearly marked a swing to the left and established the basis for upholding much of the New Deal." The Princeton professor Edward Corwin declared that *Nebbia* was "no less than revolutionary."[12] If these forecasts had been accurate, we might speak today of a "constitutional revolution of 1934" rather than 1937.

When the Court decided its first true New Deal case in early 1935, however, eight of the nine justices found the National Industrial Recovery Act unconstitutional. The NIRA, to prop up prices, authorized trade associations to draft codes of competition, which would acquire the force of law when approved by the president. The oil industry adopted one such code that sought to reduce the supply of oil by establishing production quotas for each oil company. In *Panama Refining Co. v. Ryan* (1935), the Court held that in the NIRA Congress had unconstitutionally delegated its legislative power to the president. The statute "does not state whether or in what circumstances or under what conditions the President is to prohibit the transportation of the amount of petroleum or petroleum products," Hughes noted in his opinion for the Court. Rather, the NIRA "gives to the President an unlimited authority to determine the policy and to lay down the prohibition, or not to lay it down, as he may see fit." Congress could delegate discretion to the president, Hughes explained, and indeed it had on many occasions, particularly in statutes authorizing administrative agencies under the president's control to regulate in various fields. But the NIRA was a step too far. Cardozo was the only dissenter.[13] The Court's opinion implied that all the NIRA's codes of competition were likewise unconstitutional.

Now conventional opinion swung in the opposite direction, as Court-watchers predicted the demise of other New Deal programs. "The anxiety created by the decision was profound," recalled Robert Jackson, who was then a lawyer in the Treasury Department (and who would join the Court himself a few years later). "Many thoughtful persons were unable to understand the decision except as a deliberate forewarning of what was to come." The *New York Herald Tribune* editorialized that "it would be difficult to exaggerate the importance of the decision, coming at this time as the first of the New Deal findings." The paper expected that it would "have a tonic effect upon every judge and every legislator." *Panama Refining* was "accepted in the administration as a warning in the preparation of future legislation," the *New York Times* reported. "It is clear that the highest tribunal has set a semaphore along the crowded legislative thoroughfare of the New Deal."[14]

Panama Refining was announced on a Monday. For the rest of the week, the Court heard oral argument in three cases, known collectively as the *Gold Clause Cases* (1935), that threatened to have a far greater impact on the economy. The Roosevelt administration had made several major changes to the nation's monetary system, one of which was to devalue the dollar by approximately 60% relative to gold. Many existing contracts at the time—contracts between private parties as well as the government's own contracts—included a "gold clause," which entitled creditors to choose to be paid in gold or its equivalent rather than in dollars. The purpose of a gold clause was to protect creditors against exactly what the administration had done, a devaluation of the dollar that would leave them receiving less than they had bargained for if they had to accept dollars in payment. Once the dollar had been devalued, on the other hand, enforcing a gold clause would require the debtor to pay more, in dollars, than the debtor had expected to pay. People, businesses, and even the government earned income in dollars rather than in gold, so if debtors suddenly had to pay 60% more in dollars due to a gold clause, many would have defaulted. For this reason, Congress declared all gold clauses void. The *Gold Clause Cases* were constitutional challenges to this abrogation of gold clauses, brought by creditors who argued that they had been deprived of property without due process.[15]

After *Panama Refining*, administration lawyers were so worried they would lose the *Gold Clause Cases* that Roosevelt drafted an extraordinary speech which he planned to deliver if the Court held that the Constitution barred Congress from abrogating the gold clauses. Roosevelt was ready to declare that the government would disregard the Court's decision. Under the gold clauses, he planned to say, "any attempt to collect in substance one hundred and sixty cents for every dollar owed would have brought universal bankruptcy." Enforcing the gold clauses "would automatically throw practically all the railroads of the United States into bankruptcy," because the railroads would have to pay bondholders $1,600 for every $1,000 the railroads had borrowed. "Towns, cities, counties, and states"—all would have to default on their debts. Homeowners would be unable to pay their mortgages if each payment was 60% larger than before. The federal government's own debt would swell by billions of dollars, which would make it impossible to finance relief programs occasioned by the Depression. "I do not seek to enter into any controversy with the distinguished members of the Supreme Court," Roosevelt intended to say. But "it is the duty of the Congress and the President to protect the people of the United States to the best of their ability." The speech would culminate in a defiant announcement. "To stand idly by and to permit the decision of the Supreme Court to be carried through to its logical, inescapable conclusion would so imperil the economic and political security of this nation," Roosevelt would assert, that the government would have to "look beyond the narrow letter of contractual obligations" and "immediately take such steps as may be necessary."[16]

To his great relief, Roosevelt did not have to deliver this speech. The administration won 5–4, with the Four Horsemen in dissent, in all three of the *Gold Clause Cases*. Hughes's opinion for the Court in the primary case recognized a broad power in the federal government to alter the terms of private contracts. "Contracts, however express, cannot fetter the constitutional authority of the Congress," Hughes declared. "Contracts may create rights of property, but, when contracts deal with a subject-matter which lies within the control of the Congress, they have a congenital infirmity. Parties cannot remove their transactions from the reach of dominant constitutional power by making contracts about them." The public interest, as defined by Congress, took precedence over the provisions of all contracts.[17] For decades, the Court had defended the sanctity of contracts against government interference, but now the Court had allowed the federal government to rewrite a crucial term of countless contracts in every walk of life.

In principle, the Court reached a different outcome regarding the federal government's own contracts. One of the three cases was filed by a man who had purchased Liberty Bonds during the First World War. The bonds, which came due in 1934, included a gold clause. All nine justices agreed that Congress could not eliminate the clause from the government's own obligations. When the government borrowed money on the basis of a promise, the government had to fulfill the promise. The bondholder won this point of principle, but he lost the case, because the Court determined, by the same 5–4 vote as in the other two cases, that the bondholder had suffered no loss by the abrogation of the gold clause. Another of the monetary changes implemented by the administration had been to take gold coins out of circulation, so it was no longer legally possible to be paid in gold. Dollars were the only medium of payment. "In view of the adjustment of the internal economy to the single measure of value," Hughes concluded, "the payment to the plaintiff of the amount which he demands would appear to constitute, not a recoupment of loss in any proper sense, but an unjustified enrichment." Bondholders were entitled only to the face value of their bonds, paid in newly depreciated dollars.[18]

This was "confiscation of property rights and repudiation of national obligations," McReynolds charged in his dissent from all three decisions. "Loss of reputation for honorable dealing will bring us unending humiliation; the impending legal and moral chaos is appalling." When the justices announce their decisions from the bench, they normally read excerpts of their written opinions, but McReynolds was so upset by the *Gold Clause Cases* that he was moved to speak extemporaneously for nearly half an hour. "It seems impossible to overestimate the result of what has been done here today," he lamented. "The Constitution is gone!" "I'll never forget being in the Court on that day," the journalist Marquis Childs recalled many years later. McReynolds's impassioned speech was "the last roar of an old lion who was just inveighing against Roosevelt and the New Deal and the times." Felix Frankfurter, then still a law professor but soon to join the Court himself, was appalled at McReynolds's behavior. "As for the diatribe of McReynolds," he remarked to Justice Harlan Fiske Stone, "I suppose that the poor fellow doesn't know that his kind of stuff does more to undermine public respect for the Constitution and for the Court than all the soap-box oratory of the demagogues."[19]

The *Gold Clause Cases* seemed to be another about-face for the Court. "In the space of one year," Vermont Senator Warren Austin told his mother, "our Supreme Court has changed its position from the strong protector of the citizen's property and rights against his Government to the supporter of the Government against the citizen."[20] As of February 1935, when the *Gold Clause Cases* were decided, the administration had won three of the four major challenges to the New Deal and its state analogues—*Blaisdell*, *Nebbia*, and the *Gold Clause Cases*. Its sole loss had been in *Panama Refining*, in which the Court had faulted only the NIRA's extreme delegation of authority to the president. But then the Court changed direction yet again. For the rest of 1935 and through 1936, the Court would consistently rule against the constitutionality of New Deal programs. The administration would lose one big case after another.

The first statute to fall was the Railroad Retirement Act, which set up a pension scheme for railroad employees funded by contributions from the employees and the railroads. In *Railroad Retirement Board v. Alton Railroad Co.* (1935), five justices, the Four Horsemen plus Roberts, held that the Act deprived the railroads of property without due process and exceeded Congress's power under the Commerce Clause. Harlan Fiske Stone, referring to *Lochner v. New York*, privately referred to the majority opinion as "the worst performance of the Court since the Bake Shop Case."[21]

Soon after, on a single day in May 1935, the administration lost three cases, all unanimously. In *Schechter Poultry Corp. v. United States* (1935), the Court struck down what remained of the NIRA. In *Louisville Joint Stock Land Bank v. Radford* (1935), the Court invalidated the Frazier-Lemke Act, a statute meant to protect bankrupt farmers against the foreclosure of their farms. And in *Humphrey's Executor v. United States* (1935), the Court held that Roosevelt lacked the power to remove a commissioner of the Federal Trade Commission before the expiration of the commissioner's seven-year term. Louis Brandeis, who maintained discreet communication with lawyers in the administration, immediately summoned Benjamin Cohen and Thomas Corcoran, two of Roosevelt's primary legal advisors, to the Court. "You must understand that these three decisions change everything," an agitated Brandeis told them. "The President has been living in a fool's paradise."[22]

The next year saw more New Deal programs fall. The Agricultural Adjustment Act, one of the statutes enacted in the first hundred days of Roosevelt's presidency, was a complex system of taxes and expenditures intended to support commodity prices. In *United States v. Butler* (1936), a six-justice majority held that the Act exceeded Congress's power under the Commerce Clause. The Bituminous Coal Conservation Act created a similar plan of regulation for the coal industry. A 5–4 Court struck it down, also on Commerce Clause grounds, in *Carter v. Carter Coal Co.* (1936). Meanwhile, in *Morehead v. Tipaldo* (1936), the Court held, by another 5–4 vote, that New York's minimum wage law for women violated the Due Process Clause.[23] The Four Horsemen were in the majority in each of these cases, joined by Roberts and, in *Butler*, by Hughes.

Depending on one's political views, the Court was either obstinately blocking the nation's progress or bravely defending the American way of life against socialism. After Brandeis dissented in *Butler*, he received letters from both sides. "I want to express my appreciation," wrote one rural minister. "I wonder if the Supreme Court sat in Omaha and got the Farmers' slant, if more of the Judges would not have agreed with you—as they ought." But a Philadelphian "was mortified to note you voted against the majority in the A.A.A. case. . . . As one Jew to another," he confided, "I am afraid you have placed the Jews on the spot." A history teacher from Atlanta offered a combination of praise and criticism. "I am sorry you saw it your duty to uphold the AAA, but I am glad you helped destroy the wretched NRA," she told Brandeis. "In these days when politicians are thirsting for power and dictators are the style, the only thing that safeguards the people is the Constitution." She saw "grave dangers lurking about. The so-called New Deal is harming the boys and girls of this country, because it encourages the policy of getting something for nothing."[24]

More constitutional challenges to New Deal programs were in the pipe-line, from litigants emboldened by the Court's decisions. "The aftermath of numerous recent Supreme Court decisions is a general attitude of law defi-ance," Thomas Corcoran observed. "Even in the most conservative circles," he complained, "the Constitution is simply a respectable refuge for upper-class rogues." Even New Deal statutes the Court had not invalidated, such as the two securities acts of 1933 and 1934, were getting bogged down in litiga-tion. "A law used to be *the* law until proven otherwise," Corcoran grumbled. "A law is now *the* law only after every last detail has been fought through every last court. Agencies that ought to be smoothly functioning adminis-trative institutions are completely dominated—as the price of survival—by their legal fighting machines. There isn't any civilian population down here—everyone's in the fighting forces."[25]

There had already been discussions within the Roosevelt administration about taking some kind of action to stop the Court from reaching decisions like these. Several ideas were in circulation by late 1935. One was for Congress to enact a statute withdrawing the Court's jurisdiction over the types of cases that were proving troublesome. The Court had capitulated to such a statute in *Ex parte McCardle* (1868), when Congress had prevented the Court from de-ciding the legality of Reconstruction by removing the Court's power to hear appeals in habeas corpus cases. The Justice Department advised Roosevelt, in response to his request, that the tactic would work again. A second pos-sibility was a constitutional amendment, or a group of amendments, that would grant Congress the regulatory authority the Court had found lacking. This was the strategy that had been used after the Court held in *Pollock v. Farmers' Loan & Trust Co.* (1895) that Congress could not establish an income tax. The Sixteenth Amendment, ratified in 1913, gave Congress that authority. A third option was a different sort of constitutional amendment, one that would allow Congress to reenact a statute the Court had held un-constitutional, after an intervening congressional election. "By this method," Secretary of the Interior Harold Ickes noted, "there would be in effect a ref-erendum to the country" on whether Congress's view of the Constitution would prevail over the Court's. "I think there is much to commend this idea," Ickes wrote in his diary in December 1935. "I have long believed that the Supreme Court should at the very least have the power it has usurped to de-clare laws unconstitutional seriously curtailed. As the President remarked, if all the New Deal legislation is thrown out, there will be marching farmers and marching miners and marching workingmen throughout the land."[26]

These potential measures all had shortcomings, however. A statute curtailing the Court's jurisdiction would have to be interpreted by the Court itself. The justices who repeatedly found the New Deal unconstitutional might well decide that a withdrawal of their jurisdiction was unconstitutional as well. And it was very hard to amend the Constitution. To be sure, there had been six successful amendments in the past twenty-two years, the most in such a short span of time since the original ten amendments were ratified back in 1791. But some of the recent amendments had lingered as proposals for many years before being adopted, and there had been many other proposed amendments that had failed to get the required two-thirds vote of both houses of Congress or had failed to be ratified by the requisite three-fourths of states. There was no guarantee that a constitutional amendment could be ratified quickly enough to implement the New Deal. "To get a two-thirds vote" in Congress, "this year or next year, on any type of amendment is next to impossible," Roosevelt estimated in early 1937. Even if that could be done, "the same forces which are now calling for the amendment process would turn around and fight ratification on the simple ground that they do not like the particular amendment adopted by the Congress." People who thought the administration's problems with the Court could be solved by a constitutional amendment "do not know the practical difficulties," Roosevelt concluded.[27]

One more proposal was also in circulation—a statute to expand the Court, which would allow Roosevelt to appoint several new justices all at once. This was "a distasteful idea," Ickes admitted in his diary.[28] Congress had the power to alter the number of justices and it had done so several times in the past. The expansion from six justices to seven in 1807, then to nine in 1837, and then to ten in 1863, had been to keep up with the number of circuits as the country grew larger. Twice Congress had reduced the size of the Court to prevent a president from making appointments. In 1801, the outgoing Federalist Congress shrunk the Court from six justices to five to take an appointment away from the incoming president, Thomas Jefferson, but this measure was promptly repealed by the next Congress. In 1866, Congress reduced the Court from ten justices to seven to deprive Andrew Johnson of the appointment power. Three years later, once Johnson was no longer president, Congress set the Court's size at nine. There had been nine seats on the Court ever since. These were the only episodes in which Congress had changed the size of the Court for political purposes. No president had ever tried to pack the Court by increasing the number of justices.

If Court-packing was distasteful, however, it was also the only option that could be accomplished quickly and that could not be blocked by the justices themselves. Supporters of the New Deal began encouraging Roosevelt to pack the Court. "Increase number of jurists in Supreme Court," urged a telegram from Brooklyn. Another from San Francisco reported: "Vast numbers of people on the Pacific Coast urge your immediate appointment of a sufficient increase in the membership of the Supreme Court to more nearly reflect public welfare progress and necessities." The decision to pack the Court, Roosevelt later acknowledged, "was arrived at by a process of elimination," as the least objectionable of the available alternatives.[29]

II

The 1936 election was a triumph for Roosevelt and the Democrats. Roosevelt won the electoral vote by 523 to 8. Only two states, Maine and Vermont, voted for Kansas governor Alf Landon, the Republican candidate. No president had won a greater percentage of the electoral vote since James Monroe ran unopposed in 1820. In the Senate, Democrats outnumbered Republicans 74 to 17, while in the House, the margin was 334 to 88. Congress had not been so lopsided since Reconstruction. The election was a demonstration of popular support for the New Deal. If there was ever a time to pack the Court, this was it.

Administration lawyers still had qualms, however, about expanding the Court so transparently for the purpose of adding justices who would support the constitutionality of New Deal programs. The independence of the judiciary from political manipulation was a cherished value. Of course, when vacancies arose on the Court, presidents had always sought to appoint justices who shared their views, but appointing several new justices at once, when there were no vacancies, felt different. In recent years, authoritarian governments in the Soviet Union, Italy, and Germany had forced their judiciaries to adhere to the views of the ruling party. These did not seem like good models to follow. What was needed was a way for Roosevelt to pack the Court, but for a stated reason other than his disagreement with the justices' decisions.

That reason would be the justices' age. Critics of the Court had always lampooned the justices as elderly men who were out of touch with modern conditions and who were no longer up to the job. Typical of this tradition was

The Nine Old Men, a gossipy bestseller about the Court by the Washington columnists Drew Pearson and Robert Allen, which had just been published in the fall of 1936. Pearson and Allen were steady supporters of Roosevelt in his battles with the Court. They described George Sutherland, who was then seventy-four, as "old even beyond his advanced years." Sutherland's "manner of thinking," they charged, "dates back to those days that are dead and gone. His economic and social theories are as up to date as the moldy opera house" of the Utah town in which he had grown up. Their verdict on the chief justice was similar. "To outward appearances Hughes has not aged," they smirked. "It is only when you examine Hughes's perspectives that you realize how fast he is slipping."[30] Old age was a plausible, nonpartisan reason the justices might need some help.

Roosevelt's lawyers were not the first to suggest using the justices' age as an excuse to appoint more of them. In 1869, the House of Representatives considered a bill that would have added a new justice for each sitting justice who reached the age of seventy and did not retire. The purpose of the bill was to allow President Grant to appoint two new Republican justices to counterbalance the Court's only two Democrats, Robert Grier and Samuel Nelson, the only two justices over seventy. In 1913, the Annual Report of the Attorney General made the same recommendation for the lower federal courts, ostensibly because there so many judges over seventy who could no longer handle the workload.[31] The author of this report was none other than James McReynolds, then Woodrow Wilson's fifty-one-year-old attorney general, but now a seventy-four-year-old justice the administration dearly wished to replace.

The Justice Department drafted a bill that authorized the president to appoint a new judge for each existing judge over the age of seventy who declined to retire. In its final form, the bill applied to all federal judges, not merely the justices of the Supreme Court. To avoid the infinite expansion of the judiciary (which would have happened if the new judges also stayed in office past seventy), the number of new justices was capped at six, new circuit judges were limited to two per circuit, and the number of new district judges could not exceed the existing number in any district. These provisions were combined with several other efficiency measures that would be less controversial, such as one authorizing circuit judges to be temporarily assigned to other circuits that were falling behind on their cases, so the bill could be packaged as a nonpolitical reform of the judiciary as a whole.[32] There were six justices over seventy—all but Stone, Roberts, and Cardozo—so the immediate effect of the bill, if none of the six retired, would have been to expand the Court to fifteen justices. The 5–4 majorities against the New Deal would have become 10–5 majorities in its favor.

Roosevelt announced the plan in February 1937. It was not a popular proposal. Press coverage was generally unfavorable and public opinion polling consistently found more opposition than support. "This is a bloodless coup d'etat," charged the influential columnist Walter Lippmann. By packing the Court, Roosevelt "would not have to submit amendments to the people. The new court would make the Constitution mean what he wishes it to mean." Even some of Roosevelt's closest legal advisors, who were obliged to support the plan in public, were privately opposed to it. So were many of the lawyers staffing the New Deal agencies. "None of us had any forewarning and we were appalled," remembered Milton Katz, a lawyer in the National Recovery Administration. "We reacted to it as a bewildering attack on the integrity and independence of the judiciary. We talked about it in such terms as 'This is lunacy. What's going on?'" Some of Roosevelt's old friends felt the same way. "You can't feel more strongly than I do about the majority opinions, especially AAA, Minimum Wage and Roberts J's silly talk about railroad pensions," the lawyer Charles Burlingham wrote to Roosevelt. "BUT I don't like your method." Most important of all, the plan was unpopular in Congress, even among Democrats. Just a few days after Roosevelt announced the plan, Hatton Sumners, the chair of the House Judiciary Committee, already called it "infamous."[33] Other prominent Democrats in Congress declared their opposition.

The plan's ostensible purpose, to assist the elderly justices who were behind on their work, was so clearly a fiction that some supporters of the bill abandoned the claim very quickly. Roosevelt was trying "to change the complexion of a reactionary Court," admitted Hugh Johnson, the former head of the National Recovery Administration, in a radio address only two days after the plan was announced. "What is wrong with that? This *is* a reactionary Court." In March, when Roosevelt devoted one of his "fireside chats" to the Court-packing plan, he likewise conceded that the main problem was not the justices' age but their decisions. "The Court in addition to the proper use of its judicial functions has improperly set itself up as a third house of the Congress," Roosevelt complained, "a super-legislature, as one of the justices has called it—reading into the Constitution words and implications which are not there, and which were never intended to be there."[34]

Figure 10.1 President Franklin Roosevelt promotes his Court-packing plan in a "fireside chat" on the radio in March 1937. A few weeks later, the Court began finding New Deal programs constitutional. Library of Congress, LC-DIG-hec-47304.

The justices all hated the Court-packing plan. Cardozo was "considerably shaken" when he heard the news, his law clerk recalled. When Brandeis found out, he said the president had made a great mistake. And these were Roosevelt's allies on the Court. The justices Roosevelt was trying to push off the Court were even less happy. When a person "has presented his case to a fair tribunal and lost, he should be a good sport," McReynolds argued in a widely reported speech to fellow alumni of his college fraternity. "It is difficult to understand this willful opportunism." His own decisions had been evenhanded, McReynolds insisted; he had given equal consideration to "the poorest darky in the Georgia backwoods as well as the man in the mansion of Fifth avenue." Roberts planned to resign if the bill became law, even though, as the youngest justice, he would be the last to be personally affected by it.

Hughes decided he would stick it out, no matter how large the Court became. "If they want me to preside over a convention," he grimly joked, "I can do it."[35]

In March, as the Senate Judiciary Committee prepared to hold hearings on the Court-packing bill, Senate opponents of the bill invited Hughes to testify, to explain that the Court in fact was not behind on its work and did not need any additional members. Hughes consulted Brandeis, who was strongly opposed to any justice appearing before the committee. When Hughes suggested that he could write a letter to the committee instead, Brandeis agreed, as did Willis Van Devanter, the only other justice Hughes asked. Hughes promptly advised the leaders of the Senate opposition to the bill, Burton Wheeler of Montana and William King of Utah, that he was prepared to furnish the Senate with a letter. Hughes later claimed that there was not enough time to consult any of the other justices, but this seems unlikely. They all had telephones. Even if it was too late to get agreement on the letter's precise wording, it would have been possible for Hughes to ask his other colleagues whether he should send a letter at all. The fact that he did not suggests that he suspected they might disagree. The other six justices learned of the letter only when they read about it in the newspaper.[36]

"I have here now a letter by the Chief Justice of the Supreme Court," Wheeler announced with great fanfare at the Judiciary Committee hearings. He read Hughes's letter aloud. "The Supreme Court is fully abreast of its work," Hughes informed the committee. "There is no congestion of cases upon our calendar. This gratifying condition has obtained for several years." Hughes then turned to the Court-packing plan. "An increase in the number of justices of the Supreme Court," he explained, "would not promote the efficiency of the Supreme Court." More justices would only mean "more judges to confer, more judges to discuss, more judges to be convinced and to decide. The present number of justices is thought to be large enough." Wheeler's revelation of Hughes's letter was front-page news. The letter "created a sensation," one typical story reported. It was "a serious blow to the Administration plan to enlarge the Court."[37]

The justices landed another serious blow to the Court-packing plan a week later, although, unlike Hughes's letter, the timing of this one was accidental. In *West Coast Hotel Co. v. Parrish* (1937), decided in late March, the Court astonished the legal community by holding that states could impose a minimum wage. The case had been lingering at the Court longer than usual. It had been argued back in mid-December. The Court's practice at the time was to discuss the cases and vote on them on the Saturday after the argument. But Stone was not there—he was in the midst of what would be a four-month absence from the Court caused by severe dysentery. The eight justices present divided four to four. When Stone returned to work in February, he finally cast the fifth vote in favor of the constitutionality of minimum wage laws. Now the opinions could be written. The Court's decision was published in March.[38] Had Stone not been ill, the decision would likely have been published in late January or early February, either soon before or soon after the announcement of the Court-packing plan.

It had barely been nine months since the Court had decided by a 5–4 vote in *Morehead v. Tipaldo* that a minimum wage violated the Due Process Clause. In *West Coast Hotel* the Court decided, also by a 5–4 vote, that it did not. Roberts was the justice who changed his vote. Hughes's majority opinion was explicit about the Court's new direction. The Court's earlier minimum wage cases, he declared, had been "a departure from the true application of the principles governing the regulation by the state of the relation of employer and employed." Under a proper interpretation of the Due Process Clause, Hughes reasoned, "the Legislature was entitled to adopt measures to reduce the evils of the 'sweating system,' the exploiting of workers at wages so low as to be insufficient to meet the bare cost of living." A state's decision to protect employees against exploitation "cannot be regarded as arbitrary or capricious and that is all we have to decide. Even if the wisdom of the policy be regarded as debatable and its effects uncertain, still the Legislature is entitled to its judgment."[39]

In dissent for the Four Horsemen, Sutherland criticized the majority's willingness to find new meanings in old constitutional texts. "The meaning of the Constitution does not change with the ebb and flow of economic events," he argued. To say "that the words of the Constitution mean today what they did not mean when written—that is, that they do not apply to a situation now to which they would have applied then—is to rob that instrument of the essential element which continues it in force." If the Constitution was out of date, Sutherland suggested, it could be amended. But "the judicial function is that of interpretation; it does not include the power of amendment under the guise of interpretation."[40]

West Coast Hotel was widely perceived in the press as undermining the rationale for Court-packing, because now the Court seemed favorably disposed to the constitutionality of regulation. The Court had zigged and zagged in its interpretation of the Constitution for as long as Roosevelt had been president, but not this sharply. "Wrecks Argument For Packing Supreme Court" screamed the headline in the *Chicago Daily Tribune*. To be sure, lawyers could cite a technical reason for Roberts's apparent change of heart—the Court had been asked to overrule its prior cases in *West Coast Hotel* but not in *Morehead*—but, as the *New York Times* noted, "to laymen that will seem a fine point, indeed, virtually invisible." Senate majority leader Joseph Robinson, the leading advocate for Court-packing in Congress, nevertheless planned to continue the fight. "He thinks the Supreme Court should be packed when it invalidates New Deal legislation and he thinks it should be packed when it upholds New Deal legislation," joked the columnist Franklyn Waltman. "You just cannot satisfy some people."[41]

Two weeks later, the Court did it again. In *National Labor Relations Board v. Jones & Laughlin Steel Corp.* (1937), by the same 5–4 vote, the Court rejected a Commerce Clause challenge to the National Labor Relations Act, an important New Deal statute that guaranteed the right of workers to form labor unions. Again, it was Roberts who changed his vote. For decades, the Court had drawn a distinction between commerce, which Congress could regulate, and production, the regulation of which was reserved to the states. The Court had recently struck down the National Industrial Recovery Act in *Schechter Poultry* and the Bituminous Coal Conservation Act in *Carter* on the ground that in both statutes Congress was impermissibly attempting to govern production rather than commerce. Now, however, the Court allowed Congress to set ground rules for labor relations in a wide range of industries, with little regard to the distinction between commerce and production. "The fact that the employees here concerned were engaged in production is not determinative," Hughes concluded in his majority opinion.[42]

The Four Horsemen dissented again, this time in an opinion by McReynolds, who pointed out that the decision could not be reconciled with *Schechter Poultry* or *Carter*. The employers who challenged the National Labor Relations Act "happen to be manufacturing concerns," he emphasized; they were companies that were engaged in production, not commerce. If Congress could constitutionally regulate these businesses, it could likewise regulate "a great variety of private enterprises—mercantile, manufacturing, publishing, stock-raising, mining, etc." The Act "puts into the hands of a Board power of control over purely local industry beyond anything heretofore deemed permissible." If Congress could govern activities that merely *affected* commerce, McReynolds worried, then Congress could govern nearly everything, because "almost anything—marriage, birth, death—may in some fashion affect commerce." McReynolds was so upset by the Court's decision that while announcing his dissent in court he added a great deal of material that did not appear in his text, as he had in the *Gold Clause Cases* two years before. "The raising of pigs in Iowa—whether there are more or less pigs in Iowa—may interfere with interstate commerce between Iowa and Chicago, but does that give congress the right to regulate the man who tends the pig sties?" McReynolds asked. "Whether wheat is raised in North Dakota affects interstate commerce, but does that give congress the right to say you shall raise more wheat or less wheat?" Ultimately, he wondered, "are our states obliterated?"[43]

Jones & Laughlin was argued shortly after Roosevelt announced the Court-packing plan, which meant that the justices voted on the case with knowledge of the plan, unlike in *West Coast Hotel*. Now there was even more reason to suspect that Roberts had changed his vote in an effort to defeat the plan. "This would not have happened three months ago before the agitation about the Supreme Court," the California senator Hiram Johnson complained. "I think they voted right this time, but I have damn little respect for them. In my opinion they permitted themselves to be bludgeoned into voting to sustain the Act." Felix Frankfurter likewise favored the outcome of *Jones & Laughlin*, but when he saw the decision, he sent a telegram to Roosevelt that read in its entirety: "After today I feel like finding some honest profession to enter." And now there was even less reason to increase the size of the Court. "The court has, for the second time in two weeks, taken the wind out of the court-packing plan," as one journalist put it. "Proponents of the plan have heard most of their arguments answered by the Chief Justice."[44] If a nine-justice Court was prepared to uphold the New Deal, there was no need for a fifteen-justice Court.

The final blow to the Court-packing plan came in mid-May, when Willis Van Devanter, the oldest of the Four Horsemen, announced his retirement. Van Devanter was seventy-eight years old. He had been on the Court since 1910, longer than any of his colleagues. With his departure, Roosevelt would finally be able to appoint a new justice without having to make the Court any larger.

Van Devanter's retirement was the intended result of the administration's work to alter the terms of the justices' pensions. Since 1869, a justice who reached the age of seventy and who had served for ten years was entitled to receive a pension equal to his salary when he resigned. In 1932, however, as a cost-cutting measure in the midst of the Depression, Congress reduced the salaries and pensions of all federal employees, except for "judges whose compensation may not, under the Constitution, be diminished during their continuance in office."[45] (Article III, section 1 of the Constitution says that the compensation of federal judges "shall not be diminished during their Continuance in Office.") This exception suddenly, and probably inadvertently, rendered significant a previously obscure difference between the retirement provisions for Supreme Court justices and for lower federal judges. Lower court judges could choose either to *resign* or to *retire*. If they resigned, they were no longer employed as judges. If they retired, by contrast, they were relieved of some of their duties, but they were still classified as judges who could hear cases. There was no such option for the justices of the Supreme Court. They could resign, but they could not retire. The reason for the difference was that in the lower courts, help from a retired judge was welcome, but in the Supreme Court, it would have been extremely awkward for retired justices to continue working on the Court's cases.

This difference abruptly became important in 1932 because the judges whose compensation was constitutionally protected from diminution included active judges and retired judges but not judges who had resigned. The only living ex-justice entitled to a pension at the time was Oliver Wendell Holmes, who had resigned only a few months before. His annual pension was cut in half from $20,000 to $10,000. Holmes was a wealthy man, so it was not a meaningful loss to him. "Justice Holmes probably doesn't mind," the Associated Press reported. "His private fortune is ample and his sense of humor still is keen. He is at his Summer home in Massachusetts now." But Holmes's admirers were outraged at how poorly Holmes had been treated. Some of those admirers were powerful enough to take action. "I think I have started something going which will result in a restoration of Mr. Justice Holmes's retirement allowance," Harlan Fiske Stone wrote to Felix Frankfurter. Frankfurter was glad to hear it. "He does not need the money," Frankfurter replied, "but the country's honor cannot afford the diminution of the expression of its gratitude that the pension implies." Congress restored Holmes's full pension.[46]

The episode was a sobering experience for the other justices, who realized that their pensions were at the mercy of an often-hostile Congress. Van Devanter had been planning to resign in 1932, but he changed his mind when Holmes lost half his pension. "I do not like the idea of losing half of my salary by retiring," he told his sister, "and therefore I am reconsidering my former purpose." The precarity of the justices' pensions caused George Sutherland to delay his retirement as well. Lawyers in the Roosevelt administration, who were eager to see Van Devanter and Sutherland go, were aware of the issue. While they were preparing the Court-packing bill, they also prepared a second bill that received much less attention, one that would allow justices to "retire" as well as "resign." In March 1937, while the Court-packing plan was being loudly debated in Congress and in the press, Congress quietly enacted the second bill, which granted to the justices "the same rights and privileges with regard to retiring, instead of resigning" that lower court judges already enjoyed. Retired justices would not be able to participate in Supreme Court cases, but they could serve on the circuit courts if they wished to.[47]

Van Devanter promptly *retired* (he did not resign) at the first opportunity, when the Court's 1936–1937 term came to an end. In his letter to Roosevelt, he was careful to specify that "I desire to avail myself of the rights, privileges

Figure 10.2 Willis Van Devanter speaks with the press after announcing his retirement. The opportunity to retire with a secure pension encouraged Van Devanter and George Sutherland, two consistent opponents of the constitutionality of New Deal programs, to leave the Court. Library of Congress, LC-DIG-hec-22726.

and judicial service" mentioned in the new statute. Sutherland retired less than a year later, with the same declaration.[48] The guarantee of a secure pension was the encouragement they needed to leave the Court.

With Van Devanter's retirement, there was no longer any reason to appoint extra justices. The Court drove the point home in late May with two more 5–4 decisions upholding the constitutionality of the Social Security Act, which established the nationwide system of old-age benefits that is still in existence. The Senate Judiciary Committee rejected the Court-packing bill in June, calling it "a needless, futile, and utterly dangerous abandonment of constitutional principle."[49] The Court would carry on with nine justices. The idea of Court-packing remained in disrepute for many years thereafter.

III

The Court's personnel changed almost completely in the few years after Willis Van Devanter retired. George Sutherland retired in January 1938. Benjamin Cardozo died in July 1938. Louis Brandeis retired in February 1939. Pierce Butler died in November 1939. James McReynolds, the last of the Four Horsemen, retired in January 1941. When Charles Evans Hughes retired in June 1941, Harlan Fiske Stone and Owen Roberts were the only holdovers from the Court that had bedeviled the Roosevelt administration between 1933 and 1937. Roosevelt filled seven seats on the Court in less than four years.

The seven justices Roosevelt appointed between 1937 and 1941 were all political allies with no judicial experience. "I want progressives on the Bench who will remain progressives long after I am out of office," he remarked to Clarence Dill, a senator from Washington." Hugo Black, his first appointment, was a senator from Alabama who had been a loyal supporter of Roosevelt's programs, including the Court-packing plan. The choice was controversial due to Black's partisanship and lack of relevant experience, and then it became even more controversial when he turned out to be a former member of the Ku Klux Klan. Black was so unfamiliar with the workings of the Court that his new colleagues had to correct his elementary mistakes. "It is usually inadvisable," Stone gently told him on one occasion after Black circulated a draft opinion, "to write a case reversing a state court on points involving state law which were not considered or decided by the court below." Stone ended up writing the Court's opinion himself.[50] Black would overcome this inauspicious start to become one of the Court's longest serving justices and one of its leading defenders of civil liberties.

Roosevelt appointed Stanley Reed a few months later to replace Sutherland. Reed had spent the past few years as solicitor general, the lawyer who represents the federal government in the Supreme Court, so he had argued many of the New Deal cases. He had also helped design the Court-packing plan. Few lawyers, if any, were better prepared to support New Deal measures as a justice. The same was true of Felix Frankfurter, Roosevelt's next appointee. Frankfurter, a law professor at Harvard, had been an informal advisor for many years and had placed several of his former students in important positions in the administration. By appointing Reed and Frankfurter, Roosevelt in effect placed his own lawyers on the Court.

More political allies soon followed. William Douglas was the chair of the Securities and Exchange Commission, the New Deal agency that regulated the stock market. With the retirement of Van Devanter and Sutherland, there were no longer any justices from the West. Although Douglas had spent scarcely any time in his native state of Washington since heading east for law school in the early 1920s, geographic representation on the Court had become a matter of symbolism, not substance. Administration officials were careful to check with western senators before Roosevelt chose Douglas. William Borah of Idaho, the longest-serving senator at the time, "considers William O. Douglas a Westerner," they were happy to learn. Borah assured them that Douglas "would generally be considered as in all respects satisfying the demand for the appointment of a Western man."[51] Douglas was only forty, which made him the youngest justice to join the Court since Joseph Story in 1812. With the benefit of such an early start, Douglas would set the record for tenure as a justice—more than thirty-six years.

Roosevelt's next appointment was Frank Murphy, the former governor of Michigan. Murphy had been Roosevelt's attorney general for the past year, but he did poorly in the position. "Murphy had no administrative competence. He was vain, self-conscious, and avid for publicity," recalled Francis Biddle, one of his successors. "I have no idea why the president liked Frank Murphy, but he did." Lawyers in the administration, one of them explained, thought Roosevelt meant to "kick Attorney General Murphy upstairs because of the miserable way he is running the Department of Justice." Murphy's reputation did not improve when he joined the Court. "He was way over his head in court work," remembered Robert Jackson, his successor as attorney general and later his colleague on the Court. "He didn't care greatly for the law. . . . He used to tell me that he wasn't a lawyer." The oft-told joke was that Murphy was so bad at the job that in his opinions, justice was "tempered with Murphy."[52] But appointing Murphy was prudent politics. The vacancy existed because of the death of Pierce Butler, the Court's only Catholic and only Midwesterner. Murphy ticked both boxes. When he took his seat in February 1940, five of the nine justices, a majority of the Court, were Roosevelt appointees. Only three years had passed since Roosevelt's announcement of the Court-packing plan.

When Charles Evans Hughes retired in 1941, Roosevelt appointed Harlan Fiske Stone as chief justice. Stone had been on the Court for sixteen years. He was already nearly seventy and would live only five years longer. Although he was a Republican and a close associate of Herbert Hoover—he had been part of Hoover's "medicine-ball cabinet," a group of officials who joined Hoover at the White House to exercise in the mornings—Stone had also been one of Roosevelt's teachers in law school. That experience, along with Stone's support for the constitutionality of New Deal programs, seems to have aroused genuine admiration on the part of Roosevelt. "I sat at his feet at Columbia Law School when he was a very young professor and I have never regretted it," Roosevelt told Zechariah Chafee, another law professor, shortly after he made the appointment. Stone was a popular choice within the administration. "Probably no one will tell you," Roosevelt's assistant James Rowe informed him, "but 19 out of 20 of your own New Deal lawyers hoped you would make Mr. Justice Stone the Chief Justice." The appointment briefly focused unaccustomed press attention on Stone. "At the moment I am pursued by reporters and photographers until I am nearly worn out," he complained to Hughes. "If you see a photograph of me in the bathtub don't be surprised."[53]

Roosevelt filled Stone's seat with Robert Jackson, who had replaced Murphy the year before as attorney general, after several years in other government positions. Jackson had been close with Roosevelt for a long time. Roosevelt even hoped that Jackson would succeed him as president and had unsuccessfully tried to generate support among New York Democrats to elect Jackson as governor. At nearly the same time as Jackson's appointment, Roosevelt also appointed James Byrnes to fill the vacancy created by the retirement of McReynolds. Byrnes was a senator from South Carolina who had been a staunch New Deal supporter. As New Jersey Governor A. Harry Moore urged Roosevelt, Byrnes deserved to be a justice because he "has always been your friend and, at your behest, carried many fights to victory on the floor of the Senate."[54] Of the seven new justices Roosevelt had appointed in the past four years, four (Reed, Murphy, Douglas, and Jackson) were lawyers from his own administration, two (Black and Byrnes) were senators who could be counted on to vote for the administration's measures, and one (Frankfurter) was a trusted legal advisor who was also certain to support the constitutionality of the New Deal. Roosevelt ended up packing the Court, but not in the way he expected to.

Byrnes left the Court after only a year to head the Office of Economic Stabilization, an agency created during the Second World War. Roosevelt's final appointment to the Court, as a replacement for Byrnes, was Wiley Rutledge. Rutledge had been a court of appeals judge for four years after a career as a law professor and dean at the University of Iowa and Washington University in St. Louis. As a dean, Rutledge had been a vocal proponent of the Court-packing plan. Stone, also a former law dean, urged Roosevelt— with a thinly veiled dig at Black and Murphy—to choose Rutledge because "it was important not only to appoint a liberal but a scholar who could express liberal decisions in an appropriate way."[55] After filling the Court with justices who would vote to uphold New Deal programs, Roosevelt had the luxury to pick someone who was also known for his abilities as a judge.

One candidate for the seat that went to Rutledge was Learned Hand, the most highly regarded lower court judge in the country. Hand had nearly become a justice back in 1930. When William Howard Taft retired that year, Hoover considered promoting Stone to chief justice and appointing Hand to fill Stone's seat. In the end he replaced Taft with Hughes instead. When Byrnes left the Court in 1942, Frankfurter nagged Roosevelt to appoint Hand, whom he called "*the* one choice who will arouse universal acclaim in the press." Francis Biddle told Roosevelt that Hand was "head and shoulders above the others."[56] But Hand was already seventy years old. He would have been the oldest appointee in history. And during the Court-packing controversy, Roosevelt had staked a great deal of political capital on the proposition that justices over the age of seventy were too old for the job. Had he appointed Hand, it would have been an admission that his ostensible reason for packing the Court was a lie. Wiley Rutledge was only forty-eight. As it turned out, Rutledge would die of a stroke in 1949, while Hand remained an active judge until 1961.

In the six years between 1937 and 1943, Roosevelt thus made nine appointments to the Court—eight new justices plus the elevation of Stone to chief justice. No president has ever transformed the Court so thoroughly. In 1937 the Court had been to the right of the country as a whole, but by 1943

Figure 10.3 Hugo and Josephine Black arrive at Pierce Butler's funeral in 1939. Black was one of eight new justices appointed by Franklin Roosevelt between 1937 and 1943 to succeed Butler and the Court's other conservatives. Library of Congress, LC-DIG-hec-27676.

it was to the left, and it would stay that way for some time. With all these new justices, the Court continued its repudiation of older precedents authorizing judges to assess the need for economic regulation. The Court began instead to interpret the Constitution to allow Congress and state legislatures to regulate the economy in virtually any way they saw fit. "The attitude of the Supreme Court toward constitutional questions has entirely changed," Thomas Corcoran exulted. "The personnel of the Supreme Court has been liberalized and is now made up of a majority of justices with a consistently progressive outlook."[57]

For example, in *United States v. Carolene Products* (1938), the Court upheld the Filled Milk Act, in which Congress prohibited the interstate shipment of skimmed milk mixed with any oil or fat other than milk fat. This was the kind of statute that would have vexed a majority of the Court just a few years before. The justices would have asked whether "filled milk" was truly unhealthy and whether customers were actually deceived, because a reviewing court was supposed to decide whether the statute genuinely protected the public health or whether the dairy industry was merely seeking to suppress competition. But now there was a seven-justice majority in favor of deferring to Congress. "The existence of facts supporting the legislative judgment is to be presumed," Stone declared in his opinion for the Court. He suggested in a footnote—one that would be quoted frequently in later years—that judicial review should be more searching where legislation discriminated against "discrete and insular minorities."[58] This was a declaration of a new role for the Court. It would review economic regulation deferentially, under a standard that few statutes could fail to satisfy, but it would look harder at legislation that infringed noneconomic rights.

The Court continued down this road in *United States v. Darby* (1941) by upholding the Fair Labor Standards Act, which established a nationwide minimum wage and maximum work week. Under then-existing precedent, particularly *Hammer v. Dagenhart* (1918), the Act exceeded the power of Congress. But *Darby* was decided a few days after the retirement of James McReynolds, the last justice who still followed the old doctrine. The Court unanimously overruled *Hammer*. "The reasoning and conclusion of the Court's opinion there," Stone explained, "cannot be reconciled with the conclusion which we have reached, that the power of Congress under the Commerce Clause is plenary."[59]

If there were any doubts about just how plenary Congress's power was, the Court put them to rest the following year in *Wickard v. Filburn* (1942). The Agricultural Adjustment Act imposed annual quotas on wheat production to avoid surpluses that would depress the price of wheat. Roscoe Filburn, the owner of a small farm in Ohio, grew a small quantity of wheat, all of which he either fed to his livestock or ground into flour for his own family's consumption. He contended that Congress lacked the authority to impose a production quota on *his* wheat, because his wheat never entered interstate commerce. But the Court unanimously rejected the argument. Even if Filburn's wheat never left the farm, Robert Jackson reasoned, Filburn's own consumption of wheat would reduce the overall demand for wheat, which would affect the price of wheat that was sold in interstate commerce. Filburn's "own contribution to the demand for wheat may be trivial by itself," Jackson noted, but that was "not enough to remove him from the scope of federal regulation where, as here, his contribution, taken together with that of many others similarly situated, is far from trivial." The Court had given

Congress, under its authority to regulate interstate commerce, the power to regulate all economic activity in the nation.[60]

Jackson acknowledged privately that the Court had abdicated its former role as the enforcer of constitutional limits on Congress's power over the economy. "If we were to be brutally frank," he confided to the court of appeals judge (and future justice) Sherman Minton, "I suspect what we would say is that in any case where Congress thinks there is an effect on interstate commerce, the Court will accept that judgment." As Jackson remarked to his law clerk, John Costelloe, "the interstate commerce power has no limits except those which Congress sees fit to observe." After Owen Roberts retired in 1945, he was free to make the same point in public. "In light of these decisions," he admitted in a lecture at Harvard, "it is hard to think of any local business which Congress may not regulate."[61]

A constitutional revolution had taken place, or really two simultaneous revolutions. One was in the Court's approval of economic regulation. "The day is gone when this Court uses the Due Process Clause of the Fourteenth Amendment to strike down state laws, regulatory of business and industrial conditions," Douglas wrote for a unanimous Court. "It is enough that there is an evil at hand for correction, and that it might be thought that the particular legislative measure was a rational way to correct it."[62] The other revolution was in the Court's willingness to let Congress regulate in ways that had previously been reserved to the states. It would not be long before Congress put its newfound power to use by enacting statutes governing a wide range of subjects the Court had not let it govern before.

But only a small part of this revolution occurred when Roberts had his change of heart in 1937. It began, at the latest, in 1934 with *Blaisdell* and *Nebbia*, and it was not complete until the early 1940s with *Darby* and *Filburn*. The most important cause of the change was not anything Roberts did. It was the restaffing of the Court by Roosevelt in the late 1930s and early 1940s. We will probably never know exactly why Roberts switched sides in 1937, but it hardly matters. The revolution would have taken place with or without him.

11

The Justices at War

Like everyone else, the justices were shocked by the attack on Pearl Harbor in December 1941. "I must confess I found it very difficult to concentrate on the arguments" in court, recalled James Byrnes. Two days after the nation entered World War II, the Court heard oral argument in a case that happened to be about the construction of ships twenty-five years before, during World War I. "At any other time it would have seemed important," Byrnes remembered, "but right then it appeared of little consequence in the light of the news bulletins still pouring in from Pearl Harbor." Later that week, the Court heard a case involving whether members of country clubs had to pay taxes on their club dues. "We were sitting there listening to the most affluent class in the community resisting taxes on their damn greens fees, when their very existence was at stake," Robert Jackson was to say. "It was unbearable to sit there and hear these arguments. . . . After the attack at Pearl Harbor it was impossible for one who had recently been active to serve on the court without feeling a certain sense of frustration and dissatisfaction."[1]

The United States would be at war, in one form or another, for many years thereafter. No sooner did World War II end than the nation began a different sort of war against the Soviet Union. How did these conflicts affect the Supreme Court? And what part did the Court play in them?[2]

I

When the United States entered the war, James Byrnes had been on the Court for less than six months. He had been in Congress for nearly thirty years, so he was accustomed to playing a larger role in such major events than was possible as a justice. He visited Franklin Roosevelt soon after Pearl Harbor and offered to help. For the next few months, while he was still on the Court, Byrnes participated in the planning for converting the peacetime domestic economy into one that would support production for the war. The two roles proved impossible to fulfill simultaneously. Byrnes left the Court to become director of the new Office of Economic Stabilization. He would hold similar positions for the remainder of the war and then would become secretary of state in the Truman administration.

Roosevelt also asked William Douglas to leave the Court and help coordinate the war effort. "He wants me to be the top guy in the defense work," Douglas told Hugo Black—"to take it off his neck; to be his 'alter ego'" for military matters. "I would have to resign from the Court," Douglas continued. "I have no enthusiasm for the project. In fact there is no attraction in it for me whatsoever. I can think of nothing less attractive, except practicing law in New York City."[3] Douglas stayed on the Court instead.

Other justices took on war-related responsibilities without resigning from the Court, most conspicuously Robert Jackson, who was the chief American prosecutor at the Nuremberg Trials in 1945–1946. He originally planned to be in Germany for just a few months in the summer of 1945, but the trials of Nazi war criminals took much longer to organize and carry out than he anticipated, so Jackson was away for more than a year. His colleagues grew impatient with his absence. "We are continuing to develop four-to-four votes in cases which will, for that reason, have to be reargued," Chief Justice Harlan Fiske Stone complained to Jackson in January 1946. "We are piling up quite a backlog."[4] Jackson returned to Washington in the fall of 1946. Although he spent the remaining eight years of his life on the Court, today he may be better known for his work as a prosecutor at Nuremberg than as a Supreme Court justice.

Felix Frankfurter's involvement in the war was less visible than Jackson's but more pervasive. Frankfurter had been an informal advisor to Roosevelt for many years before Roosevelt put him on the Court in 1939, and he continued in that role even afterward. As the country prepared for and then entered the war, Frankfurter spent a considerable amount of his time on war matters that had nothing to do with his work on the Court, including the conduct of behind-the-scenes diplomacy with officials of other nations.[5]

Owen Roberts chaired the presidential commission appointed in December 1941 to determine the reasons for American unpreparedness at Pearl Harbor. Roberts chaired another presidential commission in 1943 that planned for the postwar return of works of art that had been taken from their owners by the Nazis. Harlan Fiske Stone, by contrast, declined a similar appointment. In the summer of 1942, Roosevelt asked Stone to investigate what he called "this rubber matter"—the rubber shortage resulting from the Japanese control of the Dutch East Indies, which had been the source of most of the rubber in the United States. Stone refused, on the ground that a judge should not engage in extrajudicial activities, because any action he recommended "would almost certainly become the subject of political attack."[6]

In asking the justices to take on these wartime tasks, Roosevelt was following a long tradition. Presidents have often wished to capitalize on the gravity associated with Supreme Court justices, dating back to John Jay's negotiation of the eponymous treaty with England in 1794. Oliver Ellsworth served as an envoy to France a few years later. Five justices were members of the 1877 electoral commission that decided the previous year's presidential election. From time to time, justices were asked to serve as arbitrators of international disputes. John Harlan, for instance, was one of the American arbitrators of the Bering Sea dispute with Great Britain in 1893. Melville Fuller and David Brewer arbitrated a boundary dispute between British Guyana and Venezuela a few years later.[7] The same consideration would lead Lyndon Johnson to ask Earl Warren to chair the commission charged with investigating the assassination of John F. Kennedy in 1963. Supreme Court justices have a unique public image that combines fame, seriousness, and neutrality in a way that makes them perfect presidential appointees for this kind of one-time task.

Perfect for the president, that is, but not for the justices themselves, who by serving in this way have sometimes found themselves, to their horror, in the middle of political battles. Owen Roberts greatly regretted his service on the Pearl Harbor commission, which plunged him into the middle of bitter arguments over who had been to blame for the attack. Charles Evans Hughes, against his better judgment, agreed in 1911 to serve on a commission investigating postal rates. He vowed never to do any such thing again. "These administrative commissions bring the Justice into a realm of controversy with which he should not be associated," Hughes concluded. "It is best for the Court and the country that the Justices should strictly limit themselves to their judicial work." But even Hughes had to acknowledge that "after Pearl Harbor, Justice Roberts could not well decline the President's request to take part in the inquiry as to the causes of that disaster."[8]

Roosevelt's enlistment of the justices in the war effort was also a result of his personal relationships with them. Jackson and Douglas had both been trusted lawyers and close confidants in Roosevelt's administration. Byrnes had been an ally in the Senate, but he was replaceable on the Court, so it made sense for Roosevelt to have Byrnes manage the wartime economy and put Wiley Rutledge on the Court instead.

The justice who was most eager to participate in the war was the one whose assistance was least wanted. Frank Murphy had served in the Army during World War I. He had been governor of the Philippines for three years in the 1930s, so he knew the area where much of the fighting was taking place. As early as the spring of 1940, a year and a half before the United States entered the war, Murphy asked Roosevelt if he could spend the summer on war matters. "I don't relish the idea of a four months' vacation with the earth ablaze," Murphy explained. "If I can be of the slightest help to you I will be glad to remain in Washington during the summer." Roosevelt did not take him up on the offer. Murphy tried again the next year. "While I find the work of the court entirely congenial," he told Roosevelt, "in a time of crisis like the present primary consideration should be given to the nation's interests than to one's personal interests." He asked for "service in a post where my previous training and experience might be used to advantage." He had no better luck this time. The following year, in the summer of 1942, the nation was at war with Japan, and Murphy repeatedly offered to travel to the Philippines to do his part. "Nothing could distress me more," he declared, "than idleness while so many sacrifices are being made and the country is in its present grave position." He was rebuffed yet again in his attempt to reach the Pacific, but he did spend the summer in Georgia training in the army reserve. When Murphy requested another posting to the Pacific for the summer of 1943, Roosevelt finally asked Henry Stimson, the secretary of war, whether it would be possible to find Murphy something to do. The military did not want to send a Supreme Court justice anywhere near the fighting. Stimson consulted with George Marshall, the Army chief of staff, who offered Murphy a trip to Alaska instead, to give talks to soldiers stationed there. "He's been hanging on my neck and wanting me to send him to the Philippines in a submarine," Roosevelt complained to Robert Jackson. "If he can land out of a submarine, he thinks he can organize the resistance there and save MacArthur and save the Philippines." When Jackson jokingly asked, "Mr. President, haven't you got an old submarine?" Roosevelt chuckled and said, "I thought of that, but it wouldn't be fair to the crew." The indefatigable Murphy asked again in 1944 whether he might do something war-related in the Philippines during the summer. He got the same answer. If Murphy went to the Philippines, Marshall warned, the Japanese would find out, "which would result in a special effort to capture him."[9] Murphy reluctantly spent the war in the United States.

Even the justices who did not personally engage in the war effort participated indirectly. Hugo Black's sons served in the army, while his wife volunteered at a military hospital. Stanley Reed had a son in the navy. Wiley Rutledge was an air raid warden in his Washington neighborhood.[10] Like virtually all Americans, the justices were participants in the war, not merely spectators. This personal sense of mobilization would influence the Court's war-related decisions.

During the Second World War, as in the Civil War, the Court decided several cases in which people alleged that the government was conducting the war in an unconstitutional way. The fact that these cases even arose was remarkable. In no other country was the lawfulness of the war considered a judicial question. In these cases, the Court reached the same pattern of outcomes as in the Civil War cases. While the war was ongoing, the Court did not challenge the government's authority. After the war was over, by contrast, when an adverse decision no longer risked weakening the war effort, and when it was no longer likely that the administration would simply ignore an adverse decision, the Court was willing to rule against the government.

The first of these cases, *Ex parte Quirin* (1942) arrived at the Court soon after the US entered the war. In June 1942, Germany send two submarines to the United States, each carrying four saboteurs. One group landed on Long Island, the other in Florida. Both groups carried explosives and had instructions to blow up civilian targets such as factories and bridges. Neither group succeeded, because one of the Germans turned himself in to the FBI and the others were arrested soon after. All eight were tried by a military tribunal in July. The saboteurs, represented by military lawyers, challenged the authority of the military to try them. The Court agreed to hear the case and quickly scheduled oral argument for late July, before the trial had even finished. The justices rushed back to Washington from their summer homes, except for Frank Murphy, who rushed back from his summer military training at Fort Benning, Georgia. When Murphy showed up at the Court for oral argument in his army uniform, Frankfurter convinced him to recuse himself. As his law clerk recalled, Murphy had to admit that "it would not look too well for the Court if he participated in an appeal from a military tribunal" while he was conspicuously serving in the military himself.[11]

The saboteurs' principal argument against military jurisdiction rested on a Civil War precedent. In *Ex parte Milligan* (1866), the Court had held that the Constitution does not permit the military to try defendants for crimes while the ordinary civilian courts are open. "There was a troublesome Civil

NAZI SABOTEUR TRIAL, WASHINGTON, D.C.

Figure 11.1 The trial of the Nazi saboteurs before a military commission in a conference room in the Department of Justice in the summer of 1942. The Court rejected the defendants' claim of a right to be tried in a civilian court. Library of Congress, LC-USE623-D-OA-000144.

War case that seemed to stand in our way," recalled Attorney General Francis Biddle, who led the prosecution. "We thought we could overrule or get around *Ex parte Milligan*" by arguing that "it had no application to modern war in a case in which saboteurs, members in fact of the enemy's armed forces, penetrated our line of defense. When that happened, captives had always been subject to the swift penalty of military trial."[12] The government's argument prevailed. The Court unanimously upheld the military's authority to try the saboteurs. The Court announced its decision on July 31, the day after oral argument concluded, so that the trial could be completed. All eight defendants were convicted. Six were executed in early August. The other two had their sentences commuted to prison terms and were returned to Germany after the war.

The Court did not issue an opinion in the case for another three months, in part because of disagreement among the justices as to the rationale for the

Court's decision, and in part because they returned to their summer homes after announcing the decision. Finally, in late October, after the justices had reconvened in Washington, the Court published a unanimous opinion authored by Chief Justice Harlan Fiske Stone. Stone distinguished between ordinary crimes like the one at issue in *Milligan*, for which the Constitution guarantees a right to a trial by jury, and violations of the law of war, for which the Constitution provides no such guarantee. When lawful combatants—members of the regular armed forces—were captured, they were to be held as prisoners of war. Unlawful combatants, like the saboteurs, were "likewise subject to capture and detention, but in addition they are subject to trial and punishment by military tribunals for acts which render their belligerency unlawful." Stone provided a long catalogue of historical examples, dating back to the Revolution, in which the American military had tried and punished enemy spies. This uninterrupted practice demonstrated that "those who during time of war pass surreptitiously from enemy territory into our own, discarding their uniforms upon entry, for the commission of hostile acts involving destruction of life or property, have the status of unlawful combatants punishable as such by military commission," Stone concluded.[13]

Any other result would have been unthinkable in the summer of 1942, when the nation had just been attacked and the newspapers carried frightening stories that more German saboteurs were already in the United States. The Court's decision was "little more than a ceremonious detour to a predetermined goal," the political scientist Edward Corwin observed. The idea that the saboteurs should be tried at all, rather than simply killed on the spot, was controversial enough. "Just what would Germany, Italy or Japan do to our men or women if they were discovered landing on their shores with destructive material to sabotage their war industries?" asked one correspondent to the *Atlanta Constitution*. "Firing squad at dawn." And "What do we do?" she continued. "Call a special commission of generals, real United States Army men to try them, even though these men were caught with more than $100,000 of our American money to use in sabotage against our essential industries." As the *Los Angeles Times* editorialized, "the theory that an alien invader has civil rights is absurd on its face." The justices were well aware, moreover, that if they ruled in favor of the saboteurs, there was a substantial possibility that Roosevelt would ignore their decision. When the justices met in conference to discuss the case, Owen Roberts told his colleagues that Biddle, the attorney general, had confided his fear that Roosevelt would order the prisoners executed no matter what the Court did.[14] Viewed from one perspective, *Ex parte Quirin* was an extraordinary demonstration of the power of the Supreme Court, in that the government was compelled to appear before the Court in the midst of a war to defend the execution of captured enemy agents. Viewed from another perspective, however, the preordained outcome of *Quirin* was a revealing indication that the Court was not as powerful as it seemed.

A far more controversial group of cases began to reach the Court the following year.[15] In early 1942, shortly after the attack on Pearl Harbor, the government issued an increasingly harsh series of orders directed at people of Japanese ancestry living in the western United States. Ultimately, more than 100,000 Japanese Americans were interned in concentration camps during the war. The Supreme Court had a few occasions to consider the legality of these orders.

The first two cases, *Hirabayashi v. United States* (1943) and *Yasui v. United States* (1943), argued and decided together, were constitutional challenges to the curfew imposed in March 1942 on people of Japanese ancestry, which required them to stay home after 8:00 pm. Gordon Hirabayashi, a law student at the University of Washington, had been born in Seattle. He had never been to Japan. He violated the curfew deliberately and turned himself in to the FBI so he could bring a test case. Minoru Yasui, an Oregon-born lawyer and an army reservist, did the same. In both cases, their lawyers argued that the curfew unconstitutionally discriminated against Japanese Americans.

The Court unanimously held that the curfew did not violate the Constitution. Harlan Fiske Stone began his opinion in *Hirabayashi* by cautioning that courts could not second-guess military decisions. Where wartime "conditions call for the exercise of judgment and discretion and for the choice of means by those branches of the Government on which the Constitution has placed the responsibility of warmaking," he noted, "it is not for any court to sit in review of the wisdom of their action or substitute its judgment for theirs." Stone then proceeded, for most of the opinion, to endorse the wisdom of the curfew. "In the critical days of March, 1942," he recalled, officials had good cause to fear "the danger to our war production by sabotage and espionage" on the part of Japanese Americans. "At a time of threatened Japanese attack upon this country, the nature of our inhabitants' attachments to the Japanese enemy was consequently a matter of grave concern." A long history of anti-Japanese prejudice had "prevented their assimilation as an integral part of the white population. In addition, large numbers of children of Japanese parentage are sent to Japanese language schools outside the regular hours of public schools in the locality. Some of these schools are generally believed to be sources of Japanese nationalistic propaganda, cultivating allegiance to Japan." Government officials "could reasonably have concluded that these conditions have encouraged the continued attachment of members of this group to Japan and Japanese institutions."[16]

Stone acknowledged that "distinctions between citizens solely because of their ancestry are by their very nature odious to a free people." For this reason, in normal circumstances, "legislative classification or discrimination based on race alone has often been held to be a denial of equal protection." But matters were different in wartime, Stone concluded. "The fact alone that attack on our shores was threatened by Japan rather than another enemy power set these citizens apart from others who have no particular associations with Japan," he reasoned. "We cannot close our eyes to the fact, demonstrated by experience, that in time of war residents having ethnic affiliations with an invading enemy may be a greater source of danger than those of a different ancestry." The curfew was discriminatory, but it was not therefore unconstitutional. The Court reached the same conclusion in Yasui's case as well.[17]

No justice disagreed with the outcomes of these cases, but Douglas, Rutledge, and Murphy were all sufficiently troubled to write short concurring opinions. "Today is the first time," Murphy regretted, "that we have sustained a substantial restriction of the personal liberty of citizens of the United States based upon the accident of race or ancestry." He noted the irony that the curfew "bears a melancholy resemblance to the treatment accorded to members of the Jewish race in Germany and in other parts of Europe." It was a measure that "goes to the very brink of constitutional power." But even Murphy could not bring himself to say that the curfew violated the Constitution. In light "of the critical military situation which prevailed on the Pacific Coast area in the spring of 1942," he agreed, "the military authorities should not be required to conform to standards of regulatory action appropriate to normal times."[18]

The following year, in Korematsu v. United States (1944), the Court approved the exclusion of Japanese Americans from the western states. The Court's rationale was the same: discrimination based on Japanese ancestry was necessary while the nation was at war with Japan, even if it would be unconstitutional during peacetime. "Pressing public necessity may sometimes justify the existence of such restrictions," Hugo Black declared in his opinion for the Court, but "racial antagonism never can." The same logic that justified a curfew also justified barring people of Japanese ancestry from their homes. "True, exclusion from the area in which one's home is located is a far greater deprivation than constant confinement to the home from 8 p.m. to 6 a.m.," Black conceded. "But exclusion from a threatened area, no less than curfew, has a definite and close relationship to the prevention of espionage and sabotage." Black concluded: "To cast this case into outlines of racial prejudice, without reference to the real military dangers which were presented, merely confuses the issue. Korematsu was not excluded from the Military Area because of hostility to him or his race. He was excluded because we are at war with the Japanese Empire."[19]

This was too much for three of the justices. "This is not a case of keeping people off the streets at night," Owen Roberts insisted. "On the contrary, it is the case of convicting a citizen as a punishment for not submitting to imprisonment in a concentration camp, based on his ancestry, and solely because of his ancestry, without evidence or inquiry concerning his loyalty and good disposition towards the United States." Frank Murphy accused the government of having fallen "into the ugly abyss of racism." People who were disloyal to the United States could certainly be incarcerated, he recognized. "But to infer that examples of individual disloyalty prove group disloyalty and justify discriminatory action against the entire group is to deny that under our system of law individual guilt is the sole basis for deprivation of rights. Moreover, this inference, which is at the very heart of the evacuation orders, has been used in support of the abhorrent and despicable treatment of minority groups by the dictatorial tyrannies which this nation is now pledged to destroy." Robert Jackson reached the same conclusion. "If any fundamental assumption underlies our system," he declared, "it is that guilt is personal and not inheritable." But by incarcerating every person whose ancestors had come from Japan, the government had made "an otherwise innocent act a crime merely because this prisoner is the son of parents as to whom he had no choice, and belongs to a race from which there is no way to resign."[20] In 1943, the Court had been unanimous in upholding the constitutionality of a curfew, but in 1944, the Court divided 6–3 on the constitutionality of exclusion.

One cause of the difference, as Roberts suggested, was that exclusion was much more severe than a curfew. But no doubt another cause, one that remained unspoken, was the progress of the war. When the Court decided *Hirayabashi* and *Yasui*, the outcome of the war with Japan was still very much in doubt. Japan's expansion throughout the Pacific was near its peak.

By the time the Court decided *Korematsu* in December 1944, by contrast, the United States had taken the offensive. With an extra year and a half of experience, it was harder to make the case that it was necessary to incarcerate every American of Japanese descent. Nevertheless, six of the nine justices were still willing to defer to the army's judgment.

Although the justices were unaware of it at the time, the government was not telling the truth about its assessment of disloyalty among Japanese Americans. While Justice Department lawyers were litigating *Hirayabashi*, the War Department refused to give them full information about the ostensible threat posed by Japanese Americans. The lawyers found out later that they had been provided only with selected facts that would make the threat seem credible. Worse, while they were writing the government's brief in *Korematsu*, the lawyers discovered that some of the War Department's

Figure 11.2 Japanese Americans in San Francisco register to be sent to internment camps during World War II. In *Korematsu v. United States*, the Court upheld the constitutionality of excluding Japanese Americans from the western states. Photograph by Dorothea Lange, April 1942. Library of Congress, LC-USZ62-117317.

published justifications for internment were untrue. For example, the War Department claimed to have detected frequent radio signals from Japanese Americans on shore to Japanese submarines at sea, but in fact there had been no such signals. The War Department claimed that many Japanese Americans had been found with weapons and ammunition in their homes, but in fact, despite thousands of raids by the FBI, there had not been a single case in which any weapons or ammunition had been found.[21] Government lawyers could have informed the Court of these discrepancies in *Korematsu*, but they did not. Rather, the Justice Department concealed this information and allowed the Court to decide *Korematsu* based on claims that government lawyers knew to be false.

On the same day as *Korematsu*, the Court reached a very different result in *Ex parte Endo* (1944). Without addressing any constitutional issues, the Court unanimously decided that the executive order establishing the internment program did not authorize the government to intern citizens who were loyal to the United States. "A citizen who is concededly loyal presents no problem of espionage or sabotage," William Douglas insisted. "Loyalty is a matter of the heart and mind not of race, creed, or color." *Korematsu* and *Endo* could be reconciled in a formal sense. Strictly speaking, *Korematsu* approved the lawfulness only of excluding Japanese Americans from the West, not imprisoning them, while *Endo* only prohibited the incarceration of loyal citizens. Yet there was obviously considerable tension between the two decisions. In any event, the government had already decided to close the internment camps once the 1944 presidential election was over, but this move had not yet been announced. The Roosevelt administration received advance notice of the date of the *Endo* decision, apparently because Felix Frankfurter tipped off John McCloy, the assistant secretary of war. In a rare Sunday press release issued the day before the Court published its opinion in *Endo*, the War Department announced that most of the incarcerated Japanese Americans would soon be free to head home.[22]

Korematsu was a controversial case in its own day. The *Washington Post* editorial on the decision, headlined "Legalization of Racism," called it "peculiarly odious." The columnist Westbrook Pegler wondered whether it meant that the government could also imprison the millions of Americans with German ancestry, since the nation was at war with Germany too. The law professor Eugene Rostow called *Korematsu* and *Hirabayashi* "a disaster." Because of the Court's "acceptance of ethnic differences as a criterion for discrimination," he predicted, "these cases will make it more difficult to resolve one of the central problems in American life—the problem of minorities. They are a breach, potentially a major breach, in the principle of equality."[23]

With the passage of time, the conventional view came to be that the government grossly overreacted by incarcerating Japanese Americans during the war. A congressional commission concluded in 1982 that internment was "a policy conceived in haste and executed in an atmosphere of fear and anger at Japan." A few years later, the government awarded reparations to all the internees who were still alive. Some of the officials who designed and implemented the internment program regretted their wartime decisions, including Attorney General Francis Biddle, who admitted in his memoirs that "the program was ill-advised, unnecessary, and unnecessarily cruel." The Court's decisions upholding the program came to be seen in the same negative light. In the 1980s, with the consent of the Justice Department, lower courts invalidated the convictions of Gordon Hirabayashi, Minoru Yasui, and Fred Korematsu. In 2011, the Justice Department issued a public apology for the department's suppression of evidence that the justification for internment was not as strong as the military claimed it was. And in 2018, the Court declared that Korematsu was "gravely wrong the day it was decided" and that the decision had been "overruled in the court of history."[24] The Court's internment cases were now placed in the same category as Dred Scott and Plessy v. Ferguson, two other relics of the racist past.

Prejudice against the Japanese was no doubt a big part of the reason the Court went along with internment. "They all look alike to a person not a Jap," Hugo Black insisted many years later in defense of his vote. "People were rightly fearful of the Japanese." But much of the Court's acquiescence can be also be attributed to a deep-seated reluctance to second-guess the military during wartime. Racial prejudice may have diminished since the 1940s, but deference to the military has not. Despite the present-day condemnation of Korematsu, in the event of a war, if the military once again urged the necessity of discriminating against members of a particular racial or religious group, it is not at all obvious that the Court would stand in the way. "Of course Korematsu was wrong," Justice Antonin Scalia cautioned in 2014, but "you are kidding yourself if you think the same thing will not happen again."[25]

The Court was equally deferential to the government's management of the wartime economy, by approving regulatory measures that would almost certainly have been held unconstitutional in peacetime. Under the Emergency Price Control Act of 1942, enacted a few weeks after the attack

on Pearl Harbor, an official called the "price administrator" was granted
the power to set maximum prices for virtually all items. The Court rejected
constitutional challenges to several aspects of this program. "Congress has
constitutional authority to prescribe commodity prices as a war emergency
measure," Stone explained in *Yakus v. United States* (1944). "There was grave
danger of war-time inflation and the disorganization of our economy from
excessive price rises. Congress was under pressing necessity of meeting
this danger." Rutledge agreed that "judged by normal peacetime standards,
over-all nation-wide price control hardly has [an] accepted place in our
institutions." But he had no doubt that "it can be supported in the present
circumstances."[26] The demands of the war made the Court more deferential to the government, even in some areas linked only indirectly with the
fighting.

In one well-known pair of cases, by contrast, the perceived imperatives of
the war had the opposite effect: they strengthened the justices' commitment
to individual freedom from government coercion. In these cases, the Court
reached contrary rulings on the constitutionality of requiring schoolchildren
to salute the American flag and to recite the Pledge of Allegiance.[27]

Before the United States entered the war, in *Minersville School District
v. Gobitis* (1940), the justices voted 8–1 in the government's favor. The case
was brought by a family belonging to the Jehovah's Witnesses, a Christian
denomination whose beliefs proscribed saluting the flag. Felix Frankfurter's
majority opinion exhibited little sympathy for them. "National unity is the
basis of national security," Frankfurter declared. "The flag is the symbol of
our national unity, transcending all internal differences." He concluded that
if the government thought unity could best be achieved by a compulsory flag
salute, the courts had no business saying otherwise. "The wisdom of training
children in patriotic impulses by those compulsions which necessarily per-
vade so much of the educational process is not for our independent judgment," Frankfurter explained. "The court-room is not the arena for debating
issues of educational policy." Stone was the only dissenter.[28]

As with the internment of Japanese Americans, however, there was an unmistakable echo of Nazi Germany in the punishment of Jehovah's Witnesses
for refusing to salute the flag. Just a few years earlier, the German government had dissolved the Jehovah's Witnesses in Germany and confiscated
their property. A year after the Court ruled against the Jehovah's Witnesses,
an editorial in an American Bar Association publication summed up the
profession's reaction to the case. "No decision of recent years has aroused

so much informed discussion," the ABA observed, "and it is interesting to note that the critical comment has been largely adverse to the soundness of the decision." The editors shared the prevailing view. "National unity is important, even vital in these days," they concluded, "but the penalizing of religious beliefs held by a few school children is hardly the way to promote it." Frankfurter noted in his diary that he was "literally flooded with letters" disagreeing with the decision. A wave of mob violence committed against Jehovah's Witnesses after the decision, caused by the mistaken but apparently widespread belief that their refusal to salute the flag indicated their opposition to the war effort, added to the sense within the legal profession that in *Gobitis* the Court had been too deferential to the government.[29] Expelling children from school for their failure to salute the flag came to seem less like the promotion of national unity than like the persecution of the Jehovah's Witnesses for their religious beliefs.

Some of the justices began to have second thoughts. Within a few months of *Gobitis*, according to Douglas, Black had already changed his mind. "Why, has he reread the Constitution during the summer?" Frankfurter asked. "No," Douglas replied, "but he has read the papers." Douglas himself changed his mind soon after, as did Murphy. *Jones v. City of Opelika* (1942) was another constitutional challenge brought by Jehovah's Witnesses—this time to the annual licensing fees charged by several cities for selling books, which hindered the Witnesses' ability to distribute religious literature. The Court rejected the Witnesses' argument once again, but only by a vote of 5–4. In dissent, Black, Douglas, and Murphy explained that they now believed *Gobitis* had been wrongly decided.[30] Along with Stone, that made four votes to overrule *Gobitis*. A year later, after Robert Jackson also had a change of heart and Wiley Rutledge replaced James Byrnes, there were six.

In *West Virginia State Board of Education v. Barnette* (1943), the Court overruled *Gobitis* and held that the government could not compel schoolchildren to salute the flag or recite the Pledge of Allegiance. Jackson's majority opinion would become a classic statement of the importance of the freedom of thought. "We set up government by consent of the governed, and the Bill of Rights denies those in power any legal opportunity to coerce that consent," he declared. "Authority here is to be controlled by public opinion, not public opinion by authority." Readers could not have missed the implicit contrast with Nazi Germany, but Jackson nevertheless emphasized that even the Boy Scouts objected to the required salute as "being too much like Hitler's." In words that would be quoted repeatedly over the next several decades,

Jackson concluded: "If there is any fixed star in our constitutional constellation, it is that no official, high or petty, can prescribe what shall be orthodox
in politics, nationalism, religion, or other matters of opinion." Frankfurter
dissented, in an opinion that began with an unusually personal reference to
his own religious faith. "One who belongs to the most vilified and persecuted
minority in history is not likely to be insensible to the freedoms guaranteed
by our Constitution," he suggested. "Were my purely personal attitude relevant I should whole-heartedly associate myself with the general libertarian
views in the Court's opinion, representing as they do the thought and action
of a lifetime. But as judges we are neither Jew nor Gentile." Frankfurter had
attained prominence as a progressive by criticizing the conservative justices of
the *Lochner* era for reading their own preferred policies into the Constitution.
But as the Court swung to the left, he found himself on the conservative side,
criticizing the liberal justices of the Roosevelt Court for the same sin. "I want
to avoid the mistake comparable to that made by those whom we criticized
when dealing with the control of property," Frankfurter insisted. He preferred
"the true democratic faith of not relying on the Court for the impossible task
of assuring a vigorous, mature, self-protecting and tolerant democracy."[31]

There were doctrinal differences between the flag salute cases and the
internment cases, but the most important difference was likely a practical
one. The justices believed that Japanese Americans were a real threat to the
nation's security, but they recognized that the children of Jehovah's Witnesses
were not. When there was no perceived danger, the Court was less willing to
defer to the government's balance of national interest and personal freedom.

This became clear when the war ended. Hawaii was under martial law
from the day of the Pearl Harbor attack until near the end of 1944.[32] During
this period, the military conducted many trials that would normally have
been in the civilian courts, including the trials of Lloyd Duncan, a civilian
pipefitter convicted of brawling with Marines, and Harry White, a stock-
broker convicted of embezzling from a client. In *Duncan v. Kahanamoku*
(1946), the Court considered whether the military had the authority to
conduct such trials. (The respondent was Duke Kahanamoku, the sheriff
of Honolulu and perhaps the most famous law enforcement official in the
country. Kahanamoku had won Olympic medals in swimming in 1912,
1920, and 1924, and had been the person most responsible for popularizing
surfing beyond Hawaii. When his sporting career ended, he was sheriff for
nearly thirty years.)

If *Duncan* had come to the Court a few years earlier, at the height of the war in the Pacific, the justices would likely have deferred to the military as they did in *Ex parte Quirin* and in the Japanese internment cases. By 1946, however, the war was over. The Court held that the military lacked the power to supplant the civilian courts. Although the decision rested on statutory grounds—the Court found that the statute the government claimed as authority for the military trials in fact did not authorize them—Black's majority opinion emphasized the case's constitutional dimension as well. "We are aware that conditions peculiar to Hawaii might imperatively demand extraordinarily speedy and effective measures in the event of actual or threatened invasion," Black acknowledged. "But this also holds true for other parts of the United States. Extraordinary measures in Hawaii, however necessary, are not supportable on the mistaken premise that Hawaiian inhabitants are less entitled to Constitutional protection than others." Harold Burton, joined by Frankfurter, dissented. They accused the majority of 20/20 hindsight. "It is all too easy in this postwar period to assume that the success which our forces attained was inevitable and that military control should have been relaxed," Burton cautioned. But after the bombing of Pearl Harbor, "every inch of the Territory of Hawaii was like a frontier stockade under savage attack with notice that such attack would not be restrained by the laws of civilized nations. Measures of defense had to be taken on the basis that anything could happen."[33] Burton's dissent was a sharp reminder of how the presence or absence of war could influence the Court's interpretation of the Constitution.

The Court reached a similar result in *Oyama v. California* (1948), when it struck down a California law that barred people ineligible for citizenship from owning land, a law with the intent and effect of discriminating against those born in Japan. Had the case arisen during the war, the Court might well have upheld the law. By 1948, however, the Court had little trouble holding that it constituted impermissible race discrimination. Indeed, Murphy wrote a lengthy concurring opinion so critical of anti-Asian prejudice in the United States that his colleagues urged him not to publish it because of its implications for the Cold War. "You are 100 per cent right," Chief Justice Fred Vinson told him. "The difficulty is that I fear your opinion as written will be translated by the Russians into Korean, Chinese and Japanese and widely circulated in the Orient" as a propaganda tool.[34] Murphy was undeterred. He published his separate opinion anyway.

The Court was thus profoundly affected by the national mood during the war. How could it not have been? When the needs of the military seemed pressing, the justices were extraordinarily deferential to the government—so deferential as to permit the incarceration of Japanese Americans, in a decision that today is almost universally classified as among the Court's greatest mistakes. But laws that could be rationalized as military necessities during wartime lost that grounding once the danger had passed.

II

It was the war that gave Lucile Lomen her place in the Court's history. In the 1944–1945 term, she was the Court's first female law clerk. There would not be a second for more than twenty years.

By the 1940s, the justices' clerks were all junior lawyers, most just a year or two out of law school. The justices were allowed to hire two clerks beginning in 1941, but until the end of the decade most of the justices preferred to hire only one. A clerkship lasted for a year or two and was understood as an elite entry point into the profession. Walter Gellhorn, one of Harlan Fiske Stone's clerks, recalled that Stone "made one feel a co-worker—a very junior and subordinate co-worker, to be sure, but nevertheless one whose opinions counted and whose assistance was valued." Clerks were responsible for analyzing the certiorari petitions and recommending which cases the Court should hear, for helping the justices decide the cases, and for polishing (and sometimes drafting) the justices' opinions. A clerk was an "assistant associate justice," as Wiley Rutledge put it.[35]

The justices each tended to rely on a law school dean or a professor to choose their clerks for them. "A law clerkship is something to which a man is called, and for which he does not apply," proclaimed Erwin Griswold, the dean of Harvard Law School. Fred Vinson's clerks were selected by Willard Pedrick, a professor at Northwestern who had been his first clerk when Vinson was a judge on the DC Circuit. Hugo Black pursued a different strategy. Black "was taking Alabama boys on for a year at a time" as clerks, Sherman Minton explained, because "he hoped they would return to Alabama with a bit of liberalism in their souls and help spread the gospel." As Black advised a disappointed applicant from New York, "I have felt that it might be helpful to the South for boys from that region to have the advantage of the broad national viewpoint which is taken by the Court."[36] But while Black's clerks tended to be Alabamans, they usually attended the same few elite law schools as the clerks for the other justices. Jerome Cooper, who went on to become a distinguished civil rights lawyer in Birmingham, went to Harvard; Louis Oberdorfer, later a federal judge, grew up in Birmingham and attended Yale; and Truman Hobbs, who also became a federal judge, was a Yale graduate from Selma.

To become a law clerk at the Supreme Court thus required access to a closed, clubby world of white men at a handful of law schools. One can get a good sense of this process from the annual correspondence between Harlan Fiske Stone and Young Berryman Smith, who was Stone's successor as the dean of Columbia Law School. Each winter, Stone would ask Smith to recommend Columbia students, and Smith would respond with descriptions of a few students. Stone would choose someone from this list. Smith was careful to describe the students' social characteristics as well as their academic qualifications. In the winter of 1931, for example, Smith advised that Columbia's top student was Herbert Wechsler, "the best man we have graduated in many years." Smith assured Stone that "although he is a Jew, he is a very agreeable person." Wechsler got the job. In the winter of 1934, Smith discussed three students. One, Aaron Lewittes, had excellent grades. "He is a Jew," Smith cautioned. "He is not offensive but at times exhibits a lack of tact." The second candidate was Milton Klein, who had achieved distinction as the editor in chief of the school's law review. But Smith was similarly lukewarm about Klein. "He is a Jew," Smith explained. "He is an unusually timid person and sometimes gives the impression of being indifferent or queer. He undoubtedly has first rate intellectual ability but I am somewhat doubtful of his personality." Smith's third option, the one he recommended, was Thomas Everett Harris, who "is a gentile" with "a pleasing personality." Stone chose Harris. The next year, the options again included "Aaron Lewittes (Jew)"— "He is not a particularly impressive person to look at but is an extraordinarily able man"—along with "Charles C. Tillinghast, Jr. (Gentile)." Smith's bottom line was that "Lewittes is the abler, although for personal reasons you might prefer Tillinghast." Another year, Stone could pick between Howard Williams, "a Gentile" with "a very pleasant personality," and Edward Friedman, "a Jew" who was "a rather shy person but very able."[37] The evident understanding between Stone and Smith was that intelligence and ability as a lawyer were not the only desirable traits in a law clerk. Being Jewish was not a disqualification, but it was an obstacle a candidate had to overcome. To gain entry to this rarefied world, one also needed to fit in socially.

William Douglas was the one justice willing to look more widely for law clerks. Douglas had no interest in socializing with his law clerks or even in treating them like human beings. Clerking for Douglas was "like 52 weeks of boot camp," one clerk winced. Douglas's secretary recalled that "ten thousand dollars a year did not seem enough for what those boys had to put up with." She thought "they, and we for that matter, should get combat pay in addition."[38] Douglas, a native of Washington state, sought law clerks from schools in the West, which were then less prestigious than the better-established Eastern schools. In his first decade on the Court, Douglas took a few clerks from the University of Washington, a few from the University of California at Berkeley, and one from Stanford. The latter was Warren Christopher, who would go on to be secretary of state in the Clinton administration.

Before the Second World War, no justice appears to have considered hiring a woman as a law clerk. But law school enrollment plummeted during the war, as men of appropriate age entered military service instead. Harvard, for example, had 1,393 law students in the fall of 1939, but only 98 in the fall of 1943, and only 48 in the fall of 1944.[39] The justices' source of law clerks largely dried up. They had to think more broadly about where to find talented young lawyers.

In the spring of 1943, Harlan Fiske Stone remarked to Wiley Rutledge that he was having trouble finding qualified candidates. Rutledge urged him to consider Virginia Morsey, who had recently graduated from Washington University in St. Louis and was now a lawyer for the Rural Electrification Administration. Rutledge had planned to hire Morsey as his clerk when he was a Court of Appeals judge, but when he joined the Supreme Court in place of James Byrnes, he kept Victor Brudney, who had been Byrnes's clerk. Rutledge, the former dean at Washington University, told Stone that he trusted the judgment of the faculty members who informed him that Morsey was "one of the most capable students that school has produced." Morsey ranked number one in the class of 1942 and was the first woman to edit the school's law review. "At that time the war had not depopulated the school, as it has during the last year," Rutledge explained. Morsey "did excellent work as editor of the review in addition to maintaining her high scholastic standing."[40] Stone was not interested in interviewing Morsey. She would go on to become a lawyer for the World Bank.

William Douglas was also having difficulty hiring a law clerk in the spring of 1943. Judson Falknor, the law dean at the University of Washington, had sent Douglas clerks before, but he told Douglas he had no one to recommend for the coming year. Douglas responded: "When you say that you have 'no available graduates' whom you could recommend for appointment as my clerk, do you include women? It is possible that I may decide to take one if I can find one who is absolutely first-rate." The following year, Falknor suggested Lucile Lomen. Lomen was at the top of her graduating class despite also working nearly full-time as Falknor's secretary. Like Douglas, she had attended Whitman College in Walla Walla, Washington. She also had "a pleasing appearance," Falknor advised in his letter of recommendation. Before taking the unprecedented step of hiring Lomen, Douglas checked with Vern Countryman, a former clerk who was now in the army. Countryman and Lomen had been at the University of Washington Law School together. "She is a very intelligent woman and she is also an indefatigable worker," Countryman told Douglas. "She appears to be a very healthy young woman, with stamina enough to keep on working long and busy hours. In addition, she is a very pleasant girl, and gets along well with everyone." Countryman added a bit of advice. "As to how a girl would fare on the job," he continued, "I can't see that the sex would make any difference except on the point of maintaining contact with the other offices—on that score, she would not be able to keep as well informed on what your brethren were doing as a man could, unless, of course, your brethren also employ female clerks. But I doubt if that point is of any great importance—certainly not enough to warrant choosing a man instead unless you are satisfied that the man is absolutely first rate, because I am sure that Miss Lomen is just that."[41] Douglas hired her.

Lomen's clerkship was national news. "Attractive, soft-spoken Miss Lomen will smash a precedent of 154 years' standing," announced a wire service story. When she began working at the Court, the *Christian Science Monitor* ran a large photograph of Lomen in front of a wall of case reports. Like all of Douglas's law clerks, she worked extraordinarily hard for a year and saw little of the justice.[42] At the end of the clerkship, she returned to Seattle and worked for a few years in the state attorney general's office before spending most of her career at General Electric.

Lomen finished her clerkship just as the war was ending. Law school enrollment and the legal job market were once again dominated by men. It would be a very long time before another woman clerked at the Court. Perhaps inspired by Lomen, the law professors who sent clerks to the justices recommended more women in the next few years, but the justices did not hire any of them. In 1946, the faculty at the University of Indiana urged Wiley Rutledge to hire Ruth Smalley. "I am not much given to enthusiasm about most law school graduates," the law professor John Frank told Rutledge, "but this girl has something. She has brilliance approaching genius; she is indefatigable; she has grace and charm; and she is a 100% sound liberal." Frank added that "Ruth will not, in all likelihood, have children, and she intends to make law a career. . . . She may even be able to crack the usual bar against women law teachers." Jerome Hall, another professor at Indiana, advised Rutledge that "I do not believe you will find her equal among any of the graduates of the law schools." Rutledge was not interested. The following year, in Willard Pedrick's annual letter introducing Fred Vinson to the top student at Northwestern, Pedrick reported that "it happens that she is a woman." Pedrick identified her only as "Mrs. Culmer." (It was Marjorie Culmer, who would later be the national president of the Girl Scouts.) He explained that she was "in her thirties" and "married to a physician who believes in advancing his wife's professional career as well his own." Vinson was not interested either. In 1950, Hugo Black received an application from Sarah Livingston Davis, who was clerking on the Third Circuit after graduating from Columbia Law School. Black told her that he had "no objection whatever to appointing a woman clerk provided she met the qualifications desired."[43] But he did not hire her.

Now that the war was over and male law graduates were plentiful, the justices no longer perceived any need to hire women. There would be no more female law clerks until the late 1960s, when conventional attitudes toward the role of women in the legal profession began to change.

III

Wartime did not end with the formal conclusion of the Second World War. Next came the Cold War with the Soviet Union, which spawned local proxy wars all over the world. The justices were participants in the Cold War as well, as high officials in a government that devoted considerable attention to rooting out communist infiltrators. When Robert Jackson received mail from people who seemed sympathetic to communism, he forwarded the letters to the Federal Bureau of Investigation. "It occurs to me that they might be of some use to you in identifying persons following the party line," he suggested to J. Edgar Hoover, the FBI's director. Jackson had been Hoover's nominal boss not long before, when Jackson was attorney general. So had Frank Murphy and Tom Clark, two other justices who had served as attorney general. Clark, as attorney general in the late 1940s, had led the Truman administration's intensive efforts to purge the government of people who had been affiliated with communist organizations. Even William Douglas declared: "There is no doubt in my mind of the need for the Chief Executive and the Congress to take strong measures against any Fifth Column worming its way into government—a Fifth Column that has access to vital information and the purpose to paralyze and confuse."[44] And Douglas was one of the justices most willing to side with members of communist organizations in cases against the government.

An episode that took place in 1952 illustrates the justices' personal stake in the war against communism. Early that year, Chief Justice Fred Vinson hired Roland Whitman as his law clerk for the 1952–1953 term. Whitman was a recent graduate of Northwestern Law School who came highly recommended from the school's faculty. He had served in the army between college and law school. Vinson interviewed him and offered him a clerkship. Before Whitman could begin working at the Court, however, he had to fill out the routine form that all federal employees were required to submit. One of the questions was "Are you now, or have you ever been, a member of the Communist Party, U.S.A., or any Communist organization?" Whitman truthfully checked the box for "No." But he inserted a note explaining that sixteen years earlier, during his freshman year at the University of Chicago, he had attended some meetings of the Young Communist League. To Whitman's shock, when he showed up at the Court for his first day of work, Vinson revoked the clerkship. "I was only seventeen at the time," Whitman told Vinson in a long letter he wrote the following day, "a college freshman curious to learn what any campus group had to say about the social problems of the day." He had thought the group advocated "no more than a liberal, new deal philosophy," and he stopped attending meetings when he discovered the group's true nature. Vinson was unmoved. "I regret that I have been injected into this situation through no fault of my own," was all he could tell Whitman. "A moment's reflection upon your part should convince you that the Supreme Court of the United States as an institution, and I as Chief Justice should not be embarrassed by any discussions pertaining to your appointment."[45] Only two years earlier, Alger Hiss, a former law clerk to Oliver Wendell Holmes, had been convicted of perjury for denying his connections to the Soviet Union. Vinson was evidently determined—whether for reasons of principle or political prudence—not to let anyone else with any taint of communism work at the Court.

The justices' own backgrounds in government made them particularly sensitive to the presence of communists in government positions. All of Roosevelt's appointees except for Felix Frankfurter and Wiley Rutledge came from the Senate or from Roosevelt's own administration. All four of the justices appointed by Harry Truman likewise came from the Senate or the Truman administration. Harold Burton, appointed in 1945 when Owen Roberts retired, was a senator from Ohio. He was a career politician with no judicial experience. As he acknowledged to Stone shortly after he was confirmed by his colleagues in the Senate, "I shall need plenty of generous assistance in taking up my duties." Truman's next two appointments came from his own cabinet. Fred Vinson, the treasury secretary, became chief justice in 1946 after the death of Harlan Fiske Stone, and when Frank Murphy died in 1949, his replacement was Tom Clark, Truman's attorney general. Truman's final appointment was Sherman Minton, who also joined the Court in 1949, after Rutledge died. Minton was a court of appeals judge, but before that he had been a senator and another close friend of Truman's.[46]

All four of Truman's appointees remained close to Truman while they were on the Court. "As far as you are concerned I am just as approachable as I was when we sat together in the Senate," Truman wrote to Minton shortly after he became president. Minton repeatedly offered Truman advice on matters as disparate as the Voice of America, the new Air Force Academy, and the staffing of the lower courts. After Clark joined the Court, he continued to play poker with Truman—or as Truman referred to it when planning one of their games, "an eight-member session for a round-table on probabilities." Truman often sought Vinson's counsel on political matters. When Vinson died in 1953, his obituary reported that "the President and the Chief Justice had telephones by their beds, and regularly held long talks late at night, in which the President received Mr. Vinson's advice and counsel on many problems. Throughout the Truman administration Mr. Vinson was regarded as one of the real inner circle at the White House."[47]

In some of the most important cases arising from the Cold War, the justices were called upon to be arbiters between individual rights and the government's demand for security, but most of the justices were government men themselves, who were accustomed to seeing these issues from the government's point of view. As with the Second World War, so with the Cold War: the justices were participants, not merely outside observers.

Fred Vinson and William Douglas had an additional reason not to endorse the rights of communists. Both contemplated presidential campaigns while they were on the Court. Robert Jackson said in 1950 that Vinson "is on intimate terms with the President and is generally believed here to be the 'heir apparent.'" Throughout 1951, political insiders predicted that Vinson would be the Democratic candidate in the next presidential election. "Talk of nominating Chief Justice Vinson for the Presidency on the Democratic ticket is gaining momentum," the *Washington Post* reported in November. "It is often said that the President, with himself out of the picture, would favor Mr. Vinson as his successor." Vinson did not withdraw from the race until early 1952.[48]

Douglas flirted with politics far longer. He considered running for president in 1944 and came close to being Roosevelt's choice for vice president in both the 1940 and 1944 elections. If Douglas had been elected vice president in 1944, he, rather than Truman, would have become president a few months later. Before the 1948 election, Truman asked Douglas to be his running mate. Douglas declined. He seems to have regretted this decision, however, because he again considered running for president in 1952. At the time, however, he was in the midst of divorcing his first wife and he was in a relationship with the woman who would become his second, which in that era was enough of a political liability to discourage him from running. Douglas sought elective office one last time in 1960, by supporting Lyndon Johnson's candidacy for the Democratic nomination in the hope that Johnson would select him as his vice president.[49] When this last plan went awry, Douglas, now in his sixties, finally gave up on running for office.

Douglas's political aspirations infuriated some of the other justices, who believed that Douglas wrote his opinions with future campaigns in mind. For example, in an otherwise humdrum 1943 case about whether a railroad was liable for the death of one of its employees, Douglas included in the Court's opinion a paragraph extolling the importance of the right to a trial by jury. Owen Roberts complained to Frankfurter that Douglas had turned the opinion into "a stump speech on a soapbox which really makes the Court a laughing stock." Frankfurter replied that it was "the opinion of a judge who has political ambitions, and who is not thinking about the Court or his Court job." Stanley Reed lamented that Douglas "is a politician now."[50]

In the early years of the Cold War, the Court consistently allowed the government to punish people for their political views. Clyde Summers, for example, was a law school graduate who was denied admission to the Illinois bar because he had been a conscientious objector during World War II. He argued that the state violated the First Amendment by preventing him from becoming a lawyer. "The so-called 'misconduct' for which petitioner could be reproached," Summer argued, "is his taking the New Testament too seriously. Instead of merely reading or preaching the Sermon on the Mount, he tries to practice it." The Court was unpersuaded. Stanley Reed's opinion in *In re Summers* (1945) accepted the state's argument that lawyers had to swear to uphold the state constitution, one clause of which required men of Summers's age to fight in the state militia during wartime, and that Summers was therefore unfit to be a lawyer.[51] Summers became a lawyer in New York instead. He would go on to become a prominent professor of labor law.

There were many similar cases in the late 1940s and early 1950s. The Court upheld a federal law requiring the officers of labor unions to swear that they were not affiliated with the Communist Party. The Court permitted New York to fire public school teachers who belonged to organizations that advocated the overthrow of the government.[52] During the second Red Scare, after World War II, the Court was no more receptive to First Amendment claims than it had been during the first one, after World War I.

In the best known of these cases, *Dennis v. United States* (1951), the Court upheld the constitutionality of the Smith Act, which provided prison terms of up to twenty years for advocating the overthrow of the government. The defendants in *Dennis* were the leaders of the US Communist Party, who had been convicted of violating the Smith Act after a high-profile nine-month-long trial. "Overthrow of the Government by force and violence is certainly a substantial enough interest for the Government to limit speech," Fred Vinson declared. "Indeed, this is the ultimate value of any society, for if a society cannot protect its very structure from armed internal attack, it must follow that no subordinate value can be protected." He reasoned that the government need not "wait until the putsch is about to be executed" before imprisoning the party's leaders. "If Government is aware that a group aiming at its overthrow is attempting to indoctrinate its members," Vinson concluded, "action by the Government is required." Robert Jackson added that the communists of the 1950s were far more dangerous than the radicals of the 1920s, who had been limited to "a hot-headed speech on a street corner, or circulation of a few incendiary pamphlets, or parading by some zealots behind a red flag." Unlike their predecessors, he warned, the *Dennis* defendants led "a well-organized, nation-wide conspiracy" with "no scruples against sabotage, terrorism, assassination, or mob disorder."[53]

In light of the Court's wartime deference to the executive branch, it is all the more remarkable that the Court ruled *against* the president in the Cold

Figure 11.3 Robert Thompson and Benjamin Davis, two Communist Party leaders, surrounded by supporters outside the federal courthouse in New York during their trial for violating the Smith Act. The Court affirmed their convictions in *Dennis v. United States*. Photograph by C. M. Stieglitz. Library of Congress, LC-USZ62-111434.

War decision that would have the most enduring effect in later years. In 1952, during the Korean War, the United Steelworkers union was about to go on strike. The strike would have shut down all steel production in the nation. Steel was an important component of many weapons needed for the war. President Harry Truman directed Charles Sawyer, the Secretary of Commerce, to take control of most of the country's steel mills so the production of weapons would not be disrupted. In *Youngstown Sheet and Tube Company v. Sawyer* (1952), better known as the "Steel Seizure Case," the Court had to decide whether the Constitution permitted Truman to do so. Truman's decision to seize the steel mills may have been influenced by advice from Chief Justice Fred Vinson. According to John Snyder, who was secretary of the treasury, and Margaret Truman, the president's daughter, Truman asked Vinson for his view of the matter, and Vinson assured him that the seizure would be lawful and that the Court would uphold Truman's authority.[54]

But Vinson misjudged his colleagues. The Court voted 6–3, with Vinson in dissent, that Truman had exceeded his power. "The order cannot properly be sustained as an exercise of the President's military power as Commander in Chief of the Armed Forces," Hugo Black held in his majority opinion. If the government was to seize private property to prevent a labor dispute from halting production, he observed, "this is a job for the Nation's lawmakers, not for its military authorities." Nor could the order be based on the president's general authority as the head of the executive branch. "The President's power to see that the laws are faithfully executed refutes the idea that he is to be a lawmaker," Black insisted. "The Constitution limits his functions in the law-making process to the recommending of laws he thinks wise and the vetoing of laws he thinks bad."[55]

Robert Jackson concurred, in an opinion that would exert more influence than Black's. Jackson divided actions of the president into three categories. Where the president acts with the authorization of Congress, "his authority is at its maximum, for it includes all that he possesses in his own right plus all that Congress can delegate." Where Congress has not spoken, Jackson continued, the president's power is smaller, because it includes only his inherent authority under the Constitution. And "when the President takes measures incompatible with the expressed or implied will of Congress," Jackson concluded, "his power is at its lowest ebb, for then he can rely only upon his own constitutional powers minus any constitutional powers of Congress over the matter." Jackson determined that the Steel Seizure Case fell within the third category, because Congress had enacted statutes allowing the president to take control of private property, but none of them authorized the seizure of the steel mills. Jackson, who as attorney general had helped the government prepare for World War II, worried that "no doctrine that the Court could promulgate would seem to me more sinister and alarming than that a President whose conduct of foreign affairs is so largely uncontrolled, and often even is unknown, can vastly enlarge his mastery over the internal affairs of the country by his own commitment of the Nation's armed forces to some foreign venture."[56] Truman relinquished the government's control of the steel mills. The strike shut down the steel mills for nearly two months before it ended.

To smooth over relations, Black—Truman's former colleague in the Senate—invited Truman to his house for dinner with some of the other justices a couple of weeks later. Truman was "a bit testy at the beginning of the evening," according to Douglas. "But after the bourbon and canapés were passed, he turned to Hugo and said, 'Hugo, I don't much care for your law but, by golly, this bourbon is good.'" A few years later, when Truman, now out of office, was asked about his relationship with the Court, the Steel Seizure Case still rankled. "They charged Roosevelt with 'trying to pack the court' to suit himself," Truman recalled. "Well, that can't be done, because I've tried it. It won't work." The Court's decision barring him from taking over the steel industry had proved to his satisfaction that "whenever you put a man on the Supreme Court, he ceases to be your friend, you can be sure of that."[57] Today, when the 1952 steelworkers' strike has become a historical footnote, the Steel Seizure Case remains one of the Court's most important decisions regarding the balance of power between the president and Congress.

IV

While the justices were fighting World War II and the Cold War, they were also fighting with each other. There was so much feuding among the justices that accounts of the Court during this period nearly all resort to the same metaphor, one that was apparently coined by the law professor Alexander Bickel, who clerked for Felix Frankfurter in the early 1950s. As the saying goes, the justices were like nine scorpions in a bottle.[58]

Some of the scorpions bore more of the blame than others. Frankfurter was dismissive of his colleagues' intellectual capacity, sometimes to their faces. He protested that the justices' discussion of the cases was inadequate. His own contributions to these discussions often took the form of speeches so longwinded that the chief justice would cut him off. "If FF talked too long," Frank Murphy recalled, Harlan Fiske Stone "would say 'the list is long the hour is late we will have to curtail our remarks.'" Frankfurter accused his colleagues of being "influenced in decisions by considerations extraneous to the legal issues" and complained that their opinions had "fallen short of requisite professional standards." The other justices were often exasperated with him. "We all know what a great burden your long discourses are," Douglas wrote to Frankfurter after one especially excruciating conference. He registered "a protest at your degradation of the Conference and its deliberations"— and then circulated the protest to all their colleagues. Interviewed years later, Douglas recalled that Frankfurter "was utterly dishonest intellectually" and that he "was very, very devious. None of us had known him very well, but he spent his time going up and down the halls putting poison in everybody's spring, setting, trying to set one justice against another, going to my office and telling me what a terrible person Reed was or Black, going to Reed's office telling Reed what a stupid person somebody else was, and so on."[59] Felix Frankfurter was not an easy man to work with.

Neither was William Douglas. He dashed off his opinions extraordinarily quickly. They were often "superficial or just plain sloppy," an otherwise-admiring biographer concedes. "Nobody doubted that Douglas could have done a more thorough, scholarly job if he had chosen to. But he did not choose to and that indifference to detail was more infuriating than a showing of incompetence would have been." No one was more infuriated than Frankfurter, who called Douglas one of the "two completely evil men I have ever met." Douglas spent as little time as possible at the Court, often leaving Washington, DC, before the Court's term ended. During the term, he devoted much of his attention to matters other than Court business. He wrote many books, including several about his travels around the world. He was an ardent environmentalist. And to his colleagues' amusement and embarrassment, he was a notorious womanizer. When Sherman Minton was hospitalized with a back sprain, he wrote to Robert Jackson that he was eager to get back home. "I can understand how Bill Douglas with his mountain goat gonads could have fun around a hospital," Minton joked, "but it is a frustrating experience for an old man like me." Minton was only a few years older than Douglas. Douglas would marry four times. He was the first sitting justice to be divorced, and the second, and the third. Douglas met Joan Martin, his third wife, when he was sixty-three and she was a senior in college. Cathy Heffernan, his fourth, was a junior in college when she met Douglas, who was sixty-five. "Who is this child?" wondered the actress Joan Crawford when she met Heffernan at a White House dinner. A congressman from Georgia asked the House Judiciary Committee to investigate Douglas's moral character, as a prelude to possible impeachment. Douglas's response was a sly reference to the many congressmen who kept mistresses: "Well, at least I married mine!"[60]

The mutual loathing between Douglas and Frankfurter was matched by that between Hugo Black and Robert Jackson. The two men were at odds almost as soon as Jackson joined the Court in 1941. Their conflict was exacerbated when the Court decided a 1945 dispute between a coal company and the mine workers' union. Jackson accused Black of manipulating the timing of the Court's decision to help the miners in their negotiations with the coal companies, and later, when he learned that the union's lawyer was Black's former law partner, Jackson was angry with Black for his failure to recuse from the case.[61]

The animosity between Jackson and Black boiled over in 1946, when Chief Justice Harlan Fiske Stone died. Jackson hoped to be his successor, and Black may have as well. It was widely reported that each threatened to resign if the other became chief justice. Truman sidestepped the controversy by appointing Fred Vinson instead. But Jackson, who was still in Nuremberg, could not let the matter rest. He cabled Truman from Germany to repeat his accusations against Black from the previous year's coal mining case. "The controversy within the court over that case is more than a mere personal vendetta," Jackson insisted. "It affects the reputation of the court as a disinterested, non-political tribunal." He told Truman that "the impression has been created" that Truman would have appointed Jackson as chief justice, had it not been for Black's opposition. Truman promptly sent a return telegram. "I am afraid you have been grossly misinformed," he told Jackson. "I have not discussed the question of the appointment of a new chief justice with any member of the Court." Jackson, perhaps suffering from the strain of the Nuremberg trials, then released his accusations against Black to the press. Black and the other justices were astonished. So was Truman. "It sure is a lucky thing I did not make Jackson Chief Justice," Truman told his wife. "He has surely gone haywire. You never can tell how men will react. He was so dead sure he would be Chief that he had to take it out on somebody." Truman called Black and urged him not to respond.[62] Black never did, at least not in public.

These disputes among the justices could reach extraordinary levels of pettiness, perhaps never more so than in 1945, when Owen Roberts retired. It was customary for a departing justice to receive a short, courteous letter, signed by all his colleagues, made up of platitudes about the retiring justice's service to the Court. But the justices could not even cooperate to that extent. When Chief Justice Harlan Fiske Stone drafted a letter, Black objected to two passages, one that expressed the justices' regret that their association with Roberts had come to an end, and another that said: "You have made fidelity to principle your guide to decision." Black refused to sign the letter unless these passages were omitted. When Stone recirculated the letter with the offending sentences left out, Jackson refused to sign the shorter version. "I think the deletions leave the letter so colorless that it would be better to omit the letter entirely," he told Stone. He urged Stone to send Roberts the original version without Black's signature. "If we are obliged to sacrifice either una-nimity or good will," he reckoned, "I should let unanimity go." Frankfurter was willing to omit the first passage, but not the second, about Roberts's fi-delity to principle. In his characteristic style, however, Frankfurter could not praise Roberts without insulting him as well. It was important to include the line about "fidelity to principle," Frankfurter told Stone, because "if there's one thing true about Roberts, that's it! He had, from my point of view, se-rious intellectual limitations—above all, a lack of a more or less coherent ju-ristic or social philosophy." But Frankfurter thought fidelity to principle "was his outstanding characteristic—often misconceiving of course the relevance of principles or their conditioned limits." In the end, only five justices were willing to sign Black's shorter version of the letter, and Frank Murphy, who was one of the five, preferred Stone's original longer version.[63] Stone threw in the towel. Roberts received no letter at all.

While this may have been a trivial incident, it illustrates how poorly the justices got along during this period, and that turned out not to be trivial at all. The justices' mutual hatreds would have an enduring effect on how the Court functioned. Dissenting opinions, once rare, became common.

Justices had always disagreed, but the norm had been to publish dissenting opinions only rarely, in cases where the dissenter thought it especially im-portant to do so. Dissenting more often would have been impractical before the Court gained control of its docket in 1925, because the caseload was too large, but dissents remained unusual even afterward. In the 1920 term, there were dissenting opinions in 7% of the Court's cases. The percentage had not changed much in a century. In the 1930 term, a few years after the Court gained control of its caseload, that figure was only 8%, and as late as the 1940 term it was still just 16%. Then it skyrocketed. In the 1943 term, there were dissents in 52% of the cases. In 1949, 72% of the cases. And in 1952, the dis-sent rate hit 80%, the highest it has ever been. The longstanding norm of dissenting only in exceptional cases had been replaced, in just a few years, with a new norm, according to which justices were expected to publish a dissenting opinion every time they disagreed with the majority. The Court has followed the new norm ever since. Dissent rates since the 1950s have hovered between 50% and 70%, with only a few years slightly below 50%.[64]

This transformation was caused by several related factors. So many new justices had been appointed in such a short span of time that there were no old-timers on the Court to enforce its traditions. When Stone died in 1946,

Harold Burton realized, to his surprise, that it was the first time in the Court's history when there had been no justice who had served longer than thirteen years (except of course during the Court's first thirteen years). His longest-serving colleague, Black, was only in his tenth year. Burton noted in his diary that "it is the most junior court since 1799 when it was ten years old."[65] These new justices had very little judicial experience. They had not been socialized in the norm of suppressing dissent. Instead, they had been law professors, senators, or high-ranking officials in the Justice Department—positions in which one was expected to state one's views. But it was probably more important that some of the new justices—especially Frankfurter, Douglas, Jackson, and Black—had such prickly personalities. They were men who *enjoyed* disagreement and had few inhibitions about disagreeing in public. And some of them hated each other. They welcomed opportunities to display their colleagues' errors to the public.

The sudden proliferation of dissents drew considerable criticism from lawyers. One Dallas attorney wrote to Stone to complain that nine of the Court's last fifteen cases had included dissenting opinions. "I believe that I speak for the lawyers generally," he affirmed, "when I say that what we would like is a statement of the law as decided by a majority of the Supreme Court, shorn of the statements of what is not the law." Another lawyer took his grievance straight to President Truman. "We have four professors of law, or former professors, on the Supreme Court," he observed. "In my humble opinion one would be too many! They usually divide two and two." A New York lawyer told the *Herald Tribune* that all these dissents were causing the Court to lose the respect of the bar and the public. "There seems to be a growing tendency to disagree," he lamented. He blamed Stone, because "it is one of the essential functions of a chief justice to persuade his associates not to insist on differences which can be adjusted."[66]

Stone did try, gingerly, to persuade his colleagues to dissent less often. "I do not think it is the appropriate function of a Chief Justice to attempt to dissuade members of the Court from dissenting in individual cases," he began. "Nevertheless I feel free to say that there is considerable scope for judicial self-restraint in the matter of dissent, lest its usefulness and effectiveness be impaired by its abuse." He worried that "the more numerous the dissents, the more trivial the matters with which they deal, the less likely are any to be read, and the more the public is likely to gain the impression that we are obsessed with trivialities rather than the larger issues which the Court is called on to decide." Fred Vinson, Stone's successor as chief justice, also tried to convince the justices to dissent less often. "I do feel that the Bench, the Bar and the public generally have a right to be critical of the many opinions that sometimes appear," he suggested. "I know that the Bench and Bar have great difficulty, at times, in knowing what to do when we get through with some cases."[67]

But these admonitions fell on deaf ears. Frankfurter even suggested reviving the Court's eighteenth-century custom of having each justice write an opinion in every case, a practice he noted was still followed in England. He thought that "dissents are more often unwisely suppressed than unwisely uttered." If the bar or the public had trouble parsing multiple opinions, he insisted, the fault lay with them, not with the Court. "If there is one thing that the history of this Court proves," Frankfurter declared, "it is that very little attention should be paid to the ephemeral griping of an uninformed laity and, too often, of an unlearned or narrowly preoccupied bar."[68] Publishing the justices' disagreements remained the norm.

Jackson died in 1954. Frankfurter retired in 1962. Black and Douglas would remain on the Court until 1971 and 1975 respectively. Their successors were less cantankerous. There would never again be so much ill will at the Court, despite the wide political gulf between some of the justices. But the return of good feelings did not bring back the custom of suppressing dissent and speaking with one voice. The change was permanent. Ever since, justices who disagree with the majority have been expected to explain why.

12

Desegregation

The Supreme Court was a profoundly conservative institution before the mid-twentieth century. When Congress tried to legislate racial equality after the Civil War, the Court brought this effort to an abrupt end. When state legislatures experimented with reforms like minimum wages and maximum working hours, the Court held these measures unconstitutional. In the early twentieth century, when the federal government assumed new powers to regulate a newly national economy, the Court forced it to back down. The Court always blocked social change rather than encouraging it. Tocqueville had described American lawyers as "the opponents of innovation."[1] Until the mid-twentieth century, this was certainly true of the Supreme Court.

And then, for a brief period, the Court became a force for social change. If there is any decision that best represents this transformation in the Court's role, it is *Brown v. Board of Education* (1954), the case in which the Court required the desegregation of schools throughout the country. Seventy years later, *Brown* remains perhaps the Court's most famous case. *Brown* is now met with almost universal approval, but it was intensely controversial in its day. Integration was extraordinarily unpopular among white people in the South. And even many who supported integration thought it was a goal that should be accomplished through political means, not by the decree of nine unelected judges. *Brown* has thus become a symbol, not just of high hopes for racial equality, but of a particular vision of the Court's role in bringing about social change.

I

The Court did not take any interest in desegregation until the late 1930s. By then, however, three interrelated developments were underway that would combine to bring the issue to the top of the Court's agenda.

The first was the establishment of civil rights organizations devoted to litigation campaigns and political activism. The most important of these organizations from the Court's perspective was the NAACP Legal Defense and Educational Fund, or the LDF. Originally the legal department of the National Association for the Advancement of Colored People, the LDF became a separate entity in 1940 under the leadership of Thurgood Marshall. The LDF planned and litigated virtually all the challenges to segregation that reached the Court in the 1940s and 1950s, and these cases were just the tip of an iceberg of litigation in the lower courts.[2] In earlier eras, there had been no specialized civil rights lawyers and no system of paying for them. Cases involving civil rights were handled on an ad hoc basis, typically by white lawyers who had never litigated any such cases before. The LDF, by contrast, raised funds to employ a small group of lawyers, some black and some white, who were experts in the field and who were strongly committed to racial equality. Without this infrastructure, it would not have been possible to maintain the decades-long program of litigation that propelled a handful of high-profile cases to the Supreme Court.

Second, a set of institutional changes at the Court itself made the environment better for desegregation than it had ever been before. The end of circuit-riding and the attendant weakening of the tradition of regional representation meant the Court was no longer majority-southern, as it had been before the Civil War. Four of the justices were from the South in the 1940s and early 1950s, and when Earl Warren replaced Fred Vinson as chief justice in 1953 there were only three—Hugo Black, Stanley Reed, and Tom Clark. Greater representation from the South would have made it harder for the Court to find segregation unconstitutional. The Judiciary Act of 1925, by giving the Court control over which cases it would hear, allowed the Court to create new constitutional rights without worrying about being swamped by all the new cases that would come before it. The Court could recognize a right to integrated schools, for example, without overloading its docket with appeals from every school district in the South. Franklin Roosevelt's long tenure as president allowed him to fill the Court with justices amenable to arguments for racial equality. By the mid-1940s the Court was farther to the left of the contemporary political spectrum than it had ever been. Finally, in the previous two decades the Court had gradually become more receptive to new kinds of noneconomic constitutional rights, including rights to free speech and to fair criminal trials. The justices were developing habits of thought that would smooth the path toward an expanded conception of a constitutional right to equality.

Third, elite white opinion regarding segregation began to change at midcentury, outside the South. This development had many causes, including the growing civil rights movement, the great black migration from the South to northern cities, the years of war against an enemy whose distinguishing feature was an extreme form of race discrimination, and the Cold War concern with the image of the United States in other countries. In the 1940s, major national institutions that had long been segregated commenced a long, slow process of integration. The American Bar Association accepted its first black member in decades, the New York judge James S. Watson, in 1943, after adopting a resolution declaring that race should not be a factor in determining its membership. In 1949, the New York gynecologist Peter Marshall Murray became the first black member of the American Medical Association's House of Delegates.[3] Baseball, by far the most popular professional sport at the time, began desegregating in 1945, when the Brooklyn Dodgers signed Jackie Robinson to a minor league contract. Robinson played his first game for the Dodgers in 1947. Professional football integrated in 1946, when Kenny Washington joined the Los Angeles Rams, and professional basketball followed suit in 1950. The armed forces began desegregating in 1948, when President Harry Truman signed an executive order requiring racial equality in the military.

The justices were caught up in this trend, as demonstrated by two events that took place at the Court during the winter of 1947–1948. The first involved the Court's annual Christmas party. Jobs at the Court were divided by race (and by sex). The justices and their law clerks were white men, the justices' secretaries were white women, and the justices' messengers were black men. As Marquis Childs, a reporter who covered the Court at the time, explained, "each justice has of course a sort of Negro attendant who is a kind of faithful body servant." In December 1947, a group of law clerks proposed inviting the messengers, for the first time, to the Christmas party. The law clerks suggested that while no institution should exclude employees from an office party based on their race, it was especially wrong for the Supreme Court to do it. The clerks' proposal was opposed by the secretaries, who refused to attend the party if the messengers would be there. Thomas Waggaman, the Court's marshal, was the person responsible for granting permission to use one of the Court's conference rooms for the party, but he refused to do so if the messengers would be invited, unless he was so instructed by Chief Justice Fred Vinson. Vinson was reluctant to approve without conferring with his colleagues. So it was that the justices gathered in December 1947, not to discuss one of their cases, but to resolve a dispute closer to home. Who would be invited to the Christmas party?[4]

Vinson, Black, and Reed, all southerners, favored inviting the messengers, although Reed declared that he would not attend the party himself. Frankfurter thought that anyone holding a social function at the Court should be allowed to invite anyone they chose, without oversight from the justices. Jackson was the only justice who sided with the secretaries. He pointed out that "our hostesses, our wives, don't have our servants, and our messengers, as guests at our parties." Jackson proposed adopting a rule prohibiting the use of the Court's conference rooms for social events, but only Frankfurter agreed. Vinson and Reed were afraid the Court would look bad if the news should leak that the justices had closed off the conference rooms to prevent black employees from attending a Christmas party. In the end, there was no Christmas party in 1947. There would not be another until 1959.[5] Desegregation was just as difficult inside the Court as anywhere else.

Soon after the Christmas party debate, Frankfurter hired the Court's first black law clerk. William Coleman had the highest grades in Harvard Law School's class of 1946. He was clerking for Judge Herbert Goodrich on the Court of Appeals in Philadelphia. Frankfurter's former Harvard colleagues were unusually tentative in recommending Coleman, but Frankfurter brushed their reservations aside. "I don't care what color a man has, any more than I care what religion he professes or doesn't," he told the Harvard professor Paul Freund. Frankfurter's decision to make Coleman his clerk was front-page news in papers all over the country. "Frankfurter's Negro Clerk to be First in Court History," read the headline in the *Washington Post*. The black-owned *Atlanta Daily World* called Coleman's hiring "a splendid beginning." Frankfurter received admiring letters from all over the country. "At the very time we Negro citizens are being made to feel we are second and third class citizens, some *noble soul* like you enters the scene and our morale ascends to great heights," wrote the Chicago musician James Mundy. "Thank God! His truth is marching on!" A judge in Denver told Frankfurter that the example he set would do more to bring about racial equality than any legislation could possibly accomplish—and proudly added that "a member of the Syrian race is now serving as my law clerk."[6] After clerking for Frankfurter during the 1947–1948 term, Coleman would go on to a long and distinguished legal career.

These developments inside and outside the Court set the stage for a series of cases in which the Court would try to chip away at long-established patterns of segregation. The first significant case, *Missouri ex rel. Gaines v. Canada* (1938), was a challenge brought by the NAACP to the exclusion of black students from the University of Missouri's law school. Lloyd Gaines had recently graduated from Lincoln University, the state's black college. Gaines wished to attend law school, but Lincoln University had no law school. The only public law school in the state was at the white-only University of Missouri. Rather than admitting black law students, the state would pay the tuition for black Missourians to attend law school in other states. The NAACP argued that even under the "separate but equal" formula of *Plessy v. Ferguson*, an out-of-state legal education was inherently unequal to one in Missouri, because a student hoping to practice law in Missouri needed to learn about the state's law and to gain experience in the state's courts, and because prospective clients in Missouri accorded more prestige to the University of Missouri than to law schools in other states.[7]

Chief Justice Charles Evans Hughes's opinion for the Court went even farther. It made no difference whether an out-of-state law school was as good as the University of Missouri, the Court held, because the state had an obligation to provide an equal education for all its residents, a duty it could not foist on other states. If Missouri had a law school for white students, it had to have one for black students too. The only dissenters were Pierce Butler and the defiantly racist James McReynolds, the last remaining members of the Court's conservative wing. The Court's decision would "break down the settled practice concerning separate schools and thereby, as indicated by experience, damnify both races," McReynolds predicted. He insinuated that Gaines did not even want to attend law school and that the real impetus behind the case came from the NAACP. "The State has offered to provide the negro petitioner opportunity for study of the law—if perchance that is the thing really desired—by paying his tuition at some nearby school of good standing," and that was enough, McReynolds insisted. "The State should not be unduly hampered through theorization inadequately restrained by experience." *Gaines* itself had little effect on segregation, even in law schools. The state responded, not by admitting black students to the University of Missouri's law school, but by establishing a black law school at Lincoln University. It would be many years before the University of Missouri would admit its first black law student. But if *Gaines* accomplished little on its own, it was the Court's first step on a long road toward prohibiting segregation. In 1940, well before the Court decided its most important civil rights cases, the black political scientist and future diplomat Ralph Bunche already told

Hugo Black that "among Negro intellectuals it was widely believed that the Supreme Court is the strongest bulwark against the oppression of the Negro."[8]

The Court took a more substantial step a few years later in *Smith v. Allwright* (1944). One device that southern states used to prevent black people from voting was to allow political parties to set their own rules for primary elections, rather than establishing the rules by state law. Because the political parties were private organizations rather than arms of the government, they were not constrained by the Constitution. In *Grovey v. Townsend* (1935), for this reason, the Court had unanimously permitted the Texas Democratic Party to limit its primaries to white voters. So-called white primaries were standard throughout the South. But the Court's membership turned over almost completely in the next few years. In *Smith*, the Court overruled *Grovey* and held that although the Texas Democratic Party was nominally a private organization, the role of its primaries in the state's electoral system required treating the party as if it were a branch of the state. "If the state requires a certain electoral procedure," the Kentuckian Stanley Reed concluded for the Court, "it endorses, adopts and enforces the discrimination against Negroes, practiced by a party entrusted by Texas law with the determination of the qualifications of participants in the primary. This is state action within the meaning of the Fifteenth Amendment." Owen Roberts, the author of *Grovey*, was the only dissenter. "The reason for my concern," he explained, in a phrase that would be quoted often in later years, "is that the instant decision, overruling that announced about nine years ago, tends to bring adjudications of this tribunal into the same class as a restricted railroad ticket, good for this day and train only." If the Court was so willing to overrule a case decided only a few years earlier, Roberts wondered, what would become of its opinion in *Smith* a few years hence?[9]

Chief Justice Harlan Fiske Stone deliberately assigned the *Smith* opinion to Reed in the hope that the decision would be received more favorably in the South if it were written by a southerner. He initially assigned it to Frankfurter, but he reconsidered after Robert Jackson suggested that Stone had "overlooked some of the ugly factors in our national life which go to the wisdom of having Mr. Justice Frankfurter act as the voice of this Court." The justices all recognized that *Smith* was "a delicate matter," as Jackson put it. "We deny the entire South the right to a white primary, which is one of its most cherished rights." Jackson feared that the Court's decision "may be greatly weakened if the voice that utters it is one that may grate on Southern sensibilities." Frankfurter, as everyone knew, "unites in a rare degree factors which unhappily excite prejudice" in the South. He was Jewish. He was an immigrant. He was a northerner. "I suggest that the Court's decision, bound to arouse bitter resentment, will be much less apt to stir ugly reactions if the news that the white primary has been outlawed is broken to it, if possible, by a Southerner who has been a Democrat and is not a member of one of the minorities which stir prejudices kindred to those against the Negro," Jackson advised. Stone agreed.[10]

But *Smith* came as a shock in the South, despite the messenger. Texas had employed the white primary for nearly a century, a Fort Worth lawyer complained to Reed, "yet this new Court, self endowed with super-human intellect, has looked back one hundred and fifty years and decided that our forefathers who founded this country never intended to allow the people of the states to prescribe any limitation whatsoever upon the voting privilege." The Court's decision "has already led to racial strife," the lawyer continued. "It will grow worse with the further encouragement of negro radicals." If the white primary was unconstitutional, he worried, then "our laws preventing the inter-marriage of negroes with white persons are unconstitutional. The owners of our hotels, restaurants, drug stores, and barber shops will become subject to damage suits if they refuse to serve the negroes. Our schools are certain to be invaded by negroes. We may even see the Federal bayonet used to enforce some such decision by the Supreme Court of the United States."[11] The lawyer may have intended to depict a string of absurdities he thought could never happen. But every single one of his predictions would come to pass in the next twenty-five years.

Soon after deciding *Smith*, the Court struck another blow at another pervasive form of segregation in *Shelley v. Kraemer* (1948). Ever since *Buchanan v. Warley* (1917), in which the Court had held that zoning ordinances requiring segregation were unconstitutional, residential segregation had been enforced primarily through restrictive covenants, agreements among white neighbors not to sell or rent their properties to nonwhites. These were so common that three of the justices—Reed, Jackson, and Rutledge—had to recuse themselves from *Shelley* because the deeds to their own houses included restrictive covenants. The Court decided in *Corrigan v. Buckley* (1926) that because such agreements involved only private landowners, they did not violate the Equal Protection Clause of the Fourteenth Amendment, which prohibits discrimination only by state governments, not by private parties. *Shelley* raised the same issue only a couple of decades later. Indeed, because the constitutionality of discriminatory covenants was so clearly settled, the justices' law clerks recommended that the Court decline to hear the case. "No one who has had any experience with urban housing conditions can doubt that the restrictive covenant has resulted in a great many substantial social evils," acknowledged Francis Allen, who was clerking for Chief Justice Fred Vinson. But Allen suggested that "an abrupt and sweeping judicial invalidation of all restrictive covenants might well create about as many problems as it would solve." Harris Weston, Justice Harold Burton's clerk, agreed. "This case troubles me," he advised Burton. "The covenant enforced is obviously undemocratic and contrary to the theory of the Constitution." But "no case, apparently, has held that enforcement of a contract between private parties, even by way of injunction, amounts to state action. I doubt that it does."[12]

The Court nevertheless agreed to hear *Shelley v. Kraemer*, which suggests that at least some of the justices were already inclined to hold discriminatory covenants unconstitutional. This inclination received an unexpected boost when the United States government, for the first time in its history, filed an amicus brief in the Supreme Court condemning race discrimination. The idea originated with Philip Elman, a lawyer in the Solicitor General's office, who recognized that the time was right to persuade his superiors—Solicitor General Philip Perlman, Attorney General Tom Clark, and ultimately President Harry Truman—that the government should weigh in on the side of racial equality. "Truman's Gallup poll ratings at that time were very low," Elman recalled. "It looked as though whoever was going to run against him in 1948, probably Dewey, would beat him badly. Tom Clark was attorney general, and he and Perlman were political animals, very much aware of the Negro vote." Elman got permission to draft a brief, which, as he described it, "contained a lot of high-blown rhetoric about liberty and equality and so on." Elman took the unusual step of including Tom Clark's name among the brief's signatories, "because I wanted this brief—which broadly condemned governmental support of all forms of racial discrimination—to be as authoritative a statement of the position of the United States as possible. If I could have, I'd have put Truman's name on it." The initial draft of the brief also, more customarily, bore the names of the four Justice Department lawyers who had worked on it—Hilbert Zarky, Oscar Davis, Stanley Silverberg, and Elman himself. Deputy Solicitor General Arnold Raum kept Clark's name on the brief but deleted the names of the four lawyers who had actually written it. "It's bad enough that Perlman's name has to be there, to have one Jew's name on it," Raum explained, "but you have also put four more Jewish names on. That makes it look as if a bunch of Jewish lawyers in the Department of Justice put this out." In the end, as Elman recalled, this first-of-its-kind brief, in which the government of the United States argued to the Supreme Court for an end to race discrimination, "itself involved an ironic bit of religious discrimination. The names of the four Jewish lawyers who wrote the brief were stricken by their Jewish superior."[13] Just as the Court worried about making Frankfurter the spokesman for civil rights, the Justice Department worried that the identity of its messengers might weaken the force of its message.

In *Shelley*, the Court unanimously held that discriminatory covenants are unconstitutional. Vinson's opinion for the Court explained that while the covenants themselves did not constitute state action, the fact that the covenants were ultimately enforced by the courts meant that the state was involved in the discrimination. "These are not cases in which the States have merely abstained from action, leaving private individuals free to impose such discriminations as they see fit," Vinson reasoned. "Rather, these are cases in which the States have made available to such individuals the full coercive power of government to deny to petitioners, on the grounds of race or color, the enjoyment of property rights."[14] This rationale, if taken to its logical conclusion, would have extended the constitutional prohibition to all kinds of private discrimination, because all private claims are ultimately enforced by the courts. But the rationale of *Shelley* would never be taken that far. To this day, *Shelley* remains a one-time exception to the general principle that the constitution limits only action by the government, an exception the Court created because of the developing consensus among elite non-southern lawyers that discriminatory covenants should be outlawed.

No sooner had the Court decided *Shelley* than it confronted two new challenges to segregated graduate schools. A lower court had forced the University of Oklahoma to admit George McLaurin to its graduate school of education, but the state had complied with the court's order as grudgingly as possible, by requiring McLaurin to sit apart from the white students in a separate room adjoining the classroom, to eat separately from the white students in the cafeteria, and to study alone at a designated table in the library. The University of Texas had refused to admit Heman Sweatt to its law school. Instead, the university created an entirely new law school just for a handful of black students. Both cases tested the limits of *Plessy*'s "separate but equal" doctrine, because they posed the question whether education segregated by space (as in *McLaurin*) or by institution (as in *Sweatt*) could ever truly be equal. The cases also tested the willingness of the justices to reach a decision that was sure to be vociferously denounced throughout the South.[15]

Before the cases were argued, the law clerks to the Court's newest justice, Tom Clark, summarized the range of views held on these questions by Clark's colleagues. Some of the justices, they reported, thought that "the *Plessy* rule is a desirable one which should be left on the books." Other justices, by contrast, "say that the *Plessy* rule should be overruled entirely." This was also the position taken by the Truman administration, which filed another amicus brief in the two cases urging that "racial segregation is itself a manifestation of inequality and discrimination." But if *Plessy* were completely overruled, the clerks cautioned, "there is likely to be some degree of social unrest and dislocation" in the South, because it would imply that segregation was unconstitutional in all walks of life. They preferred a "compromise solution" proposed by Frankfurter, "which would interpret the Constitution in the 'right' way and would avoid, at least for the interim, most of the possibilities

Figure 12.1 George McLaurin was required to sit in a separate room from the white students at the University of Oklahoma's graduate school of education. In *McLaurin v. Oklahoma*, the Court found this requirement unconstitutional. Library of Congress, LC-DIG-ds-14150.

of defiance in the South." The compromise was merely to say that segregation was unconstitutional in graduate schools, and to leave the thornier questions for another day. "This may seem artificial," they acknowledged, "but perhaps it isn't. The only cases before us concern graduate schools, and in graduate schools, more than anywhere else, the student needs the free discussion and seminar classes, the give and take which only the large, well-established law or graduate school can provide."[16]

This was the strategy the Court adopted. In two short, unanimous opinions by Vinson, the Court required Oklahoma and Texas to integrate their schools based on rationales that were specific to graduate school. In *McLaurin*, Vinson emphasized that the separation of McLaurin from the white students would "impair and inhibit his ability to study, to engage in discussions and exchange views with other students, and, in general, to learn his profession." In *Sweatt*, Vinson highlighted the intangible aspects of legal education that gave value to a law degree—the "reputation of the faculty, experience of the administration, position and influence of the alumni, standing in the community, traditions and prestige" that made the University of Texas inherently superior to any brand-new law school. "Since these cases arise in 'my' part of the country," Clark suggested to his colleagues, he could assure them that the Court's carefully drawn opinions would not cause too much controversy. "The 'horribles' following reversal of the cases pictured by the States . . . are highly exaggerated," he told them. "There would be no 'incidents,' in my opinion, if the cases are limited to their facts, *i.e.*, graduate schools." The southern states' real concern, he observed, "was the extension of the doctrine to the elementary and secondary schools. Certainly this is not required now. I would be opposed to such extension at this time and would vote against taking a case involving same." Clark's colleagues shared his sense that the Court should proceed slowly and carefully in changing the law regarding segregation. "I certainly would not want to have anything in the opinion which would stir up feeling of anger and resentment in any portion of the country," Vinson told Frankfurter. Frankfurter agreed that "the shorter the opinion, the more there is an appearance of unexcitement and inevitability about it, the better."[17]

Between the late 1930s and the early 1950s, the Court had taken significant steps toward re-interpreting the Constitution to prohibit segregation. These decisions—*Gaines, Smith, Shelley, McLaurin,* and *Sweatt*—would scarcely have been imaginable a decade or two earlier. Just as remarkable was that some of the justices involved were southerners—Clark was from Texas,

Black was from Alabama, and Vinson and Reed were Kentuckians. The prospect of integrated primaries, integrated graduate schools, and especially integrated residential neighborhoods could not have been welcomed by many of their friends and family members back home. "It took not only wisdom about the law but also vast courage for a chief justice from Kentucky to hold fast to his beliefs," Justice Frank Murphy rightly told Vinson after the Court decided *Shelley*.[18]

Most aspects of life in the South were still segregated by law, however, including areas that white people cared much more about than anything the Court had addressed so far. One of these, as Clark recognized, was elementary and secondary education. Would the Court go so far as to hold that the Constitution required integrated schools for children too?

II

The case we remember as *Brown v. Board of Education* was actually four different cases, all brought by the LDF. In *Brown* itself the plaintiffs were black elementary school students in Topeka, Kansas. The other cases involved elementary and high school students in Clarendon County, South Carolina, high school students in Prince Edward County, Virginia, and elementary and high school students in New Castle County, Delaware. The Court consolidated all four cases and heard them all together in 1952, as one big challenge to the constitutionality of segregated schools.[19]

In the narrowest sense, the cases raised a legal question: Did the Equal Protection Clause forbid school districts from operating separate schools for black students and white students? To answer this question, however, required the justices to grapple with a set of broader political and sociological issues. Was it within the Supreme Court's role to order the complete reorganization of public education in much of the country—the Court had never done anything so transformative in its 160-year history—or was that a task properly left to Congress and state legislatures? If the Court did order school districts to integrate, would they comply, or would overwhelming white opposition render the Court's decree meaningless? In *Brown* the justices had to do much more than simply interpret the Constitution; they had to think about their own place in American government and they had to read the national mood for clues as to how their decision would be received.

The LDF offered the Court a two-level argument: first, that the Court should overrule *Plessy v. Ferguson* and hold segregation itself unconstitutional; and second, that these segregated schools were unconstitutional even under *Plessy* because they were not equal. The federal government, in the waning days of the Truman administration, once again filed an amicus brief urging the Court to find segregation unconstitutional. On the other side of the case, the school districts reminded the Court that decades of precedent were in their favor. The Court had repeatedly affirmed the constitutionality of school segregation. Schools in much of the country had always been segregated. The oral argument in December 1952 pitted Thurgood Marshall and his LDF colleagues against a diverse assortment of white lawyers. In the South Carolina case, the government was represented by the seventy-nine-year-old John W. Davis, the former solicitor general and the Democratic candidate for president in the 1924 election. Davis, the most highly regarded appellate advocate of his day, had appeared before the Court more than a hundred times. He was a veteran of high-profile cases, including most recently the *Steel Seizure Case*, which he had won just the year before. Davis, a firm believer in the rightness and the constitutionality of segregation, defended the South Carolina school district at the request of the state's governor, James Byrnes, the former justice, despite objections from the partners in Davis's New York law firm and even his daughter. *Brown* would be his last argument in the Supreme Court. In the Kansas case, by contrast, the government was represented by a young state attorney named Paul Wilson. *Brown* was the first appellate case of his career.[20]

When the justices first met to discuss the case after the arguments, the outcome was uncertain. There are differing accounts of the justices' initial views because they engaged in a free-form conversation rather than a formal vote, but every account describes a Court that was nearly evenly divided. According to William Douglas, only four of the justices were prepared to vote that school segregation was unconstitutional—Hugo Black, Harold Burton, Sherman Minton, and Douglas himself. Fred Vinson, Stanley Reed, and Tom Clark took the view that the separate-but-equal doctrine of *Plessy v. Ferguson* should still apply to schools. Felix Frankfurter and Robert Jackson thought that segregation was probably constitutional but that the Court should avoid deciding the issue if possible. Frankfurter recalled a similar lineup, but he placed himself on the other side, to make a 5–4 majority for requiring integration. Burton counted six votes for requiring integration, and Jackson thought there might be as many as seven or as few as five, depending on how the opinion was written.[21]

When Jackson asked his law clerks for their advice, he learned that they were likewise divided. One clerk, Donald Cronson, thought *Plessy* was wrong. Jackson's other clerk was William Rehnquist, who would join the Court himself two decades later. "I realize that it is an unpopular and unhumanitarian position, for which I have been excoriated by 'liberal' colleagues," Rehnquist wrote, "but I think *Plessy v. Ferguson* was right and should be re-affirmed." He drew an analogy between the view that segregation was unconstitutional and the view of the early twentieth-century Court (which he personified in Justice James McReynolds) that much economic regulation was unconstitutional. If the Court, "because its members individually are 'liberal' and dislike segregation, now chooses to strike it down," Rehnquist argued, "it differs from the McReynolds court only in the kinds of litigants it favors and the kinds of special claims it protects."[22] When Rehnquist's memo came to light at his 1971 confirmation hearings, he insisted that the views he presented were Jackson's rather than his own, but this seems unlikely. Where the memo says that "I have been excoriated by 'liberal' colleagues" for thinking *Plessy* was rightly decided, the "I" is almost certainly Rehnquist himself, and the "liberal colleagues" the law clerks for the other justices, who were indeed more liberal than Rehnquist. In any event, Jackson would not follow Rehnquist's advice.

The justices were divided in *Brown*, but one thing for which there was a clear majority was that it would be wise to delay deciding the case. To gain time, they adopted Frankfurter's suggestion to order a new round of briefing and a new set of oral arguments on a group of questions about two topics: first, whether the Fourteenth Amendment had been understood to abolish school segregation when it was ratified back in the 1860s, and second, what the precise remedy should be if the Court found segregation unconstitutional. This maneuver allowed the justices to sit on the case for another year until it was reargued in December 1953.

In the interim, during the Court's summer recess, Chief Justice Fred Vinson died suddenly of a heart attack at the age of sixty-three. "Vinson smoked about three packages of cigarettes a day," recalled William Oliver, his law clerk that year. "He went to all the Embassy Row parties and apparently couldn't resist the good food. He was very much overweight. He was probably fifty, sixty, seventy pounds overweight." When Frankfurter returned to Washington to attend Vinson's funeral, his former law clerk Philip Elman picked him up at the train station. "Phil," Frankfurter told Elman, "this is the first solid piece of evidence I've ever had that there really is a God." Elman explained that what Frankfurter "meant was that Vinson's departure from the Court was going to remove the roadblock in *Brown*. As long as Vinson was chief justice, they could never get unanimity or anything close to it. If Vinson dissented, Reed would surely join him, Tom Clark probably would too, and Jackson would write that the issue should be left to Congress."[23] Much would now depend on who would take Vinson's place.

A few months earlier, Dwight Eisenhower, the new president, had promised Earl Warren the next open seat on the Court. Warren had been the governor of California since 1943. He was the Republican candidate for vice president in 1948, when Thomas Dewey lost to Harry Truman. Warren competed with Eisenhower and Robert Taft to be the party's presidential candidate in 1952. At the Republican convention, when it became apparent that Warren would not win the nomination, he supported Eisenhower over Taft, and then he campaigned for Eisenhower in the general election, so Eisenhower felt obliged to offer Warren a position, and the Supreme Court was the position Warren wanted. While he waited for a vacancy on the Court, Warren agreed to serve as solicitor general, but Vinson died just as Warren prepared to leave California for Washington to take up the post. Now Warren would go straight from governor to chief justice.

Eisenhower and his attorney general, Herbert Brownell, considered Warren the ideal person for the job. They thought the chief justice "should not only be qualified in the law," Brownell explained, "but should be someone who was held in high esteem by the American people for past public service," like Charles Evans Hughes and William Howard Taft, two former chief justices who had held prominent elective offices. They also thought that "broad administrative experience" had become a "necessity for the chief justice," who sat as the head of the entire federal judiciary. Meanwhile, the justices were sending word to Eisenhower and Brownell that it was important to appoint a new chief justice quickly, before the Court's new term began, because *Brown* was waiting for them when they took the bench.[24] The Senate was in recess, so Warren promptly received a recess appointment in October 1953 and was confirmed by the Senate the following spring.

Political office had once been a more common route to the Court than experience as a lower court judge, but that tradition was on the wane. Warren's appointment was met with considerable skepticism in some quarters because he was a politician who had never been a judge on any court. "Nobody ever thought of him as a lawyer," recalled Clarence Manion, an official in the Eisenhower administration. Among the Court's law clerks, "there was a lot of feeling that he didn't have the qualifications and the background for it," William Oliver explained. "There was a lot of feeling that it was a political deal out of the '52 Republican convention." One former clerk, William Rehnquist, now a lawyer in Phoenix, reported to Robert Jackson that "everyone here was quite disappointed by the nomination of Warren." Rehnquist thought that "an ability to handle the administrative side and to compromise dissidence would be an asset to an able, experienced lawyer in the job, but they certainly are no substitute for some experience" as a judge. (Seventeen years later, Rehnquist himself would become a justice despite having no experience as a judge.) The letters that Eisenhower received were even blunter in their disapproval. "I had hoped that under Republican leadership, appointment to the Supreme Court would be on the basis of qualification and not as a means of paying off a political debt at the expense of the public," wrote one disappointed New Jerseyan. Another correspondent suggested that "it would have been just as sensible had you appointed the man a General in the Army." An editorial in the *Richmond News Leader* was headlined simply: "Next Time, a Judge!"[25]

But if there was any case for which political experience was more useful than judicial experience, it was *Brown v. Board of Education*. The second round of briefing and argument, concluded in December 1953, added little to what the justices already knew. When they met again to discuss the case, they did not formally vote, but this time it was clear that Warren made a fifth vote to hold that segregated schools were unconstitutional. Reed wanted to affirm the constitutionality of segregation, and Clark, Frankfurter, and Jackson were still uncertain. When Warren's short opinion for the Court was published a few months later, however, the decision was unanimous. "Everyone thought that at least Justice Reed was going to write a dissent," Douglas recalled, "but he finally agreed to leave his doubts unsaid and to go along." Reed did begin writing a dissent, but he abandoned it when he realized that a statement of opposition by a southern justice would only do harm by inspiring resistance to desegregation in the South. Jackson wrote a long separate opinion, which although technically a concurring opinion, expressed so much doubt about the Court's decision that it would have been widely interpreted as a dissent, had it been published. But Jackson did not publish it, a decision that may have been influenced by the fact that he suffered a major heart attack in March 1954 and was hospitalized until May.

Jackson only left the hospital so he could be in the courtroom when Warren announced the Court's decision. Frankfurter likewise suppressed his own ambivalence so the Court could speak with a single voice.[26] The Court's unanimity in *Brown* is often attributed to Warren's leadership skills, but just as important was his colleagues' willingness—an uncharacteristic willingness in the case of Jackson and Frankfurter—to stay quiet.

Warren tried to make the *Brown* opinion "short, readable by the lay public, non-rhetorical, unemotional and, above all, non-accusatory." The Court's opinion in *Brown* is indeed unusual in that it reads as if it were written for the general public rather than for lawyers. It is about education, not about law. "Education is perhaps the most important function of state and local governments," Warren began. "It is required in the performance of our most basic public responsibilities, even service in the armed forces. It is the very foundation of good citizenship. Today it is a principal instrument in awakening the child to cultural values, in preparing him for later professional training, and in helping him to adjust normally to his environment. In these days, it is doubtful that any child may reasonably be expected to succeed in life if he is denied the opportunity of an education." Warren then turned to the crux of the case. "Does segregation of children in public schools solely on the basis of race, even though the physical facilities and other 'tangible' factors may be equal, deprive the children of the minority group of equal educational opportunities?" he asked. "We believe that it does." This was because separating black children "from others of similar age and qualifications solely because of their race generates a feeling of inferiority as to their status in the community that may affect their hearts and minds in a way unlikely ever to be undone." The Court accordingly concluded that "in the field of public education the doctrine of 'separate but equal' has no place. Separate educational facilities are inherently unequal." And that was all. In just a few paragraphs, in a style that rested on common-sense justice rather than on conventional legal analysis, the Court decided that segregated schools were unconstitutional.[27]

The justices were well aware of the decision's importance. As Warren finished announcing the Court's opinion, Felix Frankfurter passed him a note to say: "This is a day that will live in glory. It is also a great day in the history of the Court." Harold Burton scribbled a note with a similar message. "Today I believe has been a great day for America and the Court," he told Warren. "I expect there will be no more significant decision made during our service on the Court. I cherish the privilege of sharing in this."[28]

Figure 12.2 Outside the Supreme Court, the lawyers George E. C. Hayes, Thurgood Marshall, and James M. Nabrit celebrate their victory in *Brown v. Board of Education*. Library of Congress, LC-DIG-ppmsca-38654.

Warren promptly arranged a public gesture of integration by hiring fourteen-year-old Charles Bush as the Court's first black page. The Court had long employed a few teenagers as pages each year to carry books and documents to the justices, but Bush was the first page whose selection made the national headlines. The Court's pages attended the Capitol Page School along with the pages who worked in Congress, who were then all white, so Bush's appointment caused the immediate integration of one high school. As Bush later reflected, Warren's "intent was to demonstrate to the world that the Supreme Court was indeed serious about the school integration decision."[29]

But what would happen next? What exactly would segregated school districts be required to do? The justices all had "qualms . . . about how we were going to implement it," Clark recalled. "This is a situation that had been existing, you know, over a hundred years." White parents were clearly not going to welcome black children into their schools with open arms. The justices ordered a third round of briefing and argument, this time devoted to the remedy the Court should order. In another unanimous opinion authored by Warren, this one even shorter than the first, the Court was deliberately vague about what school districts had to do. The cases were remanded to the trial courts to work out the details. "Full implementation of these constitutional principles may require solution of varied local school problems," Warren explained. "Because of their proximity to local conditions and the possible need for further hearings, the courts which originally heard these cases can best perform this judicial appraisal." The Court's only guidance was that schools should be desegregated "with all deliberate speed," a selfcontradictory phrase suggested by Frankfurter.[30]

But schools were not desegregated with any kind of speed, deliberate or otherwise. White political leaders throughout the South were virtually uniform in refusing to comply with *Brown*. In 1956, an anti-*Brown* manifesto was signed by nineteen of the twenty-two southern senators (all but the three with national political aspirations, Lyndon Johnson of Texas and Albert Gore and Estes Kefauver of Tennessee) and seventy-seven of the 105 southern representatives. Opposition to *Brown* propelled the political careers of segregationist state officials like Alabama Governor George Wallace, whose 1963 inaugural address lambasted "a group of men on the Supreme Court" who persecuted the "white minority to the whim of the international colored majority," before concluding with a call for "segregation now, segregation tomorrow, segregation forever." "The Court expected some resistance from the South," Warren reflected. "But I doubt if any of us expected as much as we got." In the early 1960s, schools were nearly as segregated as ever. Ten years after *Brown*, only 1.2% of southern black children attended a school with white students.[31]

Some of the opposition to integrating schools was directed personally to the justices themselves, especially to the justices from the South. "How can you, a white man and a former Southerner, ever face your Southern friends again after you have betrayed the race that bore you by signing a paper that will release hordes of dirty, diseased, illiterate, ill-mannered niggers to sit in schools along with our white daughters?" one irate Marylander asked of Hugo Black. A white resident of Selma, Alabama, who had helped Black in his Senate campaigns wrote to offer counsel. "It is evident you have been away from your native state so long that you have forgotten how the rural negro thinks and acts," he advised. "These so-called citizens still break the rules of sanitation, knife each other, menace the laws, carry a filthy stink, and by no stretch of the imagination are ready for enrollment in white schools." Two white ninth-graders from Alabama who had learned about *Brown* in their civics class assured Black that integration was unnecessary, because "in Alabama, the Negroes seem to be content the way they are, as are the white people, and we're sure that everyone would prefer to remain as they are."[32]

Segregationists were not the only opponents of *Brown*. Some of the most distinguished judges and lawyers of the period, men who deplored segregation, nevertheless criticized the Court for crossing the line that separated law from politics. Judge Learned Hand lamented that the Court had become "a third legislative chamber" that approved or disapproved legislation based on nothing more than the justices' own values. The Columbia law professor Herbert Wechsler saw *Brown* as a clash between competing constitutional rights—on one hand, the right of black people to equality, and on the other, the right of white people to choose with whom they would associate. "If the freedom of association is denied by segregation, integration forces an association upon those for whom it is unpleasant or repugnant," Wechsler reasoned. "Given a situation where the state must practically choose between denying the association to those individuals who wish it or imposing it on those who would avoid it, is there a basis in neutral principles for holding that the Constitution demands that the claims for association should prevail?" Wechsler suggested that the choice was political, not legal, and that the Court had accordingly strayed from its proper role in choosing integration.[33]

Brown might have had a greater effect if desegregation efforts had received more support from the Eisenhower administration and from Congress. But Congress could muster only the weakest civil rights legislation before the mid-1960s, and the administration took only a sporadic interest in the subject. Eisenhower himself was ambivalent about desegregation. "These are not bad people," he told Warren while *Brown* was pending in the Court, referring to southern whites. "All they are concerned about is to see that their sweet little girls are not required to sit in school alongside some big overgrown Negroes." The administration did offer support at one crucial moment. When Arkansas Governor Orval Faubus ordered the state militia to prevent black students from entering a Little Rock high school at the start of the 1957 school year, Eisenhower sent federal troops to Little Rock to ensure that the students could attend school. The following year, in *Cooper v. Aaron* (1958), the Court rebuffed the Little Rock school board's efforts to postpone desegregation for another two and a half years. Although the Court's opinion was primarily written by one of the Court's newest justices, William Brennan, it was signed by all nine justices, for the only time in the Court's history, to emphasize their unanimity. "The federal judiciary is supreme in the exposition of the law of the Constitution," they declared. "It follows that the interpretation of the Fourteenth Amendment enunciated by this Court in the Brown case is the supreme law of the land," which state officials could not disobey.[34]

Apart from *Cooper*, however, southern resistance to desegregation caused the Court to proceed very cautiously in the years after *Brown*. Because the *Brown* opinion had relied on the unique attributes of schools to hold segregated education unconstitutional, it was still an open question whether segregation was also unconstitutional in public parks, beaches, transportation, and the like. The Court avoided discussing the subject. Instead, when cases arrived posing constitutional challenges to segregation in fields other than education, rather than explaining why the Constitution prohibited segregation, the Court merely issued one-sentence orders either affirming the lower court (where it had found segregation unconstitutional) or reversing the lower court (where it had not). When a case arrived challenging a Virginia law barring interracial marriage, a case within the surviving remnant of the Court's mandatory jurisdiction and thus one it was required to hear, the Court nevertheless ducked the case with a single sentence unconvincingly asserting that the case did not present a federal question. We "shunted it away," Frankfurter admitted to Learned Hand, "and I pray we may be able to do it again, without being too brazenly evasive."[35] For ten years after *Brown*, the Court denied review in every school segregation case that came before it, except for *Cooper v. Aaron*.[36] The Court had gone out of the desegregation business.

Meanwhile, however, the civil rights movement was gaining strength, and the Court helped by protecting the movement from southern state laws meant to undermine it. In *NAACP v. Alabama* (1958), the Court unanimously held that Alabama could not compel the NAACP to reveal the names and addresses of its members. "On past occasions revelation of the identity of its rank-and-file members has exposed these members to economic reprisal, loss of employment, threat of physical coercion, and other manifestations of public hostility," the Court explained. Compelled disclosure of its membership lists would infringe its members' freedom of association, because "it may induce members to withdraw from the Association and dissuade others from joining it because of fear of exposure of their beliefs." In *NAACP v. Button* (1963), the Court invalidated a Virginia law prohibiting lawyers from soliciting clients. The law had been enacted specifically to target the NAACP, which often sought out black parents to serve as plaintiffs in school desegregation cases. In the NAACP's hands, litigation was "a means for achieving the lawful objectives of equality of treatment by all government, federal, state and local, for the members of the Negro community in this country," the Court reasoned. "It is thus a form of political expression" which the state could not suppress. In *Edwards v. South Carolina* (1963), the Court held that black students had a First Amendment right to march in protest to the state capitol. And in *New York Times v. Sullivan* (1964), the Court used the First Amendment to shield civil rights activists from potentially ruinous libel suits filed by southern state officials. Four black clergymen had published a full-page advertisement in the *New York Times* that included criticism of the violent tactics of the police in Montgomery, Alabama. Even if the criticism was mistaken, the Court held, the clergymen were not liable for the error unless they published the advertisement with a reckless disregard for its truth.[37] These decisions were not as high-profile as *Brown*, but in the short run they accomplished much more.

In *Brown*, the Court was out ahead of national opinion. It held segregated schools unconstitutional, but ten years later scarcely any desegregation had taken place. The lesson, as Frankfurter acknowledged, was that "the elements of public opinion" had "to be kept in mind by us in the procedures we adopt . . . and in how we express what we do."[38] But public opinion was catching up. In the 1960s, the Court would get back to desegregation, and this time it would have the support of the other two branches of the federal government.

III

The Civil Rights Act of 1964 was Congress's first significant civil rights legislation in nearly a century. The statute prohibited discrimination by private actors in a wide range of contexts, including employment and places of public accommodation like hotels and restaurants. It prohibited discrimination on several bases—not just race but also sex and religion. It authorized the Justice Department to file enforcement suits, which gave the law a much greater deterrent effect than was possible from suits by discrimination victims alone, because the United States government was a deep-pocketed litigant with skilled attorneys. And it denied federal funding to programs, including schools, that discriminated on the basis of race. The Civil Rights Act was one of the most consequential pieces of legislation in American history.

But was it constitutional? Congress had tried to outlaw private discrimination once before, back in 1875, but the Court held the statute unconstitutional in the *Civil Rights Cases* (1883) on the ground that the Thirteenth and Fourteenth Amendments authorized Congress to ban discrimination only by state governments. For this reason, the 1964 Act's ban on private discrimination was based instead on the Commerce Clause, as an exercise of Congress's power to regulate interstate commerce. Constitutional challenges were filed almost immediately. Two reached the Court quickly enough to be argued in October 1964, only three months after the statute was enacted. One suit was filed by an Atlanta lawyer named Moreton Rolleston, who owned the Heart of Atlanta Motel. Rolleston watched President Lyndon Johnson sign the Civil Rights Act into law on television and filed his suit two hours later. Rolleston argued the case himself in the Supreme Court. The other suit was filed by Ollie McClung, the owner of Ollie's Barbecue, a restaurant in Birmingham. Unlike Rolleston, who was committed to segregation, McClung had his doubts. "Many Negroes occupy a higher station in the eyes of God than whites do," he told *Life* magazine. But when the Civil Rights Act went into effect, McClung worried that he would lose all his white customers if he let black people into his restaurant. He went to see a lawyer right away.[39]

In *Heart of Atlanta Motel v. United States* (1964) and *Katzenbach v. McClung* (1964), the Court unanimously decided that Congress's power to regulate interstate commerce allowed it to bar privately owned businesses from discriminating. Segregation was primarily "a moral problem," Tom Clark acknowledged. "But that fact does not detract from the overwhelming evidence of the disruptive effect that racial discrimination has had on commercial intercourse." Most of the guests of the Heart of Atlanta Motel were from states other than Georgia, and the motel advertised nationally. Nearly half the meat barbecued by Ollie McClung's employees came from states other than Alabama. By 1964 these were easy cases under the Commerce Clause. But they were not easy cases in the South as a political matter. Another of the constitutional challenges to the Civil Rights Act was mounted by the Pickrick Restaurant of Atlanta.[40] When the restaurant lost its case, its owner, Lester Maddox, closed it rather than serve black customers. Maddox's public stand in favor of segregation was so popular among Georgia's white voters that he was elected governor in 1966.

Shortly after the Court upheld the Civil Rights Act of 1964, Congress enacted another momentous statute, the Voting Rights Act of 1965. The Voting Rights Act included several measures intended to prevent southern states from denying black citizens their right to vote. This law too was immediately challenged as unconstitutional. In *South Carolina v. Katzenbach* (1966), the Court held that the Fifteenth Amendment authorized Congress to enact the Voting Rights Act. The decision was nearly unanimous. Hugo Black thought one provision of the statute, the section requiring southern states to get permission from the federal government before changing their voting rules, exceeded the power of Congress. But the justices all agreed on the constitutionality of the other challenged provisions, which included prohibitions of literacy tests, poll taxes, and other devices which southern states had used for years to prevent black people from voting. "Congress exercised its authority under the Fifteenth Amendment in an inventive manner when it enacted the Voting Rights Act of 1965," Warren's opinion explained, because "Congress had found that case-by-case litigation was inadequate to combat widespread and persistent discrimination in voting, because of the inordinate amount of time and energy required to overcome the obstructionist tactics invariably encountered in these lawsuits." He concluded that "after enduring nearly a century of systematic resistance to the Fifteenth Amendment, Congress might well decide to shift the advantage of time and inertia from the perpetrators of the evil to its victims."[41]

Unlike the Court's decision in *Brown v. Board of Education*, the two statutes had an immediate effect. Southern schools began to integrate after the Civil Rights Act of 1964 withheld federal funding from segregated school districts. In 1964, only 1.2% of black children in the South attended a school with white children. That figure rose dramatically in the next few years, until by 1971 it had reached 85.9%. In 1964, twenty years after the Court prohibited white primaries in *Smith v. Allwright*, only 40% of voting-age black people in the South were registered to vote. By 1970, after the Voting Rights Act had been in effect for five years, 66.9% were registered.[42] There has long been debate over how best to characterize the Court's role in the civil rights revolution, but one point on which virtually all commentators agree is that the Court cannot engineer much social change without the co-operation of the other two branches of government.

In this new political climate, the Court re-entered the field of school desegregation. In the early cases up through *Brown*, "the politicians all stepped out and left it in the Court's lap to determine those things," Warren explained. "All the Court was doing was filling a vacuum because Congress had not acted." But now that Congress *had* acted, the Court's job became much easier. The two civil rights acts, Warren continued, "greatly helped the Court. . . . That's one reason that I think President Johnson rendered such a distinct service, because he put on the books the legislation that should have been there almost a hundred years before."[43]

Prince Edward County, Virginia, had been one of the school districts involved in *Brown v. Board of Education*. Rather than integrating its public schools, the county simply closed them. White residents of the county formed a private foundation to operate segregated schools, funded in part by private contributions and in part by the state and county governments. In *Griffin v. County School Board* (1964), the Court unanimously held this arrangement unconstitutional. The southern states could not evade *Brown* by shutting down their public schools. The justices had grown impatient with southern resistance. "The time for mere 'deliberate speed' has run out," Hugo Black declared. Rather than leaving the remedy to the discretion of the trial court, the Court made clear that the trial court was empowered to order the school district to reopen the public schools and even to raise taxes, if that was necessary to provide integrated education.[44]

Griffin was just the first in a series of school desegregation cases over the next decade that would test the limits of the courts' remedial authority. New Kent County, Virginia, had two schools, one for black students and one for white students. Rather than integrating the schools, which could have been accomplished simply by drawing a line down the middle of the county, local officials allowed residents to choose which school they would attend. Very little integration resulted. Out of approximately 1,300 students, divided roughly evenly between black and white, only thirty-five black students attended the formerly white school, while no white students attended the formerly black one. The same "freedom of choice" tactic was adopted by so many school districts throughout the South that by the mid-1960s the LDF had more than one hundred cases challenging it, including the one from New Kent County, which reached the Court in 1968.[45] These cases raised a basic question about the meaning of *Brown*. Was the government merely obliged to stop requiring segregation? If so, the southern school districts that adopted "freedom of choice" plans were following the law. Or did the government have an affirmative duty to provide integrated schools? If so, these school districts had failed miserably.

In *Green v. County School Board* (1968), the Court unanimously held that school districts were obliged to provide integrated schools. Segregation was unconstitutional whether or not it was required by state law. *Brown* "was a call for the dismantling of well-entrenched dual systems" of schools, Justice William Brennan explained. School districts had an "affirmative duty to take whatever steps might be necessary to convert to a unitary system in which racial discrimination would be eliminated root and branch." The burden was on the school board to "fashion steps which promise realistically to convert promptly to a system without a 'white' school and a 'Negro' school, but just schools." Again, the Court's hesitancy in *Brown* had been replaced by an aggressive effort to end school segregation. "When this opinion is handed down," Warren optimistically joked with Brennan, "the traffic light will have changed from *Brown* to *Green*. Amen!" In Georgia, meanwhile, Governor Lester Maddox ordered the flag outside the state capitol lowered to half-staff as a gesture of mourning for what he called "another attack by the U.S. Supreme Court."[46]

But many schools remained effectively segregated, in large part because neighborhoods were often segregated and students were normally assigned to their neighborhood schools. In *Swann v. Charlotte-Mecklenburg Board of Education* (1971), the Court approved the remedy of integrating schools by busing students to schools outside their own neighborhoods. Despite the political controversy surrounding busing, which was unpopular in many white neighborhoods, the Court was once again unanimous. Looking back at *Brown*, Warren Burger, the new chief justice, reflected that "nothing in our national experience prior to 1955 prepared anyone for dealing with changes and adjustments of the magnitude and complexity encountered since then." But Burger insisted that "the objective today remains to eliminate from the public schools all vestiges of state-imposed segregation." And if the best way to end segregation was to break the link between neighborhood and school, courts had the power to send students to schools in other parts of the district. "All things being equal, with no history of discrimination, it might well be desirable to assign pupils to schools nearest their homes," Burger noted. "But all things are not equal in a system that has been deliberately constructed and maintained to enforce racial segregation. The remedy for such segregation may be administratively awkward, inconvenient, and even bizarre in some situations and may impose burdens on some; but all awkwardness and inconvenience cannot be avoided in the interim period when remedial adjustments are being made to eliminate the dual school systems."[47] In the ensuing years, court-ordered busing became a common feature of desegregation plans.

Two years later, in *Keyes v. School District No. 1* (1973), the Court held that even non-Southern school districts, which had never required segregation by law, were nevertheless also obliged to integrate their schools. The Denver school district had been segregated not by law but by the discretionary decisions of school board officials, who gerrymandered school attendance zones to ensure that some schools were identifiably white and others were identifiably black and Hispanic. The Court held that this kind of segregation had to be remedied as well. But the tide was beginning to turn. For the first time in any of the Court's school desegregation cases since *Brown*, there were dissenters. The two newest justices, William Rehnquist and Lewis Powell, expressed considerable skepticism about the Court's desegregation project. Rehnquist suggested that he disagreed with the Court's assertion in *Green v. County School Board* that the Constitution required school districts to provide integrated schools rather than merely to refrain from requiring segregated ones. Powell was the Court's only member with experience administering a school system. He had chaired the Richmond, Virginia, school board in the 1950s, the years before and after *Brown*, and then he served for several years on Virginia's state board of education. In both positions, he mediated between the Court's command to desegregate and the adamant opposition of white residents. Powell had misgivings about *Swann*'s authorization of busing as a remedy for segregation.[48]

Swann and *Keyes* would be the high-water mark of the Court's efforts to desegregate the nation's schools. Between 1964 and 1973 the Court had gone considerably farther than it had in *Brown* in requiring school districts to take affirmative measures to eliminate segregation. As the surrounding political environment changed in favor of desegregation, so did the Court's decisions.

One indication of this shift was the Court's new willingness to confront southern laws banning interracial marriage. The Court had ducked the issue in 1956, shortly after *Brown*, for fear of arousing even more resistance in the South. But in *Loving v Virginia* (1967), the Court unanimously held these laws unconstitutional. The improbably but aptly named Mildred and Richard Loving were a black woman and a white man from Virginia who had been married in the District of Columbia, which permitted interracial marriage. When they returned to Virginia, they were promptly convicted of violating state law. "Almighty God created the races white, black, yellow, malay and red, and he placed them on separate continents," the trial judge explained. "The fact that he separated the races shows that he did not intend for the races to mix." The state supreme court added that the statute served the legitimate purposes of preserving "the racial integrity of its citizens" and preventing "the corruption of blood." Sixteen states, all in the South, still had similar statutes, while fourteen other states had repealed their laws banning interracial marriage only within the past fifteen years. Virginia argued that its law did not discriminate because members of both races were punished equally, and that the courts should defer to the legislature because "the scientific evidence is substantially in doubt" as to the propriety of interracial marriage. The Court rejected both arguments. "There is patently no legitimate overriding purpose independent of invidious racial discrimination which justifies this classification," Warren concluded. "The fact that Virginia prohibits only interracial marriages involving white persons demonstrates that the racial classifications must stand on their own justification, as measures designed to maintain White Supremacy."[49] An issue too hot to handle in the mid-1950s had become an easy case barely more than a decade later.

IV

The day after the Court decided *Loving*, a different kind of desegregation took place at the Court itself. President Lyndon Johnson nominated Thurgood Marshall, the country's pre-eminent civil rights lawyer, to become the Court's first black justice.[50]

Marshall had left the LDF in 1961, when President John Kennedy appointed him to the New York-based Court of Appeals for the Second Circuit. Marshall was the third black federal judge, following William Hastie, Marshall's professor at Howard Law School, who had been a court of appeals

judge in Philadelphia since 1949, and James Parsons, whom Kennedy appointed to the district court in Chicago just a few months before Marshall's
appointment. Southern senators were so adamantly opposed to Marshall
that they delayed his confirmation to the Second Circuit for nearly a year.

Marshall became solicitor general in 1965 at the request of Lyndon
Johnson, who intended the position to be a stepping-stone on the way to the
Supreme Court. "He would tell us how he got Thurgood Marshall appointed
to the Supreme Court by first appointing him solicitor general," recalled
James Davis, an employee at Johnson's Texas ranch. "He told us that he knew
if he appointed him as a Supreme Court justice they would say he had no
experience. So he appointed him solicitor general and he'd win most of the
cases that came before him so they couldn't say he wasn't qualified." In two
years as solicitor general, Marshall personally argued eighteen cases at the
Court on a wide range of topics and won most of them. One of his rare losses
was in the best-known of the cases, *Miranda v. Arizona* (1966)—ironically,
after a long career representing countless criminal defendants, Marshall
found himself on the government's side in one of the most important criminal cases of the century.[51]

Both the Kennedy and Johnson administrations contemplated appointing
a black justice. William Hastie had been one of the candidates for the seat
that opened in 1962 when Charles Whittaker retired, but Kennedy chose
Byron White, the deputy attorney general. At the time, Marshall's nomination to the Second Circuit was still being delayed in the Senate, and Kennedy
may reasonably have worried that the prospect of a black justice would provoke even more opposition. To make matters worse, when Hastie's name was
run by Earl Warren, the chief justice thought Hastie was too conservative.
Meanwhile, Kennedy planned to make the longtime government official
Robert Weaver the first black cabinet member. "You cannot appoint both
Hastie and Weaver," suggested Kennedy's advisor Ted Sorensen, "without
appearing to be guilty of reverse racism." Sorensen proposed that Kennedy
"save Hastie for the next vacancy before 1964," an election Kennedy would
not live to see.[52]

Johnson chose Marshall over Hastie. "Bill Hastie was a better lawyer,"
explained the civil rights lawyer Morris Abram, who knew both men well.
But Marshall "was symbolic of the victory and a long struggle." In 1967, when
Johnson decided it was time to appoint Marshall to the Court, there were no
vacancies, so Johnson manufactured one. He persuaded Attorney General
Nicholas Katzenbach to move to the State Department, which allowed

Johnson to name Ramsey Clark as attorney general, which caused Clark's father, Justice Tom Clark, to retire from the Court to avoid the appearance of bias. "I should not let my being here interfere with Ramsey's future," Tom Clark confided to a colleague. "There are many judges who have sons and I would not want to be used as an example or excuse for them."[53] With Clark out of the way, Johnson nominated Marshall.

Marshall's Senate confirmation hearing in the summer of 1967 was a full-blown congressional performance of the old white supremacist South. "Are you prejudiced against white people?" asked James Eastland of Mississippi. Strom Thurmond of South Carolina peppered Marshall with a series of absurdly difficult questions Thurmond could never have answered himself:

Figure 12.3 Thurgood Marshall and Lyndon Johnson at the White House on June 13, 1967, the day Johnson announced Marshall's nomination to the Court. Photograph by Frank Wolfe. LBJ Presidential Library, C5706-1.

THURMOND: Do you know who drafted the 13th amendment to the U.S. Constitution?

MARSHALL: No, sir; I don't remember. I have looked it up time after time, but I just don't remember.

THURMOND: Do you know from what provision of the prior law the language of this amendment was copied?

MARSHALL: I do not.

THURMOND: Turning to the provision of the 13th amendment forbidding involuntary servitude, are you familiar with any pre-1860 cases which interpreted this language?

MARSHALL: Well, Senator, I might say, frankly, I don't know of any case I had that involved the 13th amendment.[54]

This "Yahoo-type hazing," as *Time* magazine put it, "might have been a Southern county courthouse in the bad old days, with a white registrar administering a literacy test designed to confound even the best-educated Negro." The *New York Times* agreed that the senators "taunting Mr. Marshall are doing so only because he is a Negro." It was clear to all, however, that "this performance for the benefit of the rednecks back home exposes the vitriol of the Senators, not the knowledge of Mr. Marshall."[55] Marshall received no votes from any of the senators from North Carolina, South Carolina, Georgia, Florida, Alabama, Mississippi, or Louisiana. But he had so much support from the rest of the Senate that he was confirmed by 69 votes to 11, a wider margin than Hugo Black, Charles Evans Hughes, or Louis Brandeis had achieved.

It was impossible to avoid reflecting on how the times had changed. The very first sentence of the wire service account of Marshall's confirmation described him as "Thurgood Marshall, the great-grandson of a slave." His ascension to the Court "symbolizes a milestone in the progress of human relations," one paper marveled. "A half-century ago, when Thurgood Marshall was a little boy, he might have been ridiculed if he had dared to dream aloud of wearing, someday, the robes of a Supreme Court Justice." "This is an event of tremendous significance for Negro citizens," exclaimed the civil rights leader Whitney Young, the head of the National Urban League. Marshall's "appointment is proof that, whatever the obstacles, Negroes can fight their way to the top."[56] Just thirteen years earlier, when Marshall had argued *Brown v. Board of Education*, it would have been hard to imagine that the Court would be desegregated sooner than many school districts. Seven years before that, when the justices could not even agree on whether to invite the black messengers to the Court's Christmas party, a black justice had scarcely been conceivable. As Marshall took his seat on the Court in the fall of 1967, it was possible to hope that further progress lay ahead.

13

The Liberal Court

The desegregation cases of the 1940s and 1950s, most notably *Brown v. Board of Education*, cast the Court in an unaccustomed role as a progressive law-changing institution. This role soon expanded to domains beyond segregation. From the late 1950s through the early 1970s, the Court interpreted the Constitution to guarantee a wide variety of individual rights that had not previously been recognized, rights that could now be wielded against the government by political and religious dissenters, by penniless criminal defendants, and by others who lacked influence in their own communities. This brief period of liberal constitutional reinterpretation lasted scarcely a decade and a half, but it produced some of the Court's most famous—and still most controversial—decisions, including *Engel v. Vitale* (1962), which outlawed prayer in public schools, *Miranda v. Arizona* (1966), which placed strict limits on the power of the police to obtain confessions from suspects, and *Roe v. Wade* (1973), which recognized a constitutional right to abortion. A textbook of constitutional law written in the early 1960s was hopelessly out of date a decade later. To this day, some consider the era the Court's best, others its worst. But there is no doubt that it was extraordinarily unusual. Neither before nor since has there been a period in which the Court changed the law so much, or in which the Court was so concerned to defend the weak against the strong.

I

The institution that decided all these cases is often referred to as "the Warren Court," but the name is a bit misleading. Chief Justice Earl Warren was hardly the most liberal member of the Court, and several of the most important cases were decided after he retired in 1969. Earl Warren was, in any event, an unlikely figurehead for any liberal movement or institution. Before joining the Court, he was a prominent Republican politician. He had been the governor of California and the Republican candidate for vice president in 1948. When President Dwight Eisenhower nominated Warren as chief justice, he praised Warren's "middle-of-the-road philosophy." As a justice, however, Warren proved to be farther to the left of the road than Eisenhower expected. He would be in the majority in many of the Court's most politically salient cases. Years later, Eisenhower was widely quoted, including by Warren himself, as calling Warren's appointment "the biggest damn fool thing I ever did."[1]

The Court's most liberal member was William Douglas, who had been appointed by Franklin Roosevelt back in 1939. Douglas was well known for his willingness to interpret the Constitution in untraditional ways. At a 1964 dinner to celebrate his twenty-fifth anniversary on the Court, President Lyndon Johnson joked that "for us to amend the Constitution we need a 2/3 majority in Congress and then a vote of 3/4 of the states. Bill can do it in one afternoon." But Johnson added a more serious note that captured Douglas's tendency to decide cases in favor of powerless people and against the government. "Bill Douglas is the symbol of individual freedom in this Nation which cherishes the rights of one man to be an individual, whatever the crowd may demand," Johnson declared. "He is the symbol of the free conscience—the ultimate source of truth and freedom."[2] Douglas would be in the majority in virtually all the Court's high-profile liberal decisions.

Typically joining Douglas in the majority was Hugo Black, another long-serving Roosevelt appointee. "I have the very highest regard for Justice Douglas," Black remarked. "In fact, our views are so nearly the same that it would be almost like self praise for me to write what I feel about his judicial career." In 1964, when the cover story of *Time* magazine was titled "That Activist Supreme Court," *Time* put Black's picture on the cover. Black espoused the strongest possible version of the constitutional freedom of speech. The First Amendment says "Congress shall make no law" abridging the freedom of speech. Black, alone among his colleagues, interpreted the First Amendment literally to bar any regulation of speech under any circumstances, even in contexts, such as libel or obscenity, where regulation had traditionally been permitted. "I believe that 'no law' means no law," he explained. "And being a rather backward country fellow, I understand it to mean what the words say."[3]

By the late 1950s, the only other holdover from Franklin Roosevelt's presidency was Felix Frankfurter. Frankfurter had been a prominent progressive a generation before, when the constitutional battle was about whether judges should use the Constitution to invalidate economic regulation. The progressive position then was one of judicial deference to the legislature. Frankfurter remained deferential to legislation for the rest of his life, but in the new climate of the 1950s and 1960s, when the battle was about whether judges should use the Constitution to protect individual rights, deference became the conservative position. Frankfurter increasingly found himself in dissent. He grew ever more bitter about the Court's new direction. "Most of my years on the Court have been years not of gladness but of sadness," he told John Harlan shortly after he retired, "and not primarily because of the outrageous decisions that have been rendered in my time but because of the atmosphere of disregard for law." He complained that Warren's "crude, heavy-handed, repetitive moralizing make me feel like eating rancid butter" and that Warren "has the bias of a sansculotte." At times, when the Court orally announced its decisions, Frankfurter's dissatisfaction spilled into public view in the form of extemporaneous critical comments that did not appear in his written dissents, comments so sharp that they sometimes provoked Warren into extemporaneous remarks of his own in defense of the decisions.[4]

Frankfurter was older than Black and considerably older than Douglas. His worsening health forced him to retire in 1962. President John Kennedy replaced Frankfurter with Arthur Goldberg, the secretary of labor, who had spent most of his career as a lawyer representing labor unions. Goldberg was a reliably liberal vote during his not-quite-three years on the Court. In 1965 he resigned to become the US ambassador to the United Nations, a move so unusual that many suspected that President Johnson had somehow forced him to leave the Court. Goldberg himself always denied that Johnson had twisted his arm; he maintained that he went to the UN in the hope of preventing the country from getting enmeshed in the war in Vietnam, and that he had an understanding that Johnson would reappoint him to the Court when he was finished at the UN. Goldberg may also have felt constrained in his new role as a justice. "After a rather hectic life as Secretary of Labor," he confided to friends in 1963, "service on the Court is regarded to be quiet."[5]

Goldberg's successor was Abe Fortas, a leading Washington lawyer who had long been one of Johnson's closest advisors. Johnson would most likely never have been president without Fortas, who devised the legal strategy that had enabled Johnson to reach the Senate in a famously corrupt election in 1948. At first Fortas declined the appointment to the Court. In a handwritten letter to Johnson, he cited his desire for "a few more years to try to be of service to you." More likely, Fortas's wife objected to the severe salary cut he would suffer in leaving private practice. He accepted the nomination when Johnson offered it again.[6] Fortas would be as reliably liberal as Goldberg, although his tenure on the Court would not be much longer than Goldberg's, as we will see in the next chapter.

Warren, Douglas, Black, Goldberg, and Fortas were part of the Court's liberal majority, but it was William Brennan who became the Court's liberal icon. Brennan's career on the Court could scarcely have been expected when Eisenhower appointed him. Brennan was a judge on the New Jersey Supreme Court. He was fifty years old. He was Catholic. And although he was a lifelong Democrat, he had not participated in politics and his state court opinions had no particular ideological slant. In the fall of 1956, Eisenhower was in the stretch run of what seemed to be a close reelection campaign when Justice Sherman Minton announced his retirement. There had been no Catholic justice since Frank Murphy's death a few years earlier, after more than half a century during which Catholics were always represented on the Court. Eisenhower and his advisors determined that for campaign purposes, the ideal nominee to take Minton's place would be a Catholic with judicial experience who was not too old. Brennan satisfied all three criteria. "I used to play golf sometimes with Eisenhower," Justice Tom Clark recalled more than a decade later. Eisenhower had conferred with Arthur Vanderbilt, the chief justice of the New Jersey Supreme Court, who "told him that Brennan was more of a conservative judge." Eisenhower would be sorely disappointed. Brennan would lead the Court's liberal wing for the next thirty-four years. When he retired in 1990, among the many fan letters he received was one from a law student who identified himself as "Barack Obama, President"—not yet president of the United States but president of the Harvard Law Review. Obama credited Brennan with having inspired him to attend law school and spoke of "the debt that many of us owe to you in helping America live up to its ideals of opportunity for all its citizens."[7]

When Thurgood Marshall replaced Clark on the Court in 1967, he moved the Court even farther to the left, the farthest it would ever be. At that point there were six consistent progressive votes—Warren, Douglas, Black, Fortas, Brennan, and Marshall. The tide would turn soon after. Warren and Fortas would be gone within two years and Black within four, all to be replaced by Republicans nominated by President Richard Nixon.

The Court's leftward drift was facilitated by the fact that even apart from Warren and Brennan, Eisenhower's other three appointments were not especially conservative by the standards of the era. While they dissented in some of the Court's best-known cases, they joined the majority in others. John Marshall Harlan had spent most of his career as a corporate lawyer in New York. Like his grandfather and namesake, the first Justice Harlan, he would be remembered primarily for his dissenting opinions. Potter Stewart had been a court of appeals judge in Cincinnati. Only forty-three when he joined the Court, Stewart would remain a justice until 1981. Charles Whittaker, a lower court judge from Kansas City, suffered a nervous break-down and had to retire only five years after he was appointed. Whittaker's lifelong struggles with depression gave rise to debilitating feelings of inferi-ority when he joined the Court, which made it difficult, and eventually im-possible, for him to reach decisions in cases on which his colleagues were divided. As was typical of the era, Whittaker's illness was not disclosed to the public. His early retirement was attributed instead to overwork. There was "no Plimsoll line for him," Clark explained, using a nautical term referring to the line indicating when a ship is submerged too far into the water. "Others might leave their official duties behind as the courtroom doors closed, but for him there was no escape from their power nor flight from their presence." All three appointees reflected Eisenhower's preference for justices with, as he put it in a note to his attorney general William Rogers, "a middle-of-the-road political and governmental philosophy."[8]

The Court would have moved even farther to the left had Kennedy ap-pointed someone like Goldberg or Fortas to replace Whittaker in 1962. Instead, Kennedy chose Byron White. White had been a football star as a young man, first at the University of Colorado and later as a professional. After several years as a lawyer in Denver and after chairing Kennedy's presi-dential campaign in Colorado, White served as deputy attorney general, the second-ranking position in the Justice Department. White's voting pattern on the Court proved to be as surprising as that of Warren or Brennan, but in the opposite direction. He dissented in virtually all the major law-changing cases during his first decade on the Court.[9]

The justices of the 1960s were thus a left-leaning group of people. At least as important, they all moved comfortably within the world of nationally elite lawyers. Most of the big cases of the period, regardless of their specific subject matter, involved a clash of two sets of values. On one side were the cosmopol-itan, urbane, secular values of educated elites in the nation's largest cities, including Washington. On the other were the traditional, rural, religious values of less-educated white people, most conspicuously in the South. This opposition was perhaps most apparent in the school segregation cases, but

Figure 13.1 The justices posed for this photograph in November 1962, near the beginning of an extraordinary decade and a half in which the Court recognized a wide variety of new constitutional rights. From left to right: Tom Clark, Byron White, Hugo Black, William Brennan, Earl Warren, Potter Stewart, William Douglas, Arthur Goldberg, and John Harlan. Photograph by Warren K. Leffler. Library of Congress, LC-DIG-ppmsca-41069.

it would also characterize the Court's cases involving the freedom of speech and religion, the cases involving the rights of criminal defendants, and the cases about abortion and other individual rights. The justices were decidedly in the elite camp. Of the justices appointed in the 1950s and 1960s, all but Whittaker and Marshall attended prestigious universities, either for college, for law school, or for both. All lived most of their adult lives in big cities outside the South. All were enmeshed in national networks of likeminded people. In these respects, the justices were much like the top officials in the Kennedy and Johnson administrations. "The Court was a functioning part of the Kennedy-Johnson liberalism of the mid and late 1960s," as the historian Lucas Powe concludes. "The Warren Court demanded national liberal values be adopted in outlying areas of the United States."[10]

II

In the late 1940s and early 1950s, as we have seen, the Court had been unreceptive to the free speech claims of communists. In the best-known of these First Amendment cases, *Dennis v. United States* (1951), the Court had affirmed the constitutionality of the Smith Act of 1940, the federal statute that prescribed prison terms up to twenty years merely for belonging to an organization, such as the Communist Party, that urged revolution. But the Court's view of these cases began to change in the mid-1950s. John Harlan told his clerks in 1956 about "the feeling of some members of the Court that we should take a new look at these Smith Act conspiracies in light of the accumulated post-*Dennis* experience."[11] The justices had ample opportunity to reconsider the balance between national security and the freedom of speech, because, in the Cold War atmosphere of the era, the federal government's interest in ferreting out communists was shared by virtually all public institutions, from state governments down to local school boards. There were plenty of cases in the pipeline featuring petitioners who had been convicted of crimes or who had lost their jobs because of their political beliefs.

The Court proceeded gradually at first, by ruling in favor of communists for reasons other than the freedom of speech. In *Pennsylvania v. Nelson* (1956), the Court reversed a conviction under Pennsylvania's Sedition Act, not because of any constitutional right to espouse communism, but on the ground that state statutes targeting communists were superseded by the federal statutes that served the same purpose. In *Slochower v. Board of Higher Education* (1956), the Court held that New York City could not summarily fire a college professor who refused to say whether he had been a member of the Communist Party—again, not because the professor had a First Amendment right to be a communist, but because he had a right under the Fifth Amendment not to be punished for refusing to admit to a crime. Neither decision included any suggestion that the freedom of speech included the advocacy of communism, but the cases nevertheless alarmed the members of Congress most concerned about the issue. "The Court reached a new low in judicial irresponsibility," Senator Joseph McCarthy charged. "It has handed another solid victory to the Communist Party."[12]

The following year, the Court ruled in favor of communists in four cases on a single day in June 1957, quickly known as "Red Monday." In *Sweezy v. New Hampshire*, the Court reversed the conviction of a university professor for refusing to answer questions about his allegedly subversive political views. "Our form of government is built on the premise that every citizen shall have the right to engage in political expression and association. This right was enshrined in the First Amendment," Warren declared in his opinion for the Court. "Mere unorthodoxy or dissent from the prevailing mores is not to be condemned. The absence of such voices would be a symptom of grave illness in our society." Freedom of thought was especially important in a university,

Warren explained, because "scholarship cannot flourish in an atmosphere of suspicion and distrust. Teachers and students must always remain free to inquire, to study and to evaluate, to gain new maturity and understanding; otherwise our civilization will stagnate and die." Strictly speaking, the decision rested on procedural grounds rather than on the First Amendment, but no one could miss Warren's implication that the Court now frowned upon government efforts to suppress the expression of radical political views. Frankfurter made the point more directly in his concurring opinion. "In the political realm, as in the academic, thought and action are presumptively immune from inquisition by political authority," he insisted.[13]

In two of the other Red Monday cases, the Court likewise strengthened the freedom of speech despite basing its decisions on other grounds. In *Watkins v. United States*, the Court reversed the conviction of a labor union official for refusing to tell the House Committee on Un-American Activities whether several of his associates were members of the Communist Party. Warren warned that "abuses of the investigative process may imperceptibly lead to abridgment of protected freedoms." In *Yates v. United States*, the Court reversed the Smith Act convictions of fourteen Communist Party members on the ground that the Smith Act itself did not prohibit the mere advocacy of overthrowing the government, as distinct from actual efforts toward that goal. In his opinion for the Court, Harlan relied on the text of the statute rather than on the First Amendment, but he added that Congress would "disregard a constitutional danger zone" if it tried to prohibit speech divorced from action. In the final case, *Service v. Dulles*, the Court held that the State Department violated its own regulations when it fired a diplomat alleged to have been a secret communist.[14]

These decisions were extraordinarily controversial. "Not since the Nine Old Men shot down Franklin Roosevelt's Blue Eagle in 1935 has the Supreme Court been the center of such general commotion," *Time* magazine noted. (A blue eagle was the symbol of the National Recovery Administration, one of the New Deal agencies whose work the Court had found unconstitutional.) Those who agreed with the Red Monday decisions praised the Court for its "scrupulous affirmation and reaffirmation of the Bill of Rights," as the *New York Times* put it. On the other side of the debate, the national commander of the American Legion accused the Court of helping communists. The Michigan Representative Clare Hoffman complained on the floor of the House that "this Warren Court has now thrown its protective cloak around the fellow travelers and Communists. The Court is simply blind to the reality of our times." The Indiana Senator William Jenner accused the Court of making the United States appear to the rest of the world as "a nation of credulous fools." Jenner introduced a bill to strip the Court of jurisdiction over several categories of cases involving subversive activities and domestic security, categories that precisely matched the issues in the cases of 1956 and 1957.[15] The bill was defeated by a narrow margin.

Segregationists already despised the Court because of *Brown v. Board of Education*. Now they were joined by anti-communists. The John Birch Society, an organization formed in 1958 to fight communism in the United States, financed a campaign to impeach Warren. Soon motorists all over the country could see billboards urging "Save Our Republic! Impeach Earl Warren." The John Birch Society also held an essay contest for college students, with a prize of $1,000 for the best argument for Warren's impeachment. The prize was won by a UCLA student named Eddie Rose, who told the press that although he was not a member of the society, he shared "about 98 percent of their views." The impeachment cry was taken up by other right-wing organizations as well. Warren had sided with communists in thirty-six out of thirty-nine cases, one anonymous pamphlet charged, a record that "clearly puts him on the side of those who wittingly or unwittingly give aid and comfort to the International Communist Conspiracy." An organization called Arizona Mothers for Earl Warren's Impeachment declared that "not only is this impeachment necessary, but the careful analysis of future Supreme Court Justices is imperative."[16] This campaign lasted for several years, but Warren survived unscathed.

Over the next few years, the Court invalidated several anti-communist measures but upheld several others. The vote was usually close. In *Kent v. Dulles* (1958), for example, a 5–4 Court held that the State Department lacked statutory authority to deny passports to communists. The winning petitioner was the artist Rockwell Kent, whom the government viewed with suspicion because he urged cooperation with the Soviet Union. In *Scales v. United States* (1961), by contrast, the Court, again by a 5–4 vote, affirmed a conviction under the Smith Act of a man whose only crime was to have been a member of the Communist Party. Finally, in the mid-1960s, with the replacement of Frankfurter by Goldberg and then Fortas, the Court began to rule consistently against the constitutionality of punishing people for their belief in communism. The Court struck down a statute authorizing the Postal Service to restrict the mailing of "communist political propaganda." The Court prohibited Arizona and New York from firing state employees who belonged to communist organizations. The Court even invalidated a federal statute that barred communists from working in defense facilities.[17] These decisions were all grounded explicitly on the First Amendment freedom of speech, which now protected a much greater range of political dissent than it ever had before.

The justices did not always practice what they preached. In 1965 Brennan offered a clerkship for the 1966–1967 term to Michael Tigar, who ranked first in his class at the University of California, Berkeley. In First Amendment cases, Brennan was a steady vote in favor of radical political advocates, and Tigar was himself a student radical. As he reminded Brennan when he accepted the position as a clerk, "there may be a little stir in the press as reporters with long memories recall student politics in Berkeley a couple of years ago." But Brennan did not mind—until the following summer, as Tigar was about to start working at the Court, when student politics at Berkeley became a major issue in California's gubernatorial election. The conservative journalist James Kilpatrick, editor of the *Richmond News Leader*, wrote an editorial criticizing Brennan's hiring of Tigar. "We couldn't believe it until we checked it out with unimpeachable Washington sources," Kilpatrick declared, "because Tigar makes no bones about his Communist activities." Kilpatrick's editorial turned an obscure personnel decision into national news. The editorial was reproduced in newspapers throughout the country. It was entered into the *Congressional Record* by Representative William Tuck of Virginia, who proclaimed that "there is a communistic infiltration of the U.S. Supreme Court itself." Brennan was swamped with letters from outraged members of Congress, such as one from Robert Michel of Illinois, who reported that many of his constituents had complained of "Mr. Tigar's Marxist background."[18]

Under this intense pressure, Brennan revoked Tigar's job offer. (Tigar's last-minute replacement was Abraham Sofaer, who had just finished a clerkship on the court of appeals and who would go on to a distinguished career as a law professor, as a judge, and as the State Department's chief lawyer.) Brennan escaped further vilification from the right for hiring Tigar, but now he faced criticism from the left for failing to live up to the principles he espoused in his opinions. Brennan's support for the First Amendment "seems to stop short in his own office," charged the *New Republic*. The American Civil Liberties Union's lawyer in San Francisco wrote Brennan to say that "the pressures you bowed to (in violation of your own concept of freedom as expressed in your opinions for the Court) were created by fear and could have been neutralized by reason. The damage you have done yourself will not save the Court embarrassment but will furnish fuel for future attacks." Tigar took a job with a prominent Washington law firm and went on to become a well-known law professor and an advocate for unpopular criminal defendants. Brennan lived to regret the episode. He told his biographers that he wished "that I'd had guts enough to tell them all to go to hell and then taken them on. It'd all have blown over, of course, if I had." When Brennan retired, he admitted to Tigar: "I've often wondered whether I overreacted. I must say in all candor that, given the circumstances, I probably did."[19]

But the Court's First Amendment opinions betrayed no similar timidity. By the end of the decade, the Court held that the government could not prohibit the advocacy of lawbreaking or even violence "except where such advocacy is directed to inciting or producing imminent lawless action and is likely to incite or produce such action." This pronouncement came from the prosecution not of a communist but of a Ku Klux Klan member, who advocated violence not against the government but against black and Jewish people. But the principle was broad enough to protect virtually all forms of political engagement, no matter how upsetting to mainstream sensibilities. Communists, Klan members—the marketplace of ideas was open to all.[20]

Pornographers too. Government officials had long wielded broad authority to suppress books and pictures they deemed obscene. In *Roth v. United States* (1957), however, the Court held for the first time that the First Amendment limits the government's power to prohibit the depiction of sexual matters. Obscenity was not protected by the First Amendment, Brennan acknowledged in his opinion for the Court. But "sex and obscenity are not synonymous," he cautioned. "The portrayal of sex, e.g., in art, literature and scientific works, is not itself sufficient reason to deny material the constitutional protection of freedom of speech and press." A work of art or literature could be banned only if it portrayed "sex in a manner appealing to prurient interest."[21]

It was no easy matter to figure out which works were protected under this standard and which were not. In several cases over the next few years, the justices found themselves in the awkward position of watching allegedly obscene films to decide whether the government could prohibit them. In *Jacobellis v. United States* (1964), for example, the Court considered the French film *Les Amants* (The Lovers), one of the early films of the director Louis Malle. *Les Amants* "involves a woman bored with her life and marriage who abandons her husband and family for a young archaeologist with whom she has suddenly fallen in love," Brennan reported. "There is an explicit love scene in the last reel of the film, and the State's objections are based almost entirely upon that scene." He noted that the film was "favorably reviewed in a number of national publications, although disparaged in others, and was rated by at least two critics of national stature among the best films of the year in which it was produced." Brennan concluded that *Les Amants* "is not obscene within the standards enunciated in *Roth v. United States*." Potter Stewart added that "criminal laws in this area are constitutionally limited to hard-core pornography. I shall not today attempt further to define the kinds of material I understand to be embraced within that shorthand description; and perhaps I could never succeed in intelligibly doing so," he continued, in what would become one of the most frequently quoted passages in any of the Court's opinions. "But I know it when I see it, and the motion picture involved in this case is not that." Black and Douglas refused to participate in these reviews of films and books, because their view was that all depictions of sex were protected by the First Amendment. "If despite the Constitution this Nation is to embark on the dangerous road of censorship," Black suggested, "this Court is about the most inappropriate Supreme Board of Censors that could be found."[22]

But the rest of the Court soldiered on well into the 1970s, duly watching the films claimed to be obscene. On a Monday morning in December 1969, for instance, most of the justices and law clerks gathered to see *I, a Woman* and *I Am Curious (Yellow)*, two Swedish films, the latter of which was one of the most popular films in the United States at the time. (The Court would decide the case on procedural grounds, so it never determined whether the films were obscene.) "Nearly all of those films were the same," Justice Harry Blackmun recalled years later. "They weren't very good films. They weren't intended to be." In John Harlan's later years, his vision was so poor that he would pull his chair up as close to the screen as possible. Blackmun sat behind Harlan on one such occasion. "As the film moved on," Blackmun remembered, "he'd lean over and say to his law clerk, 'And what are they doing now?' And the law clerk would describe it, and Justice Harlan would say, 'You don't say. You don't say.'" In 1974 the justices gave their blessing to *Carnal Knowledge*, starring Jack Nicholson and Candice Bergen. "Our own viewing of the film satisfies us that 'Carnal Knowledge' could not be found" obscene, Justice William Rehnquist explained. "While the subject matter of the picture is, in a broader sense, sex, and there are scenes in which sexual conduct including 'ultimate sexual acts' is to be understood to be taking place, the camera does not focus on the bodies of the actors at such times. There is no exhibition whatever of the actors' genitals, lewd or otherwise, during these scenes. There are occasional scenes of nudity, but nudity alone is not enough to make material legally obscene."[23] Eventually, as standards of taste changed throughout the country, prosecutions for obscenity withered away, and these film screenings at the Court were no longer necessary.

Although the justices were elderly men, they were not blind to the dramatic change in the acceptance of sexual expression that took place in the 1960s. In *Stanley v. Georgia* (1969), the Court unanimously reversed a conviction for possessing obscene films, on the ground that "the mere private possession of obscene matter cannot constitutionally be made a crime." The state made the traditional argument that it had an interest in the morality of its residents, but the argument no longer carried any weight. It was nothing "more than the assertion that the State has the right to control the moral content of a person's thoughts," Marshall scoffed in his opinion for the Court. "To some, this may be a noble purpose, but it is wholly inconsistent with the philosophy of the First Amendment."[24] The notion of a constitutional right to view pornography would have been astonishing twenty years earlier—and even more astounding to the eighteenth-century drafters of the Bill of Rights. The justices had greatly expanded the freedom of speech.

By the late 1960s and early 1970s, all sorts of free speech claims prevailed at the Court that would have failed just a decade or two before. Did high school students have a First Amendment right to wear black armbands in school to protest the Vietnam War, despite their teachers' concern that the armbands would be disruptive in the classroom? Yes, because "undifferentiated fear or apprehension of disturbance is not enough to overcome the right to freedom of expression," Fortas explained for the Court. Did a man have a First Amendment right to walk through a courthouse wearing a jacket that said "Fuck the Draft" in letters big enough to be read by everyone in the corridor? Yes, Harlan wrote for the Court, because the state could not punish the defendant for his message, and those who objected to his language could simply avert their eyes.[25]

Of all these cases involving the freedom of speech, the one that may have been the most important was the one the Court decided the fastest. On a Sunday morning in June 1971, the justices, like anyone else who read the *New York Times*, saw a front-page article describing a multivolume top-secret study of American policy regarding Vietnam, a copy of which had been leaked to the *Times* by Daniel Ellsberg, one of the study's many authors.

The *Washington Post* published portions as well. The government promptly sought a court order barring further publication of the volumes—soon to be known as the Pentagon Papers—on the ground that their publication would be damaging to national security. "Discussion of these cases began in most chambers the day after the Government filed its initial request for a temporary restraining order," Justice Brennan's clerks recalled. "In the meantime, law clerks were busy counting votes." A mere two weeks later, and only four days after hearing argument, the Court decided by a 6–3 vote that the government had not made a sufficient showing to overcome the First Amendment's strong presumption against prior restraints on speech. Each of the justices wrote a separate opinion to avoid the delays that would have been caused by negotiations over language. "Every moment's continuance of the injunctions against these newspapers amounts to a flagrant, indefensible, and continuing violation of the First Amendment," Black declared. But most of the justices took a more measured position: the government did not have an absolute right to suppress information, but neither did the press have an absolute right to publish information that might damage the war effort. It all depended on whether the government could demonstrate that its fears were well grounded.[26]

The Pentagon Papers case, like all the Court's cases involving the freedom of speech, required the justices to balance individual liberty against some form of public order—national security, sexual morality, or general decorum. Between the late 1950s and the early 1970s, the Court shifted the balance decidedly toward the individual. In this respect, the justices mirrored the broader culture, where the balance was moving in the same direction.

III

The Court also played an important role in reframing the relationship between church and state. Protestant Christianity had long been intertwined with American government. Legislators and schoolchildren often began the day with prayer. Public school curricula often included Protestant religious content. Businesses were often required to close on Sunday, while employees who observed a different sabbath day were often required to work on that day. The Court itself had famously declared that "this is a Christian nation," based on a "view of American life, as expressed by its laws, its business, its customs, and its society."[27] In the 1960s and early 1970s, however, the Court decided several cases that granted new constitutional rights to religious dissenters.

The first of these cases was *Engel v. Vitale* (1962), in which the Court held that New York could not prescribe a prayer for teachers and schoolchildren to recite at the beginning of each day. The prayer was written by the state agency that governed public education, in consultation with a team of ministers, priests, and rabbis. It deliberately omitted any reference to any denomination because of the state's religious diversity. The prayer simply read: "Almighty God, we acknowledge our dependence upon Thee, and we beg Thy blessings upon us, our parents, our teachers and our Country." The Court was nearly unanimous in holding that the prayer violated the Establishment Clause of the First Amendment. "The constitutional prohibition against laws respecting an establishment of religion must at least mean that in this country it is no part of the business of government to compose official prayers for any group of the American people to recite as a part of a religious program carried on by government," Hugo Black wrote for the Court. "Neither the fact that the prayer may be denominationally neutral nor the fact that its observance on the part of the students is voluntary can serve to free it from the limitations of the Establishment Clause." Potter Stewart was the only dissenter. He contended that by prescribing an optional short prayer, New York was not "establishing" any religion, but was merely acknowledging "the spiritual heritage of our Nation." He pointed out that the Senate, the House of Representatives, and indeed the Court itself did the same—in the Court's case, by beginning each day with a pronouncement from a Court official that ended "God save the United States and this Honorable Court."[28]

Engel drew extreme appraisals on both sides. "Supreme Court Hailed as Guardian of Liberties," read the headline in one Virginia newspaper. Meanwhile, the Long Island families who were plaintiffs in the case received death threats. Members of Congress took turns denouncing the Court, including the local New York congressman, Frank Becker, who called *Engel* "the most tragic decision in the history of the United States." George Wallace, the governor of Alabama, declared that *Engel* was "the bitter fruit of the liberal dogma that worships human intelligence and scorns the concept of divinity." He accused the justices of having "a deliberate design to subordinate the American people, their faith, their customs, and their religious traditions to a godless state."[29] Strictly speaking, the Court had only barred state-scripted prayer from the schools, not all prayer, but the decision was widely understood, especially by its opponents, as having banished God from the classroom completely.

They were right about that. The next year, in *Abington School District v. Schempp* (1963), the Court struck down a Pennsylvania law that required the reading of Bible verses in public schools at the beginning of each day. Once again, all the justices but Stewart found the law unconstitutional on the ground that the Establishment Clause prohibits not merely state promotion of one religion over another but state promotion of religion in general. For a state law to satisfy the Constitution, Tom Clark explained in his opinion for the Court, the law must have "a secular legislative purpose and a primary effect that neither advances nor inhibits religion."[30] Prayer and religious instruction had no place in the public schools.

Schempp was as unpopular as *Engel*. Seventy percent of people polled disagreed with the decisions. More than seventy members of Congress introduced constitutional amendments to allow prayer and Bible reading in public schools. None of these amendments made it out of the Judiciary Committee, but widespread disagreement with the Court persisted for decades. In a Gallup poll conducted in 1999, thirty-six years after *Schempp*, 70% of respondents still favored daily prayer in the classroom.[31]

The Court also limited the extent to which religious schools could receive public funds. In *Board of Education v. Allen* (1968), the Court allowed New York to provide secular books to parochial schools. But in *Lemon v. Kurtzman* (1971), the Court barred Pennsylvania and Rhode Island from supplementing the salaries of teachers in parochial schools. As government spending on education and other social services grew, knotty questions arose as to exactly what kinds of funding could be allocated to religiously affiliated institutions without running afoul of the Establishment Clause. In *Lemon* the Court tried to lay down a rule: to satisfy the Constitution, a law required a secular purpose, the law's primary effect could not be to advance religion, and the law could not foster "excessive government entanglement" with religion.[32] But this formula merely restated the problem. Most laws had multiple effects; how could one tell which was primary? And how much "entanglement" was "excessive"? These questions would recur in a wide variety of contexts.

On the same day that the Court strengthened the Establishment Clause in *Schempp*, it also strengthened the First Amendment's other provision regarding religion, the Free Exercise Clause. *Sherbert v. Verner* (1963) was a challenge to South Carolina's scheme of unemployment benefits, which denied eligibility to applicants who refused to work on Saturdays. Adell Sherbert was a member of the Seventh-Day Adventist church, a denomination that observed the sabbath on Saturdays. Just two years earlier, the Court had rejected the free exercise claim of a Jewish store owner who argued that a Sunday closure law discriminated against Jews, whose faith required closing on Saturdays as well, because their businesses could open only five days a week while their Christian competitors could stay open for six. Brennan had dissented in that case, but in *Sherbert* he spoke for a majority. "Not only is it apparent that appellant's declared ineligibility for benefits derives solely from the practice of her religion, but the pressure upon her to forego that practice is unmistakable," Brennan concluded. The state's law "forces her to choose between following the precepts of her religion and forfeiting benefits, on the one hand, and abandoning one of the precepts of her religion in order to accept work, on the other hand. Governmental imposition of such a choice puts the same kind of burden upon the free exercise of religion as would a fine imposed against appellant for her Saturday worship." The state could restrict the practice of religion only to advance a "compelling state interest," but South Carolina had no such interest, because it could administer unemployment benefits just as efficiently if it allowed state residents to designate Saturdays rather than Sundays as their sabbath.[33]

Sherbert opened up all sorts of questions, because there were many laws that were not intended to suppress religious practice but that nevertheless imposed greater burdens on adherents of some religions than others. For example, peyote was an illegal drug, but a religious group in California, the Native American Church, used peyote in its rituals. Did the prohibition of peyote infringe the free exercise of religion? The California Supreme Court relied on *Sherbert* to hold that members of the Church could not be prosecuted for possessing peyote. Jury service was mandatory, but a Minnesota resident insisted that her religious scruples barred her from judging others. Before *Sherbert*, the Minnesota Supreme Court rejected her claim for an exemption, but after *Sherbert*, the court changed its view and held that she could not be punished for refusing to serve on a jury.[34]

What about compulsory school attendance? The Old Order Amish stopped sending their children to school after the eighth grade for religious reasons. In *Wisconsin v. Yoder* (1972), the Court held that the Constitution required the state to excuse Amish children from its requirement that children attend high school. "It is one thing to say that compulsory education for a year or two beyond the eighth grade may be necessary when its goal is the preparation of the child for life in modern society as the majority live," Chief Justice Warren Burger wrote for the Court, "but it is quite another if the goal of education be viewed as the preparation of the child for life in the separated agrarian community that is the keystone of the Amish faith." As Stewart observed in a short concurring opinion, "Wisconsin has sought to brand these parents as criminals for following their religious beliefs."[35] Religious minorities had acquired a new constitutional right to an exemption from many generally applicable laws.

In the Court's religion cases, as in its free speech cases, the Court had to balance the claims of small dissenting groups against the interest of the majority in maintaining uniformity. As in the speech cases, the Court of the 1960s placed greater weight on the side of the dissenters than it had in previous eras. But this balance was trickier for religion than for speech because the First Amendment includes two clauses about religion, not just one. As the Court was interpreting the Establishment Clause to *bar* the government from giving certain preferences to religious people, it was also interpreting the Free Exercise Clause to *require* the government to give other preferences to religious people. The justices were aware of this tension. In *Sherbert*, Stewart worried that if the state were required to pay unemployment compensation to Seventh-Day Adventists who refused to work on Saturdays, but not to other state residents who refused to work on Saturdays, the state would violate the Establishment Clause by giving an advantage to Seventh-Day Adventists.[36] The more robustly the Court enforced both clauses, the more difficulty governments would face in navigating between their demands.

IV

The Court dramatically expanded religious freedom and the freedom of speech, but the changes it made to criminal procedure were even more far-reaching. In the span of just a few years, the Court granted criminal defendants several new and important constitutional rights.

One was an effective right to stop the police from conducting unlawful searches. The Fourth Amendment and its state constitutional analogues prohibit unreasonable searches, but for many years the police had little incentive to abide by this restriction. In principle a police officer who conducted an unlawful search could face disciplinary charges at work or a civil suit filed by the person who was illegally searched, but in practice these events were extraordinarily rare. For this reason, in *Weeks v. United States* (1914), the Court had barred the use of illegally obtained evidence in federal criminal cases. The states, however, not the federal government, prosecuted most criminal cases. In *Wolf v. Colorado* (1949), the Court had declined to apply this exclusionary rule in state courts, many of which did not exclude such evidence under state law either.[37]

In *Mapp v. Ohio* (1961), the Court overruled *Wolf* and required the state courts to exclude illegally obtained evidence. Dollree Mapp's experience illustrated the exclusionary rule's importance. The Cleveland police thought a suspect in a recent bombing was hiding in Mapp's house. (The bomb exploded beneath a different house, the residence of a young man named Don King, who would later be a famous boxing promoter.) Mapp would not let them in without a warrant, so the police broke down her door and ransacked her house. Her lawyer arrived midway through the search, but the police kept him outside during the search. They never found the bombing suspect. Instead, they found obscene books and photographs. At Mapp's trial for possessing them, the books and photographs were introduced as evidence despite the illegality of the search, because the exclusionary rule was not part of Ohio law. She was convicted and sentenced to spend up to seven years in prison. If the books and photographs had not been admitted at trial, Mapp would not have been convicted.[38]

On appeal, including at the Supreme Court, the primary issue argued by Mapp's lawyers was that Ohio's obscenity statute violated the First Amendment. They barely even mentioned the search of Mapp's house and they did not argue that *Wolf* should be overruled. When the justices met to discuss the case, they voted unanimously to reverse Mapp's conviction for the reason urged by her lawyers—that the state's obscenity law was unconstitutional. But in the elevator after the justices' conference, Clark, Warren, Brennan, Douglas, and Black agreed that the case was a good opportunity to overrule *Wolf* and require the states to follow the exclusionary rule. Clark's opinion for the Court did just that. Without the exclusionary rule, he suggested, the Constitution's protection from unlawful searches would be "valueless and undeserving of mention in a perpetual charter of inestimable human liberties." Without the rule, "the State, by admitting evidence unlawfully seized, serves to encourage disobedience to the Federal Constitution which it is bound to uphold." Clark acknowledged Benjamin Cardozo's well-known criticism of the exclusionary rule, that it made no sense to say that "the criminal is to go free because the constable blundered." But he disagreed with Cardozo. "The criminal goes free, if he must, but it is the law that sets him free," Clark insisted. "Nothing can destroy a government more quickly than its failure to observe its own laws, or worse, its disregard of the charter of its own existence." He noted that the exclusionary rule had been in operation in the federal courts for nearly half a century without preventing federal law enforcement agents from conducting searches, and that some states had likewise adopted the rule without hindering their police officers, so he predicted that the Court's decision would not be unduly disruptive.[39]

In approximately half the states, those that had previously lacked the exclusionary rule, *Mapp* gave police officers a powerful new incentive to follow the law by obtaining a search warrant in circumstances where one was required. *Mapp* also had an impact in states that already employed the exclusionary rule, as Douglas discovered a few months later when he ran into Stanley Mosk, the attorney general of California. "Thank the good Lord for *Mapp v. Ohio*," Mosk exclaimed. He told Douglas that because judges were elected in California, they faced great pressure to see that criminal defendants were convicted, so they did their best to avoid the state's own exclusionary rule. The effect of *Mapp*, Mosk reported, was "to take the pressure off the local judges" by letting them blame the Supreme Court.[40]

Two years later, in *Gideon v. Wainwright* (1963), the Court held that criminal defendants who cannot afford a lawyer must be provided one for free. In a pair of cases more than twenty years before, the Court had required the federal government to provide lawyers to indigent defendants but had refused to require the states to do so. In *Gideon*, as in *Mapp*, the Court now held the states to the same standard it had long applied to the federal government. "In our adversary system of criminal justice," Black wrote for the Court, "any person haled into court, who is too poor to hire a lawyer, cannot be assured a fair trial unless counsel is provided for him. This seems to us to be an obvious truth." No justice disagreed with his conclusion that "lawyers in criminal courts are necessities, not luxuries." *Gideon* became one of the Court's best-known cases after it was chronicled in *Gideon's Trumpet*, a popular book by the journalist Anthony Lewis, which was later adapted as a film starring Henry Fonda as Clarence Gideon, the Florida inmate whose conviction the Court reversed. But *Gideon*'s practical effect was not commensurate with its fame, because most states already provided free lawyers to defendants who could not afford them. *Gideon* changed the nature of trials in only a handful of southern states, where indigent defendants had not previously been given lawyers.[41]

Far more consequential was a series of decisions that limited the power of the police to interrogate suspects. In *Massiah v. United States* (1964), the Court held that the police could not elicit information from a suspect who had already been charged with a crime unless his lawyer was present. In *Escobedo v. Illinois* (1964), the Court prohibited the police from interrogating a suspect who had not yet been charged but who had requested to speak with his lawyer. And in the best-known of these cases, *Miranda v. Arizona* (1966), the Court required the police to inform suspects of their right to counsel and their right to remain silent before conducting a custodial interrogation. Motivating these decisions was the concern that the police often used violence and psychological coercion while questioning suspects. In *Miranda*, Warren referred to cases in which "the police resorted to physical brutality—beatings, hanging, whipping—and to sustained and protracted questioning incommunicado in order to extort confessions." He concluded that "unless a proper limitation upon custodial interrogation is achieved . . . there can be no assurance that practices of this nature will be eradicated in the foreseeable future." The Court's solution was to craft the detailed "Miranda warnings" that millions of Americans would learn from films and television shows. The suspect must be "warned prior to any questioning that he has the right to remain silent," Warren declared, "that anything he says can be used against him in a court of law, that he has the right to the presence of an attorney, and that if he cannot afford an attorney one will be appointed for him prior to any questioning if he so desires."[42]

Miranda was a 5–4 decision. Harlan, one of the dissenters, argued that the Court had deprived the police of an important tool—the suspect's own confession. The Court's new "rules impair, if they will not eventually serve wholly to frustrate, an instrument of law enforcement that has long and quite reasonably been thought worth the price paid for it," Harlan contended. "There can be little doubt that the Court's new code would markedly decrease the number of confessions." Harlan concluded that "the Court is taking a real risk with society's welfare in imposing its new regime on the country. The social costs of crime are too great to call the new rules anything but a hazardous experimentation." White, also in dissent, was even more explicit about what he saw as the consequences of the Court's decision. "In some unknown number of cases," he predicted, "the Court's rule will return a killer, a rapist or other criminal to the streets and to the environment which produced him, to repeat his crime whenever it pleases him."[43]

Like White, many law enforcement officials foresaw disaster. "We've lost the right to interrogate suspects," lamented the police chief of New Haven, Connecticut. "Confessions are almost the sole basis for convictions." The Memphis police chief complained that *Miranda* "has tied our hands" because "the first thing we have to tell a suspect is that he doesn't have to answer our questions." A Pittsburgh police officer expected that "we probably will lose 60 to 70 percent of the confessions we used to get. The crime rate will go up. If that's what society wants, that's what we'll give it." Members of Congress sounded the same theme. Senator Gordon Allott of Colorado, a former prosecutor, wondered "whether it is possible to make an arrest that will stand up in court." He worried that the job of the police "is daily becoming more difficult and nearly impossible." Senator James Cleveland of New Hampshire blamed *Miranda* and similar cases for a recent rise in crime rates.[44]

Congress even enacted a statute that purported to negate *Miranda* by permitting confessions to be used at trial where the *Miranda* warnings had not been given. The statute was necessary, a Senate committee report explained, because "the rigid and inflexible requirements of the majority opinion in the *Miranda* case are unreasonable, unrealistic, and extremely harmful to law enforcement." In "instance after instance . . . the most vicious criminals have gone unpunished, even though they had voluntarily confessed their guilt." The Court eventually held this statute unconstitutional.[45]

Of all the Court's criminal cases during this period, the one that provoked the most opposition was *Furman v. Georgia* (1972), in which the Court found the death penalty unconstitutional. Capital punishment had been an important part of the American criminal justice system for the nation's entire history. Yet popular support for the death penalty seemed to be waning, measured by polling results and by the annual number of executions carried out in the United States, which had been generally declining since the 1930s. In earlier eras of diminished support for capital punishment, some states had abolished it by legislation. In *Furman*, by a 5–4 vote, the Court abolished it nationwide by determining that the death penalty was cruel and unusual punishment in violation of the Eighth Amendment. The vote was a glimpse of the future, in that the four dissenters were the justices who had been recently appointed by President Richard Nixon.[46]

The justices in the majority did not agree as to why the death penalty was unconstitutional, so they each wrote separately. For Brennan and Marshall, capital punishment was cruel and unusual regardless of how it was implemented. The Eighth Amendment "prohibits the infliction of uncivilized and inhuman punishments," Brennan reasoned. "The State, even as it punishes, must treat its members with respect for their intrinsic worth as human beings. A punishment is 'cruel and unusual,' therefore, if it does not comport with human dignity." Marshall surveyed the already-voluminous research about the death penalty's effects and concluded that "capital punishment serves no purpose that life imprisonment could not serve equally well." He added that "even if capital punishment is not excessive, it nonetheless violates the Eighth Amendment because it is morally unacceptable to the people of the United States at this time in their history." He concluded that if people understood "all the facts presently available regarding capital punishment, the average citizen would, in my opinion, find it shocking to his conscience and sense of justice."[47]

For the other three members of the majority, however, the problem was not the death penalty itself but rather how the death penalty was implemented in practice. The decision whether to sentence criminals to death was left to the discretion of juries, who were given no guidance as to how to perform the task. It was common knowledge that black defendants, especially in the South, were more likely to be sentenced to death than similarly situated white defendants. "These discretionary statutes are unconstitutional in their operation," Douglas concluded. "They are pregnant with discrimination and discrimination is an ingredient not compatible with the idea of equal protection of the laws that is implicit in the ban on 'cruel and unusual' punishments." Stewart focused not on race discrimination but on the rarity of executions relative to the number of crimes for which capital punishment was nominally available. "These death sentences are cruel and unusual in the same way that being struck by lightning is cruel and unusual," he declared. The Eighth Amendment "cannot tolerate the infliction of a sentence of death under legal systems that permit this unique penalty to be so wantonly and so freakishly imposed." White agreed that the problem was "that the death penalty is exacted with great infrequency even for the most atrocious crimes and that there is no meaningful basis for distinguishing the few cases in which it is imposed from the many cases in which it is not."[48]

The four Nixon appointees also each wrote separate opinions, but there was considerable overlap in what the opinions said. The dissenters emphasized the incongruity of declaring unconstitutional a punishment that had been a staple of American law for two centuries and that indeed seemed to be contemplated by the Constitution itself, which prohibited the states from taking life only in certain circumstances. They criticized the justices in the majority for exceeding the proper role of judges by making law rather than interpreting it. "This decision holding unconstitutional capital punishment is not an act of judgment, but rather an act of will," insisted William Rehnquist, the newest justice.[49]

Furman v. Georgia would be the farthest the Court would go in reinventing criminal procedure. The backlash was immediate. The day after *Furman* was decided, legislators in five states announced they would introduce bills to bring back the death penalty. Within a few years, thirty-five states and the federal government had new statutes authorizing capital punishment. Popular support for the death penalty skyrocketed. Fifty percent of respondents favored capital punishment in a Gallup poll conducted a few months before *Furman* was decided. A few months after *Furman*, the figure had grown to 57%, and within a few years it reached 65%. In every part of the country, the death penalty became more popular than it had been in many years, as people who had not given much thought to capital punishment now decided that the Supreme Court was wrong to abolish it.[50]

Between the early 1960s and the early 1970s, the Court revolutionized criminal procedure by developing constitutional rules that granted new rights to people charged with crimes and that sharply limited the discretion once exercised by the police, by prosecutors, by trial judges, and by jurors. Jan Deutsch, one of Potter Stewart's former law clerks, taught a law school course on the subject. He told Stewart that he had to revise his course every year. "Still, there's hope for us poor teachers yet," Deutsch joked. "As long as the tradition of saving bombshells for June is maintained, we at least have the summer over which to reorient ourselves."[51]

Crime rates were on the rise during this period. The Court's critics blamed the justices. "I am convinced that many of the problems that have plagued America in the last few years are a direct result of some of the extreme rulings of the Court, especially in the field of criminology," the minister Billy Graham complained to President Lyndon Johnson in the summer of 1968, after riots took place in cities throughout the country. Graham urged Johnson to consider "balancing the Court with a strong conservative." Another of the Court's most caustic critics, a court of appeals judge named Warren Burger, despaired that "the crime situation" was getting "far worse." The solution, he argued, was "putting LAWYERS on this court" to replace its current members.[52] Enterprising political candidates joined in, none more enthusiastically than Richard Nixon, who, as we will see in the next chapter,

made the Court's criminal cases a major issue in his 1968 campaign for president. When Nixon won the election, he would appoint Burger as chief justice.

V

Perhaps the most fundamental change the Court made to the American legal
system during this period was to require equality in political representation.
Part of the issue involved blatant race discrimination, as when Alabama re-
drew the boundaries of the city of Tuskegee—changing its shape "from a
square to an uncouth twenty-eight-sided figure," as Felix Frankfurter put
it—for the purpose of removing nearly all the black voters from the city. In
Gomillion v. Lightfoot (1960), the Court unanimously held that this kind of
racial gerrymandering is unconstitutional.[53]

But unequal voting power was and always had been pervasive in the
United States, even apart from the race of the voters, because voting districts
were often of drastically different sizes. In 1946, for example, the smallest
of Illinois's congressional districts had a population of 112,000, while the
largest congressional district in the state had a population of 914,000, which
meant that a voter in the first district had more than eight times the representation in Congress as a voter in the second. Illinois was extreme but it was
hardly alone. Virtually every state with more than one member of Congress
had districts that varied widely in size. In *Colegrove v. Green* (1946), the
Court had refused to intervene on the ground that voting was a political
matter, not a legal one. "Courts ought not to enter this political thicket,"
Frankfurter insisted. "The remedy for unfairness in districting is to secure
State legislatures that will apportion properly, or to invoke the ample powers
of Congress."[54]

In *Baker v. Carr* (1962), the Court entered the thicket; it opened the door
to constitutional challenges to inequality in political representation. Because
Tennessee had not reapportioned its state legislative districts for sixty years,
while cities had grown in population relative to rural areas, rural residents
had much more voting power than urban ones. A vote in one rural county
was worth nineteen votes in one urban county. Thirty-seven percent of the
state's voters elected twenty of the state's thirty-three senators, while 40% of
the voters elected sixty-three of the ninety-nine members of the state house
of representatives. In an opinion by Brennan, the Court held that voters
seeking to challenge this malapportionment as a violation of the Equal

Protection Clause should be given an opportunity to do so. When the decision was announced, Warren scrawled a quick note and passed it down the bench to Brennan. "Bill," he said, "it is a great day for the country."[55]

Over the next few years, the Court required several states to equalize the populations of their electoral districts. In *Gray v. Sanders* (1963), the Court struck down Georgia's voting system for primary elections, which was heavily weighted in favor of rural voters. How "can one person be given twice or 10 times the voting power of another person in a statewide election merely because he lives in a rural area or because he lives in the smallest rural county?" Douglas asked in his opinion for the Court. "The conception of political equality from the Declaration of Independence, to Lincoln's Gettysburg Address, to the Fifteenth, Seventeenth, and Nineteenth Amendments can mean only one thing," he insisted—"one person, one vote." In *Wesberry v. Sanders* (1964), the Court likewise invalidated Georgia's unequal congressional districts. "While it may not be possible to draw congressional districts with mathematical precision," Black reasoned, "that is no excuse for ignoring our Constitution's plain objective of making equal representation for equal numbers of people the fundamental goal for the House of Representatives." And in *Reynolds v. Sims* (1964), the Court forced Alabama to redraw its state legislative districts, which varied greatly in population because they had not been modified since 1900. "Legislators represent people, not trees or acres," Warren declared. "If a State should provide that the votes of citizens in one part of the State should be given two times, or five times, or 10 times the weight of votes of citizens in another part of the State, it could hardly be contended that the right to vote of those residing in the disfavored areas had not been effectively diluted."[56] In a very short time, the Court upended traditional electoral mechanisms throughout the country by requiring all votes to have equal effect.

Earl Warren's own experience as governor of California helped him appreciate the importance of enlisting courts as the enforcers of voting equality. Seats in the California state senate were apportioned by county, not by population. When Warren was governor, the four million residents of Los Angeles County had the same single senator as residents of three-county districts with populations of less than 100,000. Warren was a beneficiary of this system, so as governor he opposed a reform effort. As chief justice a decade and a half later, he regretted his position, which he admitted "was frankly a matter of political expediency." Warren approached the issue of malapportioned legislatures with the enthusiasm of a convert. Reviewing his career, he would call *Baker v. Carr* the most important case the Court decided during his tenure—even more important than *Brown v. Board of Education.* Hugo Black's political experience also colored his view of apportionment. As far back as he could remember, he told Warren, every governor of Georgia had tried to equalize representation in the state legislature, only to be defeated by the legislature itself, which was dominated by members from the smallest counties. Warren and Black drew the lesson that the problem could only be remedied by the courts, because legislatures would never vote to reapportion themselves.[57]

The Court changed the relationship of Americans with their governments in several other ways as well. The justices redefined the right to receive welfare benefits as a form of property that could not be taken away without adequate procedures such as notice and a hearing. They prohibited the states from denying public assistance to people who had only recently arrived in the state, on the ground that such waiting-period requirements infringed an unwritten constitutional right to travel. They granted expansive First Amendment rights to public employees, who could no longer be punished for criticizing their employers on matters of public importance.[58] In decisions like these, the justices placed significant new constraints on the government in its dealings with individuals.

VI

Of all the Court's liberal law-changing decisions between the late 1950s and the early 1970s, the best known and most bitterly contested was *Roe v. Wade* (1973), in which the Court recognized a constitutional right to abortion. When *Roe* was decided, abortion was not yet an issue that divided the political parties. Among the seven justices in the majority were five Republican appointees, including Harry Blackmun, the opinion's author. In a Gallup poll conducted while the Court was deciding *Roe*, 68% of Republicans—but only 59% of Democrats—agreed that "abortion should be a decision between a woman and her physician." The justices did not expect *Roe* to be particularly controversial. Indeed, when the case was first argued, the Court was down to seven justices because two recent vacancies had not yet been filled. During this three-month period, the justices heard only the cases they thought were easy enough to be decided by a Court of seven, and they postponed the others until the Court was back up to nine. They placed *Roe* in the former category. "How wrong we were," Blackmun later admitted. Even while he was writing the Court's opinion, Blackmun had no inkling that the case would be a political bombshell. "I just didn't appreciate it at the time," he reflected. "Of course, now over the years it's always been with me. I'll carry it to my grave, for what it's worth."[59]

One reason the justices treated *Roe* as just another case was that the Court's most similar previous case, *Griswold v. Connecticut* (1965), had caused little fuss. In *Griswold*, the Court struck down a Connecticut statute that prohibited the use of contraceptives, on the then-novel ground that the statute infringed a constitutional right of marital privacy. The Constitution does not explicitly include a right of privacy, but in a characteristically idiosyncratic opinion by William Douglas, the Court explained that "specific guarantees in the Bill of Rights have penumbras, formed by emanations from those guarantees that help give them life and substance." One such penumbra was the right of privacy, which Douglas derived from the First Amendment's freedom of association, the Third Amendment's prohibition on the quartering of soldiers, the Fourth Amendment's requirement that searches be reasonable, the Fifth Amendment's ban on compulsory self-incrimination, and the Ninth Amendment's instruction that the specific rights listed in the Bill of Rights are not the only ones. The married couples who sought to use contraceptives possessed "a right of privacy older than the Bill of Rights— older than our political parties, older than our school system," Douglas concluded.[60]

The Connecticut law invalidated in *Griswold* was a relic from an earlier era. When it was enacted in 1879, such laws were common. By the 1950s, only two states still had a contraceptive ban on the books, and these laws were never enforced except in the rare instances, such as *Griswold*, when plaintiffs and state officials cooperated to create a test case of the statute's constitutionality. Contraception was freely available in Connecticut, as in other states. Even the dissenters in *Griswold* agreed that the ban on contraceptives was, as Potter Stewart put it, "an uncommonly silly law" that was "obviously unenforceable." But "we are not asked in this case to say whether we think this law is unwise, or even asinine," Stewart continued. "We are asked to hold that it violates the United States Constitution. And that I cannot do," because the Constitution, in his view, did not include a right to privacy.[61]

Lawyers found fault with Douglas's unorthodox penumbras-and-emanations method of constitutional interpretation. "The actual result of *Griswold* may be applauded," one law professor wondered, "but to reach this result was it necessary to play charades with the Constitution?" There was virtually no political opposition to *Griswold*, however, because few Americans still favored prohibiting contraceptives. Nor was there much opposition to *Eisenstadt v. Baird* (1972), in which the Court held that unmarried people could not be denied the use of contraceptives either. "If the right of privacy means anything," Brennan wrote for the Court, in words with obvious implications for abortion, "it is the right of the individual, married or single, to be free from unwarranted governmental intrusion into matters so fundamentally affecting a person as the decision whether to bear or beget a child." The right of privacy in matters of childbirth was a new constitutional right, but so were most of the constitutional rights the Court had recognized over the past two decades, such as the right to attend integrated schools, the right to advocate communism, the right to an attorney during questioning by the police, or the right to a vote that was worth as much as the votes of the people in the next county. When *Roe v. Wade* arrived at the Court, it looked like it would be just another in a long line of cases applying recently established rights in new contexts. Indeed, the district court in which the pseudonymous Jane Roe filed her suit had already anticipated this outcome. The district court relied on *Griswold* to rule that Roe was entitled to obtain an abortion because the Texas law prohibiting abortion infringed her constitutional right "to choose whether to have children." In *Roe*'s companion case, *Doe v. Bolton*, another district court likewise invalidated parts of Georgia's abortion law on the ground that *Griswold* established "a right to privacy which apparently is also broad enough to include the decision to abort a pregnancy."[62] To the extent *Roe* would involve any change in the law, the heavy lifting seemed to have already been done.

Unlike contraception, however, abortion was still illegal in most states in most circumstances. And while some of these state laws were quite old, others were not. There was still considerable anti-abortion sentiment in every state. While *Roe v. Wade* was pending in the Court, the Pennsylvania and Massachusetts state houses both passed bills prohibiting abortion, in both states by overwhelming margins, and New York came very close to reinstituting a ban that had only recently been repealed.[63] A constitutional right to privacy occasioned little controversy when it merely prevented the states from banning contraception, but abortion would be another matter entirely.

After oral argument in December 1971, the seven justices then on the Court held a meandering discussion of the case that yielded a vote in favor of a right to abortion but no majority as to precisely why. Blackmun, who had spent a decade as the Mayo Clinic's lawyer before becoming a judge, was the Court's resident expert on the law governing health care, so Burger assigned the majority opinion to him. Blackmun struggled to produce an opinion. After five months, he circulated a short draft that did not even address the issue on which the justices had voted but instead found the Texas abortion law unconstitutionally vague. Blackmun's colleagues were unimpressed. They voted to start over again. The case was reargued in October 1972, this time before a full complement of nine justices now that Lewis Powell and William Rehnquist had taken their seats.[64]

The following month, Blackmun circulated an opinion very different from his first. The new draft offered a lengthy survey of the history of abortion and abruptly concluded, with little explanation, that states could prohibit abortion only after the first trimester of pregnancy, because only then did the state have a sufficiently compelling interest in protecting the potential life of the fetus. Blackmun conceded, in a memo to his colleagues but not in the opinion itself, that his use of the end of the first trimester as a dividing line "is arbitrary, but perhaps any other selected point, such as quickening or viability, is equally arbitrary." Lewis Powell suggested drawing the line instead at fetal viability outside the womb. "Once we take the major step of affirming a woman's constitutional right," he urged, "viability is a more logical and defensible time for identifying the point at which the state's overriding right to protect potential life becomes evident." He added that younger and inexperienced women, "the women who most need the benefit of liberalized abortion laws," might be unaware they are pregnant or too embarrassed to seek help during the first trimester. "If there is a constitutional right to an abortion," Powell counseled, "there is much to be said for making it effective where and when it may well be needed most." Powell's concerns resulted from personal experience. His wife's father and her two brothers were obstetricians. And shortly before joining the Court, while Powell was still in private practice, the pregnant girlfriend of a young employee of his law firm was killed when the couple tried to perform an abortion on their own. Powell had helped the employee avoid prosecution.[65]

The final, published version of the Roe opinion incorporated both dividing lines—the end of the first trimester and the point of fetal viability—in an effort to balance the right to an abortion with the state's interest in fetal and maternal health. On one hand, Blackmun reasoned, the right of privacy "is broad enough to encompass a woman's decision whether or not to

Figure 13.2 Harry Blackmun was a lawyer for the Mayo Clinic before he became a judge, so he was the justice who wrote the Court's opinion in *Roe v. Wade*. For the rest of his life, he would be lauded by those who favored legal abortion and vilified by those who did not. This photograph was taken by Robert S. Oakes in 1976, three years after the Court decided *Roe*. Library of Congress, LC-USZ62-60137.

terminate her pregnancy." On the other, "this right is not unqualified and must be considered against important state interests in regulation." These state interests included the "protection of health, medical standards, and prenatal life." Blackmun's opinion rejected the argument of Texas that the state could legitimately determine that life begins at conception. "We need not resolve the difficult question of when life begins," Blackmun explained. "When those trained in the respective disciplines of medicine, philosophy, and theology are unable to arrive at any consensus, the judiciary, at this point in the development of man's knowledge, is not in a position to speculate as to the answer." Rather, the state's interest in protecting prenatal life and maternal health depended on how long a woman had been pregnant. During the first trimester of pregnancy, when "mortality in abortion may be less than mortality in normal childbirth," a state could not prohibit abortion at all. After the first trimester, but before the point of fetal viability outside the womb, the state could regulate abortion to protect the mother's health. And after the fetus became viable, the state could prohibit abortion altogether, except when abortion was necessary to protect the mother's life or health.[66]

The short dissents of William Rehnquist and Byron White prefigured the criticism that would hound *Roe v. Wade* for decades. The Court's decision "to break pregnancy into three distinct terms and to outline the permissible restrictions the State may impose in each one," Rehnquist charged, "partakes more of judicial legislation than it does of a determination of the intent of the drafters of the Fourteenth Amendment." White emphasized that the Court had removed a difficult moral question from the process by which such questions are usually resolved. The Court's decision meant that "the people and the legislatures of the 50 States are constitutionally disentitled to weigh the relative importance of the continued existence and development of the fetus, on the one hand, against a spectrum of possible impacts on the mother, on the other hand," White observed. "As an exercise of raw judicial power, the Court perhaps has authority to do what it does today; but in my view its judgment is an improvident and extravagant exercise of the power of judicial review."[67]

News of *Roe v. Wade* reached the public before the opinions were even announced. In an issue of *Time* magazine that was available on newsstands early in the morning of January 22, 1973, a few hours before the Court session at which *Roe* was released to the public, the magazine declared that it had "learned that the Supreme Court has decided to strike down nearly every anti-abortion law in the United States." In an article titled "Abortion on Demand," *Time* accurately reported that the Court's opinion would hold that laws prohibiting abortion "represent an unconstitutional invasion of privacy." Chief Justice Warren Burger was outraged. The *Time* story "is a gross breach of security" that "goes to the very heart of the integrity of our processes," he fumed. "It is plain to me that the article could not have been written without access to a draft of the opinion. We have an obligation to find the source." If one of his own clerks had talked to a reporter, Burger promised, "I would dismiss him or them forthwith." It turned out that the *Time* reporter, David Beckwith, was a law school friend of Larry Hammond, one of Powell's clerks. The two often had lunch, including the week before, when

Hammond learned to his surprise that Beckwith somehow already knew a great deal about the case. Beckwith assured him that *Time* would not run a story about it until the opinion was public. But *Roe*'s release was delayed for a few days while everyone waited for Burger to circulate his short concurring opinion, and *Time*'s editors decided to run the story in the next issue, so *Time* ended up with a scoop of a few hours' duration. Beckwith never revealed the source of his inside knowledge, beyond noting that it took "a lot of shoe leather," which presumably included interviews with justices or clerks. And despite Burger's threats, Hammond suffered no adverse consequences from the episode; he went on to become a prominent criminal defense lawyer in Arizona.[68]

As Blackmun announced the Court's opinion, Powell dashed off a note to Blackmun's wife Dottie, who was in the courtroom for the occasion. "Harry has written an historic opinion, which I was proud to join," Powell declared. Powell was being polite. He would tell his biographer that Blackmun's opinions in *Roe* and its companion case were "the worst opinions I ever joined." Powell's view was shared by many lawyers who supported legal abortion, who were grateful for the outcome but who were uneasy about how *Roe*'s detailed restrictions on regulation seemed to lack any anchor in the Constitution. "Were I a legislator I would vote for a statute very much like the one the Court ends up drafting," the law professor John Hart Ely observed. "It is, nevertheless, a very bad decision. Not because it will perceptibly weaken the Court—it won't; and not because it conflicts with either my idea of progress or what the evidence suggests is society's—it doesn't. It is bad because it is bad constitutional law, or rather because it is *not* constitutional law and gives almost no sense of an obligation to try to be." Archibald Cox, the former solicitor general, complained that Blackmun's opinion was "like a set of hospital rules and regulations." Ruth Bader Ginsburg, who would later join the Court herself, wished the Court had grounded the decision on the importance of abortion rights for the equality of women rather than on the relationship of physicians with their female patients.[69] Among readers concerned with judicial craft, *Roe v. Wade* was almost universally panned.

Of course, most people cared only about whether abortion would be lawful. Those who liked the outcome of *Roe* rejoiced that by permitting abortions to be performed safely by trained physicians, the Court had freed women from the dangerous, sometimes-fatal procedures that had long been carried out by amateurs. *Roe* represented exactly what the Supreme Court had become known for—the defense of individual liberty against overbearing government. Blackmun himself became an improbable "icon of feminism," the journalist Linda Greenhouse reflected after his death, a man "treated worshipfully by women's rights groups."[70]

Among abortion's opponents, Blackmun became a very different sort of icon. Soon after *Roe* was announced, mail blasting the decision began pouring into Blackmun's office. "The Court's decision to deny equal protection to unborn innocents is just so much legalistic doubletalk," insisted an angry woman from Virginia Beach, "and in condemning these innocents to death you will one day be held responsible by the Supreme Judge of us all." At St. Richard Elementary School in Omaha, Nebraska, the students in room 212 discussed *Roe* in their social studies class, and they could "see no reason why any woman or doctor would want to kill a child, one of God's creations." Blackmun tried to read all these letters, but the volume of mail was so overwhelming that he had to send much of it straight to storage. When he retired twenty years later, Blackmun estimated he had received 75,000 to 80,000 letters about *Roe v. Wade*. William Brennan did not write an opinion in *Roe*, but he was the Court's lone Catholic and the Catholic Church was opposed to abortion, so he too was the target of hate mail—in his clerks' estimation, 2,000 to 3,000 letters and telegrams per day during the month after the decision, most of which they described as "extremely vitriolic."[71]

A week after *Roe*, Blackmun arrived in Cedar Rapids, Iowa, to give a speech. He had to walk through a picket line of abortion protesters to enter the auditorium. Opponents of abortion would haunt his public appearances for the rest of his life. In 1985, someone even fired a shot through the Blackmuns' living room window. The police found the bullet lodged in a chair, but they never found the person responsible.[72]

Roe v. Wade would exert a profound influence on national politics. It sparked the emergence of a political movement devoted to prohibiting abortion. Abortion would become an issue that divided Republicans from Democrats. The Court would assume an unprecedented salience in presidential elections, as candidates began to campaign on the importance of appointing justices who would overrule or reaffirm *Roe*. Abortion would become the elephant in the hearing room each time the Senate considered whether to confirm a new nominee to the Court.

Roe began a new era in American politics, but it marked the end of an era in the history of the Court, because it would be the last of the Court's major mid-century liberal decisions. The Court was already beginning a long and gradual swing back to the right, one that would proceed fitfully for the next half-century. In the two decades between *Brown v. Board of Education* and *Roe v. Wade*, the Court reinterpreted the Constitution to make dramatic changes to the law in a wide range of fields—segregation, civil rights, the freedom of speech, the relation between church and state, criminal procedure, voting, and matters involving personal privacy. For a generation of Americans, lawyers and nonlawyers alike, the Supreme Court became the part of the government that protected the powerless against the powerful. It became a creative, forward-looking, lawmaking institution. Before the mid-1950s, conservatives valued the Court as the last line of defense against unwanted change, while liberals criticized the justices for enforcing their own political preferences rather than the laws enacted by democratically elected legislatures. But for a brief span between the mid-1950s and the early 1970s, the tables turned. Now it was liberals who supported the Court's decisions and conservatives who blamed the justices for following their personal values rather than the law. In retrospect, this short period was a unique time in the Court's history—the only time in which the Court was a consistent driver of progressive legal change.

14

A Partial Counterrevolution

Between 1969 and 1991, ten consecutive justices were appointed by Republican presidents—four by Richard Nixon, one by Gerald Ford, three by Ronald Reagan, and two by George H. W. Bush. (Jimmy Carter, the lone Democrat in the White House during this period, is the only president in American history who served a full term in office but never had the opportunity to appoint a justice.) These new justices were chosen primarily to undo the Court's work of the 1960s and early 1970s. Republican officials expected that the new justices would remove Court-imposed restraints on police officers, limit the role of federal judges in remedying discrimination, reduce the separation of church and state, and allow the states once again to prohibit abortion. By 1991, eight of the nine justices were Republican appointees. Byron White was the only Democrat left on the Court, and White was the most conservative of Democrats; he had dissented in nearly all the Court's major liberal decisions. For those who deplored what they considered the excesses of the Warren Court, the future looked bright indeed.

But the Court did not fulfill these expectations. Rather than overruling the big liberal decisions, the justices merely chipped away at them. The Court created a variety of exceptions to the constitutional doctrines restricting police officers, but the police were still governed by all sorts of rules that had not existed before the 1960s. Judges had less authority to remedy some kinds of discrimination, but the Court gave them *more* authority to remedy other kinds. The Court shaved some height off the wall separating church and state, but not much—the wall was still higher than it had been before the 1960s. And, perhaps most surprising of all, *Roe v. Wade* was still standing. While the Court made it easier for states to regulate abortion in some respects, there was still a constitutional right to privacy, and abortion was still legal throughout the country. Ten straight Republican appointments had yielded only a partial counterrevolution. The ship had changed course, but it had not gone far in its new direction.

I

The Republican effort to reclaim the Court began during Richard Nixon's campaign for president in 1968. Nixon was hardly the first candidate to criticize the Court, but he did so with an unusual persistence, focusing particularly on the Court's criminal procedure decisions. The justices had given the "green light" to criminals, Nixon alleged. He complained that the effect of *Miranda v. Arizona* was to "set free patently guilty individuals on the basis of legal technicalities." Nixon's emphasis on the Court's criminal cases was smart politics. In a national poll conducted in the summer of 1968, more respondents approved than disapproved of the Court's decisions desegregating schools and establishing the principle of one person, one vote. But respondents disliked the criminal cases by a margin of seven to one. For this reason, Nixon's "campaign refrain," as one journalist reported, was that the Court had "gone too far in weakening the peace forces against the criminal forces," and that as president "he would appoint Justices who were more 'strict' in their readings of the Constitution." The platform adopted at the 1968 Republican convention included a pledge to make "a determined effort to rebuild and enhance public respect for the Supreme Court"—a promise to staff the Court with justices who would side with the police instead of the criminals.[1]

In June 1968, as the presidential campaign was entering its final months, Chief Justice Earl Warren announced that he would retire as soon as a successor was confirmed. Although he never said as much publicly, it seems clear that Warren tried to time his retirement to allow President Lyndon Johnson to appoint his successor. Contemporaries certainly thought so. Senator Roman Hruska of Nebraska "did not like the idea of Warren resigning in time to give you a chance to maintain the liberal balance on the Court," one of Johnson's aides informed him. Senator Gordon Allott of Colorado was "livid about Justice Warren resigning at this time rather than waiting until the new President takes office," another aide told Johnson.[2] Soon after Warren announced his retirement, Johnson nominated Justice Abe Fortas to take Warren's spot as chief justice. To fill Fortas's seat, Johnson nominated Homer Thornberry, an undistinguished court of appeals judge from Texas whose chief qualification was that he and Johnson had been close associates for years.

Warren's plan backfired in the Senate. A coalition of Republicans and conservative southern Democrats refused to allow the nomination of Fortas to come to a vote. Nineteen Republican senators signed a petition refusing to consider any nominee until after the election, on the ground that "the American people are in the process of choosing a new government" and the new president should be the one to appoint a chief justice. Strom Thurmond, a Democratic senator from South Carolina, issued press releases declaring that Fortas's decisions "have created revolutionary changes in the American way of life." He charged that Fortas had "freed criminals on technicalities, allowed Communists to work in defense plants, and invaded the rights of the States" (a reference to the Court's desegregation decisions), and that Fortas had ruled that "hard core pornography" was constitutionally protected. Robert Byrd of Virginia affirmed that he would do "everything in my power" to oppose the "leftist" Fortas, while Russell Long of Louisiana called Fortas "one of the dirty five who sides with the criminal against the victims of crime." It was clear almost from the start that Fortas had no hope of being confirmed.[3]

At his hearing before the Senate Judiciary Committee, where Fortas was the first sitting justice ever to testify, his opponents took turns lambasting the Court's criminal procedure decisions. The Court's "artificial rules" were "making it more difficult to bring criminals to justice," averred Sam Ervin of North Carolina. "In my humble judgment it is time for the Supreme Court members to realize that society and the victims of crime are just as much entitled to justice as an accused." Senators also grilled Fortas about his close connections with Johnson—Johnson consulted Fortas, his longtime advisor, on all sorts of issues, from the conduct of the Vietnam War to the content of the State of the Union address—and about Fortas's outside income. "It's been pretty bloody," Fortas told his colleague William Douglas. Douglas knew that the Senate's treatment of Fortas had more to do with the Court's direction in recent years—including the period before Fortas even joined the Court— than with Fortas himself. "What an ordeal you are going through!" Douglas exclaimed. "It's an attack on five of us, not you alone." (Douglas was referring to Warren, William Brennan, and Thurgood Marshall, as well as Fortas and himself.) Finally, in October, as the Court's term was about to begin, a motion to bring Fortas's nomination to a vote in the Senate fell far short of the two-thirds majority that was then required. Fortas gave up. He asked Johnson to withdraw his nomination as chief justice.[4] Fortas was the first unsuccessful nominee to the Court since John Parker, back in 1930.

Nixon won the presidential election and soon forced Fortas off the Court. Fortas's nomination as chief justice had drawn attention to the unusual amount of income he received for giving speeches and teaching courses, activities that were not part of his duties as a justice. When *Life* magazine investigated further, prodded by leaks from Nixon's Justice Department, it found more. A charitable foundation established by the financier Louis Wolfson, a client of Fortas's old law firm, had agreed to pay Fortas $20,000 per year for life, or about half of Fortas's salary as a justice, in exchange for Fortas's undefined services as a consultant. Wolfson was being investigated for securities fraud at the time; he would later be convicted and sent to prison. Fortas does not appear to have intervened in Wolfson's prosecution, and he returned the money to Wolfson when the matter became public knowledge, but the damage had been done. The Nixon administration upped the pressure on Fortas by reopening an investigation, one that had been closed under the Johnson administration, into whether Fortas's wife, Carol Agger, a partner at his old law firm, had concealed documents subpoenaed in an unrelated criminal case. "The cloud gathering over Justice Fortas makes it a good probability that he will be forced to resign after a 'decent interval,'" chortled Patrick Buchanan, Nixon's speechwriter and strategist. Fortas resigned in May 1969, still denying that he had done anything wrong. Buchanan urged Nixon not to hold a press conference on the matter until he had chosen Fortas's replacement, so "the 'judicial story' for that day" would be the new justice "and not the analysis of how we intervened." Nixon's chief of staff, H. R. Haldeman, likewise instructed that "all hands" should downplay the administration's involvement in Fortas's fall, because the "Jewish press will be after us." The White House's messaging would instead "show how responsible Mitchell's handling was"—that is, how forgiving Attorney General John Mitchell had been in allowing Fortas to bow out gracefully. After all, the administration "could have let [the case] go to [the] House"—that is, Nixon could have urged Congress to impeach Fortas.[5]

Nixon tried to push William Douglas off the Court too, but this effort failed. A few weeks after Fortas resigned, White House counsel John Ehrlichman learned that the *Washington Star* newspaper was working on "a Fortas type exposure" of Douglas. Douglas, it turned out, received an annual salary of $12,000 from a foundation established by Albert Parvin, the owner of a Las Vegas casino, for serving as the foundation's president, a position that does not seem to have entailed much work. The Justice Department began an investigation, but there was not enough evidence to charge Douglas with a crime. The Nixon administration sought to have Douglas impeached instead. In the spring of 1970, John Mitchell gave the evidence against Douglas to Gerald Ford, the House minority leader. The House began impeachment proceedings, which dragged on until December, when a House subcommittee recommended against impeachment and the matter died. Ironically, just before the impeachment effort began, Douglas had been planning to retire in the summer of 1970. "Then the storm gathered," he said later, "and I decided that was not the way to get rid of me."[6] Nixon's attempt to have Douglas impeached aroused Douglas's orneriness, which kept him on the Court for another five years, until he suffered a stroke and had to retire.

Nixon would not need to get rid of Douglas to transform the Court. He already had the opportunity to replace Warren and Fortas, and then Hugo Black and John Harlan both abruptly retired due to poor health in the fall of 1971, so Nixon was able to appoint four new justices in his first three years as president. Nixon was a lawyer who, to a degree unusual for a president, paid close attention to the Court's decisions. After he lost the 1962 California gubernatorial election, Nixon became a partner at one of the major New York law firms, and he even argued a case before the Court in 1966. (Fittingly, it was a lawsuit against the press. Nixon's side lost.)[7] Many previous presidents chose justices based on personal connections rather than political beliefs, but Nixon was primarily interested in changing the Court's direction. He wanted justices who were as conservative as possible.

Nixon's first nominee was Warren Burger to replace Earl Warren as chief justice. Burger had been assistant attorney general in Eisenhower's first term, when Nixon was vice president. Eisenhower appointed Burger to the Court of Appeals for the DC Circuit in 1956, where he had sat ever since. In Republican legal circles, Burger was known as a harsh critic of the Court's liberal decisions. When the Court, in an opinion by Potter Stewart, decided *Shelton v. Tucker* (1960), one of the First Amendment cases barring states from firing teachers based on their political beliefs, Burger referred to the decision as "Potter Stewart's latest abortion." "Read it in tomorrow's papers," he advised Herbert Brownell, who had been Eisenhower's attorney general; "it will turn your stomach." Burger offered a similar review of John Harlan's concurring opinion in *Hunter v. Erickson* (1969), in which the Court held that a city could not amend its charter to prevent the city council from implementing ordinances barring race discrimination. "John Harlan seems to have gone to Disneyland or taken LSD on this one," Burger scoffed. "It is incredible." The problem, Burger thought, was that "we have a freewheeling court which acknowledges no limits on its own power and does not begin to think in terms of self-restraint."[8] This was exactly the frame of mind Nixon was looking for in a chief justice. Burger, nominated in May 1969, sailed through the Senate in time to become chief justice at the end of the Court's term in June.

Throughout Nixon's presidency, he and Burger met regularly and spoke often on the phone. Some of these talks, which survive thanks to Nixon's habit of recording all his conversations, were about issues before the Court. In early 1973, for instance, Nixon and Burger discussed *Miller v. California*, one of the First Amendment obscenity cases. The case had recently been argued, but the Court's decision would not be published until a few months later. The two men shared an antipathy for the Court's decisions holding that pornography was entitled in some circumstances to First Amendment protection.

BURGER: I am struggling with this pornography thing. I don't know whether, I don't know how we are coming out. I am coming out hard on it.

NIXON: Good, good.

BURGER: Whether I get the support or not.

. . .

NIXON: Let's face it, it's just gone overboard, that's all. It is always a question of balance. I mean, maybe you can—they go back to this sixteenth-century stuff and say, "What's wrong with that, that was great art?" Well, the stuff today is not great art. The stuff today, its purpose—what is that term that they have—you—

BURGER: Redeeming social purpose.

NIXON: Yeah, good God.

BURGER: One of the biggest frauds—

NIXON: Oh, that was a Brennan opinion, wasn't it?

BURGER: I think so.

NIXON: Yeah, yeah.

BURGER: That was a phrase that emanated from some of the campuses in this period.

NIXON: Redeeming social purposes. [laughs]

BURGER: It is, you know, all this means is that if they have one of the outrageous orgies then if they mention Vietnam, or the condition of the ghettos, it redeems the whole thing.

NIXON: Yeah, oh boy. Well, isn't that something.[9]

Burger would be a reliable conservative vote—with the conspicuous exception of *Roe v. Wade*—until he retired in 1986.

Figure 14.1 Warren Burger and Richard Nixon at the May 1969 press conference announcing Nixon's nomination of Burger as chief justice. Burger and Nixon spoke regularly, including about cases before the Court. National Archives, 66394147.

Nixon had more trouble replacing Fortas. He wanted a conservative from the South, as part of his "southern strategy" to convert white southerners from Democrats to Republicans. His first nominee was the South Carolinian Clement Haynsworth, the chief judge of the Court of Appeals for the Fourth Circuit. But Haynsworth was opposed by labor and civil rights organizations. When it came to light that Haynsworth had not recused himself from cases involving one corporation in which he was a shareholder and another that earned revenue from a company he owned part of, opponents had enough ammunition to defeat his nomination in the Senate. These ethical breaches might not have disqualified a nominee in previous years, but in 1969, right after financial improprieties had driven Fortas off the Court, it was hard to ignore them in the judge chosen to succeed Fortas, particularly a judge with a record conservative enough that opponents were eager to pounce on any shortcoming.[10]

During the Senate debate over whether Haynsworth should have recused himself, Nixon asked Attorney General John Mitchell to "submit to him a confidential report as soon as possible as to how many justices of the Supreme

Court own stocks in corporations." If any of the sitting justices had also heard cases involving companies in which they owned shares, Haynsworth's transgressions might not look so bad. Even better from Nixon's perspective, he might be able to use this information to force one of the liberal justices to resign, as he had done to Fortas. Mitchell balked at Nixon's request "because the information can only be obtained from tax returns," an aide explained. If it ever became public knowledge that the White House was peeking at the justices' tax returns, Mitchell warned, "it would present real trouble for the President." The plan was shelved. But Nixon would not give up easily. Chief of Staff H. R. Haldeman scribbled a note—marked "Confidential"—to White House Counsel John Ehrlichman: "The P. still feels this should be checked out sometime when the issue is not so sensitive."[11]

The lesson to be drawn from Haynsworth's defeat, Nixon's advisor Leonard Garment suggested, was that "the President should make every effort to propose a candidate who is *unobjectionable* on civil rights, even if this means someone who has essentially *no* record." Sitting judges had a paper trail of opinions, Garment acknowledged, so finding such a candidate "is distinctly *more* feasible if a non-judge is appointed." Nixon did not follow Garment's advice. He nominated G. Harrold Carswell, a court of appeals judge from Florida. Carswell at least did not own any shares of corporations. But his record on civil rights was even less attractive (to those who favored civil rights) than Haynsworth's. Early in his career, while running for the state legislature, he had given a speech in which he declared: "I yield to no man as a fellow candidate, or as a fellow citizen, in the firm, vigorous belief in the principles of white supremacy, and I shall always be so governed." Carswell insisted at the hearings that he no longer felt that way, but this defense did not convince many opponents, if any, to change their vote. And Carswell was, by all accounts, a lackluster judge. "I am impelled to conclude," the dean of Yale Law School testified, "that the nominee presents more slender credentials than any nominee for the Supreme Court put forth this century." Senator Roman Hruska offered a memorable defense of Carswell: "There are a lot of mediocre judges and people and lawyers," Hruska reasoned, "and they are entitled to a little representation, aren't they? We can't have all Brandeises, Frankfurters, and Cardozos." Steve Umin, one of Potter Stewart's former clerks, joked that Carswell was so unqualified to be a justice that he would print bumper stickers that read "Bring Back Haynsworth."[12] The Senate rejected Carswell, just as it had rejected Haynsworth.

The Democrats had a majority in the Senate throughout Nixon's presidency, but the votes on Haynsworth and Carswell were more regional than partisan. Both nominees drew most of their support from the South and most of their opposition from the North. Of the fifty-five senators who opposed Haynsworth, seventeen were Republicans, and of the fifty-one who opposed Carswell, thirteen were Republicans.

Nixon gave up on appointing a southerner to fill the vacancy left by Fortas. His third nominee was Harry Blackmun, an Eighth Circuit judge in Minnesota. Blackmun had been friends with Warren Burger since childhood. He was a sixty-one-year-old Republican who had been a judge for eleven years and had compiled a record of moderation and competence. He had not written opinions or given speeches that offended any significant constituency. The Senate, no doubt relieved, held a perfunctory hearing and confirmed Blackmun unanimously. He joined the Court in June 1970, more than a year after Fortas resigned. For the rest of his life, Blackmun would refer to himself as "old number three," a name that reflected his acute awareness that he was no one's first choice for the position.[13] Blackmun would remain on the Court for twenty-four years. In his last years on the Court, he was considered the most liberal of the justices—not primarily because he had changed, but because the composition of the Court had changed around him.

The following year, when Black and Harlan retired in quick succession, the White House officials responsible for finding their successors vowed not to repeat the mistakes of Haynsworth and Carswell. "We simply can't afford to play catch up ball with a nomination again," Bud Krogh told Ehrlichman. This time, the nominees would be thoroughly vetted before they were announced, so there would be no surprises. "Experience has shown that the FBI investigations and a casual luncheon or conversation are not sufficient to extract the kind of information we need," Krogh explained. Krogh recommended "something like a CIA de-briefing" of the prospective nominee that would probe "every facet of his professional life, personal life, trips, businesses, etc." Once chosen, moreover, the nominee would no longer be left to fend for himself before the Senate. The administration would establish "a secret confirmation committee" composed of White House and Justice Department lawyers who would keep "a guiding hand on these proceedings on a daily—even hourly—basis" so that "mistaken comments by a nominee or supporter can be quickly corrected."[14] The Nixon administration's response to the defeat of Haynsworth and Carswell was the origin of the increasingly elaborate procedures the White House would employ, under

Nixon and all subsequent presidents, to select nominees and to shepherd them through Senate confirmation.

Nixon's priority was once again to appoint a conservative southerner. "I don't give a God damn if the guy can read or write, just so he votes right," Nixon declared. He settled on the Virginia congressman Richard Poff. Poff had never been a judge and he had only minimal experience as a lawyer, but he had precisely the qualifications Nixon was looking for. "He's conservative, but yet he's not considered to be racist," Nixon explained. And "he's young," only forty-seven, unlike Burger and Blackmun, who had both been in their sixties when Nixon appointed them. But the administration's beefed-up screening procedure caused concerns to surface. Like most southern elected officials, Poff had opposed school desegregation in the years after *Brown v. Board of Education* and he had voted against civil rights legislation. While in Congress, he continued to earn an income from his old law firm despite doing no legal work. If Nixon nominated Poff, warned John Dean, the new White House counsel, "we are headed for the same problem as last time," when accusations of racism and financial impropriety had doomed Haynsworth and Carswell. Poff withdrew when it became clear that his confirmation would not be easy, because he and his wife worried that controversy in the Senate would result in public disclosure that one of their young sons was adopted, a fact they had not yet told him.[15] A year later, Poff left Congress to join the Virginia Supreme Court, where he sat for the rest of his career.

The search for a young southern conservative continued. Next to be considered was Herschel Friday, an Arkansas lawyer in his late forties who was recommended by Warren Burger. Friday's most notable accomplishment was representing Arkansas school districts when they were sued for refusing to integrate. "It is evident from our experience in the Haynsworth and Carswell confirmation fights that a demonstrable 'red neck' hostility to civil rights on the part of a nominee, or a personal animus against any minority, could well prove fatal to chances for confirmation," advised Assistant Attorney General William Rehnquist. Fortunately, "Friday's public statements in these areas indicates to me that they were invariably in good taste." John Dean agreed that Friday "is not a 'red neck'—but simply a 'lawyer' who has represented civil rights defendants." But while "his instincts are conservative," Dean continued, a lengthy discussion with Friday revealed "little evidence of a reflective and strong mind that could lead on the court or articulate a substantive conservative philosophy on fundamental issues."

A committee of the American Bar Association shared Dean's skepticism; half the committee members deemed Friday unqualified for the post. At the last moment, just when Friday was expecting Nixon to call and tell him he was the nominee, John Mitchell called to let him know he had been passed over.[16]

In the end, neither of the new justices would be a young southern conservative, but one would be southern and the other would be a young conservative. The southerner was Lewis Powell, a Virginian already in his mid-sixties. Powell was unusually well known for a lawyer who had spent his entire career in private practice. As chair of the Richmond school board in the 1950s and as a member of the state's board of education in the 1960s, Powell had taken a moderate course in the battles over desegregation. (Given the time and place, Powell's moderation did not result in much integration.) As president of the American Bar Association in the 1960s, he had worked to implement reforms in professional ethics, in the administration of criminal justice, and in the provision of legal services to the poor. When the Chamber of Commerce wanted advice on how to counteract the new liberal public interest organizations that were increasingly opposing businesses in court, it was Powell to whom the Chamber turned.[17] Only one senator voted against his confirmation. At sixty-four, Powell was the oldest person to receive his first appointment to the Court since Horace Lurton, who had been sixty-five when he took office in 1910. Lurton died after only four years, but Powell served for fifteen, during which he occupied the Court's ideological center. He was often the pivotal vote in 5–4 decisions.

The young conservative was the forty-seven-year-old William Rehnquist, a man in the right place at the right time. Rehnquist led the Justice Department's Office of Legal Counsel, where one of his responsibilities was helping to choose new justices. Nixon did not think highly of him at first. "Who the hell is that clown?" he asked after his first meeting with Rehnquist, at which Rehnquist wore a pink shirt and a bright necktie. "That's a hell of a costume he's wearing." But as the administration floundered in its effort to come up with a nominee, Rehnquist's colleagues in the Justice Department put his name forward. Rehnquist was the most conservative of any of the possible nominees Nixon considered during his presidency. When he clerked for Robert Jackson, Rehnquist had been, by his own account, the only law clerk in the building who opposed *Brown v. Board of Education*. He held a similarly dim view of the Court's decisions establishing rights for criminal defendants. "Every condemned man deserves the right to a careful hearing," he wrote Jackson after his clerkship ended, "but this does not mean that the highest court of the nation must behave like a bunch of old women every time they encounter the death penalty." As a lawyer in Phoenix, Rehnquist participated in a Republican effort to deter members of minority groups from voting by challenging their qualifications while they stood in line at the polls.[18] But if there was no doubt about Rehnquist's politics or his intellectual ability, he was an obscure figure compared with most of the people who had joined the Court throughout its history, nearly all of whom had been a judge or an elected official or had (like Powell) occupied other prominent positions. Rehnquist must have been astonished when Nixon agreed to nominate him. Twenty-six senators voted against him, the most for any successful nominee since Charles Evans Hughes in 1930. Rehnquist immediately became the Court's most conservative member, a position he would occupy for many years until he was outflanked by Antonin Scalia and Clarence Thomas.

Despite a concerted effort to appoint conservative justices who would change the Court's direction, Nixon succeeded in appointing only two, Burger and Rehnquist, who were committed to overturning the decisions of the previous decade. Powell and Blackmun were centrist, pragmatic Republicans who did not share Burger's and Rehnquist's strong ideological convictions. Powell was startled when law professors complained that he lacked a judicial philosophy. "We are criticized for deciding each case on the basis of the applicable law to its facts, rather than according to some mythical 'judicial philosophy,'" he remarked. "I would hardly expect justice if I were a litigant before a court that decided cases pursuant to a 'philosophy.'" Rehnquist grew exasperated with Blackmun's focus on the details of cases rather than on the big-picture development of the law. "Harry Blackmun," he groused, "can usually find two or three sinister aspects of every case which 'disturb' him, although they have nothing to do with the merits of the question." Looking back a decade later, Peter Wallison, who served as White House counsel in the Reagan administration, summarized the four justices' records. "Were President Nixon to evaluate his appointments," Wallison reckoned, "he would be disappointed by Justice Blackmun, satisfied with Powell, highly pleased with Chief Justice Burger, and wildly enthusiastic about Rehnquist."[19]

The Court, including three of Nixon's four appointees, would play an important role in Nixon's resignation from the presidency after the Watergate scandal. (Rehnquist recused himself because before joining the Court he had worked closely with some of the Justice Department officials implicated in Watergate. He was fortunate to have left the department in December 1971, a few months before the break-in that gave rise to the scandal.) During the prosecution of the Watergate conspirators, Nixon refused to give the special prosecutor tape recordings of conversations between aides and himself. He contended that a president's confidential communications with his advisors were protected by an "executive privilege" from being disclosed in criminal proceedings. When *United States v. Nixon* arrived at the Court in the summer of 1974, the oral argument was the hottest ticket in town. Extra seating had to be placed in the courtroom to accommodate the members of Congress, journalists, Court employees, and members of the justices' own families who wished to attend, and even these seats had to be tightly rationed—for instance, only twenty-five places were allotted to each house of Congress.[20]

It took only a bit more than two weeks after oral argument for the Court to decide unanimously against Nixon, in an opinion that bore Burger's name but which represented the joint product of several justices. The president has a need for confidentiality in his communications with aides, the opinion acknowledged, but this need "cannot prevail over the fundamental demands of due process of law in the fair administration of criminal justice. The generalized assertion of privilege must yield to the demonstrated, specific need for evidence in a pending criminal trial."[21] Nixon turned over the tapes and resigned soon after. In a constitutional showdown between two branches of the federal government, the Court was once again the winner.

II

The next new justice, John Paul Stevens, was nominated by Gerald Ford to replace the retiring William Douglas in 1975. His selection was an indirect result of Watergate. Had Ford been able to, he might have followed Nixon's strategy of picking the most conservative candidate available. After all, Ford had led the failed effort to impeach Douglas just a few years earlier, a project he defended, although Douglas had committed no crime, on the ground that no crime was required because "an impeachable offense is whatever a majority of the House of Representatives considers it to be at a given moment." But Ford was greatly constrained in the aftermath of Watergate. Several of the top lawyers in the Justice Department and the White House had been convicted and sent to prison, including Attorney General John Mitchell and three people who served as White House counsel—John Ehrlichman, Charles Colson, and John Dean. To signify that he was cleaning house, Ford had to emphasize professional reputation over ideological considerations in his appointments to key legal positions. His attorney general was Edward Levi, the president of the University of Chicago and a former law professor. To replace Douglas, Levi suggested Stevens, a fellow Chicagoan and a well-regarded moderate judge on the Court of Appeals for the Seventh Circuit. The name did not ring a bell with some members of Congress. "Who?" asked Tip O'Neill of Massachusetts. "I never heard of him—who is he?" Hugh Scott of Pennsylvania wondered if Stevens was a fraternity brother of Donald Rumsfeld, Ford's chief of staff.[22] (He wasn't.) But Stevens's sterling reputation as a nonideological judge carried him through the Senate on a unanimous vote.

Stevens would serve on the Court for more than thirty-four years, the third-longest term of any justice, behind only William Douglas and Stephen Field. When he retired at the age of ninety, Stevens was the second-oldest justice in history, behind only Oliver Wendell Holmes. Stevens would join Blackmun as middle-of-the-road Republicans who occupied the left wing of a Court that had lost all its liberal members.

When Ronald Reagan became president in 1981, his administration, like Nixon's, sought to appoint justices who would overrule the liberal decisions of the 1960s and early 1970s. Like Nixon, Reagan was only partially successful. When Potter Stewart retired in the summer of 1981, Reagan chose his first nominee, Sandra Day O'Connor, not because she was the most conservative of the plausible options but because he had promised on the campaign trail to appoint the first female justice. At the time there were not many Republican women with judicial experience. O'Connor had been a judge in Arizona for six years, after five years in the state senate. And she was certainly conservative on some issues. She had a "healthy disdain for the exclusionary rule," reported an approving aide to Attorney General William French Smith, and in the state senate she had sponsored a bill to bring back the death penalty after the Court's decision in *Furman v. Georgia*. But O'Connor's nomination drew fierce opposition from anti-abortion groups, who deemed her insufficiently zealous in the crusade to overrule *Roe v. Wade*. As a state senator, she had voted for legislation that made it more difficult for women to obtain abortions, but she had voted against a resolution asking Congress to propose a constitutional amendment to prohibit abortion. "Ms. O'Connor is strongly pro-abortion," complained the president of the National Right to Life Committee, the largest anti-abortion organization. One abortion opponent accused Reagan of having "betrayed me and millions of Americans including over 8 million pre-born babies" by choosing O'Connor.[23] Such complaints had no effect on the Senate, which confirmed O'Connor unanimously. But opponents of abortion were right to worry about how she would vote in abortion cases, as they would soon find out.

They had no such concern about Antonin Scalia, Reagan's next nominee, who filled the vacancy created in 1986 when Warren Burger retired as chief justice and was replaced by William Rehnquist. Reagan himself had appointed Scalia to the DC Circuit in 1982, after Scalia had spent the previous fifteen years shuttling between academic and government posts. He was "a life-long conservative," explained an aide to White House Counsel Peter Wallison. "Supposedly, even while in law school, he chided classmates about favoring excessive government regulation. He was a hardcore Goldwater supporter and a fan of Bill Buckley and the *National Review*." And Scalia was "uniformly considered a first-rate legal scholar. Even liberal Democrats concede this. The confirmation process, consequently, should be relatively easy." It was indeed easy. Although it was evident that Scalia would become the most conservative member of the Court, the Senate confirmed him unanimously. One reason, as Patrick Buchanan predicted, was that Scalia was the first Italian American nominated to the Court—"a tremendous achievement for what is America's largest ethnic minority," Buchanan noted, "a minority which provides the GOP its crucial margins of victory in New Jersey, Connecticut, and New York."[24]

Another reason for Scalia's easy passage through the Senate was that opponents concentrated their fire on Rehnquist, whom Reagan simultaneously nominated as chief justice. Rehnquist had been on the Court for fifteen years, during which he had written plenty of opinions liberals disliked. There was much more to criticize about Rehnquist than about Scalia. All the points that had been made against him when he was first nominated in 1971 resurfaced in 1986, including his opposition to *Brown v. Board of Education* while clerking for Robert Jackson and his role in suppressing the minority vote while practicing law in Arizona. Opponents also found a new ground for criticism—in the deed to his summer home in Vermont there was a discriminatory covenant barring sale to members of "the Hebrew race," and in the deed to his former home in Phoenix there was a similar covenant barring sale to "anyone not of the white or Caucasian race." Such covenants had been unenforceable ever since the Court's decision in *Shelley v. Kraemer* (1948), but they still existed in many real estate deeds throughout the country. As Patrick Buchanan was quick to point out, many prominent Democrats likewise lived in homes with discriminatory covenants. Although Rehnquist was confirmed, thirty-three senators voted against him, the most negative votes for a successful nominee in the Court's history up to that time.[25]

Robert Bork, another judge appointed by Reagan to the DC Circuit, had been one of the finalists for the seat that went to Scalia. A year later, when Lewis Powell retired, Reagan nominated Bork to replace him. Like Scalia, before becoming a judge Bork had alternated between teaching and government. His best-known act as a government official took place in 1973, when Nixon ordered Attorney General Eliot Richardson to fire Archibald Cox, the special prosecutor investigating the Watergate scandal. Richardson refused to carry out Nixon's order and resigned, as did the deputy attorney general, William Ruckleshaus. That left Bork, the solicitor general and thus the third-ranking official in the Justice Department, as acting attorney general. Bork fired Cox. And like Scalia, Bork was an intellectual leader among conservative lawyers and judges. Bork had been on every shortlist of Republican nominees since the Ford administration.[26] Had Bork been nominated in 1986, he would likely have been confirmed as easily as Scalia was.

But the Democrats gained control of the Senate in the 1986 midterm elections, and while Scalia was a bit more conservative than Warren Burger, the justice he replaced, Bork was much more conservative than Lewis Powell. The stakes were higher than they had been the previous year. Within hours of Bork's nomination, Senator Edward Kennedy gave a speech on the Senate floor that set the Democrats' tone for the hearings to come. "Robert Bork's America is a land in which women would be forced into back-alley abortions, blacks would sit at segregated lunch counters, rogue police could break down citizens' doors in midnight raids, [and] schoolchildren could not be taught about evolution," Kennedy alleged. Bork, he argued, "stands for an extremist view of the Constitution and the role of the Supreme Court."[27] Bork did not help matters in his testimony before the Senate. Every other nominee who has testified, before and since, has taken pains to say as little as possible. Bork, by contrast, was eager to discuss his opposition to several of the Court's decisions, including *Griswold v. Connecticut*, the case establishing a right to privacy. He left no doubt as to where he stood.

Administration officials, realizing that Bork's ship was sinking, tried to rally support. "No Presidential initiative will have higher priority than the confirmation of Robert Bork," declared White House Counsel Arthur Culvahouse in a memo to the working group devoted to getting Bork through the Senate. As a young Republican congressman named Newt

Gingrich insisted in a letter to Reagan, the confirmation of Bork was "an all-out struggle to save the Supreme Court from a left-wing lynch mob" led by "an arrogant left-wing elite." ("You need to read this," one of Reagan's aides told another about Gingrich's letter. "It's a hum-dinger!") White House officials even tried to get an endorsement of Bork from Lewis Powell. Powell refused. He was so disgusted at having been asked that he dictated a lengthy memo for his files lamenting how "the White House, and perhaps the nominee himself, have taken an unprecedently active part in attempting to win public support," in a campaign "comparable in many respects to the massive media and mail campaigning that goes on in presidential elections."[28] None of these efforts could save Bork, who went down to defeat. The verb "bork" entered the American vocabulary, meaning, according to the Oxford English dictionary, "to defame or vilify (a person) systematically, esp. in the mass media, usually with the aim of preventing his or her appointment to public office." Bork was borked, but had he been nominated first and Scalia second, Scalia might have been "scaliaed" instead. A few months later, Bork resigned from the DC Circuit to take up a new career as the author of vitriolic books lamenting the decline of the United States.

After the Senate refused to confirm Bork, Reagan prepared to nominate Douglas Ginsburg, another former law professor he had appointed to the DC Circuit. Administration officials considered Ginsburg an ideal nominee. "He is generally perceived as a judge in the mold of Justice Scalia and Judge Bork," read the summary prepared by the White House counsel's office. "Unlike Judge Bork, however, Judge Ginsburg does not have a pool of writings on the issues that proved to be controversial during Judge Bork's confirmation." And Ginsburg was considerably younger than Bork. He was forty-one, while Bork was sixty. Ginsburg quickly withdrew, however, because of news accounts that he had smoked marijuana while on the Harvard law faculty in the 1970s. "The Judge is really a fine man and would have made an excellent Justice," Reagan told a supporter. "What happened was that the press talked to some people who knew him while he was teaching at Harvard and who may not have been entirely sympathetic."[29]

One of the less prominent candidates for the nominations that went to Scalia and Bork was Anthony Kennedy, a Sacramento-based judge who had been placed on the Court of Appeals for the Ninth Circuit by President Ford. Although the White House counsel's office evaluated Kennedy as "bright and conservative," the office was concerned about the "occasional significant misstep" among the cases he had decided, including an opinion that "spoke very favorably of constitutional 'privacy rights.'" Lawyers in the Justice Department were also worried about "disturbing aspects of Judge Kennedy's jurisprudence," such as a suggestion in one case that the scope of constitutional rights might change as circumstances changed. But time was running short. The 1988 presidential election was less than a year away, so if the next nominee was not confirmed soon there was a risk that the Senate would refuse to confirm anyone. Reagan chose expedience over ideological purity and nominated Kennedy, who was confirmed unanimously—the last justice to achieve that distinction. Harry Blackmun, who had also joined the Court after two nominees were defeated, sent Kennedy a cordial note welcoming him to the "very exclusive organization called 'the good old #3 club.'" Kennedy responded by reminding Blackmun that Joseph Story, one of the most respected justices in the Court's history, was a member of the same club.[30]

Reagan, like Nixon, had tried to appoint conservative justices who would transform the Court, but like Nixon, he succeeded only partially. Scalia fit the bill perfectly. But practical political considerations caused Reagan's other two nominees, O'Connor and Kennedy, to be less conservative than administration officials would have liked.

George H. W. Bush had a similar mixed record. The Court's last remaining liberals, William Brennan and Thurgood Marshall, both in their eighties and in very poor health, retired in 1990 and 1991 respectively. Bush's two appointments could have swung the Court sharply to the right. The second would. The first would not.

David Souter, Bush's first nominee, had been a judge in New Hampshire for many years, first in the state courts and then briefly on the Court of Appeals for the First Circuit. He was not well known outside the state. Nothing in his career gave much indication of how he would vote on the most contentious issues before the Supreme Court. Souter came to Bush's attention via John Sununu, the former governor of New Hampshire, who was now Bush's chief of staff, and Warren Rudman, Souter's predecessor as the state's attorney general, who was now a senator. Souter possesses a "brilliant legal intellect" and a "conservative legal philosophy," Rudman told Bush, qualities Rudman found in Souter's opinions rejecting constitutional arguments made by criminal defendants. But conservatives outside New Hampshire were less impressed. "The Souter nomination is something of a 'thud' for conservatives," one lawyer lamented. "Bush picked someone not on our 'short list.'" At a meeting in Sununu's office, the Republican lobbyist Patrick McGuigan expressed the same regret. "You guys could have hit a home run," he complained. "Instead, you've hit a blooper single which has barely cleared the mitt of the first baseman." Even Lewis Powell, now retired, admitted that he was "puzzled by the Souter nomination." Powell offered the most likely explanation. After the Bork debacle three years before, Powell suggested, "apparently the President wanted to nominate a lawyer who had not committed himself to any of the major issues of our time. It is quite remarkable that Souter, well educated and certainly able, has written virtually nothing."[31]

The difficulty of predicting Souter's views left both sides of the abortion debate unhappy. "Pro-lifers demand to know: Is Souter pro-abortion?" asked a press release issued by one anti-abortion organization. "If we discover during the hearings that Judge Souter is pro-abortion, we expect President Bush to immediately rescind his nomination and find a pro-life replacement." On the other side, the National Abortion Rights Action League worried that in one of Souter's New Hampshire opinions he "used the extremely restrictive judicial philosophy of 'original intent,'" a philosophy that might lead him to overrule *Roe v. Wade*. Souter was easily confirmed despite these concerns. He would spend nineteen years on the Court, during which the fears of conservative activists were realized, because he turned out not to be as conservative as they were. Souter was a moderate Republican who would have been on the Court's right wing during the 1960s and early 1970s, but he was on the Court's left wing throughout his career because the Court's composition had changed so much. Souter would be the last justice whose views on high-profile questions were unforeseeable at the time of nomination. "No more Souters" became a motto on the right—that is, Republicans vowed to appoint only justices who would predictably vote the right way.[32]

Conservatives would have no such reservations about Bush's second appointment, Clarence Thomas, who would be the Court's most conservative justice for a very long time. Thomas was, as the White House's analysis of his career acknowledged, a "complex and controversial" person.[33] Only forty-three years old, Thomas was already one of the most prominent black conservatives in public life, a believer in black self-help and an opponent of most legal efforts to mandate racial equality, especially affirmative action, which in his view imposed a taint of inferiority on its supposed beneficiaries. He had been chairman of the Equal Employment Opportunity Commission during the Reagan administration, and before that he had led the Education Department's Office of Civil Rights, despite his deep skepticism about some of the laws the two agencies were tasked with enforcing. Bush had appointed

Thomas to the Court of Appeals for the DC Circuit, but he had been a judge for scarcely more than a year. Thomas, only the second black justice in the Court's history, replaced Thurgood Marshall, the first, so his nomination suggested there was now an informal "black seat" analogous to the informal Jewish and Catholic seats that had once existed.

Confirmation by the Democratic-majority Senate would not have been assured even without the allegations of misconduct that would soon arise. Like Robert Bork, Thomas had an extensive record of taking conservative positions in speeches and articles on a wide variety of issues. He had, for example, repeatedly suggested that courts should use natural law to decide cases, a view shared by few American judges since the nineteenth century and one that strongly hinted that Thomas's religious beliefs might inform his decisions as a judge.[34] Asked specifically about *Roe v. Wade*, a case decided while he was in law school, Thomas claimed that he had never given any thought to it. The Judiciary Committee deadlocked on whether to recommend his nomination to the full Senate.

Before the Senate could vote, however, the press reported that several years before, Thomas had repeatedly made offensive sexual remarks to Anita Hill, one of his employees at the EEOC and the Education Department. Hill recalled that at work, Thomas "would turn the conversation to a discussion of sexual matters," including "acts he had seen in pornographic films" and "his own sexual prowess." When the Judiciary Committee reopened the hearings to examine these charges, Thomas mounted an aggressive defense. "This is a circus," he declared. "It is a national disgrace. And from my standpoint, as a black American, as far as I'm concerned, it is a high-tech lynching for uppity blacks who in any way deign to think for themselves, to do for themselves, to have different ideas, and it is a message that unless you kowtow to an old order, this is what will happen to you, you will be lynched, destroyed, caricatured by a committee of the U.S. Senate, rather than hung from a tree."[35] Thomas was confirmed by a vote of 52–48, the narrowest margin since Stanley Matthews was confirmed by a single vote in 1881.

The testimony of Hill and Thomas, watched by millions on television, made Thomas the most recognizable judge in the country. A few years later, when there was another vacancy on the Court, President Bill Clinton received letters from people satirically touting their own qualifications by contrasting themselves with Thomas. "I've never been accused of sexual harassment," one North Carolina lawyer boasted, "unlike some of our current justices." A college student from New York noted that "although I have

Figure 14.2 Anita Hill testifies before the Senate Judiciary Committee during Clarence Thomas's 1991 confirmation hearing. Thomas was confirmed by the narrowest margin in more than a century. Photograph by R. Michael Jenkins. Library of Congress, LC-DIG-ppmsca-65032.

not served on the bench, I have discussed *Roe v. Wade* with friends, which places me well ahead of some justices." But Thomas served on the Court so long that he outlasted most of his critics. He began his fourth decade as a justice in 2021, having occupied the Court's right edge all the while, often advancing legal theories so unorthodox that they were not acceptable to any of his colleagues.[36]

While Republican presidents gradually replaced the liberal justices with conservative ones, conservative lawyers and law professors were establishing a loose network of organizations devoted to pushing the Court in a conservative direction.

Foremost among these was the Federalist Society, which was founded in 1982 by law students at Yale and the University of Chicago.[37] The society began by organizing conferences at which students could hear conservative speakers. Before long, it attracted funding from conservative philanthropists and developed into an organization comprising tens of thousands of lawyers and judges. Unlike many nonprofits created to influence the law, the Federalist Society did not conduct litigation or lobby for the passage of legislation. It focused instead on bringing conservative lawyers together and on influencing the appointment of judges. One measure of the society's success is that all six of the Republican-appointed justices on the Court as of 2020 were current or former members.

Conservative lawyers also formed litigating organizations analogous to the ones that had long advanced liberal causes in the Court. The Pacific Legal Foundation was established in 1973 to defend property rights and other economic liberties. The PLF would represent property owners in most of the Court's important Takings Clause cases of the late twentieth and early twenty-first centuries. It was soon joined by counterparts in other regions, including the Southeastern Legal Foundation, the Mountain States Legal Foundation, the Washington Legal Foundation, and the Atlantic Legal Foundation. A second wave of libertarian nonprofit law firms came into existence in the late 1980s and early 1990s, including the Center for Individual Rights and the Institute for Justice. The same period saw the creation of several organizations devoted to litigating on behalf of religious freedoms, such as the American Center for Law and Justice (1990), the Alliance Defending Freedom (1993), and the Becket Fund for Religious Liberty (1994).[38] By the early 1990s, there was a new army of ideological Supreme Court litigators on the right that could match the older army on the left.

Conservative lawyers and judges began to employ two styles of argument that became newly prominent, primarily among conservatives, in the 1980s. One was originalism, the idea that the Constitution should be interpreted solely according to the intent of its eighteenth-century drafters and ratifiers, without any consideration of subsequent events. (Originalists would later shift their emphasis from the original *intent* of the Constitution's authors to the original *meaning* of the document's words among eighteenth-century readers.) The other new style of argument was textualism, the idea that legal texts, especially statutes, should be read literally, without inquiring into the purpose of the statute or the circumstances surrounding its enactment. The value of these interpretive methods, proponents argued, was that they constrained judges by preventing them from implementing their own policy views. In the most controversial liberal constitutional decisions of the 1960s and 1970s, cases like *Miranda v. Arizona* and *Roe v. Wade*, the Court had explicitly considered the policy implications of its rulings. The antidote, conservatives increasingly concluded, was not to fight liberal policy arguments with conservative ones, but to promote methods of judging that ostensibly ruled policy considerations out of bounds.[39]

Originalism and textualism were not entirely new, of course. The original intent or meaning of constitutional provisions had always been one important factor, among others, in constitutional interpretation, and the text of a statute had always been one important factor, among others, in how a judge interpreted the statute. What was new was the insistence on purity, the rejection of every other method of interpretation as illegitimate. Originalism was especially congenial to lawyers on the right because it yielded conservative outcomes in the great majority of cases. It became the house philosophy of the Reagan Justice Department. The Court should adopt "a jurisprudence of original intention," Attorney General Edwin Meese announced in a well-publicized 1985 speech to the American Bar Association.[40] Originalism gained a foothold on the Court with the appointment of Antonin Scalia in 1986 and then another when Scalia was joined by Clarence Thomas five years later.

These interpretive methods would always be controversial. Opponents, who tended to be on the left, contended that they allowed judges to conceal conservative policy preferences beneath a veneer of neutrality. Both methods would be favored by a majority of the justices in the twenty-first century, but in the 1980s and early 1990s they had not yet achieved that level of support. Apart from Scalia and Thomas, the Republican appointees of the period were conservatives of an older style. They had been trained in, and had spent their careers practicing, the eclectic mode of legal interpretation characteristic of American lawyers for two centuries, one in which original intent and literal meaning were important but not exclusive considerations. Justices like Lewis Powell and Sandra Day O'Connor saw nothing illegitimate in giving explicit attention to the policy implications of their decisions, as judges had always done. In this respect as well, the goals of conservative activists did not translate neatly into outcomes at the Court. The counterrevolution would not be fast or straightforward.

For more than twenty years, Republican presidents tried to change the Court's direction by appointing conservative justices. If we look at the ten consecutive justices appointed by Republican presidents, from Warren Burger in 1969 to Clarence Thomas in 1991, we can divide them into two groups. Four of them—Burger, William Rehnquist, Antonin Scalia, and Thomas—performed largely as administration officials and conservative activists hoped they would. But the other six—Harry Blackmun, Lewis Powell, John Paul Stevens, Sandra Day O'Connor, Anthony Kennedy, and David Souter—did not. For a variety of reasons, they proved to be more moderate. The divergence between these justices' judicial philosophies and the policy goals of the presidents who appointed them would make the Court's change of direction a slow and uneven project.

III

Among the Court's well-known liberal decisions of the 1960s and 1970s, the cases granting new rights to criminal defendants may have been the least popular. Few people in any era have much sympathy for criminals. As crime rates rose, Republican candidates regularly blamed the Court for inventing new constitutional protections that let the guilty go free. The party's platform in presidential elections repeatedly urged the appointment of justices with "an appreciation of the legitimate needs of law enforcement," as the 1972 platform described them, and "the highest regard for protecting the rights of law-abiding citizens," as the 1980 version put it. If there was any area of law in which the newly conservative Court seemed poised for a quick turnaround, it was criminal procedure.

Yet the Court did not overrule any of its famous criminal procedure decisions. Each one would be limited, with exceptions here and qualifications there that rendered the new doctrines less useful to criminal defense lawyers than they had been at first. But there was no return to the state of the law before these cases were decided. After ten consecutive Republican justices, criminal defendants still had many of the rights they had gained a generation before.

Miranda v. Arizona, for example, had been a magnet for criticism, especially from police officers who feared that guilty suspects would never confess if they were told they could halt police questioning by requesting a lawyer. Throughout the 1970s and 1980s, the Court chipped away at *Miranda* by holding that its requirements did not apply in certain situations. In *Harris v. New York* (1971), for example, a 5–4 Court allowed prosecutors to use confessions at trial that had been obtained in violation of *Miranda*, if the defendant testified at trial to facts inconsistent with those in his confession. "The shield provided by *Miranda* cannot be perverted into a license to use perjury by way of a defense," Warren Burger reasoned for the majority. A few years later, the Court held that the police could interrogate a suspect at the police station without giving the *Miranda* warnings so long as the suspect was free to leave the station afterward. In a 1981 case, the Court recognized a "public safety" exception to the requirements of *Miranda*, allowing the police to dispense with the warnings where speed was necessary. And in *Oregon v. Elstad* (1985), the Court authorized the government to use a confession obtained without the warnings, provided that the police subsequently read the warnings and reinterrogated the suspect to elicit the same information. Decisions like these reduced some of *Miranda*'s practical effect. As William Brennan worried in dissent, they undid "much of the progress made in conforming police methods to the Constitution."[41] But *Miranda* continued to govern police interrogations of most suspects who were questioned after they were arrested. The Court did not allow the police to return to pre-*Miranda* practices.

The Court took a similar course with the exclusionary rule it had enforced against the states in *Mapp v. Ohio*, prohibiting the use at trial of evidence obtained in violation of the Fourth Amendment, which usually meant evidence gathered by police officers who lacked a search warrant. Some of the new justices had grave doubts about the exclusionary rule. "My disagreement with *Mapp v. Ohio* remains so fundamental," William Rehnquist told his colleagues, "that I will seize any opportunity to limit the damage done by that case." In one line of cases, the Court whittled away at the exclusionary rule's effect by identifying several situations in which searches could be conducted without a warrant. As early as *Terry v. Ohio* (1968), for example, the Court had allowed the police, even without a warrant, to stop a suspect on the street and frisk him for weapons. Exceptions to the warrant requirement multiplied in later years. In *Schneckloth v. Bustamante* (1973), the Court held that a suspect could "consent" to a search even if he did not know he had a right not to consent. In later cases the Court dispensed with the warrant requirement in several recurring situations, including searches of cars that had been towed, searches at schools, and searches of probationers.[42]

In another line of cases, the Court etched away at the exclusionary rule from a different direction, by designating several circumstances in which the rule would simply not apply. For instance, in *United States v. Calandra* (1974), the Court refused to apply the exclusionary rule in grand jury proceedings, the stage of a prosecution that comes before a trial, because "whatever deterrence of police misconduct may result from the exclusion of illegally seized evidence from criminal trials, it is unrealistic to assume that application of the rule to grand jury proceedings would significantly further that goal." In *Nix v. Williams* (1984), the Court declined to exclude evidence that would likely have been discovered even without an unlawful search. In

United States v. Leon (1984), the Court held that the exclusionary rule should not apply where the police relied in good faith on a legally defective warrant. In cases like these, the Court identified particular situations in which it determined that the costs of applying the exclusionary rule—the escape of a guilty defendant—outweighed the rule's benefits in ensuring that police officers comply with the Constitution. This utilitarian calculus, Brennan charged, again in dissent, "reflects a startling misconception, unless it is a purposeful rejection, of the historical objective and purpose of the rule."[43]

Decisions like these authorized the police to conduct many more searches than before. But the Court never abandoned the exclusionary rule, which was still in force in the wide variety of circumstances not encompassed by one of the new exceptions. The Court did not allow the police to return to their pre-*Mapp* practices.

Furman v. Georgia, the 1972 case in which the Court held that the death penalty was unconstitutional as it was then imposed, was the criminal procedure decision that seemed most ripe for overruling. Four justices had dissented in *Furman*, and they were the four newest justices, the Nixon appointees. By 1981, when Douglas and Stewart had left the Court, only three justices remained from the *Furman* majority. *Furman* was extremely unpopular—so unpopular that it sparked a nationwide revival of support for capital punishment and led most states to rewrite their death penalty statutes in the hope that the Court would allow them to resume conducting executions. But while the Court permitted the resumption of capital punishment, it did so by imposing a host of new constitutional rules to govern the details. In *Gregg v. Georgia* (1976), the Court required the states to separate the guilt phase of a capital trial from the sentencing phase of the trial and to structure the sentencing decision by listing aggravating factors that would guide the jury's decision whether to impose a death sentence. In *Lockett v. Ohio* (1978), the Court barred the states from restricting the jury's consideration of mitigating factors that might persuade the jury not to sentence the defendant to death.[44] Decisions like these established a byzantine structure of doctrines that turned capital trials and appeals into protracted proceedings requiring specialized lawyers on both sides.

As the Court became more conservative, it grew more skeptical of arguments that aspects of the death penalty were unconstitutional. By votes of 5 to 4, the Court allowed states to execute defendants who were intellectually disabled and defendants who were sixteen years old at the time of their offenses. A few years after deciding that prosecutors could not induce juries to sentence defendants to death by presenting emotional displays of how much the victim was missed by family and friends, the Court changed its view and allowed such presentations. In the interim, Souter had replaced Brennan, turning a 5–4 vote in one direction into a 5–4 vote in the other. "Power, not reason, is the new currency of this Court's decisionmaking," Thurgood Marshall thundered in dissent, in what would be the last opinion of his career, published the day before he announced his retirement—an opinion that castigated the majority for overruling precedent, from the man who was celebrated as a lawyer for persuading the Court to overrule the separate-but-equal doctrine of *Plessy v. Ferguson*.[45]

The most important of these capital cases was *McCleskey v. Kemp* (1987), in which the justices considered statistical evidence that the death penalty was imposed in a racially discriminatory manner. Fifteen or twenty years earlier, the statistics would likely have been enough for the Court to deem capital punishment unconstitutional. Not any longer. "My understanding of statistical analysis—particularly what is called 'regression analysis' ranges from limited to zero," Lewis Powell admitted to his law clerk. But Powell was certain that discrimination across a group of cases could not call into question the propriety of a death sentence in any individual case. "Apparent disparities in sentencing," he concluded, "are an inevitable part of our criminal justice system." Antonin Scalia was even more certain. "The unconscious operation of irrational sympathies and antipathies, including racial, upon jury decisions and (hence) prosecutorial decisions is real, acknowledged in the decisions of this court, and ineradicable," he reasoned. In his view, there was simply nothing the law could do about it.[46]

But if the Court was no longer receptive to constitutional arguments against capital punishment, neither did it dismantle the complex structure of constitutional rules it had created to govern the death penalty. The Court's retreat was only partial. Capital punishment was back, but the new death penalty looked nothing like the old one.

IV

Although the southern states had resisted desegregating their public schools in the years since *Brown v. Board of Education*, there was little prospect the Court would overrule *Brown*. There was, however, a broad spectrum of constitutional questions concerning how desegregation could be accomplished, and here too the Republican restaffing of the Court began to influence the outcomes of cases in the 1970s and 1980s. The Court remained committed to the abstract goal of integration, but it had markedly less enthusiasm for requiring school officials to take concrete steps toward that goal. While it was clear that there was no going back to the era in which discrimination was lawful and pervasive, the pace of change slowed considerably.

In many cities, schools remained segregated because neighborhoods were segregated. Detroit was a stark example. The city operated a school district in which most of the students were black, while the surrounding suburbs included several districts in which most of the students were white. Detroit's schools could not be integrated unless some children who lived in the city attended suburban schools and some children who lived in the suburbs attended schools in the city. As a remedy for segregation, could a trial judge ignore school district boundaries and treat the entire metropolitan area as, in effect, one big district? In *Milliken v. Bradley* (1974), a 5–4 Court, with all four Nixon appointees in the majority, held that judges lack the power to impose such a remedy. "The notion that school district lines may be casually ignored or treated as a mere administrative convenience is contrary to the history of public education in our country," Burger wrote for the majority. "No single tradition in public education is more deeply rooted than local control over the operation of schools." In dissent, Marshall pointed out that refusing to allow inter-district remedies would mean there could be no remedy at all for unconstitutional segregation in cities like Detroit, "thereby guaranteeing that Negro children in Detroit will receive the same separate and inherently unequal education in the future as they have been unconstitutionally afforded in the past."[47] Segregated schools were still impermissible in theory, but after *Milliken* there was little that could be done about it where patterns of residential segregation were most pronounced.

In subsequent cases the Court placed additional restrictions on the authority of judges to craft remedies for unconstitutional school segregation. In *Pasadena Board of Education v. Spangler* (1976), the Court held that a judge, having once imposed a student reassignment plan to integrate schools, could not require the annual readjustment of the plan to ensure that schools stayed unsegregated. In a pair of decisions in the early 1990s, the Court made it easier for school districts to demand an end to court-supervised desegregation plans. American schools had made significant progress toward racial integration in the 1960s, but progress stalled from the 1970s onward, in part because of the Court's decisions limiting the remedial authority of trial judges.[48]

The justices divided even more sharply over "affirmative action," the term for policies that sought to undo the effects of past discrimination by favoring members of formerly discriminated-against groups. In *University of California v. Bakke* (1978), the Court split 4–1–4 on the constitutionality of a medical school admissions policy that reserved sixteen out of a hundred places in the entering class for members of disadvantaged minority groups.[49] On one side, four justices concluded that affirmative action is a permissible means of remedying the effects of past societal discrimination such as the underrepresentation of members of minority groups in the medical profession. On the other side, four justices took the view that any form of discrimination on the basis of race is unlawful, regardless of which race is discriminated against. Alone in the middle was Lewis Powell, who believed that affirmative action is unconstitutional as a means of remedying past societal discrimination but that it *is* constitutional as a method of attaining a diverse student body, so long as a school has no fixed quota for a particular race but only considers racial diversity as a "plus" factor of ambiguous magnitude in admissions decisions. Parts of Powell's opinion were joined by the four justices on one side and other parts by the four on the other side, so his unique view became the holding of the Court. It would shape university admissions policies for decades. To comply with *Bakke*, schools had to claim that diversity was their sole rationale for affirmative action and they had to blur the extent to which they favored minority applicants.

Later cases would continue this uneasy compromise, under which affirmative action was neither entirely constitutional nor entirely unconstitutional. The Court allowed fire departments and school districts to lay off white employees before black employees with less seniority, but only where the black employees had personally been victims of discrimination by the departments or districts in question—not to attain a particular racial balance among firefighters or teachers, as the employers in the two cases were attempting to do. The Court would not permit Richmond, Virginia, to set aside a percentage of the city's construction contracts for minority-owned businesses, because the underrepresentation of minority groups in the construction industry was due to a pattern of discrimination on a national scale that lasted for centuries, not to any particular acts of discrimination against individual contractors by the city of Richmond. "While there is no doubt that the sorry history of both private and public discrimination in this country has contributed to a lack of opportunities for black entrepreneurs," Sandra Day O'Connor wrote for the Court, "this observation, standing alone, cannot justify a rigid racial quota in the awarding of public contracts in Richmond."[50] Affirmative action was lawful, but only in certain circumstances and only for limited purposes.

Until the early 1970s, the Court had been receptive to new kinds of claims that discrimination was unconstitutional. This receptivity mostly ended. By a 5–4 vote, the Court rejected the argument that the local financing of public education denied equal protection to students in poor communities, where residents could not afford to spend nearly as much on their schools as could residents of affluent districts. The Court likewise rejected the claim that it was unconstitutional for a police department to use an employment test that black applicants failed more often than white ones. To be impermissible, Byron White reasoned for the majority, "the invidious quality of a law claimed to be racially discriminatory must ultimately be traced to a racially discriminatory purpose," not merely a discriminatory effect. A test that was *intended* to exclude black people from the police force was unconstitutional, but a test that merely had that effect was not.[51]

Every so often, the Court did accept the argument that a practice of long standing was newly unlawful because it was discriminatory. Single-family zoning had been around for decades, and the Court had already rebuffed the argument that it infringed anyone's constitutional rights. But in 1977 the Court held single-family zoning unconstitutional where it prohibited a grandmother from living with her grandchildren, an arrangement that, as William Brennan noted, was more common among black families than among white ones. Nonprofit organizations such as schools had traditionally been tax-exempt even if they discriminated, but the Court approved the decision of the Internal Revenue Service to deny a tax exemption to Bob Jones University because the school prohibited interracial dating. Lawyers in criminal trials had always been allowed to reject prospective jurors for any reason, and as recently as 1965 the Court had declined to find a constitutional violation where the reason was the juror's race, but in *Batson v. Kentucky* (1986) the Court overruled the earlier decision and barred lawyers from rejecting prospective jurors because of their race.[52] But such cases were becoming rarer. The Court was not cutting back on existing rights against race discrimination, but it was slower to recognize new ones.

When discrimination was based on sex, however, the Republican Court of the 1970s and 1980s was just as innovative as the Democratic Court of the

1960s had been. The first sex discrimination case to reach the Court was *Reed v. Reed* (1971), a challenge to an Idaho law that gave men preference over women in being chosen as the administrator of a deceased person's estate. In a very short opinion, the Court unanimously held that the law violated the Constitution's Equal Protection Clause.[53]

One of the lawyers representing Sally Reed was a young law professor at Rutgers named Ruth Bader Ginsburg. Ginsburg (sometimes representing the challenger, sometimes the American Civil Liberties Union as an amicus) brought a series of similar cases to the Court over the next several years and won most of them. In *Frontiero v. Richardson* (1973), the Court struck down a federal statute that made it easier for male soldiers than for female soldiers to obtain benefits for their spouses. "There can be no doubt that our Nation has had a long and unfortunate history of sex discrimination," Brennan wrote for the Court. "Women still face pervasive, although at times more subtle, discrimination in our educational institutions, in the job market and, perhaps most conspicuously, in the political arena." In *Weinberger v. Weisenfeld* (1975), the Court invalidated a provision of the Social Security Act that granted benefits to widows but not widowers. In *Craig v. Boren* (1976), the Court struck down Oklahoma's differential drinking age for men and women, a scheme that allowed women to buy low-alcohol beer at eighteen but prohibited men from buying it until they reached twenty-one. And in *Orr v. Orr* (1979), the Court held that Alabama violated the Constitution by requiring men but not women to pay alimony when they divorced.[54] Some of these cases were challenges to laws that favored women, not men, but they established the principle that the Constitution did not permit discrimination based on traditional sex roles, a principle that could be used just as effectively to attack laws that favored men. By 1980, when Ginsburg became a judge on the DC Circuit, she and her allies had persuaded the Court that sex discrimination deserved constitutional scrutiny almost as searching as that given to race discrimination.

While the Court was interpreting the Equal Protection Clause to prohibit sex discrimination, the nation was rejecting a new amendment to the Constitution that would have achieved the same end. The Equal Rights Amendment, approved by Congress in 1972, provided that "equality of rights under the law shall not be denied or abridged by the United States or by any State on account of sex." More than half the states ratified the amendment in 1972 and 1973. Powell, writing separately in *Frontiero* in early 1973, suggested that the Court should await the outcome of the ERA debate before making new law in the area. "By acting prematurely and unnecessarily," he argued, "the Court has assumed a decisional responsibility at the very time when state legislatures, functioning within the traditional democratic process, are debating the proposed Amendment."[55] The Court pressed on regardless. The ERA ultimately fell short of ratification, but by then it was no longer necessary, because the Court had reached the same goal by a different route.

Although the Court grew even more conservative in the 1980s, it continued to reach liberal outcomes in sex discrimination cases. In 1986, all nine justices accepted that the then-novel category of "sexual harassment" is a form of discrimination in violation of the Civil Rights Act. Even William Rehnquist, typically the justice least receptive to claims of the sort, agreed that "without question, when a supervisor sexually harasses a subordinate because of the subordinate's sex, that supervisor discriminates on the basis of sex." A few years later the Court decided that sex stereotyping is also a kind of unlawful discrimination. "An employer who objects to aggressiveness in women but whose positions require this trait places women in an intolerable and impermissible catch-22: out of a job if they behave aggressively and out of a job if they do not," Brennan explained. "We are beyond the day when an employer could evaluate employees by assuming or insisting that they matched the stereotype associated with their group."[56] In the 1940s and 1950s, changing societal attitudes about racial equality caused even the most tradition-minded of the justices to side with black litigants who had been treated in ways that were historically common but were increasingly viewed as unjust. In the 1970s and 1980s, the same was true of female litigants.

V

The Court's cases involving the separation of church and state had been among its most controversial in the 1960s. The Court had been attentive to the claims of religious minorities, barring prayer in public schools and exempting small sects from generally applicable laws contrary to their spiritual beliefs. Here too, the change in personnel that took place in the 1970s and 1980s had a noticeable effect on the outcomes of cases without producing a wholesale reversal. The Court did not reinstate school prayer, but it began to show less sympathy for religious minorities and more for the mainstream ceremonial Christianity that was the nation's dominant faith.

In *Marsh v. Chambers* (1983), for example, the Court considered the constitutionality of the prayer, offered by a Presbyterian minister, that opened
each daily session of Nebraska's legislature. Twenty years earlier, the Court
had not allowed a similar prayer in public schools, despite the long tradition of opening the school day with religious exercise. Now, by contrast, tradition was dispositive. Legislatures, including the United States Congress,
had always begun the day with a prayer. "In light of the unambiguous and
unbroken history of more than 200 years, there can be no doubt that the
practice of opening legislative sessions with prayer has become part of the
fabric of our society," Warren Burger explained for the Court. "To invoke
Divine guidance on a public body entrusted with making the laws is not, in
these circumstances, an 'establishment' of religion or a step toward establishment; it is simply a tolerable acknowledgment of beliefs widely held among
the people of this country."[57] The issue cut close to home for the justices, because the Court itself began each day (and indeed still does) with the ad-
monition "God save the United States and this honorable court." Prayer had
been banished from the schools, but it was alive and well in legislatures and
courts.

An analogous question was raised by the nativity scenes—displays
depicting the birth of Jesus—that were constructed annually on public land
during the Christmas season by cities all over the country. In a 1984 case, a
5–4 Court decided that Pawtucket, Rhode Island's display, in which Jesus,
Mary, and Joseph were joined by Santa Claus and his reindeer, a Christmas
tree, a clown, and an elephant, did not violate the Constitution. The metaphor of a wall of separation between church and state "is not a wholly accurate description of the practical aspects of the relationship that in fact
exists between church and state," Burger observed. The nativity scene did
not establish Christianity as an official religion, he concluded, but merely
celebrated the historical origin of the Christmas holiday. A few years later,
however, an equally fractured Court concluded that Pittsburgh's display,
which placed the infant Jesus side-by-side with a giant Chanukah menorah,
did violate the Establishment Clause. Harry Blackmun, who had dissented
in the Pawtucket case, labored to find reasons for treating the Pittsburgh
Jesus differently. Pittsburgh had configured its display to focus more attention on Jesus, Blackmun noted. Worse, above Jesus was an angel bearing a
banner that proclaimed "Gloria in Excelsis Deo!", a phrase that Pittsburghers
familiar with Latin would recognize as an endorsement of Christianity.[58]
In subsequent years, city attorneys would have to parse these not fully

consistent opinions to figure out precisely how to stage their annual nativity scenes in a manner consistent with the Establishment Clause.

A similar pattern could be found in the Court's decisions interpreting the Free Exercise Clause. The Court had excused the Amish from complying with school attendance laws because sending children to high school was inconsistent with Amish religious beliefs, but now the Court refused to exempt the Amish from another generally applicable law—the law requiring employers to pay Social Security taxes. Writing again for the Court, as he did so often in religion cases, Burger assumed that the Amish were sincere in asserting that Social Security was inconsistent with their faith, which classified support for the needy and the elderly as an obligation of the religious community, not the government. But he feared that the Social Security system, and indeed the government as a whole, would collapse if taxpayers were entitled to claim faith-based exemptions from paying for particular programs. In a similar case soon after, the Court likewise rejected the claim of a Native American father that he should be exempt from a requirement that welfare recipients have Social Security numbers because obtaining a number for his daughter would rob her of her spirit. The father "may no more prevail on his religious objection to the Government's use of a Social Security number for his daughter than he could on a sincere religious objection to the size or color of the Government's filing cabinets," Burger wrote, in a tone verging on exasperation. "The Free Exercise Clause affords an individual protection from certain forms of governmental compulsion; it does not afford an individual a right to dictate the conduct of the Government's internal procedures."[59] The view that religious minorities were in some circumstances constitutionally entitled to an exemption from generally applicable laws, the idea that motivated the Court's Free Exercise cases in the 1960s and early 1970s, was hanging by a thread.

The thread finally snapped in *Employment Division v. Smith* (1990). Peyote was an illegal drug in Oregon, but it was also a sacrament of the Native American Church, a religion that fused aspects of Christianity and indigenous North American religious beliefs. Did church members have a constitutional right to use peyote? The Court held that they did not. In an emphatic opinion by Antonin Scalia, the Court held that religious beliefs could *never* confer an exemption from generally applicable laws. Allowing such exemptions "would be courting anarchy," Scalia insisted, because Americans' faiths were so diverse that virtually any law was objectionable on religious grounds to one group or another. If the Court permitted members of the Native American Church to use peyote, its decision "would open the prospect of constitutionally required religious exemptions from civic obligations of almost every conceivable kind—ranging from compulsory military service to the payment of taxes to health and safety regulation such as manslaughter and child neglect laws."[60]

This view was controversial, both inside and outside the Court. Four justices preferred to preserve the old rule, under which religious groups were entitled to exemptions where the government lacked a compelling interest in forcing religious objectors to comply with the law. Indeed, three of them, Blackmun, Brennan, and Marshall, dissented on the ground that Oregon had not shown that allowing church members to use peyote would cause any harm. (The fourth, O'Connor, thought the state had made a sufficient showing of harm.) The Court's decision aroused so much opposition among the public, especially among religious groups, that Congress enacted a law specifically to counteract it, with no recorded opposition in the House and only three negative votes in the Senate. Under the Religious Freedom Restoration Act of 1993, the state and federal governments were barred from burdening religious exercise by generally applicable laws unless the governments were furthering a compelling interest. The Court would later find the Religious Freedom Restoration Act unconstitutional as applied to state governments, but it still constrains the federal government, and many states have enacted similar statutes of their own to constrain their own state governments.[61]

VI

The most important reason for Republican presidents to restaff the Court was to overrule *Roe v. Wade* and permit states once again to prohibit abortion.[62] It took some time for abortion to become a dividing line between the political parties. When *Roe* was decided, there was not much difference between the views of Republicans and Democrats on the issue. *Roe* had been decided by a Court with a 6–3 Republican majority. The 1976 Republican platform, adopted three years after *Roe*, acknowledged that "there are those in our Party who favor complete support for the Supreme Court decision which permits abortion on demand," while other party members "share sincere convictions that the Supreme Court's decision must be changed by a constitutional amendment prohibiting all abortions." By the next presidential election, however, the battle lines had been drawn. The party's 1980 plat-form supported a constitutional amendment to ban abortion and urged the appointment of judges who would respect "the sanctity of innocent human life." Subsequent platforms stated forthrightly that "the unborn child has a fundamental individual right to life which cannot be infringed." As we have seen, Sandra Day O'Connor's views were closely scrutinized by opponents of abortion when she was nominated in 1981, and the same would be true of every nominee thereafter.

The Court had ample opportunity to revisit *Roe v. Wade*, because there were many states in which voters favored limiting abortion as much as pos-sible. There was an inexhaustible supply of litigation from which the Court could draw. In the two decades after *Roe*, the Court would decide an impor-tant abortion case every two or three years on average.

In one line of cases, the Court held that the government, which normally funded medical procedures for patients who could not afford them, was not constitutionally required to pay for abortions. "*Roe* did not declare an un-qualified 'constitutional right to an abortion,'" Lewis Powell explained in a 1977 case, for a six-justice majority that included some of the justices who had joined the Court's opinion in *Roe*. *Roe* merely protected a "woman from unduly burdensome interference with her freedom to decide whether to ter-minate her pregnancy. It implies no limitation on the authority of a State to make a value judgment favoring childbirth over abortion, and to implement that judgment by the allocation of public funds." In dissent, Brennan accused the majority of "a distressing insensitivity to the plight of impoverished preg-nant women," who would be forced to give birth because they could not af-ford the cost of an abortion. A few years later the Court held that the federal Medicaid program was not constitutionally required to pay for abortions even when they were necessary to protect the mother's health. Poor women would suffer, Potter Stewart recognized for the majority, but Congress's re-fusal to fund abortion only "leaves an indigent woman with at least the same range of choice in deciding whether to obtain a medically necessary abortion as she would have had if Congress had chosen to subsidize no health care costs at all."[63]

The larger set of cases involved not bans on government funding but state laws placing obstacles in the path of women seeking abortions. Shortly after *Roe* was decided, Missouri imposed a host of restrictions on abortion, in-cluding requirements that married women obtain the consent of their husbands and that minors obtain the consent of their parents. In *Planned*

Figure 14.3 President Jimmy Carter poses with the justices in 1977, when the Court was once again becoming a conservative institution. From left to right: Harry Blackmun, Potter Stewart, William Rehnquist, Warren Burger, Thurgood Marshall, Carter, Lewis Powell, Byron White, William Brennan, and John Paul Stevens. Photograph by Thomas J. O'Halloran. Library of Congress, LC-DIG-ppmsca-55393.

Parenthood v. Danforth (1976), the Court found both requirements unconstitutional. The state justified the spousal consent provision as a way of strengthening the institution of marriage, but as Blackmun drily observed, "it is difficult to believe that the goal of fostering mutuality and trust in a marriage, and of strengthening the marital relationship and the marriage institution, will be achieved by giving the husband a veto power exercisable for any reason whatsoever or for no reason at all." The Court also invalidated Missouri's prohibition of the most common and safest method of abortion, a rule "designed to inhibit, and having the effect of inhibiting, the vast majority of abortions." But the Court upheld several less onerous restrictions, including a requirement that women give their consent in writing and a set of recordkeeping requirements imposed on doctors and hospitals.[64]

Danforth set the tone for subsequent cases, each of which presented the Court with another list of abortion restrictions and asked the justices to decide which were consistent with *Roe* and which were not. The city of Akron, for example, required second-trimester abortions to be performed in full-service hospitals rather than in outpatient facilities. The Court found that this rule was unconstitutional because it significantly increased the cost of abortions without contributing much to their safety. Pennsylvania required doctors to inform women of the physiological characteristics of fetuses at two-week intervals from fertilization to birth and to tell women about the resources available to help them care for newborns. The Court found these rules unconstitutional as well. Missouri, a recurring litigant in these cases, required abortion of a viable fetus to be performed by two doctors at once, the second of whom was charged with preserving the life of the unborn child. The Court held that this requirement was constitutional as a reasonable way of furthering the State's compelling interest in protecting the lives of viable fetuses. In case after case, the Court found itself micromanaging the regulation of abortion, as states and cities tested the limits of *Roe* by imposing incrementally more severe limitations. The result was "a web of legal rules that have become increasingly intricate, resembling a code of regulations rather than a body of constitutional doctrine," Rehnquist complained, leaving "this Court to serve as the country's *ex officio* medical board."[65] The Court's decisions in these cases were often splintered into multiple opinions, as different coalitions of justices formed majorities to uphold or strike down particular restrictions.

Meanwhile, of course, the composition of the Court was changing. Potter Stewart, who had joined the majority in *Roe*, was replaced in 1981 by Sandra Day O'Connor, but the hopes of abortion opponents were dashed when, in her first opinion in an abortion case, she staked out a position midway between the two views expressed in *Roe*. O'Connor agreed with the *Roe* majority that the Constitution protects a right to abortion in certain circumstances, but she thought these circumstances are narrower than explained in *Roe*. Rejecting *Roe*'s trimester framework, she suggested that a law restricting abortion is unconstitutional only where it "unduly burdens" a woman's ability to obtain an abortion. The meaning of this phrase was not self-evident, but as O'Connor elaborated upon it, it was clear that while her standard would not allow states to prohibit abortion altogether, it would allow them to place more restrictions on abortion than a majority of the Court was willing to permit.[66]

Abortion opponents were cheered in 1986 by the arrival of Antonin Scalia. In Scalia's first abortion case, *Webster v. Reproductive Health Services* (1989), he made clear that he wished to overrule *Roe*. He complained of "this Court's self-awarded sovereignty over a field where it has little proper business." Abortion, he argued, was a political issue, not a legal one. "We can now look forward," he lamented, "to at least another Term with carts full of mail from the public, and streets full of demonstrators, urging us—their unelected and life-tenured judges who have been awarded those extraordinary, undemo-cratic characteristics precisely in order that we might follow the law despite the popular will—to follow the popular will." In another case the following year, Scalia again expressed his frustration with what he viewed as the lack of any connection between the Constitution's text and the fine distinctions the Court was drawing between permissible and impermissible restrictions on abortion. "The random and unpredictable results of our consequently unchanneled individual views make it increasingly evident, Term after Term, that the tools for this job are not to be found in the lawyer's—and hence not in the judge's—workbox," he concluded. "I continue to dissent from this en-terprise of devising an Abortion Code, and from the illusion that we have authority to do so."[67]

At the time, however, Scalia was the only justice ready to take this step. Rehnquist and White had dissented in *Roe*, but they were content to chip away at *Roe* gradually, by approving each new restriction the states imposed, rather than overruling *Roe* entirely. So was Anthony Kennedy, the newest justice. In *Webster*, the Court mustered six votes to allow Missouri to impose several new requirements that made abortions even more difficult to obtain, including a ban on abortions by public employees and in public facilities and a requirement that physicians test fetuses for viability after twenty weeks. In dissent, Blackmun accused the majority of planning to overrule *Roe*. "For today," he suggested, "the women of this Nation still retain the liberty to con-trol their destinies. But the signs are evident and very ominous, and a chill wind blows."[68]

Blackmun was joined in *Webster* by Brennan and Marshall, but Brennan and Marshall both retired soon after. They were replaced by David Souter and Clarence Thomas, who were generally assumed to be prepared to over-rule *Roe*. After ten consecutive Republican appointments, there now seemed to be as many as six votes to hold that the Constitution does not include a right to abortion—Rehnquist, White, Scalia, Kennedy, Souter, and Thomas. Harry Blackmun, the author of *Roe*, was the only member of the *Roe* majority left on the Court. John Paul Stevens was *Roe*'s only other defender among the justices. The constitutional right to abortion seemed likely to last only until the next abortion case came along.

The next case arrived just a few months after Thomas joined the Court. *Planned Parenthood v. Casey* (1992) involved a familiar list of restrictions imposed by Pennsylvania, including spousal and parental consent requirements, a mandatory twenty-four-hour waiting period, and various recordkeeping and reporting requirements. *Casey* came to the Court with an odd wrinkle that made the case difficult not to hear. The court of appeals below had determined that the appropriate constitutional doctrine to apply was not the one established in *Roe* but rather Justice O'Connor's "undue burden" standard, a standard with which no other justice had agreed, and one that none of the other courts of appeals employed. "Regardless of a person's view of the legitimacy of *Roe v. Wade*," noted Stephen McAllister, one of Thomas's law clerks, "one has to admit that it is at least curious that the law of the land on the most controversial constitutional issue of this century may be a test proposed and endorsed by only one Justice and rejected (at least implicitly) by the rest of the Court."[69]

Early in a presidential election year, it was impossible not to give some thought to the political implications of deciding *Casey*. If *Roe v. Wade* was to be overruled, pro-abortion groups wanted it overruled before the election because they hoped the decision would motivate pro-abortion voters, advised Molly McUsic, Blackmun's law clerk, in a memo to the justice. On the other hand, she continued, it was by no means certain that *Roe v. Wade* was fated to be overruled. If the Court chose not to hear *Casey*, and if one or more of the anti-*Roe* justices retired (White was then in his mid-seventies) and could be replaced by a Democratic president, there might be enough votes to keep *Roe* in place.[70] The justices voted to hear the case, but even the normally mundane decision of when to announce that fact had political implications. At the mid-January conference at which the justices agreed to decide *Casey*, they also voted to defer the announcement until a later conference. Because of the Court's annual calendar, in which there are no oral arguments from May through September, delaying the announcement would have pushed argument in *Casey* from April all the way to October. An April argument would lead to a decision in June, five months before the presidential election, but an October argument would not result in a decision until several months after the election.

Blackmun was livid. He threatened to publish a first-of-its-kind opinion, a dissent from an order relisting a case for a later conference, to expose what he considered improper political maneuvering. "The obvious reason" for deferring the announcement, Blackmun fumed, "is the political repercussions of a decision by this Court in the midst of an election year. . . . This Court stands less than tall when it defers decision for political reasons." Blackmun's draft opinion was enough to shame his colleagues. They agreed to announce right away that they would hear *Casey*, which meant there was time for the case to be argued in April and decided in June.[71]

When the justices heard oral argument in April, observers assumed that the Court was, as the *Washington Post*'s Supreme Court correspondent Ruth Marcus put it, "one vote away from eliminating the constitutional right to abortion." They were right. When the vote took place at the justices' conference a couple of days later, five justices—Rehnquist, White, Scalia, Kennedy, and Thomas—agreed to overrule *Roe*. Rehnquist drafted what he expected would be the Court's majority opinion. When he circulated the opinion in late May, Blackmun wrote on his copy "Wow! Pretty extreme!" and set to work on what he thought would be a dissent.[72]

Two days later, however, Blackmun received an unexpected note from Kennedy. "Dear Harry," the note began, "I need to see you as soon as you have a few moments. I want to tell you about some developments in *Planned Parenthood v. Casey*, and at least part of what I say should come as welcome news." Kennedy had changed his mind. Now he, O'Connor, and Souter were cooperating on a joint opinion that would continue to treat abortion as a constitutional right but would adopt O'Connor's "undue burden" standard as the measure of a restriction's constitutionality. Along with the votes of Blackmun and Stevens, now there were five votes to reaffirm what the joint opinion called "the essential holding of *Roe v. Wade*," the "recognition of the right of the woman to choose to have an abortion before viability and to obtain it without undue interference from the State." Under this rule, a watered-down version of *Roe*, Pennsylvania's spousal notification requirement was unconstitutional, but the state's other restrictions were not.[73]

Rehnquist repurposed his former majority opinion as a dissent. He reiterated his view, which he had held ever since *Roe* itself, that "the Court was mistaken in *Roe* when it classified a woman's decision to terminate her pregnancy as a 'fundamental right' that could be abridged only in a manner which withstood 'strict scrutiny.'" Scalia, or "the evil nino," as one of Blackmun's clerks called him in a note to Blackmun about the case, was severely disappointed. He dissented as well, in much stronger terms. "It is difficult to maintain the illusion that we are interpreting a Constitution rather than inventing one," Scalia argued. "We should get out of this area, where we have no right to be, and where we do neither ourselves nor the country any good by remaining."[74]

The right to abortion had survived, but it was a weaker right than it had been in *Roe v. Wade*, and it was still just one vote short of being eliminated, a vote that could be cast by the next Republican appointee. "I am 83 years old," Blackmun observed in an unusually personal conclusion to his concurring opinion. "I cannot remain on this Court forever, and when I do step down, the confirmation process for my successor well may focus on the issue before us today. That, I regret, may be exactly where the choice between the two worlds will be made." Blackmun was the oldest justice. He was thirty-nine years older than Clarence Thomas and twenty-eight years older than Antonin Scalia, both of whom were likely to outlast Blackmun on the Court by many years. The future of abortion would depend on who replaced Blackmun and the other justices in the *Casey* majority. Three years later, after Blackmun and White had retired and had been replaced by two Democrats (because Bill Clinton won the 1992 presidential election), Blackmun was more confident about the future. "I think the *Casey* case has done a lot to silence the turmoil" surrounding abortion, he told an interviewer. "I think we're in a position to carry on and get on to other things now, just as *Brown against Board of Education* is an accepted fact of life, although I suppose not entirely heeded everywhere. I think *Roe against Wade* probably is ready to fade into the background and we can go on to other subjects."[75] Blackmun was wrong about that, but he would not live long enough to find out.

The outcome of *Casey* drove home the importance of the nomination decisions and confirmation battles of the previous two decades. If George Bush had placed less trust in his chief of staff in 1990, he would have passed over David Souter in favor of one of the reliably conservative court of appeals judges who made every Republican short list of the era. Any of them—Edith Jones, Patrick Higginbotham, Clifford Wallace, Ralph Winter—would likely have been the fifth vote to overrule *Roe*.[76] If Robert Bork had been confirmed in 1987, he would have been a certain fifth vote to overrule *Roe*. If Douglas Ginsburg had not smoked marijuana with his students, he might also have been the fifth vote. If Ronald Reagan had not promised in his 1980 campaign to put the first woman on the Supreme Court, he would have appointed a justice more ideological than Sandra Day O'Connor, and that person would probably have been the fifth vote. If not for Watergate, Richard Nixon would still have been president in 1975, and he would have been very unlikely to choose someone as moderate as John Paul Stevens, so there would have been one less vote to retain a constitutional right to abortion. If Nixon had succeeded in placing Clement Haynsworth or G. Harrold Carswell on the Court, Harry Blackmun would never have become a justice, so the pro-abortion side would likely have lost a vote. There were many forks in the road that led from *Roe* to *Casey*, and at each one, the Court became a bit less conservative than it might have been.

The Court's path in the abortion cases is emblematic of the long period in which Republican presidents appointed ten consecutive new justices, from Burger in 1969 through Thomas in 1991. Most of these justices were chosen specifically to overrule the high-profile liberal decisions of the 1960s and early 1970s. But somehow the big precedents were all still standing. The Court had certainly chipped away at them. The constitutional rights of criminal defendants were weaker than before, as were the rights of black people against discrimination, the rights of religious minorities, and the right to abortion. But in the mid-1990s, when the long run of Republican appointments came to an end, most of the Court's midcentury liberal decisions remained in place. How firmly in place would be a question for the future.

15

New Paths to the Court

The Supreme Court changed in some important ways in the late twentieth and early twenty-first centuries. New kinds of people became justices. The process for selecting them changed. And as the justices were taking new paths to the Court, so were the cases, as the sheer volume of work required the Court to make some significant adjustments to its personnel and to its working procedures. In each of these respects, changes at the Court reflected changes in the world outside.

I

It was never easy to become a justice. A plausible candidate had to be a person of sufficient stature within the legal profession, of course, but the candidate had to satisfy other criteria as well, criteria that changed considerably in the late twentieth and early twenty-first centuries. The justices grew more diverse in some ways and less diverse in others.

Regional diversity had once been extremely important in the selection of justices, but this tradition ended in the second half of the twentieth century. The last justice whose selection was meaningfully based on geography was Lewis Powell of Virginia, who was appointed by Richard Nixon in 1972 after a thorough search for a justice from the South. By the twenty-first century, no one paid much attention to where a justice was from. Oral arguments were dominated by accents from the New York metropolitan area, the childhood home of Antonin Scalia, Ruth Bader Ginsburg, Samuel Alito, Sonia Sotomayor, and Elena Kagan. Several of the justices, in any event, had spent most of their careers in Washington, so their association with a region of the country existed only in memory. John Roberts, for example, grew up in Indiana, but he had worked in Washington since he was in his mid-twenties. Ketanji Brown Jackson was from Miami, but she had not lived there since high school.

Religious diversity had also once been important. From the 1890s through the 1980s (except for a few years) there was at least one Catholic justice and never more than two. From 1916 through 1969 there was at least one Jewish justice and never more than two. But religion, like geography, ceased to be important. Ironically, as people stopped caring about a justice's religion, there were more Catholic and Jewish justices than ever before. When Anthony Kennedy was appointed in 1988, the Court had three Catholics for the first time, and the number kept increasing until 2009, when six of the nine justices were Catholic—Antonin Scalia, Kennedy, Clarence Thomas, John Roberts, Samuel Alito, and Sonia Sotomayor. Richard Nixon ended the custom of a "Jewish seat" when he forced Abe Fortas off the Court in 1969. "Look, there's no Jewish seat on that court," he complained to Alexander Haig, his chief of staff. "There are Jews all around this White House."[1] There would be no Jews on the Court until the appointment of Ruth Bader Ginsburg in 1993 and Stephen Breyer the following year. When Elena Kagan joined the Court in 2010, there were three Jewish justices for the first time. More remarkably, all nine justices were either Catholic or Jewish. Lawyers from a few decades earlier would have been astonished by the prospect of a Court with no Protestants. As of 2024, there have been no justices with a religion other than Christianity or Judaism and none who identify with no religion.

As regional and religious diversity on the Court lost importance, they were supplanted by the growing concern for diversity based on race and gender. Racial diversity had been an important consideration since the 1960s, when Thurgood Marshall became the first black justice. In subsequent years, presidents occasionally considered nominating a second black justice, but no black candidate made it very far in the process. So long as Marshall was on the Court, presidents perceived little political benefit from appointing another black justice. One of Richard Nixon's aides captured this attitude when he suggested maintaining a list of "possible Black nominees, should Thurgood Marshall retire." The few black candidates who did receive consideration were all women, who were in the pool because of their gender, not their race. When the Nixon administration compiled a list of women who might be nominated, the list included Constance Baker Motley, the first black woman to serve as a federal judge, as well as the Chicago lawyer Jewel Lafontant. Neither was likely to gain Nixon's favor. The White House counsel's office warned that Motley, a former civil rights litigator with the NAACP Legal Defense Fund, was "very liberal." Lafontant lacked the stature of the other candidates at the time, although Nixon would later appoint her as deputy solicitor general. Amalya Kearse, the first woman to be a judge on the Second Circuit (and the second black judge on the circuit after Marshall), was on Ronald Reagan's list in 1981 for the spot that went to Sandra Day O'Connor.[2] Once O'Connor was appointed, there was no longer as much political advantage to appointing a woman either, so Kearse dropped off the list for the next two vacancies.

As Thurgood Marshall's health deteriorated in the late 1980s, the Bush administration began preparing to appoint a black justice to take his place. The candidate pool was small because nearly all the black lawyers with conventional credentials were Democrats. In 1989, George H. W. Bush nominated Clarence Thomas to the DC Circuit, a move that was widely interpreted as positioning him for an eventual seat on the Supreme Court. When William Brennan retired in 1990, Thomas was one of the finalists to replace him, but at that point he had been a judge for less than a year, so he was not chosen. Bush nominated Thomas the following year when Marshall retired. "I don't feel he's a quota," Bush claimed at the press conference. "I don't feel that I had to appoint—nominate a black American at this time for the Court." He had selected Thomas, Bush insisted, because "I think he's the best man. And if credit accrues to him for coming up through a tough life as a minority in this country, so much the better." When Thomas was asked whether "the only reason you're being picked is because you're black," he responded: "I think a lot worse things have been said. I disagree with that, but I'll have to live with it."[3]

Once Thomas had taken Marshall's place, the familiar pattern returned. With each vacancy there were black candidates on the list, but none was appointed. The Clinton administration considered Amalya Kearse again, as well as the law professor Stephen Carter, the US representative Barbara Jordan, and Drew Days, the solicitor general. Black candidates in the George W. Bush administration included Larry Thompson, the deputy attorney general, and Janice Rogers Brown, a judge on the DC Circuit. The Obama administration considered Leah Ward Sears of the Georgia Supreme Court and Paul Watford of the Ninth Circuit. Among the names on the lists of candidates circulated by Donald Trump were Daniel Cameron, the attorney general of Kentucky, and Robert Young, formerly of the Michigan Supreme Court.[4] Of this group, Watford appears to be the only one who received serious consideration.

For fifty-five years, from 1967 to 2022, there was always one black justice. This "black seat" lasted even longer than the "Jewish seat" of 1916–1969, but it was a seat that was occupied by only two people because Marshall and

Thomas served for so long. There would not be two black justices at the same time until the day a president or a presidential candidate perceived some benefit in appointing a second one. That day came during the 2020 presidential primaries, when Joe Biden, worried that he lacked support among black voters, declared: "I'm looking forward to making sure there's a Black woman on the Supreme Court to make sure we in fact get everyone represented."[5] Two years later, when Stephen Breyer retired, Biden fulfilled his promise by appointing Ketanji Brown Jackson. The Court had two black justices for the first time.

In the late twentieth century, the largest ethnic group that had never been represented on the Court was the growing Hispanic population. ("Hispanic" was the term in common use during this period.) Presidents began to keep an eye out for Hispanic candidates. As Robert Bork was going down to defeat in 1987, the Reagan administration compiled a list of sixteen Hispanic judges who might be nominated to take his place. The United States Hispanic Chamber of Commerce and the Hispanic National Bar Association pressured Bill Clinton and George W. Bush to appoint the first Hispanic justice. When Clinton chose Ruth Bader Ginsburg instead, the Chamber's president lamented "that you did not seize the opportunity to make history by nominating a Hispanic American. As the fastest growing ethnic group, which already comprises 10% of our nation's population, Hispanic Americans deserve, and should have, a voice on the High Court." Among the candidates for the next vacancy the following year were José Cabranes, then a district judge in Connecticut, and Vilma Martinez, a Los Angeles lawyer and the former president of the Mexican American Legal Defense and Education Fund. When George W. Bush had vacancies to fill, the Hispanic Bar Association furnished a list of eight suitable candidates, one of whom was Alberto Gonzales, the attorney general. The Association reminded Bush that there were "approximately 42 million Hispanic Americans," who formed "the largest minority group in the United States of America and [the] fastest growing segment of the population." These efforts finally bore fruit in 2009, when Barack Obama appointed Sonia Sotomayor to replace the retiring David Souter. Sotomayor, a New Yorker whose parents were from Puerto Rico, had been a federal judge for seventeen years and a prosecutor before that. "Obama Chooses Hispanic Judge for Supreme Court Seat," read the headline in her hometown newspaper.[6]

Sotomayor was the third woman to join the Court. Sandra Day O'Connor, appointed in 1981, was the first, but several other women had been candidates over the previous few decades. The earliest was Florence Allen, who was elected in 1922 to a seat on the Ohio Supreme Court, becoming the first female judge on a state supreme court. In 1934, President Franklin Roosevelt appointed Allen to the US Court of Appeals for the Sixth Circuit, which made her the second woman to be a federal judge and the first to serve on an article III court. (A few years earlier, Genevieve Cline had been appointed to the US Customs Court, which was part of the Treasury Department.) Allen remained on the Sixth Circuit for the rest of her career, a perennial name in circulation whenever a vacancy opened on the Supreme Court. The *Christian Science Monitor* endorsed Allen for the Court as early as 1930. "The time has come when the presence of a woman jurist on the supreme bench must be recognized as an altogether normal and likely development," the paper urged. Allen was "eminently equipped for the responsibilities of the Nation's highest tribunal." There is no evidence that the Hoover administration took this recommendation seriously. The administration developed a list of twenty-eight candidates, all men.[7]

Women's groups made a concerted effort on Allen's behalf in 1939, when Franklin Roosevelt had the opportunity to fill three vacancies on the Court. The Women's Bar Association of the District of Columbia, the Women's Division of the Democratic National Committee, and the Young Women's Christian Association all sent letters to Roosevelt touting Allen's qualifications. So did the handful of women other than Allen who were prominent in the legal world, including the New York judge Dorothy Kenyon and the lawyer and University of Chicago professor Sophonisba Breckinridge. Even the Soviet Union had women on its highest Court, one of Allen's supporters observed, while "our own country has failed to accord American women even one-ninth representation of their sex on the highest tribunal of the land. The New Deal is in this respect incomplete."[8] But Roosevelt does not seem to have taken these suggestions any more seriously than Hoover did. Allen was passed over once again.

Allen's name came up again during the Truman administration. The journalist India Edwards, who was executive director of the Women's Division of the Democratic National Committee, frequently urged Truman to appoint women to government positions. When she suggested Allen for the Supreme Court, Edwards later recalled, Truman was open to the idea, but the justices were not. They "don't want a woman," a Truman aide told her. "They say they couldn't sit around with their robes off and their feet up and discuss their problems."[9] That ended the matter.

Figure 15.1   Florence Allen, the first woman to serve on a state supreme court and the second to serve as a federal judge, was touted as a possible Supreme Court justice during the Hoover, Roosevelt, and Truman administrations, but she was never chosen. Library of Congress, LC-DIG-ggbain-31252.

As more women occupied leadership positions in the legal profession, women started to appear regularly on lists of possible nominees to the Court. When Arthur Goldberg left the Court in 1965, Attorney General Nicholas Katzenbach provided President Lyndon Johnson with capsule biographies of eleven candidates. One was Soia Mentschikoff, a law professor at the University of Chicago, whom Katzenbach called "the only woman worthy of consideration for appointment to the Supreme Court."[10] Johnson ignored Katzenbach's list and appointed his close advisor Abe Fortas instead.

In 1971, when President Richard Nixon had two vacancies to fill at the same time, the White House Counsel's office compiled a list of thirteen female candidates, including members of both political parties. The top four candidates were Margaret Heckler (then a member of Congress, later secretary of health and human services under Reagan), Cornelia Kennedy (then a district judge, later a circuit judge), Ellen Peters (then a law professor at Yale, later a state court judge in Connecticut), and Mildred Lillie (a state court judge in California). John Dean, the White House counsel, interviewed Lillie at her home in Los Angeles and was "reasonably impressed with her as an articulate woman of considerable breadth and experience from a legal as well as personal point of view." He noted approvingly that "on the women's lib movement, she said she had stayed far away from it and personally considered it to be somewhat dangerous." Nixon preferred not to appoint a woman to the Court. When Attorney General John Mitchell told him that Chief Justice Warren Burger was "letting it be known he's not anxious to have a woman," Nixon's response was "I understand. I'm sure, no more anxious than I am." Nixon nevertheless decided to appoint Lillie. Before formally nominating her, however, he sent her name to the American Bar Association's committee on the federal judiciary for evaluation, which was then a standard practice. The committee voted eleven to one that Lillie was unqualified. This view was shared by her colleagues in the California judiciary, who, when the news of Lillie's impending nomination was leaked by the White House, tried to block it. "The Judges of the Superior Court are most disturbed over the proposed nomination," John Dean reported. "The principal complaint is that she just does not follow and/or know the law and rather renders decisions which are completely inconsistent with case law."[11] Nixon decided not to nominate Lillie.

When William Douglas retired in 1975, the Ford administration likewise compiled a list that included several women. Most were sitting judges: Sylvia Bacon, Mary Coleman, Julia Cooper, Cynthia Holcomb Hall, Margaret Haywood, Shirley Hufstedtler, Norma Hollaway Johnson, Florence Kelley, Cornelia Kennedy again, Elizabeth Kovachevich, Constance Baker Motley again, Sandra Day O'Connor, and Susie Sharp. Some were law professors: Ruth Bader Ginsburg, Herma Hill Kay, Soia Mentschikoff again, Dorothy Nelson, Ellen Peters again, Harriet Rabb, and Jean Kettleson. Some were members of Congress: Bella Abzug, Yvonne Burke, Martha Griffiths, Margaret Heckler again, Elizabeth Holtzman, Barbara Jordan again, and Patsy Mink. The list also included a cabinet member, Carla Hills, and a former United Nations representative, Rita Hauser. This was a who's-who of prominent women lawyers. Some were far too liberal to have been nominated by Gerald Ford, but the length of the list demonstrated how many women across the political spectrum were now credible candidates for the

Court. There was considerable speculation in the press that the next justice would be a woman. "Will Ford Name a Woman to Douglas Post?" asked the headline in the *Washington Star*. The *New York Times* reported that Ford "is actively considering the appointment of a woman, the first woman Justice in the Court's history."[12] It did not happen.

This pattern—several women shortlisted, none chosen—might have been repeated when the next vacancy opened in 1981, if not for a promise Ronald Reagan made while campaigning for president the previous year. With less than a month to go before the election, polls indicated that Jimmy Carter, Reagan's opponent, would receive more votes from women than Reagan would. Reagan decided he would commit to placing the first woman on the Supreme Court. "A number of false and misleading accusations have been made in this campaign," he announced at a press conference. "One of the accusations is that I am somehow opposed to full and equal opportunities for women in America." But Reagan would set the record straight. "I am announcing today that one of the first Supreme Court vacancies in my administration will be filled by the most qualified woman I can possibly find," he declared. "It is time for a woman to sit among our highest jurists."[13]

The time came sooner than he may have expected. In early March, when Reagan had been president scarcely more than a month, Attorney General William French Smith heard that Justice Potter Stewart wished to meet with him. At the meeting, Stewart told Smith in confidence that he planned to retire at the end of the Court's term in July. The Justice Department and the White House immediately began considering candidates to take Stewart's place. The list they compiled included several men and several women, including Sandra Day O'Connor, who had been an Arizona state judge since 1975 and a member of the state senate before that. Administration officials knew so little about her that the list incorrectly identified her as a judge of the superior court, a position she had left two years before, when she began serving on the court of appeals.[14]

When Stewart announced his retirement in June, Reagan's campaign promise had not been forgotten. "Last October, you pledged to the American people that you would appoint a woman to the United States Supreme Court," the National Women's Political Caucus reminded him. "With the resignation of Justice Potter Stewart, we urge you to fulfill that promise now." Lyn Nofziger, Reagan's political director, advised that "it is imperative that you appoint a woman to the Supreme Court." Doing so "means that you will live up to a commitment that you made and have that behind you," he reasoned, and "it will go a long way towards solving the problem we have with the lack of women in this Administration," which was giving "the impression, however unjustified, that you and your senior staffers are anti-women." And "one more thing," Nofziger added—"it's the right thing to do."[15]

O'Connor quickly rose to the top of the list. The two Justice Department attorneys who flew to Phoenix to meet her were impressed. (One was a young Kenneth Starr, who became well known in the 1990s even to nonlawyers as the independent counsel leading a several-year investigation of President Bill Clinton.) By early July, Reagan was ready to nominate O'Connor. The response from the press reflected the importance of the announcement. It was "a landmark for the Court," one paper headlined its editorial. Another observed that "it was important as a symbol of the nation's new sensitivity toward equal rights that a woman be appointed to the U.S. Supreme Court for the first time in its 191-year history." A third recognized that "other presidents have had the will, or the opportunity, but never both. The very presence of a woman in the cloister will have a healthy effect on justice." O'Connor was unanimously confirmed by the Senate. On the Court she joined her law school classmate and long-ago ex-boyfriend William Rehnquist, who remarked to one of his law clerks that "since everybody from Ronald Reagan to Warren Burger to Strom Thurmond milked the publicity of the historical event for all it was worth, she had her work cut out for her."[16]

O'Connor's new colleagues at the Court had already made one change to prepare for her arrival. Their traditional title was "Mr. Justice." The Court's printed opinions, for example, would say "Mr. Justice Brennan filed an opinion concurring in the judgment" or "Mr. Justice White filed a dissenting opinion." At oral argument, lawyers would address the justices as "Mr. Justice Marshall" or "Mr. Justice Harlan." Sometime around 1980, however, about a year before Potter Stewart retired, he had a sudden realization. "Stewart panicked," Harry Blackmun was to say. "He came in one day, was all upset. He said 'You know, we're going to have a woman on this Court, and we might as well confront the fact, and we shouldn't be calling each other Mr. Justice.'" The justices agreed to drop the "Mr." from their titles. By the time O'Connor took Stewart's place, they were simply called "Justice Blackmun" or "Justice O'Connor." But there was one change that had not occurred to the justices before O'Connor arrived. Behind the courtroom there was a men's bathroom but no women's bathroom, so during recesses she had to make the long walk back to her own chambers. Eventually, after John Paul Stevens pointed out the inequity, a second bathroom was added.[17]

Ruth Bader Ginsburg became the second woman on the Court in 1993. Ginsburg was far better known before joining the Court than O'Connor had been. For the past thirteen years she had been a judge on the Court of Appeals for the DC Circuit, the lower court that has produced more Supreme Court justices in recent times than any other. Before that, as a law professor, she had been a prominent Supreme Court advocate who was largely responsible for the Court's recognition of sex discrimination as a violation of the Constitution. When Byron White retired in 1993, the Clinton administration was inundated with recommendations to appoint Ginsburg. "Quite literally, it was Ruth Ginsburg's voice, raised in oral argument before the United States Supreme Court, that opened new opportunities for the women of this country," wrote Herma Hill Kay, the dean of the law school at the University of California-Berkeley. As Barbara Babcock, another law professor, described Ginsburg, she "is rightfully called the Thurgood Marshall of the women's movement."[18] Indeed, no justice since Marshall had been so well known before being nominated to the Court.

Ginsburg was not Clinton's first choice for the job. That was Mario Cuomo, the governor of New York, who would have been a throwback to the days when justices routinely came directly from political office. But Cuomo declined the appointment so he could seek a fourth term as governor. Clinton then came very close to nominating Bruce Babbitt, the secretary of the interior and a former governor of Arizona. White House aides even called key senators to sound out whether they would vote for Babbitt. In the end, though, Clinton chose Ginsburg from a list of approximately thirty candidates that included several women who, like Ginsburg, were experienced lower court judges.[19]

When O'Connor announced her intention to retire in 2005, President George W. Bush nominated Harriet Miers to take her place. Miers had been the first woman to lead a large Texas law firm, the first woman to serve as president of the Dallas bar association, and the first woman to be president of the state bar of Texas. She was Bush's personal lawyer when he was governor of Texas. When Bush became president in 2001, Miers held a series of White House posts, eventually becoming White House counsel. "Like Justice O'Connor," the Bush administration's promotional materials declared, "Ms. Miers has been a female trailblazer." Assistant Attorney General Rachel Brand suggested that Miers's background most closely resembled that of William Rehnquist, who, like Miers, had never been a judge but who had experience in private practice and in the executive branch.[20] Unlike Rehnquist, however, Miers had no experience with the Supreme Court or with most of the issues that came before it. And while Republicans in 1981 were willing to forgive O'Connor's lack of such experience, the atmosphere was very different when Miers was nominated, in three respects. First, there were many more alternatives—women who had established clear conservative records over long tenures as judges—than there had been a quarter-century earlier. Second, Miers's long professional relationship with Bush suggested that he had not weighed the merits of alternative candidates but rather that he chose her because of her loyalty to him. And third (as we will see in more detail later), the choice of a justice had become more sharply partisan than it was when O'Connor was nominated. Bush's choice of Miers was unwelcome on both sides of the political divide.

Republicans were appalled that Bush had nominated someone who had taken no public positions on any of the contentious issues the Court would decide. "Not good enough. She's not good enough," complained the conservative commentator David Frum, a former Bush speechwriter. "There aren't articles, aren't records. She's not taken an active role in legal philosophy." After years of disappointment with Republican nominees—Blackmun, Stevens, O'Connor, Kennedy, Souter—who had proven not to be as conservative as appointing presidents expected them to be, Republicans had no patience for another justice whose degree of conservatism was uncertain. When former Vice President Dan Quayle appeared on Fox News to defend the nomination, he was met with skeptical questions. "What is it about her that gives you assurance . . . that she is a judicial conservative?" wondered an incredulous Brit Hume. "Because, outwardly, there's not—nothing to look at." Robert Bork pronounced Miers "a disaster on every level." Miers did not help her own cause by performing poorly in meetings with senators. After weeks of this kind of hammering from members of her own party, it was clear that Miers would have trouble being confirmed by the Senate. She withdrew from consideration.[21] In her place Bush nominated Samuel Alito, whose conservatism was not in doubt.

Ginsburg was thus the only woman on the Court when O'Connor retired, but she was soon joined by Sonia Sotomayor in 2009 and Elena Kagan in 2010. Ginsburg died in 2020 and was replaced by Amy Coney Barrett. When Ketanji Brown Jackson joined the Court in 2022, four of the nine justices were women. For the first time in the Court's history, less than half the justices were white men. By then, the number of women in the upper reaches of the legal profession, and thus the number of women who were plausible nominees to the Court, was many times greater than it had been a generation earlier when O'Connor and Ginsburg were appointed. It had become so normal for women to be justices that presidents and presidential candidates no longer accrued as much political capital for selecting them. Other demographic characteristics became more salient. When Sotomayor became a justice, she was hailed not as the third woman on the Court but as the first Hispanic justice.[22] When Jackson joined the Court, the headlines declared that she was the first black woman on the Court, not the sixth woman.

A justice's race or gender had no necessary connection to the justice's politics or to the outcomes of cases. Thurgood Marshall and Clarence Thomas held views at opposite ends of the political spectrum. So did Ruth Bader Ginsburg and Amy Coney Barrett. There was no black position, no female position, on the issues that came before the Court, not even in cases involving race or gender discrimination. Rather, as Joe Biden made clear when he announced his intention to nominate a black woman, the justification for race and gender diversity was a concern about representation, a sense that all groups of sufficient size should see that one of their own was on the Court. O'Connor's nomination, for example, was an inspiration to countless women and girls who could now envision a career that seemed unattainable before. "Because of her, I realized this is something I could do," recalled Michelle Friedland, who was nine years old when O'Connor joined the Court. Friedland would grow up to become a law clerk for O'Connor and eventually a judge herself.[23]

The rationale for the older forms of diversity had been just the same. There was no Jewish or Catholic view of the law. The Jewish and Catholic seats existed so presidents could gain the favor of groups of voters who valued representation on the Court. Regional diversity on the Court was likewise a way for presidents to assure blocs of voters that they were being heard. As the public interest in different aspects of identity has risen or fallen over time, the concern with the demographics of the justices has followed suit. In 1940, for example, Stephen Breyer would have been identified as either a Jewish Californian (based on his childhood) or a Jewish New Englander (based on where he spent most of his adult years). When he was appointed in 1994, he was a white man.

As the public becomes interested in other dimensions of diversity, these too are likely to become important considerations in selecting new justices. Sexual orientation, for example, is a category that for most of the Court's history was unthinkable as a criterion. There has never been an openly gay justice. Until the late twentieth century, to come out as gay would have ended the career of anyone who might hope to become a justice. It was nevertheless an open secret among well-placed Washingtonians that Frank Murphy, who was on the Court from 1940 to 1949, was gay. Murphy cultivated a public image as a ladies' man and was often seen at Washington parties with glamorous women. But it was widely understood that this was for show. Insiders joked about Murphy's sexuality. "I remember sitting in Harry Hopkins's bedroom one morning about 10:00 a.m.," the columnist Drew Pearson recalled, "when Liz Whitney phoned to say: 'Harry, I bet you don't know where I am. I'm in Frank Murphy's apartment. I spent the night with him. I was out with Frank until three a.m., and he couldn't get rid of me so he brought me home here. He still can't get rid of me.' 'Well, there's no place where you could be safer,' said Harry." The journalist John Boettiger, who was married to Franklin Roosevelt's daughter, privately referred to Murphy as a "pansy" who "lacked some important manly physical characteristic."[24]

Murphy lived his entire adult life with Edward Kemp, who had been a college and law school classmate. Kemp went along with Murphy at each stage of Murphy's career. When Murphy was mayor of Detroit, Kemp was his assistant. When Murphy became governor general of the Philippines, Kemp followed him to Manila to serve as his legal advisor. When Murphy moved to Washington to be attorney general, Kemp once again became Murphy's assistant. When Murphy joined the Court, Kemp was appointed as general counsel of the Bureau of the Budget. At each posting, including at the Court, Kemp seems to have helped Murphy with his work. "Edward Kemp was his closest friend, and I think the best influence on him officially," Robert Jackson tactfully remarked after Murphy's death. "Kemp saved him from many a mistake and worked him out of others." In 1943, Murphy tried to persuade the other justices that the Court should hire Kemp in some capacity—it is not clear for what position—but they evidently declined. The following year, Murphy urged Franklin Roosevelt to appoint Kemp as a district judge, but this effort was also unsuccessful. Murphy's former secretary tried again to secure a judgeship for Kemp after Murphy died. "You know, I am sure, how dear Mr. Kemp was to the Justice," she wrote to Chief Justice Fred Vinson. "They shared an apartment from the time the Justice came to Washington. I have often heard my Chief say that no man in the Capital was of finer judicial timber than Ed Kemp."[25] But Kemp never became a judge.

The most direct evidence of Murphy's sexuality, from an era in which people as prominent as Murphy were normally careful not to leave any evidence at all, is a congratulatory letter Murphy received when he was appointed to the Court. The letter was from Abe Garfinkel, an army officer in the Philippines. Garfinkel was Murphy's aide-de-camp when Murphy was governor general. "After all is said and done," Garfinkel wrote, "I have always felt since that 13th day of June 1933 in Hong Kong, that you belonged to me. And although I was given the gate, so to speak, thrown out and relegated to my soldiering job these past four years, I assure you, there has not been a gathering at which I was present that your name didn't come up in some form or other."[26] In June 1933, Murphy was on his way to the Philippines to take up his post as governor general. It seems likely that Edward Kemp joined him there later, and that Murphy's brief relationship with Garfinkel ended when Kemp arrived.

Figure 15.2 Frank Murphy (right) and his lifelong companion Edward Kemp (center) prepare for Murphy's testimony at a congressional hearing in 1939, when Murphy was attorney general. At left is Joseph Keenan, the assistant attorney general. Library of Congress, LC-DIG-hec-25838.

If there were other justices who lived secret gay lives, they were better than Murphy at concealing them. One hint of what may lie beneath the surface is the story of G. Harrold Carswell, the court of appeals judge who was nominated to the Court by Richard Nixon in 1970 but who was rejected by the Senate. In 1976, Carswell pleaded no contest to a charge of making a sexual advance on a male vice squad officer in the restroom of a Tallahassee shopping mall. In 1979, he was beaten in his Atlanta hotel room by a man he had met at a skating rink and invited back to the hotel.[27] Carswell had a wife and four children. He appeared to lead a conventional life. Despite all the media attention focused on him during his confirmation hearings, there were no whispers of homosexuality. Of course, the same could be said of virtually all the justices who have served on the Court, so it is possible that Murphy was not the only gay justice. Today, by contrast, there are many openly gay judges on the lower courts and there are many openly gay voters. Sexual orientation may be the next kind of diversity that will considered important in choosing justices.

As the justices became more diverse in some ways, they became less diverse in others. Many justices throughout the Court's history were former elected officials, but this practice stopped completely in the late twentieth century. The Court that decided *Brown v. Board of Education* in 1954, for example, included three former US senators (Hugo Black, Harold Burton, and Sherman Minton) and one former state governor (Earl Warren). But Minton would be the last justice appointed who had served in Congress and Warren would be the last governor. Except for Sandra Day O'Connor, who spent a few years in the Arizona state senate before becoming a judge, there would be no more justices who had held elective office. Some had been lawyers in the political world—Stephen Breyer was counsel to the Senate Judiciary Committee, while John Roberts and Brett Kavanaugh both worked in the White House—but none had been politicians themselves.

As judging came to be a career path separate from politics, service on a federal court of appeals became a virtual prerequisite to an appointment as a justice. The Court that decided *Brown* in 1954 included only one member who had been a lower court judge—Minton, who had been on the Seventh Circuit for eight years after leaving the Senate. (There were two if we count Hugo Black's brief early stint as a police court judge in Alabama.) In 2009, by contrast, all nine justices were former court of appeals judges. Thirteen of the fourteen justices appointed between 1986 and 2022, everyone except Elena Kagan, came from the court of appeals. Political experience had once been considered useful on the Supreme Court, but now it was judicial experience that mattered.

Another kind of judicial experience, clerking for a justice, also became a common credential. When Byron White joined the Court in 1962, he was the first justice to have been a law clerk at the Court. (White clerked for Fred Vinson.) There were gradually more justices who were former clerks—William Rehnquist (for Robert Jackson) and John Paul Stevens (for Wiley Rutledge). Eventually, most of the justices had clerked earlier in their careers. Beginning with Stephen Breyer in 1994, seven of the next nine justices were former clerks at the Court—Breyer (for Arthur Goldberg), John Roberts (for Rehnquist), Kagan (for Thurgood Marshall), Neil Gorsuch (for Anthony Kennedy), Brett Kavanaugh (for Kennedy), Amy Coney Barrett (for Antonin Scalia), and Ketanji Brown Jackson (for Breyer). As clerking for a justice became the first step toward becoming a justice oneself, the pool of candidates became much smaller.

The justices had once come from a variety of educational backgrounds. The justices on the *Brown* Court attended seven different law schools, and one member of the Court, Stanley Reed, had no law degree at all. (Until the early twentieth century, it was common to become a lawyer without attending law school. Reed was the last-serving Supreme Court justice without a law degree.) Harold Burton and Felix Frankfurter were Harvard graduates, but several of the other justices attended schools that were less highly regarded, including Hugo Black, who went to the University of Alabama, Sherman Minton, a graduate of Indiana University, and Robert Jackson, who became a lawyer after only one year of classes at the Albany Law School. This wide range of backgrounds diminished considerably. When Elena Kagan joined the Court in 2010, all nine justices had gone to law school either at Yale or Harvard.

In some ways, then, the justices of the late twentieth and early twenty-first centuries were a less diverse group of people than they had ever been. All went to elite law schools. Most clerked at the Court. None held elective office. Virtually all were judges on the federal courts of appeals. As the path to the Court widened in some respects, it narrowed in others.

II

As the kinds of people who became justices changed, so did the process by which the Senate decided whether to confirm them. For most of the Court's history, confirmation was normally a short procedure in which the nominee scarcely participated. There were occasional exceptions when the nominee was unusually controversial, such as the lengthy Judiciary Committee hearings on the nomination of Louis Brandeis in 1916. But the Senate typically held no hearings and voted quickly. The Senate vote was often reported as "by acclamation"—that is, without any recorded disagreement. Hearings became routine only in the 1940s. Even when the committee held hearings, the nominee normally did not testify. In 1925, Harlan Fiske Stone became the first nominee to appear before the committee, and that was at Stone's own request. Stone was the attorney general and his Justice Department had recently indicted a sitting senator. Stone wanted to explain this delicate matter to the committee in person to forestall potential opposition to his confirmation. When Felix Frankfurter testified at the committee's request in 1939, he emphasized that it was unprecedented for a nominee to do so. "I, of course, do not wish to testify in support of my own nomination," he explained. "While I believe that a nominee's record should be thoroughly scrutinized by this committee, I hope you will not think it presumptuous on my part to suggest that neither such examination nor the best interests of the Supreme Court will be helped by the personal participation of the nominee itself."[28] It was only in the 1950s that the nominee's own testimony became a routine part of the proceedings.

As late as the 1960s, Byron White, Arthur Goldberg, and Abe Fortas were all confirmed by acclamation, after only one or two days of hearings. And even when hearings began to be televised and became longer, the ultimate Senate votes on successful nominees tended to be unanimous or nearly so. Sandra Day O'Connor, the first nominee whose confirmation hearings were broadcast live on television, was confirmed 99–0. Antonin Scalia was confirmed 98–0, and Anthony Kennedy 97–0. After the controversial 1991 nomination of Clarence Thomas, who squeaked through the Senate by a vote of 52–48, Ruth Bader Ginsburg was confirmed 96–3, and Stephen Breyer 87–9. The hearings were sometimes acrimonious, as senators from the opposing party regularly tried to induce nominees to state their views on issues that might come before the Court and nominees (except for Robert Bork) just as regularly refused to do so. Most nominees, however, were confirmed by overwhelming margins after receiving the support of senators from both parties.

After Breyer was confirmed in 1994, however, more than eleven years elapsed before the next justice, John Roberts, was nominated, the

Figure 15.3   Felix Frankfurter testifies at his confirmation hearing in 1939, the first nominee to the Court to testify at the request of the Judiciary Committee. Library of Congress, LC-DIG-hec-25811.

second-longest such span in the Court's history. (The longest gap was between Joseph Story in 1811 and Smith Thompson in 1823, at a time when the Court had only seven justices.) In the interim, the Senate became much more polarized.[29] It had once been possible for a senator to be a liberal Republican or a conservative Democrat, but now every Republican was more conservative than every Democrat. Roberts, who would likely have been confirmed nearly unanimously at any previous time in the Court's history, was confirmed in 2005 by a vote of only 78–22, when half the Democrats voted against him. The following year, Samuel Alito was confirmed by a vote of only 58–42. Only four Democrats voted in his favor. It became the new norm for almost every senator not of the president's party to oppose *any* nominee. In every subsequent vote, the Senate split almost perfectly along party lines. Sonia Sotomayor received 31 negative votes, all from Republicans, while every Democrat (plus only nine Republicans) voted for her. Elena Kagan received 37 negative votes; only six senators, five Republicans and one Democrat, crossed party lines. Neil Gorsuch received 45 negative votes, with only three Democrats voting in his favor. Brett Kavanaugh received 48 negative votes, with only one Democrat supporting him. And Amy Coney Barrett was confirmed 52–48 with no Democratic votes at all. The days of approval by acclamation or near-unanimous votes were long gone.

One striking illustration of the new political environment was the Senate's refusal to consider President Barack Obama's nomination of Merrick Garland in 2016. Antonin Scalia died in office in February of that year. The Republicans were the majority party in the Senate. On the day Scalia died, Senate majority leader Mitch McConnell announced that the Senate would not consider any nominee until after the next president took office in January 2017, eleven months later. In March 2016, Obama nominated Garland, the highly regarded and politically moderate chief judge of the Court of Appeals for the DC Circuit. But the Senate took no action. When Donald Trump became president in 2017, he nominated Neil Gorsuch instead, who was promptly confirmed by a Senate that still had a Republican majority.

There was a great deal of debate at the time about whether the Republicans' refusal to consider Garland was a departure from the traditions of the Senate. Before Garland, the last person nominated during a presidential election year when the president and the Senate were of opposite parties was Melville Fuller, who was nominated in April 1888 and confirmed in June. This situation also occurred in 1828, 1844, and 1852, and on each occasion the Senate let one or more nominations lapse, as with Garland, but none of the nominations took place as early in the year as Garland's. These nominations were of John Crittenden in December 1828, Reuben Walworth and Edward King in June 1844, and Edward Bradford in August 1852. During these years, the nomination closest to Garland's in timing was that of John Spencer in January 1844. The Senate voted on party lines to reject Spencer rather than letting his nomination lapse. If there was any lesson to be drawn from these episodes, perhaps it was that the more traditional thing for the Senate to do would have been to hold a vote on Garland's nomination, a vote at which there would have been nothing untraditional about voting against Garland because of his party affiliation. But it was hard to draw any lesson at all from a small set of nominations that took place so long ago.

The Senate Republicans' stated reason for refusing to consider Merrick Garland was to "give the people a voice in the filling of this vacancy" by

awaiting the results of the presidential election.[30] It was generally understood, however, that the Republicans would have taken a different view had
the president been a member of their own party, and this understanding
was confirmed when Ruth Bader Ginsburg died only two months before the
2020 presidential election. The Republicans were still the majority party in
the Senate, but now the president, Donald Trump, was a Republican as well.
Rather than giving the people a voice in choosing Ginsburg's replacement,
the Senate hurried to confirm Trump's nominee, Amy Coney Barrett, before
the election. Ginsburg died on September 18. Trump announced Barrett's
nomination on September 26. She was confirmed by the Senate on October
26, just eight days before election day. Never in the Court's history had a justice been nominated or confirmed so soon before a presidential election.

The Senate took another step in the direction of partisanship when it
abolished the filibuster for Supreme Court nominees in 2017. The Senate's
rules on filibusters have changed over time. Before 1917, there was no limit
on the use of extended debate to delay a vote. The Senate adopted a rule in
1917 allowing for "cloture"—the end of debate—by a two-thirds vote, and
this fraction was reduced to three-fifths in 1975. But filibusters have been
attempted only rarely for votes to confirm Supreme Court justices. The
only successful occasion was the nomination of Abe Fortas to be chief justice in 1968, when, as we have seen, the Senate fell short of the votes needed
for cloture. There were also cloture votes for both of William Rehnquist's
nominations, in 1971 and again in 1986 when Rehnquist was nominated as
chief justice, and for Samuel Alito's nomination in 2006. The Senate voted
against cloture in 1971, but it made no difference because the Senate voted
to confirm Rehnquist soon after. The Senate voted in favor of cloture on the
other two occasions.

As votes on judicial nominees became more politically polarized, however, the filibuster became a more powerful weapon. It took only forty-one
votes to block cloture, and there were rarely fewer than forty-one senators of
the minority party. In 2013, after several years in which the parties had taken
turns filibustering the other party's nominees to the courts of appeals and to
executive branch positions, the Senate, then controlled by the Democrats,
effectively abolished the filibuster for all nominations except those to the
Supreme Court, by lowering the cloture threshold to a simple majority. But
when Donald Trump nominated Neil Gorsuch in 2017 for the position that
Democrats believed should have gone to Merrick Garland the previous year,
forty-five senators voted against cloture. To bring Gorsuch's nomination to

a vote, the Senate, now controlled by the Republicans, lowered the cloture threshold to a simple majority for Supreme Court justices too. Since then, every nominated justice has been opposed by at least forty-five senators, so without the abolition of the filibuster for Supreme Court nominations, the Senate might have been too polarized to confirm any new justices at all.

Polarization within the Senate was accompanied by polarization in the world outside, as interest groups mobilized for and against each nomination. The participation of interest groups was not entirely new, but it had previously been only episodic. As we have seen, labor unions and the NAACP successfully lobbied against the nomination of John Parker in 1930. The nomination of Tom Clark in 1949 was opposed unsuccessfully by several organizations on the left, including the Civil Rights Congress and the Communist Party, because when Clark was attorney general, he had led the Truman administration's prosecution of alleged communists. By 1987, when Robert Bork was nominated, interest group participation had become routine and the roster of groups on both sides was much longer. Howard Baker, the former senator who served as Ronald Reagan's chief of staff, devoted the summer and early fall of 1987 to Bork's confirmation. He gave speeches to several organizations, including the NAACP, the American Farm Bureau, and a group of business leaders. He held meetings with several more, including the Chamber of Commerce and a group of Jewish leaders. On the other side, a wide array of groups worked to defeat Bork, including civil rights organizations, women's groups, and labor unions. The coalition assembled against Bork was "the largest ever to be mobilized for any Capitol Hill battle," according to its organizers.[31] Supreme Court confirmations came to resemble political campaigns, with speeches and advertisements on both sides, but these were campaigns in which the only voters were the one hundred members of the Senate.

As opponents of prospective justices scrutinized their lives for incidents that might discredit them, it was inevitable that information embarrassing to the nominees would surface. One of William Rehnquist's former law clerks recalled that the liberal journalist Nina Totenberg was "running around Arizona during your confirmation hearings trying to find someone who would say that you had unflattering things to say about a minority group." Clarence Thomas's hearings were dominated by the accusation of Anita Hill, then a law professor at the University of Oklahoma, that Thomas had repeatedly made offensive sexual remarks to her when she worked for him at the Equal Employment Opportunity Commission. As sensational as Thomas's hearings were, they seemed tame by comparison to Brett Kavanaugh's, when the primary question was whether he had committed sexual assault in high school. Thomas and Kavanaugh angrily denied these allegations, which they insisted were politically motivated. Kavanaugh called the assault charge "a calculated and orchestrated political hit fueled with apparent pent-up anger about President Trump and the 2016 election, fear that has been unfairly stoked about my judicial record, revenge on behalf of the Clintons, and millions of dollars in money from outside left-wing opposition groups."[32] Supporters of the nominations professed to believe the nominees, while opponents credited their accusers. These tawdry and emotional proceedings in the Senate stood in stark contrast with the courteous, ritualized atmosphere across the street at the Supreme Court.

Nominees had once been left to navigate the confirmation process on their own, but as the path to Senate approval became more treacherous, they needed assistance from the White House. Each administration prepared what Bill Clinton's legal advisor called an "announcement strategy" to present the nominee in the best light, a plan requiring tight "message control" and employing "spinners" to speak with representatives of the media. The campaign also required a "Hill strategy" of identifying key supporters and opponents among the senators and "mobilizing early endorsements" from supporters. And it required a "constituencies strategy" of "selling [the] nomination to interested groups" who could bring political pressure to bear on senators.[33]

It became standard practice for the president's aides to shepherd nominees to individual meetings with senators, especially the crucial senators on the Judiciary Committee. The Nixon administration inaugurated this custom with the nomination of Harry Blackmun in 1970, after the failed nominations of Clement Haynsworth and G. Harrold Carswell, and it has been followed by all administrations since. When Sandra Day O'Connor made the rounds of senators' offices in 1981, for example, she was given a binder with detailed information about the interests of each senator. She was warned that Edward Kennedy of Massachusetts "was active in opposing the confirmations of Haynsworth, Carswell and Rehnquist," and that Robert Byrd of West Virginia "devotes considerable attention to Supreme Court nominations" because he "considers himself well qualified for membership on the Supreme Court." The White House normally also arranged mock hearings at which the nominee could practice answering questions posed by lawyers pretending to be hostile senators. In 2005, for instance, John Roberts underwent at least ten "murder boards," as they were called, each lasting two to three hours at the Justice Department or the Old Executive Office Building next to the White House, at which colleagues and friends peppered him with difficult questions. At the end of each session, Roberts and his questioners discussed how he might improve his answers.[34]

One of Bill Clinton's aides recalled that the administration assembled fifteen-member teams to work on the confirmations of Ruth Bader Ginsburg and Stephen Breyer, confirmations that were not particularly controversial. "The confirmation team consisted of members from the Counsel's Office, Legislative Affairs, Communications, the Press Office, Office of Public Liaison, a coordinator from the Department of Justice and four outside lawyers and consultants," the Clinton aide explained. The team was given office space in the Senate and in the Old Executive Office Building and was assisted by "a coordinator from the Counsel's Office, a detailee secretary from the Department of Justice, and a full time intern."[35] Once, nominees simply showed up in the committee room and answered the senators' questions, but now prospective justices needed all the help they could get.

It took justices longer to join the Court, and it took them much longer to leave. The average age at which justices are appointed—in their early fifties—has not changed much since the late nineteenth century. The average length of the justices' tenure has risen considerably, however, because almost every justice in recent times has stayed on the Court until a ripe old age.[36] This is mostly a result of better medical care and a run of good luck. In earlier eras, justices, like all people, sometimes died young or became too ill to work. Wiley Rutledge and Frank Murphy both died in office in 1949. Rutledge was fifty-five, Murphy fifty-nine. A few years later, Fred Vinson died in office at sixty-three and Robert Jackson died in office at sixty-two. No justices have died so young since then. Sherman Minton retired in 1956 after only seven years on the Court due to anemia, and Charles Whittaker left in 1962 after only five years because of his depression. Since then, health issues have not caused any of the justices to leave the Court so quickly. And there are no longer any justices who leave the Court for political posts. The last to do so was Arthur Goldberg, who left in 1965, after less than three years, to become ambassador to the United Nations and run for governor of New York. Such early departures were once not unusual. James Byrnes lasted only a year before leaving to direct the Office of Economic Stabilization during World War II; he would later be secretary of state and governor of South Carolina. Charles Evans Hughes left in 1916, after less than six years, to run for president. As justices stopped leaving the Court early, whether voluntarily or involuntarily, the average age of retirement (or death in office) climbed. The twelve justices appointed between 1940 and 1957 left the Court at an average age of sixty-six, having served an average of only twelve years. By contrast, the twelve justices who left the Court between 1990 and 2022 did so at an average age of eighty-one. They had served for an average of twenty-eight years.

As in earlier eras, justices often timed their retirements to enable a president of their party to choose their successors. Byron White and Harry Blackmun both acknowledged that they retired while Bill Clinton was president so a Democrat could take their places. (Blackmun was nominally a Republican but by the end of his career his views were closer to the Democratic party than to the Republican party.) Anthony Kennedy retired while Donald Trump was president and encouraged Trump to appoint Brett Kavanaugh, his former law clerk, to succeed him. At an election day party in 2000, when the television networks predicted that the Democrat Al Gore would defeat George W. Bush, Sandra Day O'Connor was heard to exclaim "this is terrible." Her husband John explained to the other guests that O'Connor hoped to retire but would not leave the Court while a Democrat was president. He did not tell the partygoers that the reason she wished to retire was that he had recently been diagnosed with Alzheimer's disease. Bush became president, but because the Court played an important part in his victory, O'Connor felt constrained not to retire during his first term. By the time she announced her retirement in 2005, at the beginning of Bush's second term, John O'Connor's dementia was so advanced that they were unable to enjoy the retirement they had planned.[37]

Of course, not all justices had the luxury of choosing when they left the Court. Thurgood Marshall was in such poor health that he had to retire during the presidency of George H. W. Bush, a man he loathed, and he was even more unhappy when his replacement turned out to be Clarence Thomas.[38] Ruth Bader Ginsburg, as we have seen, died at the age of eighty-seven less than two months before the 2020 presidential election. She would doubtless have been dismayed that Donald Trump was left with enough time to choose her successor. The justices were lasting longer in office, but the end could still be unpredictable.

As the nation and the rest of the government became divided by political party, so did the Court. The justices had always divided along political lines, as far back as the split between Federalists and Jeffersonians in the early nineteenth century, but party affiliation was only imprecisely aligned with the justices' votes on the outcomes of cases. In the mid-twentieth century, for example, Democratic appointees like Felix Frankfurter and Byron White tended to vote on the conservative side in many areas, while Republican appointees like William Brennan and Harry Blackmun tended to vote on the liberal side. In *Roe v. Wade*, as we have seen, the seven justices in the majority included five Republicans, and the two dissenters included one justice from each party. But when White retired in 2002, the Court lost its last conservative Democrat, and when John Paul Stevens retired in 2010, the Court lost its last liberal Republican. Ever since, the Court has resembled Congress, in that every Democratic appointee is to the left of every Republican appointee.

Once, the justices all got their news from the same newspapers and television networks. This no longer appears to be the case. "We used to get the *Washington Post,* but it just . . . went too far for me. I couldn't handle it anymore," Antonin Scalia explained in a 2013 interview. "It was slanted and often nasty. And, you know, why should I get upset every morning? I don't think I'm the only one. I think they lost subscriptions partly because they became so shrilly, *shrilly* liberal." Scalia and his wife decided to read only newspapers with a conservative perspective, the *Wall Street Journal* and the *Washington Times.* Once, the justices all socialized with the same elite lawyers and journalists, but this too seems to have diminished. "In my early years on this Court," Scalia said in the same interview, "I used to go to a lot of dinner parties at which there were people from both sides. Democrats, Republicans. Katharine Graham used to have dinner parties that really were quite representative of Washington. It doesn't happen anymore." Now there are two different camps of elites, one made up Democrats and one made up of Republicans, and the justices belong to one or the other. The Court, like the nation it governs, has become increasingly divided by political party.[39]

III

The Court's caseload ballooned in the second half of the twentieth century. Approximately 1,200 cases were filed in the Court in 1950. By 1980 there were more than four thousand. And by the first decade of the twenty-first century, each year brought roughly eight thousand new cases.[40] As had happened several times before in its history, the Court was swamped.

What could be done to handle the rising tide of cases? One possibility, discussed seriously all through the 1970s and 1980s, was to add a new court to the federal court system, just below the Supreme Court, to absorb some of the Court's overflow. In the early 1980s, Chief Justice Warren Burger proposed creating an "Intercircuit Tribunal" that would decide cases raising questions of statutory interpretation on which the courts of appeals had reached divergent conclusions. These tended to be the least politically salient of the Court's cases, so they were the ones most amenable to being delegated, and the Court would still have the authority to review the Tribunal's decisions if the justices wished to. The idea was to free up the justices' time for the more important and controversial cases. The Justice Department endorsed Burger's proposal and suggested experimenting with it for five years. But the plan drew opposition from judges, from the press, and from the White House. Ruth Bader Ginsburg, then a judge on the DC Circuit, predicted that "distributing Supreme Court jurisdiction between two bodies in this way" would merely "undermine the operation of both." The *New York Times* worried that another layer of federal courts would cause even more delay in deciding cases than already existed. In the White House, a young lawyer named John Roberts thought the proposed tribunal was "exceedingly ill-advised." If the Court had reached the limits of its capacity, he suggested, that was a good thing, because "those limits are a significant check preventing the Court from usurping even more of the prerogatives of the other branches" of government. Roberts had little patience, in any event, for the justices' complaints of an excessive workload. "While some of the tales of woe emanating from the Court are enough to bring tears to the eyes," he joked, "it is true that only Supreme Court Justices and schoolchildren are expected to and do take the entire summer off."[41] The plan for an Intercircuit Tribunal was never implemented.

Congress did provide some relief by giving the Court more control of its caseload. The Judiciary Act of 1925 had authorized the Court to decide for itself whether to hear most kinds of cases, but there were still a few pockets of the Court's old mandatory jurisdiction. In a series of statutes aimed at stemming the flow of cases, Congress gradually gave the Court the power to refuse to hear most of these types of cases as well. In 1988, in the most significant of these statutes, the Court was relieved of having to hear all the cases in which lower courts held statutes unconstitutional.[42] But these measures were drops in the bucket, compared with the heavy volume of cases that arrived each year. The Court would be left to address the caseload problem largely on its own. Without much help from Congress, the rising tide of cases would lead to several important changes at the Court.

One change was that it became much harder to get a case before the Court. In 1926, the first year in which the Court exercised its new power to decline to hear cases, the justices granted only 20% of the certiorari petitions filed. (A certiorari petition is the document in which litigants ask the Court to hear a case.) By 1950 this figure had already declined to 10%. In 1980 it was down to 4%. And by 2009 the Court heard fewer than 1% of the cases presented to it.[43] The Court had become inaccessible to all but a few litigants.

Part of this sharp decline was attributable to the greater number of certiorari petitions filed each year. The rest was engineered by the justices themselves, who gradually reduced the number of cases they decided each year. In the 1970s, the Court decided approximately 150 cases per year. By the 1990 term it was only 121. In 2000 it was just eighty-three. And in the 2021 term, the Court decided only sixty-eight cases, or less than half of what had once been the norm. Scholars disagree about the causes of this decline.[44] The justices have not offered any explanation. Whatever the reason, it became much harder to persuade the Court to decide a case.

The difficulty of getting cases into the Court contributed to the development of a specialized Supreme Court bar. In the early nineteenth century, when litigation in the Court consisted primarily of oral argument, and when travel to and from Washington was expensive and time-consuming, there had been a small cadre of lawyers with a regular Supreme Court practice, but this specialized bar ceased to exist when printed briefs became the norm and when railroads and other new forms of transportation facilitated travel to Washington. For most of the Court's history, there were no specialized Supreme Court lawyers except for the staff of the solicitor general's office, who represented the federal government in the Court, and except for occasional individuals such as Thurgood Marshall who practiced before the Court repeatedly. Most lawyers who appeared in the Court were there for the first time. They were the same lawyers who had handled their cases in the lower courts. Many were not ready for the big leagues. As the legal journalist Anthony Lewis described them in the mid-twentieth century, "the average level, unfortunately, is mediocre at best—reflecting the bar generally, since there is no special group of lawyers who argue in the Supreme Court."[45]

That changed in the late twentieth century, when litigants began hiring specialists who possessed the arcane knowledge and skills needed to get a case into the Court. The members of this new specialized bar were typically alumni of the solicitor general's office or former law clerks at the Court, the two places where a lawyer could acquire an insider's feel for the kinds of arguments the justices would find persuasive. By the early twenty-first century, most of the cases before the Court involved lawyers who had been there many times before.

To assist with all these cases, the Court acquired a larger staff. The justices had each gained a second law clerk in 1941. They added a third clerk in 1970 and a fourth in 1974.[46] The law clerks were still the top graduates of the elite law schools, who now typically clerked for a lower court judge before spending one year, occasionally two, working for one of the justices. Clerks helped the justices by wading through the thousands of certiorari petitions and recommending which ones to grant. In the cases the Court agreed to decide, the clerks researched the legal issues at stake and often wrote the first drafts of the justices' opinions. A justice's chambers came to resemble a small law firm, with one senior lawyer and four junior ones assisted by a pair of secretaries.

The added law clerks were still not enough for some of the justices. When Lewis Powell joined the Court, he was astonished that he had so little help compared with the Richmond law firm where he had spent most of his career. "I am not able—with the limited staff presently available—to discharge my responsibilities with the same care and thoroughness which major law firms (with infinitely greater resources) customarily devote to major problems," he complained. He suggested that the Court should hire staff attorneys who would work for the Court as a whole rather than for any individual justice, as some of the lower courts had done. Byron White, who also grew accustomed to a large staff during his many years at a law firm in Denver, agreed that a corps of staff attorneys would help the Court handle the tide of certiorari petitions. But the expansion of the Court's legal staff stalled at four clerks for each justice. Some members of the Court were reluctant to delegate any more of their responsibility for fear of changing the nature of the institution. William Douglas wanted no additional assistance because "the job here is so highly personal, depending upon the judgment, discretion, experience and point of view of each of the nine of us." Even some of the law clerks felt this way. When the justices were authorized to hire a fourth law clerk, one of Potter Stewart's former clerks urged him not to. "It seems to me that the expansion of the clerking crew may have the effect of devaluing the experience," he advised. "At some point you stop being a Justice's advisor and begin to be a junior associate in a medium sized law firm." Although "the workload is no picnic," he acknowledged, "I, for one, would rather work on Saturdays and evenings."[47]

As in earlier eras, the justices' complaints of overwork were sometimes derided in the world outside the Court, because most of their work was invisible to outsiders. At an event commemorating Stanley Reed's retirement in 1957, Tom Clark told an anecdote about Reed that could have been told at any point in the Court's history. "Early one morning," Clark began, Reed

> came out of his apartment at the Mayflower Hotel where the Reeds have lived since they first came to Washington and asked a cab driver to take him to the Supreme Court on Capitol Hill. The driver barked back that there wasn't any use going there, nobody would be around, the Court didn't get in until much later in the day and when they arrived, they stayed only for about four hours. And that for just eight months out of the year! "Besides," he continued, "when they came in, they didn't do anything." He knew because he had taken some of the law clerks to the Court through the years, and they said they did all the work. And, he asked, "do you know how much they get for only four hours a day and eight months a year—$25,000!"
>
> The Justice wondered aloud what he supposed they did with all that money. "I'll tell you what they do with it," the driver replied, "they keep it, judging from the size of the tips I get!"[48]

Unless one worked at the Court, it could be difficult to tell how hard the job was.

The constant increase in the number of certiorari petitions, combined with the absence of any additional staff apart from the law clerks, led to the creation of the "cert pool" in 1972. Formerly, each justice's chambers considered every certiorari petition independently. This was a time-consuming process, and since most petitions had little chance of being granted, it was a duplication of effort that several of the justices began to see as a luxury the Court could no longer afford. Five justices—Burger, White, Blackmun, Powell, and Rehnquist—agreed to divide the certiorari petitions among their chambers. For each petition, one clerk would write a short memo and send it to all five chambers. The experiment was such a success that new justices normally joined the pool as well, until by 1991, Stevens was the only nonparticipant.[49] The benefits of the cert pool were obvious: it saved the clerks and the justices an enormous amount of work and it ensured that at least one person in the building would give close attention to every certiorari petition, even the ones that seemed unpromising at first glance, such as the handwritten petitions filed by prisoners. On the other hand, the cert pool gave a great deal of influence to an individual law clerk, who could affect the votes of as many as eight justices on whether to hear a case. The clerks were inexperienced lawyers just out of school; was it right to give them so much power?

Lawyers were already worried that the justices were entrusting too much decision-making to their law clerks. In 1957, William Rehnquist, then a young Phoenix lawyer a few years removed from his clerkship with Robert Jackson, wrote a widely read essay in *U.S. News & World Report*, a popular weekly magazine, entitled "Who Writes Decisions of the Supreme Court?" His answer: too often it was the clerks, some of whom, Rehnquist charged, had "a cynical disrespect for the capabilities of anyone, including Justices, who may disagree with them." Critics ever since have shared Rehnquist's concern that the clerks were performing too many tasks that properly belonged to the justices themselves. In 1993, Kenneth Starr, another former clerk (for Warren Burger), blamed the clerks for filling the Court's scarce docket with offbeat cases raising "sexy" issues rather than the cases considered important in the business world. These critiques tended to come from people who, in truth, may have been more upset with the substance of the Court's decisions than with the clerks' role in them. Rehnquist was unhappy with then-recent liberal decisions such as *Brown v. Board of Education*, while Starr was a lawyer representing large corporations in some of the business cases that he thought the Court should have heard. Because they were former clerks themselves, with social and professional ties to some of the justices, they may have found it easier to criticize a new generation of clerks than to attack the justices directly. The justices' main reaction to these critiques seems to have been amusement. In the early 1950s, Robert Jackson already noted that "a suspicion has grown at the bar that the law clerks . . . constitute a kind of junior court." He quoted the jest of a lawyer that "the Senate no longer need bother about confirmation of Justices but ought to confirm the appointment of law clerks." Sandra Day O'Connor was blunter: "I am the one who has to make the decisions around here," she declared.[50]

But if the clerks weren't deciding the cases behind the scenes, they did change the Court in subtler ways. The justices' conferences after oral argument were once their first opportunity to discuss the cases in depth, so the conferences often featured lengthy substantive give-and-take. Now, however, the justices normally engaged in long discussions of the cases in their own chambers with their law clerks before the conferences even took place. By the time of the conference, a justice often had a clear position that had already been sharpened in conversation with the clerks. The quality of discussion in the justices' conferences deteriorated accordingly. Each justice would speak in turn without much effort to change anyone's mind. Antonin Scalia was disappointed by these conferences when he joined the Court. "To call our discussion of a case a conference is really something of a misnomer," Scalia told a group of law students. "It's much more a statement of the views of each of the nine Justices, after which the totals are added and the case is assigned. I don't like that." Scalia, who loved a good argument, wished the conferences provided an opportunity for one. "Maybe it's because I'm an ex-academic," he reflected. "Maybe it's because I'm right."[51]

With more clerks involved in the cases, the justices had more reason to worry that their internal deliberations would be disclosed to the outside world. There had always been occasional leaks of the *result* of a case. As we have seen, John Catron and Robert Grier gave President James Buchanan advance notice of the outcome of *Dred Scott*, and Ashton Embry, one of Joseph McKenna's clerks, was caught in 1919 leaking the results of business cases to speculators. Similar episodes took place in the late twentieth and early twenty-first centuries.[52] In 1992, more than two weeks before the Court published the opinions in *Planned Parenthood v. Casey*, *Newsweek* magazine, citing clerks as its source, correctly reported that there would be at least three separate opinions. Chief Justice William Rehnquist admonished the clerks not to speak to the press. In 2014, after an evangelical couple had dinner with Justice Samuel Alito and his wife, news began to spread among evangelical activists that Alito would write the Court's opinion in *Burwell v. Hobby Lobby Stores* and that the Court would hold that employers with religious objections could not be required to provide health insurance coverage for contraceptives. Three weeks later, when the Court's opinion was published, the news proved to be accurate.[53]

But if the results of cases occasionally leaked, there had never been any exposure of the Court's internal workings as revealing as *The Brethren*, a gossipy 1979 bestseller coauthored by the journalist Bob Woodward, who had recently been one of the reporters who exposed the Watergate scandal. *The Brethren* included highly unflattering portraits of Warren Burger, who was described as "petty, unpleasant and dishonest," and Thurgood Marshall, who was depicted as a lazy man whose clerks did most of his work. Some of the material in *The Brethren* came from interviews with a few of the justices themselves, especially Potter Stewart, but much seems to have come from interviews with the law clerks. The justices were aghast. They were likely even more disturbed when Edward Lazarus, a former Blackmun clerk, published a similar exposé, *Closed Chambers*, in 1998. Lazarus provided a blow-by-blow account of events inside the Court during his clerkship year of 1988–1989, highlighted by conflicts between a self-styled "cabal" of conservative clerks and their liberal counterparts. It was bad enough from the justices' perspective for a journalist like Woodward to air the Court's secrets, but it was unpardonable for the revelations to come from one of the Court's own, an insider who had exploited confidential relationships with the justices and his fellow clerks. Blackmun, now retired, cut off contact with Lazarus.[54]

Opinions in individual cases also sometimes leaked. In 1979, after a reporter for ABC news obtained prepublication copies of the opinions in two cases, the Court fired one of its print shop employees, who was apparently the source. In 1981, United Press International, a news service, obtained a copy of the Court's opinion in *County of Washington v. Gunther* a few days before it was published. In 1993, the Court received a call from one of the lawyers in *Cincinnati v. Discovery Network*, a case that had been argued but not yet decided. The lawyer had received a mysterious phone call from an unidentified man who said he had a copy of a draft of the Court's opinion, which he said he found on Prodigy, an early internet service. The call was not a hoax, Rehnquist informed his colleagues, because the two pieces of information the man provided—it was the third draft, circulated on February 4, 1993—were exactly right. It was never ascertained whether someone at the Court had uploaded the draft or whether a hacker had somehow penetrated the Court's computer system.[55]

The most famous leak of all was of a draft of Samuel Alito's majority opinion in *Dobbs v. Jackson Women's Health Organization*, the 2022 case in which the Court overruled *Roe v. Wade*. The opinion was not published until June 24, but in early May, *Politico*, a news website, posted a ninety-eight-page draft of the opinion that had been circulated in February. In early June, a man with a gun arrived at Justice Brett Kavanaugh's home with the intention of killing him before the Court could publish the opinion. He surrendered to the police when he saw that the house was guarded by law enforcement officers. Chief Justice John Roberts ordered Gail Curley, the Court's marshal, to investigate the leak. After interviewing ninety-seven Court employees, the marshal determined that in addition to the justices, eighty-two employees had access to the draft opinion, approximately half of whom must have been law clerks. But Curley could not determine who was responsible for the leak. She recommended limiting the internal distribution of such documents in the future.[56] The episode was a vivid reminder that the more people are in on a secret, the harder it is to keep, and that leaks of the Court's opinions can have serious unexpected consequences.

By the middle of the twentieth century, clerking for a justice was a first step toward the higher reaches of the legal profession, and it stayed that way even as the number of clerks doubled in the 1970s, because there were still only thirty to forty spots available each year. (The number varies slightly year to year because the active justices do not always hire the full number of clerks to which they are entitled and because the retired justices, whose numbers fluctuate with retirements and deaths, are entitled to one clerk each. Clerks for the retired justices are typically "loaned" to one of the active justices.) We have already seen that in the early twenty-first century most of the justices were former clerks themselves. Many more ex-clerks were lower court judges. The most lucrative law firms competed to hire former clerks, often paying bonuses to clerks that reached hundreds of thousands of dollars. Many clerks became professors at elite law schools. Many more held important government posts. There was no better way for a new lawyer to enter the profession than to clerk at the Supreme Court.

As the race and gender of the justices came to be considered important, so did the race and gender of the law clerks. The first black clerk, as we have seen, was William Coleman, who was hired by Felix Frankfurter in 1947. There would be few black clerks in later years. The second, Tyrone Brown, clerked in 1967–1968 for Earl Warren; the third, Karen Hastie Williams, clerked for Thurgood Marshall in 1974–1975. A study in 1998 found that William Rehnquist, Antonin Scalia, Anthony Kennedy, and David Souter had collectively hired 218 law clerks, of whom none were black; that Sandra Day O'Connor, Clarence Thomas, Ruth Bader Ginsburg, and Stephen Breyer had each hired only one black clerk; and that John Paul Stevens, the justice who had hired the most black clerks, had hired sixty-one clerks in total, of whom three were black. There were repeated calls in the media for the justices to hire more black clerks. The justices themselves tended not to respond in public. In 1980, writing privately to Potter Stewart, Lewis Powell lamented a recent *Washington Post* editorial "criticizing us for not employing 'minorities' as law clerks." Powell had no intention of changing his hiring practices. "One wonders," he fretted, "what the Post will write when vacancies on the Court occur."[57]

The justices were also slow to hire women as clerks. The first, as we have seen, was Lucile Lomen, who was a clerk for William Douglas during World War II, when most of the men who would have been eligible were in the military. It was a long time before there would be a second. Albert Sacks, a Harvard law professor and a former clerk for Felix Frankfurter, selected Frankfurter's law clerks every year. In 1959 Sacks offered a suggestion that he acknowledged was "somewhat unusual." The candidate Sacks proposed was "Mrs. Ruth Ginsburg, 26 years old, married and the mother of a child a little under five years old." Ginsburg's "qualities of mind and person would make her most attractive to you as a law clerk," Sacks advised. "The lady has extraordinary self-possession. She is the kind of person who is quiet until it is time to talk but who then reflects the fruits of solid, independent thought." And "she is a pleasantly attractive female." Sacks emphasized that Ginsburg had full-time help caring for her child, so her family obligations would not pull her away from her work.[58]

Frankfurter refused to hire Ginsburg. "As you know," he told Sacks, "I am against night work and there is very little of it in this shop." But "there are exigencies when I do not want to be worrying about the availability of a law clerk because of home responsibilities." Even if Ginsburg "may not have a young child and a potentially sick husband on her mind, I would have them on my mind. The only thing my doctors have enjoined upon me is to try to simplify my life, reduce my concerns and not add to them. Willy-nilly, to have Mrs. Ginsburg would tend to complicate it." Sacks readily agreed. "Your reasons are sound, and your conclusions fully justifiable," he assured Frankfurter. Sacks recommended Daniel Mayers instead.[59] Frankfurter hired Mayers. Mayers would have a distinguished career, but not as distinguished as that of Ruth Bader Ginsburg.

There would not be a second female clerk until 1966, when Hugo Black hired Margaret Corcoran, the daughter of Thomas Corcoran, a friend of Black's who had himself clerked for Oliver Wendell Holmes and who had been one of Franklin Roosevelt's advisors. The clerkship did not go well. Corcoran stayed out late and slept much of the day. "I did all of her work that year," recalled Stephen Susman, her co-clerk. "I didn't complain one iota because Margaret provided my wife and I with a wonderful social life in Washington." Three years after the clerkship ended, Corcoran died at the age of twenty-eight of an overdose of sleeping pills.[60]

From this inauspicious beginning, the number of women clerking at the Court steadily grew. Martha Alschuler clerked for Abe Fortas in 1968; she would spend most of her career as Martha Field, a professor at Harvard Law School. Fifteen more women clerked at the Court between 1971 and 1976, including Barbara Underwood, would become the first woman to serve as solicitor general, and three future court of appeals judges—Karen Nelson Moore, Marsha Berzon, and Diane Wood. In 1971, William Douglas became the first justice to hire two women, Carol Bruch and Janet Meik, as clerks in the same year. "That's Women's Lib with a vengeance!" Douglas exclaimed. By the turn of the century, the percentage of clerks who were women hovered between 30% and 40% each year.[61]

In the late twentieth and early twenty-first centuries, the country's political polarization influenced the selection of law clerks almost as much as it affected the selection of justices. The justices had once chosen their clerks without much regard for the clerks' politics or the politics of the lower court judges for whom the clerks had previously worked. Now, however, the conservative justices typically chose conservative clerks who had worked for lower court judges appointed by Republicans, while the liberal justices typically chose liberal clerks who had worked for lower court judges appointed by Democrats. The most extreme example was Clarence Thomas, who hired 120 clerks during his first thirty years on the Court, every single one of whom had worked for a lower court judge appointed by a Republican president. "I won't hire clerks who have profound disagreements with me," Thomas explained. "It's like trying to train a pig. It wastes your time, and it aggravates the pig."[62] In this respect, as in so many others, the Court reflected the country whose legal system it supervised.

16

Back to the Right

The Supreme Court has been a conservative institution for most of its history. Not in every case, and not on every issue, but most of the time the Court has occupied a position on the political spectrum to the right of the average American. In most eras, when the Court has struck down statutes as unconstitutional, they have been statutes favored by the left. The justices are a small group of lawyers who are older and wealthier than average and who are selected from the upper echelons of a profession that prizes conformity to precedent. Perhaps the Court's record of conservatism should not be surprising.

The middle decades of the twentieth century were an exception to this pattern. From the 1940s through the early 1970s, the Court was more liberal than the nation as a whole. The cause of this change is no mystery. Of the nineteen new justices appointed between 1937 and 1967, fourteen were appointed by Democratic presidents, and the five who were not included the liberal stalwarts Earl Warren and William Brennan.

In the late twentieth and early twenty-first centuries, the Court reverted to form. It became a conservative institution once again—not on every issue, but on most. The Court's return to the right was, again, a matter of personnel. After Republican presidents appointed ten consecutive new justices between 1969 and 1991, the Court's Republican majority was so overwhelming that it would endure, throughout alternating Democratic and Republican administrations, right up to the present.

In the mid-twentieth century, liberals extolled the Court for protecting important constitutional rights, while conservatives complained of activist justices who improperly intruded into political issues. Now the tables were turned. Now it was conservatives who praised the justices for being true to the law, while liberals accused them of squandering the Court's legitimacy by letting their political beliefs dictate the outcomes of cases.

I

Ten new justices joined the Court between 1993 and 2022, five from each political party. But because the Court entered this period with an 8–1 Republican advantage, there were never more than four Democrats on the Court at any given time. The Republicans benefited as well from some flukes of timing. Had Antonin Scalia died a few months earlier rather than in February 2016, it would have been much harder for the Republican-controlled Senate to deny Barack Obama the ability to appoint Scalia's successor. Had Ruth Bader Ginsburg lived a few months longer, rather than dying shortly before the 2020 presidential election, her replacement would have been chosen by Joe Biden rather than Donald Trump. With Trump's appointment of Amy Coney Barrett to succeed Ginsburg, the Court had a 6–3 conservative majority, but it could easily have been a 5–4 liberal majority instead. When people with life tenure wield enormous power, much can depend on precisely when they die.

In the mid-twentieth century, the Court had established new constitutional rights that were supported by the left, but the new constitutional rights of the late twentieth and early twenty-first centuries were rights preferred by conservatives. The Second Amendment, for example, had been a nearly defunct part of the Constitution for two centuries. It provides: "A well regulated Militia, being necessary to the security of a free State, the right of the people to keep and bear Arms, shall not be infringed." The Second Amendment had always been understood to protect the right to own guns only in connection with their use in a militia, and because the citizen militias of the eighteenth century were almost entirely replaced by the professional armed services, the amendment had been the subject of scarcely any litigation. In *District of Columbia v. Heller* (2008), however, the Court breathed new life into the Second Amendment. In a 5–4 decision authored by Antonin Scalia, the Court held that the conventional understanding of the amendment had been wrong all along. In fact, the Court concluded, the Second Amendment protected the right of everyone to possess guns in their homes, whether or not they were affiliated with a militia.[1]

On the surface, *Heller* was a battle of originalist readings of the Constitution. In his lengthy majority opinion, Scalia canvassed eighteenth-century sources to reach the conclusion that "in numerous instances, 'bear arms' was unambiguously used to refer to the carrying of weapons outside of an organized militia," weapons that early Americans considered "even more important for self-defense and hunting" than for militia service. John Paul Stevens countered with a dissenting opinion of nearly equal length, in which he likewise surveyed eighteenth-century sources and reached the opposite conclusion. "The Amendment is most naturally read to secure to the people a right to use and possess arms in conjunction with service in a well-regulated militia," Stevens insisted. "So far as appears, no more than that was contemplated by its drafters or is encompassed within its terms."[2]

Not far beneath the surface of this history seminar were competing views about guns. Scalia was an avid hunter. Indeed, he had inadvertently become one of the best-known hunters in the country a few years before, when, after returning from a hunting trip with Vice President Dick Cheney, he declined to recuse himself from a case to which Cheney was a party. As Scalia acknowledged, the incident became "fodder for late-night comedians" who did not normally discuss the Supreme Court.[3] His love of hunting was in the news again in 2016, when he died while on a hunting trip in Texas. The other justices in the majority were not hunters, but by the time *Heller* reached the Court, one did not need to be a hunter to oppose gun regulation. After many years of lobbying by the National Rifle Association, guns had become one of the hot-button issues dividing liberals from conservatives. The practical effect of *Heller* was to invalidate the District of Columbia's ban on the possession of handguns.

The Court expanded this new Second Amendment right in subsequent cases. In *McDonald v. Chicago* (2010), the same five-justice majority held that the Constitution protects the right to possess guns from interference by states and cities as well as by the federal government. "Self-defense is a basic right, recognized by many legal systems from ancient times to the present day," Samuel Alito reasoned in his opinion for the Court. The use of firearms for self-defense was a right "deeply rooted in this Nation's history and tradition," so Chicago's ban on handguns was unconstitutional. Alito acknowledged that a right to possess guns might make life less safe for Chicagoans, but that was true of many other constitutional rights, he suggested—all the rights that made it more difficult for criminals to be arrested and prosecuted, such as the right to *Miranda* warnings and the right to have unlawfully obtained evidence excluded from one's trial.[4]

The right to bear arms received another boost in *New York State Rifle & Pistol Association v. Bruen* (2022), when the Court held that the Second Amendment guarantees a right to carry guns in public for self-defense. At oral argument, the conservative justices exhibited considerable skepticism about a New York law that required gun owners to show a special need for a permit to carry a concealed weapon. Criminals "with illegal guns, they're on the subway," Alito worried. "They're walking around the streets, but the ordinary hard-working, law-abiding people I mentioned, no, they can't be armed?"[5] The Court divided on party lines. The six Republican appointees were in the majority, while the three Democratic appointees were in dissent.

Perhaps even more important than *Bruen*'s outcome was the new method the Court adopted for interpreting the Second Amendment. When deciding whether a law satisfies other parts of the Constitution, the Court typically considers the importance of the purpose the law is intended to achieve and whether the law is appropriately tailored to achieve that purpose. In *Bruen*, however, Clarence Thomas's opinion for the Court ruled these considerations out of bounds when deciding whether gun regulation comports with the Second Amendment. Thomas announced a much stricter test, under which gun regulation is constitutional only where it is "consistent with this Nation's historical tradition of firearm regulation." If a gun restriction is intended to prevent a particular problem, such as gun violence, that has existed for a long time, "the lack of a distinctly similar historical regulation addressing that problem is relevant evidence that the challenged regulation is inconsistent with the Second Amendment." After *Bruen*, it appears that governments at all levels lack the power to devise new methods of curbing gun violence, because traditional gun regulations are the only ones that can satisfy the Second Amendment.[6]

Another new constitutional right shielded wealthy wrongdoers from paying punitive damages. In tort cases—that is, suits for harms inflicted by one person on another—victims are entitled to be compensated for their losses, and in cases of egregious wrongdoing victims may also recover punitive damages, which are intended to punish defendants for their misconduct. The Constitution was never thought to impose any limit on punitive damages—at least not until *BMW v. Gore* (1996), in which the Court found that the Due Process Clause of the Fourteenth Amendment prohibits awards that are excessive as compared with the victim's actual loss. The case involved "about as outrageous a punitive damage award as one is likely to encounter," John Paul Stevens's law clerk noted. BMW did not tell a customer that his ostensibly new car had been repainted, so the customer overpaid for the car by approximately $4,000. For this misconduct, BMW was ordered to pay punitive damages of $2 million, a figure the Court found unconstitutional by a vote of 5–4. A few years later, the Court overturned a $145 million punitive damages award against an insurance company, where the victim's actual damages were $1 million. While "there are no rigid benchmarks that a punitive damages award may not surpass," Anthony Kennedy's opinion for the Court explained, "in practice, few awards exceeding a single-digit ratio between punitive and compensatory damages, to a significant degree, will satisfy due process." And when Philip Morris, a cigarette company, was ordered to pay $79.5 million in punitive damages for contributing to the death of a lifelong smoker by deceiving the public about smoking's safety, the Court reversed the award on the ground that the Due Process Clause permits punitive damages only for misconduct that harms victims who are parties to the case, not for the wrongdoer's other victims who are not parties.[7] The Due Process Clause has always been fertile soil for new constitutional rights, the content of which has varied along with the justices' policy preferences— liberty of contract at the turn of the twentieth century, rights to contraception and abortion in the mid-twentieth century, and freedom from excessive punitive damages at the turn of the twenty-first century.

While the Court was establishing new constitutional rights favored by conservatives, it was also beefing up some old ones. For instance, the Takings Clause of the Fifth Amendment, which bars the government from "taking" private property for public use without compensating the owner, had long been understood in principle to impose some limit on the extent to which property could be regulated. In practice, however, the Court had always allowed the government to regulate without compensation where there was a good reason, even where the regulation caused a sharp drop in the value of property. In the leading case, *Penn Central v. New York* (1978), New York City's designation of Grand Central Station as a historical landmark had the effect of barring the station's owner from building an office tower above the station. The affected parcel of land was worth much less without an office tower than with one, but the Court nevertheless held that the city did not have to compensate the owner because the preservation of historic buildings was an important goal and because the city's landmark designation program applied broadly to many properties in the city rather than singling out Grand Central.[8]

As the Court grew more conservative, however, it began to construe the Takings Clause to require compensation for property owners in various situations in which government regulation reduced the value of their property. When a New York law required the owners of apartment buildings to allow a cable television company to string a thin wire across the roof so tenants would have access to television, the Court held that the wire constituted a taking of the landlord's property. When California required the owners of a beach house, as a condition of enlarging it, to allow beachgoers to walk across their sand from one public beach to another, the Court required the state to compensate the owners. The condition was "not a valid regulation of land use," Scalia declared in his opinion for the Court, "but an out-and-out plan of extortion." When, to prevent the erosion of sand from its beaches, South Carolina prohibited new construction close to the water, the Court deemed the measure unconstitutional. And when California required the owners of farms to allow union organizers to enter their property to speak with farmworkers, the Court once again held that the law amounted to a taking of the farm owners' property.[9] In most of these cases, the more conservative justices sided with the property owner, while the more liberal justices sided with the government.

The Court's best-known Takings Clause case of the period, however, resulted in a 5–4 victory for the government. *Kelo v. New London* (2005) raised a question the Court had answered before: May the government take property from one owner (while compensating the owner for the property's market value) and give it to someone else, for the purpose of encouraging economic development? Cities have used this method to assemble land for large projects since at least the mid-twentieth century. To build the World Trade Center in New York, for example, hundreds of residents were involuntarily displaced in the 1960s. Such arrangements have been politically controversial because the beneficiaries have often been well-capitalized and well-connected businesses, while the landowners forced to sell their property and move elsewhere have typically been less wealthy and less powerful. But the constitutionality of these projects had not been in doubt. The Court gave its unanimous approval in *Berman v. Parker* (1954), when it allowed Washington, DC, to redevelop blighted areas of the city by taking land containing rundown apartment buildings and selling the land to real estate developers.[10] *Kelo* involved a similar project, in which a Connecticut city planned to take parcels owned by individual homeowners and assemble them into an office park to be used by Pfizer, a large pharmaceutical company. City officials hoped that the project would bring many new jobs to the city.

Kelo was unexpectedly controversial, both at the Court and among the public. Although the Court once again affirmed the constitutionality of taking private property for the purpose of economic development, four justices dissented, led by Sandra Day O'Connor. "The specter of condemnation hangs over all property," she charged. If the government could take property from one person and give it to another on the ground that the recipient would use it more productively, "nothing is to prevent the State from replacing any Motel 6 with a Ritz-Carlton, any home with a shopping mall, or any farm with a factory." After all, she asked, "who among us can say she already makes the most productive or attractive possible use of her property?" The Court's decision was so unpopular that within the next few years most states enacted new laws prohibiting the taking of property for economic development, at least in certain circumstances. Even people who did not usually follow the Court's decisions could sympathize with the homeowners in *Kelo*, who were ordinary people forced out of their homes to benefit a large corporation. One group of angry New Hampshire residents even proposed—in the end unsuccessfully—that the town of Weare, where Justice David Souter grew up and still lived when the Court was not in session, should condemn Souter's house and convert it into the "Lost Liberty Hotel," to punish Souter for joining John Paul Stevens's majority opinion. "David seems to be getting most of the heat for this unpopular opinion," a baffled Stevens remarked to his colleagues. He reminded them that "I was actually its author."[11]

In another group of cases praised by the right and bemoaned by the left, the Court changed the balance between the First Amendment's two religion clauses—the Establishment Clause, which limits the government's power to aid religion, and the Free Exercise Clause, which limits the government's power to restrict religion. It is easy to say, in the abstract, that the Constitution requires the government to remain neutral with respect to religion, but there are many contexts in which choices must be made between competing views of what, precisely, constitutes neutrality. The Court repeatedly sided with religious claimants who argued that the government was impermissibly disfavoring religion relative to secular pursuits.

For example, when a state university pays the printing costs for student publications, how should it treat a religious magazine published by a student Christian organization? To be neutral with respect to religion, should the university decline to pay for the magazine, on the ground that the state has no business subsidizing the expression of a religious viewpoint? Or does neutrality consist of paying equally for all student publications, whether religious or secular? The University of Virginia thought it was obliged not to pay, but in *Rosenberger v. University of Virginia* (1995), a 5–4 Court held that the university had made the wrong choice. Once it decided to fund student publications, Anthony Kennedy explained for a majority consisting of the five most conservative justices, the university could not exclude a publication because it was religious in nature. "This sort of censorship is offensive, unprecedented, and itself a serious violation of that neutrality which the Establishment Clause commands," he insisted in a memo to his colleagues. Writing for the four dissenters, David Souter argued that the university's position was the correct one. "The Court is ordering an instrumentality of the State to support religious evangelism with direct funding," he declared. "This is a flat violation of the Establishment Clause."[12]

In similar cases that followed, a similarly divided Court held that government neutrality with respect to religion requires the government to provide the same assistance to religious organizations that it provides to secular ones. In *Zelman v. Simmons-Harris* (2002), the same five-justice majority upheld Ohio's system of paying the tuition costs for children in Cleveland, a system in which most of the payments went to religious schools. William Rehnquist, writing for the majority, found that Ohio's payments were "neutral with respect to religion," because "the program challenged here was enacted for the valid secular purpose of providing educational assistance to poor children," not for the purpose of promoting religion. In *Trinity Lutheran Church v. Comer* (2017), the Court held that religious schools could not be excluded from a state program that paid for schools to install rubber playground surfaces. And in *Espinoza v. Montana Department of Revenue* (2020), the Court, by another 5–4 vote, decided that where a state provides scholarships for students to attend private schools, students must be allowed to use the scholarships to attend religious schools. "This Court continues to dismantle the wall of separation between church and state that the Framers fought to build," complained Sonia Sotomayor, who dissented in the latter two cases. By requiring states to fund religious education, she contended, "the Court leads us to a place where separation of church and state becomes a constitutional violation."[13] Neutrality with respect to religion now meant that religious organizations had to be treated at least as well as secular ones.

This principle played a big role during the Covid epidemic of 2020–2021, when states and cities throughout the country had to decide which kinds of public gatherings to allow and which to prohibit. In a series of 5–4 decisions, the Court invalidated several restrictions on religious services, all on the ground that the government was impermissibly treating religious gatherings more strictly than other kinds of gatherings. "While a synagogue or church may not admit more than 10 persons," the Court noted of a New York restriction, "businesses categorized as 'essential' may admit as many people as they wish. And the list of 'essential' businesses includes things such as acupuncture facilities, camp grounds, garages, as well as many whose services are not limited to those that can be regarded as essential, such as all plants manufacturing chemicals and microelectronics and all transportation facilities." As Neil Gorsuch observed in a separate concurring opinion, "while the pandemic poses many grave challenges, there is no world in which the Constitution tolerates color-coded executive edicts that reopen liquor stores and bike shops but shutter churches, synagogues, and mosques." The dissenters argued that this was an apples-and-oranges comparison. "Bike repair shops and liquor stores generally do not feature customers gathering inside to sing and speak together for an hour or more at a time," Sonia Sotomayor pointed out. "Justices of this Court play a deadly game in second guessing the expert judgment of health officials."[14] But the conservative justices remained vigilant in ensuring that the devout were not treated with disfavor.

The justices who formed the majorities in these cases were religious people themselves. "I am decidedly and unapologetically Catholic," Clarence Thomas declared in 2018 at the graduation ceremony of Christendom College, a Catholic institution in Virginia. His faith was "the way, the truth, and the life." They were aggrieved that religion was not taken seriously enough in the upper reaches of government and the legal profession. "The challenge for those who want to protect religious liberty in the United States, Europe and other similar places," Samuel Alito announced in a 2022 speech, "is to convince people who are not religious that religious liberty is worth special protection." He accused law professors of classifying religious faith as "just like any other passionate personal attachment, say rooting for a favorite sports team." He worried that those adhering to traditional religious beliefs such as opposition to same-sex marriage "risk being labeled as bigots." Thomas likewise bemoaned a "trendy disdain for deep religious conviction" which he thought had pushed religious freedom down to "the lowest rung of the Court's ladder of rights."[15] Their solution was to help it climb back up the ladder.

The conservative justices' solicitude for religious belief made the Court a welcoming forum for claims that government officials were denigrating religion. In *Masterpiece Cakeshop v. Colorado Civil Rights Commission* (2018), the Court held that a state agency acted unconstitutionally when it ordered a bakery not to discriminate against same-sex couples in the sale of wedding cakes. The defect in the agency's decision, the majority explained, was that commissioners had spoken disrespectfully of the baker's religious beliefs. In *Kennedy v. Bremerton School District* (2022), the Court decided that a public high school football coach had a constitutional right to lead students in prayer on the field after games. And in *303 Creative v. Elenis* (2023), the Court held that a state's anti-discrimination law could not be used to force a graphic designer who opposed same-sex marriage on religious grounds to create a website for a same-sex wedding.[16] Religious observance in the United States was in broad decline, but at the Supreme Court religion was stronger than ever.

As the Court strengthened constitutional rights favored by conservatives, it modified some of the rights that were prized by liberals. Before the late twentieth century, for example, the Court's cases involving the freedom of speech tended to involve unpopular and relatively powerless speakers such as communists and civil rights protesters. Such cases continued to reach the Court in the late twentieth and early twenty-first centuries, but now they were joined by new kinds of First Amendment cases, cases in which the freedom of speech was wielded not by dissenters but by the wealthy and powerful.

In one group of these cases, the Court used the First Amendment to allow nearly unlimited spending on political campaigns. In *Buckley v. Valeo* (1976), the Court drew a distinction between limits on how much a campaign could *spend* and limits on how much an individual could *contribute* to a campaign. A spending limit, the Court held, was tantamount to a limit on political speech, because virtually every method of communicating with voters requires spending money. A contribution limit, by contrast, restricts speech to a much smaller extent, because contributors who reach the maximum can still express their support for the candidate in other ways. In *Buckley* the Court accordingly upheld the federal limits on campaign contributions but struck down the limits on campaign spending.[17]

The Court continued down this road in *Citizens United v. Federal Election Commission* (2010). For more than a century, Congress had prohibited corporations from spending on political campaigns. The Court had upheld the constitutionality of such legislation as recently as 2003. In *Citizens United*, however, by a 5–4 vote, the Court overruled its prior cases and held that the First Amendment does not allow limits on the amounts corporations can spend on a campaign. Limits on spending were limits on speech, the majority concluded, whether the speaker was an individual or a corporation. Indeed, Anthony Kennedy noted in his majority opinion, the leading newspapers and television networks were corporations, so if the government could restrict corporate spending it could suppress their speech too. The decision happened to be published a few days before President Barack Obama delivered his annual State of the Union address. "Last week," Obama declared, "the Supreme Court reversed a century of law that I believe will open the floodgates for special interests—including foreign corporations—to spend without limit in our elections." In the audience, Justice Samuel Alito was seen on national television mouthing the words "not true." But *Citizens United* did lead to greater corporate spending in political campaigns. Republican candidates were the main beneficiaries. One study, for instance, found that after *Citizens United*, Republicans were six percentage points more likely to be elected to state legislatures.[18]

A few years later, in *McCutcheon v. Federal Election Commission* (2014), the Court held that the First Amendment prohibits the government from restricting aggregate campaign *contributions* as well as campaign spending. A federal statute allowed a single individual to contribute no more than $123,200 in total to candidates and political action committees during each two-year election cycle. The Court determined that this limit was an unconstitutional abridgment of the freedom of speech. "Congress may not regulate contributions simply to reduce the amount of money in politics, or to restrict the political participation of some in order to enhance the relative influence of others," Chief Justice John Roberts explained for the majority. Restricting campaign contributions, he reasoned, is permissible only to prevent corruption, in the sense of a literal exchange of money for services. Otherwise, limits on aggregate contributions "deny the individual all ability to exercise his expressive and associational rights by contributing to someone who will advocate for his policy preferences." Roberts was joined by the Court's other four Republican appointees. The four Democrats dissented. The majority defined "corruption" too narrowly, Stephen Breyer insisted. "In reality," he argued, "as the history of campaign finance reform shows and as our earlier cases on the subject have recognized, the anticorruption interest that drives Congress to regulate campaign contributions is a far broader, more important interest than the plurality acknowledges. It is an interest in maintaining the integrity of our public governmental institutions."[19] The freedom of speech had once protected the voices of the weak; now it was ensuring that the wealthy could bring their full power to bear in the political process.

Meanwhile, the Court also strengthened the First Amendment rights of advertisers. Advertisements had once received no First Amendment protection at all. In the 1970s, the Court first brought advertising, rebranded as "commercial speech," under the umbrella of the First Amendment. By the turn of the century, the Court made the freedom of speech in the market-place nearly as robust as the freedom of speech in other walks of life. Beer companies enjoyed a new constitutional right to advertise the alcoholic con-tent of their products. Casinos had the right to advertise on radio and tel-evision. And the First Amendment guaranteed pharmaceutical companies the ability to advertise drugs. "Speech in aid of pharmaceutical marketing," Kennedy explained, "is a form of expression protected by the Free Speech Clause of the First Amendment." All commercial transactions involve speech of one kind or another, so the liberal justices worried that the Court was inventing a new kind of immunity from commercial regulation under the cover of the First Amendment. Breyer accused his conservative colleagues of surreptitiously reviving *Lochner*-style economic liberties. "Given the sheer quantity of regulatory initiatives that touch upon commercial messages," he charged, "the Court's vision of its reviewing task threatens to return us to a happily bygone era when judges scrutinized legislation for its interference with economic liberty."[20] Advertisers, like campaign contributors, were new beneficiaries of the freedom of speech.

Another new group of beneficiaries were opponents of public sector labor unions. Unions collect dues from workers and use the money to advocate for higher wages and better working conditions. Dues are typically manda-tory. If they were optional, many workers would choose not to pay because they could get the benefit of the union's advocacy for free. The result would be the death of the union. When the workers are employed in the private sector, mandatory union dues raise no First Amendment issue, because the First Amendment limits only the power of the government. In public sector unions, by contrast, dues are mandated by the government. Does it violate the First Amendment to compel public employees to pay dues to support the union's activities? In *Abood v. Detroit Board of Education* (1977), the Court answered this question by dividing union activities into two kinds. The Court decided that employees *can* be compelled to pay dues to support the union's efforts in negotiating wages and other terms of employment, but that employees *cannot* be compelled to pay dues to support the union's advocacy on political or ideological matters.[21]

As the Court grew more conservative, opponents of public sector labor unions began to urge the overruling of *Abood*, in order to cause the death of unions by starving them of dues. This effort finally paid off in *Janus v. AFSCME* (2018), when the Court, in a 5–4 decision on straight party lines, overruled *Abood* and held that public sector employees could not be required to support labor unions for any purpose, including the unions' efforts to negotiate wages. When "speech is compelled," Samuel Alito declared, "individuals are coerced into betraying their convictions." The union negotiated on behalf of all employees, he acknowledged, but that was no reason to force the employees to pay for it. "Many private groups speak out with the objective of obtaining government action that will have the effect of benefiting nonmembers," he noted. "May all those who are thought to benefit from such efforts be compelled to subsidize this speech? Suppose that a particular group lobbies or speaks out on behalf of what it thinks are the needs of senior citizens or veterans or physicians, to take just a few examples. Could the government require that all seniors, veterans, or doctors pay for that service even if they object? It has never been thought that this is permissible." The First Amendment accordingly barred the government from making union dues mandatory for public employees.[22]

In dissent, Elena Kagan accused the majority of "weaponizing the First Amendment, in a way that unleashes judges, now and in the future, to intervene in economic and regulatory policy." The extent to which labor unions were appropriate in the public sector was a vigorously contested public policy question, she pointed out, but now "the majority has chosen the winners by turning the First Amendment into a sword, and using it against workaday economic and regulatory policy." Kagan saw dire possibilities in the conservative justices' eagerness to use the freedom of speech to intervene in policy debates on behalf of the powerful. "Speech is everywhere," she noted—"a part of every human activity (employment, health care, securities trading, you name it). For that reason, almost all economic and regulatory policy affects or touches speech. So the majority's road runs long. And at every stop are black-robed rulers overriding citizens' choices. The First Amendment was meant for better things. It was meant not to undermine but to protect democratic governance."[23] Half a century before, when the justices were more liberal than the country as a whole, freedom of speech usually helped the weak. Now it helped the powerful.

The Court engineered a similar reversal regarding the Equal Protection Clause of the Fourteenth Amendment. Once the basis of rights for black people, the Equal Protection Clause increasingly became a source of rights for white people instead.

The school desegregation cases of the mid-twentieth century, especially *Brown v. Board of Education*, had turned the justices into heroes on the left and villains among much of the right. But desegregation's momentum was flagging by the end of the century, and in *Parents Involved v. Seattle* (2007), the Court just about killed it off by deciding that school districts violate the constitutional rights of white children by taking race into account when assigning pupils to schools. To prevent its schools from being segregated due to residential patterns, the Seattle school district allocated some spots in schools to students of a race that was underrepresented at the school. By a vote of 5–4, the Court determined that the district's consideration of students' race in assigning them to schools violated the Equal Protection Clause. A school district could take students' race into account as a means of remedying past discrimination, Roberts reasoned in his opinion for the Court, but not as a means of achieving racial balance for its own sake. "Accepting racial balancing as a compelling state interest would justify the imposition of racial proportionality throughout American society," Roberts worried. He likened Seattle's attempt to integrate its schools with the earlier efforts of southern school districts to segregate theirs. "Before *Brown*," he recalled, "schoolchildren were told where they could and could not go to school based on the color of their skin. The school districts in these cases have not carried the heavy burden of demonstrating that we should allow this once again—even for very different reasons." Instead, Roberts concluded, "the way to stop discrimination on the basis of race is to stop discriminating on the basis of race." Clarence Thomas agreed that Seattle's approach was "reminiscent of that advocated by the segregationists in *Brown v. Board of Education*," an approach that was "just as wrong today as it was a half century ago."[24]

Writing for the four dissenters, Breyer insisted that "the Equal Protection Clause permits local school boards to use race-conscious criteria to achieve positive race-related goals." He concluded that the Court's decision "risks serious harm to the law and for the Nation" by depriving school districts of the ability to integrate their schools. "The last half century has witnessed great strides toward racial equality, but we have not yet realized the promise of *Brown*," Breyer noted. "To invalidate the plans under review is to threaten the promise of *Brown*." He concluded: "This is a decision that the Court and the Nation will come to regret."[25] At the Court, the old ideal of integration was being eclipsed by a newer ideal of colorblindness. Schools could still take race into account to remedy the effects of legally mandated school segregation, but as the era of legally mandated segregation receded farther into the past, schools were losing their ability to counteract the segregation that remained a persistent fact of life in much of the country.

The Court also put an end to affirmative action in university admissions. The Court nearly abolished it in a pair of 2003 cases, *Gratz v. Bollinger* and *Grutter v. Bollinger*, both of which were constitutional challenges to admissions policies at the University of Michigan. In *Gratz*, white applicants to Michigan's undergraduate program argued that their right to equal protection was violated by the university's points-based method of ranking applications, under which members of minority groups received an extra 20 points toward the 100 points needed for admission. In *Grutter*, white applicants to Michigan's law school mounted a similar challenge to the school's admissions policy, which avoided numbers but instead counted membership in a minority group as a "plus" factor of ambiguous magnitude.[26]

A narrow majority of the justices determined that the undergraduate program's numerical method of affirmative action was unconstitutional, but a different majority approved of the law school's "holistic" method. The key vote belonged to Sandra Day O'Connor, who was the only justice who joined each part of both majority opinions. "It has been 25 years since Justice Powell first approved the use of race to further an interest in student body diversity in the context of public higher education," O'Connor noted, referring to Lewis Powell's opinion for the Court in *Bakke v. University of California*. "Since that time, the number of minority applicants with high grades and test scores has indeed increased. We expect that 25 years from now, the use of racial preferences will no longer be necessary to further the interest approved today."[27]

O'Connor's estimate turned out to be five years too long. In *Students for Fair Admissions v. Harvard* (2023), the Court held affirmative action unconstitutional. "Eliminating racial discrimination means eliminating all of it," John Roberts declared for a majority made up of the Court's six Republican appointees. Universities "have concluded, wrongly, that the touchstone of an individual's identity is not challenges bested, skills built, or lessons learned but the color of their skin. Our constitutional history does not tolerate that choice." In a concurring opinion, Clarence Thomas repeated his oft-expressed distaste for affirmative action. "If our history has taught us anything," he warned, "it has taught us to beware of elites bearing racial theories." The endpoint of affirmative action would not be racial equality, he charged, but rather "a world in which everyone is defined by their skin color, demanding ever-increasing entitlements and preferences on that basis." In dissent, Sonia Sotomayor accused the majority of subverting "the constitutional guarantee of equal protection by further entrenching racial inequality in education," while Ketanji Brown Jackson predicted that the majority's decision would "forestall the end of race-based disparities in this country, making the colorblind world the majority wistfully touts much more difficult to accomplish." Affirmative action had been a hotly contested aspect of elite college admissions for nearly half a century, but now this era was over.[28]

II

As the Court moved to the right, the justices also weakened and even eliminated some of the rights that were favored by liberals. The Court whittled away at the Constitution's protections for criminal defendants. The justices reinterpreted the Voting Rights Act to make it easier to suppress the minority vote.[29] And on the issue that more people cared more deeply about than any other, the Court put an end to the constitutional right to abortion.

In *Planned Parenthood v. Casey* (1992), a coalition of five justices—Harry Blackmun, John Paul Stevens, Sandra Day O'Connor, David Souter, and Anthony Kennedy—had preserved the constitutional right to abortion. Abortion had become a political issue that sharply divided Democrats from Republicans, so it was clear that the path of the Court's abortion jurisprudence would depend on which justices left the Court and which party got to appoint their replacements. The right to abortion gained a sixth vote in 1993 when Ruth Bader Ginsburg replaced Byron White. The appointment of Stephen Breyer as Blackmun's successor in 1994 did not change the vote count, nor did the next new justice, John Roberts, who replaced William Rehnquist in 2005. Supporters of abortion lost a vote, however, in 2006, when Sandra Day O'Connor resigned and was succeeded by Samuel Alito. Alito's appointment made an immediate difference. In 2000, a 5–4 Court, with Kennedy among the dissenters, had struck down Nebraska's ban on "partial-birth" abortions on the ground that it was inconsistent with *Casey*. In 2007, when the Court evaluated the constitutionality of a similar federal statute, Alito had taken O'Connor's place. Now there were five votes to uphold the statute.[30]

But there were not five votes to abolish the right to abortion. Souter and Stevens retired in 2009 and 2010, but their places were taken by Sonia

Sotomayor and Elena Kagan, so the vote on abortion did not change. In *Whole Woman's Health v. Hellerstedt* (2016), the Court reaffirmed the right to abortion while striking down a Texas law that imposed strict qualifications for physicians and hospitals performing abortions. A five-justice majority determined that these requirements had negligible health benefits; their main effect, and likely their true purpose, was simply to make abortions more difficult to obtain.[31] Soon after, Neil Gorsuch took the seat vacated by the death of Antonin Scalia, but this was another like-for-like substitution as far as abortion was concerned. There were still five votes on the Court for a right to abortion: Kennedy, Ginsburg, Breyer, Sotomayor, and Kagan.

Kennedy's retirement in 2018 was the beginning of the end. When Brett Kavanaugh joined the Court in Kennedy's place, now there were just four votes for abortion. That number soon dropped to three when Ruth Bader Ginsburg died in 2020 and was replaced by Amy Coney Barrett. In some states, legislatures wasted no time in enacting new restrictions for the purpose of provoking litigation that could get the issue to the Court.[32] One such law was enacted in Mississippi. It prohibited nearly all abortions after fifteen weeks of pregnancy. Mississippi's new law was clearly unconstitutional under *Roe v. Wade* and *Planned Parenthood v. Casey*, but that was precisely its purpose—to give the Court a case in which it could overrule *Roe* and *Casey*. After the lower courts duly found the law unconstitutional, Mississippi asked the Court to hear the case. When the Court agreed to hear it, there was little doubt as to what the result would be.

The case was called *Dobbs v. Jackson Women's Health Organization* (2022) because the nominal parties were Thomas Dobbs, the physician and medical school professor in charge of Mississippi's department of public health, and the Jackson Women's Health Organization, the state's only abortion clinic. But once the case reached the Court it was a clash between two loose agglomerations of lawyers, one in favor of legal abortion and one opposed to it, who had been battling each other in similar cases for decades. After fifty years of abortion litigation, in any event, it scarcely mattered what the lawyers said. None of the justices was thinking about the issue for the first time. The justices, like most thoughtful people with legal training, already had views about whether the Constitution protects the right to obtain an abortion, and nothing the lawyers said was likely to change their minds.

As expected, the Court overruled *Roe* and *Casey* and held that there is no constitutional right to abortion. "The Constitution makes no reference to abortion, and no such right is implicitly protected by any constitutional provision," Samuel Alito declared in his opinion for the Court. "Until the latter part of the 20th century," he continued, "such a right was entirely unknown in American law." The same was true of other rights the Court had deemed an implicit part of the "liberty" protected by the Due Process Clause of the Fourteenth Amendment, such as the rights to use contraception and to engage in private consensual sexual relations, "but abortion is fundamentally different," Alito argued, because abortion destroys what *Roe* and *Casey* "called 'fetal life' and what the law now before us describes as an 'unborn human being.'" Alito acknowledged that the Court is ordinarily reluctant to overrule its precedents, but he insisted that this general reluctance could not save "*Roe*'s abuse of judicial authority. *Roe* was egregiously wrong from the start. Its reasoning was exceptionally weak, and the decision has had damaging consequences. And far from bringing about a national settlement of the abortion issue, *Roe* and *Casey* have enflamed debate and deepened division. It is time," he concluded, "to heed the Constitution and return the issue of abortion to the people's elected representatives."[33]

The view taken by Alito was one side of a half-century-old debate. The people on the other side, he suggested, had improperly let their preference for legal abortion guide their understanding of the Fourteenth Amendment. "We must guard against the natural human tendency to confuse what that Amendment protects with our own ardent views about the liberty that Americans should enjoy," Alito cautioned. When the Court had succumbed to that temptation in the past, he explained, "it has fallen into the freewheeling judicial policymaking that characterized discredited decisions such as *Lochner v. New York*." He finished by repeating a theme that had been emphasized for fifty years in opinions by justices such as Antonin Scalia and William Rehnquist—that in a democracy, basic moral issues should be decided by the voters and not by the nine unelected justices of the Supreme Court. "Abortion presents a profound moral question," Alito affirmed. "The Constitution does not prohibit the citizens of each State from regulating or prohibiting abortion. *Roe* and *Casey* arrogated that authority. We now overrule those decisions and return that authority to the people."[34]

Alito spoke for a majority of five justices that also included Clarence Thomas and the three newest justices—Neil Gorsuch, Brett Kavanaugh, and Amy Coney Barrett. In a separate concurring opinion, Thomas argued that Alito had not gone far enough. Rather than distinguishing *Roe* and *Casey* from the other cases in which the Court had located rights in the liberty protected by the Due Process Clause, Thomas urged the Court to overrule all the other cases as well. The Due Process Clause, in his view, was meant to protect no substantive rights at all, but "merely required executive and judicial actors to comply with legislative enactments and the common law when depriving a person of life, liberty, or property." The Clause did not protect a right to an abortion, but that was not because abortion differed from contraception or sex. It was because the Clause did not protect a right to anything.[35]

John Roberts reached the same result as the majority—he found the Mississippi law constitutional—but he did not join the majority opinion because, characteristically, he preferred to decide the case on a narrower ground. It was not necessary to abolish the constitutional right to abortion, he argued, because the state law did not infringe that right. "Mississippi's law allows a woman three months to obtain an abortion, well beyond the point at which it is considered 'late' to discover a pregnancy," Roberts reasoned. The constitutional right should "extend far enough to ensure a reasonable opportunity to choose" an abortion, but the law provided women with an adequate opportunity.[36]

Figure 16.1 Protesters outside the Supreme Court on June 24, 2022, the day of the Court's decision in *Dobbs v. Jackson Women's Health Organization.* Photograph by Ted Eytan. Available on Wikimedia Commons under Creative Commons license at creativecommons.org/licenses/by-sa/2.0/deed.en.

The Court's three Democrats—Stephen Breyer, Sonia Sotomayor, and Elena Kagan—dissented in an opinion jointly credited to all three, a nod to the joint opinion of Sandra Day O'Connor, Anthony Kennedy, and David Souter that had preserved the right to abortion in *Planned Parenthood v. Casey*. "The Court reverses course today for one reason and one reason only: because the composition of this Court has changed," the dissenters charged. The premise of the legal system was "that decisions are founded in the law rather than in the proclivities of individuals," but "today, the proclivities of individuals rule." They argued that *Roe* and *Casey* had been correctly decided, and that even if they had not been, there was no justification for overruling them because American women had relied for decades on their continued existence. "The disruption of overturning *Roe* and *Casey* will therefore be profound," they wrote. "Abortion is a common medical procedure and a familiar experience in women's lives." Two generations of women had grown to adulthood relying

> on their ability to control and time pregnancies when making countless life decisions: where to live, whether and how to invest in education or careers, how to allocate financial resources, and how to approach intimate and family relationships. Women may count on abortion access for when contraception fails. They may count on abortion access for when contraception cannot be used, for example, if they were raped. They may count on abortion for when something changes in the midst of a pregnancy, whether it involves family or financial circumstances, unanticipated medical complications, or heartbreaking fetal diagnoses. Taking away the right to abortion, as the majority does today, destroys all those individual plans and expectations. In so doing, it diminishes women's opportunities to participate fully and equally in the Nation's political, social, and economic life.

In short, they concluded, "women have relied on *Roe* and *Casey* in this way for 50 years. Many have never known anything else. When *Roe* and *Casey* disappear, the loss of power, control, and dignity will be immense."[37]

Dobbs was as deeply felt on both sides of the abortion debate as *Roe* had been a half-century before. "It seems like an answer to a prayer," exulted one abortion opponent. The archbishop of Baltimore gave his "gratitude to the Lord, and gratitude to so many people, in the church and beyond the church, who have worked and prayed so hard for this day to come." Those on the other side of the debate had expected the Court to overrule *Roe*, but *Dobbs* was still a hard blow to take. The Court's decision was "devastating," acknowledged Mini Timmaraju, the president of NARAL, the country's oldest abortion rights organization. "This decision is the worst-case scenario." The law professor Reva Siegel wrote of Alito's majority opinion that "the justices' efforts to hide their views about abortion in a story about the Constitution's history and traditions reveals to us their view of women."[38] *Roe* and *Casey* had not ended the national debate about abortion and the Constitution, and neither would *Dobbs*.

III

The conservative Court of the late nineteenth and early twentieth centuries interpreted the Constitution to limit the federal government's regulatory power. The Court abandoned this narrow view of federal authority in the 1930s and 1940s. For the next half-century and more, Congress had free rein to pass laws on just about any matter it deemed deserving of regulation. In the 1990s, however, the Court reversed course. The conservative justices revived long-dormant ideas about the Constitution's limits on federal power.

In the Gun-Free School Zones Act, for example, Congress made it a federal crime to possess a firearm at or near a school. Congress had enacted many similar statutes over the preceding decades, including laws criminalizing the possession of guns in various circumstances. The constitutional grounding for these statutes was the Commerce Clause, which gives Congress the power to regulate interstate commerce. The Court had not struck down a statute for exceeding Congress's Commerce Clause power since the 1930s, so no one paid much attention to the Commerce Clause when Congress prohibited guns near schools.

They would pay attention now. In *United States v. Lopez* (1995), the Court held, by a 5–4 vote, that Congress lacked the power to enact the Gun-Free School Zones Act. The law "has nothing to do with 'commerce' or any sort of economic enterprise, however broadly one might define those terms," William Rehnquist wrote for the Court. He rejected the notion that Congress's authority could be based on the potential economic effects of gun violence in schools. Under that reasoning, he noted, "Congress could regulate any activity that it found was related to the economic productivity of individual citizens: family law (including marriage, divorce, and child custody), for example." And that was too farfetched to contemplate. "If we were to accept the Government's arguments," Rehnquist concluded, "we are hard pressed to posit any activity by an individual that Congress is without power to regulate." In dissent, Stephen Breyer pointed out that "the statute falls well within the scope of the commerce power as this Court has understood that power over the last half century," and David Souter accused the majority of returning "to the untenable jurisprudence from which the Court extricated itself almost 60 years ago."[39] For constitutional lawyers, it was as if a dinosaur had roared back to life.

The dinosaur returned in *United States v. Morrison* (2000), when the same five-justice majority struck down the Violence Against Women Act, which provided a federal civil remedy for women who were victims of gender-motivated violence. Rehnquist's opinion for the Court repeated the majority's reasoning in *Lopez*. "Gender-motivated crimes of violence are not, in any sense of the phrase, economic activity," he again explained. Crimes against women might affect interstate commerce by preventing women from working, he acknowledged, but that was true of many crimes. "If Congress may regulate gender-motivated violence, it would be able to regulate murder or any other type of violence," Rehnquist worried. "We accordingly reject the argument that Congress may regulate noneconomic, violent criminal conduct based solely on that conduct's aggregate effect on interstate commerce. The Constitution requires a distinction between what is truly national and what is truly local." Dissenting once again, Souter observed that the Violence Against Women Act "would have passed muster at any time between *Wickard* [*v. Filburn*] in 1942 and *Lopez* in 1995," a period when the Court interpreted the Commerce Clause to allow Congress to regulate "all activity that, when aggregated, has a substantial effect on interstate commerce." Why, Souter wondered, "is the majority tempted to reject the lesson so painfully learned?"[40]

Many of the most important federal statutes of the twentieth century rested on Congress's power over interstate commerce, so the Court's decisions in *Lopez* and *Morrison* threatened to overturn wide swathes of the law. To pick one well-known example, the Civil Rights of 1964, the main federal statute prohibiting discrimination, had been an exercise of Congress's commerce power. Was discrimination closely enough related to economic activity to satisfy the Court's newly stringent test? Many federal laws prohibited the possession of drugs. The *sale* of drugs was no doubt an economic activity, but what about mere possession? The Court's revival of old constitutional limits on the federal government's authority raised all sorts of questions.

Some of these questions were answered in *Gonzales v. Raich* (2005), when the Court held that Congress does have the power to prohibit the possession of marijuana. All four of the dissenters from *Lopez* and *Morrison* were in the majority in *Raich*. Three of the five members of the *Lopez* and *Morrison* majorities dissented in *Raich*. Only Antonin Scalia and Anthony Kennedy found a difference for Commerce Clause purposes between *Raich* and the other two cases. "Drugs like marijuana are fungible commodities," Scalia reasoned. "Marijuana that is grown at home and possessed for personal use is never more than an instant from the interstate market." That was enough, he concluded, to give Congress the authority to regulate the possession of marijuana in the home, even though Congress could not regulate guns at school or violence against women.[41] The Court was once again developing an intricate Commerce Clause jurisprudence with distinctions as fine as the ones that had permeated its decisions a century before.

The Court's new (or rather, old) view of the Commerce Clause influenced one of the major political issues of the era in 2012, when the Court assessed the constitutionality of the Patient Protection and Affordable Care Act, the law better known as Obamacare. The Affordable Care Act included a complex assortment of provisions, one of which required most people to purchase health insurance. The Court held, again by a 5–4 vote, that the Commerce Clause did not give Congress the authority to enact this provision, because the clause did not empower Congress to compel people to buy a product. "The power to *regulate* commerce presupposes the existence of commercial activity to be regulated," John Roberts reasoned. But the Affordable Care Act "does not regulate existing commercial activity. It instead compels individuals to *become* active in commerce by purchasing a product." He shuddered at the implications of allowing Congress to require the purchase of insurance. "Every day individuals do not do an infinite number of things," he noted. "Allowing Congress to justify federal regulation by pointing to the effect of inaction on commerce would bring countless decisions an individual could *potentially* make within the scope of federal regulation, and—under the Government's theory—empower Congress to make those decisions for him." Roberts used an analogy that had been debated for years among foes and supporters of mandatory health insurance. Many people are unhealthy because they do not eat a balanced diet, he observed, and the cost of their medical care affects interstate commerce. "Under the Government's theory, Congress could address the diet problem by ordering everyone to buy vegetables," Roberts scoffed. "That is not the country the Framers of our Constitution envisioned."[42]

In dissent, the four Democratic appointees provided the now-familiar rejoinder: the Court's conservative majority was reviving metaphysical distinctions the Court had abandoned with good reason in the first half of the twentieth century. The majority's view bears "a disquieting resemblance to those long-overruled decisions," Ruth Bader Ginsburg lamented. She wondered why the majority would "strive so mightily to hem in Congress' capacity to meet the new problems arising constantly in our ever-developing modern economy."[43] In the end, the Court upheld the Affordable Care Act despite its narrow interpretation of the Commerce Clause. Congress did not need to rely on the Commerce Clause, Roberts explained, because the monetary penalty for failing to obtain insurance could be characterized as a tax, and the Constitution includes another clause that authorizes Congress to impose taxes. None of the other Republican appointees agreed with him, but Roberts's view of Congress's taxing power made him the fifth vote to find the Affordable Care Act constitutional.

Reinterpreting the Commerce Clause was one way the conservative justices constrained the federal government's reach. Another way was to breathe life into the Tenth Amendment, which says that powers not granted to the federal government by the Constitution are reserved to the states or to the people. The Tenth Amendment had never played much of a role in American law until the 1990s. It was understood as little more than a tautology: if the Constitution did not say the federal government could do something, then the federal government could not do it. In *New York v. United States* (1992), however, the Court gave the Tenth Amendment real bite, by holding that it bars the federal government from commanding the state governments to regulate. The effect of the case was to invalidate part of a federal statute that required states to provide for the safe disposal of radioactive waste. Applying the same new principle, the Court struck down a law requiring state officials to perform background checks on handgun purchasers, and then another law barring the states from legalizing gambling on sports.[44] In the wake of the latter decision, *Murphy v. NCAA* (2018), sports betting quickly became lawful in much of the country.

Potentially the farthest-reaching of the Court's new restraints on the power of the federal government was the "major questions" doctrine enunciated in *West Virginia v. EPA* (2022). In the early United States, when the government was smaller, Congress could govern the country without much assistance from an administrative state, but the range of matters over which Congress legislates has grown so vast and complex that in many fields, such as environmental protection, Congress now establishes general rules by statute and lets administrative agencies fill in the details by issuing regulations. In *Chevron v. NRDC* (1984), the Court facilitated this delegation of authority by requiring judges to defer to agencies' interpretations of the statutes they implemented.[45] As the Court grew more conservative, however, it became more receptive to arguments that would invalidate agency regulations.

In *West Virginia v. EPA*, the Court barred the Environmental Protection Agency from requiring coal-fired power plants to switch to cleaner forms of energy production. Congress had enacted a statute instructing the EPA to regulate power plants by setting "a standard of performance" for the plants' emission of pollutants, a standard that would reflect "the best system of emission reduction" available. The EPA, acting under what it thought was the authority of this statute, determined that the best way to reduce pollutants would be to substitute wind and solar energy for coal. But the Court held that the EPA could not impose this requirement. The six Republican appointees were in the majority, while the three Democratic appointees dissented. Ordinarily, Roberts explained for the majority, the Court would defer to an agency's interpretation of its governing statute. In cases involving "major questions," however, the Court would require "clear congressional authorization" before an agency could regulate. Roberts determined that "this is a major questions case," and that the statute was not clear enough. The result of the Court's decision, the dissenters complained, was to rob the EPA of the ability to respond to climate change, "the most pressing environmental challenge of our time."[46]

By the 2020s, the federal government's regulatory power was hemmed in by more Court-created constraints than it had been since the 1930s. In virtually all these cases the majority consisted solely of justices appointed by Republican presidents. Just as a century before, it was hard not to notice that nearly all the measures the Court invalidated were laws favored by the left and opposed by the right.

IV

In some areas, however, the Court reached decisions that could scarcely be described as conservative. The leading examples were its decisions involving the rights of gay and lesbian people.

Gay sex, or what was once called sodomy, was illegal in most of the United States until the mid-twentieth century, although this prohibition was rarely enforced. As homosexuality came to be more accepted in the second half of the twentieth century, the laws against it were gradually repealed, until by the 1980s only about half the states still had sodomy laws on the books. And as the Court established a constitutional right to privacy that encompassed matters such as contraception and abortion, it became possible to suppose that there might also be a constitutional right to private consensual same-sex intimacy. The issue first reached the Court in *Bowers v. Hardwick* (1986), a constitutional challenge to Georgia's sodomy law brought by one of the very few people who had been charged with violating it.

After oral argument in *Bowers*, the Court at first voted 5 to 4 to hold Georgia's law unconstitutional. William Brennan began writing the majority opinion. But Lewis Powell, one of the five justices in the majority, was having second thoughts. He worked out his inner conflict in anguished notes that he wrote for his own benefit, notes he did not share with his colleagues but which he left in his files for historians. "In view of my age, general background, and convictions as to what is best for society, I think a good deal can be said for the validity of statutes that criminalize sodomy," Powell began. "If it becomes sufficiently wide-spread, civilization itself will be severely weakened as the perpetuation of the human race depends on normal sexual relations just as is true in the animal world." On the other hand, he continued, "if I were in the state legislature I would vote to decriminalize sodomy. It is widely prevalent in some places (e.g., San Francisco), and is a criminal statute that is never enforced." Powell was equally torn about whether sodomy laws violated the Constitution. "There is nothing explicit in the Constitution on this subject," he noted. "Yet, this Court has frequently recognized that there are human rights that can be derived from the concept of liberty," such as the right to abortion, which Powell had supported in *Roe v. Wade*. But "if sodomy is to be decriminalized on constitutional grounds," he worried, "what about incest, bigamy and adultery," which were also widely prohibited? Would the Constitution protect them too? Powell's law clerks recalled that he had difficulty understanding why someone would be gay. He believed he had never met a gay person, but at the time few gay lawyers revealed their sexuality at work. In fact, one of Powell's clerks that year, Cabell Chinnis, was gay, as were some of Powell's clerks in previous years. After going back and forth in his own mind, Powell switched his vote.[47] Now there were five votes to uphold Georgia's sodomy law.

Chief Justice Warren Burger assigned the majority opinion to Byron White. Burger had a strong distaste for homosexuality. He urged White to discuss the history of sodomy laws in the opinion. "This surely is not merely a matter of 'sexual preference' as we might discuss preferences among art, literature, or wines," Burger insisted. "We are talking about conduct that for thousands of years has been uniformly condemned as immoral." White wrote an opinion that recited this history as support for the conclusion that the claim of a constitutional right to same-sex intimacy "is, at best, facetious." Laws prohibiting sodomy based on the community's moral disapproval "have ancient roots," he noted. "If all laws representing essentially moral choices are to be invalidated under the Due Process Clause, the courts will be very busy indeed." White's opinion in *Bowers* was "one of the worst opinions he ever wrote," Harry Blackmun was to say. "There's no analysis in it." A few years later, after he had retired, Powell regretted changing his mind. "I think I probably made a mistake in that one," he told a group of law students. But it was too late to make a difference. Powell's comments were "an instance where the old axiom 'better late than never' isn't true," remarked William Rubenstein, the director of the American Civil Liberties Union's Lesbian and Gay Rights Project. "It's good that we have his vote now. It's too bad that it's now."[48]

But societal attitudes toward homosexuality continued to change. In 1982, a Gallup poll found that only 34% of respondents considered it "an acceptable alternative lifestyle," but that figure rose to 44% in 1996 and 54% by 2003. In 1985, only 24% of respondents were aware from personal conversation that a friend, relative, or coworker was gay or lesbian. In 1998 the figure was 37%. By 2003 it reached 56%.[49] Homosexuality was losing its strangeness and its moral taint and becoming an ordinary part of life. As society changed, the Court changed too.

Ten years after *Bowers v. Hardwick*, the issue returned to the Court in *Romer v. Evans* (1996). After several Colorado cities enacted ordinances banning discrimination on the basis of sexual orientation, Coloradans voted to amend their state constitution to prohibit such ordinances. This time, a six-justice majority held that Colorado's new constitutional provision violated the federal Constitution's Equal Protection Clause. The majority included Sandra Day O'Connor, who had joined the Court's opinion in *Bowers* but whose views had evidently evolved since then. The majority opinion in *Romer v. Evans* was written by a justice who would become an unexpected champion of gay rights, Anthony Kennedy. Nothing in Kennedy's background suggested he would assume this role. But his opinion was a ringing defense of the equality of all people, whatever their sexual orientation. Colorado's new constitutional amendment "seems inexplicable by anything but animus toward the class it affects," Kennedy declared. The amendment "classifies homosexuals not to further a proper legislative end but to make them unequal to everyone else. This Colorado cannot do. A State cannot so deem a class of persons a stranger to its laws."[50]

In dissent, Antonin Scalia emphasized a point that would be his recurring theme in future cases—that the Court was unjustifiably picking a winner in the culture wars by imposing the values of secular urban elites on the rest of the country. Coloradans are "*entitled* to be hostile toward homosexual conduct," Scalia insisted. They were merely expressing their "moral disapproval of homosexual conduct, the same sort of moral disapproval that produced the centuries-old criminal laws that we held constitutional in *Bowers.*" But Scalia feared that these traditional values were under attack from a wealthy and powerful gay elite. "The problem," he reasoned, "is that, because those who engage in homosexual conduct tend to reside in disproportionate numbers in certain communities, have high disposable income, and, of course, care about homosexual-rights issues much more ardently than the public at large, they possess political power much greater than their numbers, both locally and statewide. Quite understandably, they devote this political power to achieving not merely a grudging social toleration, but full social acceptance, of homosexuality." Worst of all, the Court was helping them. "I think it no business of the courts (as opposed to the political branches) to take sides in this culture war," Scalia explained. "But the Court today has done so, not only by inventing a novel and extravagant constitutional doctrine to take the victory away from traditional forces, but even by verbally disparaging as bigotry adherence to traditional attitudes." And Scalia knew why the justices in the majority had chosen the gay side over the traditional side. It was because they had adopted

the views and values of the lawyer class from which the Court's Members are drawn. How that class feels about homosexuality will be evident to anyone who wishes to interview job applicants at virtually any of the Nation's law schools. The interviewer may refuse to offer a job because the applicant is a Republican; because he is an adulterer; because he went to the wrong prep school or belongs to the wrong country club; because he eats snails; because he is a womanizer; because she wears real-animal fur; or even because he hates the Chicago Cubs. But if the interviewer should wish not to be an associate or partner of an applicant because he disapproves of the applicant's homosexuality, *then* he will have violated the pledge which the Association of American Law Schools requires all its member schools to exact from job interviewers: "assurance of the employer's willingness" to hire homosexuals.

"Today's opinion has no foundation in American constitutional law, and barely pretends to," Scalia concluded. Colorado's constitutional amendment "is designed to prevent piecemeal deterioration of the sexual morality favored by a majority of Coloradans, and is not only an appropriate means to that legitimate end, but a means that Americans have employed before."[51]

Romer received the same mixed reviews as all the Court's decisions on divisive issues. Supporters called it "their most important victory ever," while opponents despaired that it was "truly chilling." The now-retired Harry Blackmun, who had received an enormous volume of angry letters and even death threats after writing the Court's opinion in *Roe v. Wade*, wrote to Kennedy that his opinion in *Romer* "took courage. You undoubtedly now will receive a lot of critical and even hateful mail. I have had that experience and still receive letters, some of them abusive, in almost every mail. Hang in there." Kennedy responded: "No one told us it was an easy job when we signed on."[52]

As Scalia pointed out, *Romer v. Evans* was hard to reconcile with *Bowers v. Hardwick*. If the Constitution requires treating gay and straight people equally, how could it be constitutional to criminalize homosexuality? The Court resolved this inconsistency in *Lawrence v. Texas* (2003), when the same six-justice majority overruled *Bowers* and held that the constitutional right to privacy includes a right to consensual same-sex intimacy. Kennedy spoke again for the Court. "When sexuality finds overt expression in intimate conduct with another person, the conduct can be but one element in a personal bond that is more enduring," he wrote. "The liberty protected by the Constitution allows homosexual persons the right to make this choice." Gay people "are entitled to respect for their private lives," he continued. "The State cannot demean their existence or control their destiny by making their private sexual conduct a crime." Kennedy concluded that "*Bowers* was not correct when it was decided, and it is not correct today."[53]

Scalia dissented again, with a renewed emphasis on what he saw as the Court's illegitimate intervention in a cultural debate. "Today's opinion is the product of a Court, which is the product of a law-profession culture, that has largely signed on to the so-called homosexual agenda, by which I mean the agenda promoted by some homosexual activists directed at eliminating the moral opprobrium that has traditionally attached to homosexual conduct," Scalia complained. "The Court has taken sides in the culture war, departing from its role of assuring, as neutral observer, that the democratic rules of engagement are observed. Many Americans do not want persons who openly engage in homosexual conduct as partners in their business, as scoutmasters for their children, as teachers in their children's schools, or as boarders in their home. They view this as protecting themselves and their families from a lifestyle that they believe to be immoral and destructive." Scalia foresaw dire consequences. If moral opprobrium was not a good enough reason to prohibit homosexuality, he worried, on what ground could same-sex marriage be prohibited? Kennedy protested in his majority opinion that the decision had no implications for same-sex marriage, but Scalia's prediction would be proven correct.[54]

Popular support for same-sex marriage was growing rapidly. In 1996, the year the Court decided *Romer*, only 27% of those polled thought same-sex marriages should be given official recognition. But supporters outnumbered opponents by 2011, and the trend would continue, until by 2022, 71% favored recognizing same-sex marriage. Some states began granting official recognition to same-sex marriages. In response, Congress enacted the Defense of Marriage Act, a statute barring same-sex spouses from receiving the federal benefits available to spouses in traditional marriages.[55]

A 5–4 Court held this statute unconstitutional in *United States v. Windsor* (2013). "The Constitution's guarantee of equality must at the very least mean that a bare congressional desire to harm a politically unpopular group cannot justify disparate treatment of that group," Kennedy reasoned, in an opinion much like the one he had written seventeen years before in *Romer*. The Defense of Marriage Act "undermines both the public and private significance of state-sanctioned same-sex marriages; for it tells those couples, and all the world, that their otherwise valid marriages are unworthy of federal recognition." Scalia reprised his earlier dissents. "The Constitution does not forbid the government to enforce traditional moral and sexual norms," he insisted. "It is enough to say that the Constitution neither requires nor forbids our society to approve of same-sex marriage." He warned once again that a constitutional right to same-sex marriage was just around the corner. "It takes real cheek for today's majority to assure us, as it is going out the door, that a constitutional requirement to give formal recognition to same-sex marriage is not at issue here—when what has preceded that assurance is a lecture on how superior the majority's moral judgment in favor of same-sex marriage is to the Congress's hateful moral judgment against it," Scalia scoffed. "I promise you this: The only thing that will 'confine' the Court's holding is its sense of what it can get away with."[56]

Only two years later, by the same 5–4 vote, the Court established a constitutional right to same-sex marriage in *Obergefell v. Hodges* (2015). Kennedy again wrote the majority opinion. "There is no difference between same- and opposite-sex couples," he argued. Yet because they were not allowed to marry in many states, "same-sex couples are denied the constellation of benefits that the States have linked to marriage. This harm results in more than just material burdens. Same-sex couples are consigned to an instability many opposite-sex couples would deem intolerable in their own lives." He concluded that "the limitation of marriage to opposite-sex couples may long have seemed natural and just, but its inconsistency with the central meaning of the fundamental right to marry is now manifest." He acknowledged that the Court was departing from a long tradition, but he noted that there were equally long traditions that were now deemed unconstitutional, such as race discrimination and the prohibition of homosexuality. "If rights were defined by who exercised them in the past," Kennedy reasoned, "then received practices could serve as their own continued justification and new groups could not invoke rights once denied. This Court has rejected that approach."[57]

The dissenters emphasized how undemocratic it was for the Court to take this step. "Many people will rejoice at this decision, and I begrudge none their celebration," John Roberts began. "But for those who believe in a government of laws, not of men, the majority's approach is deeply disheartening." He continued: "Five lawyers have closed the debate and enacted their own vision of marriage as a matter of constitutional law. Stealing this issue from the people will for many cast a cloud over same-sex marriage, making a dramatic social change that much more difficult to accept." The majority "invalidates the marriage laws of more than half the States and orders the transformation of a social institution that has formed the basis of human society for millennia, for the Kalahari Bushmen and the Han Chinese, the Carthaginians and the Aztecs," Roberts observed. "Just who do we think we are?"[58]

Scalia had made the same point in the Court's previous cases involving the rights of gay people. He returned to the theme in *Obergefell*, with an even greater air of exasperation. "A system of government that makes the People

Figure 16.2 Michael DeLeon and Greg Bourke with their son Isaiah outside the Court the day before oral argument in *Obergefell v. Hodges*. DeLeon and Bourke were the plaintiffs in one of the cases consolidated as *Obergefell*. Photograph by Lorie Shaull. Available on Wikimedia Commons under Creative Commons license at creativecommons.org/licenses/by-sa/2.0/deed.en.

subordinate to a committee of nine unelected lawyers does not deserve to be called a democracy," Scalia declared. "To allow the policy question of same-sex marriage to be considered and resolved by a select, patrician, highly unrepresentative panel of nine is to violate a principle even more fundamental than no taxation without representation: no social transformation without representation." He called the decision "a judicial Putsch" undertaken by the five justices in the majority, who "are entirely comfortable concluding that every State violated the Constitution for all of the 135 years between the Fourteenth Amendment's ratification and Massachusetts' permitting of same-sex marriages in 2003. They have discovered in the Fourteenth Amendment a 'fundamental right' overlooked by every person alive at the time of ratification, and almost everyone else in the time since." Scalia even mocked Kennedy's writing style. "The opinion is couched in a style that is as pretentious as its content is egotistic," he sneered. If he ever joined such an opinion, Scalia wrote, "I would hide my head in a bag. The Supreme Court of the United States has descended from the disciplined legal reasoning of John Marshall and Joseph Story to the mystical aphorisms of the fortune cookie."[59]

550 THE MOST POWERFUL COURT IN THE WORLD

The Court wasn't quite following "th' election returns," as the humorist Finley Peter Dunne said of the *Insular Cases* at the turn of the twentieth century. When the Court decided *Obergefell*, most states still did not recognize same-sex marriage. But as in all its cases in this area since *Romer*, the Court was certainly following social trends. Just as changes in conventional white attitudes about racial equality led to *Brown v. Board of Education*, and just as changes in conventional male attitudes about gender equality led to the Court's sex discrimination cases of the 1970s, changes in conventional straight attitudes toward gay people led to *Lawrence v. Texas* and *Obergefell v. Hodges*. These changes in attitudes did not occur by chance. They were the product of many years of difficult political advocacy by members of the groups seeking equality.

Perhaps the most remarkable indication of the otherwise-conservative Court's embrace of changing social norms in this area was *Bostock v. Clayton County* (2020), in which the Court considered a provision of the Civil Rights Act of 1964 that prohibits workplace discrimination on the basis of sex. Everyone agreed that when the statute was enacted, this provision was meant only to bar discrimination against women or men. No one in Congress in 1964 could possibly have intended it also to prohibit discrimination against gay or transgender people, because these issues were not yet on the horizon. In the intervening years, members of Congress had repeatedly proposed adding sexual orientation and gender identity to the list of forbidden types of discrimination, but these efforts had never been successful. Yet a six-justice majority, in an opinion by Neil Gorsuch, one of the Court's more conservative members, decided that the Civil Rights Act *does* prohibit discrimination on the basis of sexual orientation and transgender status. After all, Gorsuch reasoned, an employer treats men and women differently if he fires a male employee, but not a female employee, for being attracted to men. Speaking for the dissenters, Samuel Alito accused the majority of rewriting the statute to reflect current sensibilities rather than interpreting its text. The Court was more conservative than it had been in generations, but it nevertheless extended more legal protection to gay and transgender people than they had ever enjoyed, even more than members of Congress thought they had provided.[60]

V

Nor was the Court particularly conservative when it came to the military. One of the major political issues of the early twenty-first century involved the "war on terror" following the terrorist attacks of September 11, 2001. The government's efforts to capture and detain alleged terrorists soon gave rise to legal questions. The Court confronted several high-profile cases that raised matters of national security the Court had not considered since the Second World War. The paradigmatic conservative position would have been to defer to the military, but the justices repeatedly ruled against the government.

In the first of these cases, *Rasul v. Bush* (2004), the Court had to decide whether foreign nationals imprisoned at the Guantanamo Bay Naval Base in Cuba could challenge the lawfulness of their detention in federal court. The Guantanamo prisoners were in an ambiguous legal status. On one hand, prisoners in the United States, of any nationality, have the right to go to court with a claim that they are being held in prison illegally. On the other hand, during a war, foreign soldiers captured in battle and imprisoned outside the United States have no redress in American courts. This was why the government sent the prisoners to Guantanamo, a naval base located on land leased by the United States government from the government of Cuba. In a 6–3 decision in which Sandra Day O'Connor and Anthony Kennedy sided with the more liberal justices, the Court held that the prisoners at Guantanamo could bring their claims to federal court. "By the express terms of its agreements with Cuba," John Paul Stevens observed in his majority opinion, "the United States exercises complete jurisdiction and control over the Guantanamo Bay Naval Base, and may continue to exercise such control permanently if it so chooses." In dissent, Antonin Scalia accused the majority of hindering the war on terror by unexpectedly changing the law. "Today, the Court springs a trap on the Executive, subjecting Guantanamo Bay to the oversight of the federal courts even though it has never before been thought to be within their jurisdiction—and thus making it a foolish place to have housed alien wartime detainees," Scalia charged. Such a departure from existing law "ought to be unthinkable when the departure has a potentially harmful effect upon the Nation's conduct of a war."[61]

In *Hamdi v. Rumsfeld* (2004), decided the same day as *Rasul*, the Court held that the Constitution requires the government to give an American citizen imprisoned as an enemy combatant in the United States an opportunity to challenge the factual basis for his imprisonment before an impartial decisionmaker. "It is during our most challenging and uncertain moments that our Nation's commitment to due process is most severely tested, and it is in those times that we must preserve our commitment at home to the principles for which we fight abroad." Sandra Day O'Connor declared in the

Court's opinion. Even a person alleged to be fighting against the United States was entitled to his day in court, so "that the errant tourist, embedded journalist, or local aid worker has a chance to prove military error." The vote was again six to three. In his dissenting opinion, Clarence Thomas argued that "the Government's overriding interest in protecting the Nation" outweighed the deprivation of liberty suffered by people the government classified as enemy combatants.[62]

Two years later, in *Hamdan v. Rumsfeld* (2006), the Court once again ruled against the government, this time in a suit filed by Salim Hamdan, a man from Yemen who had worked as a chauffeur for Osama bin Laden, the organizer of the September 11 attacks. The government sought to try Hamdan before a military commission for conspiracy, but the Court held that conspiracy is not an offense triable by a military commission because it is not a violation of the laws of war. Thomas, dissenting again, scoffed at the idea "that conspiracy to massacre innocent civilians does not violate the laws of war." He feared that the Court's conclusion "would sorely hamper the President's ability to confront and defeat a new and deadly enemy."[63]

Finally, in *Boumediene v. Bush* (2008), the Court held that the Constitution guarantees the Guantanamo prisoners the right to challenge their detention in federal court, despite Congress's enactment of a statute purporting to take away that right. "It is true that before today the Court has never held that noncitizens detained by our Government in territory over which another country maintains *de jure* sovereignty have any rights under our Constitution," Kennedy acknowledged. "But the cases before us lack any precise historical parallel. They involve individuals detained by executive order for the duration of a conflict that, if measured from September 11, 2001, to the present, is already among the longest wars in American history." In his dissent, Scalia emphasized what he viewed as the dire practical effect of the Court's decision. "America is at war with radical Islamists," he declared. The Court's extension of constitutional rights to enemy combatants "will almost certainly cause more Americans to be killed."[64]

In previous wars, the Court had deferred to the military's assessment of its needs, but in this one, an otherwise conservative Court repeatedly refused to accept the government's assertions that the demands of national security should take priority over the personal liberty of people accused of being enemies. Perhaps it was because this war, despite the shock of September 11, felt less threatening than earlier wars. The Civil War and the two world wars had profound effects on the daily lives of all Americans, including the justices. The war on terror was fought against an enemy that was weaker and more remote. Despite the dire warnings of Scalia and Thomas, the risks of ruling against the government did not seem quite as serious as they did in previous wars.

<h1 style="text-align:center">VI</h1>

Selecting the justices has always been a political process, and the justices' views on policy matters—their "politics" in one sense of the word—have always influenced their decisions. But the Court has rarely been called upon to participate in "politics" in a different sense of the word, that is, to decide the outcome of an election. As we saw in Chapter 5, five of the justices were members of the fifteen-person electoral commission that decided the presidential election of 1876, but the Court as an institution was not involved in the dispute, and contemporaries did not think of the commission's decision as a decision of the Court. Some of the Court's cases had significant implications for elections, such as the decisions of the 1960s requiring equality of political representation. And some of the Court's cases had important consequences for the president, especially its 1974 decision requiring Richard Nixon to hand over tape recordings of his conversations, a decision that hastened the end of Nixon's presidency. But the Court had never determined the winner of an election.

The idea of asking the Court to decide an election would have seemed incongruous for most of American history. Elections were quintessentially political disputes, not legal ones. In the disputed presidential election of 1876, for example, it does not appear to have occurred to either side to file a lawsuit claiming a legal right to victory. In the aftermath of that controversy, when Congress was debating the bill that became the Electoral Count Act of 1887, one proposal was to have the Court decide presidential elections in which the Senate and the House disagreed on who had won. But this idea attracted little support. "There is a feeling in this country that we ought not to mingle our great judicial tribunal with political questions," Senator John Sherman explained. "It would tend to bring that court into public odium of one or the other of the two great parties."[65] The idea of using litigation to decide an election raised uncomfortable questions. Would the justices vote for the candidate of their own political party? If the incumbent president was one of the contenders, would the president expect loyalty from justices he had appointed? Would these justices prove loyal to the president? These questions were uncomfortable because affirmative answers would suggest that there is no separation between "law" and "politics"—not politics in the sense of policy preferences, but politics in the sense of affiliation with a party or a candidate.

These questions arose twice in the early twenty-first century, once when the Court was asked to decide the presidential election of 2000, and again when it was asked to decide the presidential election of 2020.

The 2000 election was so close that the outcome depended on which candidate received more votes in Florida. When the Florida votes were first counted, Texas Governor George W. Bush, the Republican candidate, won the state by only 1,784 votes over Vice President Al Gore, the Democratic candidate, a margin so narrow that state law required a machine recount. The machine recount resulted in a Bush victory by a mere 229 votes. The next month saw a flurry of litigation in which the Gore campaign sought manual recounts in some counties and the Bush campaign tried to halt the manual recounts. In courthouses throughout Florida and on televisions all over the country, the campaigns argued about all sorts of matters, including how to count a punch-card ballot through which a voter had not completely punched a hole. Eventually, in late November, the state election commission declared Bush the winner, but the Florida Supreme Court partially reversed this decision and ordered additional manual recounts. When the Bush campaign asked the US Supreme Court to review the state supreme court's decision, the Court promptly held oral argument on December 11 and issued a decision the following day. By a vote of five to four, the Court halted the manual recounts ordered by the state supreme court, a ruling that made Bush the president.[66]

The majority opinion bore the designation "per curiam"—written by the Court rather than by any individual justice—but it was largely the work of Anthony Kennedy. The Court held that Florida's manual recount violated the Constitution's Equal Protection Clause because of the absence of statewide rules about how to count ballots in which the "chad"—the bit of paper that gets punched out from a ballot—was only partially dislodged. "The standards for accepting or rejecting contested ballots might vary not only from county to county but indeed within a single county from one recount team to another," the majority worried. "Palm Beach County, for example, began the process with a 1990 guideline which precluded counting completely attached chads, switched to a rule that considered a vote to be legal if any light could be seen through a chad, changed back to the 1990 rule, and then abandoned any pretense of a *per se* rule, only to have a court order that the county consider dimpled chads legal. This is not a process with sufficient guarantees of equal treatment." The Court had never reached such a decision before, and the majority strongly suggested that it would never do so again. "Our consideration is limited to the present circumstances," the per curiam opinion cautioned, "for the problem of equal protection in election processes generally presents many complexities." The solution might have been to send the case back to the state supreme court so it could prescribe statewide rules, but the majority decided that it was too late. Under state law, the majority determined, the recount had to be complete by December 12, and that day had already arrived. The Court accordingly ended the recount.[67]

In a separate concurring opinion, the Court's three most conservative members, William Rehnquist, Antonin Scalia, and Clarence Thomas, argued that the Florida Supreme Court's decision had to be reversed for a second reason as well. The Constitution provides that each state can appoint presidential electors, the people who cast electoral votes, "in such manner as the Legislature thereof may direct." By requiring a recount, the three justices reasoned, the Florida Supreme Court had unconstitutionally adopted a method of choosing electors different from the one directed by the state legislature.[68]

The four dissenters disagreed with different parts of the majority opinion. David Souter and Stephen Breyer agreed that the disparate standards for counting ballots violated the Equal Protection Clause, but they pointed out that there were still six days remaining before the electors would cast their votes for president, time enough for Florida to conduct a manual recount under uniform standards. John Paul Stevens and Ruth Bader Ginsburg thought there was no Equal Protection violation in the first place. All four disagreed with the novel constitutional theory put forward by Rehnquist, Scalia, and Thomas. And all four agreed that, as Stevens put it, "although we may never know with complete certainty the identity of the winner of this year's Presidential election, the identity of the loser is perfectly clear. It is the Nation's confidence in the judge as an impartial guardian of the rule of law."[69]

The five most conservative justices had voted for Bush, the four most liberal for Gore. Normally it was the liberals who favored an expansive reading of the Equal Protection Clause and the conservatives who wanted to augment the power of states to make their own decisions, but in *Bush v. Gore* these usual roles were reversed. It was hard to avoid concluding that the justices' votes had been driven by their preferences as to who should win the election. Adding to this discomfort was the personal connection be-tween the Bush campaign and some of the justices in the majority. Virginia Thomas, Clarence's wife, worked at the Heritage Foundation, a conservative think tank, where she was helping to staff the incoming Bush administration. Rehnquist and O'Connor were both known to be contemplating retirement and hoping a Republican would choose their successors. Eugene Scalia, Antonin's son, was a partner at one of the law firms that represented Bush.[70]

Unsurprisingly, Republicans and Democrats reacted very differently to the decision. On the Republican side, the law professor Nelson Lund insisted that "the Supreme Court acted properly, indeed admirably," by putting an end to a recount that would have been biased in Gore's favor. Democrats did not agree. The "result can be explained only in terms of the conserva-tive majority's partisan political preferences," the legal historian Michael Klarman lamented. "Had all the other facts in the Florida election imbroglio remained the same, but the situation of the two presidential candidates been reversed, does anyone seriously believe that the conservative Justices would have reached the same result?" But there was widespread agreement across the political spectrum that whatever one's view of the result, *Bush v. Gore* was not the Court's finest hour, either as a matter of judicial craft or of political good sense. "If the five justices in the majority had joined with Justices Souter and Breyer, and remanded to the Florida courts to conduct a recount under strict constitutional standards, the near unanimity of the decision would have been vastly reassuring to the American people," concluded Michael McConnell, a prominent constitutional litigator and professor. "Whichever candidate had won would enter office with far greater public confidence in the legitimacy of his election."[71] Instead, *Bush v. Gore* became a famous ex-ample of a Supreme Court decision that seemed to be based on political par-tisanship rather than law.

Twenty years later, Donald Trump and his supporters repeatedly asked the Court to change the result of the 2020 presidential election. Trump had ap-pointed the three newest justices—Neil Gorsuch, Brett Kavanaugh, and Amy Coney Barrett. Unlike many of Trump's executive branch appointments, who lacked the conventional qualifications for their positions, Trump's justices were well-regarded court of appeals judges, not Trump loyalists. They were people who could have been appointed by any Republican president. This was because the Trump administration largely outsourced the selection of justices to the Federalist Society. To be sure, there were occasions during the confirmation process when Trump's nominees seemed to go out of their

way to express a personal attachment to Trump. At a surreal press conference, Kavanaugh implausibly praised Trump's respect for the courts. "I have
witnessed firsthand your appreciation for the vital role of the American judiciary," Kavanaugh intoned, without any audible irony.[72] When Barrett was
sworn in as a justice, a week before Election Day, she appeared with Trump on
a White House balcony on prime-time television, in a ceremony that looked
very much like a campaign commercial. Previous presidents had presented
their nominees to the public in contexts meant to emphasize their dignity
and independence rather than their subservience. Despite these incidents,
however, the justices appointed by Trump were conventional Republican
judges without prior ties to Trump. Many previous justices had joined the
Court with much closer connections to the presidents who appointed them.

By the 2020 election, the justices had already decided several unusual cases
that arose from the idiosyncratic nature of the Trump administration. One
group of cases raised a fundamental but unresolved question: What should a
court do when the government's stated reason for taking an action is plainly
not the true reason? While running for president, Trump called for a "total

Figure 16.3 Amy Coney Barrett, Donald Trump, and their spouses pose on
a White House balcony after Barrett was sworn in as a justice on October
26, 2020, the week before the presidential election. Official White House
photograph by Andrea Hanks.

and complete shutdown of Muslims entering the United States" because "Islam hates us" and the United States was "having problems with Muslims coming into the country." Sure enough, one week after Trump became president, the government barred residents of several Muslim countries from the United States. Because administration lawyers recognized that a "Muslim ban," as Trump called it, would be unlawful if motivated by animus toward Muslims, the claimed justification for the ban was that the nations involved lacked sufficient means of determining whether their own nationals were security threats. *Trump v. Hawaii* (2018), a constitutional challenge to the measure, turned on which of these justifications the Court would credit.[73]

The Court divided along party lines. The five Republicans, in an opinion by John Roberts, declined to probe the sincerity of the government's asserted national security justification. The relevant question, Roberts reasoned, was not whether the travel ban was *truly* meant to protect national security, but rather whether the ban "is plausibly related to the Government's stated objective to protect the country." Whether or not the original reason for the ban was prejudice against Muslims, the ban could also be justified as a security measure, so "it cannot be said that it is impossible to discern a relationship to legitimate state interests or that the policy is inexplicable by anything but animus." Underlying the majority decision was a concern that could arise no matter who was president. A vast number of government actions were lawful if undertaken for a valid purpose but unlawful if undertaken for a discriminatory purpose. If courts could second-guess the government's asserted reasons for doing what it did, judges might acquire an uncomfortable degree of power over government policy. Rulings that curtailed Trump's expansive conception of his power would become precedents that might then constrain all future government officials. As Roberts observed, "we must consider not only the statements of a particular President, but also the authority of the Presidency itself."[74]

The four Democrats chastised the majority for ignoring reality. The travel ban "masquerades behind a facade of national-security concerns," Sonia Sotomayor argued. "But this repackaging does little to cleanse" the ban of its true motivation. In light of Trump's repeated pledges to ban Muslims from the United States, she suggested, "a reasonable observer would readily conclude that the Proclamation was motivated by hostility and animus toward the Muslim faith."[75]

The following year brought another 5–4 case in which the Trump administration advanced a pretextual reason for a policy, and this time the administration's dishonesty was too much even for John Roberts. In 2018, the secretary of commerce announced that the upcoming census would include a question about citizenship, ostensibly at the request of the Justice Department, which would supposedly use the information to enforce the Voting Right Act. In fact, as Roberts explained in his majority opinion, the "evidence showed that the Secretary was determined to reinstate a citizenship question from the time he entered office." Roberts did not say why, but the reason was well known: asking about citizenship was expected to deter millions of noncitizens from disclosing themselves to the census, which would cause the population of Democratic-leaning states to be undercounted, which would reduce these states' representation in Congress and their share of federal funding. The secretary of commerce accordingly "instructed his staff to make it happen; waited while Commerce officials explored whether another agency would request census-based citizenship data; subsequently contacted the Attorney General himself to ask if DOJ would make the request; and adopted the Voting Rights Act rationale late in the process." Roberts determined that "unlike a typical case in which an agency may have both stated and unstated reasons for a decision, here the VRA enforcement rationale— the sole stated reason—seems to have been contrived." He concluded that "we cannot ignore the disconnect between the decision made and the explanation given. Our review is deferential, but we are not required to exhibit a naiveté from which ordinary citizens are free." The Court accordingly barred the government from including the citizenship question in the census.[76]

The other Republican justices were aghast. "For the first time ever, the Court invalidates an agency action solely because it questions the sincerity of the agency's otherwise adequate rationale," Clarence Thomas complained. He worried that "it is not difficult for political opponents of executive actions to generate controversy with accusations of pretext, deceit, and illicit motives." Samuel Alito called the decision "a license for widespread judicial inquiry into the motivations of Executive Branch officials," whose actions could be invalidated by "any one of the approximately 1,000 district court judges in this country, upon receiving information that a controversial agency decision might have been motivated by some unstated consideration."[77] The travel ban and census cases involved issues of partisan politics, but they also raised a fundamental question of judicial power that transcended partisanship, because judges of either party could interrogate the sincerity of administrations of either party. This was a question the Court had never directly confronted before because no previous administration had been so transparently insincere.

Trump's unusual business dealings also brought a pair of unusual cases to the Court, cases that once more raised profound questions because the

Court's decisions would become the law that would apply to all future presidents, not just to Trump. In both cases, Thomas and Alito were the only justices who sided with Trump. The Court's other Republicans voted against him.

Trump v. Mazars (2020) was the first case in the Court's history in which the Court considered whether Congress could issue subpoenas—orders to produce documents—for information about a sitting president. Committees of the House of Representatives issued the subpoenas to Trump's accounting firm and his banks, demanding financial and tax records relating to his business interests. The committees asserted that the records were relevant to potential legislation addressing money laundering and foreign involvement in American elections. Trump sought to block the subpoenas on the ground that they had no legitimate legislative purpose but were intended only to harass him and to reveal confidential personal information. In an opinion by Roberts, the Court adopted a view midway between the positions offered by Trump and by the House. On one hand, Roberts concluded, Congress was not entitled to whatever information it considered relevant to legislation, because virtually any document possessed by the president might be relevant to legislation, and unchecked congressional power to demand documents would allow the majority party in Congress to harass a president of the opposing party. On the other hand, the president could not withhold from Congress unprivileged documents that were genuinely relevant to legislation. After setting out some considerations that should figure in this balance, the Court sent the case back to the lower court to apply these considerations to the documents in question.[78]

The other case, *Trump v. Vance* (2020), involved a similar subpoena for Trump's financial and tax records issued to Trump's accounting firm by the district attorney of New York County, as part of an investigation into whether Trump and his business organizations violated state law. Again, the case was unprecedented: it was, as far as the justices or the parties were aware, the first time a state subpoena had ever been directed against a sitting president. The Court held that Trump was not immune from the subpoena, as he contended, but that he could raise objections to the disclosure of particular documents in the lower courts.[79]

By the 2020 presidential election, the Court had thus already considered legal arguments arising from Trump's idiosyncrasies in several cases. Thomas and Alito had voted in his favor each time. The three Democratic justices had voted against him each time. Roberts, Gorsuch, and Kavanaugh had sided with him in some cases and against him in others. Amy Coney Barrett, Trump's newest appointee, had just joined the Court.

After Trump lost the election, he and his associates filed several meritless lawsuits alleging that the election had been conducted fraudulently. Some of the suits reached the Court. One, styled *Trump v. Biden*, asked the Court to invalidate absentee ballots in Wisconsin. In another, Texas tried to prevent Pennsylvania, Georgia, Michigan, and Wisconsin from casting their electoral votes for Joe Biden. While these cases were arriving at the Court, Clarence Thomas's wife, Virginia, was urging Republican legislators in Arizona and Wisconsin to switch their states' electoral votes from Biden to Trump. Two years later, testifying before the congressional committee investigating the January 2021 attack on the Capitol, she explained that she still believed the election had been stolen from Trump.[80]

Had the justices agreed to hear one of these cases, their decision might have been even more contentious than *Bush v. Gore*. But the Court, without published dissent, refused to hear any of them. Trump characteristically expressed disappointment that Gorsuch, Kavanaugh, and Barrett had not been loyal to him. Especially Kavanaugh. "Where would he be without me?" Trump asked, referring to Kavanaugh's controversial confirmation hearings. "I saved his life. He wouldn't even be in a law firm. Who would have had him? Nobody. Totally disgraced. Only I saved him." At the rally on January 6, 2021, that preceded the attack on the Capitol, Trump declared: "You know, look, I'm not happy with the Supreme Court. They love to rule against me. I picked three people. I fought like hell for them." But "the Supreme Court they rule against me so much."[81]

It is easy to overlook the significance of this episode. The litigation that reached the Court was just one facet (and one of the less flamboyant facets) of the attempt to reinstall Trump as president, and most of the challenges to the election relied on factual claims that were clearly false. But some of these lawsuits rested as much on legal arguments as on factual arguments. They were efforts to persuade the Court to reinterpret the Constitution to make Trump president. Texas, for example, argued that the Constitution allowed state legislatures to appoint electors different from the ones chosen by the voters. A group of Republican members of Congress argued that the Electoral Count Act of 1887, the law that provided the procedure for counting electoral votes, was unconstitutional. These arguments lacked any chance of succeeding unless the Court made major changes to the law. But many of the Court's best-known cases involved lawsuits that were just as weak under then-existing law. When *Brown v. Board of Education* was filed, school segregation was legal. When *Roe v Wade* was filed, there was no constitutional right to abortion. Cases like these are famous *because* the Court changed the law while deciding them. When the challenges to the 2020 election reached the Court, one possible outcome was that five justices would change existing law and declare Trump the winner. It was this possibility that led the election law expert Richard Hasen to call the suits "garbage, but dangerous garbage."[82] Segregationists might have said just the same about *Brown*. Abortion opponents might have said just the same about *Roe*.

But the Court stayed out of the 2020 presidential election. There was an important cultural difference between the justices Trump appointed and the lawyers who helped Trump try to overturn the election. The justices were members of an elite legal culture that prizes loyalty to rules rather than loyalty to individuals, while Trump's lawyers were not. (In *Bush v. Gore*, by contrast, both candidates were represented by teams of elite lawyers who had gone to the same schools, moved in the same circles, and shared the same values as the justices, and indeed three of Bush's lawyers, John Roberts, Brett Kavanaugh, and Amy Coney Barrett, would become justices themselves.) Trump's willingness to let the Federalist Society choose his justices proved fatal to his efforts to cling to power, because it ensured that even his own appointees felt allegiance to the legal system rather than to him.

VII

In the late nineteenth and early twentieth centuries, another period in which the Court was quite conservative, progressives repeatedly proposed measures to change the Court's composition and to reduce the Court's jurisdiction. In the mid-twentieth century, when the Court was liberal, conservatives were the ones who advocated such reforms.[83] And in the early twenty-first century, when the Court was conservative again, reforming the Court once again became a progressive cause. Democrats proposed changing the Court in several ways, each of which revived an old idea that had been in circulation during previous calls for reform.

One common proposal was to institute term limits for the justices, who would then serve for a period of years or to a certain age rather than for life. This idea had considerable appeal among Democrats, who were smarting from the Republicans' good fortune in the timing of recent justices' deaths, which allowed Donald Trump to appoint three justices in four years after Barack Obama had been able to appoint only two justices in eight. Depending on how they were implemented, term limits could remove this kind of randomness and ensure that new justices were appointed on a regular schedule. Term limits could also solve the perennial, nonpartisan problem of elderly justices who remain in office despite their diminishing capacity. This same combination of partisan and nonpartisan motives elicited similar proposals from Republicans in the late 1940s and early 1950s, when the Court consisted entirely of Democrats appointed by Franklin Roosevelt and Harry Truman. The Eisenhower administration supported a constitutional amendment introduced in 1954 by the conservative Republican Senator John Marshall Butler that would have required the justices to retire at seventy-five.[84] Butler's amendment was approved by the Senate but not by the House of Representatives. Butler reintroduced the amendment the following year, but by then both houses of Congress had Democratic majorities so the proposal never reached the floor of either house. As this episode suggests, life tenure is hard to change because it is hard-wired in the Constitution. When half the country is angry at the Court, the other half is pleased with the Court's decisions, so the supermajority needed for a constitutional amendment has always been out of reach.

Another common proposal was to strip the Court of jurisdiction to decide certain kinds of cases—the ones that critics thought the justices were deciding incorrectly. After the Court overruled *Roe v. Wade*, for example, several Democratic members of Congress urged the enactment of a statute that would guarantee the right to abortion and that would specify that the Court lacks jurisdiction to assess the statute's constitutionality. Republicans offered similar proposals in the mid-twentieth century. We saw one example in Chapter 13—the bill introduced by Senator William Jenner in 1957 to strip the Court of jurisdiction in cases involving political radicals, which was a response to the Court's "Red Monday" decisions affirming the free speech rights of communists. There were many others. After the Court's reapportionment decisions of the early 1960s, the Virginia congressman William Tuck introduced a bill to deprive the Court of jurisdiction over cases involving apportionment. After the Court decided *Miranda v. Arizona*, Congress considered a bill to strip the Court of jurisdiction over cases involving confessions. The most famous example of jurisdiction-stripping in the Court's history took place after the Civil War, when, as we saw in Chapter 5, Congress prevented the Court from reviewing the constitutionality of Reconstruction by removing its jurisdiction over habeas corpus cases.[85] And as we saw in Chapter 3, Virginians were so upset by *Cohens v. Virginia* (1821) that a Virginia congressman proposed eliminating the Court's power to review *any* judgments of state courts. Because the

Constitution gives Congress the authority to define the Court's jurisdiction, members of Congress have always threatened to keep certain categories of cases away from the justices.

A third proposal offered by the Court's liberal critics was to require the justices to decide cases by a supermajority. This too was a measure that had often been proposed by opponents of the Court's decisions. More than sixty bills requiring Court supermajorities have been introduced in Congress over the years, going all the way back to the 1820s, as we saw in Chapter 3. In the mid-twentieth century, members of Congress from the South who opposed the Court's civil rights decisions tried to require supermajorities or even unanimity among the justices before they could hold state statutes unconstitutional.[86]

When Joe Biden won the 2020 presidential election, many Democrats called for a more radical reform—making the Court larger, so Biden could immediately appoint new justices.[87] Ever since Franklin Roosevelt's failed Court-packing plan of 1937, neither side of the political divide had seriously considered expanding the Court to change the outcomes of cases. But after Senate Republicans kept a seat on the Court vacant for more than a year after Antonin Scalia died so Barack Obama could not appoint his replacement, and after the same Senate Republicans hurried to confirm Amy Coney Barrett before Donald Trump's presidency ended, many Democrats were convinced that they now had to play by the same hardball tactics. So much time had passed since 1937, moreover, that some of the most ardent advocates for packing the Court may have had little sense of why Roosevelt's plan proved unpopular.

When Biden took office in early 2021, these calls to reform the Court had grown so numerous that Biden, who showed little interest in the topic, adopted a time-honored method of delay. He appointed an expert commission of law professors and lawyers to study the issue and produce a report. The commission's book-length report, published in December 2021, thoroughly canvassed the arguments for and against the reform proposals that had been circulating over the past few years.[88] In the end, as in earlier eras, nothing happened. The justices still served for life. They did not lose any of their jurisdiction. They still decided cases by a simple majority. And there were still nine of them. The Court had weathered yet another challenge to its power.

Epilogue

Over the past few years, when I told people I was working on a book about the history of the Supreme Court, I got one reaction more than any other. "Well," people would say, "that's certainly timely!" I think I know what they meant. They believed that the Court is in the news more than it used to be. They thought of the past as a time when the Court was not as controversial as it is now. I hope this book has demonstrated that this view is mistaken. The Court has changed in many ways over the years, but one thing that has not changed is that some of the Court's decisions have always aroused great controversy. In a country where nine unelected lawyers are given so much power, it is hard to imagine how things could be otherwise. Whenever anyone told me that the topic is timely, I had a standard response. "Yes," I would say, "it has been timely for more than two hundred years!"

When the Court is in the news these days, it is usually for reaching decisions that are welcomed by the right and reviled by the left. One common critique of the conservative justices is that they are exceeding the proper bounds of their own authority by crossing the line that divides law from politics. The Court is engaged in "a judicial power grab," one law professor recently argued. While signing an executive order directing federal agencies to protect access to abortion, President Joe Biden castigated "an out-of-control Supreme Court."[1] As we have seen, however, similar allegations have been levelled at the Court almost since its creation. Southerners, who were bitterly opposed to the Court's early nineteenth-century decisions affirming the federal government's primacy over the states, also accused the justices of seizing power for political reasons. So did opponents of the Court's twentieth-century decisions establishing new constitutional rights for black people, for Communists, and for criminal defendants. The Court's critics have always accused the justices of grabbing power to implement their political beliefs. When the Court decided *Roe v. Wade*, half the country thought the justices were improperly making law to suit their personal views of abortion. When the Court overruled *Roe v. Wade*, the other half thought just the same.

As I finished the book, new controversies continued to swirl around the Court. Journalists discovered that for years Justice Clarence Thomas had received extraordinarily lavish gifts from wealthy conservative benefactors, including expensive vacations on yachts and private planes. Thomas was not the first justice to accept gifts from admirers. As we have seen, the Nixon administration forced Abe Fortas off the Court for this reason and tried to do the same to William Douglas. But the largesse directed at Thomas seems to have been of an entirely different order of magnitude. The revelation of these gifts sparked a debate over whether Congress should place some limits on the practice.

Lawyers, meanwhile, pondered whether the justices were deciding too many cases without full briefing and argument.[2] Every court, including the Supreme Court, must reach some decisions extremely quickly—whether to stay an imminent execution, whether to order a party to take (or not take) some action before litigation can be completed, whether to block a lower court ruling from going into effect while an appeal is pending, and so on. The Court has always had cases like these. But these emergency matters mushroomed during the Trump administration, when the justices decided a wide range of questions at lightning speed, typically in very short opinions with little or no explanation of the Court's reasoning. The frequency of these cases subsided somewhat when Joe Biden became president and administration lawyers could no longer count on a sympathetic ear, although by then states and private litigants were also opportunistically filing emergency applications. But the question lingered: Was this a sensible way to run a high court? Would the justices do a better job by taking their time?

As the emergency docket swelled, the Court's ordinary docket continued to dwindle. In the 2022–2023 term, the justices wrote opinions in only fifty-eight cases, the smallest number since the Civil War, when the justices still spent most of their time riding circuit.[3] The Court's caseload was only about a third of what it had been in the 1970s. Thirty years ago, an argument day at the Court normally consisted of four cases, two in the morning and two in the afternoon. Now the Court hears just one or two and the session ends before lunch. The shrinking docket raised a question that would once have been unthinkable: Was the Court deciding too few cases? In the past, Congress repeatedly relieved the justices of overwork, first by creating intermediate appellate courts and then by empowering the justices to decide for themselves which cases they would hear. Had these measures gone too far?

To focus on such controversies, however, would be to overlook most of the Court's work. As always, most of the Court's cases involved technical legal questions that were important to small communities of lawyers and litigants, but which received little or no attention in the media. Justices and lawyers might disagree about how these cases should be decided, but the cases were not the subject of political debate or editorials in newspapers. The lawyers who argued the cases were not ideologically motivated; they were simply serving the interests of their clients. It was ordinary cases like these that occupied most of the justices' time.

In *Bittner v. United States* (2023), for example, the Court had to resolve an ambiguity in the Bank Secrecy Act. The law imposes a $10,000 penalty on the owner of a foreign bank account who fails to file an annual report alerting the government to the account's existence, but is that $10,000 per *account* or $10,000 per *report*? Alexandru Bittner was a man with many foreign bank accounts. He neglected to file annual reports for five years, reports that should have included 272 bank accounts. If the penalty was $10,000 per report, he would owe the government $50,000, but if it was $10,000 per account, his fine would be a whopping $2.72 million. As one might expect, the government argued for the higher amount, while Bittner urged that the lower amount was correct.[4]

Both sides had plausible arguments. Indeed, courts of appeals in different parts of the country had come out different ways, which is why the Supreme Court agreed to hear the case. Both sides were represented by lawyers who had appeared in the Court many times before, as had recently become the norm. Representing Bittner was Daniel Geyser, an appellate specialist in Colorado whose previous cases at the Court had involved similarly technical questions. Geyser argued that because the text of the Bank Secrecy Act requires the filing of reports, a person who omits several accounts from a single report violates the statute only once. On the other side was Matthew Guarnieri, who had represented the government in several cases since joining the Office of the Solicitor General a few years before. Guarnieri contended that the statutory text supports the government's view, not Bittner's, because it describes each undisclosed bank account as a separate violation.

This question was important to holders of foreign bank accounts and the lawyers who advise them. It mattered to the federal prosecutors who specialize in white collar crimes. For most people, however, the case was invisible. It was not discussed in any major newspapers. There was no liberal or conservative position. No elected officials could gain votes by taking one side or the other. Whichever way the Court decided the case, no one would accuse the justices of being out of control. No one would protest. Lawyers who pay close attention to the Supreme Court knew about the case, but hardly anyone else did.

Bittner won 5–4. Neil Gorsuch's majority opinion agreed with Geyser's interpretation of the statute. Joining Gorsuch were John Roberts, Samuel Alito, Brett Kavanaugh, and Ketanji Brown Jackson. Amy Coney Barrett wrote a dissent in which she adopted the government's view. She was joined by Clarence Thomas, Elena Kagan, and Sonia Sotomayor. Alexandru Bittner was no doubt relieved to have saved more than $2 million. Whatever he paid Geyser's law firm, it was money well spent. The justices moved on to the next case, and the next, and the next.

The justices routinely insist that they are not policymakers in robes. In cases about matters like abortion or affirmative action, it is hard to take these protestations seriously. When cases involve politically controversial questions, and when the governing law can be interpreted in more than one plausible way, the justices reach outcomes congruent with their policy preferences. This has always been true. But if one looks beyond the famous cases to the full range of the Court's work, one can better understand the justices' conception of their job. Ever since the Court was established, the justices have spent most of their time deciding routine cases like *Bittner*. The famous and controversial cases have always been the unusual ones, the rare cases in which the justices exercise their remarkable power to its fullest extent. These cases, despite their unrepresentativeness, are the ones that have always created the Court's image in the public mind. But the Court can look very different from the inside, where most workdays are consumed with the daily grind of cases that most people will never hear of. It is hard to feel powerful or political while laboring on a case like *Bittner*.

This difference in perspective was just the same two hundred years ago, when Alexis de Tocqueville rightly called the Supreme Court the most powerful court in the world, but when most of its cases were even less noteworthy. The Court's history has consisted of two parallel stories—on one hand, the oft-told tale of occasional celebrated cases raising contested political questions, and on the other, a lesser-known account of a small institution that has steadily cranked out decisions in a much larger number of obscure cases, year after year. The first story is what accounts for the Court's centrality in American life, but the second is closer to the justices' lived experience. If one wants to understand the Court, both are important.

Abbreviations

Austin Papers	Warren R. Austin Papers, Silver Special Collections Library, University of Vermont, Burlington, VT
Baker Papers	Howard H. Baker, Jr. Files, Ronald Reagan Presidential Library, Simi Valley, CA
Biddle Papers	Francis Biddle Papers, Franklin D. Roosevelt Presidential Library, Hyde Park, NY
Black Papers	Hugo LaFayette Black Papers, Library of Congress, Washington, DC
Blackmun Papers	Harry A. Blackmun Papers, Library of Congress, Washington, DC
Bonaparte Papers	Charles J. Bonaparte Papers, Library of Congress, Washington, DC
Braden Papers	George D. Braden Papers, Harry S. Truman Presidential Library, Independence, MO
Bradley Papers	Joseph P. Bradley Papers, New Jersey Historical Society, Newark, NJ
Brandeis Papers	Louis D. Brandeis Collection, University of Louisville, Louisville, KY
Brennan Papers	William J. Brennan Papers, Library of Congress, Washington, DC
Brewer Papers	Brewer Family Papers, Sterling Library, Yale University, New Haven, CT
Brownell Papers	Herbert Brownell, Jr., Papers, Dwight D. Eisenhower Presidential Library, Abilene, KS
Buchen Papers	Philip Buchen Files, Gerald R. Ford Presidential Library, Ann Arbor, MI
Bunche Papers	Ralph J. Bunche Papers, Charles E. Young Research Library, Department of Special Collections, University of California, Los Angeles, CA
Burton Papers	Harold H. Burton Papers, Library of Congress, Washington, DC
G. W. Bush Library	George W. Bush Presidential Library, Dallas, TX
Campbell Papers	Campbell Family Papers, Southern Historical Collection, Louis Round Wilson Special Collections Library, University of North Carolina, Chapel Hill, NC

CCOH	Columbia Center for Oral History, Columbia University, New York, NY
Chase Papers	Salmon P. Chase Papers, Library of Congress, Washington, DC
Cheney Papers	Richard B. Cheney Files, Gerald R. Ford Presidential Library, Ann Arbor, MI
Clark Papers (Texas)	Tom C. Clark Papers, Tarlton Law Library, University of Texas, Austin, TX
Clark Papers (Truman)	Tom C. Clark Papers, Harry S. Truman Presidential Library, Independence, MO
Clinton Library	William J. Clinton Presidential Library, Little Rock, AR
Coolidge Papers	Calvin Coolidge Papers, Library of Congress, Washington, DC
Cox Papers	C. Christopher Cox Files, Ronald Reagan Presidential Library, Simi Valley, CA
Cranch Papers	Cranch Family Papers, Library of Congress, Washington, DC
Curtis Papers	Benjamin Robbins Curtis Papers, Library of Congress, Washington, DC
Davis Papers	David Davis Papers, Chicago Historical Society, Chicago, IL
Day Papers	William R. Day Papers, Library of Congress, Washington, DC
Dean Papers	John W. Dean, III Files, Richard Nixon Presidential Library and Museum, Yorba Linda, CA
DHFFC	Linda Grant De Pauw, ed., *Documentary History of the First Federal Congress* (Baltimore: Johns Hopkins University Press, 1972–2017)
DHRC	Merrill Jensen, ed., *The Documentary History of the Ratification of the Constitution* (Madison: Wisconsin Historical Society Press, 1976–)
DHSC	Maeva Marcus, ed., *The Documentary History of the Supreme Court of the United States, 1789–1800* (New York: Columbia University Press, 1985–2007)
Duberstein Papers	Kenneth M. Duberstein Files, Ronald Reagan Presidential Library, Simi Valley, CA
Duvall Papers	Gabriel Duvall Papers, Library of Congress, Washington, DC
Ehrlichman Papers	John D. Ehrlichman Files, Richard Nixon Presidential Library and Museum, Yorba Linda, CA
Eisenhower Library	Dwight D. Eisenhower Presidential Library, Abilene, KS

EWOHP	Earl Warren Oral History Project, Bancroft Library, University of California, Berkeley, CA
Fahy Papers	Charles Fahy Papers, Franklin D. Roosevelt Presidential Library, Hyde Park, NY
Field Papers	Stephen Johnson Field Correspondence, Bancroft Library, University of California, Berkeley, CA
Fielding Papers	Fred Fielding Files, Ronald Reagan Presidential Library, Simi Valley, CA
Fortas Papers	Abe Fortas Papers, Sterling Library, Yale University, New Haven, CT
Frankfurter Papers	Felix Frankfurter Papers, Harvard Law School Library, Historical & Special Collections, Cambridge, MA
Fuller Papers	Melville Weston Fuller Papers, Library of Congress, Washington, DC
Gergen Papers	David R. Gergen Files, Ronald Reagan Presidential Library, Simi Valley, CA
Goldberg Papers	Arthur J. Goldberg Papers, Library of Congress, Washington, DC
Gray Files	C. Boyden Gray Files, George H. W. Bush Presidential Library, College Station, TX
Gray Papers	Horace Gray Papers, Library of Congress, Washington, DC
Haldeman Papers	Harry R. Haldeman Files, Richard Nixon Presidential Library and Museum, Yorba Linda, CA
Harlan I Papers	John Marshall Harlan Papers, Library of Congress, Washington, DC
Harlan II Papers	John Marshall Harlan Papers, Seeley G. Mudd Manuscript Library, Princeton University, Princeton, NJ
Holmes Papers	Mark De Wolfe Howe Research Materials Relating to the Life of Oliver Wendell Holmes, Jr., Harvard Law School Library, Historical & Special Collections, Cambridge, MA
Hoover Library	Herbert Hoover Presidential Library, West Branch, IA
Hughes Papers	Charles Evans Hughes Papers, Library of Congress, Washington, DC
Andrew Jackson Papers	Andrew Jackson Papers, Library of Congress, Washington, DC
Robert Jackson Papers	Robert H. Jackson Papers, Library of Congress, Washington, DC
Johnson Library	Lyndon B. Johnson Presidential Library, Austin, TX
Kennedy Library	John F. Kennedy Presidential Library, Boston, MA

Lamar Papers	Joseph Rucker and Clarinda Pendleton Lamar Papers, Hargrett Rare Book and Manuscript Library, University of Georgia, Athens, GA
Lash Papers	Joseph P. Lash Papers, Franklin D. Roosevelt Presidential Library, Hyde Park, NY
Liberman Papers	Lee S. Liberman Files, Clarence Thomas Subject Files, George H. W. Bush Presidential Library, College Station, TX
Lurton Papers	Horace H. Lurton Papers, Library of Congress, Washington, DC
Marshall Papers	Thurgood Marshall Papers, Library of Congress, Washington, DC
McLean Papers	John McLean Papers, Library of Congress, Washington, DC
Meese Papers	Edwin Meese III Files, Ronald Reagan Presidential Library, Simi Valley, CA
Miller Papers	Samuel Freeman Miller Correspondence, Library of Congress, Washington, DC
Moody Papers	William H. Moody Papers, Library of Congress, Washington, DC
Moore Papers	Powell Moore Files, Ronald Reagan Presidential Library, Simi Valley, CA
Murphy Papers	Frank Murphy Papers, Bentley Historical Library, University of Michigan, Ann Arbor, MI
Nixon Library	Richard Nixon Presidential Library, Yorba Linda, CA
Paterson Papers	William Paterson Papers, Library of Congress, Washington, DC
Peckham Papers	Wheeler H. Peckham Family Papers, Library of Congress, Washington, DC
Powell Papers	Lewis F. Powell Jr. Papers, Washington & Lee University, Lexington, VA
Quayle Papers	Office of Vice President Dan Quayle, Council on Competitiveness Files, George H. W. Bush Presidential Library, College Station, TX
Reagan Library	Ronald Reagan Presidential Library, Simi Valley, CA
Reed Papers	Stanley Forman Reed Papers, University of Kentucky, Lexington, KY
Regan Papers	Donald Regan Files, Ronald Reagan Presidential Library, Simi Valley, CA
Rehnquist Papers	William H. Rehnquist Papers, Hoover Institution Library and Archives, Stanford University, Stanford, CA
Rogers Papers	William P. Rogers Papers, Dwight D. Eisenhower Presidential Library, Abilene, KS
Roosevelt Library	Franklin D. Roosevelt Presidential Library, Hyde Park, NY

Rowe Papers	James H. Rowe, Jr., Papers, Franklin D. Roosevelt Presidential Library, Hyde Park, NY
Rutledge Papers	Wiley Rutledge, Jr., Papers, Library of Congress, Washington, DC
Stevens Papers	John Paul Stevens Papers, Library of Congress, Washington, DC
Stewart Papers	Potter Stewart Papers, Sterling Library, Yale University, New Haven, CT
Stone Papers	Harlan Fiske Stone Papers, Library of Congress, Washington, DC
Story Papers	Joseph Story Correspondence, Library of Congress, Washington DC
Sununu Papers	John Sununu Files, George H. W. Bush Presidential Library, College Station, TX
Sutherland Papers	George Sutherland Papers, Library of Congress, Washington, DC
Taft Papers	William Howard Taft Papers, Library of Congress, Washington, DC
Truman Library	Harry S. Truman Presidential Library, Independence, MO
Van Devanter Papers	Willis Van Devanter Papers, Library of Congress, Washington, DC
Vinson Papers	Frederick Moore Vinson Papers, University of Kentucky, Lexington, KY
Waite Papers	Morrison R. Waite Papers, Library of Congress, Washington, DC
Wallison Papers	Peter Wallison Files, Ronald Reagan Presidential Library, Simi Valley, CA
Charles Warren Papers	Charles Warren Papers, Library of Congress, Washington, DC
Earl Warren Papers	Earl Warren Papers, Library of Congress, Washington, DC
White Papers	Byron R. White Papers, Library of Congress, Washington, DC
Wilson Papers	Woodrow Wilson Papers, Library of Congress, Washington, DC

Notes

Introduction

1. *Harper's Weekly*, May 16, 1903, 812; Alexander M. Bickel, *The Least Dangerous Branch: The Supreme Court at the Bar of Politics* (Indianapolis: Bobbs-Merrill, 1962), 1.
2. See, e.g., Peter Charles Hoffer, Williamjames Hull Hoffer, and N. E. H. Hull, *The Supreme Court: An Essential History*, 2nd ed. (Lawrence: University Press of Kansas, 2018); John E. Semonche, *Keeping the Faith: A Cultural History of the U.S. Supreme Court* (Lanham, MD: Rowman & Littlefield, 1998).
3. The best histories of the Court, in my view, are the ones that take this broader perspective, including Lucas A. Powe Jr., *The Supreme Court and the American Elite, 1789–2008* (Cambridge, MA: Harvard University Press, 2009), and Robert G. McCloskey, *The American Supreme Court*, 6th ed. rev. by Sanford Levinson (Chicago: University of Chicago Press, 2016).
4. See, e.g, Bernard Schwartz, *A History of the Supreme Court* (New York: Oxford University Press, 1993). The two multivolume histories of the Court—the exhaustive Holmes Devise series now published by Cambridge University Press and the series of shorter books published by the University of South Carolina Press—are likewise divided into volumes organized by chief justiceship.
5. David J. Danelski and Artemus Ward, eds., *The Chief Justice: Appointment and Influence* (Ann Arbor: University of Michigan Press, 2016); Salmon P. Chase to Jonathan D. Van Buren, March 25, 1868, John Niven, ed., *The Salmon P. Chase Papers* (Kent, OH: Kent State University Press, 1993–1998), 5:194; Harlan Fiske Stone to Erwin Griswold, June 4, 1941, Stone Papers, box 15.
6. There is a long tradition of polemical histories of the Court, from Gustavus Myers, *History of the Supreme Court of the United States* (Chicago: C. H. Kerr, 1912), through such recent books as Adam Cohen, *Supreme Inequality: The Supreme Court's Fifty-Year Battle for a More Unjust America* (New York: Penguin, 2020).
7. Owen J. Roberts, *The Court and the Constitution* (Cambridge, MA: Harvard University Press, 1951); Arthur J. Goldberg, *Equal Justice: The Warren Era of the Supreme Court* (Evanston, IL: Northwestern University Press, 1971); William H. Rehnquist, *The Supreme Court: How It Was, How It Is* (New York: Quill, 1987).
8. Charles Warren, *The Supreme Court in United States History* (Boston: Little, Brown, 1922).

Chapter 1

1. Alexis de Tocqueville, *Democracy in America*, trans. Henry Reeve (New York: George Dearborn & Co., 1838), 130–31. Although the Court did decide disputes between states, *New York v. Ohio* was a product of Tocqueville's imagination. There was no such case. Tocqueville referred to "the seven judges" because that was the size of the Court at the time.
2. *Trustees of Dartmouth College v. Woodward*, 17 U.S. 518, 712–13 (1819).
3. Michael J. Klarman, *The Framers' Coup: The Making of the United States Constitution* (New York: Oxford University Press, 2016), 165; *DHRC*, 30:358; Federalist 80, *DHRC*, 18:98; Henry J. Bourguignon, *The First Federal Court: The Federal Appellate Prize Court of the American Revolution, 1775–1787* (Philadelphia: American Philosophical Society, 1977); Federalist 22, *DHRC*, 14:442.
4. *DHRC*, 17:335; Max Farrand, ed., *The Records of the Federal Convention of 1787* (New Haven, CT: Yale University Press, 1966), 2:37.
5. Farrand, *Records of the Federal Convention*, 1:124–25; U.S. Const. art. III, § 1; Wythe Holt, "'To Establish Justice': Politics, the Judiciary Act of 1789, and the Invention of the Federal Courts," *Duke Law Journal* 1989 (1989): 1421–1531.
6. Farrand, *Records of the Federal Convention*, 1:120.
7. Wilfred J. Ritz, *Rewriting the History of the Judiciary Act of 1789: Exposing Myths, Challenging Premises, and Using New Evidence* (Norman: University of Oklahoma Press, 1990), 27–52;

DHRC, 11:269; Herbert J. Storing, ed., *The Complete Anti-Federalist* (Chicago: University of Chicago Press, 1981), 2:434.

8. *DHRC*, 15:283, 13:389.
9. I am using "appeals" in a nontechnical sense, to encompass all the procedural vehicles by which one court can review the decision of another. Strictly speaking, an appeal was just one of them.
10. U.S. Const., art. III, § 2.
11. *DHRC*, 30:369; Federalist 81, *DHRC*, 28:109.
12. Judiciary Act of 1789, 1 Stat. 73 (1789).
13. *DHRC*, 5:639.
14. *DHFFC*, 16:928; *DHSC*, 4:539.
15. John V. Orth, "How Many Judges Does It Take to Make a Supreme Court?," *Constitutional Commentary* 19 (2002): 686; Federalist 22, *DHRC*, 14:442.
16. *DHSC*, 4:424; *DHFFC*, 16:982, 16:1181, 16:895, 9:87.
17. Scott Douglas Gerber, ed., *Seriatim: The Supreme Court Before John Marshall* (New York: New York University Press, 1998); James R. Perry, "Supreme Court Appointments, 1789–1801: Criteria, Presidential Style, and the Press of Events," *Journal of the Early Republic* 6 (1986): 372–75. Iredell was a replacement for Robert Harrison of Maryland, who was nominated and confirmed before North Carolina ratified the Constitution, but who declined the position for health reasons and died shortly thereafter.
18. James K. Polk to Gideon J. Pillow, February 4, 1846, Wayne Cutler, ed., *Correspondence of James K. Polk* (Knoxville: University of Tennessee Press, 1969–2017), 11:69.
19. *DHSC*, 1:686–89, 706.
20. Robert J. Steinfeld, *"To Save the People from Themselves": The Emergence of American Judicial Review and the Transformation of Constitutions* (New York: Cambridge University Press, 2021); William Michael Treanor, "Judicial Review Before *Marbury*," *Stanford Law Review* 58 (2005): 455–562.
21. *Holmes v. Walton* (1780) (unreported but discussed in *State v. Parkhurst*, 9 N.J.L. 427, 444 (N.J. 1802)); *Bayard v. Singleton*, 1 N.C. 5, 7 (1787); Richard M. Lambert, "The 'Ten Pound Act' Cases and the Origins of Judicial Review in New Hampshire," *New Hampshire Bar Journal* 43 (2002): 37–54; *Symsbury Case*, 1 Kirby 444 (Conn. 1785); *Rutgers v. Waddington* (N.Y. Mayor's Ct. 1784), reproduced in Julius Goebel Jr., ed., *The Law Practice of Alexander Hamilton* (New York: Columbia University Press, 1964), 1:393–419; *Commonwealth v. Caton*, 8 Va. 5 (1782).
22. Jack N. Rakove, *Original Meanings: Politics and Ideas in the Making of the Constitution* (New York: Vintage Books, 1997), 175–76.
23. *DHRC*, 11:239, 30:291; Federalist 78, *DHRC*, 18:89–90.
24. *Complete Anti-Federalist*, 2:423, 422, 437, 420, 439, 438.
25. *DHFFC*, 17:1654; Federalist 78, *DHRC*, 18:88.
26. Russell Wheeler, "The Extrajudicial Activities of the Early Supreme Court," *Supreme Court Review* (1973): 123–58; 1 Stat. 132 (1790); 1 Stat. 122–23 (1790).
27. 1 Stat. 243–45 (1792).
28. *DHSC*, 6:370; James Wilson, John Blair, and Richard Peters to George Washington, April 18, 1792, *DHSC*, 6:53–54; James Iredell and John Sitgreaves to George Washington, June 8, 1792, *DHSC*, 6:284–87.
29. 1 Stat. 324 (1793); Mark Tushnet, "Dual Office Holding and the Constitution: A View from Hayburn's Case," *Journal of Supreme Court History* (1990): 44–58.
30. *Vanhorne's Lessee v. Dorrance*, 2 U.S. 304, 309 (C.C.D. Pa. 1795).
31. *Ware v. Hylton*, 3 U.S. 199 (1796); Jeremiah Smith to William Plumer, February 7, 1795, *DHSC*, 7:320. The quotation from Iredell was attributed to him by Smith.
32. *Hylton v. United States*, 3 U.S. 171, 175 (1796).
33. John Wickham, *The Substance of an Argument in the Case of the Carriage Duties* (Richmond: Augustine Davis, 1795), 15; *Hylton*, 3 U.S. at 175; Albert Gallatin, *A Sketch of the Finances of the United States* (New York: William A. Davis, 1796), 11; *Cooper v. Telfair*, 4 U.S. 14, 19 (1800).
34. *Calder v. Bull*, 3 U.S. 386, 387 (1798).
35. *Marbury v. Madison*, 5 U.S. 137, 177–78 (1803).
36. Federalist 82, *DHRC*, 18:111.
37. Klarman, *The Framers' Coup*, 606–09.

38. Keith E. Whittington, *Political Foundations of Judicial Supremacy: The Presidency, the Supreme Court, and Constitutional Leadership in U.S. History* (Princeton, NJ: Princeton University Press, 2007); Gerald Leonard and Saul Cornell, *The Partisan Republic: Democracy, Exclusion, and the Fall of the Founders' Constitution, 1780s–1830s* (New York: Cambridge University Press, 2019); Larry D. Kramer, *The People Themselves: Popular Constitutionalism and Judicial Review* (New York: Oxford University Press, 2004).

39. *DHSC*, 5:7–20; *Van Staphorst v. Maryland*, 2 U.S. 401 (1792); *DHSC*, 5:57–67.

40. *DHSC*, 5:127–37.

41. *DHSC*, 5:161–62; Shearjashub Bourne to Robert Treat Paine, February 16, 1793, *DHSC*, 5:163 (I have expanded some abbreviations).

42. Edmund Pendleton to Nathaniel Pendleton, May 21, 1792, *DHSC*, 5:157. On the divergent understandings of how constitutional interpretation related to the Constitution's text in the first few years after it was ratified, see Jonathan Gienapp, *The Second Creation: Fixing the American Constitution in the Founding Era* (Cambridge, MA: Harvard University Press, 2018).

43. *DHSC*, 5:218; *Chisholm v. Georgia*, 2 U.S. 419, 467, 471, 450 (1793).

44. William Few to Edward Telfair, February 19, 1793, *DHSC*, 5:221; Samuel Johnston to James Iredell, April 10, 1793, *DHSC*, 5:229; *DHSC*, 5:234, 5:230; Thomas Dwight to Theodore Sedgwick, March 6, 1794, *DHSC*, 5:269.

45. On the ratification and subsequent history of the Eleventh Amendment, see John V. Orth, *The Judicial Power of the United States: The Eleventh Amendment in American History* (New York: Oxford University Press, 1987).

46. On the emergence of political parties, see Stanley Elkins and Eric McKitrick, *The Age of Federalism: The Early American Republic, 1788–1800* (New York: Oxford University Press, 1993).

47. *DHSC*, 1:765; Chauncey Goodrich to Oliver Wolcott Jr., July 30, 1795, *DHSC*, 1:774; Edmund Randolph to George Washington, July 29, 1795, *DHSC*, 1:773; William Bradford Jr., to Alexander Hamilton, August 4, 1795, *DHSC*, 1:775.; *DHSC*, 1:794.

48. James Haw, *John and Edward Rutledge of South Carolina* (Athens: University of Georgia Press, 1997), 256; John Adams to Abigail Adams, December 16, 1795, *DHSC*, 1:812; Jeremiah Smith to William Plumer, December 16, 1795, *DHSC*, 1:812; Robert R. Livingston to Edward Livingston, December 20, 1795, *DHSC*, 1:815; Thomas Jefferson to William B. Giles, December 31, 1795, *DHSC*, 1:821; *DHSC*, 1:822.

49. Richard E. Ellis, *The Jeffersonian Crisis: Courts and Politics in the Young Republic* (New York: Oxford University Press, 1971); Samuel Sewall to Cushing, February 25, 1800, *DHSC*, 4:628; Kathryn Preyer, *Blackstone in America* (New York: Cambridge University Press, 2009), 10–38.

50. 2 Stat. 89 (1801); 2 Stat. 103 (1801); Preyer, *Blackstone in America*, 59–91.

51. Monroe to Jefferson, March 3, 1801, *DHSC*, 4:720; Jefferson to John Dickinson, December 19, 1801, Julian P. Boyd, ed., *The Papers of Thomas Jefferson* (Princeton, NJ: Princeton University Press, 1950–), 36:165–66; John Fowler to his constituents, March 6, 1801, *DHSC*, 4:721.

52. 2 Stat. 132 (1802); 2 Stat. 156 (1802); R. Kent Newmyer, *John Marshall and the Heroic Age of the Supreme Court* (Baton Rouge: Louisiana State University Press, 2001), 154–56.

53. *Stuart v. Laird*, 5 U.S. 299 (1803).

54. *Marbury v. Madison*, 5 U.S. 137 (1803). There is an enormous literature of varying quality on *Marbury*. One source I found especially useful is James M. O'Fallon, "Marbury," *Stanford Law Review* 44 (1992): 219–60.

55. Ellis, *Jeffersonian Crisis*, 66; Resolutions Adopted by the Kentucky General Assembly, November 10, 1798, *Founders Online*, https://founders.archives.gov/documents/Jefferson/01-30-02-0370-0004(accessed April 10, 2024); Thomas Jefferson to Spencer Roane, September 6, 1819, *Founders Online*, https://founders.archives.gov/documents/Jefferson/03-15-02-0014 (accessed April 29, 2024).

56. Ralph Lerner, "The Supreme Court as Republican Schoolmaster," *Supreme Court Review* (1967): 127–80; *DHSC*, 2:27, 2:191.

57. *DHSC*, 2:217, 2:219, 2:283–84.

58. Thomas P. Slaughter, *The Whiskey Rebellion: Frontier Epilogue to the American Revolution* (New York: Oxford University Press, 1986); *DHSC*, 2:493, 2:495, 2:487–90.

59. *DHSC*, 3:158, 3:162; 3:177, 3:183, 3:192. On Iredell's jury charges, see Willis P. Whichard, *Justice James Iredell* (Durham, NC: Carolina Academic Press, 2000), 109–17.

60. Wendell Bird, *Press and Speech Under Assault: The Early Supreme Court Justices, the Sedition Act of 1798, and the Campaign Against Dissent* (New York: Oxford University Press, 2016); Terri Diane Halperin, *The Alien and Sedition Acts of 1798: Testing the Constitution* (Baltimore: Johns Hopkins University Press, 2016); *DHSC*, 3:333, 3:366, 3:447.
61. Samuel Johnston to James Iredell, February 27, 1796, *DHSC*, 1:840.
62. Mel Laracey, "The Impeachment of Supreme Court Justice Samuel Chase: New Perspectives from Thomas Jefferson's Presidential Newspaper," *Journal of Supreme Court History* 40 (2015): 231–48; "Report of the Trial of the Hon. Samuel Chase," *Monthly Anthology, and Boston Review* 3 (1806): 32; John Quincy Adams to Thomas Boylston Adams, February 8, 1805, *Founders Online*, https://founders.archives.gov/documents/Adams/99-03-02-1387(accessed April 10, 2024).
63. William B. Paterson (son) to William Paterson (father), March 26, 1805, Paterson Papers, box 1.

Chapter 2

1. Joseph Gordon Hylton, "The African-American Lawyer: The First Generation," *University of Pittsburgh Law Review* 56 (1994): 108.
2. Eli N. Evans, *Judah P. Benjamin: The Jewish Confederate* (New York: The Free Press, 1988), 83; Catharine MacMillan, "Judah Benjamin: Marginalized Outsider or Admitted Insider?," *Journal of Law and Society* 42 (2015): 162–63.
3. "Persecution of Roman Catholics," *Catholic Telegraph* 4 (1835): 338; "Roger B. Taney: A Papist and a Jesuit," *Religious Intelligencer* 20 (1836): 739.
4. The seven justices appointed between 2005 (John Roberts) and 2020 (Amy Coney Barrett) were on average fifty-one years old when they were appointed.
5. Josiah Quincy, *Memoir of the Life of John Quincy Adams* (Boston: Phillips, Sampson and Co., 1858), 386.
6. *Richmond Enquirer*, July 24, 1835, 3; O. H. Smith, *Early Indiana Trials; and Sketches* (Cincinnati: Moore, Wilstach, Keys & Co., 1858), 156–57; "The Judges of the U.S. Supreme Court," *New York Evangelist* 8 (1837): 28.
7. Rachel A. Shelden, "Anatomy of a Presidential Campaign from the Supreme Court Bench: John McLean, Levi Woodbury, and the Election of 1848," *Journal of Supreme Court History* 47 (2022): 241–64; Francis P. Weisenburger, *The Life of John McLean: A Politician on the United States Supreme Court* (Columbus: Ohio State University Press, 1937); Herman Lincoln to John McLean, December 28, 1854, McLean Papers, reel 11.
8. Thomas Jefferson to the Justices, July 18, 1793, *DHSC*, 6:747.
9. Stewart Jay, *Most Humble Servants: The Advisory Role of Early Judges* (New Haven, CT: Yale University Press, 1997), 10–50; Max Farrand, ed., *The Records of the Federal Convention of 1787* (New Haven, CT: Yale University Press, 1966), 2:334.
10. Justices to George Washington, August 8, 1793, *DHSC*, 6:755.
11. John Jay to George Washington, November 13, 1790, Henry P. Johnston, ed., *The Correspondence and Public Papers of John Jay* (New York: G. P. Putnam's Sons, 1890–1893), 3:405–08; Andrew Jackson to Roger Taney, October 13, 1836, Andrew Jackson Papers, reel 49; Donald G. Morgan, *Justice William Johnson: The First Dissenter* (Columbia: University of South Carolina Press, 1954), 122–24.
12. Albert Gallatin to Thomas Jefferson, February 15, 1805, *Founders Online*, https://founders.archives.gov/documents/Jefferson/01-42-02-0413 (accessed April 10, 2024); Joel Barlow to Thomas Jefferson, September 28, 1806, *Founders Online*, https://founders.archives.gov/documents/Jefferson/99-01-02-4325 (accessed April 10, 2024).
13. Levi Lincoln to James Madison, April 12, 1810, *Founders Online*, https://founders.archives.gov/documents/Madison/03-02-02-0378 (accessed April 10, 2024); "Biography: Memoirs of William Cushing," *Philadelphia Repertory* 1 (1810): 169; William C.C. Claiborne to Thomas Jefferson, October 10, 1810, *Founders Online*, https://founders.archives.gov/documents/Jefferson/03-03-02-0101-0001 (accessed April 10, 2024); Thomas Jefferson to Caesar Rodney, September 25, 1810, *Founders Online*, https://founders.archives.gov/documents/Jefferson/03-03-02-0073 (accessed April 10, 2024); Thomas Jefferson to James Madison, October 15, 1810, *Founders Online*, https://founders.archives.gov/documents/Madison/03-02-02-0734 (accessed April 10, 2024).
14. Elbridge Gerry to James Madison, September 22, 1810, *Founders Online*, https://founders.archives.gov/documents/Madison/03-02-02-0683 (accessed April 10, 2024); Thomas Jefferson to Albert Gallatin, September 27, 1810, *Founders Online*, https://founders.archives.gov/docume

nts/Jefferson/03-03-02-0077 (accessed April 10, 2024); Henry Smith and others to James Madison, October 1, 1810, *Founders Online*, https://founders.archives.gov/documents/Madison/03-03-02-0705 (accessed April 10, 2024); Thomas Jefferson to Henry Dearborn, July 16, 1810, *Founders Online*, https://founders.archives.gov/documents/Jefferson/03-02-02-0456 (accessed April 10, 2024); Thomas Jefferson to James Madison, October 15, 1810, *Founders Online*, https://founders.archives.gov/documents/Madison/03-02-02-0734 (accessed April 10, 2024); Ezekiel Bacon to Joseph Story, October 8, 1810, Story Papers, reel 1.

15. "Levi Lincoln," *National Recorder* 3 (1820): 303.

16. Leonard W. Levy, *The Law of the Commonwealth and Chief Justice Shaw* (New York: Harper & Row, 1967), 91; Edmund Burke to James Polk, April 7, 1845, Herbert Weaver and Paul H. Bergeron, eds., *Correspondence of James K Polk* (Knoxville: University of Tennessee Press, 1969–2017), 9:257; David Henshaw to James Polk, September 13, 1845, *Correspondence of James K Polk*, 10:229; Millard Fillmore to Daniel Webster, September 10, 1851, Benjamin R. Curtis, ed., *A Memoir of Benjamin Robbins Curtis, LL.D.* (Boston: Little, Brown, 1879), 1:155.

17. John P. Kennedy, *Memoirs of the Life of William Wirt* (Philadelphia: Lea and Blanchard, 1849), 2:153–55.

18. This figure includes negative votes as well as refusals to hold any vote until the Senate's session expired. The number of nominees refused by the Senate would be twelve if we include Roger Taney, whose initial nomination in January 1835 to succeed Gabriel Duvall was not voted upon by the Senate, which had an anti-Jacksonian majority. Jackson renominated Taney to succeed John Marshall as chief justice when the next Congress convened, at which time the Senate had a Jacksonian majority. The number would be thirteen if we also include Jeremiah Black, whom the Senate rejected in February 1861, during the waning days of the Buchanan administration, when several of the southern states had already seceded and thus no longer had senators.

19. David N. Atkinson, *Leaving the Bench: Supreme Court Justices at the End* (Lawrence: University Press of Kansas, 1999), 32–33; "The Late Mr. Justice Baldwin," *Pennsylvania Law Journal* 6 (1846): 4.

20. Jean Edward Smith, *John Marshall: Definer of a Nation* (New York: Henry Holt and Co., 1996), 512–13; John Marshall to Joseph Story, June 26, 1831, Herbert A. Johnson, ed., *The Papers of John Marshall* (Chapel Hill: University of North Carolina Press, 1974–2006), 12:93.

21. William Wetmore Story, ed., *Life and Letters of Joseph Story* (Boston: Charles C. Little and James Brown, 1851), 2:523; Joseph Story to Ezekiel Bacon, April 12, 1845, *Life and Letters of Joseph Story*, 2:527.

22. David Howell to James Madison, November 26, 1810, *Founders Online*, https://founders.archives.gov/documents/Madison/03–03-02–0033 (accessed April 10, 2024); Artemus Ward, *Deciding to Leave: The Politics of Retirement from the United States Supreme Court* (Albany: State University of New York Press, 2003), 60. Andrew Jackson did nominate Taney to replace Duvall, but the Senate adjourned before voting on the nomination. Marshall died soon after, and Jackson nominated Taney a second time to replace Marshall. This time he was confirmed by the Senate. Duvall would be succeeded by Philip Barbour.

23. Jean Edward Smith, *John Marshall: Definer of a Nation* (New York: Henry Holt and Co., 1996); Richard Brookhiser, *John Marshall: The Man Who Made the Supreme Court* (New York: Basic Books, 2018); Harlow Giles Unger, *John Marshall: The Chief Justice Who Saved the Nation* (Boston: Da Capo Press, 2014); Charles F. Hobson, *The Great Chief Justice: John Marshall and the Rule of Law* (Lawrence: University Press of Kansas, 1996); R. Kent Newmyer, *John Marshall and the Heroic Age of the Supreme Court* (Baton Rouge: Louisiana State University Press, 2002); Albert J. Beveridge, *The Life of John Marshall* (Boston: Houghton Mifflin, 1916–1919), 1:v, 3:v.

24. William Wirt, *The Letters of the British Spy* (Richmond: Samuel Pleasants, Jr., 1803), 20–22; John Adams to John Marshall, August 17, 1825, *Founders Online*, https://founders.archives.gov/documents/Adams/99–02–02–7989 (accessed April 10, 2024).

25. Thomas Jefferson to James Madison, May 25, 1810, *Founders Online*, https://founders.archives.gov/documents/Madison/03–02-02–0435 (accessed April 10, 2024); Charles Richard Williams, ed., *Diary and Letters of Rutherford Birchard Hayes* (Columbus: Ohio State Archaeological and Historical Society, 1922), 1:116. The latter quotation comes from the law school notes of Rutherford Hayes, who heard Story quote Jefferson when he was one of Story's students at Harvard Law School in 1843. Jefferson had died seventeen years earlier, so it is possible that Story had embellished the quotation in his memory.

26. *Bas v. Tingy*, 4 U.S. 37, 43 (1800).

27. *Brown v. Maryland*, 25 U.S. 419, 449–50 (1829).

28. Robert G. Seddig, "John Marshall and the Origins of Supreme Court Leadership," *University of Pittsburgh Law Review* 36 (1975): 800.

29. Mark R. Killenbeck, "No Bed of Roses: William Johnson, Thomas Jefferson and the Supreme Court, 1822–23," *Journal of Supreme Court History* 37 (2012): 95–124; Thomas Jefferson to William Johnson, October 27, 1822, *Founders Online*, https://founders.archives.gov/docume nts/Jefferson/98-01-02-3118 (accessed April 10, 2024).

30. William Johnson to Thomas Jefferson, December 10, 1822, *Founders Online*, https://founders. archives.gov/documents/Jefferson/98-01-02-3203 (accessed April 10, 2024).

31. Thomas Jefferson to William Johnson, March 4, 1823, *Founders Online*, https://founders.archi ves.gov/documents/Jefferson/98-01-02-3373 (accessed April 10, 2024).

32. Donald Malcolm Roper, *Mr. Justice Thompson and the Constitution* (New York: Garland Publishing, 1987), iii. For a lighthearted debate over which justice was the least significant, a debate founded on the erroneous premise that the contributions of nineteenth-century justices can be evaluated by counting the number of the opinions credited to them, see David P. Currie, "The Most Insignificant Justice: A Preliminary Inquiry," *University of Chicago Law Review* 50 (1983): 466–80 (choosing Duvall); Frank H. Easterbrook, "The Most Insignificant Justice: Further Evidence," *University of Chicago Law Review* 50 (1983): 481–503 (choosing Todd).

33. "Letters from Washington," *National Register*, May 30, 1818, 338; Joseph Story to Samuel P. P. Fay, February 25, 1808, *Life and Letters of Joseph Story*, 1:167. Story's high opinion of Washington was shared by many contemporaries. Gerard N. Magliocca, *Washington's Heir: The Life of Justice Bushrod Washington* (New York: Oxford University Press, 2022), 82–86.

34. John Stokes Adams, ed., *An Autobiographical Sketch by John Marshall* (Ann Arbor: University of Michigan Press, 1937), 30.

35. John Chipman Gray, *The Nature and Sources of the Law* (New York: Columbia University Press, 1909), 239. There are a few biographies of Story, the best of which is R. Kent Newmyer, *Supreme Court Justice Joseph Story: Statesman of the Old Republic* (Chapel Hill: University of North Carolina Press, 1985).

36. *Life and Letters of Joseph Story*, 2:117.

37. A biography of Taney is long overdue. The standard work is still Carl Brent Swisher, *Roger B. Taney* (New York: Macmillan, 1935).

38. *New York Evening Post*, March 23, 1803, 2; *New York Herald*, March 26, 1803, 1; *Commercial Advertiser*, March 28, 1803, 2.

39. Craig Joyce, "The Rise of the Supreme Court Reporter: An Institutional Perspective on Marshall Court Ascendancy," *Michigan Law Review* 83 (1985): 1291–1391; Peter DuPonceau to Joseph Story, July 19, 1824, Story Papers, reel 1; Book Review, *Monthly Anthology, and Boston Review*, March 1, 1808, 160; Book Review, *American Review, and Literary Journal* 2 (1802): 27.

40. John Adams to Charles Carroll, December 10, 1794, Cranch Papers, box 2; "Review," *The Port-Folio* 4 (1804): 386; Book Review, *North American Review and Miscellaneous Journal*, May 1817, 113.

41. John Marshall to Dudley Chase, February 7, 1817, *Papers of John Marshall*, 8:148; Daniel Webster, Book Review, *North American Review and Miscellaneous Journal*, December 1818, 69.

42. 3 Stat. 376 (1817); Book Review, *The Analectic Magazine*, June 1819, 446; Simon Greenleaf to Joseph Story, October 19, 1826, Story Papers, reel 1; 42 U.S. v (1843).

43. John Blair to John Jay, August 5, 1790, *DHSC*, 2:84; John Jay to Catharine Ridley, February 1, 1791, *DHSC*, 2:126; Hannah Cushing to a relative, Jan. 1792, *DHSC*, 2:250 n.2.

44. James Iredell to Hannah Iredell, October 2, 1791, *DHSC*, 2:212.

45. James Iredell to Hannah Iredell, November 27, 1795, *DHSC*, 3:82; James Iredell to Hannah Iredell, April 10, 1798, *DHSC*, 3:245; James Iredell to Hannah Iredell, March 11, 1796, *DHSC*, 3:94.

46. James Iredell to John Jay, William Cushing, and James Wilson, February 11, 1791, *DHSC*, 2:132; John Jay to James Iredell, March 16, 1791, *DHSC*, 2:154; James Iredell to John Jay, January 17, 1792, *DHSC*, 2:238; 1 Stat. 253 (1792); James Iredell to James Wilson, November 24, 1794, *DHSC*, 2:498; John Blair to William Cushing, June 12, 1795, *DHSC*, 3:61–62.

47. Robert Harrison to George Washington, October 27, 1789, *DHSC*, 1:36; James Haw, *John & Edward Rutledge of South Carolina* (Athens: University of Georgia Press, 1997), 224; Thomas Johnson to George Washington, January 16, 1793, *DHSC*, 2:344; Walter Stahr, *John Jay: Founding Father* (New York: Hambledon and London, 2005), 283–89; John Jay to John Adams, January

2, 1801, *DHSC*, 1:147; *DHSC*, 1:56; "A Sketch of the Life and Public Services of the Late Hon. Alfred Moore," *Literary and Scientific Repository, and Critical Review* 1 (1820): 6.

48. Justices to George Washington, ca. September 13, 1790, *DHSC*, 2:89–92 (it is not known whether this letter was ever sent to Washington); "Report of the Attorney-General to the House of Representatives," December 31, 1790, *DHSC*, 4:134; Thomas Johnson to James Iredell, March 9, 1792, *DHSC*, 2:244; James Iredell to Thomas Johnson, March 15, 1792, *DHSC*, 2:247; John Jay to James Iredell, March 19, 1792, *DHSC*, 2:249; Justices to George Washington, August 9, 1792, *DHSC*, 2:288; Justices to Congress, August 9, 1792, *DHSC*, 2:290.

49. 1 Stat. 333 (1793); Wythe Holt, "'The Federal Courts Have Enemies in All Who Fear Their Influence on State Objects': The Failure to Abolish Supreme Court Circuit-Riding in the Judiciary Acts of 1792 and 1793," *Buffalo Law Review* 36 (1987): 301–40; Justices to Congress, February 18, 1794, *DHSC*, 2:443.

50. 2 Stat. 159 (1802); Jonathan R. Nash and Michael G. Collins, "The Certificate of Division and the Early Supreme Court," *Southern California Law Review* 94 (2021): 733–85.

51. Justin Crowe, *Building the Judiciary: Law, Courts, and the Politics of Institutional Development* (Princeton, NJ: Princeton University Press, 2012), 84–131; 2 Stat. 420 (1807); 5 Stat. 176 (1837); 12 Stat. 794 (1863).

52. Steven P. Brown, *John McKinley and the Antebellum Supreme Court: Circuit Riding in the Old Southwest* (Tuscaloosa: University of Alabama Press, 2012), 112–91; S. Doc. No. 50, 25th Cong., 3rd Sess. (1839), 32, 39.

53. S. Doc. No. 99, 27th Cong., 2nd Sess. (1842), 2–3; 5 Stat. 507 (1842).

54. John P. Frank, *Justice Daniel Dissenting: A Biography of Peter V. Daniel, 1784–1860* (Cambridge, MA: Harvard University Press, 1964), 275–84; William D. Hoyt Jr., "Justice Daniel in Arkansas, 1851 and 1853," *Arkansas Historical Quarterly* 1 (1942): 160–62.

55. William D. Hoyt Jr., "Travel to Cincinnati in 1853," *Ohio State Archaeological and Historical Quarterly* 51 (1942): 63.

56. John Catron to James Polk, May 8, 1837, *Correspondence of James K. Polk*, 4:116.

57. Joseph Story to Stephen White, February 17, 1819, *Life and Letters of Joseph Story*, 1:327; Daniel R. Coquillette and Bruce A. Kimball, *On the Battlefield of Merit: Harvard Law School, The First Century* (Cambridge, MA: Harvard University Press, 2015), 157–88; Joseph Story to Daniel Webster, January 4, 1824, *Life and Letters of Joseph Story*, 1:435–36.

58. *United States v. Jacobson*, 26 F. Cas. 567, 570 (C.C.D.N.Y. 1817).

59. David Lynch, *The Role of Circuit Courts in the Formation of United States Law in the Early Republic* (Oxford: Hart Publishing, 2018), 196–97; undated manuscript filed at the end of the papers for 1853, McLean Papers, reel 11.

60. Joshua Glick, "On the Road: The Supreme Court and the History of Circuit Riding," *Cardozo Law Review* 24 (2003): 1753–1843; *Annals of Congress* 11 (1802): 82; "The Examination," No. 6 (January 2, 1802), Harold C. Syrett, ed., *The Papers of Alexander Hamilton* (New York: Columbia University Press, 1961–87), 25:485; James D. Richardson, ed., *Messages and Papers of the Presidents 1789–1897* (Washington, DC: Government Printing Office, 1896–99), 1:577; *Country Courier* [New York], December 30, 1816, 115; Thomas Todd to James Madison, July 27, 1817, David B. Mattern, J. C. A. Stagg, Mary Parke Johnson, and Anne Mandeville Colony, eds., *The Papers of James Madison: Retirement Series* (Charlottesville: University of Virginia Press, 2009–) 1:97.

61. "Judiciary Intelligence," *United States Intelligencer and Review* 1 (1829): 50.

62. Joseph Story to Stephen White, February 17, 1819, *Life and Letters of Joseph Story*, 1:327.

63. *Register of Debates* 2 (1826): 416; *Congressional Globe* 30 (1848): App. 354; *Congressional Globe* 33 (1855): 212.

64. *Register of Debates* 2 (1826): 878; *Congressional Globe* 33 (1855): 194; *Congressional Globe* 30 (1848): 594.

65. *Congressional Globe* 30 (1848): 640; Abraham Bishop, *Proofs of a Conspiracy, Against Christianity, and the Government of the United States* (Hartford: John Babcock, 1802), 157; *Congressional Globe* 30 (1848): App. 582.

66. "Summary of Events," *American Law Review* 1 (1867): 207.

67. Lynch, *The Role of Circuit Courts*; Dwight F. Henderson, *Congress, Courts, and Criminals: The Development of Federal Criminal Law, 1801–1829* (Westport, CT: Greenwood Press, 1985); Newmyer, *Supreme Court Justice Joseph Story*, 318; "The Late Mr. Justice Catron," *Legal Intelligencer* 23 (1866): 132.

68. *DeLovio v. Boit*, 7 F. Cas. 418 (C.C.D. Mass. 1815); *Sherwood v. Sutton*, 21 F. Cas. 1303 (C.C.D.N.H. 1828); *Folsom v. Marsh*, 9 F. Cas. 342 (C.C.D. Mass. 1841).
69. *Golden v. Prince*, 10 F. Cas. 542 (C.C.D. Pa. 1814); John Marshall to Bushrod Washington, April 19, 1814, *Papers of John Marshall*, 8:35; John Marshall to Joseph Story, May 23, 1831 (and editors' note afterward), *Papers of John Marshall*, 12:67–68.
70. R. Kent Newmyer, *The Treason Trial of Aaron Burr: Law, Politics, and the Character Wars of the New Nation* (New York: Cambridge University Press, 2012); John Marshall to Richard Peters, November 23, 1807, *Papers of John Marshall*, 7:165.
71. Edward J. Coale, *Trials of the Mail Robbers, Hare, Alexander and Hare* (Baltimore: Edward J. Coale, 1818); John Mortimer, *The Mail Robbers: Report of the Trials of Michael Mellon, the Lancaster Mail Robber; and George Wilson and James Porter Alias May, the Reading Mail Robbers* (Philadelphia: J. Mortimer, 1830).
72. *Documentary History of the Construction and Development of the United States Capitol Building and Grounds*, H.R. Rep. No. 646, 58th Cong., 2d Sess. (1904), at 94; Benjamin Latrobe to James Madison, September 8, 1809, John C. Van Horne, ed., *The Correspondence and Miscellaneous Papers of Benjamin Henry Latrobe* (New Haven, CT: Yale University Press, 1984–1988), 2:765–66; George S. Hilliard, ed., *Life, Letters, and Journals of George Ticknor* (Boston: James R. Osgood and Co., 1876), 1:38.
73. "United States Supreme Court," *Home Journal*, March 23, 1850, 2; Benjamin Latrobe to Thomas Jefferson, September 23, 1808, *Correspondence of Latrobe*, 2:665–66; George Watterston, *A Picture of Washington* (Washington, DC: William M. Morrison, 1840), 19; Oliver H. Smith, *Early Indiana Trials and Sketches* (Cincinnati: Moore, Wilstach, Keys & Co., 1858), 137; William Allen Butler, *A Retrospect of Forty Years 1825–1865* (New York: Charles Scribner's Sons, 1911), 49–50.
74. Francis Hall, *Travels in Canada, and the United States, in 1816 and 1817* (London: Longman, Hurst, Rees, Orme, & Brown, 1818), 325; Thomas Hamilton, *Men and Manners in America* (Edinburgh: William Blackwood, 1833), 2:127; Harriet Martineau, *Retrospect of Western Travel* (London: Saunders and Otley, 1838), 1:275; Casimir Bohn, *Bohn's Hand-Book of Washington* (Washington, DC: Taylor & Maury, 1852), 35; Alexander Mackay, *The Western World, or, Travels in the United States in 1846–47* (Philadelphia: Lea & Blanchard, 1849), 1:197; "The Supreme Court of the U.S. in 1853–4," *American Law Register* 2 (1854): 706; Robert F. Lucid, ed., *The Journal of Richard Henry Dana, Jr.* (Cambridge, MA: Harvard University Press, 1968), 1:241; *Christian Reflector*, April 22, 1840, 68.
75. Book Review, *North American Review* 15 (1823): 121–22.
76. Maurice G. Baxter, *Daniel Webster & the Supreme Court* (Amherst: University of Massachusetts Press, 1966); "Henry Clay as a Lawyer," *Monthly Law Reporter* 15 (1852): 181; Gabriel Duvall to Edmund Bryce Duvall, March 6, 1816, Duvall Papers, box 1.
77. Joseph Packard, "General Walter Jones," *Virginia Law Register* 7 (1901): 233–38.
78. William Wirt to Dabney Carr, February 27, 1817, John P. Kennedy, *Memoirs of the Life of William Wirt* (Philadelphia: Lea & Blanchard, 1849), 2:15; I. Finch, *Travels in the United States of America and Canada* (London: Longman, Rees, Orme, Brown, Green, and Longman, 1833), 206–07; "Free Remarks," *Niles' Weekly Register*, April 7, 1821, 82.
79. 1843 Rules, rules 29, 40; 1850 Rules, rule 53. The dates in this note are the publication dates of compilations of the Court's rules. The rules themselves were enacted piecemeal in preceding years.
80. Joseph Story to Nathaniel Williams, February 16, 1812, *Life and Letters of Joseph Story*, 1:214; Joseph Story to Samuel Fay, February 24, 1812, *Life and Letters of Joseph Story*, 1:215; Joseph Story to Sarah Story, March 12, 1812, *Life and Letters of Joseph Story*, 1:219.
81. John Marshall to Mary Marshall, January 30, 1831, *Papers of John Marshall*, 12:16; John Marshall to John Randolph, March 4, 1816, *Papers of John Marshall*, 8:127.
82. Edward L. Pierce, ed., *Memoir and Letters of Charles Sumner* (London: Sampson Low, Marston, Searle, & Rivington, 1878), 1:137. Gabriel Duvall's name was often spelled "Duval." His family appears to have used both spellings, but the Court's reporters spelled it "Duvall," so that is the standard spelling today.
83. *Journal of Richard Henry Dana, Jr.*, 1:245.
84. John Marshall to Bushrod Washington, December 29, 1814, *Papers of John Marshall*, 8:63.
85. John Marshall to Joseph Story, November 10, 1831, *Papers of John Marshall*, 12:124; Joseph Story to John Marshall, May 29, 1831, *Papers of John Marshall*, 12:68; Joseph Story to Charles Sumner, March 15, 1838, *Life and Letters of Joseph Story*, 2:296; Joseph Story to Sarah Story, January 16,

1842, *Life and Letters of Joseph Story*, 2:400–01; Joseph Story to John McLean, October 9, 1843, McLean Papers, reel 6.

86. Brown, *John McKinley*, 113–14; Edward Waite, *The Washington Directory, and Congressional, and Executive Register, for 1850* (Washington, DC: Columbus Alexander, 1850), 138; Benjamin Curtis to George Ticknor, December 27, 1851, *Memoir of Benjamin Robbins Curtis*, 1:163–64; Willard L. King, *Lincoln's Manager: David Davis* (Cambridge, MA: Harvard University Press, 1960), 201.

87. Donald G. Morgan, *Justice William Johnson: The First Dissenter* (Columbia: University of South Carolina Press, 1954), 168–89.

88. Undated manuscript filed at the end of the papers for 1853, McLean Papers, reel 11.

Chapter 3

1. Lee J. Epstein, Jeffrey A. Segal, Harold J. Spaeth, and Thomas G. Walker, eds., *The Supreme Court Compendium: Data, Decisions, and Developments*, 5th ed. (Los Angeles: CQ Press, 2012), 250–51.

2. Book Review, *North American Review* 18 (1824): 377.

3. *Blake v. Doherty*, 18 U.S. 359 (1820).

4. Alison L. LaCroix, *The Ideological Origins of American Federalism* (Cambridge, MA: Harvard University Press, 2010).

5. Robin L. Einhorn, *American Taxation, American Slavery* (Chicago: University of Chicago Press, 2006); Douglas A. Irwin, *Clashing Over Commerce: A History of US Trade Policy* (Chicago: University of Chicago Press, 2017), 125–75; Michael Chevalier, *Society, Manners and Politics in the United States* (Boston: Weeks, Jordan & Co., 1839), 152; *Annals of Congress*, 41 (1824): 1308.

6. *M'Culloch v. Maryland*, 17 U.S. 316 (1819); Richard E. Ellis, *Aggressive Nationalism:* McCulloch v. Maryland *and the Foundation of Federal Authority in the Young Republic* (New York: Oxford University Press, 2007); Mark R. Killenbeck, M'Culloch v Maryland: *Securing a Nation* (Lawrence: University Press of Kansas, 2006); Eric Lomazoff, *Reconstructing the National Bank Controversy: Politics and Law in the Early American Republic* (Chicago: University of Chicago Press, 2018). There are variant spellings of James McCulloch's name. The man himself appears to have spelled it McCulloh, but the official report of the case spells it M'Culloch, and today it is commonly spelled McCulloch. Printers at the time often used a backward apostrophe for the lower case "c." Michael G. Collins, *"M'Culloch* and the Turned Comma," *Green Bag* 12 (2009): 265–75.

7. *McCulloch*, 17 U.S. at 332–33, 324–25.

8. *Id.* at 407.

9. *Id.* at 408, 413–14.

10. *Id.* at 431–32.

11. "Sovereignty of the States—No. 1," *Niles' Weekly Register*, March 13, 1819, 41; Gerald Gunther, ed., *John Marshall's Defense of McCulloch v. Maryland* (Stanford, CA: Stanford University Press, 1969), 110; John Marshall to Bushrod Washington, August 3, 1819, Herbert A. Johnson, ed., *The Papers of John Marshall* (Chapel Hill: University of North Carolina Press, 1974–2006), 8:373.

12. "Conflicting Jurisdictions," *National Register*, October 2, 1819, 219; *Osborn v. Bank of the United States*, 22 U.S. 738 (1824). *Osborn* is mostly remembered today for another issue involved in the case: the Court upheld the constitutionality of a provision in the bank's charter authorizing it to sue and be sued in the federal courts.

13. David S. Schwartz, *The Spirit of the Constitution: John Marshall and the 200-Year Odyssey of McCulloch v. Maryland* (New York: Oxford University Press, 2019); Felix Frankfurter, "John Marshall and the Judicial Function," *Harvard Law Review* 69 (1955): 219; *Heart of Atlanta Motel, Inc. v. United States*, 379 U.S. 241, 258 (1964).

14. *Fairfax's Devisee v. Hunter's Lessee*, 11 U.S. 603 (1813); *Martin v. Hunter's Lessee*, 14 U.S. 304, 324 (1816).

15. *Martin*, 14 U.S. at 338, 351–52.

16. *Cohens v. Virginia*, 19 U.S. 264, 416, 423 (1821); Mark A. Graber, "The Passive-Aggressive Virtues: *Cohens v. Virginia* and the Problematic Establishment of Judicial Power," *Constitutional Commentary* 12 (1995): 67–92.

17. John Marshall to Henry Wheaton, June 2, 1821, *Papers of John Marshall*, 9:150; Joseph Story to John Marshall, June 27, 1821, *Papers of John Marshall*, 9:176; "Mr. Stevenson's Resolution,"

United States Law Journal 1 (1822): 216–17; Hugh A. Garland, *The Life of John Randolph of Roanoke* (New York: D. Appleton & Co., 1850), 2:212.

18. *Fletcher v. Peck*, 10 U.S. 87 (1810); Charles F. Hobson, *The Great Yazoo Lands Sale: The Case of Fletcher v. Peck* (Lawrence: University Press of Kansas, 2016); C. Peter Magrath, *Yazoo: Law and Politics in the New Republic* (Providence: Brown University Press, 1966).

19. *Fletcher*, 10 U.S. at 136–37.

20. *New Jersey v. Wilson*, 11 U.S. 164 (1812); *Trustees of Dartmouth College v. Woodward*, 17 U.S. 518 (1819); Francis N. Stites, *Private Interest & Public Gain: The Dartmouth College Case, 1819* (Amherst: University of Massachusetts Press, 1972); Warren Dutton, Book Review, *North American Review* 10 (1820): 83; *Dartmouth College*, 17 U.S. at 644–45.

21. *Green v. Biddle*, 21 U.S. 1 (1823); Stephen Aron, *How the West Was Lost: The Transformation of Kentucky from Daniel Boone to Henry Clay* (Baltimore: Johns Hopkins University Press, 1996), 58–101; *Annals of Congress* 38 (1822): 75.

22. *Annals of Congress* 41 (1823): 28; John Marshall to Henry Clay, December 22, 1823, *Papers of John Marshall*, 9:366; "Kentucky," *Niles' Weekly Register*, November 29, 1823, 194.

23. Jennifer Nedelsky, *Private Property and the Limits of American Constitutionalism: The Madisonian Framework and Its Legacy* (Chicago: University of Chicago Press, 1990), 220; *Sturges v. Crowninshield*, 17 U.S. 122, 205–06 (1819); "Decisions of the Supreme Court," *National Register*, March 6, 1819, 145; "Supreme Court of the United States," *Niles' Weekly Register*, February 27, 1819, 1.

24. *Niles' Weekly Register*, March 20, 1824, 45; "Mr. Barbour's Bill," *United States Intelligencer and Review* 1 (1829): 80–81; Mark A. Graber, "James Buchanan as Savior?: Judicial Power, Political Fragmentation, and the Failed 1831 Repeal of Section 25," *Oregon Law Review* 88 (2009): 95–155; Joseph Story to George Ticknor, January 22, 1831, William Wetmore Story, ed., *Life and Letters of Joseph Story* (Boston: Charles C. Little and James Brown, 1851), 2:49.

25. On Jacksonian influence on the Court, see Gerard N. Magliocca, *Andrew Jackson and the Constitution: The Rise and Fall of Generational Regimes* (Lawrence: University Press of Kansas, 2007).

26. *Ogden v. Saunders*, 25 U.S. 213, 259 (1827).

27. *Id.* at 353, 355–56.

28. *Proprietors of the Charles River Bridge v. Proprietors of the Warren Bridge*, 36 U.S. 420 (1837); Stanley I. Kutler, *Privilege and Creative Destruction: The Charles River Bridge Case* (Baltimore: Johns Hopkins University Press, 1990).

29. Theodore Sedgwick Jr., ed., *A Collection of the Political Writings of William Leggett* (New York: Taylor & Dodd, 1840), 2:7; Richard Peters to Gabriel Duvall, November 10, 1834, Duvall Papers, box 1.

30. *Charles River Bridge*, 36 U.S. at 548–49, 552–53.

31. *Id.* at 608, 615.

32. Mary M. Schweitzer, "State-Issued Currency and the Ratification of the U.S. Constitution," *Journal of Economic History* 49 (1989): 311–22; *Craig v. Missouri*, 29 U.S. 410, 432 (1830).

33. *Id.* at 433.

34. *Briscoe v. President and Directors of the Bank of the Commonwealth of Kentucky*, 36 U.S. 257, 329 (1837).

35. Thomas H. Cox, Gibbons v. Ogden, *Law, and Society in the Early Republic* (Athens: Ohio University Press, 2009); Herbert A. Johnson, Gibbons v. Ogden: *John Marshall, Steamboats, and the Commerce Clause* (Lawrence: University Press of Kansas, 2010); *Gibbons v. Ogden*, 22 U.S. 1, 209 (1824).

36. *Brown v. Maryland*, 25 U.S. 419, 447, 449 (1827). *Brown* is best remembered as the origin of the now-defunct "original package" doctrine, under which the Import-Export Clause barred states from taxing imported goods while the goods were in their original packages but allowed state taxation once the goods lost their character as imports by having been taken out of their original packages and mingled with all the other property in the state.

37. *City of New York v. Miln*, 36 U.S. 102, 146, 159 (1837).

38. Joseph Story to Harriet Martineau, April 7, 1837, *Life and Letters of Joseph Story*, 2:277; Daniel Webster to Caroline Webster, January 10, 1836, C. H. Van Tyne, ed., *The Letters of Daniel Webster* (New York: McClure, Phillips & Co., 1902), 198; Joseph Story to Ezekiel Bacon, April 12, 1845, *Life and Letters of Joseph Story*, 2:528.

39. Book Review, *North American Review* 46 (1838): 153–54; "Political Regeneration," *American Monthly Magazine* 11 (1838): 299.

40. James Kent, Book Review, *New York Review* 2 (1838): 373, 385, 402.
41. "The Supreme Court of the United States," *United States Magazine and Democratic Review* 7 (1840): 498, 513.
42. *Bank of Augusta v. Earle*, 38 U.S. 519, 590, 592 (1839); Alasdair Roberts, *America's First Great Depression: Economic Crisis and Political Disorder After the Panic of 1837* (Ithaca, NY: Cornell University Press, 2012).
43. *Swift v. Tyson*, 41 U.S. 1, 19 (1842); Tony Freyer, *Harmony & Dissonance: The Swift & Erie Cases in American Federalism* (New York: New York University Press, 1981).
44. *The Steam-Boat Thomas Jefferson*, 23 U.S. 428, 429 (1825).
45. *The Propeller Genesee Chief*, 53 U.S. 443, 453–54 (1851).
46. *Thurlow v. Massachusetts*, 46 U.S. 504, 579 (1847); *Smith v. Turner*, 48 U.S. 283 (1849); Tony Alan Freyer, *The Passenger Cases and the Commerce Clause: Immigrants, Blacks, and States' Rights in Antebellum America* (Lawrence: University Press of Kansas, 2014).
47. *Cooley v. Board of Wardens*, 53 U.S. 299 (1852).
48. *Cooley*, 53 U.S. at 319.
49. See, e.g., Douglass C. North, *The Economic Growth of the United States 1790–1860* (New York: Norton, 1966).
50. Benjamin Curtis to George Ticknor, January 14, 1853 and December 20, 1854, Benjamin R. Curtis, ed., *A Memoir of Benjamin Robbins Curtis, LL.D.* (Boston: Little, Brown, 1879), 1:172–73, 1:175–76.

Chapter 4

1. *Fletcher v. Peck*, 10 U.S. 87 (1810).
2. *Id.* at 146–47.
3. *Johnson v. M'Intosh*, 21 U.S. 543, 573–74, 588 (1823); Lindsay G. Robertson, *Conquest by Law: How the Discovery of America Dispossessed Indigenous Peoples of Their Lands* (New York: Oxford University Press, 2005).
4. *Johnson*, 21 U.S. at 590.
5. Stuart Banner, *How the Indians Lost Their Land: Law and Power on the Frontier* (Cambridge, MA: Harvard University Press, 2005), 150–90; William Wirt to James Madison, October 5, 1830, John P. Kennedy, *Memoirs of the Life of William Wirt* (Philadelphia: Lea and Blanchard, 1849), 2:301; Calvin Colton, *Tour of the American Lakes, and Among the Indians of the North-West Territory, in 1830* (London: Frederick Westley and A. H. Davis, 1833), 2:35; Reply, December 11, 1824, *American State Papers: Indian Affairs* (Washington, DC: Gales and Seaton, 1834), 2:571.
6. *Cherokee Nation v. Georgia*, 30 U.S. 1 (1831); Jill Norgren, *The Cherokee Cases: The Confrontation of Law and Politics* (New York: McGraw-Hill, 1996); Tim Alan Garrison, *The Legal Ideology of Removal: The Southern Judiciary and the Sovereignty of Native American Nations* (Athens: University of Georgia Press, 2002); Anthony F. C. Wallace, *The Long, Bitter Trail: Andrew Jackson and the Indians* (New York: Hill and Wang, 1993).
7. Robert S. Davis, "State v. George Tassel: States' Rights and the Cherokee Court Cases, 1827–1830," *Journal of Southern Legal History* 12 (2004): 41–71.
8. *Cherokee Nation*, 30 U.S. at 17–18, 15.
9. *Id.* at 21, 27–28, 25, 31–32.
10. *Id.* at 50, 80; Joseph Story to Sarah Story, January 13, 1832, *Life and Letters of Joseph Story*, 2:79.
11. "The Case of the Cherokee Indians," *American Quarterly Review* 11 (1832): 2; "The Cherokee Case," *North American Review* 33 (1831): 143.
12. *Worcester v. Georgia*, 31 U.S. 515, 559, 561 (1832); Joseph Story to Sarah Story, March 4, 1832, *Life and Letters of Joseph Story*, 2:87.
13. Horace Greeley, *The American Conflict: A History of the Great Rebellion in the United States of America, 1860–'64* (Hartford: O. D. Case, 1864–1867), 1:106.
14. *United States v. Rogers*, 45 U.S. 567 (1846).
15. *Id.* at 572.
16. *Id.* at 572–73.
17. *Fellows v. Blacksmith*, 60 U.S. 366, 371–72 (1856). One of the litigants in *Fellows* was Ely Parker, who in 1869 would go on to be the first American Indian to serve as Commissioner of Indian Affairs.
18. William M. Wiecek, *The Sources of Antislavery Constitutionalism in America, 1760–1848* (Ithaca, NY: Cornell University Press, 1977); *Jones v. Van Zandt*, 46 U.S. 215, 231 (1847).

19. Thomas D. Morris, *Southern Slavery and the Law, 1619–1860* (Chapel Hill: University of North Carolina Press, 1996).

20. *The Antelope*, 23 U.S. 66 (1825); John T. Noonan Jr., *The Antelope: The Ordeal of the Recaptured Africans in the Administrations of James Monroe and John Quincy Adams* (Berkeley: University of California Press, 1977).

21. *The Antelope*, 23 U.S. at 114–15.

22. Justin Crowe, "Westward Expansion, Preappointment Politics, and the Making of the Southern Slaveholding Supreme Court," *Studies in American Political Development* 24 (2010): 90–120.

23. William Johnson, *Nugae Georgicae: An Essay, Delivered to the Literary and Philosophical Society of Charleston, South-Carolina* (Charleston: J. Hoff, 1815), 33–34; Jean Edward Smith, *John Marshall: Definer of a Nation* (New York: Henry Holt and Co., 1996), 488–90; Gerald T. Dunne, "Bushrod Washington and the Mount Vernon Slaves," *Yearbook of the Supreme Court Historical Society* (1980): 25–29. Marshall (along with Taney and Story) is criticized for his decisions concerning slavery in Paul Finkelman, *Supreme Injustice: Slavery in the Nation's Highest Court* (Cambridge, MA: Harvard University Press, 2018).

24. *The Antelope*, 23 U.S. at 120–22.

25. Noonan, *The Antelope*, 133–52.

26. *United States v. The Amistad*, 40 U.S. 518 (1841); Howard Jones, *Mutiny on the Amistad: The Saga of a Slave Revolt and Its Impact on American Abolition, Law, and Diplomacy* (New York: Oxford University Press, 1987). The story of the case was retold in *Amistad*, a 1997 film directed by Steven Spielberg, in which retired Justice Harry Blackmun played Joseph Story.

27. *The Amistad*, 40 U.S. at 593; Jones, *Mutiny*, at 205.

28. *Groves v. Slaughter*, 40 U.S. 449, 500–03 (1841).

29. *Id.* at 504–07. On McLean's view of slavery, see Francis P. Weisenburger, *The Life of John McLean: A Politician on the United States Supreme Court* (Columbus: Ohio State University Press, 1937), 188–95.

30. *Groves*, 40 U.S. at 508, 512–13, 510.

31. *Prigg v. Pennsylvania*, 41 U.S. 539 (1842); H. Robert Baker, *Prigg v. Pennsylvania: Slavery, the Supreme Court, and the Ambivalent Constitution* (Lawrence: University Press of Kansas, 2012); Paul Finkelman, "Story Telling on the Supreme Court: *Prigg v. Pennsylvania* and Justice Joseph Story's Judicial Nationalism," *Supreme Court Review* (1994): 247–94.

32. *Prigg*, 41 U.S. at 611–26.

33. *Id.* at 656–57.

34. *Moore v. Illinois*, 55 U.S. 13 (1852); *North American* (Phila.), June 29, 1846, 1.

35. Eric Foner, *Free Soil, Free Labor, Free Men: The Ideology of the Republican Party Before the Civil War* (New York: Oxford University Press, 1970), 73–102; *Eells v. People*, 5 Ill. 498 (1843).

36. *Moore*, 55 U.S. at 18. *Moore* is also one of the foundations of the "dual sovereignty" doctrine of double jeopardy. Chase argued that federal authority had to be exclusive or else a person might be unconstitutionally punished twice for the same offense. Grier responded with the Court's first extended discussion of the view that a criminal offense is against a specific sovereign and that a defendant may therefore be punished by both the state and the federal governments for the same act. *Id.* at 19–20.

37. Salmon Chase to Alfred P. Edgerton, November 14, 1853, John Niven, ed., *The Salmon P. Chase Papers* (Kent, OH: Kent State University Press, 1993–1998), 2:371. At the time, the five southern justices were Taney, Wayne, Catron, Daniel, and Campbell. The three northern justices Chase believed had been vetted for their "soundness" on slavery were probably Nelson, Grier, and either McLean or Curtis.

38. Paul Finkelman, *An Imperfect Union: Slavery, Federalism, and Comity* (Chapel Hill: University of North Carolina Press, 1981); *Strader v. Graham*, 51 U.S. 82, 93–94 (1850).

39. *Scott v. Sandford*, 60 U.S. 393 (1857). A great deal has been written about the *Dred Scott* case. The books I found most helpful are Don E. Fehrenbacher, *The Dred Scott Case: Its Significance in American Law and Politics* (New York: Oxford University Press, 1978), and Mark A. Graber, *Dred Scott and the Problem of Constitutional Evil* (New York: Cambridge University Press, 2006).

40. *Scott v. Emerson*, 15 Mo. 576 (1852).

41. Fehrenbacher, *Dred Scott Case*, 307–12.

42. H. Jefferson Powell, "Attorney General Taney and the South Carolina Police Bill," *The Green Bag* 5 (2001): 75–100; *Scott*, 60 U.S. at 404–27.

43. 1 Stat. 50, 53 (1789); *Scott*, 60 U.S. at 450–52.

44. *Id.* at 452–53.
45. *Id.* at 454 (Wayne), 475–81, 490 (Daniel), 517 (Campbell), 525–26 (Catron), 469 (Grier).
46. John P. Frank, *Justice Daniel Dissenting: A Biography of Peter V. Daniel, 1784–1860* (Cambridge, MA: Harvard University Press, 1964), 246, 257–58, 285; *Scott*, 60 U.S. at 475.
47. Timothy S. Huebner, "Roger B. Taney and the Slavery Issue: Looking Beyond—and Before—*Dred Scott*," *Journal of American History* 97 (2010): 17–38; Roger Taney to Samuel Nott, August 19, 1857, *Proceedings of the Massachusetts Historical Society* 12 (1871–1873): 445.
48. Robert Saunders Jr., *John Archibald Campbell, Southern Moderate, 1811–1889* (Tuscaloosa: University of Alabama Press, 1997), 57–68; John Archibald Campbell, "Slavery in the United States," *Southern Quarterly Review* 12 (1847): 130, 134.
49. Alexander A. Lawrence, *James Moore Wayne: Southern Unionist* (Chapel Hill: University of North Carolina Press, 1943), 144–45; *Thirty-Seventh Annual Report of the American Colonization Society* (Washington, DC: C. Alexander, 1854), 34; Timothy S. Huebner, *The Southern Judicial Tradition: State Judges and Sectional Distinctiveness, 1790–1890* (Athens: University of Georgia Press, 1999), 61–62; *Fisher's Negroes v. Dabbs*, 14 Tenn. 119, 130–31 (1834); *United States v. Hanway*, 26 F. Cas. 105, 122 (C.C.E.D. Pa. 1851).
50. Foner, *Free Soil, Free Labor, Free Men*, 55–58; Paul Frymer, *Building an American Empire: The Era of Territorial and Political Expansion* (Princeton, NJ: Princeton University Press, 2017), 140–46.
51. Graber, *Dred Scott*, 33–34; *Congressional Globe*, 31st Cong., 1st Sess., 1155, App. 154; *Scott*, 60 U.S. at 429, 455, 469.
52. Fehrenbacher, *Dred Scott Case*, 311–13; James D. Richardson, ed., *A Compilation of the Messages and Papers of the Presidents 1789–1897* (Washington, DC: Government Printing Office, 1897), 5:431.
53. Benjamin R. Curtis, ed., *A Memoir of Benjamin Robbins Curtis, LL.D.* (Boston: Little, Brown, 1879), 1:211–30; Stuart Streichler, *Justice Curtis in the Civil War Era: At the Crossroads of American Constitutionalism* (Charlottesville: University of Virginia Press, 2005), 119–50.
54. Benjamin Curtis to George Ticknor, December 20, 1854, *Memoir of Benjamin Robbins Curtis*, 1:175; Curtis to Ticknor, July 3, 1857, *Memoir*, 1:247.
55. Fehrenbacher, *Dred Scott Case*, 417; John Appleton to Benjamin Curtis, March 15, 1857, Curtis Papers, vol. 1; *Dover Gazette and Strafford Advertiser* [New Hampshire], July 17, 1858.
56. Timothy Farrar, Review, *North American Review* 85 (1857): 414–15; "Nationalization of the U.S. Supreme Court," *National Era*, October 8, 1857 (reprinted from the *Springfield Republican*).
57. Charles Evans Hughes, *The Supreme Court of the United States* (New York: Columbia University Press, 1928), 50; *Planned Parenthood v. Casey*, 505 U.S. 833, 998 (1992).
58. Allan Nevins and Milton Halsey Thomas, eds., *The Diary of George Templeton Strong* (New York: Macmillan, 1952), 3:500–01; *Congressional Globe*, 38th Cong., 2nd Sess. (1865), 1016, 1013.
59. "Maryland State House Removes Statue of Judge Who Wrote Dred Scott Decision," NPR, August 18, 2017, https://www.npr.org/sections/thetwo-way/2017/08/18/544407092/maryland-state-house-removes-statue-of-judge-who-wrote-dred-scott-decision.
60. "The Late Chief Justice Taney," *Milwaukee Daily Sentinel*, October 17, 1864.

Chapter 5

1. Robert Saunders Jr., *John Archibald Campbell, Southern Moderate, 1811–1889* (Tuscaloosa: University of Alabama Press, 1997), 138.
2. "A View of the Confederacy from the Inside," *Century Illustrated Magazine* 38 (1889): 950 (reprinting a letter from Campbell to Benjamin Curtis, July 20, 1865); Benjamin Curtis to Andrew Johnson, August 1, 1865, Campbell Papers, folder 8.
3. Alexander A. Lawrence, *James Moore Wayne: Southern Unionist* (Chapel Hill: University of North Carolina Press, 1943), 189, 199; *The American Annual Cyclopaedia and Register of Important Events of the Year 1862* (New York: D. Appleton & Co., 1863), 2:765.
4. James F. Simon, *Lincoln and Chief Justice Taney: Slavery, Secession, and the President's War Powers* (New York: Simon & Schuster, 2006); *Ex parte Merryman*, 17 F. Cas. 144, 148 (C.C.D. Md. 1861); Brian McGinty, *The Body of John Merryman: Abraham Lincoln and the Suspension of Habeas Corpus* (Cambridge, MA: Harvard University Press, 2011); James D. Richardson, comp., *A Compilation of the Messages and Papers of the Presidents* (New York: Bureau of National Literature, 1897), 7:3226; Amanda Tyler, *Habeas Corpus in Wartime: From the Tower of London to Guantanamo Bay* (New York: Oxford University Press, 2017), 160–71.

5. *Congressional Globe*, 37th Cong., 2nd Sess. 26 (1861); *New-York Daily Tribune*, December 12, 1861, 4; 12 Stat. 576 (1862).
6. 12 Stat. 794 (1863); Paul Kens, *Justice Stephen Field: Shaping Liberty from the Gold Rush to the Gilded Age* (Lawrence: University Press of Kansas, 1997), 95–97.
7. "The Taney Fund: Proceedings of a Meeting of the Bar of the Supreme Court of the United States," *Green Bag* 11 (2008): 373–83; Ross E. Davies, "The Judiciary Funded: The Generosity of David Dudley Field," *Green Bag* 14 (2011): 435–52; John Jay (the grandson of the first chief justice) to Salmon Chase, November 12, 1864, Chase Papers, General Correspondence, Nov. 1864, images 55–59.
8. Lee J. Epstein, Jeffrey A. Segal, Harold J. Spaeth, and Thomas G. Walker, eds., *The Supreme Court Compendium: Data, Decisions, and Developments*, 5th ed. (Los Angeles: CQ Press, 2012), 251; *Documentary History of the Construction and Development of the United States Capitol Building and Grounds*, H.R. Rep. No. 646, 58th Cong., 2nd Sess. (1904), 433; S. D. Wyeth, *The Federal City* (Washington, DC: Gibson Brothers, 1865), 93; E. V. Smalley, "The Supreme Court of the United States," *Century Magazine* 25 (1882): 163–64.
9. Much has been written about the legal issues that arose during and immediately after the Civil War, many of which never reached the Supreme Court. Recent books include Stephen C. Neff, *Justice in Blue and Gray: A Legal History of the Civil War* (Cambridge, MA: Harvard University Press, 2010); John Fabian Witt, *Lincoln's Code: The Laws of War in American History* (New York: Free Press, 2012); Peter Charles Hoffer, *Uncivil Warriors: The Lawyers' Civil War* (New York: Oxford University Press, 2018); Mark E. Neely Jr., *Lincoln and the Triumph of the Nation: Constitutional Conflict in the American Civil War* (Chapel Hill: University of North Carolina Press, 2011); Laura F. Edwards, *A Legal History of the Civil War and Reconstruction: A Nation of Rights* (New York: Cambridge University Press, 2015); Timothy S. Huebner, *Liberty and Union: The Civil War Era and American Constitutionalism* (Lawrence: University Press of Kansas, 2016); and Brian McGinty, *Lincoln and the Court* (Cambridge, MA: Harvard University Press, 2008).
10. *The Prize Cases*, 67 U.S. 635 (1863).
11. *Id.* at 666–71.
12. *Id.* at 688–90.
13. Charles Francis Adams, *Richard Henry Dana: A Biography* (Boston: Houghton Mifflin, 1890), 2:266–67; Jeffrey L. Amestoy, *Slavish Shore: The Odyssey of Richard Henry Dana Jr.* (Cambridge, MA: Harvard University Press, 2015), 237–52.
14. *Ex parte Vallandigham*, 68 U.S. 243, 244–48 (1864); Mark E. Neely Jr., *The Fate of Liberty: Abraham Lincoln and Civil Liberties* (New York: Oxford University Press, 1991); Frank L. Klement, *The Limits of Dissent: Clement L. Vallandigham and the Civil War* (Lexington: University Press of Kentucky, 1970).
15. *Vallandigham*, 68 U.S. at 251–52.
16. George A. Levesque, "Boston's Black Brahmin: Dr. John S. Rock," *Civil War History* 26 (1980): 326–46; John Niven, ed., *The Salmon P. Chase Papers* (Kent, OH: Kent State University Press, 1993–1998), 1:519; Alan Nevins and Milton Halsey Thomas, eds., *The Diary of George Templeton Strong* (New York: Macmillan, 1952), 3:549.
17. *Diary of Gideon Welles* (Boston: Houghton Mifflin, 1911), 2:487; 14 Stat. 209 (1866); Salmon P. Chase to Samuel Miller, June 9, 1866, *Salmon P. Chase Papers*, 5:112; David Davis to Julius Rockwell, August 9, 1866, quoted in John Lewis Moreland, *A Law for Rulers and People: David Davis, Ex parte Milligan, and Constitutional Liberalism During the Civil War Era* (Illinois State University MA thesis, 2016), 128 (I have expanded two of Davis's abbreviations). The statute also reduced the number of circuits from ten to nine, to match the number of then-serving justices. The allocation of states among the circuits that was adopted in 1866 is the one that still exists today, except for the addition of new states and the creation of the Tenth and Eleventh Circuits.
18. 16 Stat. 44 (1869).
19. *Ex parte Milligan*, 71 U.S. 2 (1866). This was the same issue the Court lacked jurisdiction to consider two years earlier in *Ex parte Vallandigham*. The Court had jurisdiction in *Milligan* because Milligan did not seek review of the military commission's judgment directly, as Vallandigham had. Rather, Milligan sought a writ of habeas corpus in a federal circuit court, which certified the question to the Supreme Court because the two judges were divided.
20. *Id.* at 109, 121–22, 126, 131.
21. *Id.* at 136–37.

22. *Reid v. Covert*, 354 U.S. 1, 30–31 (1957); David Davis to Julius Rockwell, February 24, 1867, Davis Papers, box 15; David Davis to John F. Henry, February 3, 1867, Davis Papers, box 15.
23. *New York Times*, January 3, 1867, 4; David Davis to Julius Rockwell, April 22, 1868, Davis Papers, box 16. Despite *Milligan*, the military continued to conduct trials of civilians in the South for the next few years, although in reduced numbers. Neely, *The Fate of Liberty*, 176–79.
24. *Cummings v. Missouri*, 71 U.S. 277 (1867); *Ex parte Garland*, 71 U.S. 333 (1867); Harold Melvin Hyman, *Era of the Oath: Northern Loyalty Tests During the Civil War and Reconstruction* (Philadelphia: University of Pennsylvania Press, 1954).
25. *Cummings*, 71 U.S. at 320; *Garland*, 71 U.S. at 377, 385.
26. "Practice in the Supreme Court," *Harper's Weekly*, March 2, 1867, 130; *New York Herald*, January 16, 1867, 4; *Congressional Globe*, 39th Cong., 2d Sess. (1867), 616.
27. "United States Supreme Court Room," *Harper's Weekly*, April 27, 1867, 266.
28. *Mississippi v. Johnson*, 71 U.S. 475, 499–501 (1867).
29. *Georgia v. Stanton*, 73 U.S. 50, 76–77 (1868).
30. *Ex parte McCardle*, 74 U.S. 506, 515 (1869).
31. *Texas v. White*, 74 U.S. 700 (1869); Harold Melvin Hyman, *The Reconstruction Justice of Salmon P. Chase:* In re Turner *and* Texas v. White (Lawrence: University Press of Kansas, 1997).
32. *White*, 74 U.S. at 725, 729–31, 737.
33. Salmon Chase to Gerrit Smith, April 2, 1868 and April 19, 1868, Chase Papers, General Correspondence, January–May 1868, images 7–8, 14–16.
34. David Davis to Sarah Davis, March 4, 1868 and January 30, 1868, Davis Papers, box 16.
35. Cynthia Nicoletti, *Secession on Trial: The Treason Prosecution of Jefferson Davis* (New York: Cambridge University Press, 2017), 192–204, 293–300.
36. Daniel W. Hamilton, *The Limits of Sovereignty: Property Confiscation in the Union and the Confederacy During the Civil War* (Chicago: University of Chicago Press, 2007), 140–67; *Osborn v. Nicholson*, 80 U.S. 654, 663 (1871).
37. Richard Franklin Bensel, *Yankee Leviathan: The Origins of Central State Authority in America 1859–1877* (New York: Cambridge University Press, 1990), 152, 162. Contracts that explicitly required payment in specie could still be enforced, *Bronson v. Rodes*, 74 U.S. 229 (1868), but many contracts did not require a specific medium of payment.
38. *Hepburn v. Griswold*, 75 U.S. 603, 625 (1870).
39. *Id.* at 616–24.
40. *Id.* at 626; Samuel Miller to William Pitt Ballinger, January 19, 1868, Miller Papers, box 1; Charles Bradley, ed., *Miscellaneous Writings of the Late Hon. Joseph P. Bradley* (Newark: L. J. Hardham, 1902), 71–74.
41. *Hepburn*, 75 U.S. at 632–35.
42. *Legal Tender Cases*, 79 U.S. 457 (1871).
43. *Id.* at 553–54, 572, 634.
44. Emory Washburn to Stephen Field, May 4, 1871, Field Papers; "The Supreme Court and Legal Tender," *Harper's Weekly*, May 20, 1871, 450; "Current Topics," *Albany Law Journal*, March 26, 1870, 234; George F. Hoar, *The Charge Against President Grant and Attorney General Hoar of Packing the Supreme Court of the United States to Secure the Reversal of the Legal Tender Decision, by the Appointment of Judges Bradley and Strong, Refuted* (Worcester: Charles Hamilton, 1896); Bradley, *Miscellaneous Writings*, 45–47.
45. David Davis to W. H. Hidell, April 7, 1884, Davis Papers, box 19.
46. George H. Renton to Joseph Bradley, February 26, 1877, Robert J. Ashford to Joseph Bradley, February 27, 1877, both in Bradley Papers, box 3.
47. David Davis to Sarah Davis, January 27, 1867, Davis Papers, box 15; Artemus Ward, *Deciding to Leave: The Politics of Retirement from the United States Supreme Court* (Albany: State University of New York Press, 2003), 69–89; David N. Atkinson, *Leaving the Bench: Supreme Court Justices at the End* (Lawrence: University Press of Kansas, 1999), 48–58; Charles A. Kent, ed., *Memoir of Henry Billings Brown: Late Justice of the Supreme Court of the United States* (New York: Duffield & Co., 1915), 31.
48. *Congressional Globe*, 41st Cong., 1st Sess. (1869), 337–38.
49. Kens, *Justice Stephen Field*, 97–98.
50. Epstein et al., *Supreme Court Compendium*, 251; *Congressional Globe*, 41st Cong., 1st Sess. (1869), 208.
51. Carl Brent Swisher, *Stephen J. Field: Craftsman of the Law* (Washington, DC: Brookings Institution, 1930), 121; Michael A. Ross, *Justice of Shattered Dreams: Samuel Freeman Miller*

and the Supreme Court During the Civil War Era (Baton Rouge: Louisiana State University Press, 2003), 187, 211; Joseph Bradley to Matthew H. Carpenter, February 9, 1870, Bradley Papers, box 6; Ruth Whiteside, *Justice Joseph Bradley and the Reconstruction Amendments* (PhD diss., Rice University, 1981), 135.

52. William M. Wiecek, "The Reconstruction of Federal Judicial Power, 1863–1875," *American Journal of Legal History* 13 (1969): 333–59; David Brewer to Henrietta Brewer Karrick, May 22, 1891, Brewer Papers, box 1; Felix Frankfurter and James M. Landis, *The Business of the Supreme Court: A Study in the Federal Judicial System* (New York: Macmillan, 1927), 60; Federal Judicial Center, *Caseloads: Supreme Court of the United States, 1878–2017*, www.fjc.gov/history/courts/caseloads-supreme-court-united-states-1878-2017 (accessed April 10, 2024); "The Centennial of the Supreme Court," *Harper's Weekly*, February 8, 1890, 110; William Strong, "The Needs of the Supreme Court," *North American Review* 132 (1881): 439–40; William Strong, "Relief for the Supreme Court," *North American Review* 151 (1890): 567–75; *Centennial Celebration of the Organization of the Federal Judiciary, Held in the City of New York, February 4, 1890* (Washington, DC: s.n., 1890), 22.

53. "Relief of the Supreme Court," *Harper's Weekly*, June 17, 1882, 370; 26 Stat. 826 (1891). The 1891 statute was enacted in the closing days of the 51st Congress, which sat for the first two years of the Benjamin Harrison administration. Harrison would of course be the president nominating the new circuit judges in the 52nd Congress, and it was already known that the Republicans would have a majority in the Senate that would be confirming them.

54. Federal Judicial Center, *Caseloads*.

55. Linda Przybyszewski, *The Republic According to John Marshall Harlan* (Chapel Hill: University of North Carolina Press, 1999), 73–74; Wayne MacVeagh to Rutherford Hayes, August 21, 1877, reproduced in Malvina Shanklin Harlan, *Some Memories of a Long Life, 1854–1911* (New York: Modern Library, 2002), 88–89.

56. Wirt Armistead Cate, *Lucius Q. C. Lamar: Secession and Reunion* (Chapel Hill: University of North Carolina Press, 1935), 91–106; Joseph Angelillo, "The 'Unrepentant Secessionist': The Nomination of L. Q. C. Lamar and the Retreat from Reconstruction," *Journal of the Supreme Court Historical Society* 46(1) (2021): 42–61; Daniel J. Meador, "Lamar to the Court: Last Step to National Reunion," *Yearbook of the Supreme Court Historical Society* (1986): 27–47.

57. Terry Calvani, "The Early Legal Career of Howell Jackson," *Vanderbilt Law Review* 30 (1977): 39–72; Harvey Gresham Hudspeth, "Howell Edmunds Jackson and the Making of Tennessee's First Native-Born Supreme Court Justice, 1893–1895," *Tennessee Historical Quarterly* 58 (1999): 140–55; John Marshall Harlan to Melville Fuller, February 16, 1893, Fuller Papers, box 5; Robert Baker Highsaw, *Edward Douglass White: Defender of the Conservative Faith* (Baton Rouge: Louisiana State University Press, 1981), 19–20; David M. Tucker, "Justice Horace Harmon Lurton: The Shaping of a National Progressive," *American Journal of Legal History* 13 (1969): 223–32.

58. "The Reminiscences of John W. Davis" (1953–1954), 97, CCOH; J. C. C. Black to Joseph Rucker Lamar, August 14, 1915, Lamar Papers, box 2.

Chapter 6

1. Ward Hunt to Morrison Waite, February 8, 1874, Noah Swayne to Morrison Waite, January 26, 1874, both in Waite Papers, box 28.

2. Robert B. Highsaw, *Edward Douglass White: Defender of the Conservative Faith* (Baton Rouge: Louisiana State University Press, 1981), 55–56; "Current Topics," *Albany Law Journal* 49 (1894): 140; Elbert F. Baldwin, "The Supreme Court Justices," *Outlook* 97 (1911): 157.

3. Matthew McDevitt, *Joseph McKenna: Associate Justice of the United States* (Washington, DC: Catholic University of America Press, 1946), 103–305; Charles B. Bellinger to Melville Fuller, September 11, 1897, Fuller Papers, box 3; Barbara A. Perry, "The Life and Death of the 'Catholic Seat' on the United States Supreme Court," *Journal of Law & Politics* 6 (1989): 55–92; *Washington Post*, July 27, 1949, 12; *Washington Evening Star*, July 22, 1949, 11; Linda C. Gugin and James E. St. Clair, *Sherman Minton: New Deal Senator, Cold War Justice* (Indianapolis: Indiana Historical Society, 1997), 304.

4. "Religious Affiliations of the Members of the Supreme Court" (February 1, 1916), Wilson Papers, reel 199; Melvin I. Urofsky, *Louis D. Brandeis: A Life* (New York: Pantheon, 2009), 438–42.

5. Mike Wallace, *Greater Gotham: A History of New York City from 1898 to 1919* (New York: Oxford University Press, 2017), 384; Edward D. White to William Day, March 9, 1916, and February

18, 1916, both in Day Papers, box 31; Harlan B. Phillips, ed., *Felix Frankfurter Reminisces* (New York: Reynal & Co., 1960), 101; Dennis J. Hutchinson and David J. Garrow, eds., *The Forgotten Memoir of John Knox: A Year in the Life of a Supreme Court Clerk in FDR's Washington* (Chicago: University of Chicago Press, 2002), 36–37. While there is no doubt about McReynolds's anti-Semitism, one widely circulated story about it—that in 1924 he refused to sit for the Court's traditional group photograph because he would have to be near Brandeis— turns out not to be true. Franz Jantzen, "From the Urban Legend Department: McReynolds, Brandeis, and the Myth of the 1924 Group Photograph," *Journal of Supreme Court History* 40 (2015): 325–33.

6. Nicholas Murray Butler to Calvin Coolidge, December 4, 1924, Coolidge Papers, reel 43; Drew Pearson and Robert S. Allen, *The Nine Old Men* (Garden City, NY: Doubleday, 1936), 225. Brandeis partially corroborated this story in a letter to Frankfurter, in which he reported that McReynolds, Butler, and Van Devanter urged Attorney General William Mitchell not to nominate Cardozo. Brandeis said he had "no doubt" that the three justices would "be formally correct in their behavior," which suggests he believed they would not mention Cardozo's Judaism even if that was the true reason for their opposition. Louis Brandeis to Felix Frankfurter, February 25, 1932, in Melvin I. Urofsky and David W. Levy, eds., *"Half Brother, Half Son": The Letters of Louis D. Brandeis to Felix Frankfurter* (Norman: University of Oklahoma Press, 1991), 478.

7. Thomas du Pont to George Sutherland, September 11, 1922, Sutherland Papers, box 3.

8. William Howard Taft to Pierce Butler, November 7, 1922, quoted in David J. Danelski, *A Supreme Court Justice Is Appointed* (New York: Random House, 1964), 58–59.

9. David N. Atkinson, *Leaving the Bench: Supreme Court Justices at the End* (Lawrence: University Press of Kansas, 1999), 189–91.

10. *Historical Statistics of the United States*, Millennial Edition Online, Table Ab656-703.

11. Samuel Miller to William Pitt Ballinger, November 28, 1880, Miller Papers, box 2.

12. David Brewer to Melville Fuller, August 4, 1896, Fuller Papers, box 3; Stephen Field to Melville Fuller, March 7, 1896, Fuller Papers, box 4; David Brewer to Melville Fuller, August 21, 1897, Fuller Papers, box 3.

13. Charles Alan Wright, "Authenticity of 'A Dirtier Day's Work' Quote in Question," *Supreme Court Historical Society Quarterly* 13 (Winter 1990): 6–7. The story was first published in Charles Evans Hughes, *The Supreme Court of the United States: Its Foundation, Methods, and Achievements: An Interpretation* (New York: Columbia University Press, 1928), 76, where Hughes explains that he heard it from Harlan. On whether Wright was too quick to discount Harlan's story, see Atkinson, *Leaving the Bench*, 183–87.

14. Paul Kens, *Justice Stephen Field: Shaping Liberty from the Gold Rush to the Gilded Age* (Lawrence: University Press of Kansas, 1997), 263.

15. John Marshall Harlan to Melville Fuller, August 24, 1896, Fuller Papers, box 5; Edward White to William Day, October 16, 1911, Day Papers, box 27.

16. William Howard Taft to Horace Taft, April 17, 1922, Taft Papers, reel 241. The case may have been *Oklahoma Natural Gas Co. v. Oklahoma*, 258 U.S. 234 (1922).

17. Joel Francis Paschal, *Mr. Justice Sutherland: A Man Against the State* (Princeton, NJ: Princeton University Press, 1951); William Howard Taft to George Sutherland, September 10, 1922, Sutherland Papers, box 3.

18. Warren Harding to George Sutherland, September 13, 1922, Sutherland Papers, box 3; Willard L. King, *Melville Weston Fuller: Chief Justice of the United States, 1888–1910* (New York: Macmillan, 1950), 114–21.

19. Salmon Chase to Henry B. Walbridge, January 2, 1868, in John Niven, ed., *The Salmon P. Chase Papers* (Kent, OH: Kent State University Press, 1993–1998), 5:185; David Davis to Julius Rockwell, November 30, 1870, Davis Papers, box 16; Willard L. King, *Lincoln's Manager: David Davis* (Cambridge, MA: Harvard University Press, 1960), 277–83; Samuel Miller to William Pitt Ballinger, December 5, 1875, Miller Papers, box 1; *Harper's Weekly*, April 6, 1872, cover; Kens, *Justice Stephen Field*, 169–235; Merlo J. Pusey, *Charles Evans Hughes* (New York: Macmillan, 1951), 316–34; Oliver Wendell Holmes to John Wigmore, May 10, 1916, Holmes Papers, General Correspondence, Group II, box 18.

20. "Judges and the Presidency," *Harper's Weekly*, July 10, 1880, 434; Melville Fuller to Grover Cleveland, January 2, 1893, Fuller Papers, box 4.

21. C. Peter Magrath, *Morrison R. Waite: The Triumph of Character* (New York: Macmillan, 1963), 50–53; Joseph E. McLean, *William Rufus Day: Supreme Court Justice from Ohio* (Baltimore: Johns Hopkins Press, 1946), 20–21; Pusey, *Charles Evans Hughes*, 111.

22. "Howell E. Jackson," *Harper's Weekly*, February 18, 1893, 152; Andrew L. Kaufman, *Cardozo* (Cambridge, MA: Harvard University Press, 1998), 461–67.

23. Horace Lurton to William Day, July 22, 1906 (telegram and separate letter), Day Papers, box 21; Theodore Roosevelt to William Day, July 25, 1906, Day Papers, box 21; Horace Lurton to Horace Van Deventer, December 3, 1909, Lurton Papers, reel 1. "Judge Sanford" was Edward Terry Sanford, who was a district judge in Tennessee and would become a justice himself in 1923.

24. Francis Warren to Willis Van Devanter, April 2, 1910, and April 14, 1910, both in Van Devanter Papers, box 42; Willis Van Devanter to Francis Warren, December 4, 1910, and December 5, 1910, both in Van Devanter Papers, box 8; David J. Danelski and Joseph S. Tulchin, eds., *The Autobiographical Notes of Charles Evans Hughes* (Cambridge, MA: Harvard University Press, 1973), 171; Oliver Wendell Holmes to Frederick Pollock, May 17, 1925, Mark DeWolfe Howe, ed., *Holmes-Pollock Letters: The Correspondence of Mr. Justice Holmes and Sir Frederick Pollock 1874–1932* (Cambridge, MA: Harvard University Press, 1941), 2:161.

25. *New York Times*, May 15, 1881, 1.

26. George F. Hoar, *Autobiography of Seventy Years* (New York: Charles Scribner's Sons, 1903), 306; David Davis to Judge Drummond, May 21, 1873, December 1, 1873, and December 14, 1873, all in Davis Papers, box 18; Adrian Cook, *The Alabama Claims: American Politics and Anglo-American Relations, 1865–1872* (Ithaca, NY: Cornell University Press, 1975); Magrath, *Morrison R. Waite*, 75–91; *The Nation* 18 (1874): 51.

27. Leonard E. Curtis to Wheeler Peckham, February 16, 1894, Peckham Papers, box 2; Richard Heber Newton to Wheeler Peckham, February 16, 1894, Peckham Papers, box 2.

28. Mabel Walker Willebrandt to Herbert Hoover, February 8, 1929, Herbert Hoover Papers, Campaign and Transition Subject Files, box 75, Hoover Library; *Confirmation of Hon. John J. Parker to be an Associate Justice of the Supreme Court of the United States: Hearing before the Subcommittee of the Committee on the Judiciary* (Washington, DC: Government Printing Office, 1930), 74; Walter White to William Mitchell, April 12, 1930, W. Franklyn Clerk to William Mitchell, April 14, 1930, William Green to George W. Norris et al., April 4, 1930, and John J. Parker to David H. Blair, April 9, 1930, all in Herbert Hoover Papers, President's Subject Files, box 223, Hoover Library; untitled and undated Justice Department memo, Herbert Hoover Papers, President's Personal Files, box 183, Hoover Library.

29. Henry Cabot Lodge to William Moody, December 13, 1906, Moody Papers, vol. 15; Denis Steven Rutkus, Maureen Bearden, and R. Sam Garrett, *Supreme Court Nominations 1789–2005: Actions (Including Speed) by the Senate, the Judiciary Committee, and the President* (New York: Nova Science Publishers, 2006).

30. Kenneth W. Goings, *The NAACP Comes of Age: The Defeat of Judge John J. Parker* (Bloomington: Indiana University Press, 1990); John Anthony Maltese, *The Selling of Supreme Court Nominees* (Baltimore: Johns Hopkins University Press, 1995), 52–69.

31. Samuel Miller to William Pitt Ballinger, March 21, 1874, and December 5, 1875, both in Miller Papers, box 1; "Death of Chief Justice Waite," *American Law Review* 22 (1888): 303.

32. Joseph Bradley to Stephen Field, April 30, 1888, Bradley Papers, box 3; "Chief Justice Melville Weston Fuller," *Outlook* 95 (1910): 548; Todd Peppers, "Chief Justice Melville Weston Fuller and the Great Mustache Debate of 1888," *Journal of Supreme Court History* 45 (2020): 140–50; *New York Times*, July 5, 1910, 5.

33. Oliver Wendell Holmes to Lewis Einstein, December 19, 1910, James Bishop Peabody, ed., *The Holmes-Einstein Letters: Correspondence of Mr. Justice Holmes and Lewis Einstein 1903–1935* (New York: St. Martin's Press, 1964), 57; Oliver Wendell Holmes to Frederick Pollock, September 24, 1910, *Holmes-Pollock Letters*, 1:170.

34. *Civil Rights Cases*, 109 U.S. 3 (1883); *Plessy v. Ferguson*, 163 U.S. 537 (1896). A rough measure of a justice's reputation in a given span of time is the number of biographies of the justice published during that time. In Harlan's case, there were three in the 1990s. Linda Przybyszewski, *The Republic According to John Marshall Harlan* (Chapel Hill: University of North Carolina Press, 1999); Tinsley E. Yarbrough, *Judicial Enigma: The First Justice Harlan* (New York: Oxford University Press, 1995); Loren P. Beth, *John Marshall Harlan: The Last Whig Justice* (Lexington: University Press of Kentucky, 1992).

35. Kens, *Justice Stephen Field*; Charles W. McCurdy, "Justice Field and the Jurisprudence of Government-Business Relations: Some Parameters of Laissez-Faire Constitutionalism, 1863–1897," *Journal of American History* 61 (1975): 970–1005; *Slaughterhouse Cases*, 83 U.S. 36 (1873); *Munn v. Illinois*, 94 U.S. 113 (1877); *Allgeyer v. Louisiana*, 165 U.S. 578, 589 (1897).

36. Michael A. Ross, *Justice of Shattered Dreams: Samuel Freeman Miller and the Supreme Court During the Civil War Era* (Baton Rouge: Louisiana State University Press, 2003); Henry Strong, "Justice Samuel Freeman Miller," *Annals of Iowa* 1 (1894): 247; "Current Topics," *Albany Law Journal* 42 (1890): 321; *Ex parte Yarbrough*, 110 U.S. 651 (1884); *Wabash, St. Louis, & Pacific Railway Co. v. Illinois*, 118 U.S. 557 (1886).

37. J. Gordon Hylton, "The Perils of Popularity: David Josiah Brewer and the Politics of Judicial Reputation," *Vanderbilt Law Review* 62 (2009): 571–72; Oliver Wendell Holmes to Frederick Pollock, April 1, 1910, *Holmes-Pollock Letters*, 1:160; Michael J. Brodhead, *David J. Brewer: The Life of a Supreme Court Justice, 1837–1910* (Carbondale, Ill.: Southern Illinois University Press, 1994); Linda Przybyszewski, "Judicial Conservativism and Protestant Faith: The Case of Justice David J. Brewer," *Journal of American History* 91 (2004): 471–96; *Holy Trinity Church v. United States*, 143 U.S. 457, 471 (1892).

38. There are more biographies of Holmes than of any other justice. They began appearing in his lifetime, with the journalist Silas Bent's *Justice Oliver Wendell Holmes: A Biography* (New York: Vanguard Press, 1932). In 1942, Francis Biddle, who was then the attorney general and who had been Holmes's law clerk many years before, published *Mr. Justice Holmes* (New York: Scribner, 1942), which was made into the 1946 stage play *The Magnificent Yankee*, which was turned into the 1950 film of the same name, for which Louis Calhern was nominated for an Academy Award for his portrayal of Holmes. The film was remade for television in 1965, starring Alfred Lunt as Holmes. In 1944, Catherine Drinker Bowen's book for a popular audience, *Yankee from Olympus: Justice Holmes and His Family* (Boston: Little, Brown, 1944), made the bestseller list. New biographies of Holmes are still published regularly. At this writing, the most recent one is Stephen Budiansky, *Oliver Wendell Holmes: A Life in War, Law, and Ideas* (New York: Norton, 2019). In my view the best of the bunch is still G. Edward White, *Justice Oliver Wendell Holmes: Law and the Inner Self* (New York: Oxford University Press, 1993). On *The Common Law* and related work by Holmes, see David M. Rabban, *Law's History: American Legal Thought and the Transatlantic Turn to History* (New York: Cambridge University Press, 2013), 215–68.

39. Theodore Roosevelt to Henry Cabot Lodge, July 10, 1902, Elting E. Morison, ed., *The Letters of Theodore Roosevelt* (Cambridge, MA: Harvard University Press, 1951–1954), 3:288–89.

40. George F. Hoar to Melville Fuller, November 5, 1902, Fuller Papers, box 5; Oliver Wendell Holmes to Frederick Pollock, August 13, 1902, *Holmes-Pollock Letters*, 1:103.

41. Oliver Wendell Holmes to Frederick Pollock, December 28, 1902, *Holmes-Pollock Letters*, 1:109–110; Louis Menand, *The Metaphysical Club: A Story of Ideas in America* (New York: Farrar, Straus and Giroux, 2001); Oliver Wendell Holmes to John Chipman Gray, May 10, 1914, Holmes Papers, Major Correspondence, box 3; Brad Snyder, *The House of Truth: A Washington Political Salon and the Foundations of American Liberalism* (New York: Oxford University Press, 2017).

42. Urofsky, *Louis D. Brandeis: A Life*; Philippa Strum, *Louis D. Brandeis: Justice for the People* (Cambridge, MA: Harvard University Press, 1984); Brief for the State of Oregon, *Muller v. Oregon*, 208 U.S. 412 (1908).

43. Samuel Miller to William Pitt Ballinger, March 18, 1877, Miller Papers, box 2; William Moody to John Marshall Harlan, July 3, 1910, Harlan I Papers, reel 5; Hoyt Landon Warner, *The Life of Mr. Justice Clarke: A Testament to the Power of Liberal Dissent in America* (Cleveland: Western Reserve University Press, 1959); John Hessin Clarke to Charles Warren, September 21, 1922, Charles Warren Papers, box 1; John Hessin Clarke to George Sutherland, October 4, 1922, Sutherland Papers, box 3; William Howard Taft to Horace Taft, May 15, 1922, Taft Papers, reel 242.

44. Oliver Wendell Holmes to Frederick Pollock, February 24, 1923, *Holmes-Pollock Letters*, 2:113; Dean Acheson, *Morning and Noon* (Boston: Houghton Mifflin, 1965), 65; Robert Hale to Harlan Fiske Stone, June 29, 1929, Stone Papers, box 15.

45. George Sutherland to Carrington T. Marshall, December 4, 1924, Sutherland Papers, box 4; John W. Davis to George Sutherland, September 5, 1922, Sutherland Papers, box 3; Samuel Miller to Horace Gray, December 20, 1881, Gray Papers, box 2; John H. Clarke, *Observations and Reflections on Practice in the Supreme Court of the United States* (s.l.: s.n., 1922), 2, 3, 6.

46. Federal Judicial Center, *Caseloads: Supreme Court of the United States, 1878–2017*, https://www.fjc.gov/history/courts/caseloads-supreme-court-united-states-1878-2017(accessed April 10, 2024); Charles Henry Butler, *A Century at the Bar of the Supreme Court of the United States* (New York: G. P. Putnam's Sons, 1942), 87.

47. *Kalem Co. v. Harper Bros.*, 222 U.S. 55, 60 (1911); *Southern Pacific Co. v. Kentucky*, 222 U.S. 63 (1911); *City of Chicago v. Sturges*, 222 U.S. 313 (1911).

48. *Blinn v. Nelson*, 222 U.S. 1 (1911); *Gring v. Ives*, 222 U.S. 365 (1912); *Porto Rico Sugar Co. v. Lorenzo*, 222 U.S. 481 (1912).

49. Joseph Bradley to Morrison Waite, December 15, 1886, Waite Papers, box 26; Charles A. Kent, ed., *Memoir of Henry Billings Brown: Late Justice of the Supreme Court of the United States* (New York: Duffield & Co., 1915), 29–30.

50. Mahlon Pitney to William Day, November 22, 1916, Day Papers, box 4; Lee Epstein, Jeffrey A. Segal, and Harold J. Spaeth, "The Norm of Consensus on the U.S. Supreme Court," *American Journal of Political Science* 45 (2001): 362–77; Harlan Fiske Stone to Felix Frankfurter, June 8, 1928, and January 16, 1930, both in Stone Papers, box 13.

51. William Howard Taft to Harlan Fiske Stone, January 26, 1927, Stone Papers, box 76 (the case was *Bedford Cut Stone Co. v. Journeyman Stone Cutters' Association of North America*, 274 U.S. 37 (1928)); Thomas G. Walker, Lee Epstein, and William J. Dixon, "On the Mysterious Demise of Consensual Norms in the United States Supreme Court," *Journal of Politics* 50 (1988): 361–89.

52. Edward G. Lowry, "Justice at Zero: The Frigid Austerities Which Enrobe the Members of the United States Supreme Court," *Harper's Weekly*, May 21, 1910, 8; George Shiras III and Winfield Shiras, *Justice George Shiras, Jr., of Pittsburgh, Associate Justice of the United States Supreme Court, 1892–1903: A Chronicle of His Family, Life, and Times* (Pittsburgh: University of Pittsburgh Press, 1953), 135–36.

53. Willis Van Devanter to John Alden Riner, January 16, 1911, and Willis Van Devanter to J. A. Van Orsdel, December 19, 1910, both in Van Devanter Papers, box 8.

54. Harlan Fiske Stone to William Howard Taft, October 21, 1925, and May 25, 1925, and William Howard Taft to Harlan Fiske Stone, October 22, 1925, all in Stone Papers, box 76.

55. John Marshall Harlan to Melville Fuller, September 18, 1902, Fuller Papers, box 5; John Marshall Harlan to William Day, July 14, 1909, Day Papers, box 25; William Howard Taft to George Sutherland, July 25, 1928, Sutherland Papers, box 4; *Wisconsin v. Illinois*, 278 U.S. 367 (1929).

56. Willis Van Devanter to Elmer B. Adams, May 14, 1911, Van Devanter Papers, box 8; Matthew Hofstedt, "Afterword: A Brief History of Supreme Court Messengers," *Journal of Supreme Court History* 39 (2014): 259–63; Malvina Shanklin Harlan, *Some Memories of a Long Life, 1854–1911* (New York: Modern Library, 2002), 163; Lowry, "Justice at Zero," 8.

57. Harlan, *Some Memories*, 163; Isabel McKenna Duffield, "Washington in the 90's," *Overland Monthly and Out West Magazine*, Oct. 1929, 16; Hoftstedt, "Afterword," 261.

58. David Davis to Horace Gray, December 20, 1881, Gray Papers, box 1.

59. Todd C. Peppers, "Birth of an Institution: Horace Gray and the Lost Law Clerks," in *In Chambers: Stories of Supreme Court Law Clerks and Their Justices*, ed. Todd C. Peppers and Artemus Ward (Charlottesville: University of Virginia Press, 2012), 17–41; 24 Stat. 254 (1886).

60. Clare Cushman, "The 'Lost' Clerks of the White Court Era," in *Of Courtiers & Kings: More Stories of Supreme Court Law Clerks and Their Justices*, ed. Todd C. Peppers and Clare Cushman (Charlottesville: University of Virginia Press, 2015), 15–47; Rufus Day to William Day, August 8, 1906, Day Papers, box 21; Clare Cushman, "Sons of Ohio: William Rufus Day, Nepotism, and His Law Clerks," *Journal of Supreme Court History* 45 (2020): 236–61. After becoming a lawyer, Rufus Day returned for a second stint as his father's clerk.

61. David J. Danelski and Joseph S. Tulchin, eds., *The Autobiographical Notes of Charles Evans Hughes* (Cambridge, MA: Harvard University Press, 1973), 163; Charles F. Wilson to William Day, July 9, 1906, Day Papers, box 22; Francis Biddle, *Mr. Justice Holmes* (New York: C. Scribner's Sons, 1943), 12; Francis Biddle, *A Casual Past* (Garden City, NY: Doubleday, 1961), 262; Robert M. Mennel and Christine L. Compston, eds., *Holmes and Frankfurter: Their Correspondence, 1912–1934* (Hanover, NH: University Press of New England, 1996), 40, 178, 215.

62. John B. Owens, "The Clerk, the Thief, His Life as a Baker: Ashton Embry and the Supreme Court Leak Scandal of 1919," *Northwestern University Law Review* 95 (2000): 271–308; G. Edward White, *Alger Hiss's Looking-Glass Wars: The Covert Life of a Soviet Spy* (New York: Oxford University Press, 2004).

63. 41 Stat. 686–87 (1920); Todd C. Peppers, *Courtiers of the Marble Palace: The Rise and Influence of the Supreme Court Law Clerk* (Stanford, CA: Stanford University Press, 2006), 83–144.

Chapter 7

1. Robert J. Kaczorowski, *The Politics of Judicial Interpretation: The Federal Courts, Department of Justice, and Civil Rights, 1866–1876* (New York: Fordham University Press, 2005); Lou Falkner

Williams, *The Great South Carolina Ku Klux Klan Trials, 1871–1872* (Athens: University of Georgia Press, 1996).

2. Robert M. Goldman, *Reconstruction and Black Suffrage: Losing the Vote in Reese and Cruikshank* (Lawrence: University Press of Kansas, 2001); *United States v. Reese*, 92 U.S. 214, 217, 220–21 (1876).

3. *Id.* at 243, 242, 245.

4. Charles Lane, *The Day Freedom Died: The Colfax Massacre, the Supreme Court, and the Betrayal of Reconstruction* (New York: Henry Holt and Co., 2008).

5. *United States v. Cruikshank*, 92 U.S. 542, 551, 553, 554–56 (1876).

6. David W. Blight, *Race and Reunion: The Civil War in American Memory* (Cambridge, MA: The Belknap Press of Harvard University Press, 2001); *New York Times*, March 29, 1876, 4; "Congress and the Supreme Court," *Independent*, April 13, 1876, 14; *Chicago Daily Tribune*, March 29, 1876, 4.

7. *United States v. Harris*, 106 U.S. 629 (1883); "The Civil Rights Decision," *Harper's Weekly*, February 3, 1883, 66.

8. *Civil Rights Cases*, 109 U.S. 3, 11, 17 (1883).

9. *Id.* at 21, 24.

10. *Id.* at 25.

11. Ruth Ann Whiteside, *Justice Joseph Bradley and the Reconstruction Amendments* (PhD diss., Rice University, 1981), 264–65.

12. *Civil Rights Cases*, 109 U.S. at 26, 36–37, 61–62.

13. Loren P. Beth, *John Marshall Harlan: The Last Whig Justice* (Lexington: University Press of Kentucky, 1992), 231–32; J. P. Dolliver to John Harlan, December 19, 1909, Harlan I Papers, reel 23.

14. *New York Daily Tribune*, October 17, 1883, 4; "The End of the Civil-Rights Bill," *Nation*, October 18, 1883, 326.

15. *Proceedings of the Civil Rights Mass-Meeting Held at Lincoln Hall, October 22, 1883* (Washington, DC: C. P. Farrell, 1883), 7, 11, 12.

16. *Ex parte Yarborough*, 110 U.S. 651, 660 (1884); *James v. Bowman*, 190 U.S. 127, 139 (1903).

17. Henry Billings Brown, "The Dissenting Opinions of Mr. Justice Harlan," *American Law Review* 46 (1912): 335.

18. *Louisville, New Orleans & Texas Railway Company v. Mississippi*, 133 U.S. 587, 591, 594 (1890). The earlier case was *Hall v. De Cuir*, 95 U.S. 485 (1878).

19. *Hall*, 95 U.S. at 503.

20. *Plessy v. Ferguson*, 163 U.S. 537, 544 (1896).

21. *Id.* at 551–52.

22. *Id.* at 557, 559.

23. Steve Luxenburg, *Separate: The Story of* Plessy v. Ferguson, *and America's Journey from Slavery to Segregation* (New York: Norton, 2019), 486–87; Charles A. Lofgren, *The Plessy Case: A Legal-Historical Interpretation* (New York: Oxford University Press, 1987), 196–98. One indication of the obscurity of *Plessy* in its own day and for a considerable time thereafter is that the case is not even mentioned in Charles Warren's exhaustive three-volume history of the Court published in 1922. Charles Warren, *The Supreme Court in United States History* (Boston: Little, Brown, 1922). Indeed, while today *Plessy* is one of the Court's best-known cases during the chief justiceship of Melville Fuller, Fuller's biography, published in 1950, does not mention the case. Willard L. King, *Melville Weston Fuller: Chief Justice of the United States, 1888–1910* (New York: Macmillan, 1950).

24. D. H. Pingrey, "A Legal View of Racial Discrimination," *American Law Register* 39 (1891): 86; *Gong Lum v. Rice*, 275 U.S. 78 (1927).

25. *Berea College v. Kentucky*, 211 U.S. 45, 69 (1908); Scott Blakeman, "Night Comes to Berea College: The Day Law and the African-American Reaction," *Filson Club History Quarterly* 70 (1996): 3–26. Strictly speaking, in *Berea College* the Court held that because the college was a corporation chartered by the state, the state could restrict the college's powers in any way it chose. The Court's opinion left open the theoretical possibility that similar regulation might be unconstitutional as applied to a school maintained by an individual rather than by a corporation. But the effect of *Berea College* was to put an end to integrated private education in the South.

26. *Cumming v. Board of Education of Richmond County*, 175 U.S. 528 (1899); J. Morgan Kousser, "Separate but Not Equal: The Supreme Court's First Decision on Racial Discrimination in Schools," *Journal of Southern History* 46 (1980): 17–44.

27. *McCabe v. Atchison, Topeka, & Santa Fe Railway Co.*, 235 U.S. 151, 161, 163–64 (1914).
28. Michael Perman, *Struggle for Mastery: Disfranchisement in the South, 1888–1908* (Chapel Hill: University of North Carolina Press, 2001); *Williams v. Mississippi*, 170 U.S. 213, 221–22, 225 (1898).
29. *Giles v. Harris*, 189 U.S. 475, 488 (1903).
30. Julie Novkov, *Racial Union: Law, Intimacy, and the White State in Alabama, 1865–1954* (Ann Arbor: University of Michigan Press, 2008); *Pace v. State*, 69 Ala. 231, 232 (1881); *Pace v. Alabama*, 106 U.S. 583, 585 (1883).
31. *Strauder v. West Virginia*, 101 U.S. 303 (1880); *Smith v. Mississippi*, 162 U.S. 592 (1896); *Gibson v. Mississippi*, 162 U.S. 565 (1896); Benno C. Schmidt Jr., "Juries, Jurisdiction, and Race Discrimination: The Lost Promise of *Strauder v. West Virginia*," *Texas Law Review* 61 (1983): 1401–99.
32. *Guinn v. United States*, 238 U.S. 347, 364–65 (1915); *Myers v. Anderson*, 238 U.S. 368 (1915); Benno C. Schmidt Jr., "Principle and Prejudice: The Supreme Court and Race in the Progressive Era: Part 3: Black Disfranchisement from the KKK to the Grandfather Clause," *Columbia Law Review* 82 (1982): 879–81.
33. *Buchanan v. Warley*, 245 U.S. 60 (1917); David E. Bernstein, "Philip Sober Controlling Philip Drunk: *Buchanan v. Warley* in Historical Perspective," *Vanderbilt Law Review* 51 (1998): 797–879.
34. *Buchanan*, 245 U.S. at 70, 73–74, 80–81.
35. William B. Hixson Jr., "Moorfield Storey and the Struggle for Equality," *Journal of American History* 55 (1968): 551; *Corrigan v. Buckley*, 271 U.S. 323 (1926).
36. *Bailey v. Alabama*, 219 U.S. 219, 227–28 (1911).
37. *Id*. at 232.
38. *Id*. at 240–41, 244.
39. *United States v. Reynolds*, 235 U.S. 133, 146–47, 150 (1914); Pete Daniel, *The Shadow of Slavery: Peonage in the South, 1901–1969* (Urbana: University of Illinois Press, 1972); Douglas A. Blackmon, *Slavery by Another Name: The Re-Enslavement of Black People in America from the Civil War to World War II* (New York: Doubleday, 2008).
40. John S. Haller Jr., *Outcasts from Evolution: Scientific Attitudes of Racial Inferiority, 1859–1900* (Urbana: University of Illinois Press, 1971); George M. Frederickson, *The Black Image in the White Mind: The Debate on Afro-American Character and Destiny, 1817–1914* (New York: Harper & Row, 1971); Elting E. Morison, ed., *The Letters of Theodore Roosevelt* (Cambridge, MA: Harvard University Press, 1951–1954), 5:226.
41. Robert B. Highsaw, *Edward Douglass White: Defender of the Conservative Faith* (Baton Rouge: Louisiana State University Press, 1981), 24, 182–83; Mark E. Benbow, "Birth of a Quotation: Woodrow Wilson and 'Like Writing History With Lightning,'" *Journal of the Gilded Age and Progressive Era* 9 (2010): 514–15, 519.
42. *Mississippi in 1875: Report of the Select Committee to Inquire into the Mississippi Election of 1875* (Washington, DC: Government Printing Office, 1876), vol. 2, Documentary Evidence, 161; Eric Foner, *Reconstruction: America's Unfinished Revolution, 1863–1877* (New York: Harper & Row, 1988), 601; Horace Lurton to Theodore Roosevelt, July 23, 1906, https://www.theodoroos eveltcenter.org/Research/Digital-Library/Record?libID=o53591; Albert Lawrence, "Biased Justice: James C. McReynolds of the Supreme Court of the United States," *Journal of Supreme Court History* 30 (2005): 252–53.
43. *Plessy*, 163 U.S. at 544; *Virginia v. Rives*, 100 U.S. 313, 333 (1880). On Field's views as to race discrimination, see Paul Kens, *Justice Stephen Field: Shaping Liberty from the Gold Rush to the Gilded Age* (Lawrence: University Press of Kansas, 1997), 184–96.
44. *Berea College v. Commonwealth*, 94 S.W. 623, 626 (Ky. Ct. App. 1906); *People ex rel. King v. Gallagher*, 93 N.Y. 438, 448 (1883); *West Chester and Philadelphia Railroad Co. v. Miles*, 55 Pa. 209, 213 (1867).
45. *Plessy*, 163 U.S. at 559, 561.
46. *United States v. Wong Kim Ark*, 169 U.S. 649, 715 (1898); Carol Nackenoff and Julie Novkov, *American By Birth: Wong Kim Ark and the Battle for Citizenship* (Lawrence: University Press of Kansas, 2021).
47. J. Gordon Hylton, "The Judge Who Abstained in *Plessy v. Ferguson*: Justice David Brewer and the Problem of Race," *Mississippi Law Journal* 61 (1991): 315–64.

48. See, e.g., *Fong Yue Ting v. United States*, 149 U.S. 698 (1893); *Lem Moon Sing v. United States*, 158 U.S. 538 (1895); *United States v. Ju Toy*, 198 U.S. 253 (1905). One notable exception was *Yick Wo v. Hopkins*, 118 U.S. 356 (1886), in which the Court held that San Francisco violated the Equal Protection Clause by enforcing a restriction on laundries only against Chinese proprietors.

49. *Chae Chan Ping v. United States*, 130 U.S. 581, 595 (1889); Lon Kurashige, *Two Faces of Exclusion: The Untold Story of Anti-Asian Racism in the United States* (Chapel Hill: University of North Carolina Press, 2016); Lucy E. Salyer, *Laws Harsh as Tigers: Chinese Immigrants and the Shaping of Modern Immigration Law* (Chapel Hill: University of North Carolina Press, 1995); Charles J. McClain, *In Search of Equality: The Chinese Struggle Against Discrimination in Nineteenth-Century America* (Berkeley: University of California Press, 1994).

50. Bartholomew H. Sparrow, *The Insular Cases and the Emergence of American Empire* (Lawrence: University Press of Kansas, 2006); *Downes v. Bidwell*, 182 U.S. 244, 279–80, 384 (1901).

51. Kal Raustiala, *Does the Constitution Follow the Flag? The Evolution of Territoriality in American Law* (New York: Oxford University Press, 2009), 59; F. P. Dunne, "Mr. Dooley Reviews the Supreme Court Decisions," *Washington Post*, June 9, 1901, 27.

52. *Dorr v. United States*, 195 U.S. 138, 145, 148 (1904).

53. Sidney L. Haring, *Crow Dog's Case: American Indian Sovereignty, Tribal Law, and United States Law in the Nineteenth Century* (New York: Cambridge University Press, 1994); *Ex parte Crow Dog*, 109 U.S. 556, 571 (1883); *United States v. Kagama*, 118 U.S. 375, 384 (1886).

54. *Elk v. Wilkins*, 112 U.S. 94, 100 (1884); *Lone Wolf v. Hitchcock*, 187 U.S. 553, 564 (1903); Blue Clark, *Lone Wolf v. Hitchcock: Treaty Rights and Indian Law at the End of the Nineteenth Century* (Lincoln: University of Nebraska Press, 1994).

55. *Bradwell v. Illinois*, 83 U.S. 130, 141–42 (1873); *Minor v. Happersett*, 88 U.S. 162 (1875). The Illinois Supreme Court finally admitted Bradwell to the bar in 1890, when she was terminally ill with cancer. Jane M. Friedman, *America's First Woman Lawyer: The Biography of Myra Bradwell* (Buffalo: Prometheus Books, 1993), 30.

56. U.S. Bureau of the Census, *Negroes in the United States* (Washington, DC: Government Printing Office, 1904), 16; Michael Les Benedict, "Preserving Federalism: Reconstruction and the Waite Court," *Supreme Court Review* 1978 (1978): 39–79.

Chapter 8

1. *Lochner v. New York*, 198 U.S. 45 (1905); William G. Ross, *A Muted Fury: Populists, Progressives, and Labor Unions Confront the Courts, 1890–1937* (Princeton, NJ: Princeton University Press, 1994).

2. Laura Kalman, "In Defense of Progressive Legal Historiography," *Law and History Review* 36 (2018): 1021–88.

3. *Pollock v. Farmers' Loan & Trust Co.*, 157 U.S. 429, 607 (1895); *Appendix: Centennial Celebration of the Organization of the Federal Judiciary*, 134 U.S. 711, 744–45 (1890); Paul Kens, *Justice Stephen Field: Shaping Liberty from the Gold Rush to the Gilded Age* (Lawrence: University Press of Kansas, 1997), 10.

4. Michael A. Ross, *Justice of Shattered Dreams: Samuel Freeman Miller and the Supreme Court During the Civil War Era* (Baton Rouge: Louisiana State University Press, 2003), 241–45; Samuel F. Miller, *An Address on the Conflict in This Country Between Socialism and Organized Society: Delivered at the Commencement of State University of Iowa, June 19th, 1888* (Ames, Iowa: State University of Iowa, 1888), 8.

5. David J. Brewer, *Protection to Private Property from Public Attack: An Address Delivered Before the Graduating Class at the Sixty-Seventh Anniversary of Yale Law School* (New Haven, CT: Hoggson & Robinson, 1891), 7, 10; David J. Brewer, "The Nation's Safeguard," *Proceedings of the New York State Bar Association Sixteenth Annual Meeting* (New York: New York State Bar Association, 1893), 47.

6. Henry B. Brown, "The Distribution of Property," *Annual Report of the American Bar Association* 16 (1893): 226; Hampton L. Carson, ed., *History of the Celebration of the One Hundredth Anniversary of the Promulgation of the Constitution of the United States* (Philadelphia: J. B. Lippincott Co., 1889), 2:371; George Shiras to Melville Fuller, March 5, 1908, Fuller Papers, box 9; William Howard Taft to Horace D. Taft, November 14, 1929, Taft Papers, reel 315.

7. *In re Debs*, 158 U.S. 564 (1895); *Loewe v. Lawlor*, 208 U.S. 274 (1908).

8. William J. Novak, *The People's Welfare: Law and Regulation in Nineteenth-Century America* (Chapel Hill: University of North Carolina Press, 1996); *Holden v. James*, 11 Mass. 396, 405–06 (1814); *Bethune v. Hughes*, 28 Ga. 560, 565 (1859); *Calder v. Bull*, 3 U.S. 386, 388 (1798).

9. *Slaughter-House Cases*, 83 U.S. 36, 64 (1873); Ronald M. Labbé, *The Slaughterhouse Cases: Regulation, Reconstruction, and the Fourteenth Amendment* (Lawrence: University Press of Kansas, 2003); Catherine McNeur, *Taming Manhattan: Environmental Battles in the Antebellum City* (Cambridge, MA: Harvard University Press, 2014), 134–74; Ross, *Justice of Shattered Dreams*, 202.

10. *Slaughter-House Cases*, 83 U.S. at 87, 128.

11. Robert Saunders Jr., *John Archibald Campbell, Southern Moderate, 1811–1889* (Tuscaloosa: University of Alabama Press, 1997), 214–20; *Slaughter-House Cases*, 83 U.S. at 79–80.

12. *Id.* at 96.

13. Adam Winkler, *We the Corporations: How American Businesses Won Their Civil Rights* (New York: Liveright, 2018), 113–60.

14. *Munn v. Illinois*, 94 U.S. 113, 126–26, 131–32 (1877); William Cronon, *Nature's Metropolis: Chicago and the Great West* (New York: Norton, 1991), 109–42.

15. *Munn*, 94 U.S. at 142, 141, 148.

16. *Powell v. Pennsylvania*, 127 U.S. 678, 684, 689, 695 (1888).

17. *Davidson v. New Orleans*, 96 U.S. 97, 104 (1878); *Missouri Pacific Railway Co. v. Humes*, 115 U.S. 512, 520–21 (1885).

18. *Powell*, 127 U.S. at 684 (quoting the *Sinking Fund Cases*, 99 U.S. 700, 718 (1879)).

19. Richard F. Hamm, *Shaping the 18th Amendment: Temperance Reform, Legal Culture, and the Polity, 1880–1920* (1995); *Mugler v. Kansas*, 123 U.S. 623, 661 (1887). Field dissented in part, because he thought Kansas lacked the power to bar the importation of alcohol from other states, but he agreed that Kansas could prohibit the manufacture of alcohol.

20. *Allgeyer v. Louisiana*, 165 U.S. 578, 589 (1897); Thomas M. Cooley, *A Treatise on the Constitutional Limitations Which Rest Upon the Legislative Power of the States of the American Union* (Boston: Little, Brown, 1868), 393; *In re Jacobs*, 98 N.Y. 98, 106 (1885). The statute would almost certainly have been a violation of the Commerce Clause, but the Court had held in *Paul v. Virginia*, 75 U.S. 168, 183 (1869), that insurance is not a form of commerce.

21. *Holden v. Hardy*, 169 U.S. 366, 396, 398 (1898).

22. *Lochner v. New York*, 198 U.S. 45, 58–59 (1905); Paul Kens, *Judicial Power and Reform Politics: The Anatomy of* Lochner v. New York (Lawrence: University Press of Kansas, 1990); David E. Bernstein, *Rehabilitating* Lochner: *Defending Individual Rights Against Progressive Reform* (Chicago: University of Chicago Press, 2011).

23. *Lochner*, 198 U.S. at 63, 64, 56.

24. *Id.* at 70–73.

25. Charles Henry Butler, *A Century at the Bar of the Supreme Court of the United States* (New York: G. P. Putnam's Sons, 1942), 172.

26. *Lochner*, 198 U.S. at 75–76.

27. *Id.* at 75; Mark Francis, *Herbert Spencer and the Invention of Modern Life* (Ithaca, NY: Cornell University Press, 2007); Herbert Spencer, *Social Statics: Or, The Conditions Essential to Human Happiness Specified* (London: John Chapman, 1851), 323, 297.

28. Vivien Hart, *Bound by Our Constitution: Women, Workers, and the Minimum Wage* (Princeton, NJ: Princeton University Press, 1994); *Muller v. Oregon*, 208 U.S. 412, 421–22 (1908).

29. *Hadacheck v. Sebastian*, 239 U.S. 394, 408 (1915); *Block v. Hirsch*, 256 U.S. 135, 156 (1921); *Village of Euclid v. Ambler Realty Co.*, 272 U.S. 365, 394 (1926); Michael Allan Wolf, *The Zoning of America: Euclid v. Ambler* (Lawrence: University Press of Kansas, 2008). Present-day lawyers think of the cases discussed in this paragraph as involving the Takings Clause rather than the Due Process Clause, because that is their doctrinal relevance today, but these cases were also litigated under the Due Process Clause. At the time, doctrinal differences between the two clauses were not nearly as large as they are now.

30. *Jacobson v. Massachusetts*, 197 U.S. 11, 26 (1905); Michael Willrich, *Pox: An American History* (New York: Penguin, 2011), 285–336.

31. Keith E. Whittington, *Repugnant Laws: Judicial Review of Acts of Congress from the Founding to the Present* (Lawrence: University Press of Kansas, 2019), 146–73.

32. *Smyth v. Ames*, 169 U.S. 466, 523, 527 (1898) (citation and internal quotation marks omitted).

33. "Justice Harlan on Railroad Rates," *American Monthly Review of Reviews* 17 (1898): 402, 403.

34. *Smyth*, 169 U.S. at 547–48.
35. *Adair v. United States*, 208 U.S. 161, 169, 174–75, 191–92 (1908); George I. Lovell, "'As Harmless as an Infant': Deference, Denial, and *Adair v. United States*," *Studies in American Political Development* 14 (2000): 212–33.
36. *Coppage v. Kansas*, 236 U.S. 1, 17–19, 27 (1915).
37. *Adkins v. Children's Hospital*, 261 U.S. 525 (1923).
38. David E. Bernstein, "The Feminist 'Horseman,'" *Green Bag* 10 (2007): 379–86; *Adkins*, 261 U.S. at 553.
39. *Id.* at 554–55.
40. *Id.* at 564, 569.
41. "Validity of State Regulation of Hours of Labor," *Central Law Journal* 60 (1905): 403; Louis D. Brandeis, "The Living Law," *Illinois Law Review* 10 (1916): 463.
42. Charles Bonaparte to Baron de Chassiron, January 10, 1907, Bonaparte Papers, box 182.
43. David J. Brewer, *Two Periods in the History of the Supreme Court* (Richmond, Va.: Richmond Press, 1906), 16–17; Thomas F. Bayard to Stephen Field, March 15, 1880, Field Papers; Joseph Hodges Choate to Stephen Field, June 28, 1893, Field Papers.
44. *Wabash, St. Louis & Pacific Railway Co. v. Illinois*, 118 U.S. 557, 572–73 (1886).
45. *United States v. E. C. Knight Co.*, 156 U.S. 1, 12, 13, 14 (1895).
46. *Swift & Co. v. United States*, 196 U.S. 375 (1905); *Standard Oil Co. of New Jersey v. United States*, 221 U.S. 1 (1911); *United States v. American Tobacco Co.*, 221 U.S. 106 (1911); *Federal Baseball Club of Baltimore v. National League of Professional Base Ball Clubs*, 259 U.S. 200, 209 (1922); Stuart Banner, *The Baseball Trust: A History of Baseball's Antitrust Exemption* (New York: Oxford University Press, 2013).
47. *Northern Securities Co. v. United States*, 193 U.S. 197, 400–01 (1904). Roosevelt's banana quote may be apocryphal. It first appeared in print nearly thirty years after Roosevelt supposedly said it, in a 1932 biography of Holmes by the journalist Silas Bent. Silas Bent, *Justice Oliver Wendell Holmes* (New York: Vanguard Press, 1932), 251. When the Court decided *Northern Securities*, Bent was in St. Louis, where he was a reporter for the *St. Louis Post-Dispatch*, so if he had any knowledge of Roosevelt's reaction, it was probably second-hand at best. But it is true that Roosevelt was displeased with Holmes. "Holmes should have been an ideal man on the bench," Roosevelt wrote to Henry Cabot Lodge a couple of years after *Northern Securities*. "As a matter of fact he has been a bitter disappointment." Roosevelt to Lodge, September 4, 1906, quoted in John Garraty, "Holmes's Appointment to the U.S. Supreme Court," *New England Quarterly* 22 (1949): 301.
48. *Pollock v. Farmers' Loan & Trust Co.*, 157 U.S. 429 (1895), 158 U.S. 601 (1895); Richard J. Joseph, *The Origins of the American Income Tax: The Revenue Act of 1894 and Its Aftermath* (Syracuse: Syracuse University Press, 2004); Steven A. Bank, Kirk J. Stark, and Joseph J. Thorndike, *War and Taxes* (Washington, DC: Urban Institute Press, 2008), 35–47; Ajay K. Mehrotra, *Making the Modern American Fiscal State: Law, Politics, and the Rise of Progressive Taxation 1877–1929* (New York: Cambridge University Press, 2013), 86–140.
49. Calvin H. Johnson, "Fixing the Constitutional Absurdity of the Apportionment of Direct Tax," *Constitutional Commentary* 21 (2004): 295–353; Bruce Ackerman, "Taxation and the Constitution," *Columbia Law Review* 99 (1999): 1–58.
50. *Springer v. United States*, 102 U.S. 586, 602 (1881); *Pollock*, 158 U.S. at 583, 628, 637.
51. This question is covered extensively, although perhaps not with complete objectivity, in George Shiras III, *Justice George Shiras Jr. of Pittsburgh*, ed. Winfield Shiras (Pittsburgh: University of Pittsburgh Press, 1953), 168–83.
52. "The Supreme Court and the Income Tax," *Harper's Weekly*, May 25, 1895, 492; Christopher G. Tiedeman, "The Income Tax Decisions as an Object Lesson in Constitutional Construction," *Annals of the American Academy of Political and Social Science* 6 (1895): 274; Francis R. Jones, "Pollock v. Farmers' Loan and Trust Company," *Harvard Law Review* 9 (1895): 198; "Harper's Weekly and the Dissenting Justices," *American Law Review* 29 (1895): 745; Sylvester Pennoyer, "The Income Tax Decision, and the Power of the Supreme Court to Nullify Acts of Congress," *American Law Review* 29 (1895): 550–58.
53. *Official Proceedings of the Democratic National Convention* (Logansport, IN: Wilson, Humphreys & Co., 1896), 230, 252–53; Sheldon D. Pollack, "Origins of the Modern Income Tax, 1894–1913," *The Tax Lawyer* 66 (2013): 295–330.
54. *Hammer v. Dagenhart*, 247 U.S. 251 (1918); Logan E. Sawyer III, "Creating *Hammer v. Dagenhart*," *William & Mary Bill of Rights Journal* 21 (2012): 67–123; John A. Fliter, *Child*

Labor in America: The Epic Legal Struggle to Protect Children (Lawrence: University Press of Kansas, 2018), 69–94; *Champion v. Ames*, 188 U.S. 321 (1903) (Lottery Act); *Hipolite Egg Co. v. United States*, 220 U.S. 45 (1911) (Pure Food and Drug Act); *Hoke v. United States*, 227 U.S. 308 (1913) (Mann Act); William Draper Lewis, "The Federal Power to Regulate Child Labor in the Light of Supreme Court Decisions," *University of Pennsylvania Law Review* 62 (1914): 504.

55. *Hammer*, 247 U.S. at 271–72.

56. *Id.* at 281.

57. "States' Rights vs. the Nation," *New Republic* 15 (1918): 195; *Congressional Record* 56 (1918): 7433; *Bailey v. Drexel Furniture Co.*, 259 U.S. 20 (1922).

58. James M. Beck to William Howard Taft, May 16, 1922, Taft Papers, reel 242; Frederic R. Coudert to William Howard Taft, May 16, 1922, Taft Papers, reel 242.

59. Morton Keller, *Regulating a New Economy: Public Policy and Economic Change in America, 1900–1933* (Cambridge, MA: Harvard University Press, 1990).

60. Theodore Roosevelt, "Judges and Progress," *Outlook*, January 6, 1912, 40; Frank J. Goodnow, *Social Reform and the Constitution* (New York: Macmillan, 1911), 16; Roscoe Pound, "Mechanical Jurisprudence," *Columbia Law Review* 8 (1908): 616.

61. "Harper's Weekly and the Dissenting Justices," *American Law Review* 29 (1895): 745; Frank A. Mehling to Woodrow Wilson, March 13, 1913, Wilson Papers, reel 199.

62. W. F. Dodd, "Social Legislation and the Courts," *Political Science Quarterly* 28 (1913): 4; Robert M. La Follette, "Introduction," in Gilbert E. Roe, *Our Judicial Oligarchy* (New York: B. W. Huebsch, 1912), vi.

63. Tom S. Clark, *The Limits of Judicial Independence* (New York: Cambridge University Press, 2011), 51–52; H.J. Res. 15, 60th Cong., 1st Sess. (1907); H.R. 5148, 62nd Cong., 1st. Sess. (1911); S.J. Res. 142, 62nd Cong., 3rd Sess. (1912).

64. Leslie Marc Durant, "The Validity of State Protective Legislation for Women in Light of Title VII of the Civil Rights Act of 1964," *Suffolk University Law Review* 6 (1971): 38; "Recent Decisions," *Brooklyn Law Review* 37 (1971): 614; William O. Douglas, "Chief Judge Stanley H. Fuld," *Columbia Law Review* 71 (1971): 531; *Moore v. City of East Cleveland*, 431 U.S. 494, 502 (1977); *Obergefell v. Hodges*, 576 U.S. 644, 704 (2015); *Epic Systems Corp. v. Lewis*, 138 S. Ct. 1612, 1630 (2018).

Chapter 9

1. Federal Judicial Center, *Caseloads: Supreme Court of the United States, 1878–2017*, https://www.fjc.gov/history/courts/caseloads-supreme-court-united-states-1878-2017 (accessed April 10, 2024).

2. Henry W. Taft to William Howard Taft, April 6, 1922, Taft Papers, reel 240; William Howard Taft to Henry W. Taft, April 6, 1922, Taft Papers, reel 240; James M. Beck to William Howard Taft, December 16, 1921, Taft Papers, reel 237; William Howard Taft to James M. Beck, December 18, 1921, Taft Papers, reel 237; Thomas J. Walsh, "The Overburdened Supreme Court," in *Proceedings of the Thirty-Third Annual Meeting of the Virginia State Bar Association* (Richmond: Richmond Press, 1922), 234; William Howard Taft to Louis Brandeis, July 25, 1922, Taft Papers, reel 244; *Erie Railroad Co. v. Tompkins*, 304 U.S. 64 (1938).

3. Alpheus Thomas Mason, *William Howard Taft: Chief Justice* (New York: Simon & Schuster, 1965), 17–40; Byron S. Ambler to William R. Day, January 20, 1903, Day Papers, box 18; Charles Henry Butler, *A Century at the Bar of the Supreme Court of the United States* (New York: G. P. Putnam's Sons, 1942), 165.

4. William Howard Taft, "Delays and Defects in the Enforcement of Law in This Country," *North American Review* 187 (1908): 851–52; Alan D. Scheinkman, "The Civil Jurisdiction of the New York Court of Appeals: The Rule and Role of Finality," *St. Johns Law Review* 54 (1980): 449–54; Randall Don Sosnick, "The California Supreme Court and Selective Review," *California Law Review* 72 (1984): 726–30.

5. *Congressional Record* 46 (1910): 25; William Howard Taft, "Address of the President," *Annual Report of the American Bar Association* 37 (1914): 384; William Howard Taft, "The Attacks on the Courts and Legal Procedure," *Kentucky Law Journal* 5 (1916): 15.

6. William Howard Taft to Albert B. Cummins, November 25, 1921, Taft Papers, reel 236; William Howard Taft to James M. Beck, December 4, 1921, Taft Papers, reel 236. Taft later said that the justices' work on the bill began before he joined the Court, William Howard Taft, "Possible and Needed Reforms in Administration of Justice in Federal Courts," *American Bar Association Journal* 8 (1922): 602, but his correspondence suggests otherwise.

7. Edward A. Hartnett, "Questioning Certiorari: Some Reflections Seventy-Five Years After the Judges' Bill," *Columbia Law Review* 100 (2000): 1643–1738; Jonathan Sternberg, "Deciding Not to Decide: The Judiciary Act of 1925 and the Discretionary Court," *Journal of Supreme Court History* 33 (2008): 1–16.

8. William Howard Taft to Horace D. Taft, March 30, 1922, Taft Papers, reel 240; William Howard Taft to Sen. Knute Nelson, January 23, 1922, Taft Papers, reel 238; William Howard Taft to Sen. Albert B. Cummins, March 11, 1922, Taft Papers, reel 240; William Howard Taft to Rep. Joseph Walsh, March 11, 1922, Taft Papers, reel 240; William Howard Taft to Rep. Philip P. Campbell, April 8, 1922, Taft Papers, reel 240; William Howard Taft to House Speaker Frederick H. Gillett, April 8, 1922, Taft papers, reel 240; William Howard Taft to Rep. F. W. Mondell, June 5, 1922, Taft papers, reel 242; William Howard Taft to Willis Van Devanter, February 4, 1922, Taft Papers, reel 238; William Howard Taft to James M. Beck, April 15, 1922, Taft Papers, reel 241.

9. *Jurisdiction of Circuit Courts of Appeals and United States Supreme Court: Hearing Before the Committee on the Judiciary, House of Representatives, 67th Congress, 2nd Session on H.R. 10479* (Washington, DC: Government Printing Office, 1922), 1, 9.

10. *Procedure in Federal Courts: Hearing Before a Subcommittee of the Committee on the Judiciary, United States Senate, 68th Congress, 1st Session, on S. 2060 and S. 2061* (Washington, DC: Government Printing Office, 1924), 29, 32.

11. *Jurisdiction of Circuit Courts of Appeals*, 13; Jeremy Buchman, "Judicial Lobbying and the Politics of Judicial Structure: An Examination of the Judiciary Act of 1925," *Justice System Journal* 24 (2003): 9; 43 Stat. 936 (1925).

12. Felix Frankfurter and James M. Landis, "The Supreme Court Under the Judiciary Act of 1925," *Harvard Law Review* 42 (1928): 14; "American Law Institute Holds Seventh Annual Meeting," *American Bar Association Journal* 15 (1929): 332; Louis D. Brandeis to Felix Frankfurter, February 6, 1925, Melvin I. Urofsky and David W. Levy, eds., *Letters of Louis D. Brandeis* (Albany: State University of New York Press, 1971–1978), 5:160.

13. Harlan Fiske Stone to William O. Douglas, June 23, 1942, Stone Papers, box 74; Felix Frankfurter to Harlan Fiske Stone, August 25, 1941, Stone Papers, box 74; Felix Frankfurter to the Conference, November 23, 1951, Vinson Papers, box 161.

14. Oliver Wendell Holmes to Harold Laski, November 13, 1925, Mark De Wolfe Howe, ed., *Holmes-Laski Letters: The Correspondence of Mr. Justice Holmes and Harold J. Laski, 1916–1935* (Cambridge, MA: Harvard University Press), 2:61.

15. Ryan C. Black and James F. Spriggs II, "An Empirical Analysis of the Length of U.S. Supreme Court Opinions," *Houston Law Review* 45 (2008): 635; Lee J. Epstein, Jeffrey A. Segal, Harold J. Spaeth, and Thomas G. Walker, eds., *The Supreme Court Compendium: Data, Decisions, and Developments*, 5th ed. (Los Angeles: CQ Press, 2012), 247, 253.

16. Andrew Coan, *Rationing the Constitution: How Judicial Capacity Shapes Supreme Court Decision-Making* (Cambridge, MA: Harvard University Press, 2019).

17. Catherine Hetos Skefos, "The Supreme Court Gets a Home," *Yearbook of the Supreme Court Historical Society* (1976): 25–36; Robert Post, "The Incomparable Chief Justiceship of William Howard Taft," *Michigan State Law Review* 2020 (2020): 139–79; *Congressional Record* 21 (1890): 3537–38; *New York Times*, December 8, 1893, 9; *New York Times*, December 17, 1893, 13.

18. Joseph G. Cannon to Melville W. Fuller, December 16, 1896, Fuller Papers, box 4; Melville W. Fuller to Joseph G. Cannon, December 21, 1896, Fuller Papers, box 4; *Congressional Record* 32 (1898): 12; *The Improvement of the Park System of the District of Columbia*, S. Rep. 57-166 (1902), 38.

19. Charles E. Littlefield to Melville W. Fuller, March 3, 1905, Fuller Papers, box 6; David J. Danelski and Joseph S. Tulchin, *The Autobiographical Notes of Charles Evans Hughes* (Cambridge, MA: Harvard University Press, 1973), 161–62; *Congressional Record* 54 (1917): 1715–16.

20. Charles Moore to William Howard Taft, February 2, 1922, Taft Papers, reel 238; William Howard Taft to Charles Moore, February 3, 1922, Taft Papers, reel 238.

21. 44 Stat. 630, 631 (1926); William H. Taft, Willis Van Devanter, Pierce Butler, Edward T. Stanford, and Harlan F. Stone to Reed Smoot, June 8, 1926, Stone Papers, box 81; Louis D. Brandeis to Felix Frankfurter, May 23, 1926, Melvin I. Urofsky and David W. Levy, eds., *"Half Brother, Half Son": The Letters of Louis D. Brandeis to Felix Frankfurter* (Norman: University of Oklahoma Press, 1991), 241.

22. *New York Times*, April 22, 1928, 132; Kate Greene, "Torts Over Tempo: The Life and Career of Judge Burnita Shelton Matthews," *Journal of Mississippi History* 56 (1994): 181–210; *New York Times*, March 28, 1929, 24.

23. Geoffrey Blodgett, "Cass Gilbert, Architect: Conservative at Bay," *Journal of American History* 72 (1985): 615–36; *United States Supreme Court Building*, H. Doc. No. 36, 71st Cong., 1st Sess. (1929), 9; *Public Buildings and Grounds No. 7: Hearings Before the Committee on Public Buildings and Grounds, 70ᵗʰ Cong., 1ˢᵗ Sess., on H.R. 13665 et al.* (1928), 7–8.

24. *United States Supreme Court Building*, 10, 12.

25. Thomas Waggaman to Fred Vinson, August 7, 1948, Vinson Papers, box 166; "Marble v. Velvet," *Time*, December 16, 1935, 17; Richard K. Cook to Thomas Waggaman, August 25, 1948, Vinson Papers, box 166; Richard K. Cook to Thomas Waggaman, October 29, 1948, Vinson Papers, box 166; Thomas Waggaman to Fred Vinson, May 6, 1949, Vinson Papers, box 166; *Washington Post*, May 14, 1952, 12; *Washington Post*, October 11, 1955, 48; *New York Times*, November 4, 1959, 38; *Washington Post*, February 6, 1972, F10.

26. "Supreme Court: New Homes for Justices' Lares, Penates et al.," *Newsweek*, October 12, 1935, 20.

27. *Id.* at 10.

28. *New York Times*, March 12, 1930, 15; *New York Times*, December 8, 1934, 1.

29. David Lynn (the Architect of the Capitol) to Charles Evans Hughes, May 2, 1932, Vinson Papers, box 160; Charles Evans Hughes to David Lynn, May 21, 1932, Vinson Papers, box 160; Herbert Bayard Swope to Charles Evans Hughes, January 25, 1935, Vinson Papers, box 160; Harold M. Burton to Fred Vinson, July 6, 1950, Vinson Papers, box 160; *Hirota v. MacArthur*, 335 U.S. 876, 877 (1948).

30. "Address of Chief Justice Hughes," *American Bar Association Journal* 18 (1932): 728–29.

31. George Sutherland to A. W. Agee, June 4, 1935, Sutherland Papers, box 4; Drew Pearson and Robert S. Allen, *The Nine Old Men* (Garden City, NY: Doubleday, 1936), 15; Dean Acheson, *Morning and Noon* (Boston: Houghton Mifflin, 1965), 57; Melvin I. Urofsky, *Louis D. Brandeis: A Life* (New York: Pantheon, 2009), 587; Harlan Fiske Stone to Owen Roberts, October 26, 1939, Stone Papers, box 76; Alpheus Thomas Mason, *Harlan Fiske Stone: Pillar of the Law* (New York: Viking Press, 1956), 406; Paul A. Freund, "Mr. Justice Brandeis: A Centennial Memoir," *Harvard Law Review* 70 (1957): 788; Henry F. Pringle, "Profiles: Chief Justice—III," *New Yorker*, July 13, 1935; Merlo J. Pusey, *Charles Evans Hughes* (New York: Macmillan, 1951), 690; *New York Times*, October 13, 1935, E11.

32. *New York Times Magazine*, October 6, 1935, 7; Stanley Kay, "The Highest Court in the Land," *Sports Illustrated*, July 25, 2018.

33. Howard C. Westwood, "Mr. Justice Stone—October Term, 1933," 4–9, Stone Papers, box 48; Charles A. Reich, "A Passion for Justice: Living with and Clerking for Justice Hugo Black," in *In Chambers: Stories of Supreme Court Law Clerks and Their Justices*, ed. Todd C. Peppers and Artemus Ward (Charlottesville: University of Virginia Press, 2012), 113.

34. Graham Claytor to Felix Frankfurter, December 7, 1955, Frankfurter Papers, reel 6.

35. "Nine Mortal Men Prepare," *Literary Digest*, September 7, 1935, 5.

36. David M. Rabban, *Free Speech in Its Forgotten Years* (New York: Cambridge University Press, 1997); *Patterson v. Colorado*, 205 U.S. 454, 462 (1907); *Mutual Film Corp. v. Industrial Commission of Ohio*, 236 U.S. 230, 244 (1915); *Davis v. Massachusetts*, 167 U.S. 43, 47 (1897).

37. *Schenck v. United States*, 249 U.S. 47, 52 (1919); *Debs v. United States*, 249 U.S. 211 (1919).

38. *Abrams v. United States*, 250 U.S. 616, 619, 628, 630 (1919).

39. Oliver Wendell Holmes to Felix Frankfurter, June 14, 1925, Robert M. Mennel and Christine L. Compston, eds., *Holmes and Frankfurter: Their Correspondence, 1912–1934* (Hanover, NH: University Press of New England, 1996), 184; *Gitlow v. New York*, 268 U.S. 652, 667–68, 673 (1925); Marc Lendler, Gitlow v. New York: *Every Idea an Incitement* (Lawrence: University Press of Kansas, 2012).

40. *Whitney v. California*, 274 U.S. 357, 375–76 (1927); Philippa Strum, *Speaking Freely:* Whitney v. California *and American Speech Law* (Lawrence: University Press of Kansas, 2015). Brandeis's opinion is styled as a concurrence rather than a dissent because he did not think the Court should address Whitney's free speech argument since her lawyer did not make an appropriate objection in the state courts.

41. *Gitlow*, 268 U.S. at 666; *Whitney*, 274 U.S. at 371; *Near v. Minnesota*, 283 U.S. 697 (1931). It is sometimes said that the Court incorporated the Takings Clause of the Fifth Amendment in *Chicago, Burlington & Quincy Railroad Co. v. City of Chicago*, 166 U.S. 226 (1897), but it is not clear that this was an instance of incorporation as opposed to a straightforward application of the then-prevailing view of due process.

42. *Fiske v. Kansas*, 274 U.S. 380 (1927); *Stromberg v. California*, 283 U.S. 359, 369 (1931).

43. *Frank v. Mangum*, 237 U.S. 309, 347, 350 (1915). There is a large literature on the Leo Frank case, including Steve Oney, *And the Dead Shall Rise: The Murder of Mary Phagan and the Lynching of Leo Frank* (New York: Pantheon, 2003).

44. *Moore v. Dempsey*, 261 U.S. 86, 89–91 (1923); Richard C. Cortner, *A Mob Intent on Death: The NAACP and the Arkansas Riot Cases* (Middletown, CT: Wesleyan University Press, 1988); Grif Stockley, *Blood in Their Eyes: The Elaine Race Massacres of 1919* (Fayetteville: University of Arkansas Press, 2001).

45. *Tumey v. Ohio*, 273 U.S. 510 (1927).

46. *Powell v. Alabama*, 287 U.S. 45, 71 (1932); James Goodman, *Stories of Scottsboro* (New York: Vintage Books, 1995); *Norris v. Alabama*, 294 U.S. 587 (1935); *Patterson v. Alabama*, 294 U.S. 600 (1935).

47. *Brown v. Mississippi*, 297 U.S. 278, 282, 286 (1936); Richard C. Cortner, *A "Scottsboro" Case in Mississippi: The Supreme Court and* Brown v. Mississippi (Jackson: University Press of Mississippi, 1986).

48. William G. Ross, *Forging New Freedoms: Nativism, Education and the Constitution, 1917–1927* (Lincoln: University of Nebraska Press, 1994); Christopher Capozzola, *Uncle Sam Wants You: World War I and the Making of the Modern American Citizen* (New York: Oxford University Press, 2008), 190–97; *Meyer v. Nebraska*, 262 U.S. 390, 400 (1923).

49. *Pierce v. Society of Sisters*, 268 U.S. 510, 534–35 (1925); Paula Abrams, *Cross Purposes:* Pierce v. Society of Sisters *and the Struggle Over Compulsory Public Education* (Ann Arbor: University of Michigan Press, 2009).

50. G. Edward White, *Justice Oliver Wendell Holmes: Law and the Inner Self* (New York: Oxford University Press, 1993), 407; *Buck v. Bell*, 274 U.S. 200, 205, 207 (1927). Much has been written about the case, including Adam Cohen, *Imbeciles: The Supreme Court, American Eugenics, and the Sterilization of Carrie Buck* (New York: Penguin, 2016), and Paul A. Lombardo, *Three Generations, No Imbeciles: Eugenics, the Supreme Court, and* Buck v. Bell (Baltimore: Johns Hopkins University Press, 2008).

51. *Skinner v. Oklahoma ex rel. Williamson*, 316 U.S. 535 (1942); Felix Frankfurter, "Mr. Justice Holmes and the Constitution: A Review of His Twenty-Five Years on the Supreme Court," *Harvard Law Review* 41 (1927): 153; "Sterilization Statute Sustained," *Virginia Law Register* 13 (1927): 372.

52. Patricia Sullivan, *Lift Every Voice: The NAACP and the Making of the Civil Rights Movement* (New York: New Press, 2009); Laura Weinrib, *The Taming of Free Speech: America's Civil Liberties Compromise* (Cambridge, MA: Harvard University Press, 2016); Charles R. Epp, "External Pressure and the Supreme Court's Agenda," in *Supreme Court Decision-Making: New Institutionalist Approaches*, ed. Cornell W. Clayton and Howard Gillman (Chicago: University of Chicago Press, 1999), 255–79.

53. Herbert Wechsler, undated recollection of clerkship with Stone (circa 1947), Stone Papers, box 48; Pusey, *Charles Evans Hughes*, 383–94.

54. *New York Times*, October 8, 1935, 46; *Herndon v. Lowry*, 301 U.S. 242 (1937); Charles H. Martin, *The Angelo Herndon Case and Southern Justice* (Baton Rouge: Louisiana State University Press, 1976).

Chapter 10

1. John Q. Barrett, "Attribution Time: Cal Tinney's 1937 Quip, 'A Switch in Time'll Save Nine,'" *Oklahoma Law Review* 73 (2021): 229–43.

2. Felix Frankfurter to Franklin D. Roosevelt, March 30, 1937, in Max Freedman, ed., *Roosevelt and Frankfurter: Their Correspondence, 1928–1945* (Boston: Little, Brown, 1967), 392; Joseph Alsop and Turner Catledge, *The 168 Days* (Garden City, NY: Doubleday, 1938), 140; Felix Frankfurter, "Mr. Justice Roberts," *University of Pennsylvania Law Review* 104 (1955): 311–17; Laura Kalman, "The Constitution, the Supreme Court, and the New Deal," *American Historical Review* 110 (2005): 1052–80.

3. *Morehead v. New York ex rel. Tipaldo*, 298 U.S. 587 (1936); *West Coast Hotel Co. v. Parrish*, 300 U.S. 379 (1937).

4. There is an enormous literature on this subject. The works I have found most helpful are Laura Kalman, *FDR's Gambit: The Court Packing Fight and the Rise of Legal Liberalism* (New York: Oxford University Press, 2022); G. Edward White, *The Constitution and the New Deal* (Cambridge, MA: Harvard University Press, 2000); Barry Cushman, *Rethinking the New Deal Court: The Structure of a Constitutional Revolution* (New York: Oxford University Press,

1998); William Leuchtenburg, *The Supreme Court Reborn: The Constitutional Revolution in the Age of Roosevelt* (New York: Oxford University Press, 1995); and Richard D. Friedman, "Switching Time and Other Thought Experiments: The Hughes Court and Constitutional Transformation," *Pennsylvania Law Review* 142 (1994): 1891–1984.

5. *Bailey v. Drexel Furniture Co.*, 259 U.S. 20 (1922); *Hammer v. Dagenhart*, 247 U.S. 251 (1918); *Adkins v. Children's Hospital*, 261 U.S. 525 (1923); *Heiner v. Donnan*, 285 U.S. 312 (1932); *New State Ice Co. v. Liebmann*, 285 U.S. 262 (1932); Mitchell Dawson, "The Supreme Court and the New Deal," *Harper's Monthly Magazine* 167 (1933): 642.

6. *Home Building & Loan Association v. Blaisdell*, 290 U.S. 398, 442–45 (1934).

7. *Id.* at 448–51.

8. *Bicentennial Report: Northern District of Ohio, 1789–1989* ([Cleveland]: U.S. Dept. of Justice, 1990), 37–38; Roosevelt campaign address, Baltimore, October 25, 1932, at 3, http://www.fdr library.marist.edu/_resources/images/msf/msf00589(accessed April 10, 2024). The earliest appearance in print of "four horsemen" as a reference to the conservative justices appears to be a 1937 story by the syndicated columnists Drew Pearson and Robert Allen, who reported that the four justices "have come to be known as the Four Horsemen of Reaction." Drew Pearson and Robert S. Allen, "The Washington Merry-Go-Round," *Louisville Courier-Journal*, April 2, 1937, at 2. Pearson and Allen repeated the nickname in a book published soon afterward. Drew Pearson and Robert S. Allen, *The Nine Old Men at the Crossroads* (Garden City NY: Doubleday, 1937), 13.

9. *Nebbia v. New York*, 291 U.S. 502, 515 (1934).

10. *Id.* at 531–32, 534, 536, 537.

11. *Id.* at 554–55, 558–59.

12. *New York Times*, January 10, 1934, 20; *New York Times*, January 9, 1934, 1; *Literary Digest*, April 7, 1934, quoted in Barbara A. Perry and Henry J. Abraham, "Franklin Roosevelt and the Supreme Court: A New Deal and a New Image," in *Franklin D. Roosevelt and the Transformation of the Supreme Court*, ed. Stephen K. Shaw, William D. Pederson, and Frank J. Williams(Armonk, NY: M. E. Sharpe, 2004), 26; Edward S. Corwin, *The Twilight of the Supreme Court: A History of Our Constitutional Theory* (New Haven, CT: Yale University Press, 1934), 99.

13. *Panama Refining Co. v. Ryan*, 293 U.S. 388, 415, 421 (1935).

14. Robert H. Jackson, *The Struggle for Judicial Supremacy: A Study of a Crisis in American Power Politics* (New York: Knopf, 1949), 94; *New York Herald Tribune*, January 9, 1935, 18; *New York Times*, January 9, 1935, 18.

15. *Norman v. Baltimore & Ohio Railroad Co.*, 294 U.S. 240 (1935); *Nortz v. United States*, 294 U.S. 317 (1935); *Perry v. United States*, 294 U.S. 330 (1935); Sebastian Edwards, *American Default: The Untold Story of FDR, the Supreme Court, and the Battle Over Gold* (Princeton, NJ: Princeton University Press, 2018).

16. President's Secretary's File, box 165, Roosevelt Library.

17. *Norman*, 294 U.S. at 307–08, 309–10, 311.

18. *Perry*, 294 U.S. at 350–51, 358.

19. *Id.* at 361, 381; *New York Times*, February 19, 1935, 14; "The Reminiscences of Marquis William Childs" (recorded 1957–1958), 65, CCOH; Felix Frankfurter to Harlan Fiske Stone, February 19, 1935, Frankfurter Papers, reel 3.

20. Warren Austin to Ann Austin, February 19, 1935, Austin Papers, carton I.

21. *Railroad Retirement Board v. Alton Railroad Co.*, 295 U.S. 330 (1935); Harlan Fiske Stone to Felix Frankfurter, May 9, 1935, Frankfurter Papers, reel 3.

22. *Schechter Poultry Corp. v. United States*, 295 U.S. 495 (1935); *Louisville Joint Stock Land Bank v. Radford*, 295 U.S. 555 (1935); *Humphrey's Executor v. United States*, 295 U.S. 602 (1935); Benjamin V. Cohen, meeting notes, May 27 or 28, 1935, Lash Papers, box 1.

23. *United States v. Butler*, 297 U.S. 1 (1936); *Carter v Carter Coal Co.*, 298 U.S. 238 (1936); *Morehead v. New York ex rel. Tipaldo*, 298 U.S. 587 (1936).

24. Harry J. Findlay to Louis D. Brandeis, January 7, 1936, Max Strauss to Louis D. Brandeis, January 8, 1936, Mary Bosworth to Louis D. Brandeis, January 14, 1936, all in Brandeis Papers, reel 52.

25. Thomas Corcoran, "Litigation Involving New Deal Measures" (17 Dec. 1936), Lash Papers, box 1.

26. Franklin D. Roosevelt to Homer Cummings, January 14, 1936; Alexander Holtzoff to Homer Cummings, January 16, 1936; Homer Cummings to Franklin D. Roosevelt, January 16, 1936; all in President's Secretary's File, Box 165, Roosevelt Library; *The Secret Diary of Harold L. Ickes* (New York: Simon & Schuster, 1953–1954), 1:495–96.

27. Franklin D. Roosevelt to Charles C. Burlingham, February 23, 1937, President's Secretary's Files, box 165, Roosevelt Library.

28. *Secret Diary of Harold L. Ickes*, 1:495.

29. E. Larkin to the President, June 4, 1936, and Hankins & Hankins to the President, May 26, 1936, both in President's Official File, box 49, Roosevelt Library; Franklin D. Roosevelt to Felix Frankfurter, February 9, 1937, Max Freedman, ed., *Roosevelt and Frankfurter: Their Correspondence, 1928–1945* (Boston: Little, Brown, 1967), 381.

30. Donald A. Ritchie, *The Columnist: Leaks, Lies, and Libel in Drew Pearson's Washington* (New York: Oxford University Press, 2021), 45; Drew Pearson and Robert S. Allen, *The Nine Old Men* (Garden City, NY: Doubleday, 1936), 200–01, 93.

31. *Congressional Globe*, 41st Cong., 1st Sess. (1869), 337–38; *Annual Report of the Attorney General of the United States* (Washington, DC: Government Printing Office, 1913), 5.

32. *Reorganization of the Federal Judiciary: Hearings Before the Committee on the Judiciary, United States Senate, 75th Cong., 1st Sess., on S. 1392*, 1–3.

33. Gregory A. Caldeira, "Public Opinion and the U.S. Supreme Court: FDR's Court-Packing Plan," *American Political Science Review* 81 (1987): 1139–53; *Daily Boston Globe*, February 9, 1937, 16; William Lasser, *Benjamin V. Cohen: Architect of the New Deal* (New Haven, CT: Yale University Press, 2002), 164–68; Robert H. Jackson, *That Man: An Insider's Portrait of Franklin Roosevelt*, ed. John Q. Barrett (New York: Oxford University Press, 2003), 50; Katie Louchheim, ed., *The Making of the New Deal: The Insiders Speak* (Cambridge, MA: Harvard University Press, 1983), 128; Charles C. Burlingham to Franklin D. Roosevelt, February 19, 1937, President's Secretary's File, box 165, Roosevelt Library; Jeff Shesol, *Supreme Power: Franklin Roosevelt vs. the Supreme Court* (New York: Norton, 2010), 307–49; Stephen Early, "Confidential Memorandum for the President" (February 8, 1937), President's Secretary's File, box 165, Roosevelt Library.

34. "Address Delivered by General Hugh S. Johnson Over Columbia Broadcasting System Net Work [*sic*] Sunday, February 7, 1937, at 2:00 P.M. from New York City," President's Secretary's File, box 165, Roosevelt Library; Fireside Chat, March 9, 1937, https://millercenter.org/the-presidency/presidential-speeches/march-9-1937-fireside-chat-9-court-packing(accessed April 10, 2024).

35. Joseph L. Rauh Jr., "An Unabashed Liberal Looks at a Half-Century of the Supreme Court," *North Carolina Law Review* 69 (1990): 216; Melvin I. Urofsky, *Louis D. Brandeis: A Life* (New York: Pantheon Books, 2009), 715; *Washington Post*, March 17, 1937, 1; Merlo J. Pusey, *Charles Evans Hughes* (New York: Macmillan, 1951), 753.

36. Memoranda of telephone conversations with Burton K. Wheeler and William H. King, March 19, 1937, Hughes Papers, reel 5; David J. Danelski and Joseph S. Tulchin, eds., *The Autobiographical Notes of Charles Evans Hughes* (Cambridge, MA: Harvard University Press, 1973), 304–05; Marquis Childs, "The Supreme Court To-Day," *Harper's Monthly Magazine* 176 (1938): 587–88.

37. *Reorganization of the Federal Judiciary*, 487–88, 491; *Daily Boston Globe*, March 23, 1937, 1.

38. *West Coast Hotel Co. v. Parrish*, 300 U.S. 379 (1937); Helen J. Knowles, *Making Minimum Wage: Elsie Parrish versus the West Coast Hotel Company* (Norman: University of Oklahoma Press, 2021); Edwin McElwain, "The Business of the Supreme Court as Conducted by Chief Justice Hughes," *Harvard Law Review* 63 (1949): 17; "People," *Time*, February 8, 1937, 28; Barry Cushman, "Inside the 'Constitutional Revolution' of 1937," *2016 Supreme Court Review* (2016): 376 n.40.

39. *Morehead v. New York ex rel. Tipaldo*, 298 U.S. 587 (1936); *West Coast Hotel*, 300 U.S. at 397–99.

40. *Id.* at 402–04, 414.

41. *Chicago Daily Tribune*, March 30, 1937, 1; *New York Times*, March 30, 1937, 22; *Washington Post*, April 1, 1937, 2.

42. *NLRB v. Jones & Laughlin Steel Corp.*, 301 U.S. 1, 40 (1937).

43. *Id.* at 76, 78, 99; *Chicago Daily Tribune*, April 13, 1937, 1. Some of the justices were so unhappy with McReynolds's off-script diatribes while he was ostensibly reading his dissents that they changed their customary way of delivering opinions. Rather than reading opinions at length, Stone explained in 1938, he and several colleagues had recently begun to summarize them in just a couple of minutes. Stone had urged this reform for some time, without any success, until the other justices grew exasperated with the cases in which, as Stone delicately put it, "the dissent delivered had no relationship to the written dissent which had been previously been circulated." Harlan Fiske Stone to Felix Frankfurter, March 17, 1938, Stone Papers, box 13.

44. Hiram W. Johnson to Hiram W. Johnson Jr., April 16, 1937, in Robert E. Burke, ed., *The Diary Letters of Hiram Johnson, 1917–1945* (New York: Garland Publishing, Inc., 1983), vol. 6

(unpaginated); Felix Frankfurter to Franklin D. Roosevelt, April 12, 1937, Freedman, *Roosevelt and Frankfurter*, 397; *St. Louis Post-Dispatch*, April 13, 1937, 4.

45. Judge Glock, "Unpacking the Supreme Court: Judicial Retirement, Judicial Independence, and the Road to the 1937 Court Battle," *Journal of American History* 106 (2019): 47–71; 47 Stat. 402 (1932).

46. G. Edward White, *Justice Oliver Wendell Holmes: Law and the Inner Self* (New York: Oxford University Press, 1993), 469; *Daily Boston Globe*, August 14, 1932, A15; Harlan Fiske Stone to Felix Frankfurter, December 9, 1932, and Felix Frankfurter to Harlan Fiske Stone, December 13, 1932, both in Stone Papers, box 13; *Daily Boston Globe*, March 13, 1933, 9.

47. Willis Van Devanter to Mrs. John W. Lacey, October 26, 1932, Van Devanter Papers, box 17; Danelski and Tulchin, eds., *Autobiographical Notes of Charles Evans Hughes*, 302; Alexander Holtzoff to Homer Cummings, December 28, 1936, and Homer Cummings to Franklin D. Roosevelt, December 29, 1936, both in President's Secretary's file, box 165, Roosevelt Library; 50 Stat. 24 (1937).

48. Willis Van Devanter to Franklin D. Roosevelt, May 18, 1937, Van Devanter Papers, box 44; George Sutherland to Franklin D. Roosevelt, January 5, 1938, Sutherland Papers, box 4.

49. *Steward Machine Co. v. Davis*, 301 U.S. 548 (1937); *Helvering v. Davis*, 301 U.S. 619 (1937); S. Rep. No. 711, 75th Cong., 1st Sess. (1937), 23.

50. Clarence C. Dill to Tom Clark, August 15, 1949, Clark Papers (Truman), box 118; Roger K. Newman, *Hugo Black: A Biography* (New York: Pantheon Books, 1994), 205–19; Leuchtenburg, *The Supreme Court Reborn*, 180–212; Harlan Fiske Stone to Hugo Black, January 26, 1938, Stone Papers, box 73. The case was *Adam v. Saenger*, 303 U.S. 59 (1938).

51. Bruce Allen Murphy, *Wild Bill: The Legend and Life of William O. Douglas* (New York: Random House, 2003), 167; Jerome N. Frank to Frank Murphy, February 21, 1939, Robert Jackson Papers, box 13.

52. Francis Biddle, *In Brief Authority* (Garden City, NY: Doubleday, 1962), 93; Thomas Corcoran, Memorandum (n.d.), Lash Papers, box 1; "Reminiscences of Robert Houghwout Jackson, 1952," 790, 787, CCOH; J. Woodford Howard Jr., *Mr. Justice Murphy: A Political Biography* (Princeton, NJ: Princeton University Press, 1968), 340.

53. Franklin D. Roosevelt to Zechariah Chafee Jr., June 16, 1941, OF 41a, box 50, Roosevelt Library; James Rowe Jr., to Franklin D. Roosevelt, June 13, 1941, OF 41a, box 50, Roosevelt Library; Harlan Fiske Stone to Charles Evans Hughes, June 13, 1941, Stone Papers, box 17.

54. John Q. Barrett, "Introduction," in Jackson, *That Man*, xv–xvi; A. Harry Moore to Franklin D. Roosevelt, November 17, 1939, President's Secretary's File, box 166, Roosevelt Library.

55. John M. Ferren, *Salt of the Earth, Conscience of the Court: The Story of Justice Wiley Rutledge* (Chapel Hill: University of North Carolina Press, 2004), 122–30; Francis Biddle, Memorandum, October 28, 1942, Biddle Papers, box 3.

56. Gerald Gunther, *Learned Hand: The Man and the Judge* (New York: Knopf, 1994), 418–28; Felix Frankfurter to Franklin D. Roosevelt, November 3, 1942, Freedman, *Roosevelt and Frankfurter*, 672; Biddle, *In Brief Authority*, 194. When Frankfurter's lobbying for Hand over Rutledge was reported in the press, Frankfurter told Rutledge that the story was "sheer invention parading as information." Felix Frankfurter to Wiley Rutledge, November 6, 1942, Rutledge Papers, box 95.

57. Thomas Corcoran, Memorandum, February 11, 1938, Lash Papers, box 1.

58. *United States v. Carolene Products*, 304 U.S. 144, 152 & n.4 (1938). Strictly speaking, McReynolds was the only dissenter, but Butler's separate opinion, although denominated a concurrence, was in substance closer to a dissent.

59. *United States v. Darby*, 312 U.S. 100, 116 (1941).

60. *Wickard v. Filburn*, 317 U.S. 111, 127–28 (1942).

61. Robert Jackson to Sherman Minton, December 21, 1942, Robert Jackson Papers, box 125; "Memorandum for Mr. Costelloe, Re: *Wickard* Case" (June 19, 1942), 6, Robert Jackson Papers, box 125; Owen J. Roberts, *The Court and the Constitution* (Cambridge, MA: Harvard University Press, 1951), 58.

62. *Williamson v. Lee Optical of Oklahoma, Inc.*, 348 U.S. 483, 488 (1955).

Chapter 11

1. James F. Byrnes, *Speaking Frankly* (New York: Harper & Brothers, 1947), 12–14 (referring to *United States v. Bethlehem Steel Corp.*, 315 U.S. 289 (1942)); "Reminiscences of Robert Houghwout Jackson, 1952," 1123, 1128, CCOH (referring to *White v. Winchester Country Club*, 315 U.S. 32 (1942)).

2. For a more thorough exploration of these questions, see Cliff Sloan, *The Court at War: FDR, His Justices, and the World They Made* (New York: Public Affairs, 2023); Joshua E. Kastenberg and Eric Merriam, *In a Time of Total War: The Federal Judiciary and the National Defense—1940–1954* (London: Routledge, 2016).

3. William O. Douglas to Hugo Black, September 8, 1941, in Melvin I. Urofsky, ed., *The Douglas Letters: Selections from the Private Papers of William O. Douglas* (Bethesda, MD: Adler & Adler, 1987), 108–09.

4. Harlan Fiske Stone to Robert H. Jackson, January 2, 1946, Stone Papers, box 75.

5. Brad Snyder, *Democratic Justice: Felix Frankfurter, the Supreme Court, and the Making of the Liberal Establishment* (New York: Norton, 2022), 387–457; Bruce Allen Murphy, *The Brandeis/Frankfurter Connection: The Secret Political Activities of Two Supreme Court Justices* (New York: Oxford University Press, 1982), 186–303.

6. Franklin D. Roosevelt to Harlan Fiske Stone, July 17, 1942, Stone Papers, box 51; Harlan Fiske Stone to Franklin D. Roosevelt, July 20, 1942, Stone Papers, box 51.

7. Loren P. Beth, *John Marshall Harlan: The Last Whig Justice* (Lexington: University Press of Kentucky, 1992), 165–68; Willard R. King, *Melville Weston Fuller: Chief Justice of the United States, 1888–1910* (New York: Macmillan, 1950), 249–61.

8. Owen J. Roberts, "Now Is the Time: Fortifying the Supreme Court's Independence," *American Bar Association Journal* 35 (1949): 2; David Joseph Danelski and Joseph S. Tulchin, eds., *The Autobiographical Notes of Charles Evans Hughes* (Cambridge, MA: Harvard University Press, 1973), 166–67.

9. Frank Murphy to Franklin D. Roosevelt, May 20, 1940, OF 41a, box 49, Roosevelt Library; Frank Murphy to Franklin D. Roosevelt, July 28, 1941, April 10, 1942, and May 13, 1942, all in President's Secretary's File, box 166, Roosevelt Library; J. Woodford Howard Jr., *Mr. Justice Murphy: A Political Biography* (Princeton, NJ: Princeton University Press, 1968), 273–74; Frank Murphy to Franklin D. Roosevelt, March 25, 1943, Franklin D. Roosevelt to Henry L. Stimson, March 29, 1943, and Henry L. Stimson to Franklin D. Roosevelt, April 1, 1943, all in President's Secretary's File, box 166, Roosevelt Library; "Reminiscences of Robert Houghwout Jackson," 791; George Marshall to Franklin D. Roosevelt, March 16, 1944, President's Secretary's File, box 166, Roosevelt Library.

10. Roger K. Newman, *Hugo Black: A Biography* (New York: Pantheon Books, 1994), 308; John M. Ferren, *Salt of the Earth, Conscience of the Court: The Story of Justice Wiley Rutledge* (Chapel Hill: University of North Carolina Press, 2004), 295.

11. *Ex parte Quirin*, 317 U.S. 1 (1942); Louis Fisher, *Nazi Saboteurs on Trial: A Military Tribunal and American Law* (Lawrence: University Press of Kansas, 2003); Michal R. Belknap, "The Supreme Court Goes to War: The Meaning and Implications of the Nazi Saboteur Case," *Military Law Review* 89 (1980): 59–95; Sidney Fine, *Frank Murphy: The Washington Years* (Ann Arbor: University of Michigan Press, 1984), 218.

12. Francis Biddle, *In Brief Authority* (Garden City, NY: Doubleday, 1962), 328–30.

13. *Quirin*, 317 U.S. at 30–31, 35, 45.

14. *New York Times*, July 27, 1942, 1; Edward S. Corwin, *Total War and the Constitution* (New York: Knopf, 1947), 118; *Atlanta Constitution*, July 28, 1942, 6; *Los Angeles Times*, August 1, 1942, A4; David J. Danelski, "The Saboteurs' Case," *Journal of Supreme Court History* (1996) (1): 69.

15. Of the many books on the internment of Japanese Americans, the best on legal matters is Peter Irons, *Justice at War: The Story of the Japanese American Internment Cases* (Berkeley: University of California Press, 1983).

16. *Hirabayashi v. United States*, 320 U.S. 81, 93, 96–98 (1943).

17. *Id.* at 100–01; *Yasui v. United States*, 320 U.S. 115 (1943).

18. *Hirabayashi*, 320 U.S. at 112.

19. *Korematsu v. United States*, 323 U.S. 214, 216, 218, 223 (1944).

20. *Id.* at 225–26, 240, 243.

21. Edward J. Ennis to Charles Fahy, February 26, 1944, Fahy Papers, box 37; John L. Burling to Charles Fahy, April 13, 1944, Fahy Papers, box 37.

22. *Ex parte Endo*, 323 U.S. 283, 302 (1944); Irons, *Justice at War*, 344–45.

23. *Washington Post*, December 22, 1944, 8; *Nashville Tennessean*, February 28, 1945, 5; Eugene V. Rostow, "The Japanese American Cases—A Disaster," *Yale Law Journal* 54 (1945): 492.

24. US Commission on Wartime Relocation and Internment of Civilians, *Personal Justice Denied* (Washington, DC: Government Printing Office, 1982), 18; 102 Stat. 903 (1988); Biddle, *In Brief*

Authority, 213; *Hirabayashi v. United States*, 828 F.2d 591 (9th Cir. 1987); *Yasui v. United States*, 772 F.2d 1496 (9th Cir. 1985); *Korematsu v. United States*, 584 F. Supp. 1406 (N.D. Cal. 1984); U.S. Department of Justice, "Confession of Error: The Solicitor General's Mistakes During the Japanese-American Internment Cases" (May 20, 2011), https://www.justice.gov/archives/opa/blog/confession-error-solicitor-generals-mistakes-during-japanese-american-internment-cases; *Trump v. Hawaii*, 138 S. Ct. 2392, 2423 (2018).

25. *New York Times*, September 26, 1971, 76; Debra Cassens Weiss, "Scalia: Korematsu Was Wrong, But 'You are Kidding Yourself' If You Think It Won't Happen Again," *ABA Journal*, February 4, 2014.
26. *Yakus v. United States*, 321 U.S. 414, 422, 432, 461–62 (1944).
27. Shawn Francis Peters, *Judging Jehovah's Witnesses: Religious Persecution and the Dawn of the Rights Revolution* (Lawrence: University Press of Kansas, 2000).
28. *Minersville School District v. Gobitis*, 310 U.S. 586, 595–98 (1940).
29. *Minersville School District v. Gobitis*, 108 F.2d 683, 683 n.3 (1939); "The *Gobitis* Case in Retrospect," *Bill of Rights Review* 1 (1941): 267–68; Joseph P. Lash, ed., *From the Diaries of Felix Frankfurter* (New York: Norton, 1975), 254; Peters, *Judging Jehovah's Witnesses*, 72–177.
30. Lash, *Diaries of Felix Frankfurter*, 209; *Jones v. City of Opelika*, 316 U.S. 584, 623–24 (1942).
31. *West Virginia State Board of Education v. Barnette*, 319 U.S. 624, 641, 627, 642, 646–47 (1943); Felix Frankfurter to Harlan Fiske Stone, May 27, 1940, Frankfurter Papers, reel 4.
32. Harry N. Scheiber and Jane L. Scheiber, *Bayonets in Paradise: Martial Law in Hawai'i During World War II* (Honolulu: University of Hawai'i Press, 2016).
33. *Duncan v. Kahanamoku*, 327 U.S. 304, 318, 351, 341–42 (1946).
34. *Oyama v. California*, 332 U.S. 633 (1948); Fred Vinson to Frank Murphy, January 14, 1948, Vinson Papers, box 185.
35. Artemus Ward and David L. Weiden, *Sorcerers' Apprentices: 100 Years of Law Clerks at the United States Supreme Court* (New York: New York University Press, 2006), 36–37; Walter Gellhorn to Gertrude Jenkins, January 21, 1947, Stone Papers, box 48; "Memorandum for Harvey Levin and Norman Colquhoun" (July 19, 1949), Burton Papers, box 79; "Duties of the Law Clerk" (n.d.), Stone Papers, box 48; Wiley Rutledge to Victor Brudney, March 9, 1946, Rutledge Papers, box 12.
36. Erwin N. Griswold to Robert H. Jackson, October 17, 1946, Robert Jackson Papers, box 13; Willard H. Pedrick to Fred M. Vinson, April 24, 1947, Vinson Papers, box 162; Sherman Minton to George D. Braden, "Spring, 1941," Braden Papers, box 1; Hugo Black to H. A. Glickstein, December 13, 1955, Black Papers, box 442.
37. Young B. Smith to Harlan Fiske Stone, December 7, 1931, Stone Papers, box 30; Young B. Smith to Harlan Fiske Stone, November 20, 1934, Harlan Fiske Stone to Young B. Smith, November 24, 1934, Young B. Smith to Harlan Fiske Stone, October 21, 1935, and Young B. Smith to Harlan Fiske Stone, December 14, 1939, all in Stone Papers, box 27.
38. Bruce Allen Murphy, "Fifty-Two Weeks of Boot Camp," in *In Chambers: Stories of Supreme Court Law Clerks and Their Justices*, ed. Todd C. Peppers and Artemus Ward (Charlottesville: University of Virginia Press, 2012), 182.
39. Bruce A. Kimball and Daniel R. Coquillette, *The Intellectual Sword: Harvard Law School, The Second Century* (Cambridge, MA: Harvard University Press, 2020), 312.
40. Wiley Rutledge to Harlan Fiske Stone, June 21, 1943, Rutledge Papers, box 95.
41. William O. Douglas to Judson P. Falknor, March 24, 1943, in Urofsky, *The Douglas Letters*, 46; Jennie Berry Chandra, "Lucile Lomen: The First Female United States Supreme Court Law Clerk," in Peppers and Ward, *In Chambers*, 205; Vern Countryman to William O. Douglas, January 12, 1944, in Mary Whisner, "Douglas Hires a Woman to Clerk," *Green Bag Almanac and Reader* (2020): 300.
42. *Louisville Courier-Journal*, May 1, 1944, 11; *Christian Science Monitor*, October 31, 1944, 3; David J. Danelski, "Lucile Lomen: The First Woman to Clerk at the Supreme Court," *Journal of Supreme Court History* 24 (1999): 47.
43. John P. Frank to Wiley Rutledge, May 24, 1946, Jerome Hall to Wiley Rutledge, June 7, 1946, Wiley Rutledge to John P. Frank, June 11, 1946, and Wiley Rutledge to Jerome Hall, June 11, 1946, all in Rutledge Papers, box 141; Willard H. Pedrick to Fred Vinson, February 22, 1947, and Fred Vinson to Willard H. Pedrick, April 30, 1947, both in Vinson Papers, box 162; Sarah Livingston Davis to Hugo Black, October 4, 1950, and Hugo Black to Sarah Livingston Davis, October 17, 1950, both in Black Papers, box 442.

44. Mary L. Dudziak, *War Time: An Idea, Its History, Its Consequences* (New York: Oxford University Press, 2012); Robert H. Jackson to J. Edgar Hoover, April 8, 1950, Robert Jackson Papers, box 14; *Joint Anti-Fascist Refugee Committee v. McGrath*, 341 U.S. 123, 174 (1951).

45. "Application for Federal Employment" (July 14, 1952), Roland D. Whitman to Fred M. Vinson, July 16, 1952, and Fred M. Vinson to Roland D. Whitman, July 18, 1952, all in Vinson Papers, box 162.

46. Mary Frances Berry, *Stability, Security, and Continuity: Mr. Justice Burton and Decision-Making in the Supreme Court, 1945–1958* (Westport, CT: Greenwood Press, 1978); Harold H. Burton to Harlan Fiske Stone, September 22, 1945, Stone Papers, box 73; Mimi Clark Gronlund, *Supreme Court Justice Tom C. Clark: A Life of Service* (Austin: University of Texas Press, 2009); Linda C. Gugin and James E. St. Clair, *Sherman Minton: New Deal Senator, Cold War Justice* (Indianapolis: Indian Historical Society, 1997).

47. Harry S. Truman to Sherman Minton, May 11, 1945, PPF box 576, Truman Library; Sherman Minton to Harry S. Truman, December 13, 1948, October 23, 1951, and January 30, 1952, all in PPF box 576, Truman Library; Harry S. Truman to Tom Clark, April 3, 1950, Clark Papers (Texas), box B118; James E. St. Clair and Linda C. Gugin, *Chief Justice Fred M. Vinson of Kentucky* (Lexington: University Press of Kentucky, 2002), 190–94; *New York Times*, September 8, 1953, 18.

48. Robert H. Jackson to Herbert F. Goodrich, May 25, 1950, box 13, Robert Jackson Papers; *Baltimore Sun*, November 19, 1951, 7; *Los Angeles Times*, November 23, 1951, 22; *Washington Post*, November 22, 1951, 18; *New York Times*, January 24, 1952, 1.

49. Bruce Allen Murphy, *Wild Bill: The Legend and Life of William O. Douglas* (New York: Random House, 2003), 188–80, 212–32; William O. Douglas to Felix Frankfurter, July 2, 1940, Urofsky, *Douglas Letters*, 215; William O. Douglas to Harlan Fiske Stone, July 12, 1944, box 74, Stone Papers; Murphy, *Wild Bill*, 251–65, 314, 346–47.

50. Lash, *Diaries of Felix Frankfurter*, 229–30, 182. The case was *Bailey v. Central Vermont Railway, Inc.*, 319 U.S. 350 (1943).

51. *In re Summers*, 325 U.S. 561, 570, 571–72 (1945).

52. *American Communications Association v. Douds*, 339 U.S. 382 (1950); *Adler v. Board of Education*, 342 U.S. 485 (1952).

53. Michal R. Belknap, *Cold War Political Justice: The Smith Act, the Communist Party, and American Civil Liberties* (Westport, CT: Greenwood Press, 1977); *Dennis v. United States*, 341 U.S. 494, 509, 568, 564 (1951).

54. Maeva Marcus, *Truman and the Steel Seizure Case: The Limits of Presidential Power* (New York: Columbia University Press, 1977); St. Clair and Gugin, *Chief Justice Fred M. Vinson*, 216–18.

55. *Youngstown Sheet and Tube Co. v. Sawyer*, 343 U.S. 579, 587 (1952).

56. *Id.* at 635–42.

57. William O. Douglas, *Go East, Young Man: The Early Years: The Autobiography of William O. Douglas* (New York: Random House, 1974), 450; Harry S. Truman, *Truman Speaks* (New York: Columbia University Press, 1960), 58–59.

58. See, e.g., Max Lerner, *Nine Scorpions in a Bottle: Great Judges and Cases of the Supreme Court* (New York: Arcade Publishing, 1994); Noah Feldman, *Scorpions: The Battles and Triumphs of FDR's Great Supreme Court Justices* (New York: Twelve, 2010). The earliest published description of the Court as "nine scorpions in a bottle" appears to be in a 1975 newspaper article by the legal journalist Nina Totenberg, who attributes it to Bickel. Nina Totenberg, "Beneath the Marble, Beneath the Robes," *New York Times*, March 16, 1975, SM 14. Dennis Hutchinson also attributes it to Bickel, as the way Bickel described the Court to his students. Dennis J. Hutchinson, "The Black-Jackson Feud," *Supreme Court Review* (1988): 238. There is a long tradition of crediting Oliver Wendell Holmes for the "scorpions" line, but Noah Feldman reports that there is no evidence Holmes ever said anything of the kind. As Feldman also points out, while Bickel was clerking for Frankfurter, the nuclear physicist J. Robert Oppenheimer published an article in *Foreign Affairs* in which he described the United States and the Soviet Union as "two scorpions in a bottle," because each could kill the other but only by risking its own life. Oppenheimer's "scorpions" metaphor was widely quoted in subsequent years, so it may be where Bickel got the idea. Feldman, *Scorpions*, 437 n.1.

59. Felix Frankfurter to "Brethren," October 22, 1942, Stone Papers, box 74; "Memorandum of Mr. Justice Frankfurter for the Conference" (June 1, 1951), Clark Papers (Texas), box B48; Frank Murphy to Wiley Rutledge, n.d. (October Term 1946), Rutledge Papers, box 155; Felix

Frankfurter to Stanley Reed, June 10, 1946, Robert Jackson Papers, box 119; William O. Douglas to Felix Frankfurter, May 29, 1954, Clark Papers (Texas), box B36; Roger K. Newman, *Hugo Black: A Biography* (New York: Pantheon, 1994), 297.

60. James F. Simon, *Independent Journey: The Life of William O. Douglas* (New York: Harper & Row, 1980), 353, 217; Sherman Minton to Robert Jackson, October 16, 1951, Robert Jackson Papers, box 16; *Washington Post*, December 9, 1979, K1; *New York Times*, July 19, 1966, 42; Murphy, *Wild Bill*, 400.

61. *Jewell Ridge Coal Corp. v. Local No. 6167, United Mine Workers of America*, 325 U.S. 161 (1945); Newman, *Hugo Black*, 333–37.

62. Newman, *Hugo Black*, 343–44; Robert Jackson to Harry S. Truman, June 8, 1946, and Harry S. Truman to Robert Jackson, June 8, 1946, both in Vinson Papers, box 161; Harry S. Truman to Bess Truman, June 11, 1946, Robert H. Ferrell, ed., *Dear Bess: The Letters from Harry to Bess Truman, 1910–1959* (Columbia: University of Missouri Press, 1983), 525; Harry S. Truman to Joseph Short, December 19, 1951, WHCF, Official File, box 268, Truman Library.

63. Harlan Fiske Stone, "Memorandum for the Court" (n.d. 1945), Stone Papers, box 82; Robert Jackson to Harlan Fiske Stone, September 8, 1945, Felix Frankfurter to Harlan Fiske Stone, August 20, 1945, and unsigned account (apparently written by Frankfurter), September 27, 1945, all in Robert Jackson Papers, box 119.

64. Lee Epstein, Jeffrey A. Segal, Harold J. Spaeth, and Thomas G. Walker, eds., *The Supreme Court Compendium: Data, Decisions, and Developments*, 5th ed. (Thousand Oaks, Calif.: CQ Press, 2012), 252–55.

65. Thomas G. Walker, Lee Epstein, and William J. Dixon, "On the Mysterious Demise of Consensual Norms in the United States Supreme Court," *Journal of Politics* 50 (1988): 361–89; Harold Burton Diary, October 13, 1946, Burton Papers, reel 2. Burton was very interested in the Court's history. He had a party trick, which he performed each year at a luncheon with the law clerks, of reciting from memory, in chronological order, the names of all the eighty-odd justices who had served on the Court, their home states, and the presidents who appointed them. E. Barrett Prettyman to Felix Frankfurter, February 21, 1955, Frankfurter Papers, reel 7.

66. J. W. Akin to Harlan Fiske Stone, July 21, 1943, Rutledge Papers, box 109; Frederick L. Perry to Harry S. Truman, May 3, 1945, WHCF, Official File, box 268, Truman Library (the former professors were Stone, Douglas, Frankfurter, and Rutledge); *New York Herald Tribune*, January 10, 1944, 16.

67. Harlan Fiske Stone, "Memorandum for the Court" (January 13, 1944), Stone Papers, box 77; Fred Vinson to Felix Frankfurter, December 1, 1948, Vinson Papers, box 161.

68. Felix Frankfurter to C. C. Burlingham, January 11, 1944, Rutledge Papers, box 121 (Frankfurter sent copies of this letter to all the other justices); Felix Frankfurter to Fred Vinson, December 2, 1948, Vinson Papers, box 161.

Chapter 12

1. Alexis de Tocqueville, *Democracy in America*, trans. Henry Reeve (London: Saunders and Otley, 1835–1840), 2:178.

2. Mark V. Tushnet, *The NAACP's Legal Strategy Against Segregated Education, 1925–1950* (Chapel Hill: University of North Carolina Press, 1987).

3. Mary L. Dudziak, *Cold War Civil Rights: Race and the Image of American Democracy* (Princeton, NJ: Princeton University Press, 2000); *New York Times*, August 28, 1943, 24; *New York Times*, August 9, 1949, 28.

4. "The Reminiscences of Marquis William Childs" (recorded 1957–1958), 66, CCOH; Joseph P. Lash, ed., *From the Diaries of Felix Frankfurter* (New York: Norton, 1975), 334.

5. *Id.* at 335; Ross E. Davies, "A Christmas Gift for the Supreme Court: How a 1959 Holiday Party Eclipsed a History of Discrimination," *The Green Bag* 17 (2014): 311–54.

6. Todd C. Peppers, "William Thaddeus Coleman, Jr.: Breaking the Color Barrier at the U.S. Supreme Court," *Journal of Supreme Court History* 33 (2008): 353–70; Felix Frankfurter to Paul Freund, December 18, 1947, Frankfurter Papers, reel 9; *Washington Post*, April 27, 1948, 1; *Atlanta Daily World*, April 29, 1948, 6; James A. Mundy to Felix Frankfurter, April 27, 1948, Frankfurter Papers, reel 9; Orie L. Phillips to Felix Frankfurter, June 2, 1948, Frankfurter Papers, reel 9.

7. *Missouri ex rel. Gaines v. Canada*, 305 U.S. 337, 342–43, 349–50 (1938); James W. Endersby and William T. Horner, *Lloyd Gaines and the Fight to End Segregation* (Columbia: University of Missouri Press, 2016).

8. *Gaines*, 305 U.S. at 349–50, 353–54; Ralph Bunche, "Interview with Mr. Justice Hugo Black" (February 13, 1940), 1, Bunche Papers, box 33. I am grateful to Kal Raustiala for this reference.

9. *Grovey v. Townsend*, 295 U.S. 45 (1935); *Smith v. Allwright*, 321 U.S. 649, 664, 669 (1944); Darlene Clark Hine, *Black Victory: The Rise and Fall of the White Primary in Texas* (Columbia: University of Missouri Press, 2003); Charles L. Zelden, *The Battle for the Black Ballot:* Smith v. Allwright *and the Defeat of the Texas All-White Primary* (Lawrence: University Press of Kansas, 2004).

10. Robert H. Jackson to Harlan Fiske Stone, January 17, 1944, Stone Papers, box 75.

11. Robert W. Mickey, "The Beginning of the End for Authoritarian Rule in America: *Smith v. Allwright* and the Abolition of the White Primary in the Deep South, 1944–1948," *Studies in American Political Development* 22 (2008): 143–82; Karl A. Crowley to Stanley Reed, May 2, 1944, Reed Papers, box 80.

12. Jeffrey D. Gonda, *Unjust Deeds: The Restrictive Covenant Cases and the Making of the Civil Rights Movement* (Chapel Hill: University of North Carolina Press, 2015); Clement E. Vose, *Caucasians Only: The Supreme Court, the NAACP, and the Restrictive Covenant Cases* (Berkeley: University of California Press, 1959); John Paul Stevens, *The Making of a Justice: Reflections on My First 94 Years* (New York: Little, Brown, 2019), 65; *Buchanan v. Warley*, 245 U.S. 60 (1917); *Corrigan v. Buckley*, 271 U.S. 323 (1926); Cert memo, *Shelley v. Kraemer*, Burton Papers, box 153.

13. Norman I. Silber, ed., *With All Deliberate Speed: The Life of Philip Elman: An Oral History Memoir* (Ann Arbor: University of Michigan Press, 2004), 191–93.

14. *Shelley v. Kraemer*, 334 U.S. 1, 19 (1948).

15. David W. Levy, *Breaking Down Barriers: George McLaurin and the Struggle to End Segregated Education* (Norman: University of Oklahoma Press, 2020); Gary M. Lavergne, *Before Brown: Heman Marion Sweatt, Thurgood Marshall, and the Long Road to Justice* (Austin: University of Texas Press, 2010).

16. Memorandum for the United States as Amicus Curiae, *McLaurin v. Oklahoma State Regents* and *Sweatt v. Painter*, 9; Percy D. Williams and Thomas L. Tolan to Tom Clark, April 1, 1950, and Thomas L. Tolan to Tom Clark, August 31, 1949, both in Clark Papers (Texas), box A2.

17. *McLaurin v. Oklahoma State Regents*, 339 U.S. 637, 641 (1950); *Sweatt v. Painter*, 339 U.S. 629, 634 (1950); Tom Clark to the Conference, April 7, 1950, Clark Papers (Texas), box A2; Fred Vinson to Felix Frankfurter, May 24, 1950, and Felix Frankfurter to Fred Vinson, May 19, 1950, both in Vinson Papers, box 207.

18. Frank Murphy to Fred Vinson, n.d., Vinson Papers, box 162.

19. Of the many books and articles written on *Brown*, the ones I found most helpful were Richard Kluger, *Simple Justice: The History of* Brown v. Board of Education *and Black America's Struggle for Equality*, rev. ed. (New York: Knopf, 2004); James T. Patterson, *Brown v. Board of Education: A Civil Rights Milestone and Its Troubled Legacy* (New York: Oxford University Press, 2001); and Mark Tushnet and Katya Lezin, "What Really Happened in *Brown v. Board of Education*," *Columbia Law Review* 91 (1991): 1867–1930.

20. William Henry Harbaugh, *Lawyer's Lawyer: The Life of John W. Davis* (New York: Oxford University Press, 1973), 483–84; Paul E. Wilson, *A Time to Lose: Representing Kansas in* Brown v. Board of Education (Lawrence: University Press of Kansas, 1995).

21. Melvin I. Urofsky, ed., *The Douglas Letters: Selections from the Private Papers of Justice William O. Douglas* (Bethesda, MD: Adler & Adler, 1987), 165–66; Kluger, *Simple Justice*, 618.

22. William Rehnquist, "A Random Thought on the Segregation Cases," Robert Jackson Papers, box 184.

23. "William W. Oliver: Working in the Supreme Court: Comments on Court, Brown Decision, Warren and Other Justices" (recorded 1972), 23, EWOHP; Silber, *With All Deliberate Speed*, 219.

24. "Herbert Brownell: Earl Warren's Appointment to the Supreme Court" (1975), 1–11, EWOHP.

25. "Interview with Clarence Manion" (recorded 1976), 82–83, CCOH; "William W. Oliver," 5; William H. Rehnquist to Robert H. Jackson, April 26, 1954, Robert Jackson Papers, box 19; Alfred Christie to Dwight D. Eisenhower, September 30, 1953, and Anita Garrett to Dwight D. Eisenhower, September 30, 1953, both in WHCF, General Files, box 68, Eisenhower Library; *Richmond News Leader*, October 2, 1953, 14.

26. Urofsky, *Douglas Letters*, 166–67; Kluger, *Simple Justice*, 695–96, 702; David M. O'Brien, *Justice Robert H. Jackson's Unpublished Opinion in* Brown v. Board (Lawrence: University Press of Kansas, 2017); Felix Frankfurter to "Dear Brethren," January 15, 1954, Tom Clark Papers (Texas), box A27.

27. Earl Warren to the Members of the Court, May 7, 1954, Robert Jackson Papers, box 184; *Brown v. Board of Education*, 347 U.S. 483, 493–95 (1954).

28. Felix Frankfurter to Earl Warren, May 17, 1954, and Harold Burton to Felix Frankfurter, May 17, 1954, both in Earl Warren Papers, box 571.
29. Todd C. Peppers, "The Chief Justice and the Page: Earl Warren, Charles Bush, and the Promise of *Brown v. Board of Education*," *Journal of Supreme Court History* 47 (2022): 27–43, quotation at 30. Bush later became the first black graduate of the Air Force Academy. The Court stopped hiring high school students as pages in 1975.
30. "Oral History Interview of Justice Thomas Clark" (recorded 1972), 19, Eisenhower Library; *Brown v. Board of Education*, 349 U.S. 294, 299, 301 (1955).
31. Patterson, *Brown v. Board of Education*, 98–99; Wallace's address can be found at https://digital.archives.alabama.gov/digital/collection/voices/id/2952(accessed April 10, 2024); Earl Warren, *The Memoirs of Earl Warren* (Garden City, NY: Doubleday, 1977), 290; Gerald N. Rosenberg, *The Hollow Hope: Can Courts Bring About Social Change?* (Chicago: University of Chicago Press, 1991), 52.
32. W. J. Buckner Jr., to Hugo Black, May 19, 1954, and Gerald D. Salter to Hugo Black, July 29, 1954, both in Black Papers, box 319; Glenda Allen and Libby Finnen to Hugo Black, March 19, 1956, Black Papers, box 328.
33. Learned Hand, *The Bill of Rights* (Cambridge, MA: Harvard University Press, 1958), 55; Herbert Wechsler, "Toward Neutral Principles of Constitutional Law," *Harvard Law Review* 73 (1959): 34.
34. *Memoirs of Earl Warren*, 291; "Opinions of William J. Brennan, Jr.: October Term 1958," v, Brennan Papers, Box II:6; *Cooper v. Aaron*, 358 U.S. 1, 18 (1958).
35. *Muir v. Louisville Park Theatrical Association*, 347 U.S. 971 (1954) (parks); *Mayor and City Council of Baltimore v. Dawson*, 350 U.S. 877 (1955) (beaches and bathhouses); *Holmes v. City of Atlanta*, 350 U.S. 879 (1955) (golf courses); *Gayle v. Browder*, 352 U.S. 903 (1956) (buses); *State Athletic Commission v. Dorsey*, 359 U.S. 533 (1959) (boxing matches); *Naim v. Naim*, 350 U.S. 985 (1956); Gregory Michael Dorr, "Principled Expediency: Eugenics, *Naim v. Naim*, and the Supreme Court," *American Journal of Legal History* 42 (1998): 119–59; Gerald Gunther, *Learned Hand: The Man and the Judge* (New York: Knopf, 1994), 667.
36. See, e.g., *Slade v. Board of Education of Harford County*, 252 F.2d 291 (4th Cir. 1958), cert. denied, 357 U.S. 906 (1958); *Allen v. County School Board of Prince Edward County*, 266 F.2d 507 (4th Cir. 1959), cert. denied, 361 U.S. 830 (1959); *Kelley v. Board of Education of City of Nashville*, 270 F.2d 209 (6th Cir. 1959), cert. denied, 361 U.S. 924 (1959).
37. *NAACP v. Alabama*, 357 U.S. 449, 462–63 (1958); *NAACP v. Button*, 371 U.S. 415, 429 (1963); *Edwards v. South Carolina*, 372 U.S. 229, 235 (1963); *New York Times v. Sullivan*, 376 U.S. 254, 279–80 (1964).
38. Felix Frankfurter to John M. Harlan, September 2, 1958, Frankfurter Papers, reel 1.
39. *Civil Rights Cases*, 109 U.S. 3 (1883); *Heart of Atlanta Motel v. United States*, 379 U.S. 241 (1964); *Katzenbach v. McClung*, 379 U.S. 294 (1964); Richard C. Cortner, *Civil Rights and Public Accommodations: The Heart of Atlanta Motel and McClung Cases* (Lawrence: University Press of Kansas, 2001); *New York Times*, July 7, 1964, 1; Michael Durham, "Ollie McClung's Big Decision," *Life*, October 9, 1964, 31.
40. *Heart of Atlanta Motel*, 379 U.S. at 257, 243; *McClung*, 379 U.S. at 296; *Willis v. Pickrick Restaurant*, 231 F. Supp. 396 (N.D. Ga. 1964).
41. *South Carolina v. Katzenbach*, 383 U.S. 301, 327–28 (1966).
42. Rosenberg, *Hollow Hope*, 50, 61.
43. Earl Warren Oral History, Interview I (recorded 1971), 6, Johnson Library.
44. *Griffin v. County School Board of Prince Edward County*, 377 U.S. 218, 233–34 (1964).
45. Jack Greenberg, *Crusaders in the Courts: How a Dedicated Band of Lawyers Fought for the Civil Rights Revolution* (New York: Basic Books, 1994), 381–83.
46. *Green v. County School Board of New Kent County*, 391 U.S. 430, 437–38, 442 (1968); Earl Warren to William Brennan, May 22, 1968, Brennan Papers, box I:174; *Indianapolis Star*, May 29, 1968, 23.
47. *Swann v. Charlotte-Mecklenburg Board of Education*, 402 U.S. 1, 13, 15, 28 (1971).
48. John C. Jeffries Jr., *Justice Lewis F. Powell, Jr.* (New York: Charles Scribner's Sons, 1994), 139–82; *Keyes v. School District No. 1*, 413 U.S. 189, 200, 258, 238 (1973).
49. Peter Wallenstein, *Race, Sex, and the Freedom to Marry: Loving v. Virginia* (Lawrence: University Press of Kansas, 2014); *Loving v. Virginia*, 388 U.S. 1, 3, 6, 7, 8, 11 (1967).
50. Among the many biographies of Marshall, the ones I found most helpful are Howard Ball, *A Defiant Life: Thurgood Marshall and the Persistence of Racism in America* (New York: Crown Publishers,

1998); Juan Williams, *Thurgood Marshall: American Revolutionary* (New York: Three Rivers Press, 1998); and Mark V. Tushnet's two volumes, *Making Civil Rights Law: Thurgood Marshall and the Supreme Court, 1936–1961* (New York: Oxford University Press, 1994), and *Making Constitutional Law: Thurgood Marshall and the Supreme Court, 1961–1991* (New York: Oxford University Press, 1997). Particularly helpful on Marshall's confirmation are Laura Kalman, *The Long Reach of the Sixties: LBJ, Nixon, and the Making of the Contemporary Supreme Court* (New York: Oxford University Press, 2017), and Wil Haygood, *Showdown: Thurgood Marshall and the Supreme Court Nomination That Changed America* (New York: Knopf, 2015).

51. James Davis Oral History Transcript (recorded 1983), 23, Johnson Library. *Miranda v. Arizona*, 384 U.S. 436 (1966), comprised three separate cases, two state prosecutions and one federal prosecution. Marshall represented the federal government in the latter case, *Westover v. United States*. "I am not too optimistic as to the outcome," he reported after the argument, "but whether we win or not it was certainly worth a try." Thurgood Marshall to Clinton E. Riggs, March 4, 1966, Marshall Papers, box 26.

52. Burke Marshall Oral History Interview (recorded 1970), 16, Kennedy Library; Theodore C. Sorensen, "Memorandum for the President" (March 29, 1962), President's Office Files, box 88a, Kennedy Library. Weaver eventually did become the first black cabinet member in 1966, when he became secretary of the new Department of Housing and Urban Development.

53. Morris Abram Oral History Transcript (recorded 1984), 5, Johnson Library; Tom Clark to Potter Stewart, March 30, 1967, Clark Papers (Texas), box B111.

54. *Nomination of Thurgood Marshall: Hearings Before the Committee on the Judiciary, United States Senate*, 90th Cong., 1st Sess. (1967), 161.

55. "The Judiciary: Kite-Flying and Other Games," *Time*, July 28, 1967; *New York Times*, July 21, 1967, 23.

56. *Atlanta Constitution*, August 31, 1967, 38; *Philadelphia Inquirer*, September 1, 1967, 12; *New York Amsterdam News*, July 22, 1967, 16.

Chapter 13

1. *New York Times*, October 1, 1953, 14; Earl Warren, *The Memoirs of Earl Warren* (Garden City, NY: Doubleday, 1977), 5.

2. "Mr. Justice Douglas' Twenty-Fifth Anniversary on the Supreme Court: Dinner Proceedings" (May 14, 1964), 3, Rowe Papers, box 89.

3. Hugo Black to Alan V. Washburn, December 17, 1958, Black Papers, box 59; *Time*, October 9, 1964; *New York Times*, June 11, 1962, 1.

4. Brad Snyder, *Democratic Justice: Felix Frankfurter, the Supreme Court, and the Making of the Liberal Establishment* (New York: Norton, 2022); Felix Frankfurter to John Harlan, May 28, 1963, Harlan II Papers, box 599; Felix Frankfurter to John Harlan, December 26, 1960, Harlan II Papers, box 605; *New York Times*, March 21, 1901, 1.

5. David L. Stebenne, *Arthur J. Goldberg: New Deal Liberal* (New York: Oxford University Press, 1996), 348–51; "Arthur J. Goldberg Oral History, Interview I" (conducted March 23, 1983), 1, 19, Johnson Library; Arthur Goldberg to Nathan and Lois Bar Yaacov, December 19, 1963, Goldberg Papers, box II:28.

6. Robert A. Caro, *Means of Ascent: The Years of Lyndon Johnson* (New York: Vintage Books, 1991), 368–72; Abe Fortas to Lyndon Johnson, July 19, 1965, White House Central Files, Confidential Files, FG 535, box 34, Johnson Library; Laura Kalman, *Abe Fortas: A Biography* (New Haven, CT: Yale University Press, 1990), 241–45.

7. Seth Stern and Stephen Wermiel, *Justice Brennan: Liberal Champion* (Boston: Houghton Mifflin, 2010), 71–80; "Tom Clark Oral History, Interview I" (conducted October 7, 1969), 5, Johnson Library; Barack Obama to William Brennan, December 7, 1990, Brennan Papers, box II:49.

8. Tinsley E. Yarbrough, *John Marshall Harlan: Great Dissenter of the Warren Court* (New York: Oxford University Press, 1992); Craig Alan Smith, *Failing Justice: Charles Evans Whittaker on the Supreme Court* (Jefferson, NC: McFarland, 2005); "Charles Evans Whittaker—The Supreme Court Years," *Texas Law Review* 40 (1962): 747; Dwight Eisenhower to William Rogers, September 17, 1958, Rogers Papers, box 4.

9. Dennis J. Hutchinson, *The Man Who Once Was Whizzer White: A Portrait of Justice Byron R. White* (New York: Free Press, 1998).

10. Lucas A. Powe Jr., *The Warren Court and American Politics* (Cambridge, MA: Harvard University Press, 2000), 494.

11. *Dennis v. United States*, 341 U.S. 494 (1951); "Memorandum for Messrs. Bator and Schlei" (July 8, 1956), Harlan II Papers, box 553.
12. *Pennsylvania v. Nelson*, 350 U.S. 497 (1956); *Slochower v. Board of Higher Education*, 350 U.S. 551 (1956); *Congressional Record* 102 (1956): 6064.
13. Arthur J. Sabin, *In Calmer Times: The Supreme Court and Red Monday* (Philadelphia: University of Pennsylvania Press, 1999); *Sweezy v. New Hampshire*, 354 U.S. 234, 250–51, 265–66 (1957).
14. *Watkins v. United States*, 354 U.S. 178, 197 (1957); *Yates v. United States*, 354 U.S. 298, 319 (1957); *Service v. Dulles*, 354 U.S. 363 (1957).
15. *Time*, July 1, 1957; *New York Times*, June 25, 1957, 28; Mendel Silberberg to Earl Warren, January 12, 1959, Earl Warren Papers, box 360; *Congressional Record* 104 (1958): A1249; *Chicago Daily Tribune*, July 27, 1957, 1; Paul Freund, "Storm Over the American Supreme Court," *Modern Law Review* 21 (1958): 345–46. Senator Joseph McCarthy is often reported to have alleged after Red Monday: "I will not say that Earl Warren is a Communist, but I will say he is the best friend the Communists have in America." But McCarthy died the month before Red Monday. The quotation seems to have first appeared in Warren's memoirs, which were published twenty years later. Warren, *Memoirs*, 325. While Warren's recollection may have been faulty, the quotation no doubt reflects what McCarthy *would* have thought about Red Monday had he lived to see it.
16. *New York Times*, August 5, 1961, 1; *New York Times*, February 6, 1962, 17; "Impeach Earl Warren?" (June 12, 1961), Harlan II Papers, box 605; "Arizona Mothers for Earl Warren's Impeachment" (n.d.), Harlan II Papers, box 605.
17. *Kent v. Dulles*, 357 U.S. 116 (1958); *Scales v. United States*, 367 U.S. 203 (1961); *Lamont v. Postmaster General*, 381 U.S. 301 (1965); *Elfbrandt v. Russell*, 384 U.S. 11 (1966); *Keyishian v. Board of Regents*, 385 U.S. 589 (1967); *United States v. Robel*, 389 U.S. 258 (1967).
18. William Brennan to Michael Tigar, June 16, 1965, Michael Tigar to William Brennan, June 17, 1965, and Michael Tigar to William Brennan, July 13, 1965, all in Brennan Papers, box II:58; *Congressional Record* 112 (1966): A3226. Kilpatrick's editorial and the correspondence from members of Congress are in Brennan Papers, box II:58.
19. Michael E. Tigar, *Fighting Injustice* (Chicago: American Bar Association, 2002), 52–64; Andrew Kopkind, "Brennan v. Tigar," *New Republic*, July 1966, 21; Marshall W. Krause to William Brennan, August 8, 1966, Brennan Papers, box II:58; Stern and Wermiel, *Justice Brennan*, 274; William Brennan to Michael Tigar, November 19, 1990, Brennan Papers, box II:101.
20. *Brandenburg v. Ohio*, 395 U.S. 444, 447 (1969).
21. Whitney Strub, *Obscenity Rules: Roth v. United States and the Long Struggle Over Sexual Expression* (Lawrence: University Press of Kansas, 2013); *Roth v. United States*, 354 U.S. 476, 487–88 (1957).
22. *Jacobellis v. Ohio*, 378 U.S. 184, 195–96, 197, 196 (1964).
23. Hugo Black to John Harlan, December 10, 1969, Harlan II Papers, box 484; *Byrne v. Karalexis*, 401 U.S. 216 (1971); Oral History Transcript, 174, Blackmun Papers; William Brennan to Lewis Powell, March 10, 1986, Brennan Papers, box II:112; Oral History Transcript, 191, Blackmun Papers; *Jenkins v. Georgia*, 418 U.S. 153, 161 (1974).
24. *Stanley v. Georgia*, 394 U.S. 557, 559, 565–66 (1969).
25. *Tinker v. Des Moines Independent Community School District*, 393 U.S. 503, 508 (1969); *Cohen v. California*, 403 U.S. 15, 18, 21 (1971).
26. David Rudenstine, *The Day the Presses Stopped: A History of the Pentagon Papers Case* (Berkeley: University of California Press, 1996); "Opinions of William J. Brennan, Jr.: October Term, 1970," 51, Brennan Papers, box II:6; *New York Times v. United States*, 403 U.S. 713, 715 (1971).
27. Stuart Banner, *The Decline of Natural Law: How American Lawyers Once Used Natural Law and Why They Stopped* (New York: Oxford University Press, 2021), 96–118; *Holy Trinity Church v. United States*, 143 U.S. 457, 471 (1892).
28. Bruce J. Dierenfield, *The Battle Over School Prayer: How Engel v. Vitale Changed America* (Lawrence: University Press of Kansas, 2007), 67; *Engel v. Vitale*, 370 U.S. 421, 425, 430, 445–46 (1962).
29. *New Journal and Guide* [Norfolk, Va.], October 13, 1962, A8; Dierenfield, *Battle Over School Prayer*, 137–47.
30. *School District of Abington Township v. Schempp*, 374 U.S. 203, 222 (1963).
31. Steven K. Green, "Evangelicals and the Becker Amendment: A Lesson in Church-State Moderation," *Journal of Church and State* 33 (1991): 541–67; Rebecca Rifkin, "In U.S., Support

for Daily Prayer in Schools Dips Slightly," Gallup, September 25, 2014, https://news.gallup.com/poll/177401/support-daily-prayer-schools-dips-slightly.aspx.

32. *Board of Education v. Allen*, 392 U.S. 236 (1968); *Lemon v. Kurtzman*, 403 U.S. 602, 612–13 (1971).

33. *Braunfeld v. Brown*, 366 U.S. 599 (1961); *Sherbert v. Verner*, 374 U.S. 398, 404, 406 (1963).

34. *People v. Woody*, 394 P.2d 813 (Cal. 1964); *In re Jenison*, 120 N.W.2d 515 (Minn. 1963), 125 N.W.2d 588 (Minn. 1963).

35. Shawn Francis Peters, *The Yoder Case: Religious Freedom, Education, and Parental Rights* (Lawrence: University Press of Kansas, 2003); *Wisconsin v. Yoder*, 406 U.S. 205, 222, 237 (1972).

36. *Sherbert*, 374 U.S. at 415.

37. *Weeks v. United States*, 232 U.S. 383 (1914); *Wolf v. Colorado*, 338 U.S. 25 (1949).

38. Carolyn N. Long, Mapp v. Ohio: *Guarding Against Unreasonable Searches and Seizures* (Lawrence: University Press of Kansas, 2006), 5–22.

39. Bernard Schwartz, *Super Chief: Earl Warren and His Supreme Court—A Judicial Biography* (New York: New York University Press, 1983), 393; *Mapp v. Ohio*, 367 U.S. 643, 655, 657, 659–60 (1961).

40. William Douglas to Tom Clark, January 25, 1962, Clark Papers (Texas), box B36.

41. *Johnson v. Zerbst*, 304 U.S. 458 (1938); *Betts v. Brady*, 316 U.S. 455 (1942); *Gideon v. Wainwright*, 372 U.S. 335, 344 (1963); Anthony Lewis, *Gideon's Trumpet* (New York: Random House, 1964); Yale Kamisar, "The Right to Counsel and the Fourteenth Amendment: A Dialogue on 'the Most Pervasive Right' of an Accused," *University of Chicago Law Review* 30 (1962): 19.

42. *Massiah v. United States*, 377 U.S. 201 (1964); *Escobedo v. Illinois*, 378 U.S. 478 (1964); *Miranda v. Arizona*, 384 U.S. 436, 446–47, 479 (1966).

43. *Id.* at 516–17, 542.

44. *Hartford Courant*, August 18, 1966, 43A; *Arizona Republic*, August 14, 1966, 35; *Congressional Record* 112 (1966): 23650; *Congressional Record* 113 (1967): 11097.

45. 82 Stat. 210 (1968); S. Rep. No. 1097, 90th Cong., 2nd Sess. 46 (1968); *Dickerson v. United States*, 530 U.S. 428 (2000).

46. David M. Oshinsky, *Capital Punishment on Trial:* Furman v. Georgia *and the Death Penalty in Modern America* (Lawrence: University Press of Kansas, 2010); *Furman v. Georgia*, 408 U.S. 238 (1972).

47. *Id.* at 270, 359–60, 369.

48. *Id.* at 256–57, 309–10, 313.

49. *Id.* at 468, 470.

50. Stuart Banner, *The Death Penalty: An American History* (Cambridge, MA: Harvard University Press, 2002), 268–69.

51. Jan Deutsch to Potter Stewart, January 22, 1965, Stewart Papers, box 616.

52. Billy Graham to Lyndon Johnson, June 21, 1968, White House Central Files, FG 535/A, box 360, Johnson Library; Warren Burger to Herbert Brownell, January 12, 1969, Brownell Papers, box 107.

53. *Gomillion v. Lightfoot*, 364 U.S. 339, 340 (1960).

54. *Colegrove v. Green*, 328 U.S. 549, 557–59, 556 (1946).

55. *Baker v. Carr*, 369 U.S. 186, 245, 253, 237 (1962); Earl Warren to William Brennan, undated note filed with *Baker v. Carr* opinion, Brennan Papers, box I:64. The full note read "Bill: It is a great day for the ~~Irish~~ country." "It's a Great Day for the Irish" was a popular song from the 1940s. Brennan's parents were Irish immigrants, so Warren's joke was meant to compliment Brennan. Warren's passing of the note down to Brennan is described by Brennan's clerks in "Opinions of William J. Brennan, Jr.: October Term 1961," Brennan Papers, box II:6.

56. *Gray v. Sanders*, 372 U.S. 368, 379, 381 (1963); *Wesberry v. Sanders*, 376 U.S. 1, 18 (1964); *Reynolds v. Sims*, 377 U.S. 533, 562 (1964).

57. Warren, *Memoirs*, 306–10.

58. *Goldberg v. Kelly*, 397 U.S. 254 (1970); *Shapiro v. Thompson*, 394 U.S. 618 (1969); *Pickering v. Board of Education*, 391 U.S. 563 (1968).

59. *Washington Post*, August 25, 1972, A2; Harry Blackmun to William Rehnquist, July 20, 1987, Blackmun Papers, box 151; Oral History Transcript, 204, Blackmun Papers.

60. *Griswold v. Connecticut*, 381 U.S. 479, 484, 486 (1965).

61. John W. Johnson, Griswold v. *Connecticut: Birth Control and the Constitutional Right of Privacy* (Lawrence: University Press of Kansas, 2005), 6–7; *Griswold*, 381 U.S. at 527.

62. Robert G. Dixon Jr., "The *Griswold* Penumbra: Constitutional Charter for an Expanded Law of Privacy?", *Michigan Law Review* 64 (1965): 218; *Eisenstadt v. Baird*, 405 U.S. 438, 453 (1972); *Roe v. Wade*, 314 F. Supp. 1217, 1225 (N.D. Tex. 1970); *Doe v. Bolton*, 319 F. Supp. 1048, 1055 (N.D. Ga. 1970).

63. Leslie J. Reagan, *When Abortion Was a Crime: Women, Medicine, and Law in the United States, 1867–1973* (Berkeley: University of California Press, 1997); David J. Garrow, *Liberty and Sexuality: The Right to Privacy and the Making of* Roe v. Wade (Berkeley: University of California Press, 1998), 546–47.

64. Tinsley E. Yarbrough, *Harry A. Blackmun: The Outsider Justice* (New York: Oxford University Press, 2008), 55–62; Blackmun's first draft of *Roe v. Wade*, May 18, 1972, Powell Papers, box 374; Garrow, *Liberty and Sexuality*, 547–56.

65. Blackmun's second draft of *Roe v. Wade*, November 22, 1972, Powell Papers, box 374; Harry Blackmun to the Conference, November 21, 1972, Blackmun Papers, box 151; Lewis Powell to Harry Blackmun, December 13, 1972, Powell Papers, box 374; John C. Jeffries Jr., *Justice Lewis F. Powell, Jr.* (New York: Charles Scribner's Sons, 1994), 347.

66. *Roe v. Wade*, 410 U.S. 113, 153–55, 160, 163–64 (1973).

67. *Id.* at 174; *Doe v. Bolton*, 410 U.S. 179, 222 (1973).

68. "Abortion on Demand," *Time*, January 29, 1973, 46; Garrow, *Liberty and Sexuality*, 588; Warren Burger to the Conference, January 24, 1973, Powell Papers, box 327; Jane Mayer, "Roe-Gate," *New Yorker*, May 16, 2022; Larry Hammond to Lewis Powell, n.d., Powell Papers, box 327; Jeffries, *Powell*, 343–46.

69. Lewis Powell to Dottie Blackmun, January 22, 1973, Blackmun Papers, box 151; Jeffries, *Powell*, 341; John Hart Ely, "On the Wages of Crying Wolf: A Comment on *Roe v. Wade*," *Yale Law Journal* 82 (1973): 926, 947; Archibald Cox, *The Role of the Supreme Court in American Government* (New York: Oxford University Press, 1976), 113; Ruth Bader Ginsburg, "Some Thoughts on Autonomy and Equality in Relation to *Roe v. Wade*," *North Carolina Law Review* 63 (1985): 375–86.

70. *New York Times*, April 10, 2005, E30.

71. Julia F. Trogler to Harry Blackmun, March 21, 1973, and St. Richard School students to Harry Blackmun, March 22, 1973, both in Blackmun Papers, box 72; Oral History Transcript, 205, Blackmun Papers; "Opinions of William J. Brennan, Jr.: October Term, 1972," 69, Brennan Papers, box II:6.

72. Oral History Transcript, 204, 314, Blackmun Papers.

Chapter 14

1. Donald Grier Stephenson Jr., *Campaigns and the Court: The U.S. Supreme Court in Presidential Elections* (New York: Columbia University Press, 1999); *Chicago Tribune*, May 31, 1968, 3; *Chicago Tribune*, May 9, 1968, A7; *Atlanta Constitution*, August 12, 1968, 9; *Washington Post*, September 29, 1968, G8. Party platforms are available at https://www.presidency.ucsb.edu/documents/presidential-documents-archive-guidebook/party-platforms-and-nominating-conventions-3 (accessed April 10, 2024). There are two excellent books about Nixon's appointments to the Court, one by a participant in the process, John W. Dean, *The Rehnquist Choice: The Untold Story of the Nixon Appointment That Redefined the Supreme Court* (New York: Free Press, 2001), and the other by a historian, Laura Kalman, *The Long Reach of the Sixties: LBJ, Nixon, and the Making of the Contemporary Supreme Court* (New York: Oxford University Press, 2017).

2. G. Edward White, *Earl Warren: A Public Life* (New York: Oxford University Press, 1982), 307–13; Jim Newton, *Justice for All: Earl Warren and the Nation He Made* (New York: Riverhead Books, 2006), 491–92; Bernard Schwartz, *Super Chief: Earl Warren and His Supreme Court—A Judicial Biography* (New York: New York University Press, 1983), 681–82; Joe Califano to Lyndon Johnson, July 12, 1968, Fortas-Thornberry File, box 5, Johnson Library; Mike Manatos to Lyndon Johnson, July 2, 1968, Fortas-Thornberry File, box 4, Johnson Library.

3. *Time*, July 5, 1968, 12; "Strom Thurmond Reports to the People," July 22, 1968 and August 5, 1968, Fortas Papers, box 97; Mike Manatos to Lyndon Johnson, June 25, 1968, Fortas-Thornberry File, box 1, Johnson Library; George Reedy to Lyndon Johnson, July 30, 1968, Fortas-Thornberry File, box 7, Johnson Library.

4. *Nominations of Abe Fortas and Homer Thornberry: Hearings Before the Committee on the Judiciary, U.S. Senate*, 90th Cong., 2d Sess. (Washington, DC: Government Printing Office, 1968), 142; Abe Fortas to William Douglas, July 26, 1968, Fortas Papers, box 95; William

Douglas to Abe Fortas, September 23, 1968, Fortas Papers, box 97; Abe Fortas to Lyndon Johnson, October 1, 1968, Fortas Papers, box 95.

5. Dean, *Rehnquist Choice*, 5; Laura Kalman, *Abe Fortas: A Biography* (New Haven, CT: Yale University Press, 1990), 322–27, 359–70; Dean, *Rehnquist Choice*, 10; Patrick Buchanan to Richard Nixon, May 6, 1969, WHCF, FG51, box 1, Nixon Library; Abe Fortas to Earl Warren, May 14, 1969, Fortas Papers, box 99; Patrick Buchanan to Richard Nixon, May 19, 1969, WHCF, FG51, box 1, Nixon Library; Notes, May 17, 1969, Haldeman Papers, box 32.

6. Joshua E. Kastenberg, *The Campaign to Impeach Justice William O. Douglas: Nixon, Vietnam, and the Conservative Attack on Judicial Independence* (Lawrence: University Press of Kansas, 2019); Jack Caulfield to John Ehrlichman, June 4, 1969, Ehrlichman Papers, box 39; Bruce Allen Murphy, *Wild Bill: The Legend and Life of William O. Douglas* (New York: Random House, 2003), 366–67, 429–42; William Douglas to Charles E. Ares, February 6, 1970, Douglas Papers, box 1117; William Douglas to Thomas J. Klitgaard, May 12, 1970, Douglas Papers, box 1120.

7. *Time, Inc. v. Hill*, 385 U.S. 374 (1966); Samantha Barbas, *Newsworthy: The Supreme Court Battle Over Privacy and Press Freedom* (Stanford, CA: Stanford University Press, 2017), 175–90.

8. *Shelton v. Tucker*, 364 U.S. 479 (1960); Warren Burger to Herbert Brownell, December 12, 1960, Brownell Papers, box 107; *Hunter v. Erickson*, 393 U.S. 385 (1969); Warren Burger to Herbert Brownell, n.d., Brownell Papers, box 107; Warren Burger to Herbert Brownell, January 5, 1969, Brownell Papers, box 107.

9. John Ehrlichman to Richard Nixon, December 16, 1970, WHCF, FG51, box 1, Nixon Library; *Miller v. California*, 413 U.S. 15 (1973); Douglas Brinkley and Luke A Nichter, eds., *The Nixon Tapes: 1973* (Boston: Houghton Mifflin, 2015), 4–5.

10. David Alistair Yalof, *Pursuit of Justices: Presidential Politics and the Selection of Supreme Court Nominees* (Chicago: University of Chicago Press, 1999), 97–132; John P. Frank, *Clement Haynsworth, the Senate, and the Supreme Court* (Charlottesville: University Press of Virginia, 1991).

11. Ken Cole to H. R. Haldeman, October 23, 1969, and H. R. Haldeman to John Ehrlichman, October 27, 1969, both in Ehrlichman Papers, box 39.

12. Leonard Garment to Richard Nixon, January 9, 1970, Ehrlichman Papers, box 39; *George Harrold Carswell: Hearings Before the Committee on the Judiciary, U.S. Senate*, 91st Cong., 2nd Sess. (Washington, DC: Government Printing Office, 1970), 23–24, 242; *New York Times*, March 17, 1970, 21; Note of telephone call from Steve Umin, March 24, 1970, Stewart Papers, box 617.

13. Tinsley E. Yarbrough, *Harry A. Blackmun: The Outsider Justice* (New York: Oxford University Press, 2008), 120–38; Wanda S. Martinson, "My Twenty-Five Years with 'Old Number Three,'" *Columbia Law Review* 99 (1999): 1406–07.

14. Bud Krogh to John Ehrlichman, September 24, 1971, Ehrlichman Papers, box 27.

15. Dean, *Rehnquist Choice*, 96, 47; Leonard Garment to Richard Nixon, September 30, 1971, Ehrlichman Papers, box 27; Richard G. Kleindienst to Wallace H. Johnson, September 29, 1971, Dean Papers, box 60; David Young to John Ehrlichman, September 30, 1971, Dean Papers, box 75; Dean, *Rehnquist Choice*, 119.

16. William H. Rehnquist to John Mitchell, October 12, 1971, and John W. Dean and David R. Young to John N. Mitchell and John D. Ehrlichman, October 16, 1971, both in Dean Papers, box 75; Kalman, *Long Reach of the Sixties*, 296.

17. John C. Jeffries Jr., *Justice Lewis F. Powell, Jr.* (New York: Charles Scribner's Sons, 1994), 115–221; Ann Southworth, *Lawyers of the Right: Professionalizing the Conservative Coalition* (Chicago: University of Chicago Press, 2008), 15.

18. John A. Jenkins, *The Partisan: The Life of William Rehnquist* (New York: Public Affairs, 2012), 108–09; William Rehnquist to Robert Jackson, n.d., Robert Jackson Papers, box 19; Dean, *Rehnquist Choice*, 270–73.

19. Lewis Powell to William Rehnquist, July 23, 1979, and William Rehnquist to Lewis Powell, January 18, 1985, both in Powell Papers, box 327; Peter J. Wallison to Donald T. Regan, May 30, 1986, Regan Papers, box 6.

20. William Rehnquist to the Conference, June 12, 1974, Clark Papers (Texas), box B113.

21. *United States v. Nixon*, 418 U.S. 683, 713 (1974).

22. *Washington Post*, April 26, 1970, A4; Bill Barnhart and Gene Schlickman, *John Paul Stevens: An Independent Life* (Dekalb: Northern Illinois University Press, 2010), 182–92; Max L. Friedersdorf to Gerald Ford, November 28, 1975, Buchen Papers, box 62.

23. Hank Habicht to Herbert Ellingwood, July 7, 1981, Fielding Papers, box 37F; Evan Thomas, *First: Sandra Day O'Connor* (New York: Random House, 2019), 92–93; John C. Willke to Ronald Reagan, July 1, 1981, FG O51, box 9, Reagan Library; Marie Craven to Ronald Reagan, July 7, 1981, Gergen Papers, box OA9422.

24. Joan Biskupic, *American Original: The Life and Constitution of Supreme Court Justice Antonin Scalia* (New York: Farrar, Straus and Giroux, 2009); Alan Charles Raul to Peter J. Wallison, June 5, 1986, Regan Papers, box 6; Patrick Buchanan to Donald Regan, July 10, 1985, FG 051, box 10, Reagan Library.

25. Jenkins, *The Partisan*, 218; Patrick Buchanan to Orrin Hatch, July 31, 1986, FG 051, box 11, Reagan Library. Because the Senate has expanded with the addition of new states, and because not all senators are present for every vote, Rehnquist's 65–33 margin of victory in 1986 was larger than that of many earlier justices.

26. Peter Wallison, Memorandum for the File, August 29, 1986, Wallison Papers, box OA14287; Edward Levi to Gerald Ford, November 10, 1975, Cheney Papers, box 11.

27. *Congressional Record* 133 (1987): S9188.

28. Arthur B. Culvahouse Jr., to Howard H. Baker Jr., Kenneth M. Duberstein, and William L. Ball III, July 9, 1987, Cox Papers, box 14; Newt Gingrich to Ronald Reagan, October 13, 1987, FG051, box 21, Reagan Library; Kenneth M. Duberstein to Howard H. Baker Jr., October 14, 1987, FG051, box 21, Reagan Library; "Nomination of Judge Robert Bork" (October 14, 1987), Powell Papers, box 756.

29. "Douglas H. Ginsburg: Biographical Information," Duberstein Papers, box 1; Ronald Reagan to Alan Brown, n.d., FG 051, box 20, Reagan Library.

30. "Anthony M. Kennedy: Biographical Information," Regan Papers, box 6; Steve A. Matthews to Special Project Committee, May 23, 1986, Wallison Papers, box OA14287; Harry Blackmun to Anthony Kennedy, November 12, 1987, and Anthony Kennedy to Harry Blackmun, November 16, 1987, both in Blackmun Papers, box 1405.

31. Warren Rudman to George Bush, July 22, 1990, Sununu Papers, box 86 (the first page of this letter, but not the second, is misdated to 1989); Thomas L. Jipping to "721 Group & Allies," July 24, 1990, Sununu Papers, box 86; Patrick McGuigan to files, July 24, 1990, Quayle Papers, box 7; Lewis Powell to Gerald Gunther, September 4, 1990, Brennan Papers, box II:113. This letter is in Brennan's papers because Powell shared it with Brennan.

32. American Life Lobby Press Release (July 26, 1990), Sununu Papers, box 86; Dawn Johnsen to "Interested Parties" (August 2, 1990), Liberman Papers, box 1; Tinsley E. Yarbrough, *David Hackett Souter: Traditional Republican on the Rehnquist Court* (New York: Oxford University Press, 2005); *New York Times*, October 8, 2000, 28.

33. Untitled and undated memorandum about Clarence Thomas, Gray Files, unnumbered miscellaneous file.

34. Stuart Banner, *The Decline of Natural Law: How Americans Once Used Natural Law and Why They Stopped* (New York: Oxford University Press, 2021), 238–39.

35. *Nomination of Judge Clarence Thomas to be Associate Justice of the Supreme Court of the United States: Hearings Before the Senate Judiciary Committee*, part 4, 102nd Cong., 1st Sess. (Washington, DC: Government Printing Office, 1993), 37, 157–58.

36. Connie J. Vetter to Bill Clinton, April 8, 1994, and Tim Carvell to Bill Clinton, April 21, 1994, both in 2006-1067-F(2), box 14, Clinton Library; Corey Robin, *The Enigma of Clarence Thomas* (New York: Metropolitan Books, 2019).

37. Amanda Hollis-Brusky, *Ideas with Consequences: The Federalist Society and the Conservative Counterrevolution* (New York: Oxford University Press, 2015).

38. Steven M. Teles, *The Rise of the Conservative Legal Movement: The Battle for Control of the Law* (Princeton, NJ: Princeton University Press, 2008), 58–89, 220–64; Amanda Hollis-Brusky and Joshua C. Wilson, *Separate but Faithful: The Christian Right's Radical Struggle to Transform Law and Legal Culture* (New York: Oxford University Press, 2020).

39. Jonathan O'Neill, *Originalism in American Law and Politics: A Constitutional History* (Baltimore: Johns Hopkins University Press, 2005); Logan E. Sawyer III, "Principle and Politics in the New History of Originalism," *American Journal of Legal History* 57 (2017): 198–222; Robert Post and Reva Siegel, "Originalism as Political Practice: The Right's Living Constitution," *Fordham Law Review* 75 (2006): 545–74.

40. Edwin Meese III, "The Attorney General's View of the Supreme Court: Toward a Jurisprudence of Original Intention," *Public Administration Review* 45 (1985): 704.

41. *Harris v. New York*, 401 U.S. 222, 226 (1971); *Oregon v. Mathiason*, 429 U.S. 492 (1977); *New York v. Quarles*, 467 U.S. 649 (1981); *Oregon v. Elstad*, 470 U.S. 298 (1985); *Harris*, 401 U.S. at 232.

42. William Rehnquist to Warren Burger, March 30, 1984, Powell Papers, box 627; *Terry v. Ohio*, 392 U.S. 1 (1968); *Shneckloth v. Bustamante*, 412 U.S. 218 (1973); *South Dakota v. Opperman*, 428 U.S. 364 (1976); *New Jersey v. T.L.O.*, 469 U.S. 325 (1985); *Griffin v. Wisconsin*, 483 U.S. 868 (1987).

43. *United States v. Calandra*, 414 U.S. 338, 350 (1974); *Nix v. Williams*, 467 U.S. 431 (1984); *United States v. Leon*, 468 U.S. 897 (1984); *Calandra*, 414 U.S. at 356.

44. Carol S. Steiker and Jordan M. Steiker, *Courting Death: The Supreme Court and Capital Punishment* (Cambridge, MA: Harvard University Press, 2016); *Gregg v. Georgia*, 428 U.S. 153 (1976); *Lockett v. Ohio*, 438 U.S. 586 (1976).

45. *Penry v. Lynaugh*, 492 U.S. 302 (1989); *Stanford v. Kentucky*, 492 U.S. 361 (1989); *South Carolina v. Gathers*, 490 U.S. 805 (1989); *Payne v. Tennessee*, 501 U.S. 808, 844 (1992).

46. Lewis Powell to Leslie Gielow, September 16, 1986, Powell Papers, box 662; *McCleskey v. Kemp*, 481 U.S. 279, 312 (1987); Antonin Scalia to the Conference, January 6, 1987,

47. *Milliken v. Bradley*, 418 U.S. 717, 741, 782 (1974); Joyce A. Baugh, *The Detroit School Busing Case: Milliken v. Bradley and the Controversy Over Desegregation* (Lawrence: University Press of Kansas, 2011).

48. *Pasadena City Board of Education v. Spangler*, 427 U.S. 424 (1976); *Board of Education of Oklahoma City v. Dowell*, 498 U.S. 237 (1990); *Freeman v. Pitts*, 503 U.S. 467 (1992); James T. Patterson, *Brown v. Board of Education: A Civil Rights Milestone and Its Troubled Legacy* (New York: Oxford University Press, 2001), 228–29.

49. *Regents of the University of California v. Bakke*, 438 U.S. 265 (1978); Howard Ball, *The Bakke Case: Race, Education, and Affirmative Action* (Lawrence: University Press of Kansas, 2000).

50. *Firefighters Local Union No. 1784 v. Stotts*, 467 U.S. 561 (1984); *Wygant v. Jackson Board of Education*, 476 U.S. 267 (1986); *City of Richmond v. J.A. Croson Co.*, 488 U.S. 469, 499 (1989).

51. *San Antonio Independent School District v. Rodriguez*, 411 U.S. 1 (1973); *Washington v. Davis*, 426 U.S. 229, 240 (1976).

52. *Village of Belle Terre v. Boraas*, 416 US. 1 (1974); *Moore v. City of East Cleveland*, 431 U.S. 494, 509 (1977); *Bob Jones University v. United States*, 461 U.S. 574 (1983); *Batson v. Kentucky*, 476 U.S. 79 (1986). *Batson* overruled *Swain v. Alabama*, 380 U.S. 202 (1965).

53. *Reed v. Reed*, 404 U.S. 71 (1971).

54. *Frontiero v. Richardson*, 411 U.S. 677, 684, 686 (1973); *Weinberger v. Weisenfeld*, 420 U.S. 636 (1975); *Craig v. Boren*, 429 U.S. 190 (1976); *Orr v. Orr*, 440 U.S. 268 (1979).

55. *Frontiero*, 411 U.S. at 692.

56. *Meritor Savings Bank v. Vinson*, 477 U.S. 57, 64 (1986); *Price Waterhouse v. Hopkins*, 490 U.S. 228, 251 (1989).

57. *Marsh v. Chambers*, 463 U.S. 783, 792 (1983).

58. *Lynch v. Donnelly*, 465 U.S. 668, 673 (1984); Wayne R. Swanson, *The Christ Child Goes to Court* (Philadelphia: Temple University Press, 1990); *County of Allegheny v. American Civil Liberties Union*, 492 U.S. 573, 598 (1989).

59. *United States v. Lee*, 455 U.S. 252 (1982); *Bowen v. Roy*, 476 U.S. 693, 700 (1986).

60. *Employment Division v. Smith*, 494 U.S. 872, 888–89 (1990); Garrett Epps, *To an Unknown God: Religious Freedom on Trial* (New York: St. Martin's Press, 2001).

61. 107 Stat. 1488 (1993); *City of Boerne v. Flores*, 521 U.S. 507 (1997).

62. Mary Ziegler, *Abortion and the Law in America: Roe v. Wade to the Present* (New York: Cambridge University Press, 2020).

63. *Maher v. Roe*, 432 U.S. 464, 473–74, 483 (1977); *Harris v. McRae*, 448 U.S. 297, 317 (1980). The Court reached a similar result with respect to a different funding program in *Rust v. Sullivan*, 500 U.S. 173 (1991).

64. *Planned Parenthood of Central Missouri v. Danforth*, 428 U.S. 52, 70, 79 (1976).

65. *City of Akron v. Akron Center for Reproductive Health, Inc.*, 462 U.S. 416 (1983); *Thornburgh v. American College of Obstetricians and Gynecologists*, 462 U.S. 747 (1986); *Planned Parenthood Association of Kansas City v. Ashcroft*, 462 U.S. 476 (1983); *Webster v. Reproductive Health Services*, 492 U.S. 490, 518–19 (1989).

66. *Akron*, 462 U.S. at 452–75.

67. *Webster*, 492 U.S. at 532, 535; *Hodgson v. Minnesota*, 497 U.S. 417, 480 (1990).

68. *Webster*, 492 U.S. at 557, 560.

69. Cert pool memo, *Planned Parenthood v. Casey* (December 19, 1991), http://blackmun.wustl.edu/BlackmunMemos/1991/1991%20GRANTED-pdf/91-744.pdf.
70. Molly McUsic to Harry Blackmun, January 4, 1992, Blackmun Papers, box 602.
71. Draft dissent from relisting order, Jan. 1992, Blackmun Papers, box 602.
72. *Washington Post*, April 23, 1992, A1; First draft, *Planned Parenthood v. Casey* (May 27, 1992), Blackmun Papers, box 602.
73. Anthony Kennedy to Harry Blackmun, May 29, 1992, Blackmun Papers, box 601; *Planned Parenthood of Southeastern Pennsylvania v. Casey*, 505 U.S. 833, 846 (1992).
74. *Id.* at 953; Stephanie Dangel to Harry Blackmun, June 20, 1992, Blackmun Papers, box 602; *Casey*, 505 U.S. at 989–90, 1002.
75. *Id.* at 943; Harry Blackmun Oral History, 210, Blackmun Papers.
76. Lawyers in Bush's White House counsel's office interviewed Jones in December 1989 for the position that was eventually filled by Souter. Withdrawal/Redaction Sheet, Gray Files, no box number. Higginbotham, Wallace, and Winter were thoroughly vetted by the Reagan administration for the 1986 and 1987 vacancies that ended up going to Scalia and Kennedy. Regan Papers, box 6.

Chapter 15

1. Douglas Brinkley and Luke A. Nichter, eds., *The Nixon Tapes: 1973* (Boston: Houghton Mifflin, 2015), 738.
2. David R. Young to John D. Ehrlichman, October 20, 1971, Dean Papers, box 76; "Additional Women Candidates for Supreme Court" (October 5, 1971), Dean Papers, box 75; List of candidates, June 18, 1981, Fielding Papers, box 37F.
3. Press Conference (July 1, 1991), Liberman Papers, Clarence Thomas Subject Files, box 1.
4. Bernie Nussbaum and Ron Klain to Bill Clinton, April 5, 1993, 2006-1067-F(2), box 16, Clinton Library; Lloyd Cutler, Joel I. Klein, and Victoria L. Radd to Bill Clinton, April 26, 1994, 2006-1067-F(2), box 17, Clinton Library; Bernie Nussbaum and Ron Klain to Bill Clinton, May 4, 1993, 2006-1067-F(2), box 16, Clinton Library; Ron Klain to Bernie Nussbaum and Joel Klein, November 8, 1993, 2006-1067-F(2), box 16, Clinton Library; *New York Times*, September 29, 2005, A22; *New York Times*, May 2, 2009, A10; *New York Times*, February 15, 2016, A12; https://ballotpedia.org/Complete_list_of_Donald_Trump%27s_potential_nominees_to_the_U.S._Supreme_Court.
5. *New York Times*, January 26, 2022.
6. Rudy Beserra to Linas Kojelis, October 15, 1987, FG051, box 23, Reagan Library; José F. Niño to Bill Clinton, July 9, 1993, 2006-1067-F, box 1, Clinton Library; Lloyd Cutler, Joel I. Klein, and Victoria L. Radd to Bill Clinton, April 11, 1994, and Lloyd N. Cutler, Joel I. Klein, and Victoria L. Radd to Bill Clinton, May 2, 1994, both in 2006-1067-F(2), box 6, Clinton Library; "HNBA Provides White House with Nominee List" (July 1, 2005), 2014-0108-F[1], box 34, G. W. Bush Library; Alan M. Varela to George W. Bush, September 29, 2005, 2014-0108-F[1], box 34, G. W. Bush Library; *New York Times*, May 27, 2009, A1.
7. Renee Knake Jefferson and Hannah Brenner Johnson, *Shortlisted: Women in the Shadows of the Supreme Court* (New York: New York University Press, 2020); "A Woman on the Supreme Bench?", *Christian Science Monitor*, March 12, 1930, 18 (also endorsing Mabel Walker Willebrandt, who had been assistant attorney general for most of the preceding decade); "Supreme Court of the U.S.—Biographies of Men Considered," President's Subject Files, box 224, Hoover Library.
8. Dorothy McAllister to Stephen Early, March 9, 1939 (listing letters from several other Allen supporters), Sophonisba Breckinridge to Stephen Early, November 17, 1939, Helena Reed to Franklin Roosevelt, December 5, 1939, and James P. Slattery to Stephen Early, November 16, 1939, all in OF 41a, box 54, Roosevelt Library.
9. Jefferson and Johnson, *Shortlisted*, 33.
10. Nicholas Katzenbach to Lyndon Johnson, July 22, 1965, WHCF, FG 535/A, box 360, Johnson Library.
11. "Top Potential Women Candidates for Supreme Court" (October 5, 1971) and "Additional Women Candidates for Supreme Court" (October 5, 1971), Dean Papers, box 75; John Dean and David R. Young to John N. Mitchell and John D. Ehrlichman, October 16, 1971, Dean Papers, box 75; "President Nixon's Telephone Conversation with John Mitchell" (October 14, 1971), http://americanradioworks.publicradio.org/features/prestapes/rmn_jm_101471.html(accessed April 10, 2024); John Dean to John Ehrlichman, October 20, 1971, Dean Papers, box 75.

12. Douglas P. Bennett to Richard B. Cheney, n.d., Buchen Papers, box 62; *Washington Star*, November 13, 1975, 1; *New York Times*, November 13, 1975, 1.
13. Evan Thomas, *First: Sandra Day O'Connor* (New York: Random House, 2019), 120; "Statement by Governor Ronald Reagan" (October 14, 1980), Fielding Papers, box 37F.
14. William French Smith, "History of the Nomination of Justice Sandra Day O'Connor" (Sept. 1981), FG051, box 10, Reagan Library; List of candidates, June 18, 1981, Fielding Papers, box 37F.
15. National Women's Political Caucus to Ronald Reagan, June 18, 1981, and Lyn Nofziger to Ronald Reagan, June 22, 1981, both in FG051, box 9, Reagan Library.
16. Smith, "History"; *New York Daily News*, July 8, 1981, 45; *Los Angeles Times*, July 8, 1981, C4; *New York Times*, July 8, 1981, A26; William Rehnquist to Dean Colson, October 1, 1981, Rehnquist Papers, box 113.
17. Oral History Transcript, 317–18, Blackmun Papers; John Paul Stevens, *The Making of a Justice: Reflections on My First 94 Years* (Boston: Little, Brown, 2019), 186. Stevens told a different version of the "Mr. Justice" story in which he, not Stewart, was the one who raised the issue, after Stevens judged a law school moot court competition alongside Cornelia Kennedy and was struck by how Kennedy bristled at being called "Madame Justice." John Paul Stevens, "Fond Memory," *Ohio State Law Journal* 75 (2014): 1009.
18. Herma Hill Kay to Bill Clinton, April 24, 1993, and Barbara Babcock to Bill Clinton, May 20, 1993, both in 2006-1067-F, box 1, Clinton Library.
19. Ron Klain to Bruce Lindsey, Bernie Nussbaum, and Vince Foster, March 24, 1993, and Bernie Nussbaum and Ron Klain to Bill Clinton, April 1, 1993, both in 2006-1067-F(2), box 16, Clinton Library; *New York Times*, June 8, 1993, A20; Ron Klain to Bernie Nussbaum and Howard Paster, June 6, 1993, 2006-1067-F, box 1, Clinton Library; Bernie Nussbaum and Ron Klain to Bill Clinton, May 13, 1993, 2006-1067-F(2), box 2, Clinton Library.
20. "Harriet Miers Is Well Qualified to Serve on the United States Supreme Court" (n.d. 2005), 2014-0123-F[1], box 5, G. W. Bush Library; Rachel Brand, "Comments Regarding Release of Harriet Miers Senate Questionnaire" (n.d. 2005), 2014-0123-F[1], box 5, G. W. Bush Library.
21. Transcript of CNN interview, October 5, 2005, 2016-0183-F, box 6, G. W. Bush Library; Transcript of Fox News interview, October 14, 2005, 2016-0183-F, box 6, G. W. Bush Library; *Chicago Tribune*, October 8, 2005, A8; *Los Angeles Times*, October 28, 2005, A30; Harriet Miers to George W. Bush, October 27, 2005, 2014-0123-F[1], box 1, G. W. Bush Library.
22. Joan Biskupic, *Breaking In: The Rise of Sonia Sotomayor and the Politics of Justice* (New York: Farrar, Straus and Giroux, 2014).
23. Thomas, *First*, 134.
24. James Kirchick, *Secret City: The Hidden History of Gay Washington* (New York: Henry Holt and Co., 2022); Joyce Murdoch and Deb Price, *Courting Justice: Gay Men and Lesbians v. The Supreme Court* (New York: Basic Books, 2001), 18–21; Sidney Fine, *Frank Murphy: The Washington Years* (Ann Arbor: University of Michigan Press, 1984), 8–9, 202–03; Tyler Abell, ed., *Drew Pearson Diaries 1949–1959* (New York: Holt, Rinehart and Winston, 1974), 66 (Harry Hopkins was a top official in the Roosevelt administration, Liz Whitney a prominent socialite); Fine, *Frank Murphy*, 9.
25. "Reminiscences of Robert Houghwout Jackson, 1952," 790, 787, CCOH; Frank Murphy to Hugo Black, n.d. (1943), Black Papers, box 61; "Re: Kemp: Circulated at the Suggestion of the Chief Justice for the Consideration of the Conference" (December 4, 1943), Black Papers, box 61; Frank Murphy to Franklin Roosevelt, December 7, 1944, Vinson Papers, box 162; Eleanor Bumgardner to Fred Vinson, August 15, 1949, Vinson Papers, box 162.
26. Abe Garfinkel to Frank Murphy, January 10, 1940, Murphy Papers, reel 149.
27. *Los Angeles Times*, September 11, 1979, A2.
28. *Nomination of Felix Frankfurter: Hearings Before a Subcommittee of the Committee on the Judiciary, United States Senate*, 76th Cong., 1st Sess. (Washington, DC: Government Printing Office, 1939), 107
29. Cynthia R. Farina, "Congressional Polarization: Terminal Constitutional Dysfunction?", *Columbia Law Review* 115 (2015): 1689–1738.
30. "McConnell on Supreme Court Nomination" (March 16, 2016), https://www.republicanleader.senate.gov/newsroom/remarks/mcconnell-on-supreme-court-nomination.
31. Richard Davis, *Supreme Democracy: The End of Elitism in Supreme Court Nominations* (New York: Oxford University Press, 2017); *New York Times*, August 10, 1949, 18; John C. Tuck

to Howard Baker, October 14, 1987, Baker Papers, box 3; *New York Times*, September 14, 1987, B14.

32. Robert W. Wild to William Rehnquist, January 8, 1982, Rehnquist Papers, box 113; *Confirmation Hearing on the Nomination of Hon. Brett M. Kavanaugh to be an Associate Justice of the Supreme Court of the United States* (Washington, DC: Government Publishing Office, 2020), 683.

33. John Anthony Maltese, *The Selling of Supreme Court Nominees* (Baltimore: Johns Hopkins University Press, 1995); Ron Klain to Bernie Nussbaum, June 1, 1993, 2006-1067-F(2), box 17, Clinton Library.

34. Stevens, *Making of a Justice*, 127; "Schedule for Sandra Day O'Connor" (n.d. 1981), Moore Papers, box OA3209; *New York Times*, September 1, 2005, A12.

35. Douglas J. Band to Charles F. C. Ruff et al., June 19, 1998, 2006-1067-F(2), box 20, Clinton Library.

36. Daniel Hemel, "Can Structural Changes Fix the Supreme Court?", *Journal of Economic Perspectives* 35 (2021): 128–30.

37. Jeffrey Toobin, *The Nine: Inside the Secret World of the Supreme Court* (New York: Anchor Books, 2007), 73; Tinsley E. Yarbrough, *Harry A. Blackmun: The Outsider Justice* (New York: Oxford University Press, 2008), 323; Ruth Marcus, *Supreme Ambition: Brett Kavanaugh and the Conservative Takeover* (New York: Simon & Schuster, 2019), 3; Thomas, *First*, 323, 333–34.

38. Howard Ball, *A Defiant Life: Thurgood Marshall and the Persistence of Racism in America* (New York: Crown Publishers, 1998), 379; Juan Williams, *Thurgood Marshall: American Revolutionary* (New York: Times Books, 1998), 390–94.

39. "In Conversation with Antonin Scalia," *New York*, October 4, 2013; Neil Devins and Lawrence Baum, *The Company They Keep: How Partisan Divisions Came to the Supreme Court* (New York: Oxford University Press, 2019).

40. Federal Judicial Center, *Caseloads: Supreme Court of the United States, 1878–2017*, https://www.fjc.gov/history/courts/caseloads-supreme-court-united-states-1878-2017 (accessed April 10, 2024).

41. Ruth Bader Ginsburg and Peter W. Huber, "The Intercircuit Committee," *Harvard Law Review* 100 (1987): 1426; *New York Times*, February 9, 1983, A30; John G. Roberts to Fred F. Fielding, April 19, 1983, FG 051, box 10, Reagan Library.

42. 102 Stat. 662 (1988).

43. Lee Epstein, Jeffrey A. Segal, Harold J. Spaeth, and Thomas G. Walker, eds., *The Supreme Court Compendium: Data, Decisions, and Developments*, 5th ed. (Los Angeles: CQ Press, 2012), 79–83.

44. *Id.* at 89; Ryan J. Owens and David A. Simon, "Explaining the Supreme Court's Shrinking Docket," *William & Mary Law Review* 53 (2012): 1219–85.

45. Richard J. Lazarus, "Advocacy Matters Before and Within the Supreme Court: Transforming the Court by Transforming the Bar," *Georgetown Law Journal* 96 (2008): 1487–1564; Anthony Lewis, *Gideon's Trumpet* (New York: Random House, 1964), 47.

46. Artemus Ward and David L. Weiden, *Sorcerers' Apprentices: 100 Years of Law Clerks at the United States Supreme Court* (New York: New York University Press, 2006), 36, 45.

47. John C. Jeffries Jr., *Justice Lewis F. Powell, Jr.* (New York: Charles Scribner's Sons, 1994), 270; Lewis Powell to Warren Burger, November 1, 1973, Byron White to Warren Burger, October 30, 1973, and William Douglas to Warren Burger, July 13, 1972, all in Blackmun Papers, box 1374; Andrew Hurwitz to Potter Stewart, September 30, 1974, Stewart Papers, box 617.

48. "Stanley Forman Reed Day" (April 6, 1957), Clark Papers (Texas), box B100.

49. Warren Burger to the Conference, July 12, 1972, Blackmun Papers, box 1374; Warren Burger to the Conference, October 11, 1972, White Papers, box I:237; Lewis Powell to "Participants in the Cert Pool," November 22, 1972, White Papers, box I:237; Harry Blackmun to William Rehnquist, August 6, 1991, Blackmun Papers, box 1374.

50. William H. Rehnquist, "Who Writes Decisions of the Supreme Court?", *U.S. News & World Report*, December 13, 1957, 74, 75; Kenneth W. Starr, "Supreme Court Needs a Management Revolt," *Wall Street Journal*, October 13, 1993, A23; Tom C. Clark, "The Supreme Court Conference," *Texas Law Review* 37 (1959): 274; Todd C. Peppers, *Courtiers of the Marble Palace: The Rise and Influence of the Supreme Court Law Clerk* (Stanford, CA: Stanford University Press, 2006), 197.

51. *New York Times*, February 22, 1988, A16.

52. It is sometimes said that the *New York Tribune* reported the outcome of *Pennsylvania v. Wheeling and Belmont Bridge Co.*, 50 U.S. 647 (1852), and *Pennsylvania v. Wheeling and Belmont Bridge Co.*, 59 U.S. 421 (1856), before the opinions were published, but this appears to be a

misinterpretation that may have originated in Carl B. Swisher, *The Taney Period: 1836–64* (New York: Macmillan, 1974), 412, 416. I was unable to find any prediction of the 1852 opinion in the *Tribune*, including on the date cited by Swisher. As for the supposed leak of the 1856 opinion, the *Tribune* reported two months prior to its publication that "it is well understood that a large majority of the Court are prepared to affirm the constitutionality of the law." *New York Daily Tribune*, February 19, 1856, 4. Perhaps the *Tribune* had advance word of the decision, but it is at least equally likely that the paper's Washington correspondent was merely reporting the consensus of lawyers who correctly anticipated the outcome. Separately, Justice Robert Grier was accused of leaking the result of the 1852 case to members of the Pennsylvania legislature (the state was one of the parties) two weeks before the opinion was published. It is not clear whether he did. Daniel J. Wisniewski, "Heating Up a Case Gone Cold: Revisiting the Charges of Bribery and Official Misconduct Made Against Supreme Court Justice Robert Cooper Grier in 1854–55," *Journal of Supreme Court History* 38 (2013): 1–19.

53. *Newsweek*, June 15, 1992, 6; William Rehnquist to "all law clerks," June 10, 1992, Blackmun Papers, box 601; *New York Times*, November 19, 2022; *Burwell v. Hobby Lobby Stores, Inc.*, 573 U.S. 682 (2014).

54. Bob Woodward and Scott Armstrong, *The Brethren: Inside the Supreme Court* (New York: Simon & Schuster, 1979), 71, 258–59; David J. Garrow, "The Supreme Court and *The Brethren*," *Constitutional Commentary* 18 (2001): 303–18; Edward Lazarus, *Closed Chambers: The First Eyewitness Account of the Epic Struggles Inside the Supreme Court* (New York: Times Books, 1998); Yarbrough, *Blackmun*, 336.

55. *Washington Post*, April 25, 1979, A4; *Washington Post*, June 6, 1981, A6; *County of Washington v. Gunther*, 452 U.S. 161 (1981); William Rehnquist to the Conference, February 16, 1993, Blackmun Papers, box 1407; *City of Cincinnati v. Discovery Network, Inc.*, 507 U.S. 410 (1993).

56. "Marshal's Report of Findings & Recommendations" (January 19, 2023), 1–2, 11, 18–19, https://www.supremecourt.gov/publicinfo/press/Dobbs_Public_Report_January_19_2023.pdf.

57. Peppers, *Courtiers of the Marble Palace*, 22; Lewis Powell to Potter Stewart, August 26, 1980, Powell Papers, box 327.

58. Albert Sacks to Felix Frankfurter, November 30, 1959, Frankfurter Papers, reel 8.

59. Felix Frankfurter to Albert Sacks, December 7, 1959, and Albert Sacks to Felix Frankfurter, December 12, 1959, both in Frankfurter Papers, reel 8.

60. Todd C. Peppers, "A Family Tradition: Clerking at the U.S. Supreme Court," in *Of Courtiers and Kings: More Stories of Supreme Court Law Clerks and Their Justices*, ed. Todd C. Peppers and Clare Cushman (Charlottesville: University of Virginia Press, 2015), 342–43.

61. Ward and Weiden, *Sorcerers' Apprentices*, 90–92; William Douglas to Thomas Klitgaard, November 11, 1971, Douglas Papers, box 1120. Bruch and Meik were hired in 1971 for the Court's 1972–73 term.

62. William E. Nelson, Harvey Rishikof, I. Scott Messinger, and Michael Jo, "The Liberal Tradition of the Supreme Court Clerkship: Its Rise, Fall, and Reincarnation?", *Vanderbilt Law Review* 62 (2009): 1749–1814; *New York Times*, September 7, 2010, A1.

Chapter 16

1. *District of Columbia v. Heller*, 554 U.S. 570 (2008); Adam Winkler, *Gunfight: The Battle Over the Right to Bear Arms in America* (New York: Norton, 2011).

2. *Heller*, 554 U.S. at 584, 599, 651.

3. *Cheney v. U.S. District Court*, 541 U.S. 913, 929 (2004).

4. *McDonald v. City of Chicago*, 561 U.S. 742, 767–68 (2010).

5. Oral argument transcript, *New York State Rifle & Pistol Association v. Bruen*, No. 20-843 (November 3, 2021), 69–70.

6. *New York State Rifle & Pistol Association v. Bruen*, 142 S. Ct. 2111, 2126, 2131 (2022).

7. Gregory P. Magarian, cert memo to John Paul Stevens, *BMW of North America v. Gore*, Stevens Papers, box 727; *BMW of North America, Inc. v. Gore*, 517 U.S. 559 (1996); *State Farm Mutual Automobile Insurance Co. v. Campbell*, 538 U.S. 408, 425 (2003); *Philip Morris USA v. Williams*, 549 U.S. 346 (2007).

8. *Penn Central Transportation Co. v. City of New York*, 438 U.S. 104 (1978).

9. *Loretto v. Teleprompter Manhattan CATV Corp.*, 458 U.S. 419 (1982); *Nollan v. California Coastal Commission*, 483 U.S. 825, 837 (1987) (internal quotation marks omitted); *Lucas v. South Carolina Coastal Council*, 505 U.S. 1003 (1992); *Cedar Point Nursery v. Hassid*, 141 S. Ct. 2063 (2021).

10. *Berman v. Parker*, 348 U.S. 26 (1954).
11. *Kelo v. City of New London*, 545 U.S. 469, 503 (2005); Ilya Somin, *The Grasping Hand: Kelo v. City of New London and the Limits of Eminent Domain* (Chicago: University of Chicago Press, 2015), 135–80; *New York Times*, March 14, 2006, A27; John Paul Stevens to the Conference, September 19, 2005, Stevens Papers, box 941.
12. Anthony Kennedy to the Conference, June 21, 1995, Stevens Papers, box 698; *Rosenberger v. Rector and Visitors of the University of Virginia*, 515 U.S. 819, 840, 892 (1995).
13. *Zelman v. Simmons-Harris*, 536 U.S. 639, 652, 649 (2002); *Trinity Lutheran Church of Columbia, Inc. v. Comer*, 137 S. Ct. 2012 (2017); *Espinoza v. Montana Department of Revenue*, 140 S. Ct. 2246 (2020); *Carson v. Makin*, 142 S. Ct. 1987, 2012, 2014 (2022).
14. *Roman Catholic Diocese of Brooklyn v. Cuomo*, 141 S. Ct. 63, 66, 72, 79 (2020).
15. *Arlington Catholic Herald*, May 21, 2018; *New York Times*, August 11, 2022; *Obergefell v. Hodges*, 576 U.S. 644, 741 (2015); *Espinoza*, 140 S. Ct. at 2266, 2267. The "trendy disdain" line is a quotation from a Scalia opinion: "One need not delve too far into modern popular culture to perceive a trendy disdain for deep religious conviction." *Locke v. Davey*, 540 U.S. 712, 733 (2004).
16. *Masterpiece Cakeshop v. Colorado Civil Rights Commission*, 138 S. Ct. 1719, 1729 (2018); *Kennedy v. Bremerton School District*, 142 S. Ct. 2407 (2022); *303 Creative LLC v. Elenis*, 143 S. Ct. 2298 (2023).
17. *Buckley v. Valeo*, 424 U.S. 1 (1976). The opinions in *Buckley* take up 294 pages of the official reports, which makes *Buckley* the longest decision in the Court's history. The majority opinion alone is more than 65,000 words, longer than many books. Ryan C. Black and James F. Spriggs II, "An Empirical Analysis of the Length of Supreme Court Opinions," *Houston Law Review* 45 (2008): 631. Because of its length, the writing was divided among five justices (Burger, Brennan, Stewart, Powell, and Rehnquist) and it was designated as a per curiam opinion. Warren Burger to the Conference, November 18, 1975, Powell Papers, box 441.
18. *McConnell v. Federal Election Commission*, 540 U.S. 93 (2003); *Citizens United v. Federal Election Commission*, 558 U.S. 310 (2010); *New York Times*, January 29, 2010, A12; Adam Winkler, *We the Corporations: How American Businesses Won Their Civil Rights* (New York: Liveright, 2018), 372–73; Tilman Klumpp, Hugo M. Mialon, and Michael A. Williams, "The Business of American Democracy: *Citizens United*, Independent Spending, and Elections," *Journal of Law and Economics* 59 (2016): 1–43.
19. *McCutcheon v. Federal Election Commission*, 572 U.S. 185, 191, 204, 235–35 (2014).
20. *Valentine v. Chrestensen*, 316 U.S. 52 (1942); *Bigelow v. Virginia*, 421 U.S. 809 (1975); *Virginia State Board of Pharmacy v. Virginia Citizens Consumer Council, Inc.*, 425 U.S. 748 (1976); *Carey v. Population Services International*, 431 U.S. 678 (1977); *Central Hudson Gas & Electric Corp. v. Public Service Commission*, 447 U.S. 557 (1980); *Rubin v. Coors Brewing Co.*, 514 U.S. 476 (1995); *Greater New Orleans Broadcasting Association, Inc. v. United States*, 527 U.S. 173 (1999); *Thompson v. Western States Medical Center*, 535 U.S. 357 (2002); *Sorrell v. IMS Health Inc.*, 564 U.S. 552, 557, 591–92 (2011).
21. *Abood v. Detroit Board of Education*, 431 U.S. 209 (1977).
22. *Janus v. American Federation of State, County, and Municipal Employees*, 138 S. Ct. 2448, 2464, 2466 (2018).
23. *Id.* at 2501–02.
24. *Parents Involved in Community Schools v. Seattle School District No. 1*, 551 U.S. 701, 730, 747–48 (2007).
25. *Id.* at 823, 865, 868.
26. *Gratz v. Bollinger*, 539 U.S. 244 (2003); *Grutter v. Bollinger*, 539 U.S. 306 (2003); Barbara A. Perry, *The Michigan Affirmative Action Cases* (Lawrence: University Press of Kansas, 2007).
27. *Grutter*, 539 U.S. at 343.
28. *Students for Fair Admissions, Inc. v. President and Fellows of Harvard College*, 143 S. Ct. 2141, 2161, 2176, 2226, 2277 (2023).
29. *Hudson v. Michigan*, 547 U.S. 586 (2006); *Berghuis v. Thompkins*, 560 U.S. 370 (2010); *Shelby County v. Holder*, 570 U.S. 529 (2013); *Brnovich v. Democratic National Committee*, 141 S. Ct. 2321 (2021).
30. *Stenberg v. Carhart*, 530 U.S. 914 (2000); *Gonzalez v. Carhart*, 550 U.S. 124 (2007).
31. *Whole Woman's Health v. Hellerstedt*, 579 U.S. 582 (2016).
32. *June Medical Services LLC v. Russo*, 140 S. Ct. 2103 (2020); *Whole Woman's Health v. Jackson*, 142 S. Ct. 522 (2021).
33. *Dobbs v. Jackson Women's Health Organization*, 142 S. Ct. 2228, 2242–43 (2022).

34. *Id.* at 2248, 2284.
35. *Id.* at 2300–01.
36. *Id.* at 2310–11.
37. *Id.* at 2319–20, 2343–44, 2346.
38. *New York Times,* June 26, 2022; *New York Times,* June 24, 2022; *Washington Post,* June 25, 2022.
39. *United States v. Lopez,* 514 U.S. 549, 561, 564, 615, 608 (1995).
40. *United States v. Morrison,* 529 U.S. 598, 613, 617–18, 637, 643 (2000).
41. *Gonzales v. Raich,* 545 U.S. 1, 40 (2005).
42. *National Federation of Independent Business v. Sebelius,* 567 U.S. 519, 550, 552, 554 (2012).
43. *Id.* at 623.
44. *United States v. Darby,* 312 U.S. 100, 124 (1941); *New York v. United States,* 505 U.S. 144 (1992); *Printz v. United States,* 521 U.S. 898 (1997); *Murphy v. NCAA,* 138 S. Ct. 1461 (2018).
45. *Chevron, U.S.A., Inc. v. Natural Resources Defense Council, Inc.,* 467 U.S. 837 (1984).
46. *West Virginia v. EPA,* 142 S. Ct. 2587, 2609–10, 2626 (2022).
47. William Brennan to Warren Burger, April 4, 1986, White Papers, box II:50; John C. Jeffries Jr., *Justice Lewis F. Powell, Jr.* (New York: Charles Scribner's Sons, 1994), 514–29; Lewis Powell, undated notes, Powell Papers, box 657; *New York Times,* June 8, 2013; Lewis Powell to the Conference, April 8, 1986, White Papers, box II:50.
48. Warren Burger to Byron White, April 9, 1986, and Warren Burger to Byron White, May 13, 1986, both in White Papers, box II:50; *Bowers v. Hardwick,* 478 U.S. 186, 193, 192, 196 (1986); Oral History Transcript, 367, Blackmun Papers; *Washington Post,* October 26, 1990, A3.
49. Gallup, *LBGT Rights,* https://news.gallup.com/poll/1651/gay-lesbian-rights.aspx (accessed April 10, 2024).
50. Lisa Keen and Suzanne B. Goldberg, *Strangers to the Law: Gay People on Trial* (Ann Arbor: University of Michigan Press, 1998); *Romer v. Evans,* 517 U.S. 620, 632, 635 (1996).
51. *Id.* at 644, 645–46 (citations omitted), 652–53.
52. *Wall Street Journal,* May 22, 1996, A22; Harry Blackmun to Anthony Kennedy, May 23, 1996, and Anthony Kennedy to Harry Blackmun, May 28, 1996, both in Blackmun Papers, box 1405.
53. *Lawrence v. Texas,* 539 U.S. 558, 567, 578 (2003).
54. *Id.* at 602, 604.
55. Gallup, *LBGT Rights;* Michael J. Klarman, *From the Closet to the Altar: Courts, Backlash, and the Struggle for Same-Sex Marriage* (New York: Oxford University Press, 2013).
56. *United States v. Windsor,* 570 U.S. 744, 770, 772, 795, 798 (2013).
57. *Obergefell v. Hodges,* 576 U.S. 644, 670–71 (2015).
58. *Id.* at 687.
59. *Id.* at 717–18, 719.
60. *Bostock v. Clayton County,* 140 S. Ct. 1731 (2020).
61. *Rasul v. Bush,* 542 U.S. 466, 480, 497–98, 506 (2004).
62. *Hamdi v. Rumsfeld,* 542 U.S. 507, 532, 534, 598 (2004).
63. *Hamdan v. Rumsfeld,* 548 U.S. 557, 705 (2006).
64. *Boumediene v. Bush,* 553 U.S. 723, 770–71, 827–28 (2008).
65. *Congressional Record* 17 (1886): 817–18.
66. This account simplifies a complicated sequence of events. For a full discussion, see Howard Gillman, *The Votes That Counted: How the Court Decided the 2000 Presidential Election* (Chicago: University of Chicago Press, 2001).
67. Anthony Kennedy to the Conference, December 12, 2000, and William Rehnquist to the Conference, December 12, 2000, both in Stevens Papers, box 854; *Bush v. Gore,* 531 U.S. 98, 106–07, 109, 110 (2000).
68. *Id.* at 112–13.
69. *Id.* at 134–35, 143, 128–29.
70. Richard K. Neumann Jr., "Conflicts of Interest in *Bush v. Gore*: Did Some Justices Vote Illegally?", *Georgetown Journal of Legal Ethics* 16 (2003): 375–79; Joan Biskupic, *American Original: The Life and Constitution of Supreme Court Justice Antonin Scalia* (New York: Farrar, Straus and Giroux, 2009), 248.
71. Nelson Lund, "The Unbearable Rightness of *Bush v. Gore,*" *Cardozo Law Review* 23 (2002): 1219; Michael J. Klarman, "*Bush v. Gore* Through the Lens of Constitutional History," *California Law Review* 89 (2001): 1724, 1725; Michael W. McConnell, "Two-and-a-Half Cheers for *Bush v. Gore,*" *University of Chicago Law Review* 68 (2001): 660–61.

72. Jeffrey Toobin, "The Conservative Pipeline to the Supreme Court," *New Yorker*, April 17, 2017; Jennie Neufeld, "Trump Nominates Brett Kavanaugh to Supreme Court: Full Transcript," Vox, July 9, 2018, https://www.vox.com/2018/7/9/17550910/brett-kavanaugh-nomination-transcr ipt-supreme-court.

73. *Trump v. Hawaii*, 138 S. Ct. 2392, 2417 (2018).

74. *Id.* at 2420–21, 2418.

75. *Id.* at 2433.

76. *Department of Commerce v. New York*, 139 S. Ct. 2551, 2574–75 (2019).

77. *Id.* at 2576, 2597.

78. *Trump v. Mazars USA, LLP*, 140 S. Ct. 2019 (2020).

79. *Trump v. Vance*, 140 S. Ct. 2412 (2020).

80. *Ward v. Jackson*, 141 S. Ct. 1381 (2021); *Wood v. Raffensberger*, 141 S. Ct. 1379 (2021); *Kelly v. Pennsylvania*, 141 S. Ct. 1449 (2021); *Donald J. Trump for President, Inc. v. Degraffenreid*, 141 S. Ct. 1451 (2021); *Trump v. Biden*, 141 S. Ct. 1387 (2021); *Texas v. Pennsylvania*, 141 S. Ct. 1230 (2020); *Washington Post*, May 20, 2022; *Washington Post*, September 1, 2022; *New York Times*, September 29, 2022.

81. *Axios*, July 13, 2021; Donald Trump, "Remarks to Supporters Prior to the Storming of the United States Capitol," The American Presidency Project, https://www.presidency.ucsb.edu/docume nts/remarks-supporters-prior-the-storming-the-united-states-capitol (accessed April 10, 2024).

82. Motion for Expedited Consideration of the Motion for Leave to File a Bill of Complaint (December 7, 2020), 10, *Texas v. Pennsylvania*, No. 22O155; Emergency Application for Administrative Stay (January 6, 2021), *Gohmert v. Pence*, No. 20A115; *Texas Tribune*, December 12, 2020.

83. Tom S. Clark, *The Limits of Judicial Independence* (New York: Cambridge University Press, 2011), 46.

84. Adam Chilton, Daniel Epps, Kyle Rozema, and Maya Sen, "Designing Supreme Court Term Limits," *Southern California Law Review* 95 (2021): 1–72; David J. Garrow, "Mental Decrepitude on the U.S. Supreme Court: The Historical Case for a 28th Amendment," *University of Chicago Law Review* 67 (2000): 1028–43; Dwight Eisenhower to John W. Davis, July 7, 1954, WHCF Official File, box 321, Eisenhower Library.

85. Max Baucus and Kenneth R. Kay, "The Court-Stripping Bills: Their Impact on the Constitution, the Courts, and Congress," *Villanova Law Review* 27 (1982): 991; *Ex parte McCardle*, 74 U.S. 506 (1869).

86. David Orentlicher, "Politics and the Supreme Court: The Need for Ideological Balance," *University of Pittsburgh Law Review* 79 (2018): 422–23; Evan H. Caminker, "Thayerian Deference to Congress and Supreme Court Supermajority Rules: Lessons from the Past," *Indiana Law Journal* 78 (2003): 73–122; see, e.g., H.R. 4565, 86th Cong., 1st Sess. (1959), introduced by Watkins Abbitt of Virginia, which would have required unanimity.

87. See, e.g., Michael Klarman, "The Democrats' Last Chance to Save Democracy: Expand the Court Now," *Atlantic*, February 22, 2021.

88. Presidential Commission on the Supreme Court of the United States, *Final Report* (December 8, 2021).

Epilogue

1. Josh Chafetz, "The First Name of a Supreme Court Justice Is Not Justice," *New York Times*, June 2, 2023; *Wall Street Journal*, July 8, 2022.

2. Stephen I. Vladeck, *The Shadow Docket: How the Supreme Court Uses Stealth Rulings to Amass Power and Undermine the Republic* (New York: Basic Books, 2023).

3. Lee J. Epstein, Jeffrey A. Segal, Harold J. Spaeth, and Thomas G. Walker, *The Supreme Court Compendium: Data, Decisions, and Developments*, 5th ed. (Los Angeles: CQ Press, 2012), 251.

4. *Bittner v. United States*, 143 S. Ct. 713 (2023).

Index

For the benefit of digital users, indexed terms that span two pages (e.g., 52–53) may, on occasion, appear on only one of those pages.

Figures are indicated by an italic *f* following the page number.

640 INDEX